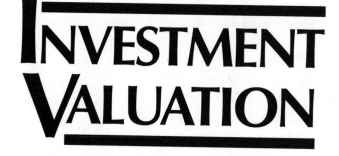

INVESTMENT VALUATION

WILEY FRONTIERS IN FINANCE

INVESTMENT VALUATION

Tools and techniques for determining the value of *any* asset

ASWATH DAMODARAN

John Wiley & Sons, Inc.

New York • Chichester • Brisbane • Toronto • Singapore

Library of Congress Cataloging-in-Publication Data:

Damodaran, Aswath.
 Investment valuation / Aswath Damodaran.
 p. cm.
 ISBN 0-471-13393-0 (cloth) ISBN 0-471-11213-5 (paper)
 1. Corporations—Valuation—Mathematical models. I. Title.
 II. Series.
 HG4028.V3D353 1996
 658.15—dc20 95-7418

This book is dedicated to Michele, whose patience and support made it possible; to Ryan and Brendan, who helped in their own way; and to Kendra, who arrived just in time to be included.

Preface

This is a book about valuation—the valuation of stocks, bonds, options, futures, and real assets. It is a fundamental precept of this book that any asset can be valued, albeit imprecisely in some cases. I have attempted to provide a sense of not only the differences among the models used to value different types of assets, but also the common elements in these models.

In the process of presenting and discussing the various models available for valuation, I have tried to adhere to four basic principles. First, I have attempted to be as comprehensive as possible in covering the ranges of valuation models that are available to an analyst doing a valuation, while presenting the common elements in these models and providing a framework that can be used to pick the right model for any valuation scenario. Second, I have used real world examples, warts and all, to capture some of the problems inherent in applying the models. There is the obvious danger that some of these valuations be proven hopelessly wrong in hindsight, but this risk is well worth the benefits. Third, in keeping with my belief that valuation models are universal and not market-specific, throught the book I have interspersed illustrations from markets outside the United States. Finally, I have tried to make the book as modular as possible, enabling a reader to pick and choose sections to read without a significant loss of continuity.

In applying valuation models to real-world examples, I have used the capital asset pricing model (CAPM) as my model for risk and beta as my measure of risk. I am well aware of the controversy surrounding the CAPM, and I have discussed its limitations as well as alternative models in Chapter 4, Estimation of Discount Rates. There are four reasons for my dependence on the CAPM in this book. First, the estimation of the cost of equity, which is where I have used the CAPM, is just one component of valuation. The valuation models described in this book require a cost of equity, and any model that provides one can be used instead of the CAPM without any loss of generality. Second,

the data that are available often determine usage. The betas of both domestic and foreign firms are estimated by a number of information services, and they are easily accessible. I could have attempted to estimate the parameters of an alternative model for the stocks that I have valued, but that would have diverted me from my primary focus, which was valuation. Third, the CAPM provides a convenient forum for discussing more general issues that are important in valuation, such as the effects of financial leverage on risk and the relationship between risk and growth opportunities. Finally, in spite of all the criticism of the CAPM, I am not convinced that alternative models do much better in predicting expected returns, although there is evidence that they do better at explaining past returns.

OUTLINE OF THE BOOK

Chapter 1 examines the general basis for valuation models and the role that valuation plays in different investment philosophies. Chapter 2 provides an overview to the three basic approaches to valuation—discounted cashflow valuation, relative valuation, and contingent claim valuation. The rest of the book delves into the details of using these models.

Basic Valuation Tools

The first section of the book presents the basic tools needed for valuation, starting with models for analyzing risk and return and for estimating discount rates in Chapters 3 and 4. Chapter 5 provides an introduction to financial statements, and the process of estimating cashflows is discussed in Chapter 6. Chapter 7 examines the process of estimating growth rates in earnings and cashflows from historical and fundamental data.

Market Efficiency and the Efficacy of Investment Screens

The next section looks at the issue of market efficiency as a vehicle for developing investment screens and developing investment strategies. Chapter 8 examines the question of how to test an investment scheme, and Chapter 9 summarizes the empirical evidence on a wide variety of investment strategies, ranging from those based upon past prices to those based upon financial fundamentals such as the PE ratio.

Discounted Cashflow Models

The next section examines different discounted cashflow models to value both equity and the firm. Chapter 10 describes the basis dividend discount model and its variants. Chapter 11 starts off with a discussion of why free cashflows to equity (FCFE) are different from dividends for most firms. The two-stage

and three-stage FCFE discounted cashflow models are described and applied to high-growth firms that do not pay dividends. Chapter 12 examines the alternative of valuing the firm by discounting free cashflows to the firm at the weighted average cost of capital. The advantages of this approach are discussed, with caveats on its usage. Chapter 13 is dedicated to the valuation of firms that do not fit easily into traditional discounted cashflow models. In particular, the problems in valuing cyclical and troubled firms are discussed, and possible solutions are suggested.

Relative Valuation Models

The section on relative valuation encompasses three chapters. Chapter 14 discusses the use and misuse of price/earnings (PE) and price/cashflow ratios, beginning with an examination of the determinants of price/earnings ratios, and continuing with an analysis of why PE ratios change over time and why earnings multiples are different across industries and countries. Chapter 15 explores the relationship between price and book value, and attempts to clear misconceptions about the relationship. The determinants of price/book value ratios are examined, and a rationale is presented for why some firms sell for less than book value while others sell for more. Finally, there is a discussion of how to use price/book value ratios sensibly in investing. Chapter 16 examines the price/sales ratio and reasons for differences across firms and industries on this multiple. The price/sales ratio is also a useful tool to examine the value of a brand name and the effects of changes in corporate strategy.

Contingent Claim Valuation Models

Contingent claim valuation is discussed in two chapters. Chapter 17 develops the basic concepts of option pricing. It describes the payoff diagrams on call and put options and provides the rationale for option pricing models. The binomial model and the Black-Scholes model are presented and contrasted, and extensions on these models and their limitations are described. Chapter 18 applies these models in pricing a number of contingent claim securities such as warrants, and explores the use of option pricing models in pricing assets that have option-like features such as equity in a firm, natural resource rights, and product patents.

Valuing Fixed Income Securities

The next section looks at the valuation of fixed-income securities in two parts. In Chapter 19, the determinants of the level of rates, the term structure, and the default premia are examined. Chapter 20 looks at special features of bonds, including conversion and call options, as well as the effect of caps and floors on floating-rate bonds.

Valuing Futures and Real Assets

Chapter 21 examines the pricing of futures contracts on perishable and storable commodities and extends the lessons to valuing futures on stock indices, bonds, and currencies. Chapter 22 provides an introduction to the use of discounted cashflow models and comparables in the valuation of real estate, while Chapter 23 analyzes the valuation of other assets, including private businesses and franchises.

CHOOSING THE RIGHT MODEL

The problem in valuation is not that there are not enough models; it is that there are too many. Consequently, the final chapter, Chapter 24, may be the most important one in this book. It provides a framework for picking the right model for any occasion, based upon the characteristics of the asset being valued.

ACKNOWLEDGMENTS

I would like to express my appreciation to Value Line and Bloomberg. Without their data the practical examples that I have worked out in this book would not have been possible.

Contents

1

Introduction to Investment Valuation

E
very asset, financial as well as real, has value. The key to successfully investing in and managing these assets lies in understanding not only what the value is, but the sources of the value. Any asset can be valued, but some assets are easier to value than others, and the details of valuation will vary from case to case. Thus, the valuation of a share of a real estate property will require different information and follow a different format from the valuation of a publicly traded stock. What is surprising, however, is not the differences in valuation techniques across assets, but the degree of similarity in basic principles. There is undeniably uncertainty associated with valuation. Often that uncertainty comes from the asset being valued, although the valuation model may add to that uncertainty.

This chapter lays out a philosophical basis for valuation, together with a discussion of how valuation is or can be used in a variety of frameworks, from portfolio management to corporate finance.

A PHILOSOPHICAL BASIS FOR VALUATION

A surprising number of investors subscribe to the "bigger fool" theory of investing, which argues that the value of an asset is irrelevant as long as there is a "bigger fool" around who is willing to buy the asset from them. While this may provide a basis for some profits, it is a dangerous game to play, since there is no guarantee that such an investor will still be around when the time to sell comes.

A postulate of sound investing is that an investor does not pay more for an asset than its worth. This statement may seem logical and obvious, but it is forgotten and rediscovered at some time in every generation and in every market. There are those who are disingenuous enough to argue that value is in the eyes of the beholder, and that any price can be justified if there are other investors willing to pay that price. That is patently absurd. Perceptions may be all that matter when the asset is a painting or a sculpture, but investors do not (and should not) buy most assets for aesthetic or emotional reasons; financial assets are acquired for the cashflows expected from owning them. Conse-

quently, perceptions of value have to be backed up by reality, which implies that the price that is paid for any asset should reflect the cashflows it is expected to generate. The models of valuation described in this book attempt to relate value to the level and expected growth of these cashflows.

There are many areas in valuation where there is room for disagreement, including how to estimate true value and how long it will take for prices to adjust to true value. But there is one point on which there can be no disagreement. Asset prices cannot be justified merely by using the argument that there will be other investors around willing to pay a higher price in the future.

GENERALITIES ABOUT VALUATION

Like all analytical disciplines, valuation has developed its own set of myths over time. This section examines and debunks some of these myths.

Myth I: Since valuation models are quantitative, valuation is objective.

Valuation is neither the science that some of its proponents make it out to be nor the objective search for true value that idealists would like it to become. The models that we use in valuation may be quantitative, but the inputs leave plenty of room for subjective judgments. Thus, the final value that we obtain from these models is colored by the bias that we bring into the process.

The obvious solution is to eliminate all bias before starting on a valuation, but this is easier said than done. Given the exposure we receive to external information, analyses, and opinions about an asset such as a firm, it is unlikely that we embark on most analyses without some bias. There are two ways of reducing the bias in the process. The first is to avoid taking strong public positions on the value of a firm before the valuation is complete. In far too many cases, the decision on whether a firm is under- or overvalued precedes the actual valuation,[1] leading to seriously biased analyses. The second is to minimize the stake we have in whether the firm is under- or overvalued, prior to the valuation.

Institutional concerns also play a role in determining the extent of bias in valuation. For instance, it is an acknowledged fact that equity research analysts are more likely to issue buy rather than sell recommendations,[2] that is, that they are more likely to find firms to be undervalued than overvalued. This can be traced partly to the difficulties they face in obtaining access to and collecting information on firms that they have issued sell recommendations on, and partly to pressure that they face from portfolio managers, some of whom might have large positions in the stock.

When using a valuation done by a third party, the biases of the analyst(s) doing the valuation should be considered before decisions are made on its basis. For instance, a self-valuation done by a target firm in a takeover is likely to be positively biased. While this does not make the valuation worthless, it suggests that the analysis should be viewed with skepticism.

Myth 2: A well-researched and well-done valuation is timeless.

The value obtained from any valuation model is affected by firm-specific as well as marketwide information. As a consequence, the value will change as new information is revealed. Given the constant flow of information into financial markets, a valuation done on a firm ages quickly and has to be updated to reflect current information. Thus, pharmaceutical companies that were valued highly in early 1992, on the assumption that the high growth from the 1980s would continue into the future, would have been valued much less in early 1993, as the prospects of health reform and price controls dimmed the future outlook. With the benefit of hindsight, the valuations of these companies (and the analyst recommendations) made in 1992 can be criticized, but they were reasonable given the information available at that time.

Myth 3: A good valuation provides a precise estimate of value.

Even at the end of the most careful and detailed valuation, there will be uncertainty about the final numbers, colored as they are by assumptions that we make about the future of the company and the economy. It is unrealistic to expect or demand absolute certainty in valuation, since cashflows and discount rates are estimated with error. This also means that analysts have to give themselves a reasonable margin for error in making recommendations on the basis of valuations.

Myth 4: The more quantitative a model, the better the valuation.

The usefulness of the models presented in this book is circumscribed by the time and effort analysts spend in coming up with the inputs to the model. If they do not do their homework and the inputs are wrong, the output from the models will reflect those errors. In general, the quality of a valuation will be directly proportional to the time spent in collecting the data and in understanding the firm being valued.

Myth 5: The market is generally wrong.

The benchmark for comparison in most valuations remains the market price. When the value from an analysis is significantly different from the market price, there are two possibilities: One is that the valuation is incorrect and the market is right; the other is that the valuation is correct and the market is not. The presumption should be that the market is correct and that it is up to the analyst to convince himself or herself (and others) that his or her valuation offers a better estimate of value than the market price. This higher standard may lead investors to be more cautious in following through on valuations, but given the difficulty of beating the market, this is not an undesirable outcome.

Myth 6: The product of valuation (i.e., the value) is what matters; the process of valuation is not important.

As valuation models are introduced in this book, there is the risk of focusing exclusively on the outcome, that is, the value of the company, and whether it

is under- or overvalued, and missing some valuable insights that can be obtained from the process of the valuation. The process can tell us a great deal about the determinants of value and help us answer some fundamental questions: What is the appropriate price to pay for high growth? What is a brand name worth? How important is it to improve returns on projects? What is the effect of profit margins on value? Since the process is so informative, even those who believe that markets are efficient (and that the market price is therefore the best estimate of value) should be able to find some use for valuation models.

THE ROLE OF VALUATION

Valuation is useful in a wide range of tasks. The role it plays, however, is different in different arenas. The following section lays out the relevance of valuation in portfolio management, in acquisition analysis, and in corporate finance.

Valuation and Portfolio Management

The role that valuation plays in portfolio management is determined in large part by the investment philosophy of the investor. Valuation plays a minimal role in portfolio management for a passive investor, whereas it plays a larger role for an active investor. Even among active investors, the nature and the role of valuation are different for different types of active investment. Active investors can be categorized as either market timers, who trust in their abilities to foresee the direction of the overall stock or bond markets, on security selectors who believe that their skills lie in funding under- or overvalued securities. Market timers use valuation much less than do investors who pick stocks, and the focus is on market valuation rather than on firm-specific valuation. Among security selectors, valuation plays a central role in portfolio management for fundamental analysts and a peripheral role for technical analysts.

The following subsections describe, in broad terms, different investment philosophies and the role played by valuation in each.

Fundamental Analysts. The underlying theme in fundamental analysis is that the true value of the firm can be related to its financial characteristics—its growth prospects, risk profile, and cashflows. Any deviation from this true value is a sign that a stock is under- or overvalued. It is a long-term investment strategy, and the assumptions underlying it are that:

(a) The relationship between value and the underlying financial factors can be measured.
(b) The relationship is stable over time.
(c) Deviations from the relationship are corrected in a reasonable time period.

Valuation is the central focus in fundamental analysis. Some analysts use discounted cashflow models to value firms, while others use multiples such as the price/earnings and price/book value ratios. Since investors using this ap-

proach hold a large number of "undervalued" stocks in their portfolios, their hope is that, on average, these portfolios will do better than the market.

Franchise Buyers. The philosophy of a franchise buyer is best expressed by an investor who has been very successful at it—Warren Buffett. "We try to stick to businesses we believe we understand," Mr. Buffett writes.[3] "That means they must be relatively simple and stable in character. If a business is complex and subject to constant change, we're not smart enough to predict future cash flows." Franchise buyers concentrate on a few businesses they understand well and attempt to acquire undervalued firms. Often, as in the case of Mr. Buffett, franchise buyers wield influence on the management of these firms and can change financial and investment policy. As a long-term strategy, the underlying assumptions are that:

(a) Investors who understand a business well are in a better position to value it correctly.
(b) These undervalued businesses can be acquired without driving the price above the true value.

Valuation plays a key role in this philosophy, since franchise buyers are attracted to a particular business because they believe it is undervalued. They are also interested in how much additional value they can create by restructuring the business and running it right.

Chartists. Chartists believe that prices are driven as much by investor psychology as by any underlying financial variables. The information available from trading—price movements, trading volume, short sales, and so forth—gives an indication of investor psychology and future price movements. The assumptions here are that prices move in predictable patterns, that there are not enough marginal investors taking advantage of these patterns to eliminate them, and that the average investor in the market is driven more by emotion than by rational analysis.

While valuation does not play much of a role in charting, there are ways in which an enterprising chartist can incorporate it into analysis. For instance, valuation can be used to determine support and resistance lines[4] on price charts.

Information Traders. Prices move on information about the firm. Information traders attempt to trade in advance of new information or shortly after it is revealed to financial markets, buying on good news and selling on bad. The underlying assumption is that these traders can anticipate information announcements and gauge the market reaction to them better than the average investor in the market.

For an information trader, the focus is on the relationship between information and changes in value, rather than on value per se. Thus an information trader may buy an "overvalued" firm if he or she believes that the next information announcement is going to cause the price to go up because it contains better-than-expected news. If there is a relationship between how undervalued

or overvalued a company is and how its stock price reacts to new information, then valuation could play a role in investing for an information trader.

Market Timers. Market timers note, with some legitimacy, that the payoff to calling turns in markets is much greater than the returns from stock picking. They argue that it is easier to predict market movements than to select stocks and that these predictions can be based upon factors that are observable.

While valuation of individual stocks may not be of any use to a market timer, market timing strategies can use valuation in at least two ways:

(a) The overall market itself can be valued and compared to the current level.
(b) A valuation model can be used to value all stocks, and the results from the cross-section can be used to determine whether the market is over- or under-valued. For example, as the number of stocks that are overvalued using the dividend discount model increases relative to the number that are underval-ued, there may be reason to believe that the market is overvalued.

Efficient Marketers. Efficient marketers believe that the market price at any point in time represents the best estimate of the true value of the firm and that any attempt to exploit perceived market efficiencies will cost more than it will make in excess profits. They assume that markets aggregate information quickly and accurately, that marginal investors promptly exploit any inefficiencies, and that any inefficiencies in the market are caused by friction, such as transactions costs, and cannot be arbitraged away.

For efficient marketers, valuation is a useful exercise to determine why a stock sells for the price it does. Since the underlying assumption is that the market price is the best estimate of the true value of the company, the objective becomes determining what assumptions about growth and risk are implied in this market price, rather than on finding under- or overvalued firms.

Valuation in Acquisition Analysis

Valuation should play a central part in acquisition analysis. The bidding firm or individual has to decide on a fair value for the target firm before making a bid, and the target firm has to determine a reasonable value for itself before deciding to accept or reject the offer.

There are also special factors to consider in takeover valuation. First, the effects of synergy on the combined value of the two firms (target plus bidding firm) have to be considered before a decision is made on the bid. Those who suggest that synergy is impossible to value and should not be considered in quantitative terms are wrong. Second, the effects on value of changing manage-ment and restructuring the target firm will have to be taken into account in deciding on a fair price. This is of particular concern in hostile takeovers.

Finally, there is a significant problem with bias in takeover valuations. Target firms may be overly optimistic in estimating value, especially when the takeover is hostile and they are trying to convince their stockholders that the offer price is too low. Similarly, if the bidding firm has decided, for strategic reasons, to

do an acquisition, there may be strong pressure on the analyst to come up with an estimate of value that backs up the acquisition decision.

Valuation in Corporate Finance

If the objective in corporate finance is the maximization of firm value,[5] then the relationship between financial decisions, corporate strategy, and firm value has to be delineated. In recent years, management consulting firms have started offering companies advice on how to increase value.[6] Their suggestions have often provided the basis for the restructuring of these firms.

The value of a firm can be directly related to decisions that it makes—on which projects it takes, on how it finances them, and on its dividend policy. Understanding this relationship is key to making value-increasing decisions and to sensible financial restructuring.

CONCLUSION

Valuation plays a key role in many areas of finance—in corporate finance, in mergers and acquisitions, and in portfolio management. The models presented in this book will provide a range of tools that analysts in each of these areas will find of use, but the cautionary note sounded in this chapter bears repeating. Valuation is not an objective exercise, and any preconceptions and biases that an analyst brings to the process will find their way into the value.

QUESTIONS AND SHORT PROBLEMS

1. The value of an investment is
 a. the present value of the cashflows on the investment.
 b. determined by investor perceptions about it.
 c. determined by demand and supply.
 d. often a subjective estimate, colored by the bias of the analyst.
 e. all of the above.
2. There are many who claim that value is based upon investor perceptions, and perceptions alone, and that cashflows and earnings do not matter. This argument is flawed because
 a. value is determined by earnings and cashflows, and investor perceptions do not matter.
 b. perceptons do matter, but they can change. Value must be based upon something more stable.
 c. investors are irrational. Therefore, their perceptions should not determine value.
 d. value is determined by investor perceptions, but it is also determined by the underlying earnings and cashflows. Perceptions must be based upon reality.

3. You use a valuation model to arrive at a value of $15 for a stock. The market price of the stock is $25. The difference can be explained by
 a. a market inefficiency; the market is overvaluing the stock.
 b. the use of the wrong valuation model to value the stock.
 c. errors in the inputs to the valuation model.
 d. none of the above
 e. either a, b, or c.

ENDNOTES

1. This is most visible in takeovers, where the decision to acquire a firm often seems to precede the valuation of the firm. It should come as no surprise, therefore, that the analysis almost invariably supports the decision.

2. There are approximately five times as many buy recommendations issued by analysts on Wall Street as there are sell recommendations.

3. This is extracted from Mr. Buffett's letter to stockholders in Berkshire Hathaway for 1993.

4. On a chart, the *support line* usually refers to a lower bound below which prices are unlikely to move, and the *resistance line* refers to the upper bound above which prices are unlikely to venture. While these levels are usually estimated using past prices, the range of values obtained from a valuation model can be used to determine these levels; i.e., the maximum value will become the resistance level and the minimum value will become the support level.

5. Most corporate financial theory is constructed on this premise.

6. The motivation for this has been the fear of hostile takeovers. Companies have increasingly turned to "value consultants" to tell them how to restructure, increase value, and avoid being taken over.

2

Approaches to Valuation

Analysts use a wide range of models in practice, ranging from the simple to the sophisticated. These models often make very different assumptions about pricing, but they do share some common characteristics and can be classified in broader terms. There are several advantages to such a classification: It makes it is easier to understand where individual models fit into the big picture, why they provide different results, and when they have fundamental errors in logic.

In general terms, there are three approaches to valuation. The first, *discounted cashflow valuation*, relates the value of an asset to the present value of expected future cashflows on that asset. The second, *relative valuation*, estimates the value of an asset by looking at the pricing of "comparable" assets relative to a common variable like earnings, cashflows, book value, or sales. The third, *contingent claim valuation*, uses option pricing models to measure the value of assets that share option characteristics. There can be significant differences in outcome, depending upon which approach is used. One of our objectives in this book is to explain the reasons for such differences in value across different models, and to help in picking the right model to use for a specific task.

This chapter provides a short summary of each approach, its applicability, and its limitations in valuation.

DISCOUNTED CASHFLOW VALUATION

Basis for Approach

This approach has its foundation in the "present value" rule, where the value of any asset is the present value of expected future cashflows on it.

$$\text{Value} = \sum_{t=1}^{t=n} \frac{CF_t}{(1 + r)^t}$$

where n = life of the asset

CF_t = cashflow in period t

r = discount rate reflecting the riskiness of the estimated cashflows

The cashflows will vary from asset to asset—dividends for stocks, coupons

(interest), and the face value for bonds and after-tax cashflows for a real project. The discount rate will be a function of the riskiness of the estimated cashflows, with higher rates for riskier assets and lower rates for safer projects.

Equity Valuation Versus Firm Valuation

There are two paths to discounted cashflow valuation: The first is to value just the equity stake in the business, while the second is to value the entire firm, which includes, besides equity, the other claimholders in the firm (bondholders, preferred stockholders, etc.). While both approaches discount expected cashflows, the relevant cashflows and discount rates are different under each.

The value of equity is obtained by discounting expected cashflows to equity, i.e., the residual cashflows after meeting all expenses, tax obligations, and interest and principal payments, at the cost of equity, that is, the rate of return required by equity investors in the firm.

$$\text{Value of Equity} = \sum_{t=1}^{t=\infty} \frac{\text{CF to Equity}_t}{(1 + k_e)^t}$$

where CF to Equity$_t$ = expected Cashflow to Equity in period t
k_e = cost of equity

The dividend discount model is a specialized case of equity valuation, and the value of a stock is the present value of expected future dividends.

The value of the firm is obtained by discounting expected cashflows to the firm, i.e., the residual cashflows after meeting all operating expenses and taxes but prior to debt payments, at the weighted average cost of capital, which is the cost of the different components of financing used by the firm, weighted by their market value proportions.

$$\text{Value of Firm} = \sum_{t=1}^{t=\infty} \frac{\text{CF to Firm}_t}{(1 + \text{WACC})^t}$$

where CF to Firm$_t$ = expected Cashflow to Firm in period t
WACC = Weighted Average Cost of Capital

While the two approaches use different definitions of cashflow and discount rates, they will yield consistent estimates of value as long as the same set of assumptions is used for both. The key error to avoid is mismatching cashflows and discount rates, since discounting cashflows to equity at the weighted average cost of capital will lead to an upwardly biased estimate of the value of equity, while discounting cashflows to the firm at the cost of equity will yield a downwardly biased estimate of the value of the firm. This is illustrated in the following example.

Illustration 2.1: Effects of mismatching cashflows and discount rates

Assume that you are analyzing a company with the following cashflows for the next five years. Assume also that the cost of equity is 13.625% and that the firm can borrow

long term at 10%. (The tax rate for the firm is 50%.) The current market value of equity is $1,073, and the value of debt outstanding is $800.

Year	CF to Equity	Interest $(1 - t)$	CF to Firm
1	$ 50	$40	$ 90
2	60	40	100
3	68	40	108
4	76.2	40	116.2
5	83.49	40	123.49
Terminal Value	1,603.008		2,363.008

Cost of Equity = 13.625%

Cost of Debt = Pretax Rate$(1 - $ Tax Rate$) = 10\%(1 - .5) = 5\%$

Value of Equity = $1,073

Value of Debt = $800

WACC = Cost of Equity(Equity/[Debt + Equity])
 + Cost of Debt(Debt/[Debt + Equity])
 = 13.625%($1,073/1,873) + 5%($800/$1,873) = 9.94%

Method 1: Discount CF to Equity at Cost of Equity to get Present Value (PV) of Equity:

PV of Equity = $50/1.13625 + $60/1.13625^2 + $68/1.13625^3
 + $76.2/1.13625^4 + ($83.49 + $1,603)/1.13625^5 = $1,073

Method 2: Discount CF to Firm at Cost of Capital to get PV of Firm:

PV of Firm = $90/1.0994 + $100/1.0994^2 + $108/1.0994^3 + $116.2/1.0994^4
 + ($123.49 + $2,363)/1.0994^5 = $1,873
. PV of Equity = PV of Firm − Market Value of Debt
 = $1,873 − $800 = $1,073

X Method 1: Discount CF to Equity at Cost of Capital to get too high a PV of Equity:

PV of Equity = $50/1.0994 + $60/1.0994^2 + $68/1.0994^3 + $76.2/1.0994^4
 + ($83.49 + $1,603)/1.0994^5 = $1,248

X Method 2: Discount CF to Firm at Cost of Equity to get too low a PV of Firm:

PV of Firm = $90/1.13625 + $100/1.13625^2 + $108/1.13625^3
 + $116.2/1.13625^4 + ($123.49 + $2,363)/1.13625^5 = $1,613
PV of Equity = PV of Firm − Market Value of Debt
 = $1,613 − $800 = $813

The effects of using the wrong discount rate are clearly visible in the last two calculations. When the cost of capital is mistakenly used to discount the cashflows to equity, the value of equity increases by $175 over its true value ($1,073). When the cashflows to the firm are erroneously discounted at the cost of equity, the value of the firm is understated by $260.

Applicability of Approach and Limitations

Discounted cashflow valuation is based upon expected future cashflows and discount rates. Given these informational requirements, this approach is easiest to use for assets (firms) whose cashflows are currently positive and can be estimated with some reliability for future periods, and where a proxy for risk that can be used to obtain discount rates is available. The further we get from this idealized setting, the more difficult discounted cashflow valuation becomes. Following are some scenarios where discounted cashflow valuation might run into trouble and need to be adapted.

Firms in Trouble. A distressed firm generally has negative earnings and cashflows currently and expects to lose money for some time in the future. For these firms, estimating future cashflows is difficult to do, since there is a strong probability of bankruptcy. For firms which are expected to fail, discounted cashflow valuation does not work very well, since it looks at the firm as a going concern providing positive cashflows to its investors. Even for firms that are expected to survive, cashflows will have to be estimated until they turn positive, since obtaining a present value of negative cashflows will yield a negative[1] value for equity or the firm.

Cyclical Firms. The earnings and cashflows of cyclical firms tend to follow the economy—rising during economic booms and falling during recessions. If discounted cashflow valuation is used on these firms, expected future cashflows are usually smoothed out, unless the analyst wants to undertake the onerous task of predicting the timing and duration of economic recessions and recoveries. Many cyclical firms, in the depths of a recession, look like troubled firms, with negative earnings and cashflows. Estimating future cashflows then becomes entangled with analyst predictions about when the economy will turn and how strong the upturn will be, with more optimistic analysts arriving at higher estimates of value. This is unavoidable, but the economic biases of the analyst have to be taken into account before using these valuations.

Firms with Unutilized Assets. Discounted cashflow valuation reflects the value of all assets that produce cashflows. If a firm has assets that are unutilized (and hence do not produce any cashflows), the value of these assets will not be reflected in the value obtained from discounting expected future cashflows. The same caveat applies, in lesser degree, to underutilized assets, since their value will be understated in discounted cashflow valuation. While this is a problem, it is not insurmountable. The value of these assets can always be obtained externally[2] and added on to the value obtained from discounted cashflow valuation.

Firms with Patents or Product Options. Firms often have unutilized patents or product options that do not produce any current cashflows, are not expected to produce cashflows in the near future, but nevertheless are valuable. If this is the case, the value obtained from discounting expected cashflows to the firm will understate the true value of the firm. Again, the problem can be overcome by valuing

these assets in the open market or by using option pricing models and then adding on the value obtained from discounted cashflow valuation.

Firms in the Process of Restructuring. Firms in the process of restructuring often sell some of their assets, acquire other assets, and change their capital structure and dividend policy. Some of them also change their ownership structure (going from publicly traded to private status) and management compensation schemes. Each of these changes makes estimating future cashflows more difficult and affects the riskiness of the firm. Using historical data for such firms can give a misleading picture of the firm's value. However, these firms can be valued, even in the light of the major changes in investment and financing policy, if future cashflows reflect the expected effects of these changes and the discount rate is adjusted to reflect the new business and financial risk in the firm.

Firms Involved in Acquisitions. There are at least two specific issues relating to acquisitions that need to be taken into account when using discounted cashflow valuation models to value target firms. The first is the thorny one of whether there is synergy in the merger and if its value can be estimated. It can be done, though it does require assumptions about the form the synergy will take and its effect on cashflows. The second, especially in hostile takeovers, is the effect of changing management on cashflows and risk. Again, the effect of the change can and should be incorporated into the estimates of future cashflows and discount rates and hence into value.

Private Firms. The biggest problem in using discounted cashflow valuation models to value private firms is the measurement of risk (to use in estimating discount rates), since most risk/return models require that risk parameters be estimated from historical prices on the asset being analyzed. Since securities in private firms are not traded, this is not possible. One solution is to look at the riskiness of comparable firms that are publicly traded. The other is to relate the measure of risk to accounting variables that are available for the private firm.

RELATIVE VALUATION

Basis for Approach

In relative valuation, the value of an asset is derived from the pricing of "comparable" assets, standardized using a common variable such as earnings, cashflows, book value, or revenues. One illustration of this approach is the use of an industry-average price/earnings ratio to value a firm, the assumption being that the other firms in the industry are comparable to the firm being valued and that the market, on average, prices these firms correctly. Another multiple in wide use is the price/book value ratio, with firms selling at a discount on book value relative to comparable firms being considered undervalued. The price/sales ratio is also used to value firms, with the average price/sales ratios of firms with similar characteristics being used for comparison. While these three

multiples are among the most widely used, there are other ratios that also play a role in analysis—price/cashflows, price/dividends, and market value/replacement value (Tobin's Q), to name a few.

Ways of Using Multiples

There are at least two ways in which an analyst can come up with the appropriate multiple to use in valuing a firm.

1. Using Fundamentals

The first approach relates multiples to fundamentals about the firm being valued—growth rates in earnings and cashflows, payout ratios, and risk. This approach to estimating multiples is equivalent to using discounted cashflow models, requiring the same information and yielding the same results. Its primary advantage is that it shows the relationship between multiples and firm characteristics and allows us to explore how multiples change as these characteristics change. For instance, what will be the effect of changing profit margins on the price/sales ratio? What will happen to price/earnings ratios as growth rates decrease? What is the relationship between price/book value ratios and return on equity?

2. Using Comparables

The second approach estimates multiples for a firm by looking at comparable firms. The key issue in this approach is the definition of a "comparable" firm. In theory, the analyst should control for all the variables that can influence the multiple. In practice, controlling for these variables can range from the naive (using industry averages) to the sophisticated (multivariate regression models where the relevant variables are identified and controlled for).

Applicability of Multiples and Limitations

The allure of multiples is that they are simple and easy to relate to. They can be used to obtain estimates of value quickly for firms and assets, and are particularly useful when there are a large number of comparable firms being traded on financial markets and the market is, on average, pricing these firms correctly.

By the same token, they are also easy to misuse and manipulate, especially when comparable firms are used. Given that no two firms are exactly similar in terms of risk and growth, the definition of "comparable" firms is a subjective one. Consequently, a biased analyst can choose a group of comparable firms to confirm his or her biases about a firm's value (see Illustration 2.2). While this potential for bias exists with discounted cashflow valuation as well, the analyst in discounted cashflow valuation is forced to be much more explicit about the assumptions which determine the final value. With multiples, these assumptions are often left unstated.

Illustration 2.2:　The potential for misuse with comparable firms

Assume that an analyst is valuing an initial public offering of a firm that manufactures computer software. At the same time,[3] the price/earnings (PE) ratios of other publicly traded firms, manufacturing software, are as follows:

Firm	Multiple
Adobe Systems	23.2
Autodesk	20.4
Broderbund	32.8
Computer Associates	18.0
Lotus Development	24.1
Microsoft	27.4
Novell	30.0
Oracle	37.8
Software Publishing	10.6
System Software	15.7
Average PE ratio	*24.0*

While the average PE ratio using the entire sample listed is 24, it can be changed markedly by removing a couple of firms from the group. For instance, if the two firms with the lowest PE ratios in the group (Software Publishing and System Software) are eliminated from the sample, the average PE ratio increases to 27. If the two firms with the highest PE ratios in the group (Broderbund and Oracle) are removed from the group, the average PE ratio drops to 21.

The other problem with using multiples based upon comparable firms is that it builds in errors (overvaluation or undervaluation) that the market might be making in valuing these firms. In Illustration 2.2, for instance, if the market has overvalued all computer software firms, using the average PE ratio of these firms to value an initial public offering will lead to an overvaluation of its stock. In contrast, discounted cashflow valuation is based upon firm-specific growth rates and cashflows and is less likely to be influenced by market errors in valuation.

CONTINGENT CLAIM VALUATION

Basis for Approach

A contingent claim or option is an asset that pays off only under certain contingencies—if the value of the underlying asset exceeds a prespecified value for a call option or is less than a prespecified value for a put option. Much work has been done in the last twenty years in developing models that value options, and these option pricing models can be used to value any assets that have option-like features.

Figure 2.1 illustrates the payoffs on call and put options as a function of the value of the underlying asset. An option can be valued as a function of the following variables: the current value and the variance in value of the underlying asset, the strike price and the time to expiration of the option, and the riskless interest rate. This was first established by Black and Scholes (1972) and has been extended and refined subsequently in numerous variants. While the Black-Scholes option pricing model ignored dividends and assumed that options would not be exercised early, it can be modified to allow for both. A discrete-time variant, the Binomial option pricing model, has also been developed to price options.

An asset can be valued as a call option if the payoffs on it are a function of the value of an underlying asset. If that value exceeds a prespecified level, the asset is worth the difference; if not, it is worth nothing. It can be valued as a put option if it gains value as the value of the underlying asset drops below a prespecified level and if it is worth nothing when the underlying asset's value exceeds that specified level.

Applicability and Limitations

There are several direct examples of securities that are options: primes and scores, traded on the American Stock Exchange; primes entitling investors to dividends and scores providing price appreciation; contingent value rights, which provide protection to stockholders in companies against stock price declines; and warrants, which are long-term call options issued by firms.

There are other assets that generally are not viewed as options but still share several option characteristics. Equity, for instance, can be viewed as a call option on the value of the underlying firm, with the face value of debt representing the strike price and the term of the debt measuring the life of the option. A patent can be analyzed as a call option on a product, with the invest-

FIGURE 2.1 Payoffs on Options as a Function of the Underlying Asset's Value

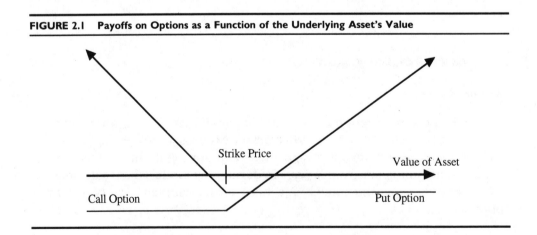

ment outlay needed to get the project going considered the strike price and the patent life becoming the time to expiration of the option.

There are limitations in using option pricing models to value long-term options on nontraded assets. The assumptions made about constant variance and dividend yields, which are not seriously contested for short-term options, are much more difficult to defend when options have long lifetimes. When the underlying asset is not traded, the inputs for the value of the underlying asset and the variance in that value cannot be extracted from financial markets and have to be estimated. Thus, the final values obtained from these applications of option pricing models have much more estimation error associated with them than do the values obtained in their more standard applications (to value short-term traded options).

CONCLUSION

There are three basic, though not mutually exclusive, approaches to valuation. The first is discounted cashflow valuation, where cashflows are discounted at a risk-adjusted discount rate to arrive at an estimate of value. The analysis can be done purely from the perspective of equity investors, by discounting expected cashflows to equity at the cost of equity, or it can be done from the viewpoint of all claimholders in the firm, by discounting expected cashflows to the firm at the weighted average cost of capital. The second is relative valuation, where the value of the equity in a firm is based upon the pricing of comparable firms relative to earnings, cashflows, book value, or sales. The third is contingent claim valuation, where an asset with the characteristics of an option is valued using an option pricing model. There should be a place for each among the tools available to any analyst interested in valuation.

QUESTIONS AND SHORT PROBLEMS

1. Discounted cashflow valuation is based upon the notion that the value of an asset is the present value of the expected cashflows on that asset, discounted at a rate that reflects the riskiness of those cashflows. Specify whether the following statements about discounted cashflow valuation are true or false, assuming that all variables are constant except for the variable discussed below:
 a. As the discount rate increases, the value of an asset increases.
 b. As the expected growth rate in cashflows increases, the value of an asset increases.
 c. As the life of an asset is lengthened, the value of that asset increases.
 d. As the uncertainty about the expected cashflows increases, the value of an asset increases.
 e. An asset with an infinite life (i.e., it is expected to last forever) will have an infinite value.

2. Why might discounted cashflow valuation be difficult to do for the following types of firms?
 a. A private firm whose owner is planning to sell it.
 b. A biotechnology firm with no current products or sales, but with several promising product patents in the pipeline.
 c. A cyclical firm during a recession.
 d. A troubled firm that has had significant losses and is not expected to get out of trouble for a few years.
 e. A firm in the process of restructuring that is selling some of its assets and changing its financial mix.
 f. A firm that owns a lot of valuable land that is currently unutilized.
3. The following are the projected cashflows to equity and to the firm over the next five years:

Year	Cashflows to Equity	Interest $(1 - t)$	Cashflows to Firm
1	$250.00	$90.00	$340.00
2	$262.50	$94.50	$357.00
3	$275.63	$99.23	$374.85
4	$289.41	$104.19	$393.59
5	$303.88	$109.40	$413.27
Terminal Value	$3,946.50		$6,000.00

(The terminal value is the value of the equity or firm at the end of year 5.)
The firm has a cost of equity of 12% and a cost of capital of 9.94%. Answer the following questions:
 a. What is the value of the equity in this firm?
 b. What is the value of the firm?
4. You are estimating the price/earnings multiple to use to value Paramount Communications by looking at the average price/earnings multiple of comparable firms. The following are the price/earnings ratios of firms in the entertainment business:

Firm	P/E Ratio	Firm	P/E Ratio
Disney (Walt)	22.09	PLG	23.33
Time Warner	36.00	CIR	22.91
King World Productions	14.10	GET	97.60
New Line Cinema	26.70	GTK	26.00

 a. What is the average P/E ratio?
 b. Would you use all the comparable firms in calculating the average? Why or why not?
 c. What assumptions are you making when you use the industry-average P/E ratio to value Paramount Communications?

ENDNOTES

1. The protection of limited liability should ensure that no stock will sell for less than zero. The price of such a stock can never be negative.

2. If these assets are traded on external markets, the market prices of these assets can be used in the valuation. If not, the cashflows can be projected, assuming full utilization of assets, and the value can be estimated.

3. These were the PE ratios for these firms at the end of 1992.

3

Risk and Return—Theory

The questions of how risk is measured, how it is rewarded, and how much risk to take on are fundamental to every investment decision, from asset allocation to valuation. It is also the area where there is the most debate among both theorists and practitioners about the right model to use. This chapter attempts to lay out, in broad terms, the different models for risk and return, including the intuition behind each model, the derivation, and implications for investors. It also provides a framework for comparative analysis across the models.

INGREDIENTS FOR A GOOD RISK AND RETURN MODEL

As a prelude to examining different models for risk and return, it is worth exploring what ingredients would make a model a good one. A good risk and return model should do the following:

(a) *Come up with a measure for risk that is universal.* A risk measure, to be useful, has to apply to all investments, whether stocks or bonds or real estate, since they all compete for the same investment dollar. A good risk and return model will come up with one measure of risk that applies to all investments, financial or real.

(b) *Specify what types of risk are rewarded and what types are not.* It is an accepted part of investments that not all risks are rewarded, and a good model should be able to distinguish between risk that is rewarded and risk that is not and provide an intuitive rationale for the distinction.

(c) *Standardize risk measures, to enable analysis and comparison.* While risk is always relative, a good risk measure should be standardized in such a way that an investor, when looking at the measure or risk for any one investment, should be able to come to a conclusion about the riskiness of that investment relative to others.

(d) *Translate the risk measure into an expected return.* One of the objectives in measuring risk is to come up with an estimate of an expected return for an investment. This expected return then becomes the benchmark which determines whether the investment is a "good" or "bad" one. It is not sufficient for a model to say that higher-risk investments should yield higher expected returns, without providing a specific estimate of the risk premium.

(e) *Work.* The ultimate test of a good model is that it works; that is, it provides a measure of risk that at least in the long term and across the cross-section of investments is positively correlated with returns. A stronger test would be to examine whether the actual returns, again in the long term, are equal to the expected returns derived from the model.

GENERAL MODELS FOR RISK AND RETURN

The awareness that risk matters is not new. Until recently, however, models for risk and return were largely subjective and varied widely across investors. Starting in the early 1950s, with the development of modern portfolio theory, risk and return models have been developed, which in addition to being more quantitative and specific in their predictions have also been more widely accepted. As the ensuing discussion will make clear, the debate has not ended and the search for a consensus, however elusive, continues.

The Capital Asset Pricing Model (CAPM)

The capital asset pricing model is still the standard against which other risk and return models are measured. Given its wide use on Wall Street and in corporate policy making, it has also become a magnet for criticism, some warranted and some not. The model itself has the advantage of being simple and intuitive, and provides some very strong and testable implications.

Derivation of the CAPM

The capital asset pricing model is built on the premise that the variance in returns is the appropriate measure of risk, but only that portion of variance that is not diversifiable is rewarded. The model measures this nondiversifiable variance using a beta estimate and links up expected returns to this beta estimate.

A. Measuring Risk

In the capital asset pricing model, investments are measured on two dimensions: The "expected return" on the investment comprises the reward, and the variance in anticipated returns comprises the risk on the investment. The variance on any investment measures the disparity between actual and expected returns. In statistical terms, the variance can be captured in the return distribution. The graph of the return distributions on two investments in Figure 3.1 illustrates this point.

In the CAPM world, variance is the only measure of risk. Investors given a choice between two investments with the same standard deviation but different expected returns will always pick the one with the higher expected return. In Figure 3.2 both investments have the same standard deviation, but investment A has a much higher expected return.

FIGURE 3.1 Return Distributions on Two Investments

FIGURE 3.2 Expected Returns on Two Investments with the Same Standard Deviation

While this choice may seem intuitive, it is not as straightforward as it seems. In the real investment world, investors often consider other dimensions of risk and return, beyond just the mean and the variance, in making their decisions. For instance, an investor may accept a higher-variance investment (over a lower-variance investment with the same expected returns) because it offers a higher probability of extraordinary payoffs. In statistical terms, this probability of a high payoff is measured by the "skewness" of returns, and there is some evidence that investors like positively skewed distributions.[1]

The assumptions about risk and return made by the CAPM are central to its derivation and implications, and have been defended by its proponents on two levels. At a theoretical level, the assumption that expected return is traded

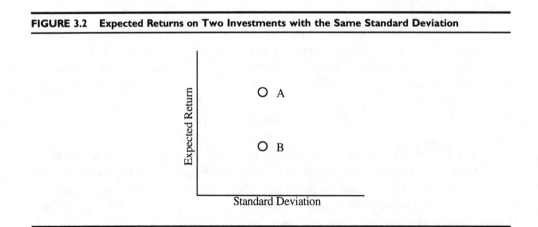

off against variance can be justified if investors possess utility functions where nothing else matters. (For instance, if investors have quadratic utility functions, they will not care about any of the other dimensions of return distributions.) This is, however, more an assumption of convenience than one that can be defended on empirical grounds, since there is no evidence that investors have such utility functions. The other way in which the expected return/variance tradeoff can be justified is by assuming that returns follow a normal distribution, in which case the entire distribution can be described in terms of the first two moments—the expected return and the variance. This assumption is also difficult to justify on empirical grounds, because the fact that investors have limited liability will result in return distributions that are positively skewed.

The other defense provided for the assumption that variance is the appropriate measure of risk is more believable, because it is based upon the empirical evidence related to average returns and variances on classes of assets over a long time period. For instance, an examination of returns on different classes of assets between 1926 and 1992 provides the results shown in Table 3.1. There is clear evidence here of a positive relationship between the variance in returns and the average returns on investment classes. It still requires a leap in logic to arrive at the CAPM assumption that variance is the only measure of risk that matters.

B. What Portion of the Risk is Rewarded?

While the capital asset pricing model defines variance as risk, not all variance is rewarded by financial markets with higher returns. The model is built on the tenet that some of the risk in any individual asset can be eliminated by diversifying across large numbers and classes of assets. This notion that diversification can reduce risk can be backed up on both intuitive and statistical grounds.

An Intuitive Rationale for the Argument that Diversification Reduces Risk. The risk in any asset comes from two sources: firm-specific actions, that affect primarily the prices of that asset, and marketwide movements, that affect all assets. The effects of firm-specific and marketwide actions can be either positive or negative. There

TABLE 3.1 Returns on Investment Categories (percent)

Series	Average Annual Return	Standard Deviation
Common stocks	12.40	20.60
Small stocks	17.60	35.00
Long-term corporate bonds	5.80	8.50
Long-term government bonds	5.20	8.60
U.S. Treasury bills	3.60	3.30
Inflation	3.20	4.70

is, however, a key difference between the two effects. The effects of firm-specific actions of individual assets in a portfolio can be either positive or negative for any period; that is, some firms can take actions that increase stock prices at the same time that other firms take actions that reduce stock prices. Thus, in large portfolios, it can be reasonably argued that this risk will average out to zero and thus not impact the overall value of the portfolio. The effects of marketwide movements are likely to be in the same direction for all investments in a portfolio, though some assets may be affected more than others. For instance, an increase in interest rates will, other things being equal, lower the values of most assets in a portfolio. Being more diversified does not eliminate this risk, though holding assets in different classes may reduce the impact.

While the argument that diversification reduces risk is incontestable, the assumption, which the CAPM makes, that diversifiable risk does not matter is not. It is based upon the presumption that the marginal investor in the market, who sets prices and therefore determines how risk is viewed, is well diversified and expects to be rewarded only for the nondiversifiable risk. If the marginal investor is not well diversified, diversifiable risk may affect prices and expected returns.

A Statistical Analysis of the Risk-Reducing Effects of Diversification. The effects of diversification on risk can be illustrated fairly dramatically by examining the effects on return variance of increasing the number of assets in a portfolio. The variance in a portfolio is determined by the variances of the individual assets in the portfolio and the covariances between pairs of assets in that portfolio. It is the covariance term, which captures how asset prices move together, that provides an insight into why and by how much diversification will reduce risk.

Variance of a Two-Asset Portfolio. Consider a portfolio of two assets. Asset A has an expected return of μ_A and a variance in returns of σ_A^2, while asset B has an expected return of μ_B and a variance in returns of σ_B^2. The correlation in returns between the two assets is ρ_{AB}. The expected returns and variance of a two-asset portfolio (p) can be written as a function of these inputs and the proportion of the portfolio going to each asset.

$$\mu_p = w_A\mu_A + (1 - w_A)\mu_B$$
$$\sigma_p^2 = w_A^2\sigma_A^2 + (1 - w_A)^2\sigma_B^2 + 2w_Aw_B\rho_{AB}\sigma_A\sigma_B$$

where w_A = proportion of the portfolio in asset A

The last term in the variance formulation is sometimes written in terms of the covariance in returns between the two assets, which is

$$\sigma_{AB} = \rho_{AB}\sigma_A\sigma_B$$

The savings that accrue from diversification are a function of the correlation coefficient. Other things remaining equal, the higher the correlation in returns between the two assets, the smaller are the potential benefits from diversification. Illustration 3.1 illustrates the savings from diversification.

Illustration 3.1: Variance of a two-asset portfolio

An investor is considering combining two assets in a portfolio and wants to evaluate the diversification benefits. Asset A has an expected return of 15% and a standard deviation in returns of 30%. Asset B has an expected return of 18% and a standard deviation in returns of 40%. The correlation in returns between the two assets is 0.25. The expected returns and variance of a portfolio of the two assets, with half of the portfolio invested in each, is as follows:

$$\mu_p = (.5 \times 15\%) + (.5 \times 18\%) = 16.5\%$$
$$\sigma_p^2 = (.5^2 \times 30^2) + (.5^2 \times 40^2) + (2 \times .5 \times .5 \times .25 \times 30 \times 40) = 775$$
$$\sigma_p = 27.84\%$$

The standard deviation of the portfolio is lower than the variances of the individual assets in the portfolio. The expected returns and standard deviation of the portfolio are graphed as a function of the portfolio weights in Figure 3.3.

A Minimum Variance Portfolio. In the example in Illustration 3.1, the variance of the portfolio of two assets was minimized when the weight on asset A was roughly 70%. A more precise estimate of the weights on the two assets needed to minimize variance can be obtained from the variance equation for the two-asset portfolio:

$$\sigma_p^2 = w_A^2\sigma_A^2 + (1 - w_A)^2\sigma_B^2 + 2w_A(1 - w_A)\rho_{AB}\sigma_A\sigma_B$$
$$\delta\sigma_p^2/\delta w_A = 2w_A\sigma_A^2 + (2w_A - 2)\sigma_B^2 + 2\rho_{AB}\sigma_A\sigma_B - 4w_A\rho_{AB}\sigma_A\sigma_B = 0$$

Solving for w_A^*, the weight on asset A which minimizes the variance of the portfolio:

$$w_A^* = (\sigma_B^2 - \rho_{AB}\sigma_A\sigma_B)/(\sigma_A^2 + \sigma_B^2 - 2\rho_{AB}\sigma_A\sigma_B)$$

FIGURE 3.3 Portfolio: Expected Returns and Standard Deviation (weights in parentheses)

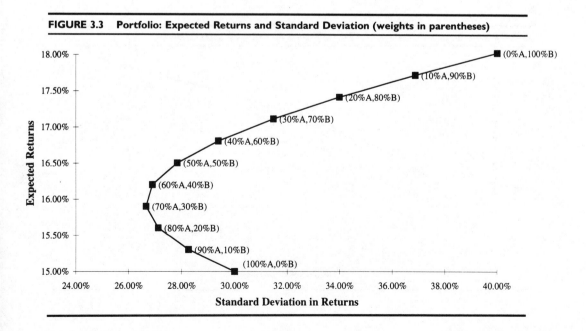

Substituting the values from Illustration 3.1:

$$w_A^* = (40^2 - [.25 \times 30 \times 40])/(30^2 + 40^2 - [2 \times .25 \times 30 \times 40])$$
$$= 1,300/(900 + 1,600 - 600) = 1,300/1,900 = 68.42\%$$

Thus, a portfolio with 68.42% invested in asset A and 31.58% invested in asset B will minimize the variance of the portfolio.

Correlation Coefficients and Portfolio Variance. The variance of the two-asset portfolio is clearly a function of the correlation in returns between the two assets. The greater the correlation in returns between the two assets, the smaller is the benefit from diversification. As long as the correlation is less than 1, there will be some benefit from diversification. Figure 3.4 shows the variance of the portfolio of two assets from Illustration 3.1, with half of the portfolio invested in each asset, as a function of the correlation in returns between the two assets.

Note, in this graph, that the standard deviation of the portfolio is halfway between the standard deviations of the individual assets (i.e., there is no gain from diversifying) when the correlation coefficient is 1. As the correlation coefficient declines, so does the standard deviation of the portfolio.

From two assets to three assets to n assets: If there is a diversification benefit of going from one asset to two, as the preceding discussion illustrates, there must be a benefit in going from two assets to three and from three to more. The variance of a portfolio of three assets can be written as a function of the variances of each of the three assets, the portfolio weights on each, and the correlations between pairs of the assets. The variance can be written as follows:

FIGURE 3.4 Standard Deviation of Portfolio as a Function of Correlation

$$\sigma_P^2 = w_A^2\sigma_A^2 + w_B^2\sigma_B^2 + w_C^2\sigma_C^2 + 2w_Aw_B\rho_{AB}\sigma_A\sigma_B + 2w_Aw_C\rho_{AC}\sigma_A\sigma_C$$
$$+ 2w_Bw_C\rho_{BC}\sigma_B\sigma_C$$

where w_A, w_B, w_C = portfolio weights on assets A, B, and C
σ_A^2, σ_B^2, σ_C^2 = variances of assets A, B, and C
ρ_{AB}, ρ_{AC}, ρ_{BC} = correlation in returns between pairs of assets (A&B, A&C, B&C)

Note that the number of covariance terms in the variance formulation has increased to three from one. This formulation can be extended to the more general case of a portfolio of n assets:

$$\sigma_P^2 = \sum_{i=1}^{i=n}\sum_{j=1}^{j=n} w_iw_j\rho_{ij}\sigma_i\sigma_j$$

Note that the covariance of an asset with itself is the variance of that asset. The number of terms in this formulation increases exponentially with the number of assets in the portfolio, largely because of the number of covariance terms that have to be considered. In general, the number of covariance terms can be written as a function of the number of assets:

Number of covariance terms = $n(n - 1)/2$

where n is the number of assets in the portfolio. Table 3.2 shows the relationship between number of covariance terms and number of assets in the portfolio.

This formulation can be used to estimate the variance of a portfolio and the effects of diversification on that variance. For purposes of simplicity, assume that the average asset has a standard deviation in returns of σ and that the average covariance in returns between any pair of assets is σ_{ij}. Furthermore, assume that the portfolio is always equally weighted across the assets in that portfolio. The variance of a portfolio of n assets can then be written as

$$\sigma_P^2 = n\left(\frac{1}{n}\right)^2\overline{\sigma}^2 + \frac{(n-1)}{n}\overline{\sigma}_{ij}$$

TABLE 3.2 Number of Covariance Terms as a Function of the Number of Assets in the Portfolio

Number of Assets	Number of Covariance Terms
2	1
5	10
10	45
20	190
100	4,950
1,000	499,500

Illustration 3.2: Variance of a portfolio as a function of the number of assets

Assume that the average asset has a variance in returns of 50% and that the average covariance in returns between any two assets is 10%. The variance of a portfolio of five assets can then be written as

$$\sigma_p^2 = (\tfrac{1}{5} \times 50\%) + (\tfrac{4}{5} \times 10\%) = 18\%$$

The variance of a portfolio of ten assets can be written as

$$\sigma_p^2 = (\tfrac{1}{10} \times 50\%) + (\tfrac{9}{10} \times 10\%) = 14\%$$

Note that as the number of assets in the portfolio increases, the variance of the portfolio approaches the average covariance, and the first term in the equation (which is the firm-specific component of risk) approaches 0. The marginal gains from diversification are illustrated in Figure 3.5, where variance is shown as a function of the number of assets in the portfolio. The marginal benefits of diversification decrease with the addition of each new asset to the portfolio. The variance of the portfolio drops from 50% to 11.60% as the number of assets increases from 1 to 25. Increasing the number of assets further provides only a small additional benefit, since the variance can drop to 10% at the minimum (with an infinite number of assets). Given that diversification can be costly, in terms of transactions and information costs, this provides a rationale for why most investors do not carry diversification to its logical limit and hold as many assets as there are available.

Return Optimization—Markowitz Portfolios. The fact that variances can be estimated for portfolios of a large number of assets suggests an approach to optimizing portfolio construction in the mean/variance framework on which the CAPM is devised. If an investor can specify the maximum amount of risk he or she is willing to take on (in terms of variance), the task of portfolio optimization becomes the maximization of expected returns subject to this level of risk.

FIGURE 3.5 Variance of Portfolio and Number of Assets

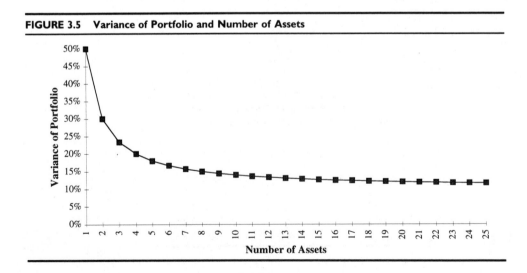

Alternatively, if an investor specifies his desired level of return, the optimum portfolio is the one that minimizes the variance subject to this level of return. These optimization algorithms can be written as follows:

Return Maximization *Risk Minimization*

Maximize Expected Return Minimize Return Variance

$$E(R_p) = \sum_{i=1}^{i=n} w_i\, E(R_i) \qquad\qquad \sigma_p^2 = \sum_{i=1}^{i=n}\sum_{j=1}^{j=n} w_i w_j \sigma_{ij}$$

$$\text{subject to } \sigma_p^2 = \sum_{i=1}^{i=n}\sum_{j=1}^{j=n} w_i w_j \sigma_{ij} \le \hat{\sigma}^2 \qquad E(R_p) = \sum_{i=1}^{i=n} w_i E(R_i) = E(\hat{R})$$

where $\hat{\sigma}^2$ = investor's desired level of variance
 $E(\hat{R})$ = investor's desired expected returns

The portfolios that emerge from this process are called Markowitz portfolios. Graphically, these portfolios are shown on the mean/standard deviation dimensions in Figure 3.6. The Markowitz approach to portfolio optimization, while intuitively appealing, suffers from two major problems. One is that it requires a very large number of inputs, since the covariances between pairs of assets are required input to estimate the variances of portfolios. While this may be manageable for small numbers of assets, it becomes less so when the entire universe of stocks or all investments is considered. The second problem is that the Markowitz approach ignores a very important asset choice that most investors have, that is, the choice of investing their money risklessly in default-free government securities in coming up with the optimum portfolios. The CAPM addresses these limitations and comes up with a far simpler approach to constructing optimal portfolios, while considering the riskless asset simultaneously.

There is one assumption that both the CAPM and the Markowitz portfolio optimization make that exposes them to some criticism. They both assume that there are no transactions and/or information costs[2] associated with diversification.

C. Optimal Portfolios with the Riskless Asset

Most investors have the choice of investing some or all of their money in a riskless asset, as a way of managing risk. By itself, the addition of one asset to the universe may seem trivial, but the riskless asset has some special characteristics that affect optimal portfolio choice for all investors.

(a) The riskless asset, by definition, has an expected return which will always be equal to the actual return; that is, there is no return variance.
(b) The absence of variance in the riskless asset, while risky assets' returns vary, make it uncorrelated with returns on any of these risky assets. As a consequence of this absence of correlation in returns, combinations of any risky asset or portfolio with the riskless asset will yield linear results for the standard deviation. To prove this, assume that the variance of the risky portfolio is

σ_r^2 and that w_r is the proportion of the overall portfolio invested to these risky assets. The balance is invested in a riskless asset, which has no variance and is uncorrelated with the risky asset. The variance of the overall portfolio can be written as

$$\sigma_p^2 = w_r^2 \sigma_r^2$$

$$\sigma_p = w_r \sigma_r$$

Note that the other two terms drop out and the standard deviation of the overall portfolio is linearly related to the proportion of the portfolio invested in the risky portfolio.

The significance of this result can be illustrated by returning to Figure 3.6 and adding the riskless asset to the choices available to the investor. The effect of this addition is shown in Figure 3.7.

Consider investor A, whose desired risk level is σ_A. This investor, instead of choosing portfolio A, the Markowitz portfolio, will choose to invest in a combination of the riskless asset and a much riskier portfolio (B), since he will be able to make a much higher return for the same level of risk. Note, however, that the expected return does not necessarily increase as the riskiness of the risky portfolio increases, and is maximized for combinations of the riskless asset and the risky portfolio (M), which is tangential to the riskless asset. Thus investor A will maximize expected returns if he puts some of his portfolio in the riskless asset and the balance in portfolio M. Investor B, whose desired risk level is σ_B, which happens to be equal to the standard deviation of the portfolio M, will choose to invest his entire portfolio in that portfolio. Investor C, whose desired risk level is σ_C, which exceed the standard deviation of portfolio M, will borrow money at the riskless rate and invest in the portfolio M.

These results are predicated on two assumptions. First, there exists a riskless asset, with the characteristics described above. Second, investors can lend and borrow at this riskless rate to arrive at their optimal allocations. There are variations of the CAPM that allow these assumptions to be relaxed and still arrive at conclusions which are consistent with the model.

Adding the riskless asset to the risky portfolios, developed using the Markowitz optimization techniques, yields very strong implications for optimal

FIGURE 3.6 Markowitz Portfolios

FIGURE 3.7 Introducing a Riskless Asset

investment strategy. All investors in this investment world described above will hold combinations of the riskless asset and the risky portfolio M, and the only difference across investors will be in the allocation decision, with more-risk-averse investors investing more in the riskless asset and less-risk-averse investors investing more in the risky portfolio M. Note, in Figure 3.7, that all the optimal portfolios lie on a straight line, emanating from the riskfree asset. This is the capital market line, and contains all possible combinations of the riskfree asset and the market portfolio.

The central role that the risky portfolio M plays in this process opens up the question of how this portfolio is constructed and what assets are incorporated in it. Since all investors in the CAPM universe are assumed to have the same information and they all hold the same portfolio, it has to include all traded assets, in proportion to their market values. Put another way, any asset that is not in this portfolio will be held by no investors and have no value. The fact that this portfolio includes all traded assets in the market is the reason this portfolio is called the "market portfolio." This should not be a surprising result, given the benefits of diversification and the absence of transactions costs in the CAPM. If diversification is good and there are no costs associated with adding more assets to the portfolio, the logical limit to diversification is to hold a small proportion of every traded asset in the economy.

Defenders of the CAPM should undoubtedly be troubled by the fact that investors in the real world hold a wide variety of portfolios and do not hold just the riskless asset and the market portfolio. Some of these variations can be ascribed to the presence of transactions costs and others to differences in information available to investors and to expectations about future returns. The question that remains, however, is whether these deviations from the predictions of the CAPM are serious enough to call into question its conclusions about how risk is measured. That remains an empirical question that will be addressed later in this chapter.

D. Measuring Nondiversifiable Risk with the Market Portfolio as the Standard

In a world where investors hold a combination of only two assets—the riskless asset and the market portfolio—the risk of any individual asset will be measured

relative to the market portfolio. In particular, the risk of any asset will be risk it adds on to the market portfolio. To arrive at the appropriate measure of this added risk, assume that σ_m^2 is the variance of the market portfolio prior to the addition of the new asset and that the variance of the individual asset being added to this portfolio is σ_i^2. The market value portfolio weight on this asset is w_i, and the covariance in returns between the individual asset and the market portfolio is σ_{im}. The variance of the market portfolio prior to and after the addition of the individual asset can then be written as

Variance prior to asset i being added $= \sigma_m^2$

Variance after asset i is added $= \sigma_{m'}^2 = w_i^2 \sigma_i^2$
$$+ (1 - w_i)^2 \sigma_m^2 + 2 w_i (1 - w_i) \text{Cov}_{im}$$

The market value weight on any individual asset in the market portfolio should be small since the market portfolio includes all traded assets in the economy. As a consequence, the first term in the equation should approach zero and the second term should approach σ_m^2, leaving the third term (Cov_{im}, the covariance) as the measure of the risk added by asset i.

Since the covariance of the market portfolio with itself is the market variance, the covariances of individual assets with the market portfolio can be standardized by dividing by the market variance. This standardized measure of nondiversifiable risk is the beta of the asset.

Beta of an asset i $= \text{Cov}_{im} / \sigma_m^2$

The beta of the market portfolio is 1 (since $\text{Cov}_{mm} = \sigma_m^2$); assets which are riskier than average (using this measure of risk) will have betas that exceed 1, and assets that are safer than average will have betas that are lower than 1. The riskless asset will have a beta of zero.

The expected return on an asset is linearly related to the beta of the asset. This follows from Figure 3.7, where all the optimal portfolios lay on the capital market line. In particular, the expected return on an asset can be written as a function of the riskfree rate, the beta of that asset:

$$E(R_i) = R_f + \beta_i (\text{risk premium on market portfolio}) = R_f + \beta_i (E[R_m] - R_f)$$

where $E(R_i) =$ expected return on asset i
$\quad R_f =$ riskfree rate
$\quad E(R_m) =$ expected return on market portfolio
$\quad \beta_i =$ beta of asset i

The relationship between betas and expected returns is captured in Figure 3.8. If the CAPM is true, all assets should fall on the security market line, which provides the expected return for any given beta.

Implications of the CAPM

The capital asset pricing model does make some strong assumptions, but it provides equally strong, and testable, implications:

FIGURE 3.8 Betas and Expected Returns: The Security Market Line (SML)

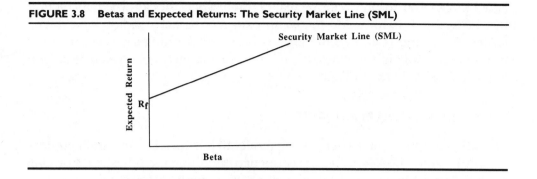

(a) All investors will allocate their wealth across two assets—the riskless asset and a market portfolio of all risky assets, held in proportion to their market value.

(b) The risk of any asset will be measured by how much risk it adds on to the market portfolio, and this added risk can be estimated using the covariance between the returns on the asset and the returns on the market portfolio. This covariance can be standardized by dividing by the market variance, to arrive at a beta for the asset.

(c) The expected return on any asset is linearly related to its beta; that is, the higher the beta, the higher the expected return.

Testing the CAPM

Does the capital asset pricing model work? Is beta a good proxy for risk and is it correlated with expected returns? The answers to these questions have been debated widely in the last two decades. The first tests that were done of the model suggested that betas and returns were positively related, though other measures of risk (such as variance) continued to explain differences in actual returns. This was attributed to limitations in the testing techniques. In 1977, Roll, in a seminal critique of the model's tests, suggested that since the market portfolio could never be observed, the CAPM could never be tested, and that all tests of the CAPM were therefore joint tests of the model and the market portfolio used in the tests.

In a more damning indictment, Fama and French (1992) examined the relationship between betas and returns between 1963 and 1990 and concluded that there is no relationship between the two. They also noted that two other variables, size and book value/market value, explain differences in returns across firms much better than beta and may in fact be better proxies for risk. These results have been contested on two fronts. First, Amihud, Christensen, and Mendelson (1992) used the same data, performed different statistical tests, and showed that betas do, in fact, explain returns during the time period. Second, Chan and Lakonishok (1993) looked at a much longer time series of returns from 1926 to 1991 and found that the positive relationship between betas and returns breaks down only in the period after 1982. They attribute this to indexing, which they argue has led the larger, lower-beta stocks in the Standard and

Poors (S&P) 500 to outperform smaller, higher-beta stocks. They also found that betas are a useful guide to risk in extreme market conditions, with the riskiest firms (the 10% with the highest betas) performing far worse than the market as a whole in the ten worst months for the market between 1926 and 1991. This is depicted in Figure 3.9.

The Arbitrage Pricing Model (APM)

The failure of the capital asset pricing model to adequately explain differences in returns across assets using betas opened the door for other asset pricing models. The leading candidate for an alternative model is the arbitrage pricing

FIGURE 3.9 Returns and Betas: Ten Worst Months Between 1926 and 1991 (all returns are negative)

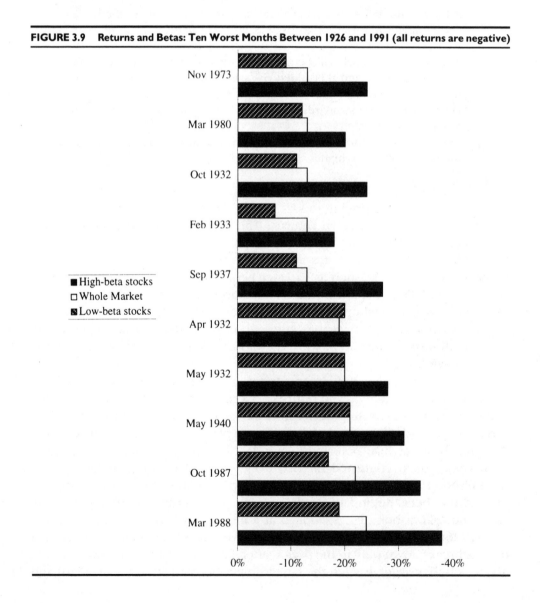

model (APM). The logic behind the APM is much the same as the logic behind the CAPM; that is, investors get rewarded for taking on nondiversifiable risk. In the CAPM, one factor (the sensitivity to the market portfolio) captures this nondiversifiable risk. The measure of this nondiversifiable risk in the APM, however, does not have to be a single factor but can come from multiple factors. The number and the identity of the factors are determined by the data on historical returns.

Derivation of the APM

The arbitrage pricing model is built on the simple premise that investors take advantage of arbitrage opportunities; that is, if two portfolios have the same exposure to risk but offer different expected returns, investors will buy the portfolio that has the higher expected returns, and in the process adjust the expected returns to equilibrium.

A. Decomposing Returns into Anticipated and Unanticipated Components

The return on any asset can be decomposed into two parts: a normal or expected return component that is predictable and an unanticipated component that is not, shown as follows:

$$R = R + U$$

where R is the expected component and U is the unexpected component of returns. It is the unanticipated component that creates the risk in investments.

B. The Source of Unanticipated Returns: Firm-Specific and Marketwide Risk

The "surprise" in returns comes from two sources. The first is firm-specific and covers information that affects primarily or only the firm. The second is marketwide and affects most or all investments, and includes unanticipated changes in a number of economic variables including gross national product, inflation rate, and interest rates. This may be incorporated into the return model above as follows:

$$R = R + m + \epsilon$$

where m is the marketwide component of unanticipated risk and ϵ is the firm-specific component. Note that this distinction is very similar to the distinction between firm-specific and marketwide risk made in the capital asset pricing model.

C. The Sources of Marketwide Risk

While both the capital asset pricing model and the arbitrage pricing model make a distinction between firm-specific and marketwide risk, they part ways when it comes to measuring the marketwide risk. The CAPM assumes that the market risk is captured in the market portfolio, whereas the APM sticks with economic fundamentals. It allows for multiple sources of marketwide risk, such

as unanticipated changes in gross national product, interest rates, and inflation, and measures the sensitivity of investments to these changes with factor betas. In general, the market component of unanticipated returns can be decomposed into economic factors, shown as follows:

$$R = R + m + \epsilon$$
$$= R + (\beta_1 F_1 + \beta_2 F_2 + \ldots + \beta_n F_n) + \epsilon$$

where β_j = sensitivity of investment to unanticipated changes in factor j
F_j = unanticipated change in factor j

Illustration 3.3: Decomposing returns using economic factors

Asset i is expected to have a return of 7% next year. There are four economic factors that drive returns, and the betas of asset i to each factor are given below:

Beta relative to factor 1 = 2.5

Beta relative to factor 2 = .5

Beta relative to factor 3 = −1.0

Beta relative to factor 4 = .8

The expected values for each of the factors are as follows:

Expected value for factor 1 = 4%

Expected value for factor 2 = 6%

Expected value for factor 3 = 0%

Expected value for factor 4 = 1.5%

Assume that the actual values for each of the factors are as follows:

Actual value for factor 1 = 6%

Actual value for factor 2 = 7%

Actual value for factor 3 = 1%

Actual value for factor 4 = 2%

The marketwide component for unanticipated returns will be as follows:

$$m = 2.5(6\% - 4\%) + .5(7\% - 6\%) - 1.0(1\% - 0\%)$$
$$+ .8(2\% - 1.5\%) = 4.9\%$$

If the firm-specific component for unanticipated returns is 3%, the total return for asset i is as follows:

$$R = 7\% + 4.9\% + 3\% = 14.9\%$$

D. The Effects of Diversification

The benefits of diversification have been discussed extensively in the section on the capital asset pricing model. The primary point of that discussion was that diversification of investments into portfolios eliminated firm-specific risk.

The arbitrage pricing model makes the same point and concludes that the return on a portfolio will not have a firm-specific component of unanticipated returns. The return on a portfolio can be written as the sum of two weighted averages: the weighted average of the anticipated returns in the portfolio and the weighted average of the factor betas, as follows:

$$R_p = (w_1 R_1 + w_2 R_2 + \ldots + w_n R_n) + (w_1 \beta_{1,1} + w_2 \beta_{1,2} + \ldots + w_n \beta_{1,n})F_1$$
$$+ (w_1 \beta_{2,1} + w_2 \beta_{2,2} + \ldots + w_n \beta_{2,n})F_2 + \ldots$$

where w_i = portfolio weight on asset i
\quad R_i = expected return on asset i
\quad $\beta_{j,i}$ = beta on factor j for asset i
\quad F_j = factor j

E. Expected Returns and Betas

The fact that the beta of a portfolio is the weighted average of the betas of the assets in the portfolio, in conjunction with the absence of arbitrage, leads to the conclusion that expected returns should be linearly related to betas. To see why, assume that there is only one factor and that there are three portfolios. Portfolio A has a beta of 2.0 and an expected return of 20%; portfolio B has a beta of 1.0 and an expected return of 12%; and portfolio C has a beta of 1.5 and an expected return of 14%. Note that the investor can put half his or her wealth in portfolio A and half in portfolio B and end up with a portfolio with a beta of 1.5 and an expected return of 16%. As a consequence, no investor will choose to hold portfolio C until the prices of assets in that portfolio drop and the expected return increases to 16%. By the same rationale, the expected returns on every portfolio should be a linear function of the beta, or there will be an opportunity for arbitrage. This argument can be extended to multiple factors, with the same results. Therefore, the expected return on an asset can be written as

$$E(R) = R_f + \beta_1(E[R_1] - R_f) + \beta_2(E[R_2] - R_f) + \ldots + \beta_n(E[R_n] - R_f)$$

where R_f = expected return on a zero-beta portfolio
\quad $E(R_j)$ = expected return on a portfolio with a factor beta of 1 for factor j and of
$\quad\quad$ 0 for all other factors

The terms in parentheses can be considered to be risk premiums for each of the factors in the model.

Note that the CAPM can be considered to be a special case of the APM where there is only one economic factor driving marketwide returns and the market portfolio is the factor.

$$E(R) = R_f + \beta_m(E[R_m] - R_f)$$

Multifactor Models for Risk and Return

The arbitrage pricing model's failure to identify specifically the factors in the model may be a strength from a statistical standpoint, but it is a clear weakness

from an intuitive standpoint. The solution seems simple: Replace the unidentified statistical factors with specific economic factors, and the resultant model should be intuitive while retaining much of the strength of the arbitrage pricing model. That is precisely what multifactor models do.

Deriving a Multifactor Model

Multifactor models are generally not based upon extensive economic rationale and are instead driven by the data. Once the number of factors has been identified in the arbitrage pricing model, the behavior of the factors over time can be extracted from the data. These factor time series can then be compared to the time series of macroeconomic variables, to see if any of the variables map on to the factors.

For instance, Chen, Roll, and Ross (1986) suggest that the following macroeconomic variables are highly correlated with the factors that come out of factor analysis: industrial production, changes in default premium, shifts in the term structure, unanticipated inflation, and changes in the real rate of return. These variables can then be correlated with returns to come up with a model of expected returns, with firm-specific betas calculated relative to each variable.

$$E(R) = R_f + \beta_{GNP}(E[R_{GNP}] - R_f) + \beta_i(E[R_i] - R_f) + \ldots + \beta_\delta(E[R_\delta] - R_f)$$

where β_{GNP} = beta relative to changes in industrial production (gross national product)

$E(R_{GNP})$ = expected return on a portfolio with a beta of 1 on the industrial production factor and 0 on all other factors

β_i = beta relative to changes in inflation

$E(R_i)$ = expected return on a portfolio with a beta of 1 on the inflation factor and 0 on all other factors

The costs of going from the arbitrage pricing model to a macroeconomic multifactor model can be traced directly to the errors that can be made in identifying the factors. The factors in the model can change over time, as will the risk premiums associated with each economic factor. For instance, oil price changes were a significant economic factor driving expected returns in the 1970s but are not as significant in other time periods. Using the wrong factor(s) or missing a significant factor in a multifactor model can lead to inferior estimates of cost of equity.

Another approach to developing multifactor models is developed in Fama and French (1992), where it is noted that actual returns over long time periods have been much more highly correlated with price/book value ratios and size. They suggest that these measures and similar ones developed from the data be used as proxies for risk and that the regression coefficients be used to estimate expected returns for investments. For instance, Fama and French report the following regression for monthly returns on stocks on the New York Stock Exchange, using data from 1963 to 1990:

$$R_t = 1.77\% - (.11 \times \ln[MV]) + (.35 \times \ln[BV/MV])$$

where MV = Market Value of equity
 BV = Book Value of equity

The values for market value of equity and book value/price ratios for individual firms, when plugged into this regression, should yield expected monthly returns. The reliability of the prediction, however, is open to question, since the regression coefficients change significantly from period to period and the variables themselves may explain returns in some periods and not in others.

A COMPARATIVE ANALYSIS OF RISK AND RETURN MODELS

All the risk and return models developed in this chapter have common ingredients. They assume that only marketwide risk is rewarded and derive the expected return as a function of measures of this risk. The capital asset pricing model makes the most assumptions but arrives at the simplest model, with only one factor driving risk and requiring estimation. The arbitrage pricing model makes fewer assumptions but arrives at a more complicated model, at least in terms of the parameters that require estimation. The CAPM can be considered to be a specialized case of the APM, where there is only one underlying factor and that underlying factor is completely measured by the market index. In general, the CAPM has the advantage of being a simpler model to estimate and to use, but it will underperform the richer APM when the company is sensitive to economic factors not well represented in the market index. For instance, oil companies, which derive most of their risk from oil price movements, tend to have low CAPM betas. Using an APM, where one of the factors may be capturing oil and other commodity price movements, will yield a better estimate of risk and higher cost of equity[3] for these firms.

The biggest intuitive block in using the APM is its failure to identify specifically the factors driving expected returns. While this may preserve the flexibility of the model and reduce statistical problems in testing, it does make it difficult to understand what the APM beta coefficients for a firm mean and how they will change as the firm changes (or restructures).

As the discussion at the end of the section on the CAPM made clear, the CAPM does not do very well at explaining differences in returns across firms, though predictions of its demise are premature. While multifactor models do better than the CAPM at explaining past returns, the comparison is a little unfair to the CAPM, since it constrains itself to explaining differences in returns using only one factor, while the other models allow themselves the freedom of more than one factor. When it comes to making predictions of expected returns in the future, the comparison provides a more ambiguous result, since the gains that can be made by having multiple factors can be offset by the errors associated with estimating both the factor loadings and the factor betas, especially for individual companies.[4] The continued use of the CAPM attests to both its intuitive appeal and its simplicity.

MODELS OF DEFAULT RISK

In contrast to the general risk and return models described previously, which focus on market risk rather than firm-specific risk, models of default risk examine the consequences of firm-specific default risk on expected returns. While the rationale for diversification can be used to explain why firm-specific risk will not be priced into expected returns, the same rationale does not apply for securities which have limited upside potential and much greater downside potential from firm-specific events. For instance, corporate bonds benefit only marginally from firm-specific events that increase the value of the firm and make it safer, while they bear the risk of any firm-specific events that lower the value of the firm and increase the probability of default. As a consequence, the expected return on a corporate bond is likely to reflect the firm-specific default risk of the firm issuing the bond.

A General Model of Default Risk

The default risk of a firm is a function, very broadly, of two variables: its capacity to generate cashflows from operations and its financial obligations[5]—including interest and principal payments. Keeping everything else equal,

- Firms which generate high cashflows relative to their financial obligations have lower default risk than firms which generate low cashflows relative to obligations. Thus, firms with significant assets in place, which generate high cashflows, will have lower default risk than firms that do not.
- The more stability there is in cashflows, the lower is the default risk in the firm. Firms which operate in predictable and stable businesses will have lower default risk than otherwise similar firms which operate in cyclicate and/or volatile businesses.

Most models of default risk use financial ratios to measure the cashflow coverage (i.e., the magnitude of cashflows relative to obligations) and control for industry effects, to capture the variability in cashflows.

Bond Ratings and Interest Rates

The most widely used measure of a firm's default risk is its bond rating, which is generally assigned by an independent ratings agency, using a mix of private and public information.

The Ratings Process

The process of rating a bond starts with the issuing company, requesting a rating from the ratings agency. The ratings agency collects information both from publicly available sources, such as financial statements, and from the company itself and makes a decision on the rating. The company, if it disagrees with the rating, is given the opportunity to present additional information. This process is presented schematically in Figure 3.10.

FIGURE 3.10 The Ratings Process

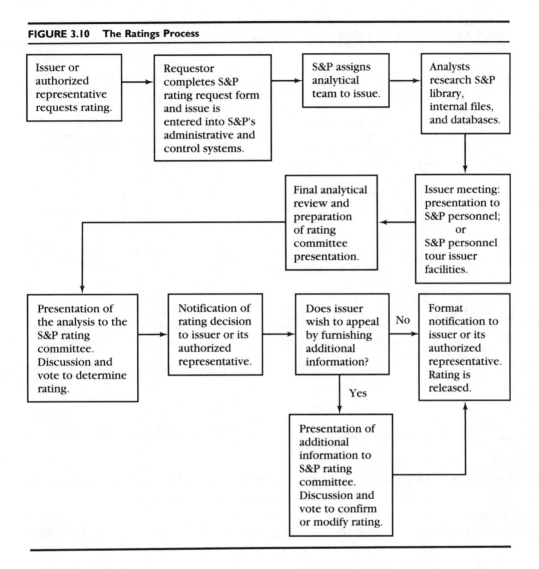

Description of Bond Ratings

The two major agencies rating corporate bonds are Standard and Poor's and Moody's. While the ratings are fairly similar, there are some differences in the ratings assigned by the two agencies. Table 3.3 provides a description of the bond ratings assigned by the two agencies. In financial markets, bonds with ratings of BBB or higher (Standard and Poor's) are considered "investment grade."

Determinants of Bond Ratings

The bond ratings assigned by ratings agencies are based primarily upon publicly available information, although private information conveyed by the firm to

TABLE 3.3 Index of Bond Ratings

Standard and Poor's		Moody's	
AAA	The highest debt rating assigned. The borrower's capacity to repay debt is extremely strong.	Aaa	Judged to be of the best quality with a small degree of risk.
AA	Capacity to repay is strong and differs from the highest quality only by a small amount.	Aa	High quality but rated lower than Aaa because margin of protection may not be as large or because there may be other elements of long-term risk.
A	Has strong capacity to repay; borrower is susceptible to adverse effects of changes in circumstances and economic conditions.	A	Bonds possess favorable investment attributes but may be susceptible to risk in the future.
BBB	Has adequate capacity to repay, but adverse economic conditions or circumstances are more likely to lead to risk.	Baa	Neither highly protected nor poorly secured; adequate payment capacity.
BB, B, CCC, CC	Regarded as predominantly speculative, BB being the least speculative and CC the most.	Ba	Judged to have some speculative risk.
		B	Generally lacking characteristics of a desirable investment; probability of payment small.
D	In default or with payments in arrears.	Caa	Poor standing and perhaps in default.
		Ca	Very speculative; often in default.
		C	Highly speculative; in default.

the rating agency does play a role. The rating that is assigned to a company's bonds will depend in large part on financial ratios that measure the capacity of the company to meet debt payments and generate stable and predictable cashflows. While a multitude of financial ratios exist, Table 3.4 summarizes some of the key ratios that are used to measure default risk.

There is a strong relationship between the bond rating a company receives and its performance on these financial ratios. Table 3.5 provides a summary of the median ratios from 1990 to 1992 for different Standard and Poor's ratings classes for manufacturing firms.

Not surprisingly, firms that generate income and cashflows that are significantly higher than debt payments, are profitable, and have low debt ratios are more likely to be highly rated than firms that do not have these characteristics. There will be individual firms whose ratings are not consistent with their financial ratios, because the ratings agency does bring subjective judgments into the final mix. Thus, a firm that performs poorly on financial ratios currently but is expected to improve its performance dramatically over the next period may receive a higher rating than justified by its current financials. For most firms, however, the financial ratios should provide a reasonable basis for guessing the bond rating.

TABLE 3.4 Financial Ratios Used to Measure Default Risk

Ratio	Description
Pretax Interest Coverage	= (Pretax Income from Continuing Operations + Interest Expense)/Gross Interest
EBITDA Interest Coverage	= EBITDA/Gross Interest
Funds from Operations/ Total Debt	= (Net Income from Continuing Operations + Depreciation)/ Total Debt
Free Operating Cashflow/ Total Debt	= (Funds from Operations − Capital Expenditures − Change in Working Capital)/Total Debt
Pretax Return on Permanent Capital	= (Pretax Income from Continuing Operations + Interest Expense)/(Average of Beginning of the year and End of the year of long and short term debt, minority interest and Shareholders Equity)
Operating Income/Sales (%)	= (Sales − COGS (before depreciation) − Selling Expenses − Administrative Expenses − R&D Expenses)/Sales
Long Term Debt/Capital	= Long Term Debt/(Long Term Debt + Equity)
Total Debt/Capitalization	= Total Debt/(Total Debt + Equity)

TABLE 3.5 Financial Ratios by Bond Rating, 1990–1992

	AAA	AA	A	BBB	BB	B	CCC
Pretax interest coverage	17.65	7.62	4.14	2.49	1.50	0.92	0.68
EBITDA interest coverage	21.03	10.52	6.17	4.24	2.60	1.87	1.16
Funds from operations/ Total debt (percent)	120.1	65.3	37.0	26.3	15.5	9.8	5.5
Free operating cashflow/ Total debt (percent)	42.3	28.0	13.6	6.1	3.2	1.6	.8
Pretax return on permanent capital (percent)	31.9	20.6	15.6	10.9	10.9	6.9	4.6
Operating income/Sales (percent)	22.2	16.3	15.1	12.6	12.7	11.9	12.1
Long-term debt/ Capital (percent)	12.5	23.3	34.7	43.8	59.3	59.9	69.3
Total debt/ Capitalization (percent)	21.9	32.7	40.3	48.8	66.2	71.5	71.2

Bond Ratings and Interest Rates

The interest rate on a corporate bond should be a function of its default risk, which is measured by its rating. If the rating is a good measure of the default risk, higher-rated bonds should be priced to yield lower interest rates than lower-rated bonds. This "default spread" will vary by maturity of the bond and can also change from period to period, depending upon economic conditions.

Multiple Discriminant Analysis of Default Risk

Since bond ratings are based primarily upon financial data, and more specifically upon financial ratios, it is not difficult to visualize other approaches to estimating default risk that use financial ratios. One approach is multiple discriminant analysis, where an attempt is made to combine several financial ratios into a predictive model. There are three basic steps involved in this approach. First, firms in a particular time period are classified into two groups: firms that defaulted on their financial obligations and firms that did not. Second, data is collected on a set of financial ratios, specified by the researcher, for firms in each group. Third, discriminant analysis derives the linear combination of these ratios which best discriminates between the groups. The most widely cited example of multiple discriminant analysis is by Altman (1968), who derived a discriminant function Z as a function of five financial ratios: working capital as a percentage of total assets, retained earnings as a percentage of total assets, earnings before interest and taxes as a percentage of total assets, market value of equity as a percentage of book value of debt, and sales as a percentage of total assets. Using a sample of 66 firms, half of which went into bankruptcy, he arrived at the following discriminant function:

$$Z = .012X_1 + .014X_2 + .033X_3 + .006X_4 + .999X_5$$

where X_1 = Net Working Capital/Total Assets
X_2 = Retained Earnings/Total Assets
X_3 = Earnings before Interest and Taxes/Total Assets
X_4 = Market Value of Equity/Book Value of Liabilities
X_5 = Sales/Total Assets

In applying this function, Altman found that Z-scores less than 1.81 indicated a high probability of bankruptcy, whereas Z-scores higher than 3.00 indicated a low probability. Z-scores between 1.81 and 3.00 were in the gray area. These Z-scores are also correlated with bond ratings. Altman and others have extended this approach to include other variables (cashflow ratios, noncapitalized leases), specialized industries, and international settings, and claim a high degree of predictive accuracy for their models. While the models have been criticized for the ad hoc way in which ratios are included (since no theory drives the choice of the ratios), the difficulty of obtaining matched pairs of bankrupt and healthy firms in the same industry, and the selection bias implicit in choosing firms that have gone bankrupt and looking backward over time, they are simple and provide signals of potential problems in the firm.

CONCLUSION

The notion that risk is a "negative" and needs to be rewarded is not contestable, though the precise model for estimating risk and reward is still a subject of debate. For equity investments, the models of risk and return that are widely used all measure risk in terms of nondiversifiable risk, although the capital asset pricing model measures it with one "market" factor, whereas the arbitrage pricing and multifactor models use several factors. For debt investments, where the holders have limited upside potential and significant downside risk, models of default risk are used to obtain estimates of appropriate returns.

While this chapter provides a background to the intuition behind and the assumptions underlying models of risk, the next chapter will look at the practical issues of how to estimate and use these models and how decisions made by firms affect their risk parameters.

QUESTIONS AND SHORT PROBLEMS

1. Assume that the assumptions underlying the CAPM hold. Evaluate whether the following statements are true or false.
 a. A firm with high variance will have a higher beta than one with lower variance.
 b. A portfolio is efficient if it has no unsystematic risk.
 c. A firm that is highly correlated with the market will have a higher beta than one that is less correlated.
 d. If the variance of the overall market goes up, the betas of all firms will go down.
 e. A well-managed firm will have a lower beta than a badly managed firm.
 f. The market portfolio is efficient and therefore contains only the best stocks in the market.
 g. A risk lover will hold the riskiest stocks in the market, whereas a risk-averse investor will hold the safest stocks.
 h. If the riskless rate increases, the slope of the capital market line will decrease.
2. You are in a world where there are only two assets, gold and stocks. You are interested in investing your money in one, the other, or both assets. Consequently, you collect the following data on the returns on the two assets over the last six years:

	Gold	Stock Market
Average return	8%	20%
Standard deviation	25%	22%
Correlation	−.4	

 a. If you were constrained to pick just one, which one would you choose?
 b. A friend argues that this wrong. He says that you are ignoring the big payoffs that you can get on gold. How would you go about alleviating his concern?
 c. How would a portfolio composed of equal proportions in gold and stocks do in terms of mean and variance?
 d. You now learn that GPEC (a cartel of gold-producing countries) is going to

vary the amount of gold it produces with stock prices in the United States. (They will produce less gold when stock prices are up and more stock prices are down.) What effect will this have on your portfolios? Explain.

3. You have just learned about the Markowitz frontier and are eager to put it into practice.
 a. What steps would you have to go through in terms of
 • defining universe?
 • data requirements?
 • calculations and statistics?
 b. Assume you have succeeded in deriving the frontier. How would you go about providing investment advice to naive investors who come to you for recommendations? If you use this as a basis for your investment recommendations, what assumptions are you making?
 c. How would the frontier that you have calculated change if
 • a massive disaster wiped out a hundred firms that used to be part of your universe?
 • you ignored foreign stocks initially, but now added them on?
 • A breakthrough in technology occurs that cuts in half the cost of making computer chips?

4. Assume that the average variance of return for an individual security is 50 and that the average covariance is 10. What is the expected variance of a portfolio of 5, 10, 20, 50, and 100 securities? How many securities need to be held before the risk of a portfolio is only 10% more than the minimum?

5. The capital asset pricing model has been attacked on several different dimensions. Summarize the criticism of the CAPM and evaluate whether it is justified.

6. You are comparing the arbitrage pricing model to the capital asset pricing model. What are the similarities between the two models? What are the differences?

7. You are estimating the expected returns for a stock using both the CAPM and the arbitrage pricing model.
 a. Under what conditions would you get the same expected return?
 b. If the expected returns are different, how would you explain the difference?

ENDNOTES

1. One rationale that has been advanced for individuals playing the lottery or indulging in other "negative-sum" games, where the expected returns are negative and the variance in returns is high, is their preference for skewness.

2. Transactions and information costs can be built into the Markowitz optimization algorithms explicitly. There are, however, both conceptual and practical problems associated with doing so, since these costs are likely to vary from asset to asset, from investor to investor, and for different investment time horizons.

3. Weston and Copeland (1992) used both approaches to estimate the cost of equity for oil companies in 1989 and came up with 14.4% with the CAPM and 19.1% using the APM.

4. Estimating these parameters for a portfolio is easier because the errors can average out over a large number of investments.

5. Financial obligation refers to any payment that the firm has legally obligated itself to make, such as interest and principal payments. It does not include discretionary cashflows, such as dividend payments or new capital expenditures, which can be deferred or delayed without legal consequences, although there may be economic consequences.

4

Estimation of Discount Rates

The models of risk and return developed in the prior chapter are useful only if the risk parameters needed for the models can be estimated with relative ease and if these parameters can then be used to predict expected returns. This chapter looks at the contexts in which these valuation models can be used, the process of estimating risk parameters in each model, and the determinants of these parameters. It also develops two alternative measures of discount rates: the cost of equity and the cost of capital, and provides a contrast between the two.

COST OF EQUITY

The cost of equity is the rate of return that investors require to make an equity investment in a firm. There are two approaches to estimating the cost of equity: The first is to use a risk and return model, and the second is to apply a dividend growth model.

Using Risk and Return Models

The Capital Asset Pricing Model

As the discussion in Chapter 3 makes clear, the CAPM measures risk in terms of nondiversifiable variance and relates expected returns to this risk measure. The nondiversifiable risk for any asset is measured by its beta, which can be used to yield an expected return.

$$E(R) = R_f + \text{Equity Beta}(E[R_m] - R_f)$$

where R_f = riskfree rate
$E(R_m)$ = expected return on the market index

The return that investors expect to make on an equity investment, given its risk, becomes the cost of equity to managers in that firm.

A. Using the CAPM

The following inputs are required to use the CAPM: the current riskfree rate, the expected return on the market index, and the beta of the asset being ana-

lyzed. There are two practical issues in using the CAPM: 1) How do we measure the risk premium to be used in calculating the expected return on the market index? 2) What is the correct riskfree rate to use in the model?

1. Measurement of the Risk Premium. The risk premium used in the CAPM is generally based upon historical data, and the premium is defined to be the difference between average returns on stocks and average returns on riskfree securities over the measurement period. Two measurement questions remain: How long should the measurement period be? Should arithmetic or geometric averages be used to compute the risk premium? While measurement periods ranging from 10 years to longer (beginning in 1926) are used in practice, the use of the longest possible historical period seems justified absent any trend in premiums over time. In much of the analysis in this book, the average premiums based upon data from 1926 to 1990 will be used for U.S. stocks.

There is just as much disagreement among practitioners on the usage of the arithmetic versus the geometric mean. Those who use the arithmetic mean argue that it is much more consistent with the mean-variance framework of the CAPM and a better predictor of the premium in the next period. Use of the geometric mean is justified on the grounds that it takes into account compounding and that it is a better predictor of the average premium in the long term. There can be dramatic differences in premiums based upon the choices made at this stage, as illustrated in Table 4.1 based upon historical data on stock and bond returns.

The geometric mean generally yields lower premium estimates than the arithmetic mean. In the context of valuation, where cashflows over a long time horizon are discounted back to the present, the geometric mean provides a better estimate of the risk premium. Thus, the premium of 5.50% (the geometric mean of the premium over Treasury bonds) is used throughout this book for calculating expected returns.

While historical data on stock returns is most easily available and accessible in the United States, the premiums for other countries are updated in Ibbotson and Brinson. Reliable historical data are not available for as long a time period as is available for the United States. Table 4.2 shows risk premiums around the world. The premium earned by stocks over Treasury bonds has been much lower in the European markets (not counting the United Kingdom) than in

TABLE 4.1 Magnitude of the Risk Premium
(percent)

Historical Period	Stocks–Treasury Bills		Stocks–Treasury Bonds	
	Arithmetic	Geometric	Arithmetic	Geometric
1926–1990	8.41	6.41	7.24	5.50
1962–1990	4.10	2.95	3.92	3.25
1981–1990	6.05	5.38	.13	.19

TABLE 4.2 Risk Premiums around the World, 1970–1990
(percent)

Country	Stocks	Government Bonds	Risk Premium
Australia	9.60	7.35	2.25
Canada	10.50	7.41	3.09
France	11.90	7.68	4.22
Germany	7.40	6.81	.59
Italy	9.40	9.06	.34
Japan	13.70	6.96	6.74
Netherlands	11.20	6.87	4.33
Switzerland	5.30	4.10	1.20
United Kingdom	14.70	8.45	6.25
United States	10.00	6.18	3.82

either the United States or Japan. There are three fundamentals that determine the size of this premium:

(a) *Variance in the underlying economy:* Risk premiums will be larger in econo-mies that have more volatility associated with them. Thus the premiums for emerging markets, with their higher-growth, higher-risk economies, will be larger than the premiums for developed markets.

(b) *Political risk:* Risk premiums will be larger in those markets where there is potential for political instability, which translates into economic instability.

(c) *Structure of the market:* There are some markets where the risk premium for investing in stocks will be lower because the companies that are listed on the exchange are large, diversified, and stable (Germany and Switzerland would be good examples). In general, as smaller and riskier companies get listed on the market, the average risk premium for investing in stocks will increase.

Using the premium for stocks over bonds of 5.50% for the United States as the benchmark, these fundamentals would point toward a larger premium for markets that are more risky than the United States on any or all of these counts and a smaller premium for markets that are less risky. The premiums that are used in this book for various markets are as follows:

Financial Market Characteristics	Premium[1] over Government Bond Rate
Emerging markets with political risk (South American, East European markets)	8.5%
Emerging markets (Asian markets other than Japan; Mexico)	7.5%
Developed markets with wide listings (United States, Japan, United Kingdom)	5.5%
Developed markets with limited listings (Western European markets other than Germany and Switzerland)	4.5–5.5%
Developed markets with limited listings and stable economies (Germany, Switzerland)	3.5–4%

2. Variants on the Riskfree Rate.

Variant 1: A short-term government security rate is used as the riskfree rate, and the historical premium earned by a broad equity market index over and above this security rate is used to estimate the expected return on the market. The cost of equity thus obtained is then used as the discount rate for each year's cashflows.

Illustration 4.1: Using the CAPM—current Treasury bill rate: Pepsi Cola

In December 1992, Pepsi Cola Corporation had a beta of 1.06.[2] The Treasury bill rate at that time was 3.35%. The cost of equity can be calculated as follows:

Cost of Equity = 3.35% + (1.06 × 6.41%) = 10.14%

The market premium of 6.41% was based upon historical data and is the premium earned by stocks, on average (geometric), over Treasury bills. The cost of equity of 10.14% will be used to discount dividends and cashflows to equity and to obtain the value of Pepsi stock.

Variant 2: The current short-term government security rate and the market's historical premium are used to calculate the cost of equity for the first period (year). The forward rates built into the term structure are used as estimates of expected riskfree rates in future time periods, which are used to calculate the cost of equity for future years.

Illustration 4.2: Using the CAPM—forward rates: Pepsi Cola

In Illustration 4.1, assume, in addition to the current Treasury bill rate of 3.35%, that the following forward rates are built into the term structure:

1 year = 4.0% 2 year = 4.4% 3 year = 4.7% 4 year = 5.0%

Using these forward rates to compute costs of equity,

Cost of Equity for year 1 = 3.35% + (1.06 × 6.41%) = 10.14%
Cost of Equity for year 2 = 4% + (1.06 × 6.1%) = 10.47%
Cost of Equity for year 3 = 4.4% + (1.06 × 5.9%) = 10.65%
Cost of Equity for year 4 = 4.7% + (1.06 × 5.8%) = 10.85%
Cost of Equity for year 5 = 5% + (1.06 × 5.7%) = 11.04%

Notice that the market premiums are lower for future years, reflecting the smaller historical premiums[3] earned by stocks over forward rates (compared to the premium over the spot Treasury bill rate).

Variant 3: The current long-term government bond rate (with the duration of the bond matched up to the duration of the asset) is used as the riskfree rate, and the historical premium earned by a broad market index above this long-term government security rate is used to estimate the expected return on the market. The cost of equity, calculated using these inputs, is used as the discount rate for each year's cashflows.

Illustration 4.3: Using the CAPM—current Treasury bond rate: Pepsi Cola

In December 1992, the 30-year bond rate was 7%. The premium that should be used here to calculate the expected return on the market is the one earned by stocks over Treasury bonds, not Treasury bills. Between 1926 and 1990, this premium was 5.5%. The cost of equity for Pepsi Cola Corporation, with a beta of 1.06, can be written as follows:

Cost of Equity $= 7\% + (1.06 \times 5.5\%) = 12.83\%$

Illustration 4.4: Comparing costs of equity across countries: Telecommunication companies

The costs of equity can be different for companies in the same line of business, operating in different countries, either because of differences in interest rates or risk premiums. The following table compares the costs of equity of telecommunication companies in different parts of the world.

Country	Company	10-year Bond Rate (percent)	Beta	Risk Premium (percent)	Expected Return (percent)
Italy	STET	8.98	1.00	4.50	13.48
Canada	BCE	7.09	.75	5.50	11.22
Spain	Telefonica	9.70	.98	5.50	15.09
United Kingdom	British Telecom	7.19	.75	5.50	11.32
United States of America	AT&T	6.50	.95	5.50	11.73
Mexico	Tele de Mexico	12.50	1.11	7.50	20.83
Japan	NT&T	4.30	1.13	5.50	10.52

Note, though, that a lower cost of equity does not necessarily translate into an advantage for a firm, since expected inflation rates and growth rates are different in these markets.

Which variant works best? There are believable rationale that can be provided, on both theoretical and intuitive grounds, for all three variants. The first variant

can be backed up by arguments that the CAPM is a one-period model of risk and return and that current short-term rates are reasonable predictors of future short-term rates. The second variant is based upon the superiority of forward rates in forecasting future short-term rates. The final variant takes a strict view of matching the duration of the riskfree security with the duration of the asset being analyzed.

At a practical level, in periods when the term structure follows historical patterns in the relationship between short rates and long rates and the beta is close to 1, all three variants will provide similar results. When the term structure deviates from historical patterns and/or the betas are significantly different from 1, the three variants will provide different answers. If the yield curve is more upward sloping than normal, the discount rates obtained from using long-term rates will be higher, leading to lower estimates of value. The reverse will be true if the yield curve is less upward sloping than normal or if it is downward sloping.

In most of the valuations done in this book, the third variant, using the long-term bond rate as the riskless rate and the historical premium between stocks and Treasury bonds as the risk premium, is used.

Standard Procedures for Estimating CAPM Parameters. The standard procedure for estimating betas is to regress stock returns (R_j) against market returns (R_m):

$$R_j = a + bR_m$$

where a = intercept from the regression
 b = slope of the regression = covariance (R_j, R_m)$/\sigma_m^2$

The *slope* of the regression corresponds to the beta of the stock and measures the riskiness of the stock. The *intercept* of the regression provides a simple measure of performance during the period of the regression, relative to the CAPM.

$$R_j = R_f + \beta(R_m - R_f)$$
$$\quad = R_f(1 - \beta) + \beta R_m \qquad \text{: Capital Asset Pricing Model}$$
$$R_j = a + bR_m \qquad \text{: Regression Equation}$$

Thus a comparison[4] of the intercept *(a)* to $R_f(1 - \beta)$ should provide a measure of the stock's performance at least relative to the CAPM.

If a $> R_f(1 - \beta)$... Stock did better than expected during regression period.
 a $= R_f(1 - \beta)$... Stock did as well as expected during regression period.
 a $< R_f(1 - \beta)$... Stock did worse than expected during regression period.

The final statistic that emerges from the regression that is useful is the *R-squared* (R^2) of the regression. While the statistical explanation of the R-squared is that it provides a measure of the goodness of fit of the regression, the financial rationale for the R-squared is that it provides an estimate of the proportion of the risk (variance) of a firm that can be attributed to market risk; the balance ($1 - R^2$) can be attributed to firm-specific risk.

FIGURE 4.1 Returns on Intel vs. S&P 500, 1989–1993

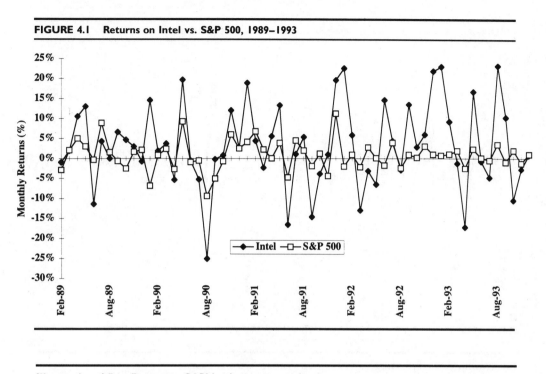

Illustration 4.5: Estimating CAPM risk parameters: Intel

Intel Corporation is one of the world's leading manufacturers of integrated circuits primarily for personal computers. Figure 4.1 graphs monthly returns on Intel against returns on the S&P 500 index from January 1989 to December 1993.

The regression statistics for Intel are as follows:

(a) *Slope of the regression = 1.39;* this is Intel's beta, based upon returns from 1989 to 1993. Using a different time period for the regression or different return intervals (weekly or daily) for the same period can result in a different beta.

(b) *Intercept of the regression = 2.09%;* this is a measure of Intel's performance, when it is compared with $R_f(1 - \beta)$. The monthly riskfree rate (since the returns used in the regression are monthly returns) between 1989 and 1993 averaged 0.4%, resulting in the following estimate for the performance:

$$R_f(1 - \beta) = .4\%(1 - 1.39) = -.16\%$$
$$\text{Intercept} - R_f(1 - \beta) = 2.09\% - (-.16\%) = 2.25\%$$

This analysis suggests that Intel performed 2.25% better than expected, where expectations are based upon the CAPM, on a monthly basis between January 1989 and December 1993. This results in an annualized excess return of approximately 30.6%.

(c) *R-squared of the regression = 22.90%;* this statistic suggests that 22.90% of the risk (variance) in Intel comes from market sources (interest rate risk, inflation risk, etc.), and that the balance of 77.10% of the risk comes from firm-specific components. The latter should be diversifiable and therefore unrewarded in the CAPM.

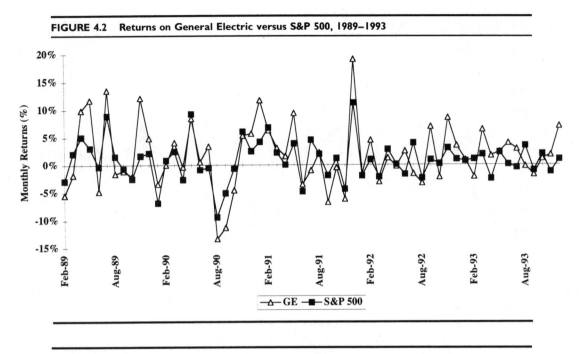

FIGURE 4.2 Returns on General Electric versus S&P 500, 1989–1993

Illustration 4.6: Estimating CAPM risk parameters: General Electric

General Electric is one of the largest and most diversified industrial companies in the world, with three core areas of business: technology, which includes aircraft engines, plastics, medical systems, and factory automation; services—financial, broadcasting, and communications; and core manufacturing, which includes appliances, lighting, and industrial and power systems. Figure 4.2 graphs monthly returns on General Electric against returns on the S&P 500 index from January 1989 to December 1993.
The regression statistics for GE are as follows:

(a) *Slope of the regression = 1.26;* this is GE's beta, based upon returns from 1989 to 1993. Using a different time period for the regression or different return intervals (weekly or daily) for the same period can result in a different beta.

(b) *Intercept of the regression = 0.69%;* this is a measure of GE's performance, when it is compared with $R_f(1 - \beta)$. The monthly riskfree rate (since the returns used in the regression are monthly returns) between 1989 and 1993 averaged 0.4%, resulting in the following estimate for the performance:

$$R_f(1 - \beta) = .4\%(1 - 1.26) = -.10\%$$
$$\text{Intercept} - R_f(1 - \beta) = .69\% - (-.10\%) = .79\%$$

This analysis suggests that GE performed 0.79% better than expected, where expectations are based upon the CAPM, on a monthly basis between January 1989 and December 1993. This results in an annualized excess return of approximately 9.90%.

(c) *R-squared of the regression = 60.99%;* this statistic suggests that 60.99% of the risk (variance) in GE comes from market sources (interest rate risk, inflation risk, etc.), and that the balance of 39.01% of the risk comes from firm-specific components.

Estimation Issues. There are four decisions that the analyst has to make in setting up the regression described above. The first one is the *length of the estimation period;* most estimates of betas, including those by Value Line and Standard and Poors, use five years of data, while Bloomberg uses two years of data. The tradeoff is simple. A longer estimation period provides more data, but the firm itself might have changed in its risk characteristics over the time period. For instance, using data from 1980 to 1992 to estimate betas for Apple Computer might increase the amount of data available, but it will lead to a beta estimate that is much higher than the true beta, since Apple was a smaller and riskier firm in the early 1980s.

The second estimation issue relates to the *return interval.* Returns on stocks are available on an annual, monthly, weekly, daily, and even an intra-day basis. Using daily or intra-day returns will increase the number of observations in the regression, but it opens the estimation process to a significant bias[5] in beta estimates related to nontrading. For instance, the betas estimated for small firms, which are more likely to suffer from nontrading, are biased downward when daily returns are used. Using weekly or monthly returns can reduce the nontrading bias[6] significantly.

The third estimation issue relates to the choice of a *market index* to use in the regression. The standard practice used by most beta estimation services is to estimate the betas of a company relative to the index of the market in which its stock trades. Thus, the betas of German stocks are estimated relative to the Frankfurt DAX, British stocks relative to the FTSE, Japanese stocks relative to the Nikkei, and U.S. stocks relative to the NYSE composite. While this may give an estimate that is a reasonable measure of risk for the parochial investor, it may not be the best approach for an international or cross-border investor, who would be better served with a beta estimated relative to an international index.

The fourth estimation issue relates to whether the betas obtained from regressions should be *adjusted* to reflect the likelihood of estimation errors and the tendency of betas to regress toward the average (either of the industry or the overall market). Most published betas use variants of a statistical technique that shrinks betas toward 1, based upon the standard error of the regression beta estimate—the larger the error, the greater the shrinkage. The gains from using these techniques are large when daily returns are used to estimate betas, but become smaller as longer return intervals are used.

Determinants of Betas. The beta of a firm is determined by three variables: the type of business(es) the firm is in, the degree of operating leverage in the firm, and the firm's financial leverage.

Type of business: Since betas measure the risk of a firm relative to a market index, the more sensitive a business is to market conditions, the higher is its beta. Thus cyclical firms can be expected to have higher betas, other things remaining equal, than noncyclical firms. When a firm operates in more than

one business area, its beta will be the weighted average of the betas of its different business lines, with the weights based upon the market value of each.

Illustration 4.7: Beta of a firm with several business lines: General Motors

In 1986, General Motors Corp. had three major divisions: the GM Automotive division, the Hughes Aircraft division, and GM Acceptance Corporation. The betas of each division and their market values are listed below:

Division	Beta	Market Value (millions)	Weight (percent)
GM Automotive	0.95	$22,269	55.25
Hughes Aircraft	.85	2,226	5.52
GM Acceptance Corporation	1.13	15,812	39.23

The weights are based upon the market values of the divisions. The beta for the entire corporation is:

GM's beta = $(.95 \times .5525) + (.85 \times .0552) + (1.13 \times .3923) = 1.02$

GM acquired Electronic Data Systems in 1986 for $2,000 million. The betas of each division and their market value weights after the acquisition are:

Division	Beta	Market Value (millions)	Weight (percent)
GM Automotive	0.95	$22,269	52.64
Hughes Aircraft	.85	2,226	5.26
GM Acceptance Corporation	1.13	15,812	37.37
Electronic Data Systems	1.25	2,000	4.73

The beta for the firm after the acquisition is:

GM's beta = $(.95 \times .5264) + (.85 \times .0526) + (1.13 \times .3737)$
$+ (1.25 \times .0473) = 1.03$

Degree of operating leverage: The degree of operating leverage is a function of the cost structure of a firm and is usually defined in terms of the relationship between fixed costs and total costs. A firm which has high operating leverage, that is, high fixed costs relative to total costs, will also have higher variability in earnings before interest and taxes (EBIT) than a firm producing a similar product with low operating leverage. The higher variance in operating income, other things remaining equal, will lead to a higher beta for the firm with high operating leverage. This is illustrated in the following example.

Illustration 4.8: Operating leverage and variability in EBIT

Consider two firms, A and B, which produce the same product. Firm A has fixed costs of $50 million and variable costs which are 40% of revenues. Firm B has fixed costs of $25 million and variable costs which are 60% of revenues. Assume three scenarios:

Expected: Revenues will be $125 million for both firms.
Boom: Revenues will be $200 million for both firms.
Recession: Revenues will be $80 million for both firms.

Firm	Fixed Costs (millions)	Variable Costs (millions)	Fixed/ Total Cost	EBIT (millions)		
				Expected	Boom	Recession
A	$50	$50	0.50	$25	$70	− $2
B	25	75	.25	25	55	7

Firm A, with the higher operating leverage, has more variable earnings before interest and taxes, which translates into a higher beta. Firm B, with lower operating leverage, has less volatile earnings and a lower beta.

Financial leverage: Other things remaining equal, an increase in financial leverage will increase the equity beta of a firm. Intuitively, the interest payments on debt increase the variance in net income, with higher leverage increasing income during good times and decreasing income during economic downturns. If all of the firm's risk is borne by the stockholders, that is, the beta of debt is 0,[7] and debt has a tax benefit to the firm, then

$$\beta_L = \beta_u(1 + [1 - t][D/E])$$

where β_L = levered beta for equity in the firm
 β_u = unlevered beta of the firm, i.e., the beta of the firm without any debt
 t = corporate tax rate
 D/E = debt/equity ratio

The unlevered beta of a firm is determined by the types of the businesses it operates in and its operating leverage.

Illustration 4.9: Effects of leverage on betas: Boeing

In 1990, Boeing Co. had a beta of 0.95, a debt/equity ratio of 1.71%, and a tax rate of 34%.

$$\beta_u = \beta/(1 + [1 - t][D/E])$$
$$= .95/(1 + [1 - .34][.171]) = .94$$

The levered beta at different levels of debt can then be estimated:

$$\beta_L = \beta_u(1 + [1 - t][D/E])$$

For instance, if Boeing were to increase its debt/equity ratio to 10%, its equity beta would be

$$\beta_L(\text{at } 10\% \text{ D/E}) = .94(1 + [1 - .34][.10]) = 1.00$$

If the debt/equity ratio were raised to 25%, the equity beta would be

$$\beta_L(\text{at } 25\% \text{ D/E}) = .94(1 + [1 - .34][.25]) = 1.10$$

Other Approaches to Estimating Betas. The standard approach for estimating betas requires market prices on an asset, which makes it difficult to apply for non-traded assets (or firms) or for assets that have only been traded for a short time period. Other approaches can be used to estimate betas for such assets:

Using comparable firms: One approach to estimating a beta for a nontraded firm is to use the betas of publicly traded firms that are comparable in terms of business risk and operating leverage. The relationship between betas and leverage, elucidated above, can be used to correct for differences in financial leverage between the firm being analyzed and the comparable firms.

Illustration 4.10: Using comparable firms to estimate betas

Assume that you are trying to estimate the beta for a private firm that disposes of environmental and medical waste for other firms. It has a debt/equity ratio[8] of 0.30 and a tax rate of 40%. The betas of publicly traded firms involved in environmental waste disposal are as follows (they face an average tax rate of 40%):

Firm	Beta	Debt/Equity
Allwaste Inc.	1.25	0.33
Browning Ferris	1.20	.24
Chemical Waste Mgmt.	1.20	.20
Rollins Environmental	1.35	.02
Waste Management	1.10	.22
Average	1.22	.20

Unlevered beta of environmental firms $= 1.22/(1 + [1 - .4][.20]) = 1.09$
Beta for private firm involved in waste disposal $= 1.09(1 + [1 - .4][.3])$
$$= 1.29$$

Using fundamental factors: This approach combines industry- and company-fundamental factors to predict betas. Income statement and balance sheet variables are important predictors of beta: High payout is predictive of low beta; high variability of earnings and covariability with economywide earnings are predictive of high beta. Researchers[9] have looked at the relationship between betas and fundamental variables. The following regression relates the betas of NYSE and AMEX stocks in 1991 to five variables: dividend yield, coefficient of variation in operating income, size, debt/equity ratio, and growth in earnings.

> Beta = .9832 + .08 CV in Operating Income − .126 Dividend Yield
>
> + .15 Debt/Equity Ratio + .034 Growth in Earnings per Share
>
> − .00001 Total Assets (in thousands)
>
> where,
> CV in Operating Income = coefficient of variation in operating income
> = standard deviation in operating income/average
> operating income

In more general terms, Rosenberg and Marathe (1979) suggest that fundamental information about a firm can be used in conjunction with historical beta estimates to provide superior predictors of future betas.

Illustration 4.11: Using fundamental information to predict betas

Assume that you are trying to estimate the beta for a private firm with the following financial characteristics (defined consistently with the regression):

CV in Operating Income = 2.2

Dividend Yield = 0.04

Debt/Equity Ratio = 0.30

Growth in Earnings per Share = 0.30

Total Assets = $10,000 (in thousands)

The estimated beta for this firm is:

Beta = .9832 + (.08 × 2.2) − (.126 × .04)
+ (.15 × .30) + (.034 × .30) − (.00001 × 10,000)

= 1.06

The Arbitrage Pricing Model

The APM, like the CAPM, defines risk to be nondiversifiable risk but, unlike the CAPM, allows for multiple economic factors in measuring this risk. While the process of estimation of risk parameters is different for the APM, many of the issues raised relating to the determinants of risk in the CAPM continue to have relevance for the APM.

Estimating Risk Parameters in the APM. The parameters of the APM are estimated from a factor analysis on historical stock returns, which yields the number of common economic factors determining these returns, the risk premium for each factor, and the factor-specific betas for each firm.

Using the APM. Once the factor-specific betas are estimated for each firm and the factor premiums are measured, the APM can be used to estimate expected returns on a stock.

$$\text{Cost of Equity} = R_f + \sum_{j=1}^{j=k} \beta_j(E[R_j] - R_f)$$

where R_f = riskfree rate
$\quad \beta_j$ = beta specific to factor j
$E(R_j) - R_f$ = risk premium per unit of factor j risk
$\quad k$ = number of factors

Illustration 4.12: Using the APM to estimate the cost of equity

Assume that the parameters for the APM have been estimated and that there are three factors.

Riskfree rate = 3.35%

$E(R_1) - R_f = 3\%$: Risk premium for factor 1
$E(R_2) - R_f = 4\%$: Risk premium for factor 2
$E(R_3) - R_f = 1.5\%$: Risk premium for factor 3

Assume that the betas specific to each of these factors are estimated for Pepsi Cola Corporation in 1992 and that the estimates are as follows:

$\beta_1 = 1.20$
$\beta_2 = .90$
$\beta_3 = 1.10$

Substituting into the APM,

$\text{Cost of Equity} = 3.35\% + (1.20 \times 3\%) + (.90 \times 4\%) + (1.1 \times 1.5\%)$
$\quad\quad\quad\quad\quad\; = 12.20\%$

Determinants of Risk Parameters in the APM. The determinants of risk parameters in the APM are the same as the determinants of risk in the CAPM, namely the type of business or businesses the firm is in, the degree of operating leverage it uses to generate earnings, and the amount of financial leverage it has taken on.

Type of business: Since factor betas in the APM measure the risk of an investment relative to specific economic factors, the type of business that a firm is in will determine in large part its exposure to factor risk. Thus, if one of the economic factors in the model is unanticipated changes in inflation, natural resource companies whose revenues and profits are much more directly linked with changes in inflation are likely to have higher betas relative to this factor.

Just as the beta of a company is the market value weighted average of the betas of its different divisions, the factor betas of a company are market value weighted averages of the factor betas of divisions which are in different business lines.

Degree of operating leverage: Higher operating leverage, by increasing the volatility of earnings, increases the betas of companies in the CAPM. By the same

rationale, they will also make firms more sensitive to specific economic conditions and increase factor betas in the APM.

Degree of financial leverage: The linear relationship between betas and the debt/equity ratio laid out in the section on the CAPM continues to hold for each factor beta in the APM:

$$\beta_{jL} = \beta_{ju}(1 + [1 - t][D/E])$$

where β_{jL} = levered beta relative to factor j (j = 1, 2, 3, ... n factors)
β_{ju} = unlevered beta relative to factor j (j = 1, 2, 3, ... n factors)

DIVIDEND GROWTH MODEL

This approach to estimating the cost of equity draws on a discounted cashflow valuation model that can be used to value a firm in stable growth.[10] For a firm which has a stable growth rate in earnings and dividends, the present value of cashflows on a share of equity can be written as:

$$P_0 = \text{Present Value of expected dividends} = DPS_1/(k_e - g)$$

where P_0 = price of the stock today
DPS_1 = expected dividends per share next year
k_e = cost of equity
g = growth rate in dividends (steady state)

A simple manipulation of this formula yields

$$k_e = DPS_1/P_0 + g$$
$$= \text{Expected Dividend Yield} + \text{Growth Rate in earnings/dividends}$$

While this approach is simple, its use is limited to firms that are in steady state. Furthermore, it is sensitive to estimates of growth in earnings and dividends.

More importantly, since the current price is a key input to the model, it is inappropriate to use this approach to value stock in a firm. There is a strong element of circular reasoning involved that will lead the analyst to conclude, using this cost of equity, that equity is fairly valued.

Illustration 4.13: Using the dividend growth model to estimate the cost of equity: Southwestern Bell

In 1992, Southwestern Bell paid dividends per share of $2.82, and the stock traded at $66 in December 1992. The estimated[11] growth rate in dividends was 5.5%, and the firm is assumed to be in steady state. The dividend growth model is used to estimate the cost of equity:

Expected Dividends in 1993 = $2.82 × 1.055 = $2.98
Cost of Equity = $2.98/$66 + 5.5% = 10%

To illustrate the circular reasoning involved in using this cost of equity to value stock,

Value of Equity $= \$2.98/(.10 - .055) = \66

Not surprisingly, the stock is found to be fairly valued.

WEIGHTED AVERAGE COST OF CAPITAL (WACC)

Intuitively, the cost of capital is the weighted average of the costs of the different components of financing, including debt, equity, and hybrid securities, used by a firm to fund its financial requirements. This section explores the estimation of the cost of capital in more detail.

Definition of the WACC

The weighted average cost of capital is defined as the weighted average of the costs of the different components of financing used by a firm:

$$WACC = k_e(E/[E + D + PS]) + k_d(D/[E + D + PS]) + k_{ps}(PS/[E + D + PS])$$

where WACC = Weighted Average Cost of Capital

k_e = cost of equity

k_d = after-tax cost of debt

k_{ps} = cost of preferred stock

$E/(E + D + PS)$ = market value proportion of Equity in funding mix

$D/(E + D + PS)$ = market value proportion of Debt in funding mix

$PS/(E + D + PS)$ = market value proportion of Preferred Stock in funding mix

Illustration 4.14: Calculating the cost of capital: Pepsi Cola

In December 1992, Pepsi Cola Corporation had a cost of equity of 12.83% and an after-tax cost of debt of 5.28%. Of the total financing for the firm, equity comprised 76.94% (in market value terms) of the funding mix and debt made up the remaining 23.06%. The cost of capital for Pepsico can then be calculated as follows:

WACC $= (12.83\% \times .7694) + (5.28\% \times .2306) = 11.09\%$

The estimation of the cost of equity has been described in detail in the preceding section. A short description of the estimation of the cost of debt, preferred stock, and hybrid securities follows.

Calculating the Cost of Debt

The cost of debt measures the current cost to the firm of borrowing funds to finance projects. In general terms, it is determined by the following variables:

(a) *The current level of interest rates:* As the level of interest rates increases, the cost of debt for firms will also increase.

(b) *The default risk of the company:* As the default risk of a firm increases, the cost of borrowing money will also increase. One way of measuring default risk is to use the bond rating for the firm, with higher ratings leading to lower interest rates and lower ratings to higher interest rates. If bond ratings are not available, as is the case in many markets outside the United States, the rates paid most recently by the firm on its borrowings may provide a measure of the default risk of the firm.

(c) *The tax advantage associated with debt:* Since interest is tax deductible, the after-tax cost of debt is a function of the tax rate. The tax benefit that accrues from paying interest makes the after-tax cost of debt lower than the pretax cost. Furthermore, this benefit increases as the tax rate increases.

$$\text{After-tax cost of debt} = \text{Pretax cost of debt} (1 - \text{tax rate})$$

Illustration 4.15: Calculating the after-tax cost of debt: Siemens

Siemens AG (Germany) had 4.244 billion DM of debt outstanding in July 1993. Due to its low leverage and substantial cash balances, its default risk was minimal and it could borrow at 6.72%. The marginal tax rate it faced on income was 38%. The after-tax cost of debt for Siemens can then be estimated as follows:

$$\text{After-tax cost of debt} = 6.72\% (1 - .38) = 4.17\%$$

What the cost of debt is not: The cost of debt is not the coupon rate on bonds that the company has outstanding nor is it the rate at which the company was able to borrow at in the past. While these may help determine the dollar interest cost that the company will have to pay in the current year, they do not determine the after-tax cost of debt. Thus a company that has debt on the books that it took on when interest rates were low cannot contend that it has a low cost of debt if the overall level of interest rates or its risk of default has increased in the meantime.

Calculating the Cost of Preferred Stock

Preferred stock shares some of the characteristics of debt—the preferred dividend is prespecified at the time of the issue and is paid out before common dividend—and some of the characteristics of equity—the payments of preferred dividend are not tax deductible. If preferred stock is viewed as perpetual, the cost of preferred stock can be written as follows:

$$k_{ps} = \text{Preferred Dividend per share/Market Price preferred share}$$

This approach assumes that the dividend is constant in dollar terms forever and that the preferred stock has no special features (convertibility, callability, etc.). If such special features exist, they will have to be separately valued to come up with a good estimate of the cost of preferred stock. In terms of risk, preferred stock is safer than common equity but riskier than debt. Consequently it should, on a pretax basis, command a higher cost than debt and a lower cost than equity.

Illustration 4.16: Calculating the cost of preferred stock: General Motors

At the end of 1992, General Motors Co. had preferred stock which paid a dividend of $2.28 annually and traded at $27 per share. The cost of preferred stock can be estimated as follows:

Cost of preferred stock = $2.28/$27 = 8.44%

At the same time, GM's cost of equity, using the CAPM, was 12.30%, its pretax cost of debt was 8%, and its after-tax cost of debt was 5.10%.

Calculating the Cost of Other Hybrid Securities

In general terms, hybrid securities share some of the characteristics of debt and some of the characteristics of equity. A good example is a convertible bond, which can be viewed as a combination of a straight bond (debt) and a conversion option (equity). Instead of trying to calculate the cost of these hybrid securities individually, they can be broken down into their debt and equity components and treated separately.

Illustration 4.17: Breaking down a convertible bond into debt and equity components:
 Unisys

At the end of 1992, Unisys Corp. had an 8.25% convertible bond, coming due in the year 2000, which was trading at $1,400. It also had straight bonds, with the same maturity, trading in December 1992 at a yield of 8.4%. The convertible bond can then be broken down into straight bond and conversion option components.

Straight Bond component = value of a straight 8.25% coupon bond due in 2000

at a yield of 8.40%

= $991.50

Conversion Option component = $1,400 − $991.50 = $408.50

The straight bond component of $991.50 is treated as debt, while the conversion option component of $408.50 is treated as equity.

Calculating the Weights of Debt and Equity Components

Market Value Versus Book Value Weights

The weights assigned to equity and debt in calculating the weighted average cost of capital have to be based upon market value, not book value. The rationale rests on the fact that the cost of capital measures the cost of issuing securities, stocks as well as bonds, to finance projects, and that these securities are issued at market value, not at book value.

There are three standard arguments against using market value, and none of them are convincing. First, it is argued that book value is more reliable than market value because it is not as volatile. While it is true that book value does not change as much as market value, this is more a reflection of weakness than

strength, since the true value of the firm changes over time as both firm-specific and marketwide information is revealed. We would argue that market value, with its volatility, is a much better reflection of true value[12] than book value is. Second, it is suggested that using book value rather than market value is a more conservative approach to estimating debt ratios. This assumes that market value debt ratios are always lower than book value debt ratios, an assumption not based upon fact. Third, it is claimed that lenders will not lend on the basis of market value, but this claim again seems to be based more upon perception than fact.[13]

Illustration 4.18: Difference between market value and book value debt ratios: Pepsi Cola

In December 1992, Pepsico had a market value of equity of $30.02 billion and a book value of equity of $6.438 billion. The market value[14] of debt at the same time was approximately $9.00 billion while the book value of debt was $8.894 billion. The debt ratios calculated on the basis of book and market values are as follows:

Book Value Debt Ratio = $8,894/($8,894 + $6,438) = 58.01%

Market Value Debt Ratio = $9,000/($9,000 + $30,020) = 23.07%

The market value debt ratio is significantly lower than the book value ratio, and it clearly is much more representative of Pepsico's financial strength.

CONCLUSION

This chapter explains the process of estimating discount rates. The cost of equity can be estimated using risk and return models: the capital asset pricing model, where risk is measured relative to a single market factor; the arbitrage pricing model, where the cost of equity is determined by the sensitivity to multiple unspecified economic factors; or a multifactor model, where sensitivity to macroeconomic variables is used to measure risk. The cost of capital is a weighted average of the costs of the different components of financing, with the weights based upon the market values of each component.

QUESTIONS AND SHORT PROBLEMS

1. You have just done a regression of monthly stock returns (on XYZ Corp) on monthly market returns over the last five years and have come up with the following regression:

 $$R_{XYZ} = 0.5\% + 1.2 R_M$$

 The variance of the stock is 50% and the variance of the market is 20%. The current T-bill rate is 3% (it was 5% one year ago). The stock is currently selling for $50, down $4 over the last year. It has paid a dividend of $2 during the last

year and expects to pay a dividend of $2.50 over the next year. The NYSE composite has gone down 8% over the last year, with a dividend yield of 3%. XYZ Corp. has a tax rate of 40%.

 a. What is the expected return on XYZ over the next year?
 b. What would you expect XYZ's price to be one year from today?
 c. What would you have expected XYZ's stock returns to be over the last year?
 d. What were the actual returns on XYZ over the last year?
 e. XYZ Corporation has $100 million in equity and $100 million in debt. It plans to issue $50 million in new equity and retire $50 million in debt. Estimate the new beta.

2. A firm that currently has $50 million in debt and $100 million in equity has a beta of 1.2. It is planning a leveraged buyout with a debt/equity ratio of 8. If the tax rate is 40%, what will the beta of the equity in the firm be after the LBO?

3. Novell, which had a market value of equity of $2 billion and a beta of 1.50, announced that it was acquiring WordPerfect, which had a market value of equity of $1 billion and a beta of 1.30. Neither firm had any debt in its financial structure at the time of the acquisition, and the corporate tax rate was 40%.

 a. Estimate the beta for Novell after the acquisition, assuming that the entire acquisition was financed with equity.
 b. Assume that Novell had to borrow the $1 billion to acquire WordPerfect. Estimate the beta after the acquisition.

4. You are analyzing the beta for Hewlett Packard and have broken down the company into four broad business groups, with market values and betas for each group.

Business Group	Market Value of Equity	Beta
Mainframes	$2.0 billion	1.10
Personal Computers	$2.0 billion	1.50
Software	$1.0 billion	2.00
Printers	$3.0 billion	1.00

 a. Estimate the beta for Hewlett Packard as a company. Is this beta going to be equal to the beta estimated by regressing past returns on HP stock against a market index? Why or why not?
 b. If the Treasury bond rate is 7.5%, estimate the cost of equity for Hewlett Packard. Estimate the cost of equity for each division. Which cost of equity would you use to value the printer division?
 c. Assume that HP divests itself of the mainframe business and pays the cash out as a dividend. Estimate the beta for HP after the divestiture. (HP had $1 billion in debt outstanding.)

ENDNOTES

1. If expected inflation is high and the government bond rate exceeds 15%, all valuation is done in U.S. dollars, using the U.S. Treasury bond rate as the riskfree rate. If the local currency is used, the premium will probably have to be increased as expected inflation increases.

2. The beta was obtained from Value Line. It was based upon a five-year regression of weekly returns on Pepsico against the NYSE Composite.

3. These were obtained by subtracting from the historical premium the average differences between spot Treasury bill rates and 1-year, 2-year, 3-year, and 4-year forward rates.

4. The regression is sometimes done using returns in excess of the riskfree rate, for both the stock and the market. In that case, the intercept of the regression should be 0 if the actual returns equal the expected returns from the CAPM, greater than 0 if the stock does better than expected, and less than 0 if it does worse than expected.

5. The nontrading bias arises because the returns in nontrading periods are 0 (even though the market may have moved up or down significantly in those periods). Using these nontrading period returns in the regression will reduce the correlation between stock returns and market returns and the beta of the stock.

6. The bias can also be reduced using statistical techniques suggested by Dimson and Scholes-Williams.

7. If debt has market risk (i.e., its beta is greater than 0), this formula can be modified to take it into account. If the beta of debt is β_D, the beta of equity can be written as:

$$\beta_L = \beta_u(1 + [1 - t][D/E]) - \beta_D(D/E)$$

8. Since private firms do not have market values for debt and equity, the book value ratio is used. This does create an inconsistency in the valuation, which can be resolved by doing a series of iterations until the value used in the debt/equity ratio converges on the value from the valuation.

9. Beaver, Kettler, and Scholes (1970) examined the relationship between betas and seven variables: dividend payout, asset growth, leverage, liquidity, asset size, earnings variability, and the accounting beta. Rosenberg and Guy (1976) did a similar analysis of the relationship between betas and financial fundamentals.

10. It can be argued that a firm in stable growth cannot be growing a rate very different from the overall economy, since the growth rate is assumed to stay constant forever. For example, if the nominal growth rate in the economy is 8%, a stable firm cannot be growing at a rate much faster than this rate.

11. This is the Value Line projected growth rate in dividends over the next five years. Since the firm is assumed to be in steady state this growth rate is expected to continue forever.

12. There are some who argue that stock prices are much more volatile than the underlying true value. Even if this argument is justified (and it has not been conclusively shown to be so), the difference between market value and true value is likely to be much smaller than the difference between book value and true value.

13. Any homeowner who has taken a second mortgage on a house that has appreciated in value knows that lenders do lend on the basis of market value. It is true, however, that the greater the perceived volatility in the market value of an asset, the lower is the borrowing potential on that asset.

14. Not all of Pepsico debt is traded. An approximate valuation of debt was made based upon coupon rates and market interest rates in 1992.

APPENDIX I Historical Returns on Stocks, Treasury Bills, and Treasury Bonds, 1926–1990
(percent)

Year	Stocks	Treasury Bills	Treasury Bonds	Year	Stocks	Treasury Bills	Treasury Bonds
1926	11.62	3.27	7.77	1960	−.47	2.66	13.78
1927	37.49	3.12	8.93	1961	26.89	2.13	.97
1928	43.61	3.24	.10	1962	−8.73	2.73	6.89
1929	−8.42	4.75	3.42	1963	22.80	3.12	1.21
1930	−24.90	2.41	4.66	1964	16.48	3.54	3.51
1931	−43.34	1.07	−5.31	1965	12.45	3.93	.71
1932	−8.19	.96	16.84	1966	−10.06	4.76	3.65
1933	53.99	.30	−.08	1967	23.98	4.21	−9.19
1934	−1.44	.16	10.02	1968	11.06	5.21	−.26
1935	47.67	.17	4.98	1969	−8.50	6.58	−5.08
1936	33.92	.18	7.51	1970	4.01	6.53	12.10
1937	−35.03	.31	.23	1971	14.31	4.39	13.23
1938	31.12	−.02	5.53	1972	18.98	3.84	5.68
1939	−.41	.02	5.94	1973	−14.66	6.93	−1.11
1940	−9.78	.00	6.09	1974	−26.47	8.00	4.35
1941	−11.59	.06	.93	1975	37.20	5.80	9.19
1942	20.34	.27	3.22	1976	23.84	5.08	16.75
1943	25.90	.35	2.08	1977	−7.18	5.12	−.67
1944	19.75	.33	2.81	1978	6.56	7.18	−1.16
1945	36.44	.33	10.73	1979	18.44	10.38	−1.22
1946	−8.07	.35	−.10	1980	32.42	11.24	−3.95
1947	5.71	.50	−2.63	1981	−4.91	14.71	1.85
1948	5.50	.81	3.40	1982	21.41	10.54	40.35
1949	18.79	1.10	6.45	1983	22.51	8.80	.68
1950	31.71	1.20	.06	1984	6.27	9.85	15.43
1951	24.02	1.49	−3.94	1985	32.16	7.72	30.97
1952	18.37	1.66	1.16	1986	18.47	6.16	24.44
1953	−.99	1.82	3.63	1987	5.23	5.47	−2.69
1954	52.62	.86	7.19	1988	16.81	6.35	9.67
1955	31.56	1.57	−1.30	1989	31.49	8.37	18.11
1956	6.56	2.46	−5.59	1990	−3.17	7.81	6.18
1957	−10.78	3.14	7.45	1991	32.84	7.45	15.45
1958	43.36	1.54	−6.10	1992	7.87	5.50	12.16
1959	11.96	2.95	−2.26				

Means of Historical Returns
(percent)

	Stocks	Treasury Bills	Treasury Bonds
		1926–1992	
Arithmetic	12.40	3.60	5.20
Geometric	10.30	3.70	4.80
		1962–1992	
Arithmetic	10.80	6.70	6.88
Geometric	9.62	6.67	6.36
		1981–1992	
Arithmetic	14.63	8.58	14.50
Geometric	13.93	8.55	13.74

5

Understanding Financial Statements

Much of the information that is used in valuation and corporate finance comes from financial statements. An understanding of the basic financial statements and some of the financial ratios that are used in analysis is therefore a necessary first step for either pursuit. This chapter provides a background to how income statements, balance sheets, and statements of cashflows are constructed, as well as the generally accepted accounting principles that underlie their construction. It also examines a range of widely used financial ratios and provides a framework for their understanding. Finally, it explores differences in accounting standards across the world and how these differences may affect an analysis.

PRINCIPAL FINANCIAL STATEMENTS

There are three basic financial statements: the income statement, that measures the revenues and expenses of the firm; the balance sheet, that reports on the assets and liabilities of the firm; and the statement of cashflows, that examines the sources and the uses of cash.

Income Statement

An income statement provides information about a firm's operating activities over a specific time period. The net income of a company is equal to the revenues minus expenses, where revenues measure the inflows from selling goods or services and expenses measure the outflows from the firm to generate revenues.

Classification: A Typical Income Statement

Since income can be generated from a number of different sources, generally accepted accounting principles (GAAP) require that income statements be classified into four sections: income from continuing operations, income from discontinued operations, extraordinary gains or losses, and adjustments for changes in accounting principles. A typical income statement starts with reve-

nues and adjusts for the cost of the goods sold, depreciation on assets used to produce the revenues, and any selling or administrative expenses to arrive at an operating profit. The operating profit, when reduced by interest expenses, yields the taxable income, which when reduced by taxes yields net income.

<div align="center">Income Statement</div>

Revenues
- Cost of Goods Sold
- Depreciation
- Selling Expenses
- Administrative Expenses
= Earnings before interest and taxes (EBIT)
- Interest Expenses
= Earnings before taxes
- Taxes
= Net Income before extraordinary items
+ Gains (Losses) from discontinued operations
+ Extraordinary Gains (Losses)
+ Net Income Changes caused by changes in accounting methods
= Net Income after extraordinary items

Accrual versus Cash Basis: Income Statements

Firms often expend resources to acquire materials or manufacture goods in one period but do not sell them until the following period. Alternatively, they often provide services in one period but do not get paid until the following period. In accrual-based accounting the revenue from selling a good or service is recognized in the period in which the good is sold or the service is performed (in whole or substantially). A corresponding effort is made on the expense side to match[1] expenses to revenues. Under a cash-based system of accounting, revenues are recognized when received, while expenses are recorded when paid. Since there is no matching of revenues and expenses, GAAP requires that firms use accrual-based accounting in income statements.

GAAP: Recognizing Income

Generally accepted accounting principles require the recognition of revenues when the service for which the firm is getting paid has been performed in full or substantially and has received in return either cash or a receivable that is both observable and measurable. For expenses that are directly linked to the production of revenues (like labor and materials), expenses are recognized in the same period in which revenues are recognized. Any expenses that are not directly linked to the production of revenues are recognized in the period in which the firm consumes the services.

While accrual accounting is straightforward in firms that produce goods and sell them, there are special cases where accrual accounting can be complicated by the nature of the product or service being offered.

- *Long-term contracts:* Long-term contracts span several accounting periods, and customers often make periodic payments as the contract progresses (for example,

home or commercial building). When a long-term contractor has a contract with a buyer with an agreed-upon price, revenue during the period of construction is recognized on the basis of the percentage of the contract that is completed. As the revenue is recognized on a percentage-of-completion basis, a corresponding proportion of the expense is also recognized. An alternative is to wait until the contract is completed, and recognize the total revenue and expense upon completion. Since this delays the payment of income taxes, it is not permitted under the Internal Revenue Code for tax purposes.

- *Uncertainty about cash collections:* When there is considerable uncertainty about the capacity of the buyer of a good or service to pay for a service, the firm providing the good or service may recognize the income only when it collects portions of the selling price under the installment method. While this is similar to revenue recognition in the cash method, the expenses under the installment method are recognized only when the cash is collected, even though payment may be made in the period of the initial sale. An alternative to this approach is the cost-recovery-first method, where cash receipts and expenses are matched dollar for dollar (thus generating no profits) until all the expenses are covered, after which any additional revenues are reported as profits.

Illustration 5.1: Examples of income statements: General Motors and The Home Depot

The following table summarizes income statements for fiscal year 1993 for General Motors Corporation and The Home Depot.

	General Motors	The Home Depot
Revenues	$138,220.00	$9,238.00
− Cost of Goods Sold	$108,996.00	$6,596.00
− Depreciation	$ 9,442.00	$ 90.00
− Selling Expenses	$ 6,132.00	$1,624.00
− Administrative Expenses	$ 5,400.00	$ 220.00
= Earnings before interest and taxes (EBIT)	$ 8,250.00	$ 708.00
+ Interest Income	$ —	$ 61.00
− Interest Expenses	$ 5,637.00	$ 31.00
= Earnings before taxes	$ 2,613.00	$ 738.00
− Taxes	$ 110.00	$ 280.00
= Net Income before extraordinary items	$ 2,503.00	$ 458.00
+ Gains (Losses) from discontinued operations	—	$ —
+ Extraordinary Gains (Losses)	—	$ —
+ Income changes from changes in accounting methods	—	$ —
Net Income after extraordinary items	$ 2,503.00	$ 458.00
− Preferred Dividends	$ 357.00	$ —
= Profit to Common Stockholders	$ 2,146.00	$ 458.00

Balance Sheet

Unlike the income statement, which measures flows over a period of time, the balance sheet provides a summary of what the firm owns in terms of assets and what it owes to both its lenders and its equity investors. The balance sheet is built around the equality

Assets = Liabilities + Shareholders' Equity

Assets and liabilities can be further broken down into current and noncurrent portions.

Assets	Liabilities & Equity
Current Assets	Current Liabilities
Cash and Marketable Securities	Accounts Payable
Accounts Receivable	Short-Term Borrowing
Inventories	Other Current Liabilities
Other Current Assets	Long-Term Debt
Investments	Other Noncurrent Liabilities
Property, Plant, & Equipment (Fixed Assets)	Stockholders' Equity
Intangible Assets	Preferred Stock
	Common Stock
	Retained Earnings
	Treasury Stock

Assets

An asset is any resource that has the potential to either generate future cash inflows or reduce future cash outflows. For a resource to be an asset, therefore, a firm has to have acquired it in a prior transaction and be able to quantify future benefits with reasonable precision. Assets can be classified on several bases—into fixed and current assets, into monetary assets (like cash and notes receivable) and nonmonetary assets—and GAAP on valuation varies from asset to asset.

Fixed Assets. Generally accepted accounting principles in almost all countries require the valuation of fixed assets at historical costs, adjusted for any depreciation charges on these assets. The rationale that is often provided for this practice is that

(a) Book value is easier to obtain than market value for most assets, since an active secondary market does not exist for most assets.
(b) Book value can be more objectively valued than market value and is less likely to be manipulated by firms to suit their purposes.
(c) Book value is a more conservative estimate of true value than is market value.

All these arguments are open to challenge, and it is quite clear that the book value of many fixed assets bears little resemblance to the market value.

Since fixed assets are valued at book value and are adjusted for depreciation provisions, the value of a fixed asset is strongly influenced by both its deprecia-

ble life and the depreciation method used. Since firms estimate the depreciable life, and lengthening the depreciable life can increase[2] earnings, this provides an opportunity for firms to manage earnings. Firms are also offered an opportunity to manage earnings through the choice of a depreciation method, since GAAP allows firms to use either straight-line depreciation (where depreciation is spread evenly over the life of the asset) or accelerated depreciation methods (where more depreciation is taken in the initial years, and less later on). Most U.S. firms use straight-line depreciation for financial reporting, while they use accelerated depreciation for tax purposes, since firms can report better earnings with the former, at least in the years right after the asset is acquired. In contrast, Japanese and German firms often use accelerated depreciation for both tax and financial reporting purposes, leading to income that is understated relative to their U.S. counterparts.

Inventory. There are three basic approaches to valuing inventory that are allowed by GAAP:

(a) *First-in, First-out (FIFO):* Under FIFO, the cost of goods sold is based upon the cost of material bought earliest in the period, while the cost of inventory is based upon the cost of material bought later in the year. This results in inventory being valued close to current replacement cost. During periods of inflation, the use of FIFO will result in the lowest estimate of cost of goods sold among the three approaches, and the highest net income.

(b) *Last-in, First-out (LIFO):* Under LIFO, the cost of goods sold is based upon the cost of material bought toward the end of the period, resulting in costs that closely approximate current costs. The inventory, however, is valued on the basis of the cost of materials bought earlier in the year. During periods of inflation, the use of LIFO will result in the highest estimate of cost of goods sold among the three approaches, and the lowest net income.

(c) *Weighted average:* Under the weighted average approach, both inventory and the cost of goods sold are based upon the average cost of all units bought during the period. When inventory turns over rapidly, this approach will more closely resemble FIFO than LIFO.

Firms often adopt the LIFO approach for the tax benefits during periods of high inflation, and studies indicate that firms with the following characteristics are more likely to adopt LIFO: rising prices for raw materials and labor, more variable inventory growth, an absence of other tax loss carry-forwards, and large size. When firms switch from FIFO to LIFO in valuing inventory, there is likely to be a drop in net income and a concurrent increase in cashflows (because of the tax savings). The reverse will apply when firms switch from LIFO to FIFO.

Given the income and cashflow effects of inventory valuation methods, it is often difficult to compare firms that use different methods. There is, however, one way of adjusting for these differences. Firms that choose to use the LIFO approach to value inventories have to specify in a footnote the difference in inventory valuation between FIFO and LIFO, and this difference is termed the

LIFO reserve. This can be used to adjust the beginning and ending inventories and consequently the cost of goods sold, and to restate income based upon FIFO valuation.

Intangible Assets. Intangible assets include a wide array of assets ranging from patents and trademarks to goodwill. GAAP requires that intangible assets be accounted for as follows:

(a) The costs incurred in developing the intangible asset are expensed in that period, even though the asset might have a life of several accounting periods. Thus, the research and development expenditure that creates a patent (the intangible asset) is expensed nevertheless in the period it is incurred.

(b) When an intangible asset is acquired from an external party, the expenditure is treated as an asset, in contrast to the treatment of expenditures incurred in internally developing the same asset.

(c) Intangible assets have to be amortized over their expected lives, with a maximum amortization period of 40 years. The standard practice is to use straight-line amortization. For tax purposes, however, firms are not allowed to amortize goodwill and other intangible assets with no specific lifetime.

Intangible assets are often byproducts of acquisitions. When a firm acquires another firm, the purchase price is first allocated over tangible assets, and the excess price is then allocated to any intangible assets such as patents or trade names. Any residual becomes goodwill. While accounting principles suggest that goodwill captures the value of any intangibles that are not specifically identifiable, it is really a reflection of the difference between the book value of assets and their market value.

Liabilities

For an obligation to be recognized as a liability, it must meet three requirements: It is expected to lead to a future cash outflow or the loss of a future cash inflow at some specified or determinable date; the firm cannot avoid the obligation; and the transaction giving rise to the obligation has happened.

Degree of Certitude. Liabilities vary in the degree to which they create a future obligation. At one extreme, a straight bond creates an obligation to make fixed payments on fixed dates and results in a very specific and certain obligation. At the other extreme, an option contract entered into by a firm creates a contingent obligation, where the amount and the timing of the obligation is unclear. Along the continuum, GAAP recognizes as accounting liabilities those obligations that create future payments that can be both quantified and timed, even if the amount and the timing have to be estimated by the firm. It does not recognize as accounting liabilities purchase or employment commitments or contingent contracts.

As firms enter into more and more complex arrangements to manage their financial and operating risk, a number of gray areas are emerging, where generally accepted accounting principles do not provide sufficient guidance on the

right path to take. One example is the use of hybrid securities by firms, possessing some of the properties of debt and some of equity, making a classification into liabilities and stockholders' equity very difficult. Another is the use of off-balance-sheet financing by firms, where a liability is created but not recognized. The evolving attitude toward this phenomenon is that firms must disclose information[3] about the off-balance-sheet risk of any financial instruments or agreements that they have entered into.

Dealing with Leases. Firms often choose to lease long-term assets rather than buy them, for a variety of reasons: The tax benefits are greater to the lessor than the lessee, and leases offer more flexibility in terms of adjusting to changes in technology and capacity needs. Lease payments create the same kind of obligation that interest payments on debt create, and have to be viewed in a similar light. If a firm is allowed to lease a significant portion of its assets and keep them off its financial statements, a perusal of the statements will give a very misleading view of the company's financial strength. Consequently, accounting rules have been devised to force firms to reveal the extent of their lease obligations on their books.

There are two ways of accounting for leases. In an **operating** lease, the lessor (or owner) transfers only the right to use the property to the lessee. At the end of the lease period, the lessee returns the property to the lessor. Since the lessee does not assume the risk of ownership, the lease expense is treated as an operating expense in the income statement, and the lease does not affect the balance sheet. In a **capital** lease, the lessee assumes some of the risks of ownership and enjoys some of the benefits. Consequently, the lease, when signed, is recognized both as an asset and as a liability (for the lease payments) on the balance sheet. The firm gets to claim depreciation each year on the asset and also deducts the interest expense component of the lease payment each year. In general, capital leases recognize expenses sooner than equivalent operating leases.

Since firms prefer to keep leases off the books, and sometimes prefer to defer expenses, there is a strong incentive on the part of firms to report all leases as operating leases. Consequently, the Financial Accounting Standards Board (FASB) has ruled that a lease should be treated as a capital lease if it meets any one of the following four conditions:

(a) If the lease life exceeds 75% of the life of the asset.
(b) If there is a transfer of ownership to the lessee at the end of the lease term.
(c) If there is an option to purchase the asset at a "bargain price" at the end of the lease term.
(d) If the present value of the lease payments, discounted at an appropriate discount rate, exceeds 90% of the fair market value of the asset.

The lessor uses the same criteria for determining whether the lease is a capital or operating lease and accounts for it accordingly. If it is a capital lease, the lessor records the present value of future cashflows as revenue and recognizes

expenses. The lease receivable is also shown as an asset on the balance sheet, and the interest revenue is recognized over the term of the lease as paid.

From a tax standpoint, the lessor can claim the tax benefits of the leased asset only if it is an operating lease, though the revenue code uses slightly different criteria[4] for determining whether the lease is an operating lease.

Employee Benefits. Employers provide pension and health care benefits to their employees. In many cases, the obligations created by these benefits are extensive, and a failure by the firm to adequately fund these obligations needs to be revealed in financial statements.

Pension plans: In a pension plan, the firm agrees to provide certain benefits to its employees, either by specifying a "defined contribution" (where a fixed contribution is made to the plan each year by the employer, without any promises on the benefits which will be delivered in the plan) or a "defined benefit" (where the employer promises to pay a certain benefit to the employee). Under the latter, the employer has to put sufficient money into the plan each period that the amounts with reinvestment are sufficient to meet the defined benefits.

Under a defined contribution plan, the firm meets its obligation once it has made the prespecified contribution to the plan. Under a defined benefit plan, the firm's obligations are much more difficult to estimate, since they will be determined by a number of variables, including the benefits that employees are entitled to, which will change as their salaries and employment status change; the prior contributions made by the employer and the returns they have earned; and the rate of return that the employer expects to make on current contributions. As these variables change, the value of the pension fund assets can be greater than, less than, or equal to pension fund liabilities (which include the present value of promised benefits). A pension fund whose assets exceed its liabilities is an overfunded plan, whereas one whose assets are less than its liabilities is an underfunded plan, and disclosures to that effect have to be included in financial statements, generally in the footnotes.

When a pension fund is overfunded, the firm has several options: It can withdraw the excess assets from the fund, or it can discontinue contributions to the plan, or it can continue to make contributions on the assumption that the overfunding is a transitory phenomenon that could well disappear by the next period. When a fund is underfunded, the firm has a liability, though the FASB rule requires that firms reveal only the excess of accumulated[5] pension fund liabilities over pension fund assets on the balance sheet.

Health care benefits: A firm can provide health care benefits in one of two ways: by making a fixed contribution to a health care plan, without promising specific benefits (analogous to a defined contribution plan); or by promising specific health benefits and setting aside the funds to provide these benefits (analogous to a defined benefit plan). The accounting for health care benefits is very similar to the accounting for pension obligations. The key difference

between the two is that firms do not have to report the excess of their health care obligations over the health care fund assets as a liability on the balance sheet, though a footnote to that effect has to be added to the financial statement.

Income Taxes. Firms often use different methods of accounting for tax and financial reporting purposes, leading to a question of how tax liabilities should be reported. Since the use of accelerated depreciation and favorable inventory valuation methods for tax accounting purposes leads to a deferral of taxes, the taxes on the income reported in the financial statements will be much greater than the actual tax paid. The same principles of matching expenses to income that underlie accrual accounting suggest that the "deferred income tax" be recognized in the financial statements. Thus a company which pays $55,000 on its taxable income based upon its tax accounting, and which would have paid $75,000 on the income reported in its financial statements, will be forced to recognize the difference ($20,000) as deferred taxes. Since the deferred taxes will be paid in later years, they will be recognized as paid.

The question of whether the deferred tax liability is really a liability is an interesting one. Firms do not owe the amount categorized as deferred taxes to any entity, and treating it as a liability makes the firm look more risky than it really is.

Reserves in Financial Statements. Reserves can appear in financial statements as a deduction from an asset, as a liability, or as a reduction of stockholders' equity. While reserves have to be for specific purposes in the United States, firms in Germany and Japan are allowed to create general reserves to equalize income across time periods. Reserve accounts are created for a number of different reasons:

(a) *To match expenses with benefits.* A firm can create a reserve for an expense that is expected to arise from an activity from the current period and reduce the income in the current period by the expense. When the expense actually occurs, the reserve is reduced by the amount, and the net income in the future period is not affected by the expense. Thus, a bank which expects 1% of its loans to go uncollected may create a reserve for bad debts in the period the loan is made, and charge income in that period with a charge transferring funds to the reserve. Any subsequent loan defaults will be charged to the reserve.

(b) *To keep expenses out of income statements.* Firms can keep some expenses out of the income statement by directly reducing the stockholders' equity, by a reserve created to meet the expense. While the net effect on stockholders' equity is the same as if the expense had been shown in the income statement, it results in an overstatement of net income for that period.

The varied uses to which reserves are put, and the wise diversity of accounting standards relating to reserves in different countries, suggests that analysts should be careful about how they factor in reserves when comparing the profitability of companies in different countries using different accounting standards.

Statement of Cashflows

The statement of cashflows is based upon a reformulation of the basic equation relating assets to liabilities:

$$\text{Assets} = \text{Liabilities} + \text{Stockholders' Equity}$$
$$\triangle\text{ Assets} = \triangle\text{ Liabilities} + \triangle\text{ Stockholders' Equity}$$
$$\triangle\text{ Cash} + \triangle\text{ Noncash Assets} = \triangle\text{ Liabilities} + \triangle\text{ Stockholders' Equity}$$
$$\triangle\text{ Cash} = \triangle\text{ Liabilities} + \triangle\text{ Stockholders' Equity} - \triangle\text{ Noncash Assets}$$

A statement of changes in cashflows classifies all changes into one of three categories: operating, investing, or financing activities. The final step in preparing a statement of changes in cashflows is to classify changes in liabilities, stockholders' equity, and noncash assets into one of these three categories, though some items will not fit easily into one or another. Once categorized, the statement of cashflows provides a breakdown of the changes in the cash balance over the period.

Illustration 5.2: Statement of cash flows: General Motors and The Home Depot

The following table summarizes the statement of cash flows at The Home Depot in 1993.

Cash Provided from Operations:	
Net Earnings	$ 457,401.00
Reconciling Net Earnings to Net Operating Cash	
Depreciation and Amortization	$ 89,839.00
Deferred Income Tax Expense	$ 12,578.00
Increase in Receivables	$ (36,658.00)
Increase in Merchandise Inventory	$(353,653.00)
Increase in Accounts Payable and Accrued Expenses	$ 200,977.00
Increase in Income Taxes Payable	$ 36,143.00
Other	$ (10,120.00)
Total	$ (60,984.00)
Net Cash Provided by Operations	$ 396,507.00
Cash Flows from Investing	
Capital Expenditures	$(864,158.00)
Proceeds from Sale of Property & Equipment	$ 35,070.00
Sale of Short-Term Investments	$ 14,903.00
Purchase of Long-Term Investments	$(840,361.00)
Proceeds from Maturities of Long-Term Investments	$ 269,988.00
Proceeds from Sale of Long-Term Investments	$ 935,279.00
Net Cash Used in Investing Activities	$(449,279.00)
Cash Flows from Financing	
Proceeds from Long-Term Borrowing	$ —
Repayments of Notes Receivables from ESOP	$ 6,585.00
Principal Repayments of Long-Term Debt	$ (2,006.00)

Proceeds from Sale of Common Stock	$ 76,789.00
Cash Dividends Paid to Stockholders	$ (50,343.00)
Net Cash Provided by Financing Activities	$ 31,025.00
Increase (Decrease) in Cash and Equivalents	$ (21,747.00)
Cash and Equivalents at the beginning of year	$ 121,744.00
Cash and Equivalents at end of the year	$ 99,997.00

FINANCIAL RATIOS

Financial ratios are a useful byproduct of financial statements and provide standardized measures of a firm's profitability and riskiness. In this section, we will consider a number of financial ratios and provide a framework for categorizing and understanding them.

Profitability Ratios

There are a number of ways of measuring the profitability of an enterprise. One is to examine the profitability relative to the capital employed to get a rate of return on investment. This can be done either from the viewpoint of just the equity investors or by looking at the entire firm. Another is to examine profitability relative to sales, by estimating a profit margin.

Return on Assets (ROA)

The return on assets of a firm measures its operating efficiency in generating profits from its assets, prior to considering the effects of financing.

ROA = Earnings before interest and taxes(1 − tax rate)/Total Assets

Alternatively, the ROA can be written as

ROA = [Net Income + Interest Expenses(1 − tax rate)]/Total Assets

By separating the financing effects from the operating effects, this measure provides a cleaner measure of the true value of these assets.

This measure can also be computed on a pretax basis with no loss of generality, by using the earnings before interest and taxes and not adjusting for taxes:

Pretax ROA = Earnings before interest and taxes/Total Assets

This measure is useful if the firm or division is being evaluated for purchase by an acquirer with a different tax rate.

Illustration 5.3: Estimating pretax and after-tax ROA: General Electric

In 1993, General Electric (not including GE Capital Services) reported earnings before interest and taxes of $13,564 million on total assets of $251,506 million. The tax rate applicable for 1993 was 36%. The following table summarizes the pretax and after-tax ROA for GE for 1992 and 1993.

	1993	1992
EBT	$3,927	$4,238
+ Interest expenses	$525	$768
EBIT	$4,452	$5,006
Tax rate	36%	36%
EBIT(1 − t)	$2,849	$3,204
Total assets	$51,134	$48,075
Pretax ROA	8.71%	10.41%
ROA	5.57%	6.66%

Comparisons of ROA. The return on assets, once computed, can be used in a number of different ways. It can be used to compare different firms in the same business, to evaluate operating efficiency. In making these comparisons, care has to be taken to account for significant differences in accounting standards across the companies. The ROA can also be compared to the cost of capital of the firm, to get a measure of realized returns on projects. Though the ROA is based upon the book value of assets, a firm that picks good projects (with positive net present values) should have an ROA that exceeds its cost of capital. Note that both the ROA and cost of capital are concepts that measure returns to the firm, rather than just to equity investors.

Determinants of ROA. The return on assets of a firm can be written as a function of the operating profit margin that it has on its sales and its asset turnover ratio.

$$\text{ROA} = \text{EBIT}(1 - t)/\text{Total Assets}$$
$$= \text{EBIT}(1 - t)/\text{Sales} \times \text{Sales}/\text{Total Assets}$$
$$= \text{Pretax Operating Margin}(1 - t) \times \text{Asset Turnover Ratio}$$

> Pretax Operating Margin = EBIT/Sales

Thus, a firm can arrive at a high ROA by either increasing its profit margin or more efficiently utilizing its assets to increase sales. There are likely to be technological constraints on the latter and competitive constraints on the firm, but firms still have some freedom within these constraints to choose the mix of profit margin and asset turnover that maximizes their ROA.

The advantage of this decomposition of ROA is that it helps explain why some businesses have high ROA while others have low ROA, and it helps relate the ROA to strategic decisions that the firm makes on whether it wants to be a low-margin, high-volume producer or a high-margin, low-volume competitor.

Illustration 5.4: Decomposition of ROA: General Electric

General Electric had revenues of $29,533 million in 1993. Incorporating this with the numbers provided in Illustration 5.1 for earnings and total assets, the pretax ROA in 1993 can be decomposed into profit margin and asset turnover components:

Profit Margin = Earnings before interest and taxes/Revenues

 = $4,452/$29,533

 = 15.07%

Asset Turnover = Revenues/Total Assets

 = $29,533/$51,134

 = 57.76%

Pretax ROA = .1507 × .5776 = .0871 or 8.71%

After-tax ROA = .0871 (1 − .36) = 5.57%

Comparing ROA across Industries. The return on assets varies widely across firms in different businesses, largely as a consequence of differences in profit margins and asset turnover ratios. Table 5.1 provides returns on assets for major industry groups in 1994.

Note that differences in ROA across industries exist for two reasons: differences in risk, which are likely to persist over time, and differences in competitive pressure, which are likely to lead to new firms entering businesses with high profit margins and ROA and to existing firms leaving businesses with low profit margins and ROA.

Changes in ROA over Time. The return on assets of a firm can change for a number of reasons. Since it is largely a function of the operating profit, any factors that affect operating profit, positively or negatively, will also affect ROA.

Changes in sales: As sales increase or decrease, in response to economic cycles and the firm's own actions, the after-tax operating profit is likely to change, leading to changes in the ROA. The operating leverage measures the sensitivity of operating profit to changes in sales:

Operating Leverage = percentage change in Operating Profit/percentage

change in Sales

The operating leverage of a firm will be determined, in large part, by its cost structure. The operating income of firms with high fixed costs and low variable costs per unit is likely to be much more sensitive to changes in sales. On the other hand, a firm with high variable costs per unit and small fixed costs will have operating income which is not as sensitive to changes in sales.

Illustration 5.5: Operating Leverage: The Home Depot and Toys 'R Us

The Home Depot reported an increase of 28.6% in operating income from 1992 to 1993, while revenues increased by 29.2% over the same period. The operating leverage,

TABLE 5.1 Return on Assets by Industry Group
(Industry averages, end of 1994)

Industry	ROE (percent)	ROA (percent)	Payout (percent)	Debt Ratio (percent)	Beta	CE/Dep (percent)	WC/Rev (percent)
Agricultural Products	15.28	11.78	38.99	37.67	0.74	119	36.45
Mining	11.07	9.03	43.16	40.21	0.64	201	51.09
Petroleum Production & Refining	13.35	10.08	44.31	44.43	0.59	227	25.23
Building Contractors & Related Areas	11.84	10.09	39.20	30.04	1.08	148	22.47
Food Production	17.31	13.03	40.61	37.87	0.85	164	15.26
Beverages	17.55	12.80	39.22	41.14	0.95	218	24.59
Tobacco	32.65	19.22	61.90	50.39	1.11	133	11.52
Textile & Clothing Manufacturers	13.45	11.41	29.45	27.42	0.98	173	27.43
Furniture	14.73	12.52	25.18	25.34	0.93	138	24.62
Paper & Plastic Production	15.48	11.41	43.80	42.96	1.03	153	13.77
Publishing	17.34	13.44	34.69	34.41	0.99	102	20.10
Chemicals	18.64	13.89	38.64	37.61	1.34	170	49.84
Pharmaceuticals	28.40	20.82	44.53	33.83	1.36	222	71.49
Consumer Products	28.81	18.60	32.96	44.78	1.06	137	21.00
Autos & Related	18.12	13.31	27.65	39.69	0.99	143	21.55
Miscellaneous Manufacturing	16.42	12.72	32.76	35.51	1.07	139	23.36
Equipment Manufacturing	13.89	11.01	30.32	36.47	1.02	138	30.70
Computers & Office Equipment	14.84	12.14	30.79	30.49	1.27	143	43.82
Consumer Electronics	15.00	12.60	23.04	26.65	1.26	125	38.45
Other Consumer Durables	17.51	14.15	27.18	29.18	1.08	159	34.24
Transportation	12.79	9.51	29.33	48.29	1.10	199	14.48
Telephone Utilities	16.10	11.38	51.96	46.70	1.20	182	35.96
Entertainment (TV & Movies)	23.00	14.64	20.85	49.20	1.25	199	36.47
Electric & Gas Utilities	11.41	8.25	70.77	58.35	0.58	174	16.72
Wholesalers	16.50	12.82	29.84	35.01	1.08	138	22.14
Retailers	14.04	11.38	30.16	33.12	1.19	222	17.81
Restaurants & Eating Places	17.51	13.83	31.62	31.94	1.20	423	16.34
Banks & Financial Services	17.09	13.83	21.43	29.37	1.23	159	45.37
Insurance	23.62	18.22	35.84	30.66	0.85	108	22.05
Real Estate	19.69	14.43	33.42	38.44	0.69	130	36.53
Other Services	18.11	13.34	34.35	39.39	1.05	144	21.77
Computer Software & Services	20.66	19.31	25.30	9.18	1.33	155	43.35
Health Services	14.33	12.02	33.41	27.78	1.32	155	29.82
AVERAGE	15.44	11.63	38.05	40.35	1.03	165	31.67

based upon 1992–1993 data, is

$$\text{Operating Leverage}_{\text{Home Depot}} = 28.6\%/29.2\% = .98$$

In contrast, Toys 'R Us reported an increase of 27.15% in operating income, while revenues increased by only 17.06% from 1992 to 1993. The operating leverage, based upon 1992–1993 data, is

$$\text{Operating Leverage}_{\text{Toys 'R Us}} = 27.15\%/17.06\% = 1.59$$

Based only upon 1992–1993 data, it can be argued that Toys 'R Us has much higher operating leverage than the Home Depot.

Restructuring and ROA: One of the objectives in restructuring a firm is to increase operating efficiency, thus increasing either profit margin or asset turnover or both, leading to a healthier return on assets. Some of these changes happen immediately after the restructuring, but others take much longer to be reflected in operating profits. Consequently, even in a successful restructuring, the increase in ROA happens over an extended period of time.

Illustration 5.6: Restructuring and ROA: ARCO

Atlantic Richfield went through a major restructuring in 1985, changing both its asset and liability mixes. All of the company's refining and marketing operations east of the Mississippi River were sold. An $800 million reduction in capital outlays in areas where returns were low was also planned. All nonoil mineral operations were also sold. This was expected to increase the profit margin and the asset turnover.

	Pretax Profit Margin	Asset Turnover	Pretax ROA
Before restructuring	20.20%	1.675433231	33.84%
After restructuring	26.20%	1.934795699	50.69%

Strategic decisions: The decomposition of ROA into the profit margin and the asset turnover ratio provides a simple framework for evaluating shifts in corporate strategy. If a firm shifts from high profit margins to lower profit margins, hoping to generate more sales (higher asset turnover), the effects on the ROA can be estimated. Generally speaking, the asset turnover ratio will have to increase proportionately to the decrease in profit margins for the firm to maintain its ROA.

Illustration 5.7: Pricing strategy and ROA: Procter and Gamble

Procter and Gamble decided to reduce prices on its disposable diapers in April 1993 to better compete with low-price private label brands. The preinterest, after-tax profit margin was expected to drop from 7.43% to 7% as a consequence, and the asset turnover ratio was expected to increase from 1.6851 to 1.80. The following table

provides projections in profit margins, asset turnover, and growth rates after the shift in corporate strategy:

	1992	After Shift in Strategy
EBIT(1 − tax rate)	$2,181	
Sales	$29,362	
Preinterest, after-tax profit margin	7.43%	7.00%
Total assets	$17,424	
Asset turnover	1.6851	1.80
ROA	12.52%	12.60%

ROA of a Firm versus Divisional ROA. The return on assets of a firm can be further decomposed by division, and each division's ROA can be estimated separately.

Divisional ROA = EBIT of Division(1 − t)/Total Assets of Division

If the earnings and the assets of each division are clearly delineated, this statistic is easy to estimate. If assets are used by more than one division (headquarters expenses), and earnings are generated by multiple divisions, the analyst has to allocate the assets and earnings to the divisions before computing the ROA.

The advantage of computing ROA by division is that it can then be compared to the cost of capital for that division (the cost of capital can be different for different divisions because of risk and financing mix differences), to arrive at a conclusion about where the firm is creating wealth (those divisions where ROA exceeds the cost of capital) and where it is losing wealth (where ROA is less than the cost of capital). It can also provide a basis for restructuring the firm by focusing attention on those divisions that need change the most.

Illustration 5.8: ROA by division: General Electric, 1993

In 1993, General Electric reported operating profit, by segment, for its different operations. The following table provides ROA estimates[6] for the different segments:

Operating Segment	Operating Income	Total Assets	ROA
Aircraft engines	$ 798	$8,294	9.62%
Appliances	372	7,002	5.31%
Broadcasting	264	3,910	6.75%
Industrial	782	9,301	8.41%
Materials	834	6,355	13.12%
Power systems	1,143	8,435	13.55%
Technical products	706	5,261	13.42%

Return on Equity (ROE)

While the return on assets measures the profitability of the overall firm, the return on equity examines profitability from the perspective of the equity investor, by relating profits to the equity investor (net profit after taxes and interest) to the book value of the equity investment.

> Return on Equity = Net Income/Book Value of Equity

Since preferred stockholders have a different type of claim on the firm than do common stockholders, the return on equity should be cleansed of the effects of preferred stock. This can be accomplished by using net income after preferred dividends in the numerator and the book value of common equity in the denominator.

Comparisons of ROE. Since the return on equity is computed from the viewpoint of common stockholders, the comparison, when made, should be to the cost from the same viewpoint; that is, the cost of equity. Generally speaking, a firm that takes good projects should have an ROE that exceeds its cost of equity. This is, however, based upon the presumption that the book value of equity is a good approximation of the market value of equity in existing assets[7] and that the realized returns during the period being examined are a good measure of the returns that the projects will make over their lifetime. Since the ROE can vary widely from year to year, analysts often look at an average ROE over a longer time period and compare this average to the cost of equity.

Determinants of ROE. Since the return on equity is based upon earnings after interest payments, it is affected by the financing mix that the firm uses to fund its projects. In general, a firm that borrows money to finance projects and earns an ROA on those projects that exceeds the after-tax interest rate it pays on its debt will be able to increase its ROE by borrowing. The ROE can be written as follows[8]:

$$ROE = ROA + D/E(ROA - i[1 - t])$$

where ROA = EBIT$(1 - t)$/(BV of Debt + BV of Equity)
 D/E = BV of Debt/BV of Equity
 i = Interest on Debt/BV of Debt
 t = tax rate on ordinary income

The second term captures the benefit of financial leverage.

Since increased leverage also increases[9] the cost of equity, the ROE will have to increase by more than the cost of equity for higher leverage to be in the best interest of the firm.

Illustration 5.9: ROE and leverage: Boeing

In 1993, Boeing had a book value of equity of $8,983 million and a book value of debt of $2,630 million. It had interest expenses of $140 million. The company faced a tax rate of 31.69%. Boeing reported earnings before interest and taxes of $1,821 million. Based upon these numbers

ROA = $1,821(1 - .3169)/($8,983 + $2,630) = 10.71%

Debt/equity ratio = $2,630/$8,983 = 29.28%

Interest rate on debt = $140/$2,630 = 5.32%

ROE = 10.71% + .2928 (10.71% − 5.32%[1 − .3169]) = 12.78%

This can be confirmed by dividing the net income ($1,148 million) by the book value of equity:

ROE = $1,148/$8,983 = 12.78%

Profit Variability, Profitability Ratios, and Risk

One limitation of profitability ratios is that they measure profitability based upon the earnings in a period. Since earnings can vary significantly from period to period, the level of a profitability ratio can be a misleading indicator of future profitability. Furthermore, the risk/return tradeoff would suggest that it would be useful to know both the level and the variance in profitability ratios (ROE and ROA). If two firms have the same ROE but one has a much lower variability in ROE than the other, the lower-variance ROE firm would be considered to be the superior firm from a profitability standpoint.

Before analysts start using variability in ROA and ROE as a measure of risk, it has to be emphasized that this variability comes from both firm-specific and market sources. Only the latter is rewarded in most risk and return models, though there is some correlation between total risk and market risk; that is, firms that have high total risk also tend to be exposed to high market risk. Studies indicate that there is statistically significant correlation between ROE and market rates of return, though ROE explains only a small portion of the return.

Financial Ratios Measuring Risk

Firms face significant risk in their operations from a variety of sources, some specific to the industry in which the firm operates and some marketwide. A number of financial ratios measure a firm's exposure to risk, both from short-term liquidity pressures and long-term solvency needs.

Short-Term Liquidity Risk

Short-term liquidity risk arises primarily from the need to finance current operations. To the extent that the firm has to make payments to its suppliers before it gets paid for the goods and services it provides, there is a cash shortfall that has to be met, usually through short-term borrowing. Though this financing of working capital needs is routinely done in most firms, financial ratios have been devised to keep track of the extent of the firm's exposure to the risk that it will not be able to meet its short-term obligations.

Current Ratio. The current ratio is the ratio of current assets (cash, inventory, accounts receivable) to current liabilities (obligations coming due within the next period).

> Current Ratio = Current Assets/Current Liabilities

A current ratio below 1, for instance, would indicate that the firm has more obligations coming due in the next year than assets that it can expect to turn into cash. That would be an indication of liquidity risk.

While traditional analysis suggests that firms maintain a current ratio of 2 or greater, there is a tradeoff here between minimizing liquidity risk and tying up more and more cash in working capital. (Working Capital = Current Assets − Current Liabilities.) In fact, it can be reasonably argued that a very high current ratio is indicative of an unhealthy firm, which is having problems reducing its inventory. In recent years, firms have worked at reducing their current ratios and managing their working capital better.

The use of current ratios has to be tempered by a number of concerns. First, the ratio can be easily manipulated by firms, insofar as financial reporting dates, to give the illusion of safety. Second, current assets and current liabilities can change by an equal amount, but the effect on the current ratio will depend upon its level[10] before the change.

Quick Ratio. The quick or acid test ratio is a variant of the current ratio. It distinguishes between current assets that can be converted quickly into cash (cash, marketable securities) from those that cannot (inventory, accounts receivable).

> Quick Ratio = (Cash + Marketable Securities)/Current Liabilities

The exclusion of accounts receivable and inventory is not a hard and fast rule. If there is evidence that either can be converted into cash quickly, they can be included as part of the quick ratio.

Working Capital Turnover Ratios. The management of working capital is often a key component of the management of cash and liquidity risk. One measure of the efficiency of working capital is the magnitude of inventory and accounts receivable, relative to annual cost of goods sold and sales:

> Accounts Receivable Turnover = Sales/Average Accounts Receivable
>
> Inventory Turnover = Cost of Goods Sold/Average Inventory

These statistics can be interpreted as measuring the speed with which the firm turns accounts receivable into cash or inventory into sales. These ratios are often expressed in terms of the number of days outstanding:

> Days Accounts Receivable Outstanding = 365/Accounts Receivable Turnover
>
> Days Inventory Held = 365/Inventory Turnover

A similar pair of statistics can be computed for accounts payable, relative to purchases:

> Accounts Payable Turnover = Purchases/Average Accounts Payable
>
> Days Accounts Payable Outstanding = 365/Accounts Payable Turnover

Since accounts receivable and inventory are assets and accounts payable is a liability, these three statistics (standardized in terms of days outstanding) can be combined to get an estimate of how much financing the firm needs to raise to fund working capital needs.

> Required Financing Period = Days Accounts Receivable Outstanding
> + Days Inventory Held
> − Days Accounts Payable Outstanding

The longer the financing period for a firm, the greater is its short-term liquidity risk.

Illustration 5.10: Working capital turnover ratios: General Electric

The following table provides a computation of working capital ratios for General Electric and the Home Depot:

Item	GE	Home Depot
Current assets	$13,921	$1,966
Current liabilities	$14,359	$972
Current ratio	.97	2.02
Cash and marketable securities	$1,536	$100
Current liabilities	$14,359	$972
Quick ratio	.11	.10
Sales	$29,533	$9,238
Accounts receivable	$8,561	$198
Accounts receivable turnover	3.45	46.66
Days accounts receivable outstanding	105.81	7.82
Cost of goods sold	$22,630	$6,685
Average inventory	$3,824	$1,293
Inventory turnover	5.92	5.17
Days inventory held	61.68	70.60

The differences between the two firms reflect the different businesses they are in. The Home Depot sells few items on credit and hence has a much lower accounts receivable, relative to GE.

Long-Term Solvency and Default Risk

Measures of long-term solvency attempt to examine a firm's capacity to meet interest and principal payments in the long term. Clearly, the profitability ratios discussed earlier in the section are a critical component of this analysis. The ratios specifically designed to measure long-term solvency try to relate profitability to the level of debt payments, to see the degree of comfort with which the firm can meet these payments.

Interest Coverage Ratio. The interest coverage ratio measures the capacity of the firm to meet interest payments from predebt, pretax earnings.

Interest Coverage Ratio = Earnings before interest
and taxes/Interest expenses

The higher the interest coverage ratio, the more secure is the firm's capacity to make interest payments from earnings. This argument, however, has to be tempered by the recognition that earnings before interest and taxes is volatile and can drop significantly if the economy enters a recession. Consequently, two firms can have the same interest coverage ratio but can be viewed very differently in terms of risk.

The denominator in the interest coverage ratio can be easily extended to cover other fixed obligations such as least payments. If this is done, the ratio is called a fixed charges coverage ratio:

Fixed Charges Coverage Ratio = Earnings before interest,
fixed charges,
and taxes/Fixed Charges

Finally, this ratio, while stated in terms of earnings, can be restated in terms of cashflows, by using earnings before interest, taxes, and depreciation (EBITDA) in the numerator and cash fixed charges in the denominator.

Cash Fixed Charges Coverage Ratio = EBITDA/Cash Fixed Charges

Both interest and fixed charges coverage ratios are open to the criticism that they do not consider capital expenditures, cashflows that may be discretionary in the very short term but not in the long term, if the firm wants to maintain growth. One way of capturing the extent of this cashflow, relative to operating cashflows, is to compute a ratio of the two:

> Operating Cashflow/Cap. Ex. Ratio = Cashflows from Operations/Capital
> Expenditures

While there are a number of different definitions of cashflows from operations, the most reasonable way of defining it is to measure the cashflows from continuing operations, before interest but after taxes and after meeting working capital needs.

$$\text{Cashflow from Operations} = \text{EBIT}(1 - \text{tax rate}) - \triangle \text{Working Capital}$$

Debt Ratios. Interest coverage ratios measure the capacity of the firm to meet interest payments but do not examine whether it can pay back the principal on outstanding debt. Debt ratios attempt to do this, by relating debt to total capital or to equity. The two most widely used debt ratios are:

> Debt/Capital Ratio = Debt/(Debt + Equity)
> Debt/Equity Ratio = Debt/Equity

The first ratio measures debt as a proportion of the total capital of the firm, and cannot exceed 100%. The second measures debt as a proportion of the book value of equity in the firm, and can be easily derived from the first, since

$$\text{Debt/Equity Ratio} = (\text{Debt/Capital Ratio})/(1 - \text{Debt/Capital Ratio})$$

Variants on debt ratios: There are two close variants of these ratios. In the first, only long-term debt is used rather than total debt, with the rationale being that short-term debt is transitory and will not affect the long-term solvency of the firm.

> Long-Term Debt/Capital Ratio = Debt/(Debt + Equity)
> Long-Term Debt/Equity Ratio = Debt/Equity

Given the ease with which firms can roll over short-term debt and the willingness of many firms to use short-term financing to fund long-term projects, these variants can provide a misleading picture of the firm's financial leverage risk.

The second variant of these ratios uses market value instead of book value, primarily to reflect the fact that some firms have a significantly greater capacity to borrow than their book values indicate.

> Market Value: Debt/Capital Ratio = MV of Debt/
> (MV of Debt + MV of Equity)
> MV Debt/Equity Ratio = MV of Debt/MV of Equity

Many analysts disavow the use of market value in their calculations, contending that market values, in addition to being difficult to get for debt, are volatile and hence unreliable. These contentions are open to debate. It is true that the market value of debt is difficult to get for firms which do not have publicly traded bonds, but the market value of equity is not only easy to obtain, it is constantly updated to reflect marketwide and firm-specific changes. Furthermore, using the book value of debt as a proxy for market value in those cases where bonds are not traded does not significantly shift[11] most market-value-based debt ratios.

Illustration 5.11: Debt ratios and variants: Boeing

In 1993, Boeing reported a book value of equity of \$8,983 million and a book value of debt of \$2,630 million (all long term). The market price per share at the end of 1993 was \$42, and there were 349 million shares outstanding. The market value of the outstanding debt was \$2,750 million.

Market Value of Equity = 349 million shares × \$42 = \$18,148 million

Book Value of Equity = \$8,983 million

Book Value of Debt = \$2,630 million

Market Value of Debt = \$2,750 million

Book Value − Debt/Capital Ratio = \$2,630/(\$8,983 + \$2,630) = 22.65%

Market Value − Debt/Capital Ratio = \$2,750/(\$18,148 + \$2,750) = 13.16%

Book Value − Debt/Equity Ratio = \$2,630/\$8,983 = 29.28%

Market Value − Debt/Equity Ratio = \$2,750/\$18,148 = 15.15% ·

What to include in debt: There are a number of recent trends in financing that have made the estimation of the debt to include in debt ratios much more difficult.

(a) *Hybrid securities.* The first is the use of hybrid securities, part debt and part equity, like convertible bonds and preferred stock. The standard practice in calculating debt ratios has been all or nothing—a security is classified as debt if it has more debt characteristics than equity characteristics, which is itself a subjective judgment. The problem in this approach is that it leads to large shifts in debt ratios, depending upon whether a security is included in debt or not, and sudden changes in years in which a security is converted into equity. A more sensible way of dealing with hybrid securities would be to estimate the debt and equity components separately for hybrid securities and add these components to their respective sides.

(b) *Off-balance-sheet commitments.* The second area of controversy is in the classification of off-balance-sheet commitments, such as contingent liabilities. The general rule to follow is to ignore contingent liabilities that hedge against risk, since the obligations on the contingent claim will be offset[12] by benefits elsewhere.

(c) *Leases.* The third area of debate is the treatment of leases. While capitalized leases are now shown as part of debt, operating leases are not. Since a fine line separates the two, the conservative approach to estimating debt ratios will capitalize operating leases and show them as part of debt.

(d) *Pensions.* Firms generally include in their debt the excess of accumulated benefit obligation over the pension fund assets. Here again, a conservative estimate of the debt ratio will consider projected benefit obligation over pension fund assets.

(e) *Debt of nonconsolidated entities.* Firms generally do not have to show as a liability that debt that is owed by their nonconsolidated subsidiaries, even though they may have guaranteed and stand liable for that borrowing. The conservative approach to estimating debt ratios will add this debt to the firm's total debt and compute the debt ratio on that basis.

A Note of Caution on Financial Ratios

Financial ratios are easy to compute and often useful in evaluating a firm's health and profitability and comparing firms in the same business. Financial ratios are also used widely as intermediate statistics to compute other measures, like the Altman Z score, and in estimating levered betas. Like all financial statistics, they have to be used with caution, since firms can and do manipulate them to suit their needs. They are also often based upon the financial statements of one period and do not reflect the variability in the underlying numbers.

OTHER ISSUES IN ANALYZING FINANCIAL STATEMENTS

There are two more issues that bear consideration before concluding this section on financial statements. The first relates to differences in accounting standards and practices and how these differences may color comparisons across companies, and the second relates to accounting for acquisitions and how this can affect both the acquisition method and price.

Differences in Accounting Standards and Practices

There are differences in accounting standards across countries that affect the measurement of earnings. These differences, however, are not as great as they are made out to be and cannot be used to explain away radical departures from fundamental principles of valuation.[13] Choi and Levich (1990) in a survey of accounting standards across developed markets, note that most countries subscribe to basic accounting notions of consistency, realization, and historical cost principles in preparing accounting statements. Appendix 1 summarizes accounting standards in six major financial markets and reveals that the common elements vastly outnumber those areas where there are differences.

The two countries that offer the strongest contrast to the United States are Germany and Japan. The key differences and their implications are as follows.

First, companies in the United States generally maintain separate tax and financial reporting books, which in turn generates items like deferred taxes to cover differences between the two books and leads to different depreciation methods—straight line in the financial reports and accelerated in the financial reports. Companies in Germany and Japan do not maintain separate books. Consequently, depreciation methods in financial reports are much more likely to be accelerated and hence reduce stated income. Second, the requirement that leases be capitalized and shown as a liability is much more tightly enforced in the United States. In Japan, leases are generally treated as operating leases and do not show up as liabilities in the balance sheet. In Germany, firms can capitalize leases but have more leeway in classifying leases as operating and capital leases than do U.S. companies. Third, goodwill once created can be amortized over 40 years in the United States, compared with much shorter time periods in Germany and Japan, again depressing stated income. Fourth, reserves in the United States can be created only for specific purposes, whereas German and Japanese companies can use general reserves to equalize income across periods, leading to income being understated during the good years and overstated during bad years.

Most of these differences can be accounted and adjusted for when comparisons are made of companies in the United States and those in other financial markets. Statistics such as price/earnings ratios, which use stated and unadjusted earnings, can be misleading when accounting standards vary widely across the companies being compared.

Accounting for Acquisitions

There are two basic approaches to accounting for acquisitions. In the purchase method, the acquiring firm records the assets and liabilities of the acquired firm at market value, with goodwill capturing the difference between market value and the value of the assets acquired. This goodwill is then amortized, though the amortization is not tax deductible. If a firm pays cash on an acquisition, it has to use the purchase method to record the transaction.

In a pooling of interests approach, the book values of the assets and liabilities of the merging firms are added up to arrive at the values for the combined firm. Since the market value of the transaction is not recognized, there is no goodwill created or amortized. This approach is allowed only if the acquiring firm exchanges its common stock for common stock of the acquired firm. Since earnings are not affected by the amortization of goodwill, the reported earnings per share under this approach will be greater than the reported earnings per share in the purchase approach.

CONCLUSION

Financial statements remain the primary source of information for most investors and analysts. While an understanding of every detail and FASB rule may

not be necessary, it is important that the basics be understood. This chapter attempts to explain the basics of financial statements and the generally accepted accounting principles that underlie their construction, and the various financial ratios that often accompany financial analyses. As long as there is a recognition that financial statements and financial ratios are a means to an end, which is understanding and valuing the firm, they are useful.

QUESTIONS AND SHORT PROBLEMS

The following were the financial statements for Eaton Corp. in 1993 and 1994.

Income Statements			Balance Sheets		
Sales	1993	1994	Assets	1993	1994
− Cost of Goods Sold	$4,300	$4,900	Fixed Assets		
− Depreciation	$3,578	$4,063	Current Assets	1114	1340
= Earnings Before Interest & Taxes	$ 185	$ 200	Inventory	439	450
− Interest Expenses	$ 537	$ 637	Receivables	599	630
= Earnings Before Taxes	$ 70	$ 72	Other	443	420
− Taxes	$ 467	$ 565	Liabilities		
= Net Income	$ 177	$ 215	Current Liabilities	732	780
Dividends Paid	$ 290	$ 350	Debt	788	820
Stock Price	$ 80	$ 84	Equity	1075	1240
	$ 51	$ 60			

There were 71 million shares outstanding in each year. The debt traded at 95% of book value.

1. Prepare a statement of cashflows for 1994 for Eaton Corp.
2. Estimate the following profitability measures for Eaton Corp. in 1994:
 a. Pretax and after-tax returns on assets.
 b. Return on equity.
 c. Pretax and after-tax operating margin.
 d. Net profit margin.
3. Based upon 1993 and 1994 earnings and revenues, estimate the operating leverage for Eaton Corp.
4. Estimate the following leverage measures for Eaton Corp.:
 a. Book value debt to equity ratio.
 b. Market value debt to equity ratio.
 c. Book value debt to capital ratio.
 d. Market value debt to capital ratio.
5. Estimate the following working capital measures for Eaton Corp.:
 a. Dollar working capital in 1993 and 1994.
 b. Current ratio.
 c. Asset turnover ratios.
 d. Number of days sales in inventory.

ENDNOTES

1. If a cost (such as an administrative cost) cannot be easily linked with a particular revenue, it is usually recognized as an expense in the period in which it is consumed.

2. It has the opposite effect on cashflows, since lengthening the depreciable life reduces depreciation and increases both taxable income and taxes.

3. The FASB statement (105) requires that the following be disclosed: the face value or notional principal amount, the terms of the instrument and the credit and market risk involved, and the accounting loss that the firm would incur if any party to the agreement does not perform.

4. The requirements for an operating lease in the revenue code are as follows: (a) The property can be used by someone other than the lessee at the end of the lease term; (b) the lessee cannot buy the asset using a bargain purchase option; (c) the lessor has at least 20% of its capital at risk; (d) the lessor has a positive cashflow from the lease independent of tax benefits; and (e) the lessee does not have an investment in the lease.

5. The accumulated pension fund liability does not take into account the projected benefit obligation, where actuarial estimates of future benefits are made. Consequently, it is much smaller than the total pension liabilities.

6. While General Electric did not provide a breakdown of total assets by division, the assets were assumed to be in proportion to the revenues of the divisions.

7. The market value of equity includes both the market value of equity in assets in place and market value of equity in anticipated future growth. The book value of equity reflects the book value of equity of assets in place, and the ROE measures returns on those assets.

8. $\text{ROA} + D/E(\text{ROA} - i[1 - t]) = (NI + \text{Int}[1 - t])/(D + E) + D/E\{NI + \text{Int}[1 - t]/$
$$(D + E) - \text{Int}(1 - t)/D\}$$
$$= \{(NI + \text{Int}[1 - t])/(D + E)\}(1 + D/E) - \text{Int}(1 - t)/E$$
$$= NI/E + \text{Int}(1 - t)/E - \text{Int}(1 - t)/E = NI/E = \text{ROE}$$

9. The relationship between financial leverage and betas is explored in the chapter on risk and return. As the leverage increases, the beta increases, leading to a higher cost of equity.

10. If the current assets and current liabilities increase by an equal amount, the current ratio will go down if it was greater than 1 before the increase and go up if it was less than 1.

11. Deviations in the market value of equity from the book value are likely to be much larger than those for debt, and are likely to dominate in most debt ratio calculations.

12. This assumes that the hedge is set up competently. It is entirely possible that a hedge, if sloppily set up, can end up costing the firm money.

13. At the peak of the Japanese market, there were many investors who explained away the price/earnings multiples of 60 and greater in the market by noting that Japanese firms are conservative in measuring earnings. Even after taking into account the general provisions and excess depreciation used by many of these firms to depress current earnings, the price/earnings multiples were greater than 50 for many firms, suggesting either extraordinary expected growth in the future or overvaluation.

APPENDIX 1 Comparison of Accounting Principles

Accounting Principle	UK	USA	France	Germany	Netherlands	Sweden	Switzerland	Japan
1. Consistency—accounting principles and methods are applied on the same basis from period to period.	Yes	Yes	Yes	Yes	Yes	PP	PP	Yes
2. Realization—revenue is recognized when realization is reasonably assured.	Yes	Yes	Yes	Yes	Yes	Yes	PP	Yes
3. Fair presentation of the financial statement is required.	Yes	Yes	Yes	Yes	Yes	Yes	Yes	Yes
4. Historical cost convention—departures from the historical cost convention are disclosed.	Yes	Yes	Yes	Yes	Yes	Yes	RF	Yes
5. Accounting policies—a change in accounting principles and methods without a change in circumstances is accounted for by a prior year adjustment.	Yes	No	Yes	MP	RF	MP	MP	No
6. Fixed assets—revaluation—in historical cost statements, fixed assets are stated at an amount in excess of cost which is determined at irregular intervals.	MP	No	Yes	No	RF	PP	No	No
7. Fixed assets—revaluation—when fixed assets are stated, in historical cost statements, at an amount in excess of cost, depreciation based on the revaluation amount is charged to income.	Yes	No	Yes	No	Yes	Yes	No	No
8. Goodwill amortized.	MP	Yes	Yes	Yes	M	Yes	MP	Yes
9. Finance leases capitalized.	Yes	Yes	No	No	No	Yes	RF	No
10. Short-term marketable securities at the lower of cost or market value.	Yes	Yes	Yes	Yes	Yes	Yes	Yes	Yes
11. Inventory values at the lower of cost or market value.	Yes	Yes	Yes	Yes	Yes	Yes	Yes	Yes
12. Manufacturing overhead allocated to year-end inventory.	Yes	Yes	Yes	Yes	Yes	Yes	Yes	Yes
13. Inventory costed using FIFO.	PP	M	M	M	M	PP	PP	M
14. Long-term debt includes maturities longer than one year.	Yes	Yes	Yes	No	Yes	Yes	Yes	M
15. Deferred tax recognized where accounting income and taxable income arise at different times.	Yes	Yes	Yes	No	Yes	No	No	Yes

#	Item	C1	C2	C3	C4	C5	C6	C7
16.	Total pension fund assets and liabilities excluded from a company's financial statements.	Yes	Yes	Yes	No	Yes	Yes	Yes
17.	Research and development expensed.	Yes	Yes	Yes	Yes	Yes	Yes	Yes
18.	General purpose (purely discretionary) reserves allowed.	No	No	Yes	Yes	Yes	Yes	Yes
19.	Offsetting—assets and liabilities are offset against each other in the balance sheet only when a legal right of offset exists.	Yes	Yes	Yes	Yes	Yes	PP	Yes
20.	Unusual and extraordinary gains and losses are taken in the income statement.	Yes	Yes	Yes	Yes	Yes	Yes	Yes
21.	Closing rate method of foreign currency translation employed.	Yes	No	Yes	Yes	No	Yes	No
22.	Currency translation gains or losses arising from trading are reflected in current income.	MP	MP	MP	MP	MP	MP	No
23.	Excess depreciation permitted.	Yes	Yes	Yes	Yes	Yes	Yes	Yes
24.	Basic statements reflect a historical cost valuation (no price level adjustment).	Yes	Yes	Yes	M	Yes	Yes	Yes
25.	Supplementary inflation—adjusted financial statements adjusted.	MP	MP	No	MP	No	No	No
26.	Accounting for long-term investments:							
(a)	less than 20% ownership—cost method.	Yes	Yes	Yes	No	Yes	Yes	Yes
(b)	20–50% ownership—equity method.	Yes	Yes	No	Yes	MP	M	Yes
(c)	More than 50% full consolidation.	Yes	Yes	Yes	Yes	Yes	Yes	Yes
27.	Both domestic and foreign subsidiaries consolidated.	Yes	Yes	M	Yes	Yes	MP	MP
28.	Acquisition accounted for under the purchase cost method.	PP	Yes	PP	Yes	Yes	PP	Yes
29.	Minority interest excluded from consolidation income.	Yes	Yes	Yes	Yes	Yes	Yes	Yes
30.	Minority interest excluded from consolidated owners' equity.	Yes	Yes	Yes	Yes	Yes	Yes	Yes

Key: PP—Predominant practice
MP—Minority practice
M—Mixed practice
RF—Rarely or not found

Estimation of Cashflows

Much of the tedium in valuation is a direct result of having to estimate cashflows. There can be no discounted cashflow valuation without this, though. This chapter examines the process of estimating cashflows and establishes some general principles that should be adhered to in all valuation. The one overriding principle governing cashflow estimation is to match cashflows to discount rates—equity cashflows to cost of equity, firm cashflows to cost of capital, pretax cashflows to pretax rates, posttax cashflows to posttax rates, nominal cashflows to nominal rates, and real cashflows to real rates. The process of estimating these cashflows is explained in detail in the pages that follow.

CASHFLOWS TO EQUITY

Equity investors in an asset receive a residual claim on its cashflows; that is, they are entitled to any cashflows left over after meeting all financial obligations including debt payments and after meeting the reinvestment needs of the firm. The cashflow to equity is therefore the cashflow remaining after operating expenses, interest and principal payments, and any capital expenditure needed to maintain the growth rate in projected cashflows.

Cashflows to Equity for an Unlevered Firm

An unlevered firm has no debt and hence no interest and principal repayments. To compensate, it also finances all capital expenditure and working capital needs with equity. The cashflow to equity for an unlevered firm can then be calculated as follows:

Revenues

- − Operating Expenses
- = Earnings before interest, taxes, depreciation, and amortization (EBITDA)
- − Depreciation and Amortization
- = Earnings before interest and taxes (EBIT)
- − Taxes

= Net Income
+ Depreciation and Amortization
= Cashflows from Operations
− Capital Expenditures
− Working Capital Change
= Free Cashflows to Equity

The cashflow to equity is the residual cashflow after meeting all of the firm's financial needs. It can be negative, in which case the firm has to raise new equity, either by issuing stock or warrants.[1] If it is positive, it could be, but is not always, paid out as dividend to equity investors. The key items that distinguish this measure from net income, which is more commonly used to measure returns to equity investors, are the following.

Depreciation and Amortization

While depreciation and amortization are treated as tax-deductible expenses in an income statement, they are different from other expenses because they are noncash charges; that is, there are no cash outflows associated with either. They provide a benefit by reducing the taxable income of the firm and create a savings in taxes which is a function of the tax rate of the firm:

Tax Benefit from depreciation $=$ Depreciation \times Marginal Tax Rate of the firm

The cashflows from operations will be much higher than the net income for capital-intensive firms that have high depreciation allowances.

Capital Expenditures

Equity investors cannot withdraw the entire cashflow from operations from the firm, since some or all of this cashflow will have to be reinvested to maintain existing assets and to create new assets to generate future growth. Since the benefits of growth are usually reflected in cashflow forecasts, the cost of creating this growth will also have to be considered in estimating cashflows. It would be inconsistent, for instance, for a manufacturing firm to have a high growth rate in cashflows and have no or low capital expenditures.

The relationship between depreciation and capital expenditures is a complex one, and it will be different for firms in different stages of growth and in different business areas. Firms in a high growth phase generally have capital expenditures which exceed depreciation, while there is more parity between the two for firms in stable growth. Many analysts assume, for example, that depreciation is equal to capital spending for firms in a stable growth phase. This implies that the ratio of capital expenditures to depreciation should decrease as the firm moves through the growth cycle from high growth to stable growth.

Working Capital Requirements

The working capital of a firm is the difference between its current assets and its current liabilities. Since funds tied up in working capital cannot be used

elsewhere in the firms, changes in working capital affect the cashflows to the firm—increases in working capital are cash outflows and decreases in working capital are cash inflows. In the context of valuation, the working capital needs of the firm have to be taken into account in calculating cashflows to equity.

The accounting definition of working capital includes cash in current assets. This is appropriate as long as the cash is necessary for the day-to-day operations of the firm. Increases in cash beyond this requirement should not be considered in calculating working capital for purposes of cashflow calculation, since an increase in working capital as a consequence of cash accumulating in the firm is not a cash outflow to the firm.

The working capital needs of a firm will in large part be determined by the type of business it is in. Retail firms have a much higher need for working capital, as a percent of revenues, since they have higher inventory and credit needs than do service firms. Furthermore, the changes in working capital will be correlated to the growth rate of the firm. In general, higher-growth firms can expect to have much larger increases in working capital than lower-growth firms in the same line of business.

The failure to consider working capital needs in valuation will result in the over estimation of cashflows to equity and the value of equity in the firm.

Illustration 6.1: Estimating the cashflows to equity on an unlevered firm: Cypress Semiconductor

Cypress Semiconductor Corporation is an unlevered firm that designs, develops, and manufactures a broad line of integrated circuits used in workstations, mainframes, and personal computers. It had net income of $34.2 million in 1991 and $3.0 million in 1992. The following table estimates free cashflows to equity in each year (in millions):

	1991	1992
Net Income	$34.2	$ 3.0
+ Depreciation	41.5	45.0
= Cashflows from Operations	75.7	48.0
− Capital Expenditures	64.1	36.5
− Working Capital Change	12.5	−6.3
= Free Cashflows to Equity	−.9	17.8

The free cashflows to equity present a different picture from the net income. The drop in capital expenditures and working capital in 1992 increased free cashflows to equity, though net income was much lower.

Cashflows to Equity for a Levered Firm

A levered firm has to, in addition to making all of the outlays that an unlevered firm makes, also generate cashflows to cover interest expenses and principal

repayments. A levered firm, however, also finances some of its capital expenditures and working capital needs with debt, thus reducing the equity investment needed.

 Revenues
 − Operating Expenses
 = Earnings before interest, taxes, depreciation, and amortization (EBITDA)
 − Depreciation and Amortization
 = Earnings before interest and taxes (EBIT)
 − Interest Expenses
 = Earnings before taxes
 − Taxes
 = Net Income
 + Depreciation and Amortization
 = Cashflows from Operations
 − Preferred Dividends[2]
 − Working Capital Change
 − Principal Repayments
 + Proceeds from New Debt Issues
 = Free Cashflows to Equity

There is a difference in the tax treatment of debt payments—interest is tax deductible while principal payments are not. The amount of new debt issued by the firm will depend upon whether it views itself as being at, above, or below its desired[3] leverage.

Levered Firm at Desired Leverage

If a levered firm is at its desired leverage, that is, it has a debt ratio that it views as acceptable for future financing, the calculation of the cashflows to equity is simplified. For a firm with a desired debt ratio (debt/total capital) of δ,

 Net Income
 − $(1 - \delta)$(Capital Expenditures − Depreciation)
 − $(1 - \delta)$Working Capital Change
 = Free Cashflows to Equity

For this firm,

 Proceeds from new debt issues = Principal Repayments
 + δ(Capital Expenditures − Depreciation + Working Capital Change)

Since the firm is at its desired capital structure, principal repayments are made with proceeds from new debt issues. Capital expenditures and working capital needs are financed with the desired mix of debt and equity.

Illustration 6.2: Estimating the cashflow to equity for a firm at its desired leverage:
Warner-Lambert

The following is an estimation of free cashflows to equity for Warner-Lambert, a large
pharmaceutical company, in 1994 and for 1995 (projected):

- The company had $1.5 billion in debt outstanding and $9 billion in market value
 of equity, leading to a debt-to-capital ratio ("debt ratio") of 14%. This debt ratio
 was assumed to be stable.[4]
- The company reported net income of $695 million in 1994 and was projected
 to have a net income of $765 million in 1995.
- The company reported depreciation of $180 million in 1994 and was expected
 to have depreciation of $200 million in 1995.
- The company had capital expenditures of $362 million in 1994 and was expected
 to have capital expenditures of $400 million in 1995.
- The company's working capital increased to $225 million in 1994 from $203
 million in 1993. It was expected to maintain working capital at the same percent-
 age of sales in 1995, and sales were expected to increase from $6,420 million
 in 1994 to $7,100 million in 1995.

	1994	Estimated 1995	
Net Income	$695.00	$765.00	
−(Capital Expenditures − Depreciation)			
$(1 - \partial)$	156.52	172.00	$(\partial = 14\%)$
−(Change in Working Capital) $(1 - \partial)$	18.92	20.50	$(\partial = 14\%)$
Free Cashflows to Equity	519.56	572.50	

Proposition: The Free Cashflow to Equity will increase as the amount of
debt financing used by the firm increases. Thus FCFE will be an increasing
function of ∂.

Sensitivity of FCFE to Debt Ratio

The following are the cashflows to equity for Warner-Lambert, using a debt
ratio of 40% instead of a debt ratio of 14%.

	1994	Estimated 1995	
Net Income	$695.00	$765.00	
−(Capital Expenditures − Depreciation)			
$(1 - \partial)$	109.20	120.00	$(\partial = 40\%)$
−(Change in Working Capital) $(1 - \partial)$	13.20	14.30	$(\partial = 40\%)$
Free Cashflows to Equity	572.60	630.70	

Figure 6.1 illustrates the effect on free cashflows to equity of changing the debt ratios
from 0% to 100%. It has to be pointed out, however, that this increase in cashflows
to equity comes at a price—the risk to equity investors will increase concurrently.
The net effect on value may not be positive.

FIGURE 6.1 Debt Ratios, FCFE, and Betas

Levered Firm at Debt Ratio Below Optimal

A levered firm that is operating at a debt ratio below its desired level (δ) can afford to use more debt in financing its capital expenditures and working capital needs, at least until it reaches its targeted debt level. The cashflows to equity can then be calculated as follows:

Net Income
+ Depreciation and Amortization
= Cashflows from Operations
− Capital Expenditures
− Working Capital Change
− Principal Repayments
+ Proceeds from new debt issues
= Free Cashflows to Equity

If the firm decides to increase its leverage toward the targeted level, then

Proceeds from new debt issues > Principal Repayments
+ δ(Capital Expenditures + Working Capital Change)

During the period when a firm finances its investment needs disproportionately with debt, the free cashflows to equity of this firm will exceed the free cashflows to equity of a firm that does not have this financing slack. The principal repayments are still financed with new debt issues and hence do not affect cashflows to equity.

Illustration 6.3: Estimating the cashflows to equity for a firm with debt slack;
E-Systems

E-Systems makes electronic products for use in defense and information processing. The net income in 1992 was $120 million and the projected net income in 1993 was $130 million. The capital expenditure in 1992 was $75 million and was projected to be $80 million in 1993. The working capital increased by $24 million in 1992 and was expected to increase by $25 million in 1993. E-Systems had debt of $101.8 million in 1992 and a market value of equity of $1,170 million, yielding a debt ratio of 8%. Assume that E-Systems plans to increase its debt ratio to 15% by 1996. To reach this debt level, it plans to finance 30% of its capital expenditures and working capital requirements between 1993 and 1996 with debt. The projected free cashflows to equity (in millions) in 1993 are:

	1992	Projected 1993
Net Income	$120.0	$130.0
+ Depreciation	53.0	58.0
= Cashflows from Operations	173.0	188.0
− Capital Expenditures	75.0	80.0
− Working Capital Change	24.0	25.0
− Principal Repayments	10.0	10.0
+ Proceeds from new debt issues	20.0	41.5
= Cashflows to Equity	84.0	114.5

New Debt Issues in 1993 = Principal Repayments + 30% of Capital Expenditure
and Working Capital Change = $10 + .3($80 + $25) = $41.5 million

Levered Firm at Debt Ratio Above Desired Level

A levered firm that is operating at a debt ratio above its desired level will have to use disproportionately more equity in financing its investment needs if it wants to lower its debt ratio. It might also have to generate funds from equity to meet some or all of its principal repayments. The cashflows to equity can then be calculated as follows:

Net Income

+ Depreciation and Amortization

= Cashflows from Operations

− Capital Expenditures

− Working Capital Change

− Principal Repayments

+ Proceeds from new debt issues

= Free Cashflows to Equity

If the firm decides to reduce its leverage toward the optimal, then

Proceeds from new debt issues < Principal Repayments
+ δ(Capital Expenditure
+ Working Capital Change)

In the time period when disproportionately more equity is used in financing investment needs and to meet principal repayments by the firm, the free cashflows to equity will be lower than the free cashflows to equity of an otherwise similar firm at its desired laverage.

Illustration 6.4: Estimating the cashflows to equity for a firm with too much debt: IBM

In 1992, IBM had net income of $1,417 million (excluding extraordinary charges and a one-time accounting change), capital expenditures of $5,800 million, and depreciation of $6,259 million. For 1993, the projected net income was $1,130 million, the projected capital expenditure was $4,500 million, and the projected depreciation was $6,350 million. The working capital increased by $1,500 million in 1992 and was expected to increase by $200 million in 1993. IBM had debt outstanding of $30,000 million in 1992 and a market value of equity of $30,000 million. Assume that IBM plans to reduce its debt ratio from 50% to 40% by 1996 by financing its capital expenditures and working capital increases primarily with equity (90% equity and 10% debt) and by repaying long-term debt with cashflows from equity.

	1992	Projected 1993
Net Income	$1,417	$1,140
+ Depreciation and Amortization	6,259	6,350
= Cashflows from Operations	7,676	7,480
− Capital Expenditures	5,800	4,500
− Working Capital Change	1,500	200
− Principal Repayments	10,735	5,000
+ Proceeds from new debt issues	14,244	4,070
= Cashflows to Equity	3,885	1,850

New Debt Issues in 1993 = Short-Term Debt Refinanced
 + 10% of Capital Expenditure and Working Capital Change = $3,600
 + .1($4,500 + $200) = $4,070.0 million

This implies that all principal payments on long-term debt ($1,400 million) coming due in 1993 will be met by cashflows from equity investors. The drop in free cashflows to equity in 1993 is a consquence of the reduction in new debt issues.

Cashflows to Equity versus Net Income

The standard measure of the returns to equity investors, in accounting terms, remains net income, and it plays a significant role in many valuation models. In discounted cashflow valuation, the focus is on cashflows. The free cashflows to equity are different from net income for a number of reasons. First, all noncash charges are added back to net income to arrive at the cashflows from operations. Thus, the earnings reported by firms that take significant noncash charges against current income might be lower than cashflows. Second, cashflows to equity are residual cashflows after meeting capital expenditures and working capital needs, whereas net income does not include either. Thus, high-

growth firms that have significant capital expenditures and working capital needs might report positive and growing earnings while facing negative cashflows to equity.

A basic question in valuation is whether investors care more about net income or cashflows in setting market prices for securities. There are circumstances where actions taken by a firm increase earnings while reducing cashflows, or vice versa. For instance, when firms switch the depreciation method they use from accelerated to straight line, they increase the reported earnings while decreasing cashflows.[5] Kaplan and Roll (1972) examine firms that switch depreciation methods from accelerated to straight line and vice versa and find that financial markets react negatively to firms that increase earnings at the expense of cashflows and positively to firms that increase cashflows at the expense of earnings. In a similar vein, firms that switch inventory valuation methods can affect reported earnings and cashflows. In inflationary periods, firms that switch from using First-in First-out (FIFO) to Last-in First-out (LIFO) accounting will report higher costs of goods sold and lower net income while lowering their tax liability and increasing cashflows. Sunder (1973, 1975) examined 110 firms that switched from FIFO to LIFO between 1946 and 1966 and concluded that stock prices did not react negatively to the lower earnings reported by these firms.

For the most part, increases (decreases) in earnings lead to increases (decreases) in cashflows, and the attention that analysts pay to forecasting future earnings is justified. By focusing only on earnings, however, analysts might develop a misleading picture of a firm especially when cashflows and earnings diverge.

Net Income and Extraordinary Items

Net income is also affected by extraordinary gains and losses that are taken in individual years. Since these extraordinary items can cause reported earnings to deviate significantly from operating earnings during that year, they have to be eliminated from consideration when forecasting future earnings. For example, IBM, which reported a net loss of $4.965 billion in 1992, had restructuring charges of $11.645 billion and a one-time gain from an accounting change of $1.9 billion. Without the restructuring charges and the gain from accounting changes, IBM would have reported earnings of about $1.417 billion, which is a much more reasonable base to use for forecasting future earnings and cashflows.

The implication is not, however, that extraordinary items do not affect value. Extraordinary gains and/or losses often are the result of both financial restructuring (i.e., changing the capital structure) and asset restructuring (i.e., selling assets or divisions). The results of this restructuring have to be factored into projected cashflows and discount rates in the valuation and can make a significant difference in value.

CASHFLOWS TO THE FIRM

A firm is composed of all its claimholders and includes, in addition to equity investors, bondholders and preferred stockholders. The cashflows to the firm are therefore the accumulated cashflows to all these claimholders.

Estimating Cashflows to the Firm

In general terms, the cashflows to the firm are those cashflows left over after meeting operating expenses and taxes but before making payments to any claimholders. There are two ways in which these cashflows can be calculated. One way is to accumulate the cashflows to different claimholders in the firm:

Claimholder	Cashflows to Claimholder	Discount Rate
Equity investors	Free Cashflows to Equity	Cost of Equity
Debtholders[6]	Interest Expenses (1 − tax rate) + Principal Repayments − New Debt Issues	After-Tax Cost of Debt
Preferred stockholders	Preferred Dividends	Cost of Preferred Stock
Firm = equity investors + debtholders + preferred stockholders	Free Cashflows to Firm = Free Cashflows to Equity + Interest Expenses (1 − tax rate) + Principal Repayments − New Debt Issues + Preferred Dividends	Weighted Average Cost of Capital

The other approach, which should yield an equivalent number, starts with the earnings before interest and taxes.

> EBIT(1 − tax rate)
> + Depreciation
> − Capital Expenditures
> − Working Capital Needs
> = Cashflows to the Firm

The cashflows to the firm will generally be greater than the cashflows to equity for any levered firm and equal to it for an unlevered firm.

Illustration 6.5: Estimating the expected cashflows to the firm: Siemens

Siemens AG, a German-based multinational involved in a wide range of businesses, reported earnings before interest and taxes of 3,482 million DM in 1992, prior to general provisions and extraordinary charges. It had depreciation of 4,613 million DM and capital expenditures of 5,560 million DM in 1992. In addition, the working capital increased from 14,306 million DM in 1991 to 15,405 million DM in 1992. The earnings before interest and taxes is expected to increase to 3,967 million DM in 1993. Capital

expenditures, depreciation, and working capital are all expected to increase by 5% in 1993. The firm had a tax rate of 38% in 1992. The free cashflows to the firm (in millions) for 1992 and 1993 (estimated) are as follows:

	1992	Projected 1993
EBIT(1 − tax rate)	2,159	2,460
+ Depreciation	4,613	4,844
− Capital Expenditures	5,560	5,838
− Working Capital Change	1,099	770
Free Cashflows to Firm	114	696

Cashflows to the Firm, Leverage, and Value

Since the cashflows to the firm are before debt payments, they are unaffected by the amount of debt that the firm takes on. This does not imply, however, that the value of the firm, obtained by discounting cashflows to the firm at the weighted average cost of capital, is unaffected by leverage. As a firm takes on more debt, the weighted average cost of capital can change, causing the value of the firm to change. If the weighted average cost of capital decreases, the value of the firm will increase.

Intuitively, it might seem reasonable that the cashflows to the firm should reflect the tax benefits from interest expenses. However, the tax benefit from debt is already reflected in the weighted average cost of capital, through the use of after-tax cost of debt, and will be double-counted if it is also shown in the cashflows.

INFLATION, CASHFLOWS, AND VALUE

The effects of inflation on value will depend, in part, upon whether the inflation is expected or unanticipated. Expected inflation can be incorporated into cashflows and discount rates at the time of the analysis, and value can be conditioned on it.

Nominal and Real Cashflows/Discount Rates

Nominal cashflows incorporate expected inflation. The process of estimating nominal cashflows requires the analyst to make estimates not only of expected inflation in the general price level but also of expected price increases in the specific goods and services that the firm either sells or uses. Thus, an analyst making nominal cashflow predictions for an airline would have to predict price increases in airline tickets to obtain revenues and the inflation rate in the price of oil to estimate costs. The process of estimating nominal discount rates is much simpler. If financial market rates are used as the basis for estimating discount rates, the resulting rates will be nominal. In the capital asset pricing model, for instance, using the Treasury bill or bond rate as the riskfree rate

will result in a nominal discount rate, since these rates incorporate expected inflation.[7]

The relationship between nominal and real cashflows is determined by expected inflation:

Real Cashflow$_t$ = Nominal Cashflow$_t$/$(1 + E[I])^t$

where $E(I_t)$ = expected inflation rate in the general price level

The effects of inflation on real cashflows will depend, in part, on the difference, if any, between the expected inflation in the prices of the goods that the firm sells and that in the cost of the resources that the firm uses. If a firm can expect to increase prices on goods that it sells at a rate faster than the rate at which it costs go up, the real cashflows will increase with inflation. If not, the real cashflows will go down.

The relationship between nominal and real discount rates also depends upon the expected inflation rate:

Real Discount Rate = $(1 + $ Nominal Discount Rate$)/(1 + E[I]) - 1$

where $E(I)$ = expected inflation rate in the general price level

When the expected inflation rate is low, the difference between the nominal discount rate and expected inflation can be used as an approximation for the real discount rate.

Illustration 6.6: The effect of inflation on cashflows and discounts rates

Consider a firm that has cashflows to equity currently of $100 million and is expected to grow, in real terms, at 5% a year for the next three years and 3% a year after that. The firm has a beta of 1.0, and the current Treasury bond rate is 6.5%. The expected inflation rate is 3% in both the firm's cashflows and the general economy. The valuation of this firm can be done on either a real or a nominal basis. The estimates of growth on a real and nominal basis are done first:

	Real	Nominal
Growth rate in first 3 years	5%	$(1.05 \times 1.03) - 1 = 8.15\%$
Growth rate after year 3	3%	$(1.03 \times 1.03) - 1 = 6.09\%$

The discount rate can similarly be estimated on a real and nominal basis:

	Real	Nominal
Discount rate	$1.12/1.03 - 1 = 8.74\%$	$E(R) = 6.5\% + 1(5.5\%) = 12\%$

The expected nominal return is estimated using the CAPM, with a historical premium earned by stocks over Treasury bonds of 5.5%.

Using these growth rates the cashflows can be generated in both nominal and real terms (in millions):

	Real Cashflows		Nominal Cashflows	
Year	Cashflows to Equity	Terminal Value	Nominal Cashflows	Terminal Value
1	$105		$108	
2	110		117	
3	116	$2,078	126	$2,271

The terminal values are calculated as follows for real and nominal cashflows:

Terminal Value (using real cashflows)

= $116 \times 1.03/(.0874 - .03)$ = $2,078 million

Terminal Value (using nominal cashflows)

= $126 \times 1.0609/(.12 - .0609)$ = $2,271 million

The calculation assumes that the growth rates after year 3 are steady state growth rates and will continue through infinity.

The present values of the cashflows to equity and the terminal value can then be calculated using the appropriate discount rate:

Present Value (using real cashflows)

= $105/1.0874 + $110/1.0874^2 + ($116 + $2,078)/1.0874^3$ = $1,896 million

Present Value (using nominal cashflows)

= $108/1.12 + $117/1.12^2 + ($126 + $2,271)/1.12^3$ = $1,896 million

Thus the value of equity is the same whether real cashflows are discounted at real discount rates or nominal cashflows are discounted at nominal rates.

The Discounting Rule for Inflation-Adjusted Cashflows

The simple rule on expected inflation is to be consistent about matching cashflows and discount rates. If the cashflows being discounted are nominal cashflow, that is, cashflows have expected inflation built into them, the appropriate discount rate is a nominal rate, that is, a discount rate with an expected inflation component. If the cashflows discounted are real cashflows (i.e., cashflows are based upon constant dollars), the appropriate discount rate is a real rate.

The effect on value of mismatching cashflows and discount rates can be substantial. If nominal cashflows are discounted at real discount rates, the resulting value will be higher than the true value. If, on the other hand, real cashflows are discounted at nominal rates, the resulting value will be lower than the true value.

Illustration 6.7: The effect of mismatching cashflows and discount rates

Illustration 6.6 showed how the use of nominal discount rates to discount real cashflows or real discount rates to discount nominal cashflows will result in biased estimates of value. The following table illustrates the effect (amounts in millions):

Year	Real Cashflows at Nominal Rate		Nominal Cashflows at Real Rate	
	Cashflows to Equity	Terminal Value	Nominal Cashflows	Terminal Value
1	$105		$108	
2	110		117	
3	116	$1,325	126	$5,068

The terminal values are miscalculated because cashflows and discount rates are not matched.

Terminal Value (using nominal rate and real cashflows)
= $116 \times 1.03/(.12 - .03) = \$1,325$ million

Terminal Value (using real rate and nominal cashflows)
= $126 \times 1.0609/(.0874 - .0609) = \$5,068$ million

If real cashflows are discounted at the nominal discount rate, the present value is:

Present Value (real cashflows discounted at nominal rates)
$= \$105/1.12 + \$110/1.12^2 + (\$116 + \$1,325)/1.12^3$
$= \$1,207$ million < True Value of $1,896 million

If nominal cashflows are discounted at the real discount rate, the present value is:

Present Value (nominal cashflows discounted at real rates)
$= \$108/1.0874 + \$117/1.0874^2 + (\$126 + \$5,068)/1.0874^3$
$= \$4,293$ million > True Value of $1,896 million

Inflation, Depreciation, and Value

The primary benefit from depreciation is a tax benefit. The depreciation allowance in many countries is based upon book value and is not adjusted for inflation. If the dollar tax benefits from depreciation are fixed, the value of the tax benefits will decrease as expected inflation increases. This negative effect on value can be neutralized if depreciation is indexed to inflation, as it is in some high-inflation environments.

Illustration 6.8: Inflation, Depreciation, and Value

Consider an asset that cost $24,000 and is depreciated straight line over a 4-year lifetime. The asset creates cash savings of $10,000 (in real dollars) a year, and income is taxed at 50%. In an economy with no inflation, the cashflows are as follows, and the discount rate is 8%. (Since there is no inflation, this is both the real and the nominal rate.)

Year	Cash Savings	Depreciation	Taxes	Cashflows
1	$10,000	$6,000	$2,000	$8,000
2	10,000	6,000	2,000	8,000
3	10,000	6,000	2,000	8,000
4	10,000	6,000	2,000	8,000

$$\text{Value of Asset} = \$8,000 \, (1 - 1.08^{-4})/.08 = \$26,497$$

Consider now a situation in which inflation is at a rate of 7% per annum and cash savings are expected to grow at this overall rate of inflation. The depreciation is unaffected because it is based upon book value.

Year	Cash Savings	Depreciation	Taxes	Nominal Cashflows
1	$10,700	$6,000	$2,000	$8,350
2	11,449	6,000	2,725	8,724
3	12,250	6,000	3,125	9,125
4	13,108	6,000	3,554	9,554

The nominal rate can be calculated based upon the real rate of 8% and expected inflation of 7%:

$$\text{Nominal Rate} = (1.08 \times 1.07) - 1 = .1556 \text{ or } 15.56\%$$

This nominal rate can be used to discount nominal cashflows:

$$\text{Value of Asset} = \$8,350/1.1556 + \$8,724/1.1556^2 + \$9,125/1.1556^3$$
$$+ \; \$9,554/1.1556^4 = \$25,030$$

Thus the value of the asset drops from $26,497 to $25,030 because of the loss of present value of tax benefits from depreciation.

PERSONAL TAXES AND CASHFLOWS

The cashflow estimates so far have taken into account corporate taxes but have ignored the effect of personal taxes. Since the receipt of a cashflow from an asset can expose an investor to a tax liability, the valuation can be done on the basis of cashflows after personal taxes. The effect, however, on value is largely neutralized by the adjustment of discount rates for personal taxes.

Pretax and Posttax Cashflows

The effect of personal taxes on cashflows depends upon three factors: what portion, if any, of the cashflows on an asset are taxable, at what rate the cashflows will be taxed, and when the tax has to be paid. The question of whether a cashflow is taxable or not is determined largely by the tax code. In the United

States, interest on state and local bonds is not taxable, but dividends on stocks is. Even with the same asset, some cashflows may be tax exempt while others are taxable. For instance, the price appreciation on a tax-exempt bond is taxable. The rate at which cashflows are taxed will depend upon the tax status of the investor doing the analysis and can vary depending upon whether the investor is an individual or a corporation and on the investor's income bracket.[8] The timing of cashflows matters in calculating present values, and the present value of deferred taxes is lower than an equivalent amount in current taxes. With stocks, for example, dividends are taxed when received, whereas price appreciation is taxed only when the security is sold.

Pretax and Posttax Discount Rates

The after-tax discount rates (cost of equity and cost of capital) used hitherto are after corporate taxes but before personal taxes. To preserve consistency in discounting, cashflows adjusted for personal taxes have to be discounted at discount rates also adjusted for personal taxes.

Cost of Equity after Personal Taxes

The capital asset pricing model, as described in the previous chapter, does not consider the effect of personal taxes. The simplest approach to estimating the cost of equity after personal taxes is to apportion the pretax returns from the CAPM to dividends (γ) and capital gains (λ) and to adjust the components by the respective tax rates.

$$\text{After-Tax Cost of Equity} = \gamma(1 - t_0) + \lambda(1 - t_{cg})$$

where γ = expected dividend yield
t_0 = tax rate on ordinary income (dividends)
γ = expected price appreciation
t_{cg} = tax rate on capital gains

When dividends are taxed at a higher rate than capital gains, this adjustment for personal taxes will result in lower after-tax expected returns on equity for firms that pay higher dividends than for firms, with the same pretax expected returns, that pay no or lower dividends. To compensate for this tax disadvantage, investors may demand higher pretax returns on stocks that pay high dividends. Brennan (1970) investigated the effects of differential taxes on dividends and capital gains on the equilibrium model and concluded that while beta was still the appropriate measure of risk, there is an additional term in the model reflecting the dividend yield of the stock. In his model, the expected pretax return on an investment can be written as:

$$E(R_i) = R_f + \delta_0 + \delta_1\beta_i + \delta_2(\gamma_i - R_f)$$

where $E(R_i)$ = expected pretax return on asset i
R_f = riskfree rate
β_i = beta of asset i

γ_i = dividend yield of asset i
δ_0 = a constant term
δ_1 = market premium for systematic risk
δ_2 = influence of dividend payout on expected returns

Litzenberger and Ramaswamy (1979) tested this model and concluded that risk-adjusted returns are higher for securities with higher dividend yields. Bethke and Boyd (1983) calculated a yield-tilt factor of 0.29, meaning that the required pretax rate of return increases by 0.29% for every 1% increase in dividend yield, and confirmed this with empirical estimates of the factor from 1980–1982. Since marginal tax rates on capital gains and dividends were equalized in the United States after 1986, it is not clear whether this yield-tilt factor can be generalized to current investments.

Cost of Debt after Personal Taxes

The interest expense on debt to the firm is interest income to the bondholder and hence can be taxed at his or her personal tax rate.

Cost of Debt after personal and corporate taxes = Interest Rate$(1 - t_0)(1 - t)$

where t_0 = personal tax rate on ordinary income
 t = corporate tax rate

Illustration 6.9: Effect of personal taxes on cashflows and discount rates: Eli Lilly

The expected dividends and the terminal price were estimated for Eli Lilly at the beginning of 1992 for the next five years (before personal taxes). The firm had a beta of 1.05, and the Treasury bond rate was 7.15%. The following example values Eli Lilly on the basis of cashflows after personal taxes for an investor with a tax rate of 40% for ordinary income and 28% for capital gains. The cashflows on a pre- and posttax basis are as follows:

Year	Before Personal Taxes		After Personal Taxes	
	Dividends per Share	Terminal Price	Dividends per Share	Terminal Price
1	$2.27		$1.36	
2	2.60		1.56	
3	2.98		1.79	
4	3.41		2.05	
5	3.91	$93.43	2.35	$84.41

The discount rate can be estimated before personal taxes and used to calculate the present value per share:

Discount Rate before personal taxes = 7.15% + 1.05(5.5%) = 12.93%

Present Value per share (based upon pretax cashflows and pretax discount rates)
$$= \$2.27/1.1293 + \$2.60/1.1293^2 + \$2.98/1.1293^3 + \$3.4/1.1293^4$$
$$+ (3.91 + \$93.43)/1.1293^5 = \$62.20$$

The initial price is assumed to be $62.20. The cashflows after personal taxes are estimated as follows:

Dividends per share after taxes
= Dividends per share before taxes $(1 - \text{Ordinary Tax Rate})$
Terminal Price after taxes = Terminal Price before taxes
$- (\text{Terminal Price} - \text{Initial Price}) \times \text{Capital Gains Tax Rate}$
$= \$93.43 - (\$93.43 - \$62.20) \times .28 = \84.41

The discount rate before personal taxes can be apportioned into dividend yield and price appreciation:

Expected Dividend Yield = Expected Dividends next year/Initital Price
 $= \$2.27/\$62.20 = 3.71\%$
Expected Price Appreciation = Expected Return $-$ Expected Dividend Yield
 $= 12.93\% - 3.71\% = 9.22\%$
Discount Rate after personal taxes $= 3.71\%(1 - .40)$
 $+ 9.22\%(1 - .28) = 8.86\%$
Present Value per share (based upon after-tax cashflows and after-tax discount rates)
$= \$1.36/1.0886 + \$1.56/1.0886^2 + \$1.79/1.0886^3 + \$2.05/1.0886^4$
$+ (\$2.35 + \$84.41)/1.0886^5 = \$62.20$

Thus the value is unaffected by whether cashflows are before or after personal taxes, as long as the discount rates are adjusted accordingly.

Exploiting Differences in Tax Rates

Introducing personal taxes into the analysis complicates affairs since the same asset can yield different after-tax returns to different investors. The question of which investors' tax rates are reflected in the market price is an important one, since the answer will determine whether an investor will find an asset to be under- or overvalued. Market prices are generally determined by the marginal investor's tax preferences. If the marginal investors are tax-exempt institutions, the market price will be based upon their expected returns, which are unaffected by tax preferences. If the marginal investors are individuals in the highest tax bracket, the market prices will be based upon their expected returns, which incorporate tax preferences.

Differences in tax rates can create arbitrage opportunities for investors whose tax rates are different from those of the marginal investor. Thus, a tax-exempt investor may be able to buy an asset for less than estimated value (obtained by discounting cashflows) if the marginal investor in that asset is a high-tax-rate individual. There are limits to profits from this type of arbitrage, since these tax-exempt investors will move the price upward by buying the asset and can end up supplanting the high-rate individuals as the marginal investors in the asset.

The effect on value of introducing personal taxes will be greater for some investments than for others, especially for high-tax-rate individuals. In an environment where dividends are taxed at a higher rate than capital gains, the negative effects, on cashflows, of personal taxes will be greater for high-dividend-yield firms than for firms that pay no or low dividends. This might explain the existence of dividend clienteles, with investors with similar tax rates congregating in firms which best fit their tax profile.

CASHFLOWS AND ASSET LIFE

The principles for estimating cashflow developed in this chapter apply for all kinds of assets—financial assets such as stocks and bonds as well as real investments in property and projects. One characteristic in which there are differences across assets is in the life of the asset—many assets have finite lifetimes, whereas some, like stock in a publicly traded firm, have infinite lifetimes. This section examines some estimation issues related to whether an asset has a finite or infinite lifetime.

Salvage Value versus Terminal Value

Most valuations, whether for finite- or infinite-lived assets, are done over a finite time horizon. There is a difference, however, in the treatment of the two types of assets at the end of the time horizon. Valuing a finite-lived asset requires assumptions about the life of the asset and the value of the asset at the end of the lifetime. This salvage value is usually a fraction of the initial cost of the asset since its value is depleted during its lifetime. Valuing an asset with an infinite lifetime requires estimation of the value of the asset at the end of the finite horizon. This "terminal value" reflects the expected future cashflows on the asset and is usually significantly higher than the initial value because of growth in the cashflows. Often, a significant portion of the present value comes from this terminal value, making its estimation a key part of the valuation.

Depreciation and Capital Expenditure

The depreciation on a finite-lived asset follows the depreciation method used—a uniform amount each year with straight-line depreciation and declining amounts over time with accelerated depreciation. For an investment with an infinite lifetime, depreciation is generally not on one asset but on a series of asset investments made over time, and hence should not decline over the estimation period.

The expected capital expenditures, which affect cashflows, also serve different purposes for the two types of assets. In a finite-lived asset, the capital expenditure is the investment needed to maintain the asset's cashflows until the

end of its lifetime. In an infinite-lived asset, capital expenditure is the investment needed not only to maintain existing assets but also to create new assets and future growth—the higher the projected future growth, the greater the capital expenditure provision.

Working Capital Needs

The working capital needs during the lifetime of both finite- and infinite-lived assets usually follows the pattern of growth in revenues and/or costs. With a finite asset, however, the working capital has to be liquidated at the end of the asset's lifetime and accounted for. With an infinite-lived asset, the working capital will be in use for the long term and will never be entirely liquidated, though it may be reduced as the growth rate in revenues declines over time.

CONCLUSION

This chapter establishes the basic principles for estimating cashflows and using them in discounted cashflow valuation. The fundamental rule in discounting is to match up cashflows with the appropriate discount rate—cashflows to equity with the cost of equity, cashflows to the firm with the cost of capital, nominal cashflows with a nominal discount rate, real cashflows with a real discount rate, pretax cashflows with a pretax discount rate, and posttax cashflows with a posttax discount rate.

QUESTIONS AND SHORT PROBLEMS

1. Which of the following is the best description of the free cashflow to equity?
 a. It is the cash that equity investors can take out of the firm.
 b. It is the dividend that is paid to stockholders.
 c. It is the cash that equity investors can take out of the firm after financing investment needed to sustain future growth.
 d. It is the cash left over after meeting debt payments and paying taxes.
 e. None of the above.
2. Answer true or false to the following statements:
 a. The free cashflow to equity will always be higher than the net income of the firm, because depreciation is added back.
 b. The free cashflow to equity will always be higher than the dividend.
 c. The free cashflow to equity will always be higher than cashflow to the firm, because the latter is a predebt cashflow.
 d. The entire free cashflow to equity cannot be paid out as dividends because some of it has to be invested in new projects.
3. Diebold Incorporated manufactures, markets, and services automated teller machines in the United States. The following are selected numbers from the financial statements for 1992 and 1993:

	1992	1993
Revenues	$544.0 million	$620.0 million
Operating Expenses	$465.1 million	$528.5 million
Depreciation	$ 12.5 million	$ 14.0 million
Earnings Before Interest and Taxes	$ 66.4 million	$ 77.5 million
Interest Expenses	$ 0.0 million	$ 0.0 million
Taxes	$ 25.3 million	$ 29.5 million
Net Income	$ 41.1 million	$ 48 million
Working Capital	$175 million	$240 million

The firm had capital expenditures of $15 million in 1992 and $18 million in 1993. The working capital in 1991 was $180 million.
a. Estimate the cashflows to equity in 1992 and 1993.
b. What would the cashflows to equity in 1993 have been if working capital had remained at the same percentage of revenue it was in 1992?
4. Ryder System is a full-service truck leasing, maintenance, and rental firm with operations in North America and Europe. The following are selected numbers from the financial statements for 1992 and 1993:

	1992	1993
Revenues	$5,192.0 million	$5,400.0 million
− Operating Expenses	$3,678.5 million	$3,848.0 million
− Depreciation	$ 573.5 million	$ 580.0 million
= EBIT	$ 940.0 million	$ 972.0 million
− Interest Expenses	$ 170.0 million	$ 172.0 million
− Taxes	$ 652.1 million	$ 670.0 million
= Net Income	$ 117.9 million	$ 130.0 million
Working Capital	$ 92 million	⟨$ 370 million⟩
Total Debt	$ 2.0 million	$ 2.2 million

The firm had capital expenditures of $800 million in 1992 and $850 million in 1993. The working capital in 1991 was $34.8 million, and the total debt outstanding in 1991 was $1.75 billion. There were 77 million shares outstanding, trading at $29 per share.
a. Estimate the cashflows to equity in 1992 and 1993.
b. Estimate the cashflows to the firm in 1992 and 1993.
c. Assuming that revenues and all expenses (including depreciation and capital expenditures) increase 6% and that working capital remains unchanged in 1994, estimate the projected cashflows to equity and the firm in 1994. (The firm is assumed to be at its optimal financial leverage.)
d. How would your answer in (c) change if the firm planned to increase its debt ratio in 1994 by financing 75% of its capital expenditures (net of depreciation) with new debt issues?
5. Watts Industries, a manufacturer of valves for industrial and residential use, had the following projected free cashflows to equity per share for the next five years, in nominal terms:

Year	FCFE/share	Terminal Value
1	$1.12	
2	$1.25	
3	$1.40	
4	$1.57	
5	$1.76	$23.32

The terminal price is based upon a stable nominal growth rate of 6% a year after year 5. The discount rate, based upon financial market rates, is 14%, and the expected inflation rate is 3%.

 a. Estimate the value per share, using nominal cashflows and the nominal discount rate.

 b. Estimate the value per share, using real cashflows and the real discount rate.

ENDNOTES

1. For a private firm, the funds will have to be raised from the owners of the firm or from venture capitalists.

2. This applies only if the firm has preferred stock. Preferred dividends are not tax deductible and hence have to be paid for with after-tax cashflows.

3. This statement can be made much stronger by replacing "desired" with "optimal." However, this requires that firms (a) know what their optimal debt levels are and (b) would like to get to that optimal level.

4. Very few firms state that they are at their optimal leverage, but indicate it more through their actions—they finance their new investments using roughly the same mix of debt and equity that they have in their current structure.

5. This assumes that the switch in depreciation methods applies for tax calculations as well. If a firm uses two depreciation methods, straight line for reporting to stockholders and accelerated for tax calculations, the switch will not affect cashflows.

6. The tax benefit from interest expenses is already reflected in the free cashflows to equity. To prevent double counting of this tax benefit, only the after-tax interest expense is considered as a cashflow to debt holders.

7. There is substantial evidence that Treasury bill rates are determined largely by expectations about inflation. Between 1926 and 1990, the average Treasury bill rate was 3.4% while the inflation rate was 3.3%.

8. Even for an individual, investments made in a pension fund or an Individual Retirement Account (IRA) are exempt from taxes.

<div style="text-align: right">

7

</div>

Estimation of Growth Rates

he value of a firm is ultimately determined not by current cashflows but by expected future cashflows. The estimation of growth rates in earnings and cashflows is therefore central to doing a reasonable valuation. Growth rates can be obtained in many ways—they can be based upon past growth, drawn from estimates made by other analysts who follow the firm, or related to the firm's fundamentals. Since each of these approaches yields some valuable information, it makes sense to blend them to arrive at one composite growth rate to use in the valuation. This chapter examines different approaches to estimating future growth and discusses the determinants of growth.

THE USE OF HISTORICAL GROWTH RATES

There is a connection between past growth rates and expected future growth rates, but the reliability of this connection is open to question. This section explores various ways of using historical growth rates to predict future growth.

Using Average Growth Rates from the Past

This approach uses the average growth rate from the past as the predicted growth rate for the future. There are several estimation issues related to coming up with an average growth rate. Some of these are discussed herein.

Arithmetic Average versus Geometric Average

The average growth rate can be very different depending upon whether it is an arithmetic average or a geometric average. The arithmetic average is the mean of past growth rates, while the geometric average takes into account the compounding effect. The latter is clearly a much more accurate measure of true growth in past earnings, especially when year-to-year growth has been erratic. This can be illustrated with a simple example.

Illustration 7.1: Using arithmetic average versus geometric average: Glaxo Inc.

The following are the earnings per share at Glaxo Pharmaceuticals, starting in 1989 and ending in 1994:

Year	EPS	Growth Rate (percent)
1989	$0.66	
1990	0.90	36.36
1991	0.91	1.11
1992	1.27	39.56
1993	1.13	−11.02
1994	1.27	12.39

Arithmetic average = (36.36% + 1.11% + 39.56% − 11.02% + 12.39%)/5

= 15.68%

Geometric average = ($1.27/$.66)$^{1/5}$ − 1 = 13.99%

The arithmetic average will be lower than the geometric average, and the difference will increase with the variability in earnings.

An alternative to the standard calculation of the arithmetic average is a weighted average, with growth rates in more recent years being weighted more heavily than growth rates in earlier years. This would lead to a much lower estimate of the average for Glaxo.

Estimation Period

The average growth rate is sensitive to the starting and ending periods for the estimation. Thus, the growth rate in earnings over the last five years may be very different from the estimated growth rate over the last six years. The length of the estimation period is subject to the analyst's judgment, but the sensitivity of historical growth estimates to the length of the period should be a factor considered in deciding how much to weight these past growth rates in predictions.

Illustration 7.2: Sensitivity of historical growth rates to the length of the estimation period: Glaxo Inc.

The following table provides earnings per share at Glaxo, starting in 1988 instead of 1989 and uses six years of growth rather than five to estimate the arithmetic and geometric averages.

Time (t)	Year	EPS	Growth Rate (percent)
1	1988	$0.65	
2	1989	0.66	1.54
3	1990	0.90	36.36
4	1991	0.91	1.11
5	1992	1.27	39.56
6	1993	1.13	−11.02
7	1994	1.27	12.39

Arithmetic average = 13.32%

Geometric average = $(\$1.27/\$.65)^{1/6} - 1 = 11.81\%$

The growth rate drops significantly if earnings per share starting in 1988 are used rather than earnings starting in 1989, with the arithmetic average dropping from 15.68% to 13.32%.

Linear and Log-Linear Regression Models

The arithmetic average weights percentage changes in earnings in each period equally and ignores compounding effects in earnings. The geometric average considers compounding but focuses on the first and the last earnings observations in the series—it ignores the information in the intermediate observations and any trend in growth rates that may have developed over the period. These problems are at least partially overcome by using OLS[1] regressions of earnings per share against time. The linear version of this model is:

$$EPS_t = a + bt$$

where EPS_t = earnings per share in period t

t = time period t

The slope coefficient on the time variable is a measure of earnings change per time period. The problem, however, with the linear model is that it specifies growth in terms of dollar EPS and is not appropriate for projecting future growth, given compounding.

The log-linear version of this model converts the coefficient into a percentage change:

$$\ln(EPS_t) = a + bt$$

where $\ln(EPS_t)$ = natural logarithm of earnings per share in period t

The coefficient b on the time variable becomes a measure of the percentage change in earnings per unit time.

Illustration 7.3: Linear and log-linear models of growth: Glaxo.

The earnings per share from 1988 to 1994 are provided for Glaxo, and the linear and log-linear regressions are done below:

Time(t)	Year	EPS	ln(EPS)
1	1988	$0.65	−0.43
2	1989	0.66	−0.42
3	1990	0.90	−0.11
4	1991	0.91	−0.09
5	1992	1.27	0.24
6	1993	1.13	0.12
7	1994	1.27	0.24

Linear regression: EPS $= .5171 + .1132t$

Log-linear regression: $\ln(\text{EPS}) = -.55536 + .1225t$

The slope from the log-linear regression (0.1225) provides an estimate of growth rate of 12.25% in earnings. The slope from the linear regression is in dollar terms. The prediction for 1995 from each regression is as follows:

Expected EPS (1995): linear regression $= .5171 + .1132(8) = \$1.42$

Expected EPS (1995): log-linear regression $= e(-.55536 + .1225\,(8))$

$$= \$1.53$$

Dealing with Negative Earnings

Measures of historical growth are distorted by the presence of negative earnings numbers. The percentage change in earnings on a year-by-year basis is defined as:

Percentage changes in EPS in period t $= (\text{EPS}_t - \text{EPS}_{t-1})/\text{EPS}_{t-1}$

If EPS_{t-1} is negative, this calculation yields a meaningless number. This extends into the calculation of the geometric mean. If the EPS in the initial time period is negative or 0, the geometric mean is not meaningful.

Similar problems arise in log-linear regressions, since the EPS has to be greater than 0 for the log transformation to exist. There are at least two ways of trying to get meaningful estimates of earnings growth for firms with negative earnings. One is to run the linear regression of EPS against time specified in the previous regression:

$\text{EPS} = a + bt$

The growth rate can then be approximated as follows:

Growth Rate in EPS $=$ b/average EPS over the time period of the regression

This assumes that the average EPS over the time period is positive. Another approach to estimating growth for these firms, suggested by Arnott (1985), is as follows:

Percentage change in EPS $= (\text{EPS}_t - \text{EPS}_{t-1})/\text{Max}(\text{EPS}_t, \text{EPS}_{t-1})$

Note that these approaches to estimating historical growth do not provide any information on whether these growth rates are useful in predicting future growth. It is not incorrect and, in fact, may be appropriate to conclude that the historical growth rate is "not meaningful" when earnings are negative, and to ignore it in predicing future growth.

Illustration 7.4: Dealing with negative earnings: Sterling Chemicals

The following series lists earnings per share from 1988 to 1994 for Sterling Chemicals.

Time(t)	Year	EPS	log(EPS)	Growth Rate	Modified Growth Rate
1	1988	$3.56	1.27		
2	1989	1.77	0.57	−50.28%	−50.28%
3	1990	1.07	0.07	−39.55%	−39.55%
4	1991	0.67	−0.40	−37.38%	−37.38%
5	1992	0.08	−2.53	−88.06%	−88.06%
6	1993	(0.10)	NMF	−225.00%	−225.00%
7	1994	0.34	−1.08	−440.00%	129.41%

Approach 1: Using the slope coefficient from the linear regression

EPS = 3.1114 − .5139t

Average EPS (1988–1994) = $1.06

Growth rate = −.5139/1.06 = −48.48%

Approach 2: Using the minimum or maximum of earnings as the denominator

Arithmetic average, using modified growth rates = −51.81%

Per Share versus Total Earnings

The growth rate in net income can be misleading for firms that have issued substantial amounts of new equity during the estimation time period. The funds raised from these equity issues will generate income that, in turn, will create growth in total net income. Hence, it makes sense to adjust income for the number of shares issued and to look at growth in earnings per share, rather than net income.

The number of shares to be used in calculating earnings per share is also an issue since accountants measure earnings per share relative to both the actual number of shares outstanding (primary EPS) as well as in terms of the potential number of shares that could be outstanding, assuming conversion of warrants and convertible bonds (diluted EPS). The primary earnings per share, using the actual number of shares outstanding, is the appropriate number to use in calculating earnings growth. The potential dilution effects of convertible bonds and warrants on value can be better assessed using option pricing models to value these securities.

Time Series Models to Predict Earnings per Share

Time series models use the same historical information as the simpler models described in the previous section. They attempt to extract better predictions from this data, however, through the use of sophisticated statistical techniques.

Box-Jenkins Models

Box and Jenkins (1976) developed a procedure for analyzing and forecasting univariate time series data using an autoregressive integrated moving average (ARIMA) model. ARIMA models model a value in a time series as a linear combination of past values and past errors (shocks). Since historical data are used,

these models are appropriate as long as the data do not show deterministic behavior, such as a time trend or a dependence on outside events or variables. ARIMA models are usually denoted by the notation:

ARIMA(p,d,q)

where p = degree of the autoregressive part
 d = degree of differencing
 q = degree of the moving average process

The mathematical model can then be written as follows:

$$w_t = \phi_1 w_{t-1} + \phi_2 w_{t-2} + \ldots + \phi_p w_{t-p} + \theta_0 - \theta_1 a_{t-1} - \theta_2 a_{t-2} - \ldots$$
$$- \theta_q a_{t-q} + \epsilon_t$$

where w_t = original data series or difference of degree d of the original data
 $\phi_1, \phi_2, \ldots \phi_p$ = autoregressive parameters
 θ_0 = constant term
 $\theta_1, \theta_2, \ldots \theta_q$ = moving average parameters
 ϵ_t = independent disturbances, random error

ARIMA models can also adjust for seasonality in the data, in which case the model is denoted by the notation

SARIMA(p,d,q) X(p,d,q)$_{s=n}$

where s = seasonal parameter of length n

Time Series Models in Earnings

Most time series models used in forecasting earnings are built around quarterly earnings per share. In a survey paper, Bathke and Lorek (1984) pointed out that three time series models have been shown to be useful in forecasting quarterly earnings per share. All three models are seasonal ARIMA (SARIMA) models, since quarterly earnings per share have a strong seasonal component. The first model, developed by Foster (1977), allows for seasonality in earnings and is as follows:

Model 1: SARIMA(1,0,0) X(0,1,0)$_{s=4}$
$$EPS_t = \phi_1 EPS_{t-1} + EPS_{t-4} - \phi_1 EPS_{t-5} + \theta_0 + \epsilon_t$$

This model was extended by Griffin and Watts (1975, 1977) to allow for a moving average parameter:

Model 2: SARIMA(0,1,1) X(0,1,1)$_{s=4}$
$$EPS_t = EPS_{t-1} + EPS_{t-4} - EPS_{t-5} - \theta_1 \epsilon_{t-1} - \Theta \epsilon_{t-4} - \Theta \theta_1 \epsilon_{t-5} + \epsilon_t$$

where θ_1 = first-order moving average parameter
 Θ = First-order seasonal moving average parameter
 ϵ_t = disturbance realization at the end of quarter t

The third time series model, developed by Brown and Rozeff (1979), is similar in its use of seasonal moving average parameters:

Model 3: SARIMA(1,0,0) X(0,1,1)$_{s=4}$
$$EPS_t = \phi_1 EPS_{t-1} + EPS_{t-4} - \phi_1 EPS_{t-5} + \theta_0 - \Theta \epsilon_{t-4}$$

How Good Are Time Series Models at Predicting Earnings?

Time series models do better than naive models (using past earnings) in predicting earnings per share in the next quarter. The forecast error, that is, the difference between the actual earnings per share and the forecasted earnings per share, from the time series models is, on average, smaller than the forecast error from naive models (such as simple averages of past growth). The superiority of these models over naive estimates declines with longer-term forecasts, suggesting that the estimated time series parameters are not stationary.

Among the time series models themselves, there is no evidence that any one model is dominant, in terms of minimizing forecast error, for every firm in the sample. The gain from using the firm-specific best models, relative to using the same model for every firm, is relatively small.

Limitations in Using Time Series Models in Valuation

In most studies, time series models provide superior forecasts relative to naive models. There are several concerns, however, in using these models for forecasting earnings in valuation. First, time series models require a lot of data, which is why most of them are built around quarterly earnings per share. In most valuation, the focus is on predicting annual earnings per share and not quarterly earnings. Second, even with quarterly earnings per share, the number of observations is limited for most firms 10 to 15 years of data (40 to 60 quarters of data), leading to large estimation errors[2] in time series model parameters and in the forecasts. Third, the superiority of earnings forecasts from time series models declines as the forecasting period is extended. Given that earnings forecasts in valuation have to be made for several years rather than for a few quarters, the value of time series models may be limited. Finally, studies indicate that analyst forecasts dominate even the best time series models in forecasting earnings.

In conclusion, time series models are likely to work best for firms that have a long history of earnings and where the parameters of the models have not shifted significantly over time. For the most part, however, the cost of using these models is likely to exceed their benefits, at least in the context of valuation.

The Value of Past Growth in Predicting Future Growth

Past growth rates are useful in forecasting future growth but can seldom be considered sufficient information. In a study of the relationship between past growth rates and future growth rates, Little (1960) coined the term "higgledy piggledy growth" because he found little evidence that firms that grew fast in one period continued to grow fast in the next period. In the process of running a series of correlations between growth rates in consecutive periods of different length, he frequently found negative correlations between growth rates in the two periods and the average correlation across the two periods was close to 0 (0.02). We update his study using growth rates in two more recent five-

year time periods—1981–1985 and 1986–1990—and find that the correlation coefficient in earnings growth, while positive, is still not significantly different from 0.

The value of past growth in predicting future growth is determined by a number of factors, including the following.

Variability in growth rates: The usefulness of past growth rates in predicting future growth is inversely related to the variability in these growth rates. This variability can be measured in a number of ways. A simple measure is the standard deviation in growth rates in past EPS:

$$\sigma_g = \frac{\sum_{t=1}^{n} (g_t - \bar{g})^2}{n - 1}$$

where σ_g = standard deviation in growth rate in earnings per share
\quad g_t = growth rate in earnings per share in year t
\quad \bar{g} = average growth rate in earnings per share over n periods
\quad n = number of periods of historical data

In the linear and log-linear regressions of earnings per share described in the earlier section, the variability can be measured by the standard error of the coefficient estimates as well as the R-squared of the regression. In general, analysts should be cautious about using past growth rates in forecasting future growth rates if there is significant volatility in these rates.

Size of the firm: Since the growth rate is stated in percentage terms, the role of size has to be weighed in the analysis. It is easier for a firm with $10 million in earnings to generate a 50% growth rate than it is for a firm with $500 million in earnings. Since it becomes harder for firms to sustain high growth rates as they become larger, past growth rates for firms that have grown dramatically in size and profits may be difficult to sustain in the future.

Illustration 7.5: The effect of size on growth: Amgen

Amgen increased its net income from $19.1 million in 1989 to $430 million in 1994. The following table shows the growth in net income for Amgen from 1989 to 1994, in both percentage and dollar terms.

Year	Net Income	% Growth Rate	Δ Net Income
1989	$ 19.10		
1990	86.30	351.31	$ 67.10
1991	186.30	116.13	100.10
1992	306.70	64.63	120.40
1993	354.90	15.72	48.20
1994	430.00	21.16	75.10

Geometric Average Growth Rate = 86.42%

Assuming that this growth rate continues for the next five years:

Year	Net Income	% Growth Rate	Δ Net Income
1995	$ 801.60	86.42%	$ 371.60
1996	1,494.32	86.42%	$ 692.72
1997	2,785.67	86.42%	$1,291.35
1998	5,192.98	86.42%	$2,407.31
1999	9,680.63	86.42%	$4,487.65

The dollar increase in net income needed each year to sustain an 86.42% growth rate becomes larger and larger and rises to $4.487 billion by 1999. Even if Amgen remains a well-run and successful firm, it will become progressively more difficult over time to deliver these high growth rates.

Cyclicality in economy: Historical growth rates for cyclical firms are strongly influenced by where in the business cycle the economy is at the time of the estimation. If historical growth rates for cyclical firms are estimated in the middle of a recession, the growth rates are likely to be very negative. The reverse is generally true if the estimation of historical growth is done at an economic peak. These growth rates are of little value, however, in predicting future growth.[3] It would be more useful to estimate growth across two or more economic cycles for these firms.

Changes in fundamentals: The observed growth rate is the result of fundamental decisions made by the firm on business mix, project choice, capital structure, and dividend policy. If a firm changes in any or all of these dimensions, the historical growth rate may not be a reliable indicator for future growth. For instance, the restructuring of a firm often changes both its asset and its liability mix, and makes past growth rates fairly meaningless in predicting future growth.

The other problem with using past growth rates arises when the business in which the firm is operating changes, either as a result of market forces or government regulation. These changes in fundamentals may cause a shift upward or downward in growth for all companies in that business and have to be factored into predictions. For instance, pharmaceutical companies at the end of 1992 had enjoyed a decade of high growth as medical technology advanced and health care costs surged. Looking into the future, however, market forces and the potential for health care reform make it unlikely that these growth rates would continue.

Quality of earnings: All earnings growth is not equal. Earnings growth created by changes in accounting policy or acquisitions is inherently less reliable than growth created by increasing units sold, and should be weighted less in forecasting future growth. Bernstein and Seigel (1978) presented some guidelines for assessing future quality:

(a) Earnings growth reported by firms with more liberal accounting policies[4]

is less reliable (and of lower quality) than growth reported by firms with conservative accounting policies.

(b) The integrity of the reporting period (i.e., the extent to which current earnings benefit from past earnings or borrow from future earnings) is important for earnings quality. The earnings growth rates for firms that use accounting techniques to increase current earnings at the expense of future earnings should be used cautiously in analyses.

(c) Earnings quality is also affected by whether proper provisions are made for discretionary costs needed to maintain assets and earnings power.

THE USE OF ANALYSTS' FORECASTS OF EARNINGS

Few firms are valued in a vacuum. In most cases, an analyst valuing a firm has access to estimates of growth in earnings and cashflows made by other analysts who follow the same firm. Should the growth forecasts of other analysts be incorporated into the valuation? If so, how? The answers to these and other questions will be considered in this section.

What Information Do Analysts Use in Making Earnings Forecasts?

There is a simple reason why analyst forecasts should be better than mechanical models, which use only past earnings data. Analysts, in addition to using historical data, can avail themselves of other information that may be useful in predicting future growth:

(a) *Firm-specific information that has been made public since the last earnings report.* Analysts can use information that has come out about the firm since the last earnings report to make predictions about future growth. This information can sometimes lead to significant reevaluation of the firm's expected cashflows. For instance, Leslie Fay, a leading women's apparel manufacturer, reported net income of $23.9 million in 1992. It revealed on January 29, 1993, that false entries had been made on the books and that it had really lost $13.7 million in 1992. Analysts following Leslie Fay proceeded to significantly lower expectations of future earnings, and this, in turn, led to a drop in the stock price from $12 on January 29 to $3.50 on April 8, 1993.

(b) *Macroeconomic information that may impact future growth.* The expected growth rates of all firms are affected by economic news on GNP growth, interest rates, and inflation. Analysts can update their projections of future growth as new information comes out about the overall economy and about changes in fiscal and monetary policy. Information, for instance, that shows the economy growing at a faster rate than forecast will result in analysts increasing their estimates of expected growth for cyclical firms.

(c) *Information revealed by competitors on future prospects.* Analysts can also condition their growth estimates for a firm on information revealed by competitors on pricing policy and future growth. Analysts following tobacco companies in March 1993 were forced to reevaluate expectations of growth following

the decision by Philip Morris to cut prices on its Marlboro brand and therefore reduce profit margins. A similar action by American Airlines in the summer of 1992 on airline fares led to a reestimation of growth and value for the airlines.

(d) *Private information about the firm.* Analysts sometimes have access to private information about the firms they follow that may be relevant in forecasting future growth. This avoids answering the delicate question of when private information becomes illegal inside information. There is no doubt, however, that good private information can lead to significantly better estimates of future growth.

(e) *Public information other than earnings.* Models for forecasting earnings that depend entirely upon past earnings data may ignore other publicly available information that is useful in forecasting future earnings. It has been shown, for instance, that other financial variables such as earnings retention, profit margins, and asset turnover are useful in predicting future growth. Analysts can incorporate information from these variables into their forecasts.

How Good Are Analysts at Forecasting Future Growth?

The ability of analysts to provide superior forecasts of future growth has been studied extensively. The results can be categorized on the basis of the time horizon for the forecasts—short term versus long term.

The Accuracy of Short-Term Forecasts

The general consensus from studies that have looked at short-term forecasts (one quarter ahead to four quarters ahead) of earnings is that analysts provide better forecasts of earnings than do models that depend purely upon historical data. The following table summarizes the results from three studies of analyst forecasts:

		Mean Relative Absolute Error*	
Study	Analyst Group	Analyst Forecasts	Mechanical Models
Collins & Hopwood (1976)	Value Line Forecasts 1970–1974	31.7%	34.1%
Brown & Rozeff (1978, 1980)	Value Line Forecasts 1972–1975	28.4%	32.2%
Fried & Givoly (1982)	Earnings Forecaster 1969–1979	16.4%	19.8%

*The mean relative absolute error measures the absolute difference between the actual earnings and the forecast for the next quarter, in percentage terms. The mechanical models are all based upon historical data.

Two other studies shed further light on the value of analyst forecasts. Crichfield, Dyckman, and Lakonishok (1978) examined the relative accuracy of forecasts in the *Earnings Forecaster,* a publication from Standard and Poors that summarizes forecasts of earnings from more than 50 investment firms. They measured the squared forecast errors by month of the year and computed the

ratio of analyst forecast error to forecast error from time series models of earnings. They found that the time series models actually outperform analyst forecasts from April until August but underperform them from September through January. They hypothesize that this is because there is more firm-specific information available to analysts during the latter part of the year. The other study, by O'Brien (1988), compares consensus analyst forecasts from the Institutions Brokers Estimate System (I/B/E/S) with time series forecasts from one quarter ahead to four quarters ahead. The analyst forecasts outperform the time series model for one quarter ahead and two quarters ahead forecasts, do as well as the time series model for three quarters ahead forecasts, and do worse than the time series model for four quarters ahead forecasts. Thus, the advantage gained by analysts from firm-specific information seems to deteriorate as the time horizon for forecasting is extended.

The Accuracy of Long-Term Forecasts

In valuation, the focus is more on long-term growth rates in earnings than on next quarter's earnings. There is little evidence to suggest that analysts provide superior forecasts of earnings when the forecasts are over three or five years. An early study by Cragg and Malkiel (1965) compared long-term forecasts by five investment management firms in 1962 and 1963 with actual growth over the following three years, to conclude that analysts were poor long-term forecasters. This view is contested by Vander Weide and Carleton (1988), who found that the consensus prediction of five-year growth in the I/B/E/S is superior to historically oriented growth measures in predicting future growth.

There is an intuitive basis for arguing that analyst predictions of growth rates must be better than time series or other historical-data-based models simply because they use more information. The evidence indicates, however, that this superiority in forecasting is surprisingly small for long-term forecasts and that past growth rates play a significant role in determining analyst forecasts.

Analyst Forecasts and Stock Prices

There is evidence from financial markets that analyst forecasts have informational value. Hawkins, Chamberlin, and Daniel (1984) found that revisions in forecasts seem to predict subsequent stock price movements and that portfolios of stocks that had the largest upward revisions in consensus earnings forecasts had a risk-adjusted abnormal return of 14.2% in the following 12 months. Richards and Martin (1979) classified revisions by quarter of the year and found that revisions made in the first quarter contain more new information and lead to higher abnormal returns than revisions made later in the year. Other studies confirm the findings in these two studies that revisions in analyst forecasts contain new information and that financial markets do not impound this information in prices effectively.

How Do You Use Analyst Forecasts in Estimating Future Growth?

The information in the growth rates estimated by other analysts can and should be incorporated into the estimation of expected future growth. There are sev-

eral factors that determine the weight assigned to analyst forecasts in predicting future growth.

(a) *Amount of recent firm-specific information.* Analyst forecasts have an advantage over historical-data-based models because they incorporate more recent information about the firm and its future prospects. This advantage is likely to be greater for firms in which there have been significant changes in management or business conditions in the recent past, for example, a restructuring or a shift in government policy relating to the firm's underlying business.

(b) *Number of analysts following the stock.* Generally speaking, the larger the number of analysts following a stock, the more informative is their consensus forecast, and the greater should be the weight assigned to it in analysis. The informational gain from having more analysts is diminished somewhat by the well-established fact that most analysts do not act independently and that there is a high correlation across analysts' revisions of expected earnings.

(c) *Extent of disagreement between analysts.* While consensus earnings growth rates are useful in valuation, the extent of disagreement between analysts, measured by the standard deviation in growth predictions, is also a useful measure of the reliability of the consensus forecasts. Givoly and Lakonsihok (1980) found that the dispersion of earnings is correlated with other measures of risk such as beta and is a good predictor of expected returns.

(d) *Quality of analysts following the stock.* This is the hardest of the variables to quantify. One measure of quality is the size of the forecast error made by analysts following a stock relative to models that use only historical data—the smaller this relative error, the larger the weight that should be attached to analyst forecasts. Another measure is the effect on stock prices of analyst revisions—the more informative the forecasts, the greater the effect on stock prices. There are some who argue that the focus on consensus forecasts misses the point that some analysts are better than others in predicting earnings and that their forecasts should be isolated from the rest and weighted more.

Analyst forecasts may be useful in coming up with a predicted growth rate for a firm, but there is a danger in blindly following consensus forecasts. Analysts often make significant errors in forecasting earnings, partly because they depend upon the same data sources (which might have been erroneous or misleading) and partly because they sometimes overlook significant shifts in the fundamental characteristics of the firm. The secret to successful valuation often lies in discovering inconsistencies between analysts' forecasts of growth and a firm's fundamentals. The next section examines this relationship in more detail.

THE DETERMINANTS OF EARNINGS GROWTH

While growth in a firm may be measured using history or analyst forecasts, it is determined by fundamental decisions that a firm makes on product lines, profit margins, leverage, and dividend policy.

Retention Ratio and Return on Equity

The simplest relationship determining growth is one based upon the retention ratio (percentage of earnings retained in the firm) and the return on equity

on its projects (Return on Equity = Net Income/Book Value of Equity). To establish this, note that

$$g_t = (NI_t - NI_{t-1})/NI_{t-1}$$

where g_t = growth rate in net income
NI_t = net income in year t

Given the definition of return on equity, the net income in year $t - 1$ can be written as:

$$NI_{t-1} = \text{Book Value of Equity}_{t-1} \times ROE_{t-1}$$

where ROE_{t-1} = return on equity in year $t - 1$

The net income in year t can be written as:

$$NI_t = (\text{Book Value of Equity}_{t-1} + \text{Retained Earnings}_{t-1})ROE_t$$

Assuming that the return on equity is unchanged, that is, that $ROE_t = ROE_{t-1} = ROE$,

$$g_t = \text{Retained Earnings}_{t-1}/NI_{t-1} \times ROE$$
$$= \text{Retention Ratio} \times ROE$$
$$= b \times ROE$$

where b is the retention ratio.

In this relationship, growth in earnings is an increasing function of both the retention ratio and the return on equity. Table 7.1 provides approximate growth rates for a firm given different retention ratios and return on equity. This calculation of the growth rate assumes that the return on equity is unchanged over time. If it changes over time, the growth rate in period t can be written as follows:

$$g_t = (\text{BV of Equity}_{t-1} [ROE_t - ROE_{t-1}]/NI_{t-1}) + b \times ROE_t$$

The first term captures the effect of changing return on equity on the existing

TABLE 7.1 Growth Rate as a Function of Retention Ratios and Return on Equity (percent)

ROE	Retention Ratio				
	0%	25%	50%	75%	100%
4%	0.00	1.00	2.00	3.00	4.00
6%	0.00	1.50	3.00	4.50	6.00
8%	0.00	2.00	4.00	6.00	8.00
10%	0.00	2.50	5.00	7.50	10.00
12%	0.00	3.00	6.00	9.00	12.00
14%	0.00	3.50	7.00	10.50	14.00
16%	0.00	4.00	8.00	12.00	16.00
18%	0.00	4.50	9.00	13.50	18.00
20%	0.00	5.00	10.00	15.00	20.00

equity base—increases (decreases) in ROE make it more (less) profitable and create a higher (lower) growth rate.

Illustration 7.6: Effects of changes in return on equity—Merck

The following table provides information on the retention ratio and the return on equity for Merck for 1994 and projections for 1995.

	1994	1995
BV of Equity	11700	
Net Income	3010	
Retention Ratio	52.00%	52%
Return on Equity	26.0%	25.5%
Growth Rate	= 0.52*0.26	= (11700*[.255 − .26]/3010)
	= 13.52%	+ 0.52*0.255 = 11.32%

A drop in the return on equity of 0.5% translates into a drop in the growth rate of 2.20%. If the ROE drops by 2% the expected growth rate in 1995 would be 3.72%. If the return on equity after 1994 remains at 26%, the growth rate in earnings will also stay unchanged at 13.52% (assuming the retention ratio is 52%) after 1994.

Return on Equity and Leverage

The return on equity and, by implication, the growth rate are affected by the leverage decisions of the firm. In the broadest terms, increasing leverage will lead to a higher return of equity if the preinterest, after-tax return on projects (assets) exceeds the after-tax interest rate paid on debt. This is captured in the following formulation of return on equity:

$$ROE = ROA + D/E(ROA - i[1 - t])$$

where ROA = (Net Income + Interest[1 − tax rate])/BV of Total Assets
 = EBIT(1 − t)/BV of Total Assets
 D/E = BV of Debt/BV of Equity
 i = Interest Expense on Debt/BV of Debt
 t = tax rate on ordinary income

Note that BV of Assets = BV of Debt + BV of Equity.

The derivation is simple and is provided in the footnote.[5] Using this expanded version of ROE, the growth rate can be written as:

$$g = b\{ROA + D/E(ROA - i[1 - t])\}$$

The advantage of this formulation is that it allows explicitly for changes in leverage and the consequent effects on growth. It is a useful way of analyzing the effects of restructuring on growth and value. There are generally three dimensions to restructuring:

(a) *Restructuring assets/projects:* Asset restructuring generally takes the form of eliminating unprofitable projects and divisions and/or acquiring new assets. The objective in asset restructuring is to increase the firm's return on assets, which in turn increases growth. The changing of a firm's asset mix also leads to a change in the riskiness of the firm, which causes discount rates to shift. The net effect of these changes in growth and risk will determine the change in firm value. The effect of changing ROA on growth can be obtained fairly simply using the growth formulation above:

$$\delta g/\delta ROA = b(1 + D/E)$$

Thus, the effect of a change in the ROA on growth will depend upon the firm's retention ratio (b) and debt/equity ratio (D/E).

(b) *Changing capital structure:* Another component in financial restructuring is a change in leverage—an increase or decrease in the debt financing in the firm. The effect on future growth can be captured by changing the debt/equity ratio and interest rate in the growth rate formulation, and recalculating the growth rate. The change in leverage will also lead to a change in risk—increases in leverage will increase risk while decreases in leverage will reduce risk—and in discount rates. Again, the net effect can be either positive or negative.

$$\delta g/\delta(D/E = ROA - i(1 - t) - (\delta i/\delta D/E)(\text{New } D/E)(1 - t)$$

where $\delta i/\delta D/E$ = change in interest rate as a result of the debt/equity change
New D/E = debt/equity ratio after the change in leverage

(c) *Changing dividend policy:* The final aspect of financial restructuring is changing dividend policy. A decrease (increase) in dividends will lead to an increase (decrease) in the retention ratio and an increase in the expected growth rate. This has to be offset, however, by the effects of changing payout ratio on the expected dividends. The tradeoff usually takes the form of higher growth for lower dividends, and the net effect on value can again be either positive or negative.

$$\delta g/\delta \text{Payout} = -1\{ROA + D/E(ROA - i[1 - t])\}$$

In general terms, this formulation of expected growth rates ties value to corporate financial policy—capital budgeting, capital structure, and dividend policy decisions.

Illustration 7.7: Effects of restructuring on expected growth rate and risk: ARCO

Atlantic Richfield went through a major restructuring in 1985, changing both its asset and liability mixes. The effects of these changes on the growth rate and the beta are shown below.

Investment Policy. All of the company's refining and marketing operations east of the Mississippi River were sold. An $800 million reduction in capital outlays in areas where returns were low was also planned. All nonoil mineral operations were also sold. This was expected to increase the return on assets from 12% to 16%.

	Before	Planned Changes	After
After-tax ROA	12.0%	Improve project choice. Eliminate unprofitable divisions.	16%

Financing Policy. ARCO planned to borrow $4 billion and repurchase $4 billion in equity.

D/E	.45	Increase long-term debt.	1.00
Beta	.60	Leverage increases β.	.76
Interest rate	7.00%		8.00%

Dividend Policy. An increase in quarterly dividends to $1 per share from $0.75 per share was planned.

Payout	.50	Reinvest less in company.	.60
Retention	.50	Reinvest less in company.	.40
Earnings growth rate	7.76%		10.88%

The expected growth rate in earnings can be expected to increase from 7.76% to 10.88% as a consequence of the restructuring. ARCO's stock price went up $5.25 to $58.25 after the restructuring was announced, representing a total gain of $1.3 billion to stockholders.

Return on Assets, Profit Margin, and Asset Turnover

The analysis of return on assets can be carried forward one step if it is related to profit margins and sales.

$$\text{ROA} = \text{EBIT}(1 - t)/\text{Total Assets}$$
$$= (\text{EBIT}[1 - t]/\text{Sales} \times (\text{Sales/Total Assets})$$
$$= \text{Preinterest Profit Margin} \times \text{Asset Turnover}$$

The return on assets is an increasing function of both the preinterest profit margin and the asset turnover. The relationship is made more interesting, however, by the tradeoff between the two variables—increasing profit margins will generally reduce asset turnover, and reducing profit margins will increase asset turnover. The net effect will depend upon the elasticity of demand for the product. Thus, the effects on ROA of the decision by Philip Morris to reduce prices (and hence profit margins) on its Marlboro brand cigarettes cannot be evaluated without making some assumptions about the effect of lower prices on sales.

This extension of the growth formulation allows for the linkage of value to corporate strategy. For instance, Sears, in 1991, decided that it was going to reduce prices and profit margins on products to increase sales. The effects of this lower-margin, higher-turnover strategy on value could have been analyzed by estimating the effects of the shift on growth and consequently on value.

Illustration 7.8: Evaluating the effects of corporate strategy on growth rate and value: Procter and Gamble

Procter and Gamble decided to reduce prices on its disposable diapers in April 1993 to compete better with low-price private label brands. The preinterest, after-tax profit margin is expected to drop from 7.43% to 7% as a consequence, and the asset turnover is expected to increase from 1.6851 to 1.80. The following table provides projections of profit margins, asset turnover, and growth rates after the shift in corporate strategy:

	1992	After Shift in Strategy
EBIT$(1 - $ tax rate$)$	$2,181	
Sales	$29,362	
Preinterest, after-tax profit margin	7.43%	7.00
Total assets	$17,424	
Asset turnover	1.6851	1.80
Return on assets	12.52%	12.60%
Retention ratio	58.00%	58.00%
Debt/equity (book value) ratio	0.7108	0.7108
Interest rate on debt$(1 - $ tax rate$)$	4.27%	4.27%
Growth rate	10.66%	10.74%

The shift in corporate strategy will increase the expected growth rate in earnings marginally. This is of course conditioned on the assumption that sales will increase enough to cause the turnover to increase to 1.8.

Product Line Analysis

One criticism that is often leveled at analysts is that by focusing on aggregates at the firm level, they might be missing significant trends in the profitability of individual product lines. Thus, a firm with an aging product line mix may look healthy in terms of historical growth and current profitability, but it is not likely to sustain this growth into the future. The analysis of growth for a firm can be made more complete by looking at its individual product lines and examining where they stand in terms of the product life cycle. The classical analysis of the product life cycle suggests that as products go through the different growth phases from high growth to decline, the profit margins vary systematically with each phase. The growth rates across time for individual product lines can then be estimated as follows:

$$g_{jt} = b\{\pi_{jt} \times \tau_{jt} - D/E(\pi_{jt} \times \tau_{jt} - i[1 - t])\}$$

where g_{jt} = growth rate in year t for product line j

π_{jt} = preinterest, after-tax profit margin in year t for product line j

τ_{jt} = asset turnover in year t for product line j

D/E = debt/equity ratio for the firm

i = interest rate on debt

t = tax rate on ordinary income

Figure 7.1 adapts a classical life cycle chart to growth analysis, with profit margins and revenues in each stage.

Some General Issues Relating to "Fundamental" Models

There are clearly benefits to examining the determinants of growth and estimating growth rates in terms of financial fundamentals. There are issues, however, in their usage that need to be considered.

Estimation of Inputs

One of the costs of using fundamental models of growth is the increase in the

FIGURE 7.1 Product-Line Analysis

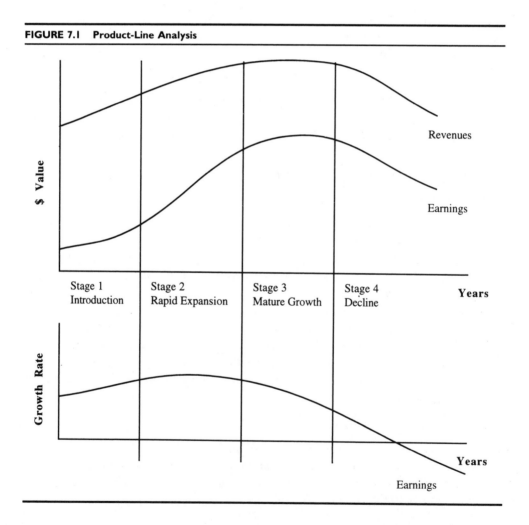

number of inputs needed to estimate growth and value a firm. There are several estimation issues that arise in this context.

Current versus Projected Values. The current values of most of the inputs used in these models are generally easily available. Given that the objective in valuation is the forecasting of future growth rates, the real inputs that are needed are projected values for these variables. The current values may be a useful starting point, but they seldom provide sufficient information for making good predictions.

Emphasis on Book Value. The emphasis placed on book value in all these models is troublesome, though it is much less of a factor for future projections than it is for current values for the variables. For instance, if a firm has a current debt/equity ratio of 50% in book value terms and a target debt/equity ratio of 100% in market value terms, the use of the latter may provide a better estimate of future growth in earnings. For those who are still squeamish about the use of book value, the growth rate can be stated entirely in market value terms:

$$g_t = b(ROA_m + (D/E)_m(ROA_m - i_m[1 - t]))$$

where ROA_m = return on assets in place (in market value terms)
$$= EBIT(1 - t)/MV \text{ of Assets in Place}$$
$(D/E)_m$ = MV of Debt/(MV of Assets in Place − MV of Debt)
i_m = market interest rate on the firm's debt

The difficulty in applying this version of the model lies in separating out the market value of assets in place from the total market value of the firm.

Level of Detail. The fundamental models for growth described in this section can be carried to higher and higher levels of detail. While there are gains to increasing detail, there is a cost. The number of inputs needed increases, and the "noise" in the valuation created by errors in estimating these inputs has to be weighed against the potential benefits. In some cases, where the product lines of the firm are distinct and in different growth phases, and where the analyst has the time and the experience to analyze these product lines, the estimates of growth are likely to become more accurate with more detail. In other cases, where any or all of these conditions do not apply, additional detail may actually result in inferior estimates of growth and less accurate valuation.

Consistency of Inputs with Firm Type. It is important that analysts, when forecasting inputs to these models, ensure that the values they use are consistent with their description of the firm. For instance, if an analyst considers a firm to be a high-growth firm in a profitable, albeit risky, business, it is likely to have a low payout ratio, high return on assets, and low leverage during the growth period. As it grows larger and becomes more stable, it is likely to increase dividend payout, its projects will no longer be generating super-normal returns, and it will generally increase leverage. Though individual firms may deviate from these generalities, a good reason has to be provided for these deviations.

Illustration 7.9:　Adjusting inputs for firm type: Neutrogena

The following table provides estimates of return on assets, retention ratio, and interest rates for Neutrogena Inc., a cosmetics manufacturer. Neutrogena is expected to grow at an extraordinary rate in the first five years (growth phase) and at a stable rate after that (steady state).

	Growth Phase	Steady State
Retention ratio	76%	50%
Return on assets	19.5%	15%
Debt/equity ratio	0%	25%
Interest rate on debt	10%	8.00%
Growth rate	14.82%	8.375%

Note that the retention ratio decreases, the return on assets decreases, and the debt/equity ratio increases after the firm enters steady state. The firm is also expected to have lower default risk and pay a lower interest rate on borrowing. The steady state values for inputs were obtained from the cross-sectional averages for larger (and presumably more stable) firms in the cosmetic industry.

The questions of what is reasonable for a firm in the long term will in large part be determined by the cross-section not only in the firm's industry but across all industries. Thus a firm that has a profit margin of 22% in an industry where the average profit margin is 10% is unlikely to maintain that margin after it reaches stable growth, by which point it has presumably exhausted some or all of the differential advantage that gave it the high margin in the first place. In forecasting values for fundamental variables, it is useful to know where other firms stand in terms of the same inputs. The following table gives the average values in percent for the retention ratio, return on assets, and debt/equity ratio for large manufacturing firms between 1987 and 1991:

Year	Retention Ratio	Return on Assets	Debt/Equity Ratio
1987	72.49	10.41	25.68
1988	70.95	9.93	21.84
1989	68.38	9.23	25.62
1990	68.70	9.22	24.48
1991	68.84	5.96	25.85

GENERAL ISSUES IN ESTIMATING GROWTH

There are several approaches to estimating growth, and the analyst should exploit the information in each approach. This section examines two issues: the weighting of the growth rates obtained from historical data, analyst fore-

casts, and fundamentals; and the smoothing of future growth for firms that have had volatile earnings in the past.

Weighting Different Estimates of Growth

There are three possible ways of estimating growth: use historical data in either naive or time series models, use the consensus forecasts made by other analysts, or use growth rates estimated from the firm's fundamentals. From a practical standpoint, the three approaches often overlap. Analysts use historical data in forecasting earnings, and analyst estimates of fundamentals (such as profit margins) as well as historical data drive many fundamental models of growth. This does not imply, however, that the approaches always yield similar values. On the contrary, they often provide very different estimates of growth, leaving the analyst with the difficult decision of which growth rate or what combination of growth rates to use in valuation.

If only one of these three growth rates is to be used, the appropriate one will depend upon the firm being analyzed. If the firm is going through a complex restructuring, the growth rate from fundamentals is the best choice because it can be conditioned on the planned changes in the asset and liability mix. If the firm is relatively stable in terms of its fundamentals and is heavily followed by analysts, their long-term forecasts are likely to dominate forecasts from the other approaches. If a firm has established a stable pattern of historical growth and the fundamentals of the business have not changed, the time series models based upon historical data will provide accurate forecasts of future growth.

There is no reason, however, to use only one of these growth rates. Each approach provides a forecast of future growth and is informative. A weighted average of these growth rates, with the weight based upon the informativeness of each growth rate, may provide a superior estimate of future growth to any one of the three. The tricky part is measuring the informativeness of each growth rate. One approach is to calculate the standard errors for each of the estimates and to weight them based upon these errors—the larger the error, the smaller the weight. For models based upon historical data, this will be measured by the standard error in data series or in the time series models. For analyst forecasts, it will be determined by the extent of disagreement between analysts, and measured by the standard deviation across their forecasts. For fundamental models, it will be driven by standard errors in the inputs to the model.

Illustration 7.10: Weighting based upon standard deviations: Glaxo Inc.

Consider the example of Glaxo, with earnings per share available from 1989 to 1994. The following table also provides analyst forecasts of expected growth over the next five years from nine analysts following Glaxo.

Historical EPS		
Year	EPS	Growth Rate
1989	$0.66	
1990	0.90	36.36%
1991	0.91	1.11%
1992	1.27	39.56%
1993	1.13	− 11.02%
1994	1.27	12.39%

Analyst Estimates	
Analyst Number	Estimated Growth
1	10.00%
2	10.50%
3	12.00%
4	12.50%
5	13.00%
6	16.00%
7	16.00%
8	18.00%
9	20.00%

Arithmetic average = 15.68% Consensus Forecast = 14%

Standard Deviation = 13.99% Standard Deviation = 3.45%

The analyst forecast will be weighted more, because of its lower standard deviation.

The problem with this approach is that it assumes that the standard errors in the different estimates are comparable and provide good measures of the informativeness of the estimates. Consider, for instance, a firm that has been in a regulated business where its earnings have grown at 10% a year for the last decade, with very low variability (assume that the standard error is 2%). Now, assume that this firm has just announced its entry into an unregulated risky business, where analysts forecast that it will grow much faster but disagree on how fast (consensus forecast of growth = 25%; standard error = 20%). A weighting based purely upon standard error would weight the historical growth rate more and the analyst forecast less. Common sense suggests that the analyst forecasts should be weighted more because they impound valuable information on changes in the underlying business of the firm.

The more satisfactory, though subjective, way of dealing with the weighting is to assign weights based upon both the standard errors and other factors. Since it is subjective, there will be room for reasonable analysts to disagree and for biased analysts to build in their bias. Figure 7.2 lists some of the factors that should be considered in coming up with a weighting.

Smoothing Future Growth

Analysts generally use smoothed forecasts of earnings, even for firms that have had volatile earnings in the past. This is often criticized as unrealistic. It is true that forecasts of earnings that incorporate future business cycles accurately are more realistic than those that use smoothed growth rates (and hence do not

Figure 7.2 Factors Determining Weights for Different Forecasts

Growth Forecast Method	Factors to Consider	Weight Assigned Higher ↔ Lower
Historical	1. How much history is available?	More ↔ Less
	2. How variable are past earnings?	Less ↔ More
	3. How cyclical is the firm?	Less ↔ More
	4. Has the firm made any fundamental changes in business or leverage?	No ↔ Yes
	5. Has the firm's size changed much over time?	No ↔ Yes
Analyst	1. How much firm-specific information has come out since the last earnings report?	Less ↔ More
	2. How many analysts follow the stock?	More ↔ Less
	3. How much agreement is there between analysts?	More ↔ Less
	4. How good are the analysts?	Good ↔ Poor
Fundamental	1. How much change has there been in firm fundamentals?	More ↔ Less
	2. How well can the inputs to the model be estimated?	Well ↔ Poorly

attempt to forecast either the timing or the effects of future recessions or recoveries). It is also true, however, that analysts who try to predict cyclical movements in the economy three or four years into the future are unlikely to succeed in making accurate predictions. Thus, it might be prudent to accept the less realistic approach of smoothing earnings rather than expose the analysis to the error inherent in forecasting economic cycles. While the smoothed earnings will not reflect the volatility of the firm's income stream, the discount rate will. Firms with variable earnings will, in general, have higher discount rates.[6]

CONCLUSION

The estimation of future growth rates plays a key role in valuation. This chapter looked at three approaches to estimating these growth rates. The first uses past earnings, the second is built on forecasts made by other analysts who follow the same firm, and the third relates growth rates to fundamentals. Each approach has some informational value, and the estimates from all three can be incorporated into the final analysis, with the weight attached to each a function of its informativeness. This informativeness can be measured using both statistical measures (such as standard error) and subjective factors.

QUESTIONS AND SHORT PROBLEMS

1. Walgreen Company reported the following earnings per share from 1989 to 1994:

Year	EPS
1989	$1.28
1990	1.42
1991	1.58
1992	1.78
1993	1.98
1994	2.30

 a. Estimate the arithmetic average and geometric average growth rate in earnings per share between 1989 and 1994. Why are they different? Which is more reliable?

 b. Estimate the growth rate using a linear growth model.

 c. Estimate the growth rate using a log-linear growth model.

2. Cobra Electronics reported the following earnings per share from 1989 to 1994:

Year	1989	1990	1991	1992	1993	1994
EPS	$0.77	−$0.26	−$0.90	−$1.39	−$0.65	$0.10

Estimate a historical growth rate in earnings for Cobra Electronics.

3. BIC Corporation reported a return on equity of 20% in 1994 and paid out 37% of its earnings as dividends in that year. Assuming that these fundamentals do not change, estimate the expected growth rate in earnings per share. How sensitive is this growth rate to changes in these fundamentals?

4. Gillette Company reported earnings before interest and taxes of $1,488 million in 1994, on debt (in book value) of $1,330 million and equity (in book value) of $1,790 million. Gillette had interest expenses that amounted to $90 million in that year and paid out 30% of its earnings as dividends. Allowing for a 40% tax rate,

 a. estimate the expected growth rate in earnings per share from fundamentals.

 b. estimate how much the growth rate would change if Gillette doubled its debt (assume that the interest rate on debt will increase by 1%).

If you were valuing Gillette, and you anticipated that the firm would become stable after 10 years, would you expect these fundamentals to change over time?

5. B.A.T. Industries had a pretax operating margin of 10% on revenues of $34,500 million in 1994 and reported an asset turnover ratio of 3.0 in that year.

 a. If the tax rate is 36%, estimate the return on assets for B.A.T. Industries.

 b. If the pretax operating margin drops to 8% of revenues and the asset turnover ratio remains unchanged, estimate the new return on assets.

ENDNOTES

1. An ordinary least squares (OLS) regression estimates regression coefficients by minimizing the squared differences of predicted from actual values.

2. Time series models generally can be run as long as there are at least 30 observations, but the estimation error declines as the number of observations increases.

3. The earnings of cyclical firms are likely to be depressed, relative to normal levels, during a recession. As the economy improves, these earnings can be expected to rebound strongly. Thus, at the same time that historical growth is negative, the expected growth is likely to be strongly positive.

4. In the aftermath of IBM's fall from grace, with the stock price dropping from $170 in 1986 to $50 in 1992, *The Wall Street Journal* revealed that accounting policies in the firm during the 1980s had been liberal in recognizing income (though their actions were not illegal).

5. ROA + D/E(ROA $-$ i [1$-$t]) = (NI + Int[1$-$t])/(D+E)

$$+ D/E\{(NI + Int[1-t])/(D + E) - Int(1-t)/D\}$$

$$= \{(NI + Int[1-t])/(D + E)\}(1 + D/E) - Int(1-t)/E$$

$$= NI/E + Int(1-t)/E - Int(1-t)/E = NI/E = ROE$$

6. There is a high correlation between variance in earnings and betas of stocks. Firms with more variable earnings tend to have higher betas and therefore higher expected returns.

8

Market Efficiency—Definition and Tests

What is an efficient market? What does it imply for investment and valuation models? Clearly, market efficiency is a concept that is controversial and attracts strong views, pro and con, partly because of differences between individuals about what it really means and partly because it is a core belief that in large part determines how an investor approaches investing. This chapter provides a simple definition of market efficiency, considers the implications of an efficient market for investors, and summarizes some of the basic approaches that are used to test investment schemes, thereby proving or disproving market efficiency.

MARKET EFFICIENCY AND INVESTMENT VALUATION

The question of whether markets are efficient and, if not, where the inefficiencies lie is central to investment valuation. If markets are, in fact, efficient, the market price provides the best estimate of value, and the process of valuation becomes one of justifying the market price. If markets are not efficient, the market price may deviate from the true value, and the process of valuation is directed toward obtaining a reasonable estimate of this value. Those who do valuation well, then, will be able to make "higher" returns than other investors, because of their capacity to spot under- and overvalued firms.

There is also much that can be learned from studies of market efficiency which highlights segments where the market seems to be inefficient. These "inefficiencies" can provide the basis for screening the universe of stocks to come up with a subsample that is more likely to have undervalued stocks. Given the size of the universe of stocks, this not only saves time for the analyst but significantly increases the odds of finding under- and overvalued stocks. For instance, some efficiency studies suggest that stocks that are "neglected" by institutional investors are more likely to be undervalued and earn excess returns. A strategy that screens firms for low institutional investment (as a percentage of the outstanding stock) may yield a subsample of neglected firms, which can then be valued using valuation models to arrive at a portfolio of

undervalued firms. If the research is correct, the odds of finding undervalued firms should increase in this subsample.

WHAT IS AN EFFICIENT MARKET?

An efficient market is one where the market price is an unbiased estimate of the true value of the investment. Implicit in this definition are several key concepts:

(a) Contrary to popular view, market efficiency does not require that the market price be equal to true value at every point in time. All it requires is that errors in the market price be unbiased, that is, that prices can be greater than or less than true value as long as these deviations are random.[1]

(b) The fact that the deviations from true value are random implies, in a rough sense, that there is an equal chance that a stock is under- or overvalued at any point in time, and that these deviations are uncorrelated with any observable variable. For instance, in an efficient market, stocks with lower price/earnings ratios should be no more or less likely to be undervalued than stocks with high price/earnings ratios.

(c) If the deviations of market price from true value are random, it follows that no group of investors should be able to consistently find under- or overvalued stocks using any investment strategy.

Definitions of market efficiency have to be specific not only about the market that is being considered but also about the investor group that is covered. It is extremely unlikely that all markets are efficient to all investors, but it is entirely possible that a particular market (for instance, the New York Stock Exchange) is efficient with respect to the average investor. It is also possible that some markets are efficient while others are not, and that a market is efficient with respect to some investors and not to others. This is a direct consequence of differential tax rates and transactions costs, which confer advantages on some investors relative to others.

Definitions of market efficiency are also linked up with assumptions about what information is available to investors and reflected in the price. For instance, a strict definition of market efficiency that assumes that all information, public as well as private, is reflected in market prices would imply that even investors with precise inside information will be unable to beat the market. One of the earliest classifications of levels of market efficiency was provided by Fama (1971), who argued that markets could be efficient at three levels, based upon what information was reflected in prices. Under weak-form efficiency, the current price reflects the information contained in all past prices, suggesting that charts and technical analyses that use past prices alone would not be useful in finding undervalued stocks. Under semistrong-form efficiency, the current price reflects not only the information contained in past prices but all public information (including financial statements and news reports), and no approach that is predicated on using and massaging this information would

be useful in finding undervalued stocks. Under strong-form efficiency, the current price reflects all information, public as well as private, and no investors will be able to consistently find undervalued stocks.

IMPLICATIONS OF MARKET EFFICIENCY

An immediate and direct implication of an efficient market is that no group of investors should be able to consistently beat the market using a common investment strategy. An efficient market would also carry very negative implications for many investment strategies and actions that are taken for granted:

(a) In an efficient market, equity research and valuation would be a costly task that provides no benefits. The odds of finding an undervalued stock would always be 50:50, reflecting the randomness of pricing errors. At best, the benefits from information collection and equity research would cover the costs of doing the research.

(b) In an efficient market, a strategy of randomly diversifying across stocks or indexing to the market, carrying little or no information cost and minimal execution costs, would be superior to any other strategy that created larger information and execution costs. There would be no value added by portfolio managers and investment strategists.

(c) In an efficient market, a strategy of minimizing trading, that is, creating a portfolio and not trading unless cash was needed, would be superior to a strategy that required frequent trading.

It is therefore no wonder that the concept of market efficiency evokes such strong reactions on the part of portfolio managers and analysts, who view it, quite rightly, as a challenge to their existence.

It is also important that there be clarity about what market efficiency does not imply. An efficient market does *not* imply that

(a) stock prices cannot deviate from true value. In fact, there can be large deviations from true value. The only requirement is that the deviations be random.

(b) no investor will "beat" the market in any time period. To the contrary, approximately half[2] of all investors, prior to transactions costs, should beat the market in any period.

(c) no group of investors will beat the market in the long term. Given the number of investors in financial markets, the laws of probability would suggest that a fairly large number are going to beat the market consistently over long periods, not because of their investment strategies but because they are lucky. It would not, however, be consistent if a disproportionately large number[3] of these investors used the same investment strategy.

In an efficient market, the expected returns from any investment will be consistent with the risk of that investment over the long term, though there may be deviations from these expected returns in the short term.

NECESSARY CONDITIONS FOR MARKET EFFICIENCY

Markets do not become efficient automatically. It is the actions of investors, sensing bargains and putting into effect schemes to beat the market, that make markets efficient. The necessary conditions for a market inefficiency to be eliminated are as follows:

(a) The market inefficiency should provide the basis for a scheme to beat the market and earn excess returns. For this to hold true,
 (1) The asset that is the source of the inefficiency has to be traded.
 (2) The transactions costs of executing the scheme have to be smaller than the expected profits from the scheme.
(b) There should be profit-maximizing investors who
 (1) Recognize the "potential for excess return."
 (2) Can replicate the beat the market scheme that earns the excess return.
 (3) Have the resources to trade on the stock until the inefficiency disappears.

The internal contradiction of claiming that there is no possibility of beating the market in an efficient market and requiring profit-maximizing investors to constantly seek out ways of beating the market and thus make it efficient has been explored by many. If markets were, in fact, efficient, investors would stop looking for inefficiencies, which would lead to markets becoming inefficient again. It makes sense to think about an efficient market as a self-correcting mechanism, where inefficiencies appear at regular intervals but disappear almost instantaneously as investors find them and trade on them.

PROPOSITIONS ABOUT MARKET EFFICIENCY

A reading of the conditions under which markets become efficient leads to general propositions about where investors are most likely to find inefficiencies in financial markets.

Proposition 1. The probability of finding inefficiencies in an asset market decreases as the ease of trading on the asset increases. To the extent that investors have difficulty trading on a stock, because open markets do not exist or there are significant barriers to trading, inefficiencies in pricing can continue for long periods.

This proposition can be used to shed light on the differences between asset markets. For instance, it is far easier to trade on stocks than it is on real estate, since stock markets are much more open, prices are in smaller units (reducing the barriers to entry for new traders), and the asset itself does not vary from transaction to transaction (one share of IBM is identical to another share, whereas one piece of real estate can be very different from another piece a stone's throw away). Based upon these differences, there should be a greater likelihood of finding inefficiencies (both under- and overvaluation) in the real estate market.

Proposition 2. The probability of finding an inefficiency in an asset market increases as the transactions and information costs of exploiting the inefficiency increase. The costs of collecting information and of trading vary widely across markets and even across investments in the same market. As these costs increase, it pays less and less to try to exploit these inefficiencies.

Consider, for instance, the perceived wisdom that investing in "loser" stocks, that is, stocks that have done very badly in some prior time period, should yield excess returns. This may be true in terms of raw returns, but transactions costs are likely to be much higher for these stocks, since

(a) They tend to be low-priced stocks, leading to higher brokerage commissions and expenses.
(b) The bid-ask spread, a transaction cost paid at the time of purchase, becomes a much higher fraction of the total price paid.
(c) Trading is often thin on these stocks, and small trades can cause prices to change, resulting in a higher "buy" price and a lower "sell" price.

Corollary 1: Investors who can establish a cost advantage (either in information collection or in transactions costs) will be more able to exploit small inefficiencies than other investors who do not possess this advantage.

There are a number of studies that look at the effect of block trades on prices and conclude that while they affect prices, investors will not exploit these inefficiencies because of the number of times they will have to trade and because of their transactions costs. These concerns are unlikely to hold for a specialist on the floor of the exchange, who can trade quickly, often, and at no or very low cost. It should be pointed out, however, that if the market for specialists is efficient, the value of a seat on the exchange should reflect the present value of potential benefits from being a specialist.

This corollary also suggests that investors who work at establishing a cost advantage, especially in relation to information, may be able to generate excess returns on the basis of these advantages. Thus a John Templeton, who started investing in Japanese and other Asian markets well before other portfolio managers, might have been able to exploit the informational advantages he had over his peers to make excess returns on his portfolio.

Proposition 3. The speed with which an inefficiency is resolved will be directly related to how easily the scheme to exploit the inefficiency can be replicated by other investors. The ease with which a scheme can be replicated itself is inversely related to the time, resources, and information needed to execute it. Since very few investors single-handedly possess the resources to eliminate an inefficiency through trading, it is much more likely that an inefficiency will disappear quickly if the scheme used to exploit the inefficiency is transparent and can be copied by other investors.

To illustrate this point, assume that stocks are consistently found to earn excess returns in the month following a stock split. Since firms announce stock splits publicly and any investor can buy stocks right after these splits, it would be surprising if this inefficiency persisted over time. This can be contrasted to

the excess returns made by some "arbitrage funds" in index arbitrage, where index futures are bought (sold) and stocks in the index are sold short (bought). This strategy requires that investors be able to obtain information on index and spot prices instantaneously, have the capacity (in terms of margin requirements and resources) to buy and sell index futures and to sell short on stocks, and have the resources to take and hold very large positions until the arbitrage unwinds. Consequently, inefficiencies in "index futures pricing" are likely to persist at least for the most efficient arbitrageurs, with the lowest execution costs and the speediest execution times.

TESTING MARKET EFFICIENCY

Tests of market efficiency look at whether specific investment strategies earn excess returns. Some tests also account for transactions costs and execution feasibility. Since an excess return on an investment is the difference between the actual and expected return on that investment, there is implicit in every test of market efficiency a model for this expected return. In some cases, this expected return adjusts for risk using the capital asset pricing model or the arbitrage pricing model, and in others the expected return is based upon returns on similar or equivalent investments. In every case, a test of market efficiency is a joint test of market efficiency and the efficacy of the model used for expected returns. When there is evidence of excess returns in a test of market efficiency, it can indicate that markets are inefficient or that the model used to compute expected returns is wrong or both. While this may seem to present an insoluble dilemma, if the conclusions of the study are insensitive to different model specifications, it is much more likely that the results are being driven by true market inefficiencies and not just by model misspecifications.

There are a number of different ways of testing for market efficiency, and the approach used will depend in great part on the investment scheme being tested. A scheme based upon trading on information events (stock splits, earnings announcements, or acquisition announcements) is likely to be tested using an "event study" where returns around the event are scrutinized for evidence of excess returns. A scheme based upon trading on an observable characteristic of a firm (price/earnings ratio, price/book value ratio, or dividend yield) is likely to be tested using a "portfolio" approach, where portfolios of stocks with these characteristics are created and tracked over time to see if, in fact, they make excess returns. The following discussion summarizes the key steps involved in each of these approaches and some potential pitfalls to watch out for when conducting or using these tests.

Event Study

An event study is designed to examine market reactions to and excess returns around specific information events. The information events can be marketwide,

such as macroeconomic announcements, or firm specific, such as earnings or dividend announcements. The steps in an event study are as follows:

1. The event to be studied is clearly identified and the date on which the event was announced pinpointed. The presumption in event studies is that the timing of the event is known with a fair degree of certainty. Since financial markets react to the information about an event, rather than to the event itself, most event studies are centered around the announcement date for the event.

<div align="center">

Announcement Date

</div>

2. Once the event dates are known, returns are collected around these dates for each of the firms in the sample. In doing so, two decisions have to be made. First, the analyst has to decide whether to collect weekly, daily, or shorter-interval returns around the event. This will, in part, be decided by how precisely the event date is known (the more precisely, the more likely it is that shorter return intervals can be used) and by how quickly information is reflected in prices (the faster the adjustment, the shorter the return interval to use). Second, the analyst has to determine how many periods of returns before and after the announcement date will be considered as part of the "event window." That will also be determined by the precision of the event date, since more imprecise dates will require longer windows.

$$R_{-jn} \cdots \cdots \qquad R_{jo} \qquad \cdots \cdots R_{+jn}$$

Return window: $-n$ to $+n$

where R_{jt} = returns on firm j for day $t(t = -n \ldots 0 \ldots +n)$

3. The returns, by period, around the announcement date are adjusted for market performance and risk to arrive at excess returns for each firm in the sample. For instance, if the capital asset pricing model is used to control for risk,

$$ER_{jt} = R_{jt} - \text{Beta} \times R_{mt}$$

$$ER_{-jn} \cdots \cdots \qquad ER_{jo} \qquad \cdots \cdots ER_{+jn}$$

Return window: $-n$ to $+n$

where ER_{jt} = excess returns on firm j for day $t(t = -n \ldots 0 \ldots +n)$
R_{mt} = returns on market for day t

4. The excess returns, by day, are averaged across all firms in the sample and a standard error is computed.

$$\text{Average ER}_t = \sum_{j=1}^{j=N} \frac{ER_{jt}}{N}$$

where N = number of events in the event study

5. The question of whether the excess returns around the announcement are differ-

ent from 0 is answered by estimating the t statistic for each day, by dividing the average excess return by the standard error:

T statistic for excess return on day t = Average Excess Return/

Standard Error

If the t statistics are statistically significant,[4] the event affects returns; the sign of the excess return determines whether the effect is positive or negative.

Illustration 8.1: Example of an event study: Effects of option listing on stock prices

Academics and practitioners have long argued about the consequences of option listing for stock price volatility. On the one hand, there are those who argue that options attract speculators and hence increase stock price volatility. On the other hand, there are those who argue that options increase the available choices for investors and increase the flow of information to financial markets, and thus lead to lower stock price volatility and higher stock prices.

One way to test these alternative hypotheses is to do an event study, examining the effects of listing options on the underlying stocks' prices. Conrad (1989) did such a study, following these steps:

Step 1: The date on which the announcement that options would be listed on the Chicago Board of Options on a particular stock was collected.

Step 2: The prices of the underlying stock (j) were collected for each of the ten days prior to the option listing announcement date, the day of the announcement, and the ten days after.

Step 3: The returns on the stock (R_{jt}) were computed for each of these trading days.

Step 4: The beta for the stock (β_j) was estimated using the returns from a time period outside the event window (using 100 trading days before the event and 100 trading days after the event).

Step 5: The returns on the market index (R_{mt}) were computed for each of the 21 trading days.

Step 6: The excess returns were computed for each of the 21 trading days:

$$ER_{jt} = R_{jt} - \beta_j R_{mt} \qquad t = -10, -9, -8 \dots +8, +9, +10$$

The excess returns were accumulated for each trading day.

Step 7: The average and the standard error of excess returns across all stocks with option listings were computed for each of the 21 trading days. The *t* statistics were computed using the averages and standard errors for each trading day. The following table summarizes the average and cumulative excess returns (in percent) and *t* statistics around option listing announcement dates:

Trading Day	Average Excess Return	Cumulative Excess Return	T Statistic
−10	0.17	0.17	1.30
−9	.48	.65	1.66
−8	−.24	.41	1.43
−7	.28	.69	1.62

Trading Day	Average Excess Return	Cumulative Excess Return	T Statistic
−6	.04	.73	1.62
−5	−.46	.27	1.24
−4	−.26	.01	1.02
−3	−.11	−.10	.93
−2	.26	.16	1.09
−1	.29	.45	1.28
0	.01	.46	1.27
1	.17	.63	1.37
2	.14	.77	1.44
3	.04	.81	1.44
4	.18	.99	1.54
5	.56	1.55	1.88
6	.22	1.77	1.99
7	.05	1.82	2.00
8	−.13	1.69	1.89
9	.09	1.78	1.92
10	.02	1.80	1.91

Based upon these excess returns, there is no evidence of an announcement effect on the announcement day alone, but there is mild[5] evidence of a positive effect over the entire announcement period.

Portfolio Study

In some investment strategies, firms with specific characteristics are viewed as more likely to be undervalued, and therefore have excess returns, than firms without these characteristics. In these cases, the strategies can be tested by creating portfolios of firms possessing these characteristics at the beginning of a time period and examining returns over the time period. To ensure that these results are not colored by the idiosyncracies of any one time period, this is repeated for a number of periods. The steps in doing a portfolio study are as follows:

1. The variable on which firms will be classified is defined, using the investment strategy as a guide. This variable has to be observable, though it does not have to be numerical. (Examples would include market value of equity, bond ratings, stock price, price/earnings ratios, price/book value ratios, etc.)
2. The data on the variable are collected for every firm in the defined universe[6] at the *start* of the testing period, and firms are classified into portfolios based upon the magnitude of the variable. Thus, if the price/earnings ratio is the screening variable, firms are classified on the basis of PE ratios into portfolios from lowest PE to highest PE classes. The number of classes will depend upon the size of the universe, since there have to be sufficient firms in each portfolio to get some measure of diversification.

3. The returns are collected for each firm in each portfolio for the testing period, and the returns for each portfolio are computed, generally assuming that the stocks are equally weighted.

4. The beta of each portfolio is estimated, either by taking the average of the betas of the individual stocks in the portfolio or by regressing the portfolio's returns against market returns over a prior time period (for instance, the year before the testing period).

5. The excess returns earned by each portfolio are computed, in conjunction with the standard error of the excess returns.

6. There are a number of statistical tests available to check whether the average excess returns are, in fact, different across the portfolios. Some of these tests are parametric[7] (they make certain distributional assumptions about excess returns) and some are nonparametric.[8]

7. As a final test, the extreme portfolios can be matched against each other to see whether there are statistically significant differences across these portfolios.

Illustration 8.2: Example of a portfolio study: Price/earnings ratios

Practitioners have claimed that low price/earnings ratio stocks are generally bargains and do much better than the market or stocks with high price/earnings ratios. This hypothesis can be tested using a portfolio approach:

Step 1: Using data on price/earnings ratios from the end of 1987, firms on the New York Stock Exchange were classified into five groups, the first group consisting of stocks with the lowest PE ratios and the fifth group consisting of stocks with the highest PE ratios. Firms with negative price/earnings ratios were ignored.

Step 2: The returns on each portfolio were computed using data from 1988 to 1992. Stocks that went bankrupt or were delisted were assigned a return of -100%.

Step 3: The betas for each stock in each portfolio were computed using monthly returns from 1983 to 1987, and the average beta for each portfolio was estimated. The portfolios were assumed to be equally weighted.

Step 4: The returns on the market index were computed from 1988 to 1992.

Step 5: The excess returns on each portfolio were computed using data from 1988 to 1992. The following table summarizes the excess returns (in percent) for each year from 1988 to 1992 for each portfolio:

PE Class	1988	1989	1990	1991	1992	1988–1992
Lowest	3.84	−0.83	2.10	6.68	0.64	2.61
2	1.75	2.26	0.19	1.09	1.13	1.56
3	0.20	−3.15	−0.20	0.17	0.12	−0.59
4	−1.25	−0.94	−0.65	−1.99	−0.48	−1.15
Highest	−1.74	−0.63	−1.44	−4.06	−1.25	−1.95

Based upon this, we would conclude that low PE ratio stocks did outperform the market and high PE ratio stocks between 1988 and 1992.

THE CARDINAL SINS IN TESTING MARKET EFFICIENCY

In the process of testing investment strategies, there are a number of pitfalls that have to be avoided. Some of them are discussed here.

Using "anecdotal evidence" to support/reject an investment strategy: Anecdotal evidence is a double-edged sword. It can be used to support or reject the same hypothesis. Since stock prices are noisy and all investment schemes (no matter how absurd) will succeed sometimes and fail at other times, there will always be cases where the scheme works or does not work.

Testing an investment strategy on the same data and time period from which it was extracted: This is the tool of choice for the unscrupulous investment advisor. An investment scheme is extracted from hundreds through an examination of the data for a particular time period. This investment scheme is then tested on the same time period, with predictable results. (The scheme does miraculously well and makes immense returns.)

An investment scheme should always be tested out on a time period different from the one it is extracted from or on a universe different from the one used to derive the scheme.

Choosing a biased universe: The universe is the sample on which the test is run. Since there are thousands of stocks that could be considered part of this universe, researchers often choose to use a smaller universe. When this choice is random, this does limited damage to the results of the study. If the choice is biased, it can provide results that are not true in the larger universe.

Failure to control for market performance: A failure to control for overall market performance can lead one to conclude that one's investment scheme works just because it makes good returns (most schemes will make good returns if the overall market does well; the question is did they make better returns than expected?) or does not work just because it makes bad returns (most schemes will do badly if the overall market performs poorly). It is crucial therefore that investment schemes control for market performance during the period of the test.

Failure to control for risk: A failure to control for risk leads to a bias toward accepting high-risk investment schemes and rejecting low-risk investment schemes, since the former should make higher returns than the market and the latter lower, without implying any excess returns.

SOME LESSER SINS THAT CAN BE A PROBLEM

Survival bias: Most researchers start with an existing universe of publicly traded companies and work back through time to test investment strategies. This can create a subtle bias since it automatically eliminates firms that failed during the period, with obvious negative consequences for returns. If the invest-

ment scheme is particularly susceptible to picking firms that have high bankruptcy risk, this may lead to an "overstatement" of returns on the scheme.

For example, assume that the investment scheme recommends investing in stocks that have very negative earnings, using the argument that these stocks are most likely to benefit from a turnaround. Some of the firms in this portfolio will go bankrupt, and a failure to consider these firms will overstate the returns from this strategy.

Not allowing for transactions costs: Some investment schemes are more expensive than others because of transactions costs—execution fees, bid/ask spreads, and price impact. A complete test will take these into account before it passes judgment on the strategy. This is easier said than done, because different investors have different transactions costs and it is unclear which investor's trading cost schedule should be used in the test. Most researchers who ignore transactions costs argue that individual investors can decide for themselves, given their transactions costs, whether the excess returns justify the investment strategy.

Not allowing for difficulties in execution: Some strategies look good on paper but are difficult to execute in practice, either because of impediments to trading or because trading creates a price impact. Thus a strategy of investing in very small companies may seem to create excess returns on paper, but these excess returns may not exist in practice because the price impact is significant.

CONCLUSION

The question of whether markets are efficient will always be a provocative one, given the implications that efficient markets have for investment management and research. If an efficient market is defined as one where the market price is an unbiased estimate of the true value, it is quite clear that some markets will always be more efficient than others and that markets will always be more efficient to some investors than to others. The capacity of a market to correct inefficiencies quickly will depend, in part, on the ease of trading, the transactions costs, and the vigilance of profit-seeking investors in that market.

While market efficiency can be tested in a number of different ways, the two most widely used tests of efficiency are "event studies," which examine market reactions to information events, and "portfolio studies," which evaluate the returns of portfolios created on the basis of observable characteristics. It does make sense to be careful, because bias can enter these studies, intentionally or otherwise, in a number of different ways and can lead to unwarranted conclusions and, worse still, wasteful investment strategies.

QUESTIONS AND SHORT PROBLEMS

1. Which of the following is an implication of market efficiency? (There may be more than one right answer.)

 a. Resources are allocated among firms efficiently (i.e., put to best use).

 b. No investor will do better than the market in any time period.

 c. No investor will do better than the market consistently.

 d. No investor will do better than the market consistently after adjusting for risk.

 e. No investor will do better than the market consistently after adjusting for risk and transactions costs.

 f. No group of investors will do better than the market consistently after adjusting for risk and transactions costs.

2. Suppose you are following a retailing stock that has a strong seasonal pattern to sales. Would you expect to see a seasonal pattern in the stock price as well?

3. Tests of market efficiency are often referred to as joint tests of two hypotheses—the hypothesis that the market is efficient and an expected returns model. Explain. Is it ever possible to test market efficiency alone (i.e., without jointly testing an asset pricing model)?

4. You are in a violent argument with a chartist. He claims that you are violating the fundamental laws of economics by trying to find intrinsic value. "Price is determined by demand and supply . . . not by some intrinsic value." Is finding an intrinsic value inconsistent with demand and supply?

5. You are testing the effect of merger announcements on stock prices. (This is an event study.) Your procedure goes through the following steps:

Step 1: You choose the twenty biggest mergers of the year.

Step 2: You isolate the date the merger became effective as the key day around which you will examine the data.

Step 3: You look at the returns for the five days after the effective merger date.

By looking at these returns (.13%), you conclude that you could not have made money on merger announcements. Are there any flaws that you can detect in this test? How would you correct for them? Can you devise a stronger test?

6. In an efficient market, the market price is defined to be an "unbiased estimate" of the true value. This implies that

 a. the market price is always equal to true value.

 b. the market price has nothing to do with true value.

 c. markets make mistakes about true value, and investors can exploit these mistakes to make money.

 d. market prices contain errors, but the errors are random and therefore cannot be exploited by investors.

 e. no one can beat the market.

7. Evaluate whether the following actions are likely to increase stock market efficiency, decrease it, or leave it unchanged, and explain why.

 a. The government imposes a transaction tax of 1% on all stock transactions.

 b. The securities exchange regulators impose a restriction on all short sales to prevent rampant speculation.

 c. An options market, trading call and put options, is opened up, with options traded on many of the stocks listed on the exchange.

 d. The stock market removes all restrictions on foreign investors acquiring and holding stock in companies.

8. The following is a graph of cumulative abnormal returns around the announcement of asset divestitures by major corporations:

How best would you explain the

a. market behavior before the announcement?

b. market reaction to the announcement?

c. market reaction after the announcement?

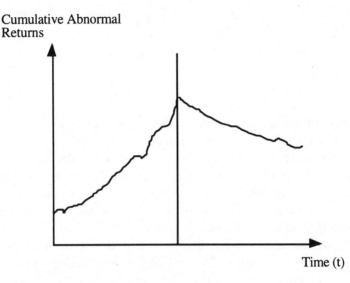

Cumulative Abnormal
Returns

Time (t)

ENDNOTES

1. Randomness implies that there is an equal chance that stocks are under- or overvalued at any point in time.

2. Since returns are positively skewed, that is, large positive returns are more likely than large negative returns (since this is bounded at -100%), less than half of all investors will probably beat the market.

3. One of the enduring pieces of evidence against market efficiency is the performance records posted by many of the investors who learned their lessons from Ben Graham in the 1950s. No probability statistics could ever explain the consistency and superiority of their records.

4. The standard levels of significance for a t statistic are:

Level	Two-tailed	One-tailed
1%	2.33	1.96
5%		

5. The t statistics are marginally significant at the 5% level.

6. Though there are practical limits on how big the universe can be, care should be taken to ensure that no biases enter at this stage of the process. An obvious one would be picking only stocks that have done well over the time period for the universe.

7. One parametric test is an F test, which tests for equality of means across groups. This test can be conducted assuming either that the groups have the same variance or that they have different variances.

8. An example of a nonparametric test is a rank sum test, which ranks returns across the entire sample and then sums the ranks within each group to check whether the rankings are random or systematic.

Market Efficiency—
The Evidence

Market efficiency has been tested in hundreds of studies over the last three decades. The evidence from these studies has sometimes been contradictory, as researchers have looked at the same questions in a variety of ways, using different statistical techniques and different time periods for their tests. The pendulum of consensus opinion has swung back and forth between the view that markets are mostly efficient and the view that there are significant inefficiencies in financial markets.

This chapter attempts to summarize the evidence from studies of market efficiency. Without claiming to be comprehensive, the evidence is classified into four sections: the study of price changes and their time series properties, the research on the efficiency of market reaction to information announcements, the existence of return anomalies across firms and over time, and the analysis of market behavior in response to insider trading, analyst recommendations, and money managers.

TIME SERIES PROPERTIES OF PRICE CHANGES

Investors have used price charts and price patterns as tools for predicting future price movements for as long as there have been financial markets. It is not surprising, therefore, that the first studies of market efficiency focused on the relationship between price changes over time, to see if in fact such predictions were feasible. Some of this testing was spurred by the "random walk" theory of price movements, which contended that price changes over time followed a random walk. As the studies of the time series properties of prices have proliferated, the evidence can be classified into two classes: studies that focus on short-term (intraday, daily, and weekly price movements) price behavior and research that examines long-term (annual and five-year returns) price movements.

Short-Term Price Movements

The notion that today's price change conveys information about tomorrow's price change is deep-rooted in most investors' psyches. There are several ways in which this hypothesis can be tested in financial markets.

Serial Correlation

The serial correlation measures the correlation between price changes in consecutive time periods, whether hourly, daily, or weekly, and is a measure of how much the price change in any period depends upon the price change over the previous time period. A serial correlation of 0 would therefore imply that price changes in consecutive time periods are uncorrelated with each other, and can thus be viewed as a rejection of the hypothesis that investors can learn about future price changes from past ones. A serial correlation that is positive, and statistically significant, could be viewed as evidence of price momentum in markets, and would suggest that returns in a period are more likely to be positive (negative) if the prior period's returns were positive (negative). A serial correlation that is negative, and statistically significant, could be evidence of price reversals, and would be consistent with a market where positive returns are more likely to follow negative returns and vice versa.

From the viewpoint of investment strategy, serial correlations can be exploited to earn excess returns. A positive serial correlation would be exploited with a strategy of buying after periods with positive returns and selling after periods with negative returns. A negative serial correlation would suggest a strategy of buying after periods with negative returns and selling after periods with positive returns. Since these strategies generate transactions costs, the correlations have to be large enough to allow investors to generate profits to cover these costs. It is therefore entirely possible that there be serial correlation in returns without any opportunity to earn excess returns for most investors.

Table 9.1 summarizes the evidence from a number of studies that have looked at the serial correlation of returns in short periods in financial markets.

As the evidence indicates, the serial correlation in most markets is small. While there may be statistical significance associated with some of these correlations, it is unlikely that there is enough correlation to generate excess returns.

The serial correlation in short-period returns is also affected by price measurement issues and the market microstructure characteristics. The serial correlation in market index returns in short periods is affected by nontrading in some of the components of the index. Since the trading in these nontraded stocks in the next time period can create a carryover effect from the prior time period, this can result in positive serial correlation in the index returns. The bid/ask spread creates a bias in the opposite direction, if transactions prices are used to compute returns, since prices have an equal chance of ending up at the bid or the ask price. The bounce that this induces in prices will result in negative serial correlations in returns. Roll (1984) provides a simple measure of this relationship:

$$\text{Bid/Ask Spread} = -\sqrt{2(\text{Serial Covariance in returns})}$$

where the serial covariance in returns measures the covariance between return changes in consecutive time periods. For very short return intervals, this bias induced in serial correlations might dominate and create the mistaken view that price changes in consecutive time periods are negatively correlated.

Filter Rules

In a filter rule, an investor buys an investment if the price rises X% from a previous low and holds the investment until the price drops X% from a previous high. The magnitude of the change (X%) that triggers the trades can vary from filter rule to filter rule, with smaller changes resulting in more transactions per period and higher transactions costs. This is illustrated in Figure 9.1.

This strategy is based upon the assumption that price changes are serially correlated and that there is price momentum; that is, that stocks that have gone up strongly in the past are more likely to keep going up than go down. Table 9.2 summarizes results from a study on returns, before and after transactions costs, on a trading strategy based upon filter rules ranging from 0.5% to 20%. (A 0.5% rule implies that a stock is bought when it rises 0.5% from a previous low and sold when it falls 0.5% from a prior high.)

The only filter rule that beats the returns from the buy and hold strategy is the 0.5% rule, but it does so before transactions costs. This strategy creates

TABLE 9.1 Serial Correlation in Short-Period Returns

Author (*)	Data	Variable	Time Intervals	Correlation
Kendall & Alexander (28)	19 indices—U.K.	Price	1 week	0.131
			2 weeks	.134
			4 weeks	.006
Moore (28)	30 companies—U.S.	Log prices	1 week	−.056
Cootner (28)	45 companies—U.S.	Log prices	1 week	−.047
Fama (46)	30 companies—U.S.	Log prices	1 day	.026
			4 days	−.039
			9 days	−.053
King (28)	63 companies—U.S.	Log prices	1 month	.018
Niarchos (119)	15 companies—Greece	Log prices	1 month	.036
Praetz (128)	16 indices	Log prices	1 week	.000
	20 companies		1 week	−.118
Griffiths (73)	5 companies—U.K.	Prices	9 days	−.026
			1 month	.011
Jennergren (90)	15 companies—U.K.	Log prices	1 day	.068
			2 days	−.070
			5 days	−.004
Jennergren & Kosvold (91)	30 companies—Sweden	Log prices	1 day	.102
			3 days	−.021
			5 days	−.016

* The number in brackets after the authors' names is the number of firms in that study.

FIGURE 9.1 Illustration of Filter Rule

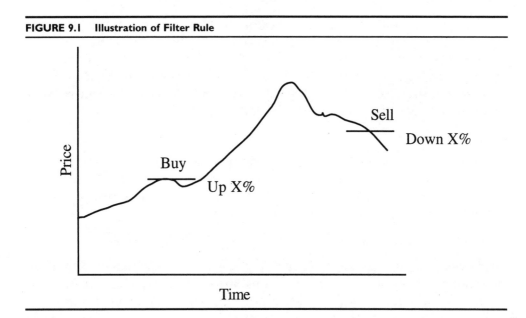

12,514 trades during the period, which generate enough transactions costs to wipe out the principal invested by the investor.

While this test is dated, it also illustrates a problem with basic strategies that require frequent short-term trading. Even though these strategies may earn excess returns prior to transactions costs, adjusting for these costs can wipe out the excess returns.

TABLE 9.2 Returns on Filter Rule Strategies

Value of X (percent)	Return with Strategy (percent)	Return with Buy and Hold (percent)	Number of Transactions with Strategy	Return after Transactions Costs (percent)
0.5	11.5	10.4	12,514	− 103.6
1.0	5.5	10.3	8,660	− 74.9
2.0	.2	10.3	4,764	− 45.2
3.0	− 1.7	10.1	2,994	− 30.5
4.0	.1	10.1	2,013	− 19.5
5.0	− 1.9	10.0	1,484	− 16.6
6.0	1.3	9.7	1,071	− 9.4
7.0	.8	9.6	828	− 7.4
8.0	1.7	9.6	653	− 5.0
9.0	1.9	9.6	539	− 3.6
10.0	3.0	9.6	435	− 1.4
12.0	5.3	9.4	289	2.3
14.0	3.9	10.3	224	1.4
16.0	4.2	10.3	172	2.3
18.0	3.6	10.0	139	2.0
20.0	4.3	9.8	110	3.0

One popular indicator among investors that is a variant on the filter rule is the relative strength measure, which relates recent prices on stocks or other investments to either average prices over a specified period, say six months, or the price at the beginning of the period. Stocks that score high on the relative strength measure are considered good investments. This investment strategy is also based upon the assumption of price momentum.

Runs Tests

A runs test is a nonparametric variation on the serial correlation, and it is based upon a count of the number of runs, that is, sequences of price increases or decreases, in the price changes. Consider the following time series of price changes, where U is an increase and D is a decrease:

UUU DD U DDD UU DD U D UU DD U DD UUU DD UU D UU D

There were 18 runs in this time series of 33 periods. The actual number of runs in the price series is compared against the number that can be expected[1] in a series of this length, assuming that price changes are random. If the actual number of runs is greater than the expected number, there is evidence of negative correlation in price changes. If it is lower, there is evidence of positive correlation. A study of price changes in the Dow 30 stocks, assuming daily, four-day, nine-day, and sixteen-day return intervals, provided the following results:

	Daily	4-Day	9-Day	16-Day
Actual runs	735.1	175.7	74.6	41.6
Expected runs	759.8	175.8	75.3	41.7

Based upon these results, there is evidence of positive correlation in daily returns but no evidence of deviations from normality for longer return intervals.

Again, while the evidence is dated, it serves to illustrate the point that long strings of positive and negative changes are, by themselves, insufficient evidence that markets are not random, since such behavior is consistent with price changes following a random walk. It is the recurrence of these strings that can be viewed as evidence against randomness in price behavior.

Long-Term Price Movements

While most of the earlier studies of price behavior focused on shorter return intervals, more attention has been paid to price movements over longer periods (one year to five years) in recent years. Part of this attention can be attributed to the fact that there is substantial negative correlation in longer-term return intervals, suggesting that markets reverse themselves over very long periods. Since such behavior, if true, would be a serious challenge to market efficiency, the phenomenon has been examined in extensive detail. Studies that break down stocks on the basis of market value have found that the serial correlation is more negative in five-year returns than in one-year returns and is much more

negative for smaller stocks than larger stocks. Figure 9.2 summarizes one-year and five-year serial correlation by size class for stocks on the New York Stock Exchange.

This phenomenon has also been examined in other markets, and the findings have been similar. There is evidence that returns reverse themselves over long time period.

Winner and Loser Portfolios

Since there is evidence that prices reverse themselves in the long term for entire markets, it might be worth examining whether such price reversals occur on classes of stock within a market. For instance, are stocks that have gone up the most over the last period more likely to go down over the next period and

FIGURE 9.2 One-Year and Five-Year Serial Correlations, by Size Class

Source: E. F. Fama and K. R. French, "Permanent and Temporary Components of Stock Prices, " *Journal of Political Economy* (April 1988).

vice versa? To isolate the effect of such price reversals on the extreme portfolios, DeBondt and Thaler (1985, 1987) constructed a winner portfolio of 35 stocks, which had gone up the most over the prior year, and a loser portfolio of 35 stocks, which had gone down the most over the prior year, for each year from 1933 to 1978, and examined returns on these portfolios for the 60 months following the creation of the portfolio. Figure 9.3 summarizes the excess returns for winner and loser portfolios.

This analysis suggests that loser portfolios clearly outperform winner portfolios in the 60 months following creation. This evidence is consistent with market overreaction and correction in long return intervals.

There are many, academics as well as practitioners, who suggest that these findings may be interesting but that they overstate potential returns on loser portfolios. For instance, there is evidence that loser portfolios are more likely to contain low-priced stocks (selling for less than $5), which generate higher transactions costs and are also more likely to offer heavily skewed returns; that is, the excess returns come from a few stocks making phenomenal returns rather than from consistent performance. One study of the winner and loser portfolios attributes the bulk of the excess returns of loser portfolios to low-priced stocks and also finds that the results are sensitive to when the portfolios are created. Loser portfolios created every December earn significantly higher returns than portfolios created every June.

FIGURE 9.3 Excess Returns for Winner and Loser Portfolios*

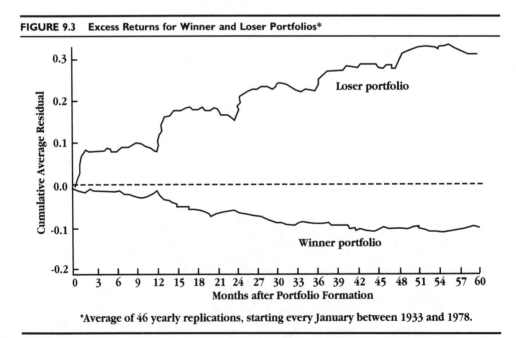

Average of 46 yearly replications, starting every January between 1933 and 1978.

Cumulative average residuals for winner and loser portfolios of 35 stocks, one to 60 months after portfolio formation; length of formation periods: 5 years.
Source: W. F. M. DeBondt and R. Thaler, "Does the Stock Market Overreact?" *Journal of Finance* (July 1985).

Speculative Bubbles, Crashes, and Panics

Historians who have examined the behavior of financial markets over time have challenged the assumption of rationality that underlies much of efficient market theory. They point to the frequency with which speculative bubbles have formed in financial markets, as investors buy into fads or get-rich-quick schemes, and the crashes with which these bubbles have ended, and suggest that there is nothing to prevent the recurrence of this phenomenon in today's financial markets. There is some evidence in the literature of irrationality on the part of market players.

Experimental Studies of Rationality

Some of the most interesting evidence on market efficiency and rationality in recent years has come from experimental studies. While most experimental studies suggest that traders are rational, there are some examples of irrational behavior in some of these studies.

One such study was done at the University of Arizona. In an experimental study, traders were told that a payout would be declared after each trading day, determined randomly from four possibilities—0, 8, 28, or 60 cents. The average payout was 24 cents. Thus the share's expected value on the first trading day of a 15-day experiment was \$3.60 (.24 × 15), on the second day \$3.36, . . . The traders were allowed to trade each day. The results of 60 such experiments are summarized in the graph in Figure 9.4.

There is clear evidence here of a "speculative bubble" forming during days 3 to 5, when prices exceed expected values by a significant amount. The bubble ultimately bursts, and prices approach expected value by the end of the period.

FIGURE 9.4 Trading Price by Trading Day

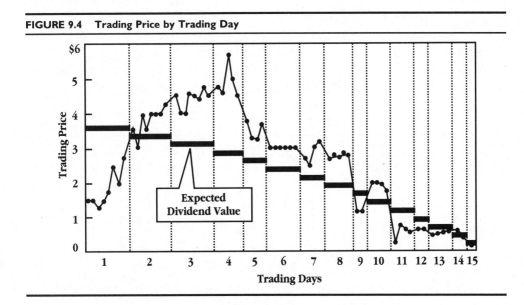

If this is feasible in a simple market, where every investor obtains the same information, it is clearly feasible in real financial markets, where there is much more differential information and much greater uncertainty about expected value.

It should be pointed out that some of the experiments were run with students and some with Tucson businessmen, with "real world" experience. The results were similar for both groups. Furthermore, when price curbs of 15 cents were introduced, the booms lasted even longer because traders knew that prices would not fall by more than 15 cents in a period. Thus, the notion that price limits can control speculative bubbles seems misguided.

Chaos and Nonlinear Dynamics in Prices

The recent use of chaos theory to explain natural phenomena (such as weather patterns) has also generated some interest in its potential uses in explaining stock price behavior. Peters (1991), for instance, has tried to model price behavior using the nonlinear models that underlie much of chaos theory with mixed results.

MARKET REACTION TO INFORMATION EVENTS

Some of the most powerful tests of market efficiency are event studies where market reaction to informational events (such as earnings and takeover announcements) has been scrutinized for evidence of inefficiency. While it is consistent with market efficiency for markets to react to new information, the reaction has to be instantaneous and unbiased. This point is made in Figure 9.5 by contrasting three different market reactions to information announcements.

Of the three market reactions pictured, only market A is consistent with an efficient market. In market B, the information announcement is followed by a gradual increase in prices, allowing investors to make excess returns after the announcement. This is a slow-learning market where some investors will make excess returns on the price drift. In market C, the price reacts instantaneously to the announcement but corrects itself in the days that follow, suggest-

FIGURE 9.5 Contrasting Market Reactions to Information Announcements

ing that the initial price change was an overreaction to the information. Here again, an enterprising investor could have sold short after the announcement and expected to make excess returns as a consequence of the price correction.

Earnings Announcements

When firms make earnings announcements, they convey information to financial markets about their current and future prospects. The magnitude of the information, and the size of the market reaction, should depend upon how much the earnings report exceeds or falls short of investor expectations. In an efficient market, there should be an instantaneous reaction to the earnings report, if it contains surprising information, and prices should increase following positive surprises and decrease following negative surprises.

Since actual earnings are compared to investor expectations, one of the key parts of an earnings event study is the measurement of these expectations. Some of the earlier studies used earnings from the same quarter in the prior year as a measure of expected earnings; that is, firms that report increases in quarter-to-quarter earnings provide positive surprises and those that report decreases in quarter-to-quarter earnings provide negative surprises. In more recent studies, analyst estimates of earnings have been used as a proxy for expected earnings and compared to the actual earnings.

Figure 9.6 provides a graph of price reactions to earnings surprises, classified on the basis of magnitude into different classes from "most negative" earnings reports (group 1) to "most positive" earnings reports (group 10).

The evidence contained in this graph is consistent with the evidence in most earnings announcement studies:

(a) The earnings announcement clearly conveys valuable information to financial markets; there are positive excess returns (cumulative abnormal returns) after positive announcements and negative excess returns around negative announcements.

(b) There is some evidence of a market reaction in the day immediately prior to the earnings announcement that is consistent with the nature of the announcement; that is, prices tend to go up on the day before positive announcements and down in the day before negative announcements. This can be viewed either as evidence of insider trading or as a consequence of getting the announcement date wrong.[2]

(c) There is some evidence, albeit weak, of a price drift in the days following an earnings announcement. Thus, a positive report evokes a positive market reaction on the announcement date, and there are mildly positive excess returns in the days following the earnings announcement. Similar conclusions emerge for negative earnings reports.

The management of a firm has some discretion on the timing of earnings reports, and there is some evidence that the timing affects expected returns. A study of earnings reports, classified by the day of the week that the earnings are reported, reveals that earnings and dividend reports on Fridays are much

FIGURE 9.6 Price Reactions to Quarterly Earnings Reports

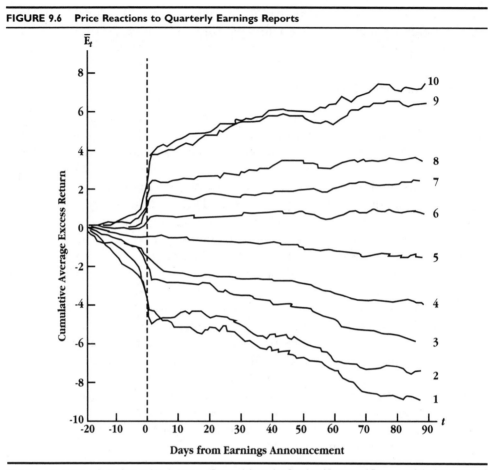

Source: R. J. Rendleman, C. P. Jones, and H. A. Latané, "Empirical Anomalies Based on Unexpected Earnings and the Importance of Risk Adjustment," Journal of Financial Economics (November 1982).

more likely to contain negative information than announcements on any other day of the week. This is shown in Figure 9.7.

There is also some evidence that earnings announcements that are delayed, relative to the expected announcement date, are much more likely to contain bad news than earnings announcements that are early or on time. This is graphed in Figure 9.8.

Earnings announcements that are more than six days late, relative to the expected announcement date, are much more likely to contain bad news and evoke negative market reactions than earnings announcements that are on time or early.

Investment and Project Announcements

Firms frequently make announcements of their intentions of investing resources in projects and research and development. There is evidence that financial markets react to these announcements. The question of whether market have a long-term or short-term perspective can be partially answered by looking at

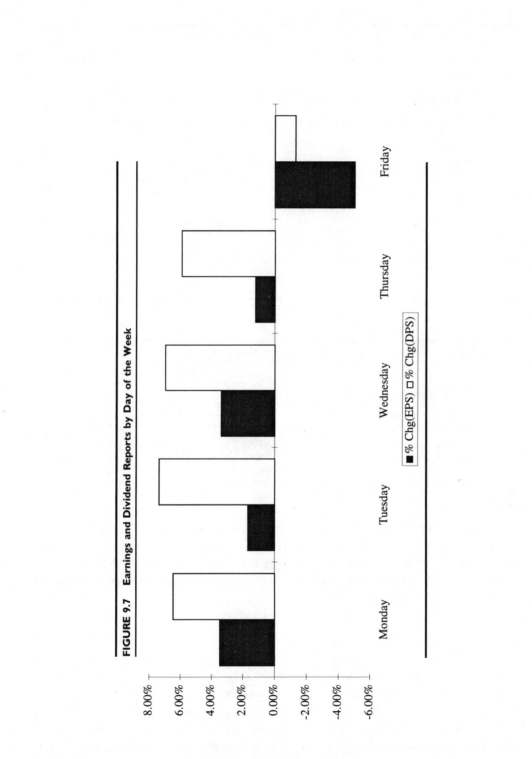

FIGURE 9.7 Earnings and Dividend Reports by Day of the Week

■ % Chg(EPS) □ % Chg(DPS)

FIGURE 9.8 Cumulative Abnormal Returns and Earnings Delay (Day 0 is earnings announcement date.)

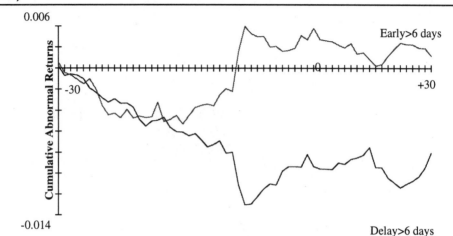

TABLE 9.3 Market Reactions to Investment Announcements

Type of Announcement	Abnormal Returns on	
	Announcement Day	Announcement Month
Joint-venture formations	0.399%	1.412%
R&D expenditures	.251%	1.456%
Product strategies	.440%	−.35%
Capital expenditures	.290%	1.499%
All announcements	.355%	.984%

these market reactions. If financial markets are as short term as some of their critics claim, they should react negatively to announcements by the firm that it plans to invest in research and development. The evidence suggests the contrary. Table 9.3 summarizes market reactions to various classes of investment announcements made by the firm.

MARKET ANOMALIES

Webster's Dictionary defines an anomaly as a "deviation from the common rule." Studies of market efficiency have uncovered numerous examples of market behavior that are inconsistent with existing models of risk and return and often defy rational explanation. The persistence of some of these patterns of behavior suggests that the problem, in at least some of these anomalies, lies in the models being used for risk and return rather than in the behavior of financial markets. The following section summarizes some of the more widely noticed anomalies in financial markets in the United States and elsewhere.

Anomalies Based upon Firm Characteristics

There are a number of anomalies that have been related to observable firm characteristics, including the market value of equity, price/earnings ratios, and price/book value ratios.

The Small Firm Effect

Studies have consistently found that smaller firms (in terms of market value of equity) earn higher returns than larger firms of equivalent risk, where risk is defined in terms of the market beta. Figure 9.9 summarizes returns for stocks in ten market value classes, for the period from 1927 to 1983.

The size of the small firm premium, while it has varied across time, has been generally positive, as measured in Figure 9.10, which summarizes small stock premiums from 1926 to 1990.

This has led to several possible explanations for the phenomenon:

(a) The transactions costs of investing in small stocks is significantly higher than the transactions costs of investing in larger stocks, and the premiums are estimated prior to these costs. While this is generally true, the differential transactions costs are unlikely to explain the magnitude of the premium across time, and are likely to become even less critical for longer investment horizons. The difficulties of replicating the small firm premiums that are observed in the studies in real time are illustrated in Figure 9.11, which compares the returns on a hypothetical small firm portfolio (CRSP Small Stocks) with the

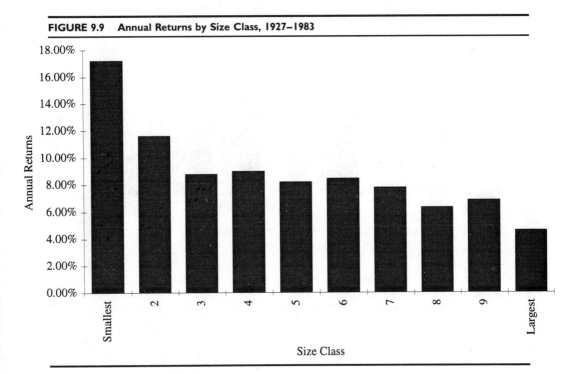

FIGURE 9.9 Annual Returns by Size Class, 1927–1983

FIGURE 9.10 Small Stock Premiums, 1926–1990

FIGURE 9.11 Returns on CRSP Small Stocks versus DFA Small Stock Fund

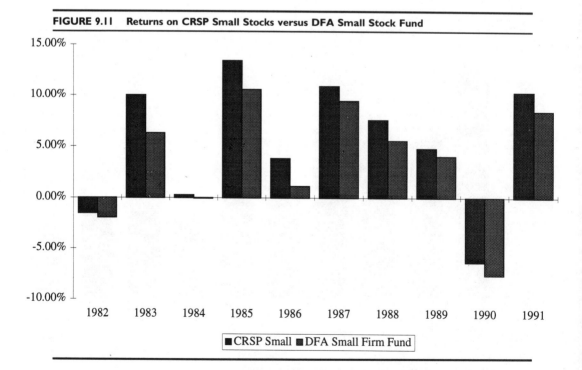

■CRSP Small ■DFA Small Firm Fund

actual returns on a small firm mutual fund (DFA Small Stock Fund), which passively invests in small stocks.

(b) The capital asset pricing model may not be the right model for risk, and betas underestimate the true risk of small stocks. Thus, the small firm premium is really a measure of the failure of beta to capture risk. The additional risk associated with small stocks may come from several sources. First, the estimation risk associated with estimates of beta for small firms is much greater than the estimation risk associated with beta estimates for larger firms. The small firm premium may be a reward for this additional estimation risk. Second, there may be additional risk in investing in small stocks because far less information is available on these stocks. In fact, studies indicate that stocks that are neglected by analysts and institutional investors earn an excess return that parallels the small firm premium.

There is evidence of a small firm premium in markets outside the United States as well. Dimson and Marsh (1990) examined stocks in the United Kingdom from 1955 to 1984 and found that the annual returns on small stocks exceeded that on large stocks by 7% annually over the period. Bergstrom, Frashure, and Chisholm (1991) reported a large size effect for French stocks (small stocks made 32.3% per year between 1975 and 1989, while large stocks made 23.5% a year), and a much smaller size effect in Germany. Hamao (1989) reported a small firm premium of 5.1% for Japanese stocks between 1971 and 1988.

Price/Earnings Ratios

Investors have long argued that stocks with low price/earnings ratios are more likely to be undervalued and earn excess returns. For instance, Ben Graham, in his investment classic *The Intelligent Investor,* uses low PE ratios as a screen for finding undervalued stocks. Studies that have looked at the relationship between PE ratios and excess returns confirm this hypothesis. Figure 9.12 summarizes annual returns by PE ratio classes for stocks from 1967 to 1988.

Firms in the lowest PE ratio class earned an average return of 16.26% during the period, while firms in the highest PE ratio class earned an average return of only 6.64%.

The excess returns earned by low PE ratio stocks also persist in other international markets. Table 9.4 summarizes the results of studies looking at this phenomenon in markets outside the United States.

The excess returns earned by low PE ratio stocks are difficult to justify using a variation of the argument used for small stocks, that is, that the risk of low PE ratio stocks is understated in the CAPM. Low PE ratio stocks generally are characterized by low growth, large size, and stable businesses, all of which should work toward reducing their risk rather than increasing it. The only explanation that can be given for this phenomenon, which is consistent with an efficient market, is that low PE ratio stocks generate large dividend yields, which would have created a larger tax burden in those years when dividends were taxed at higher rates.

FIGURE 9.12 Annual Returns by PE Ratio Class, 1967–1988

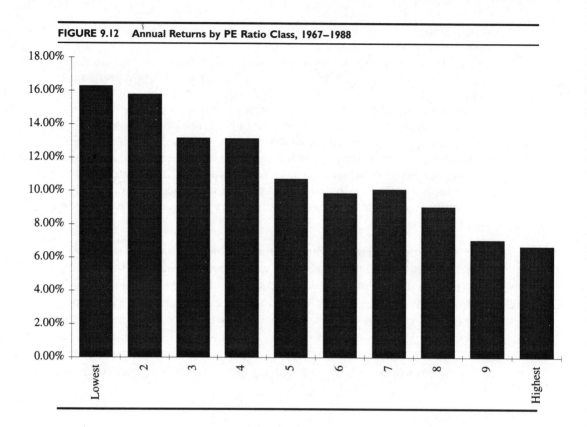

TABLE 9.4 Excess Returns on Low PE Ratio Stocks by Country: 1989–1994

Country	Annual Premium* Earned by Lowest PE Stocks (bottom quintile) (percent)
Australia	3.03
France	6.40
Germany	1.06
Hong Kong	6.60
Italy	14.16
Japan	7.30
Switzerland	9.02
United Kingdom	2.40

* Premium earned over an index of equally weighted stocks in that market between January 1, 1989 and December 31, 1994. These numbers were obtained from a Merrill Lynch Survey of Proprietary Indices.

Price/Book Value Ratios

Another statistic that is widely used by investors in investment strategy is the price/book value ratios. A low price/book value ratio has been considered a reliable indicator of undervaluation in firms. In studies that parallel those done on price/earnings ratios, the relationship between returns and price/book value ratios has been studied. The consistent finding from these studies is that there is a negative relationship between returns and price/book value ratios—that is, low price/book value ratio stocks earn higher returns than high price/book value ratio stocks.

Rosenberg, Reid, and Lanstein (1985) find that the average returns on U.S. stocks are positively related to the ratio of a firm's book value to market value. Between 1973 and 1984, the strategy of picking stocks with high book value/price ratios (low price/book value ratios) yielded an excess return of 36 basis points a month. Fama and French (1992), in examining the cross-section of expected stock returns between 1963 and 1990, established that the positive relationship between book value/price ratios and average returns persists in both the univariate and multivariate tests, and is even stronger than the size effect in explaining returns. When they classified firms on the basis of book value/price ratios into twelve portfolios, firms in the lowest book value/price (higher P/BV) class earned an average monthly return of 0.30%, while firms in the highest book value/price (lowest P/BV) class earned an average monthly return of 1.83% for the 1963–1990 period.

Chan, Hamao, and Lakonishok (1991) found that the book value/market ratio has a strong role in explaining the cross-section of average returns on Japanese stocks. Capaul, Rowley, and Sharpe (1993) extended the analysis of price/book value ratios across other international markets and conclude that value stocks, that is, stocks with low price/book value ratios, earned excess returns in every market that they analyzed between 1981 and 1992. Their annualized estimates of the return differential earned by stocks with low price/book value ratios, over the market index, were as follows:

Country	Added Return to Low P/BV Portfolio
France	3.26%
Germany	1.39%
Switzerland	1.17%
United Kingdom	1.09%
Japan	3.43%
United States	1.06%
Europe	1.30%
Global	1.88%

A caveat is in order. Fama and French (1992) pointed out that low price/book value ratios may operate as a measure of risk, since firms with prices well below book value are more likely to be in trouble and go out of business. Investors therefore have to evaluate for themselves whether the additional re-

turns made by such firms justify the additional risk taken on by investing in
them.

Temporal Anomalies

There are a number of peculiarities in return differences across calendar time
that are not only difficult to rationalize but are also suggestive of inefficiencies.
Furthermore, some of these temporal anomalies are related to the small firm
effect described in the previous section.

The January Effect

Studies of returns in the United States and other major financial markets consis-
tently reveal strong differences in return behavior across the months of the
year. Figure 9.13 reports average returns by month of the year from 1926 to
1983.

Returns in January are significantly higher than returns in any other month
of the year. This phenomenon is called the year-end or January effect, and it
can be traced to the first two weeks in January.

The relationship between the January effect and the small firm effect adds
to the complexity of this phenomenon. The January effect is much more accen-
tuated for small firms than for larger firms, and roughly half of the small firm
premium, described in the prior section, is earned in the first two days of
January. Figure 9.14 graphs returns in January by size and risk class for data
from 1935 to 1986.

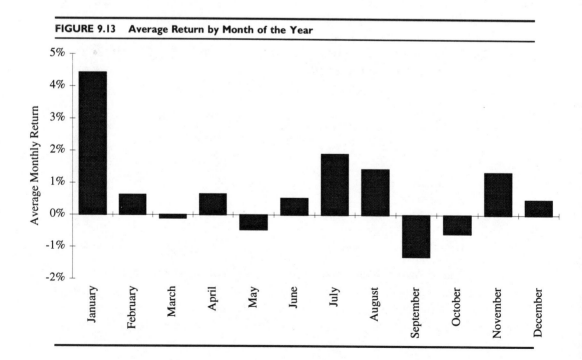

FIGURE 9.13 Average Return by Month of the Year

FIGURE 9.14 Returns in January by Size and Risk Class, 1935–1986

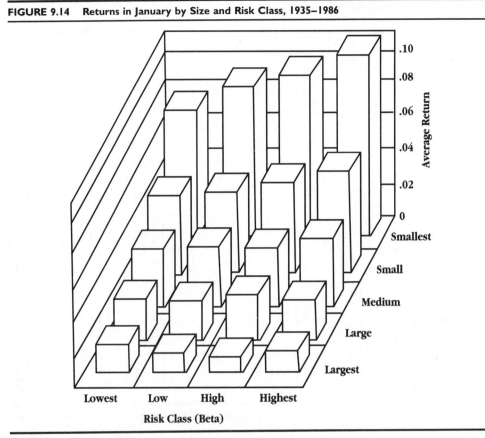

Source: R. Haugen and J. Lakonishok, The Incredible January Effect (Homewood, IL: Dow Jones-Irwin, 1988).

A number of explanations have been advanced for the January effect, but few hold up to serious scrutiny. One is that there is tax loss selling by investors at the end of the year on stocks that have "lost money" to capture the capital loss, driving prices down, presumably below true value, and a buying back of the same stocks[3] in January, resulting in the high returns. The fact that the January effect is accentuated for stocks that have done worse over the prior year is offered as evidence for this explanation. There are several pieces of evidence that contradict it, though. First, there are countries, like Australia, that have a different tax year but continue to have a January effect. Second, the January effect is no greater, on average, in years following bad years for the stock market than in other years.

A second rationale is that the January effect is related to individual trading behavior around the turn of the year. It has been noted, for instance, that the ratio of buys to sells for individuals drops significantly below average in the days before the turn of the year and picks up to above average in the months that follow. This is illustrated in Figure 9.15.

It is argued that the absence of individual buying pushes down prices in the days before the turn of the year and pushes up prices in the days after.

FIGURE 9.15 Individual Buying/Selling Around Yearend

Source: J. J. Ritter, "The Buying and Selling Behavior of Individual Investors at the Turn of the Year," *Journal of Finance* (July 1988).

The universality of the January effect is illustrated in Figure 9.16, which examines returns in January versus the other months of the year in several major financial markets, and finds strong evidence of a January effect in every market.

The Weekend Effect

The weekend effect is another return phenomenon that has persisted over extraordinarily long periods and over a number of international markets. It refers to the differences in returns between Mondays and other days of the week. The significance of the return difference is brought out in Figure 9.17, which graphs returns by day of the week from 1962 to 1978.

The returns on Mondays are significantly negative, whereas the returns on every day of the week are not. There are a number of other findings on the Monday effect that have fleshed it out. First, the Monday effect is really a weekend effect since the bulk of the negative returns is manifested in the Friday close to Monday open returns. The returns from intraday returns on Monday are not the culprits in creating the negative returns. Second, the Monday effect is worse for small stocks than for larger stocks. Third, the Monday effect is no worse following three-day weekends than two-day weekends.

FIGURE 9.16 Returns in January versus Other Months—Major Financial Markets

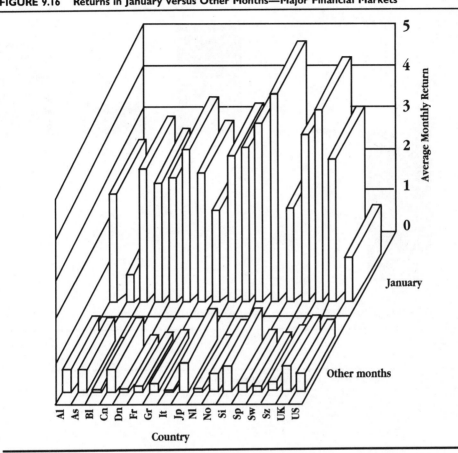

Source: R. Haugen and J. Lakonishok, *The Incredible January Effect* (Homewood, IL: Dow Jones-Irwin, 1988).

There are some who have argued that the weekend effect is the result of bad news being revealed after the close of trading on Friday and during the weekend. They point to available evidence which reveals that more negative earnings reports are revealed after close of trading on Friday. Even if this were a widespread phenomenon, the return behavior would be inconsistent with a rational market, since rational investors would build in the expectation of the bad news over the weekend into the price before the weekend, leading to an elimination of the weekend effect.

The weekend effect is fairly strong in most major international markets, as shown in Figure 9.18.

The presence of a strong weekend effect in Japan, which allowed Saturday trading for a portion of the period studied here, indicates that there might be a more direct reason for negative returns on Mondays than bad information over the weekend.

As a final note, the negative returns on Mondays cannot be just attributed to the absence of trading over the weekend. The returns on days following

FIGURE 9.17 Average Daily Returns by Day of the Week: 1962–1978

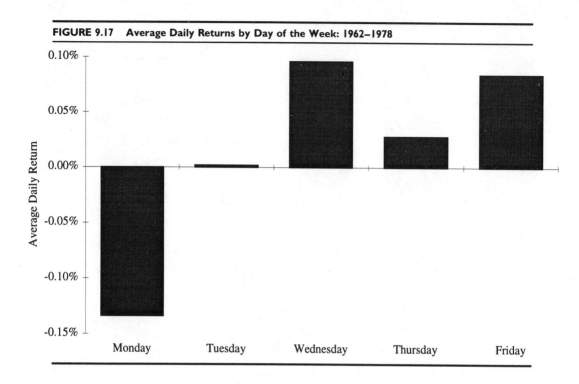

FIGURE 9.18 Weekend Effect in International Markets

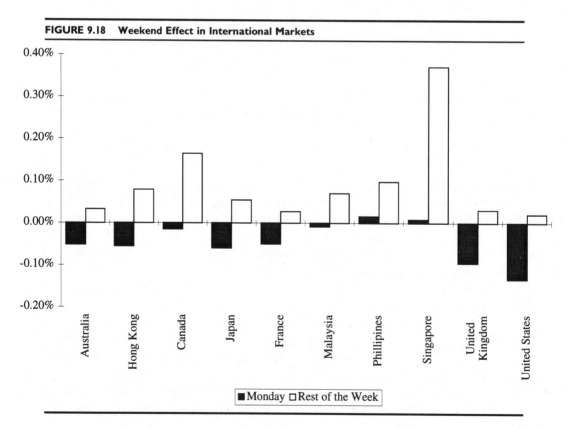

trading holidays, in general, are characterized by positive, not negative, returns. Figure 9.19 summarizes returns on trading days following major holidays and confirms this pattern.

EVIDENCE ON INSIDERS AND INVESTMENT PROFESSIONALS

There is a sense that insiders, analysts, and portfolio managers must possess an advantage over the average investors in the market and be able to convert this advantage into excess returns. The evidence on the performance of these investors is actually surprisingly mixed.

Insider Trading

The SEC defines an insider to be an officer or director of the firm or a major stockholder (holding more than 5% of the outstanding stock in the firm). Insiders are barred from trading in advance of specific information on the company and are required to file with the SEC when they buy or sell stock in the company. If it is assumed, as seems reasonable, that insiders have better information about the company, and consequently better estimates of value, than other investors, the decisions by insiders to buy and sell stock should affect stock prices. Figure 9.20, derived from an early study of insider trading by Jaffe, examines excess returns on two groups of stock, classified on the basis of insider trades. The "buy group" includes stocks where buys exceeded sells by the biggest margin, and the "sell group" includes stocks where sells exceed buys by the biggest margin.

While it seems like the buy group does significantly better than the sell group in this study, advances in information technology have made this informa-

FIGURE 9.19 Average Market Returns on Holidays—A Holiday Effect?

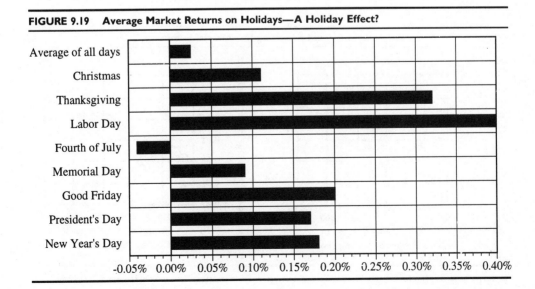

FIGURE 9.20 Cumulative Abnormal Returns Following Insider Trading: Buy Versus Sell Group

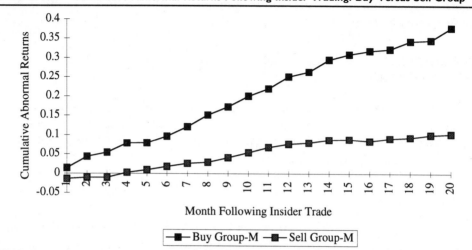

Source: J. F. Jaffe, "Special Information and Insider Trading," *Journal of Business* (July 1974).

tion on insider trading available to more and more investors. A more recent study of insider trading examined excess returns around both the date the insiders report to the SEC and the date that information becomes available to investors in the official summary. Figure 9.21 presents the contrast between the two event studies.

Given the opportunity to buy on the date the insider reports to the SEC, investors could have marginal excess returns, but these returns diminish and become statistically insignificant if investors are forced to wait until the official summary date.

None of these studies examine the question of whether insiders themselves make excess returns. The reporting process, as set up now by the SEC, is biased

FIGURE 9.21 Abnormal Returns Around Reporting Day/Official Summary

Source: H. N. Seyhun, "Insiders' Profits, Costs of Trading, and Market Efficiency," *Journal of Financial Economics* (June 1986).

FIGURE 9.22 Returns Around Buy and Sell Recommendations

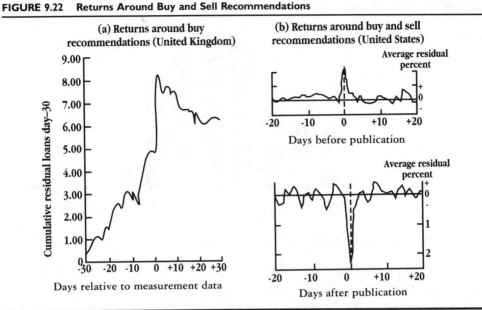

(a) Returns around buy recommendations (United Kingdom)

Cumulative residual loans day–30

Days relative to measurement data

(b) Returns around buy and sell recommendations (United States)

Average residual percent

Days before publication

Average residual percent

Days after publication

Source: P. Lloyd-Davies and M. Canes, "Stock Prices and the Publication of Second-Hand Information," *Journal of Business* (1978).

toward legal and less profitable trades and away from illegal and more profitable trades. Though direct evidence cannot be offered for this proposition, insiders trading illegally on private information must make excess returns.

Analyst Recommendations

Analysts clearly hold a privileged position in the market for information, operating at the nexus of private and public information. Using both types of information, analysts issue buy and sell recommendations to their clients, who trade on its basis. Figure 9.22 reveals the price impact that analyst buy and sell recommendations have on stock prices.

FIGURE 9.23 Average Returns by Analyst Class

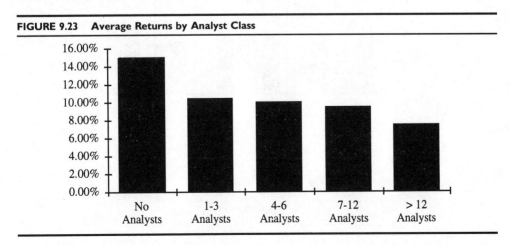

FIGURE 9.24 Mutual Fund Performance, 1955–1964—The Jensen Study

Intercept [Actual Return - E(R)]

While both recommendations affect stock prices, sell recommendations affect prices much more adversely than buy recommendations affect them positively. The price effect is restricted to the day of the recommendation, and there is no evidence in the prices of front running or drifts.

Though analysts provide a valuable service in collecting private information, or maybe because they do, there is a negative relationship in the cross-section

FIGURE 9.25 Performance of Equity Funds, 1983–1990

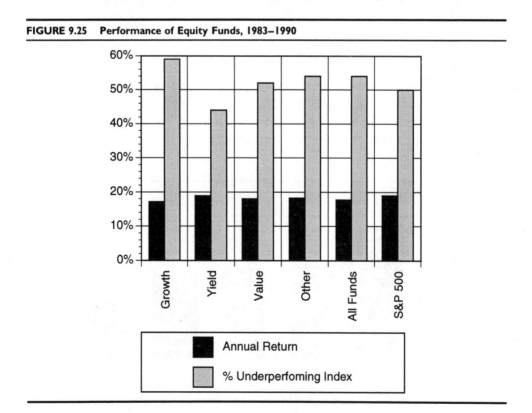

between returns earned by stocks and the number of analysts following the stock. This phenomenon, known as the "neglect" effect, is illustrated in Figure 9.23.

The same kind of relationship exists between another proxy for interest, institutional ownership, and returns.

Money Managers

Professional money managers operate as the experts in the field of investments. They are supposed to be better informed, smarter, have lower transactions costs, and be better investors overall than smaller investors. The earliest study of mutual funds by Jensen (1968) suggested that this supposition might not hold in practice. His findings, summarized in Figure 9.24 as excess returns on mutual funds, were that the average portfolio manager actually underperformed the market between 1955 and 1964.

These results have been replicated with mild variations in the conclusions. In the studies that are most favorable for professional money managers, they break even against the market after adjusting for transactions costs, and in those that are least favorable they underperform the market even before adjusting for transactions costs.

The results, when categorized on a number of different bases, do not offer much solace. For instance, Figure 9.25 shows excess returns from 1983 to 1990 and the percentage of money managers beating the market, categorized by investment style. Money managers in every investment style underperform the market index.

Figure 9.26, from the same study, looks at the payoff to active portfolio management by looking at the added value from trading actively during the

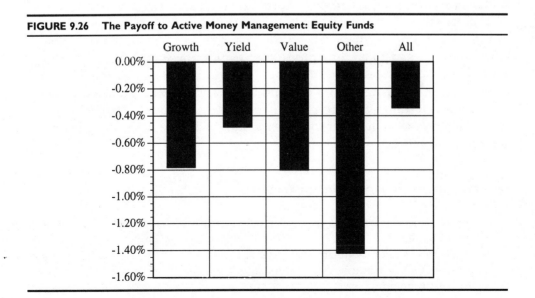

FIGURE 9.26 The Payoff to Active Money Management: Equity Funds

TABLE 9.5 Probabilities of Transition from One Quartile to Another

Ranking This Period	Ranking Next Period			
	1	2	3	4
1	26%	24%	23%	27%
2	20%	26%	29%	25%
3	22%	28%	26%	24%
4	32%	22%	22%	24%

course of the year, and finds that returns drop from 0.5% to 1.5% a year as a consequence. The payoff was measured by looking at the difference between the actual return on equity funds and the return on a hypothetical portfolio frozen at the beginning of the period.

Finally, the study, like others before it, found no evidence of continuity in performance. It classified money managers into quartiles and examined the probabilities of movement from one quartile to another each year from 1983 to 1990. The results are summarized in Table 9.5.

This table indicates that a money manager who was ranked in the first quartile in a period had a 26% chance of being ranked in the first quartile in the next period and a 27% chance of being ranked in the bottom quartile. There is some evidence of reversal in the portfolio managers in the lowest quartile, though some of that may be a reflection of the higher risk portfolios that they put together.

CONCLUSION

There is substantial evidence of irregularities in market behavior, related to systematic factors such as size, price/earnings ratios, and price/book value ratios, as well as to time—the January and weekend effects. While these irregularities may be inefficiencies, there is also the sobering evidence that professional money managers, who are in a position to exploit these inefficiencies, have a very difficult time consistently beating financial markets. Read together, the persistence of the irregularities and the inability of money managers to beat the market is testimony to the gap between empirical tests on paper and real world money management, in some cases, and the failure of the models of risk and return in others.

QUESTIONS AND SHORT PROBLEMS

1. What is the phenomenon of the size effect in stock performance? How does it relate to the "turn-of-the-year" effect? Can you suggest any good reasons why small stocks, after adjusting for beta, still do better than large stocks? What strategy would you follow to exploit this anomaly? What factors do you have to keep in mind?

2. A study examining market reactions to earnings surprises found that prices tend to drift after earnings surprises. What does this tell you about the market's capacity to learn from events and new information? What cross-sectional differences would you expect to find in this learning behavior? (I.e., Would you expect to see a greater price drift in some types of firms than in others? Why?) How would you try to exploit this anomaly? What possible costs would you have to keep in mind?

3. One explanation of the "turn-of-the-year" or January effect has to do with sales and purchases related to the tax year.
 a. State the tax effect hypothesis.
 b. Studies have shown that the January effect occurs internationally, even in countries where the tax year does not start in January. Speculate on a good reason for this.

4. The following are the expected price appreciation and dividend yield components of returns on two portfolios—a "high dividend yield" portfolio and a "low dividend yield" portfolio.

Portfolio	Expected Price Appreciation	Expected Dividend Yield
High Yield	9%	5%
Low Yield	12%	1%

You are a taxable investor who faces a tax rate of 40% on dividends. What would your tax rate on capital gains need to be for you to be indifferent between these two portfolios?

5. Answer true or false to the following questions:
 a. Low price/earnings stocks, on average, earn returns in excess of expectations, while high price/earnings stocks earn less than expected. This is primarily because lower P/E ratio stocks have lower risk.
 b. The small firm effect, which refers to the positive excess returns earned, on average, by small firms, is primarily caused by a few small firms that make very high positive returns.
 c. Investors generally cannot make money on analyst recommendations, because stock prices are not affected by these recommendations.

6. You are examining the performance of two mutual funds. AD VALUE Fund has been in existence since January 1, 1988, and invests primarily in low price/earnings ratio stocks with high dividend yields. AD GROWTH Fund has also been in existence since January 1, 1988, but it invests primarily in high growth stocks, with high P/E ratios and low or no dividends. The performance of these funds over the last five years is summarized in the following table:

	Average from 1988–1992		
	Price Appreciation	Dividend Yield	Beta
NYSE Composite	13%	3%	1.0
AD VALUE	11%	5%	0.8
AD GROWTH	15%	1%	1.2

The average risk-free rate during the period was 6%. The current risk-free rate is 3%.
 a. How well or badly did these funds perform after adjusting for risk?

b. Assume that the front-end load on each of these funds is 5% (i.e., if you put $1,000 in each of these funds today, you would only be investing $950 after the initial commission). Assume also that the *excess returns* you have calculated in part (a) will continue into the future and that you choose to invest in the fund that outperformed the market. How many years would you have to hold this fund to break even?

ENDNOTES

1. There are statistical tables that summarize the expected number of runs, assuming randomness, in a series of any length.

2. *The Wall Street Journal* and COMPUSTAT are often used as information sources to extract announcement dates for earnings. For some firms, news of the announcement may actually cross the newswire the day before *The Wall Street Journal* announcement, leading to a misidentification of the report date and the drift in returns the day before the announcement.

3. Since wash sales rules would prevent an investor from selling and buying back the same stock within 45 days, there has to be some substitution among the stocks. Thus investor 1 sells stock A and investor 2 sells stock B, but when it comes time to buy back the stock, investor 1 buys stock B and investor 2 buys stock A.

10

Dividend Discount Models

The basic model for valuing equity is the dividend discount model—the value of a stock is the present value of expected dividends on it. This chapter explores the general model as well as specific versions of it tailored for different assumptions about future growth. It also examines issues in using the dividend discount model and the results of studies that have looked at its efficacy.

THE GENERAL MODEL

When investors buy stock, they generally expect to get two types of cashflows: dividends during the period they hold the stock and an expected price at the end of the holding period. Since this expected price is itself determined by future dividends, the value of a stock is the present value of dividends through infinity:

$$\text{Value per share of stock} = \sum_{t=1}^{t=\infty} \frac{DPS_t}{(1 + r)^t}$$

where DPS_t = expected dividends per share
r = required rate of return on stock

The rationale for the model lies in the present value rule—the value of any asset is the present value of expected future cashflows, discounted at a rate appropriate to the riskiness of the cashflows being discounted.

There are two basic inputs to the model: expected dividends and the required rate of return on equity. To obtain the expected dividends, we make assumptions about expected future growth rates in earnings and payout ratios. The required rate of return on a stock is determined by its riskiness, measured differently in different models—the market beta in the capital asset pricing model and the factor betas in the arbitrage pricing model and multifactor models. The model is flexible enough to allow for time-varying discount rates, where the time variation is because of expected changes in interest rates or risk across time.

VERSIONS OF THE MODEL

Since projections of dollar dividends cannot be made through infinity, several versions of the dividend discount model have been developed based upon different assumptions about future growth.

The Gordon Growth Model

The Gordon growth model can be used to value a firm that is in "steady state" with dividends growing at a rate that is expected to stay stable in the long term.

The Model

The Gordon growth model relates the value of a stock to its expected dividends in the next time period, the required rate of return on the stock, and the expected growth rate in dividends.

$$\text{Value of Stock} = \frac{DPS_1}{r - g}$$

where DPS_1 = expected dividends one year from now
r = required rate of return for equity investors
g = growth rate in dividends forever

What Is a Stable Growth Rate?

While the Gordon growth model is a simple and powerful approach to valuing equity, its use is limited to firms that are growing at a stable growth rate. There are two insights worth keeping in mind when estimating a "stable" growth rate. First, since the growth rate in the firm's dividends is expected to last forever, the firm's other measures of performance (including earnings) can also be expected to grow at the same rate. To see why, consider the consequences in the long term of a firm whose earnings grow 6% a year forever, while its dividends grow 8%. Over time, the dividends will exceed earnings. If a firm's earnings grow at a faster rate than dividends in the long term, the payout ratio, in the long term, will converge toward 0, which is also not a steady state. Thus, though the model's requirement is for the expected growth rate in *dividends,* analysts should be able to substitute the expected growth rate in *earnings* and get precisely the same result, if the firm is truly in steady state.

The second issue relates to what growth rate is reasonable as a "stable" growth rate. Again, the assumption in the model that this growth rate will last forever establishes rigorous constraints on "reasonableness." A firm cannot in the long term grow at a rate significantly greater than the growth rate in the economy in which it operates. Thus, a firm that grows at 12% forever in an economy growing at 6% will eventually become larger than the economy. In practical terms, the stable growth rate cannot be larger than the nominal (real) growth rate in the economy in which the firm operates, if the valuation is done

in nominal (real) terms. (If the firm's operations are restricted to the domestic arena, this will be the expected growth rate in the domestic economy. For multinationals, the relevant benchmark will be the growth rate in the world economy.) The nominal growth rate in the economy is determined by expected inflation and the real growth rate in GNP. Thus, in 1993, in the United States, the expected nominal growth in the economy, assuming expected inflation[1] in the long term of 4% a year and real growth[2] of 2%, would have been:

Expected Nominal Growth in U.S. economy = Expected Inflation
+ expected Real Growth
= 4% + 2% = 6%

By definition, therefore, a stable firm is one whose growth rate does not exceed 6% by a significant amount. Given the uncertainty associated with estimates of expected inflation and real growth, there can be differences in the benchmark growth rate used by different analysts; that is, analysts with higher expectations of inflation in the long term may project a nominal growth rate in the economy that is higher.

There is another instance in which an analyst may be able to stray from a strict limit imposed on the "stable growth rate." If a firm is likely to maintain a few years of "above-stable" growth rates, an approximate value for the firm can be obtained by adding a premium to the stable growth rate, to reflect the above-average growth in the initial years. Even in this case, the flexibility that the analyst has is limited. The sensitivity of the model to growth implies that the stable growth rate cannot be more than 1% or 2% above the growth rate in the economy. If the deviation becomes larger, the analyst will be better served using a two-stage or three-stage model to capture the "super-normal" or "above-average" growth, and restricting the Gordon growth model to when the firm becomes truly stable.

Can a stable growth rate be much lower than the growth rate in the economy? There are no logical or mathematical limits on the downside. Firms that have a stable growth rate much lower than the growth rate in the economy will become smaller in proportion to the economy over time. Since there is no economic basis for arguing that this cannot happen, there is no reason to prevent analysts from using a stable growth rate much lower than the nominal growth rate in the economy.

Does a stable growth rate have to be constant over time? The assumption that the growth rate in dividends has to be constant over time is a difficult assumption to meet, especially given the volatility of earnings. If a firm has an average growth rate that is close to a stable growth rate, the model can be used with little real effect on value. Thus, a cyclical firm that can be expected to have year-to-year swings in growth rates, but has an average growth rate that is 6%, can be valued using the Gordon growth model without a significant loss of generality. There are two reasons for this result. First, since dividends are smoothed even when earnings are volatile, they are less likely to be affected

by year-to-year changes in earnings growth. Second, the mathematical effects of using an average growth rate rather than a constant growth rate are small.

Limitations of the Model

The Gordon growth model is a simple and convenient way of valuing stocks, but it is extremely sensitive to the inputs for the growth rate. As the growth rate converges on the discount rate, the value goes to infinity. This is illustrated in the following example.

Illustration 10.1: Sensitivity of value to expected growth rate in the Gordon growth model

Consider a stock, with an expected dividend per share next period of $2.50, a discount rate of 15%, and an expected growth rate of 8% forever. The value of this stock is:

Value = $2.50/(.15 − .08) = $35.71

Note, however, the sensitivity of this value to estimates of the growth rate in Figure 10.1.

This issue is tied to the question of what comprises a stable growth rate. If an analyst follows the constraints discussed in the previous section in estimating stable growth rates, it is unlikely that the value from the model will approach the absurd. In this example, for instance, an analyst who uses a 14% growth rate and obtains a $250 value would have been violating a basic rule on what comprises stable growth. The value of the firm, however, will be sensitive to different growth rates even within what comprises a reasonable range for stable growth.

FIGURE 10.1 **Value of Stock and Expected Growth**

Suitability of the Model

In summary, the Gordon growth model is best suited for firms growing at a rate comparable to or lower than the nominal growth rate in the economy and that have well-established dividend payout policies that they intend to continue into the future. The dividend payout of the firm has to be consistent with the assumption of stability, since stable firms generally pay substantial dividends.[3]

Illustration 10.2: Suitability to a regulated firm: Consolidated Edison

Consolidated Edison is the electric utility that supplies power to homes and businesses in New York and its environs. It is a monopoly whose prices and profits are regulated by the State of New York.

Rationale for using the model:
- The firm is in stable growth, based upon size and the area that it serves. Its rates are also regulated; it is unlikely that the regulators will allow profits to grow at extraordinary rates.
- The beta is 0.75 and has been stable over time.
- The firm is in stable leverage.
- The firm pays out dividends that are roughly equal to its free cashflows to equity (FCFE).

> Average Annual FCFE between 1990 and 1994 = $460 million
>
> Average Annual Dividends between 1990 and 1994 = $442 million
>
> Dividends as a percentage of FCFE = 96.08%

Background information:
Earnings per share in 1994 = $3.00
Dividend Payout Ratio in 1994 = 68.00%
Dividends per share in 1994 = $2.04
Expected Growth Rate in Earnings and Dividends = 5%
Long-Term Bond Rate = 7.50%
Beta = .75
Cost of Equity = $7.5\% + (.75 \times 5.5\%) = 11.63\%$

> Value of Equity = $\$2.00 \times 1.05/(.1163 - .05) = \31.67

Con Ed was trading for $26.75 on the day of this analysis (March 1995).

What growth rate would Con Ed have to attain to justify the current stock price? Figure 10.2 estimates value as a function of the expected growth rate (assuming a beta of 0.75 and current dividends per share of $2.04).

Solving for the expected growth rate that provides the current price,

$$\$26.75 = \$2.04(1 + g)/(.1163 - g)$$

FIGURE 10.2 Con Ed: Value versus Expected Growth

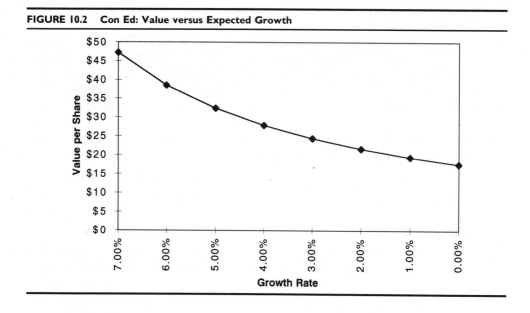

Solving for g,

$$g = (.1163 \times \$26.75 - \$2.04)/(\$26.75 + \$2.04) = 3.72\%$$

The growth rate in earnings and dividends would have to be 3.72% a year to justify the stock price of $26.75.

While utilities, with their regulated prices, stable growth, and high dividends, are particularly well suited for the Gordon growth model, the model can be applied to other firms as well. The following application illustrates this point.

Illustration 10.3: Suitability to a financial service firm: Chemical Bank

Chemical Bank is one of the largest commercial banks in the United States, and it also derives considerable revenues from providing other financial services and from trading.

Rationale for using the model:
- As a large financial service firm in a competitive environment, it is unlikely that Chemical's earnings are going to grow much faster than the economy over the long term. Allowing for international expansion, the expected growth rate used is 7%.
- As a financial service firm, free cashflows to equity are difficult to estimate; hence the dependence on dividends.
- The leverage of financial service firms is high and unlikely to change over time.

Background information:
 Current Earnings per share = $4.90
 Current Dividend Payout Ratio = 35.91%

Dividends per share = \$1.76
Expected Growth Rate in Earnings and Dividends = 7%
Long-Term Bond Rate = 7.50%
Stock Beta = 1.25
Cost of Equity = 7.5% + (1.25 × 5.5%) = 14.38%

Value of Equity = \$1.76 × 1.07/(.1438 − .07) = \$25.52

Chemical Bank was trading for \$39.38 on the day of this analysis (March 1995).

Two-Stage Dividend Discount Model

The two-stage growth model allows for two stages of growth: an initial phase where the growth rate is high and a subsequent steady state where the growth rate is stable and is expected to remain so for the long term.

The Model

The model allows for an extraordinary-growth phase that lasts n years and a stable-growth phase that lasts forever after that:

Extraordinary-growth rate: g% each year for n years Stable-growth rate: g_n forever

Value of the Stock = PV of Dividends during extraordinary phase + PV of Terminal Price

$$P_0 = \sum_{t=1}^{t=n} \frac{DPS_t}{(1 + r)^t} + \frac{P_n}{(1 + r)^n}, \quad \text{where } P_n = \frac{DPS_{n+1}}{r_n - g_n}$$

where DPS_t = expected dividends per share in year t
r = required rate of return (cost of equity) in high-growth period
P_n = price at the end of year n
g = extraordinary-growth rate for the first n years
g_n = growth rate forever after year n
r_n = required rate of return in steady state

In the case where the extraordinary-growth rate (g) and payout ratio are unchanged for the first n years, this formula can be simplified as follows:

$$P_0 = \frac{DPS_0(1 + g)\left(1 - \frac{(1 + g)^n}{(1 + r)^n}\right)}{r - g} + \frac{DPS_{n+1}}{(r_n - g_n)(1 + r)^n}$$

where the inputs are as defined above.

Calculating the Terminal Price

The same constraint that applies to the growth rate for the Gordon growth rate model, that is, that the growth rate in the firm is comparable to the nominal growth rate in the economy, applies for the terminal growth rate (g_n) in this

model as well. In addition, the payout ratio has to be consistent with the estimated growth rate. If the growth rate is expected to drop significantly after the initial growth phase, the payout ratio should be higher in the stable phase than in the growth phase. (A stable firm can pay out more of its earnings in dividends than can a growing firm.) One way of estimating this new payout ratio is to use the fundamental growth model described in Chapter 5:

$$g = b \{ROA + D/E(ROA - i[1 - t])\}$$

where b = retention ratio = 1 − payout ratio
 ROA = return on assets = (Net Income + Interest Expense[1 − t])/Total Assets
 D/E = Debt/Equity (in book value terms)
 i = Interest Expense/Book Value of Debt

Manipulating this growth rate equation yields the payout ratio as a function of the expected growth rate:

$$\text{Payout ratio} = 1 - b = 1 - \left[g/\{ROA + D/E(ROA - i[1 - t])\} \right]$$

where the inputs for this equation will be those for the stable-growth period.

Illustration 10.4: Estimating the payout ratio during the stable-growth period

Assume you have a firm that has the following parameters for the ROA, payout ratios, debt/equity ratios, and interest rates in the initial high-growth phase and in the stable-growth phase:

	Initial-Growth Phase	Stable-Growth Phase
ROA	20%	16%
Payout ratio	20%	?
D/E	1.00	1.00
i	10%	8%
Growth rate	?	8%

The tax rate for the firm is 40%.

Growth rate in first five years = $(1 - .2)\{20\% + 1(20 - 10[1 - .04])\} = 27.2\%$

Payout ratio after year five = $1 - \left[8/\{16 + 1(16 - 8[1 - .4])\} \right] = 70.59\%$

As the growth rate drops in the stable-growth period, the payout increases from 20% to 70.59%.

The characteristics of the firm in the stable period should be consistent with the assumption of stability. While this point has been emphasized with payout ratios in the example above, it applies to other characteristics as well. For instance, it is reasonable to assume that a high-growth firm has a high beta

but unreasonable to assume that this beta will remain unchanged when the firm becomes stable. Similarly, the return on assets, which can be high during the initial-growth phase, should come down to levels commensurate with a stable firm in the stable-growth phase. Failure to adjust these inputs for stability can lead to significant errors in valuation.

Limitations of the Model

There are three problems with the two-stage dividend discount model. The first practical problem is in defining the length of the extraordinary-growth period. Since the growth rate is expected to decline to a stable level after this period, the value of an investment will increase as this period is made longer. While, in theory, the duration of the growth phase can be linked to product life cycles and project opportunities, it is difficult in practice to convert these qualitative considerations into a specific time period.

The second problem with this model lies in the assumption that the growth rate is high during the initial period and is transformed overnight to a lower stable rate at the end of the period. While these sudden transformations in growth can happen, it is much more realistic to assume that the shift from high growth to stable growth happens gradually over time. Third, since a significant component of the present value in the two-stage model comes from the terminal price, which is calculated using the Gordon growth model, the value is sensitive to assumptions about the stable growth. Overestimating or underestimating this growth rate can lead to significant errors in value.

Suitability of the Model

Since the two-stage dividend discount model is based upon two clearly delineated growth stages—high growth and stable growth—it is best suited for firms that are in high growth and expect to maintain that growth rate for a specific time period, after which the sources of the high growth are expected to disappear. One scenario, for instance, in which this may apply is when a company has patent rights to a very profitable product for the next few years and is expected to enjoy super-normal growth during this period. Once the patent expires, it is expected to settle back into stable growth. Another scenario in which it may be reasonable to make this assumption about growth is when a firm is in an industry that is enjoying super-normal growth, because there are significant barriers to entry (either legal or as a consequence of infrastructure requirements), which can be expected to keep new entrants out for several years.

The assumption that the growth rate drops precipitously from its level in the initial phase to a stable rate also implies that this model is more appropriate for firms with modest growth rates in the initial phase. For instance, it is more reasonable to assume that a firm growing at 12% in the high-growth period will see its growth rate drop to 6% after, than for a firm growing at 40% in the high-growth period.

Illustration 10.5: Valuing a firm with the two-stage dividend discount model: American
Express

In February 1995, Warren Buffett announced that he was increasing his stake in American Express from 5% to 9.8%, leading to a surge in the stock price. As a large financial service firm, American Express would be a good candidate for a two-stage dividend discount model.

Rationale for using the model:
 • *Why two-stage?* While American Express is a large financial service firm in a competitive marketplace, normally not a candidate for above-stable growth, it has gone through an extended period of depressed earnings (EPS in 1994 was $2.70 while earnings five years earlier was $3.52). It is expected that the recovery in earnings will create higher growth over the next five years.
 • *Why dividends?* As a financial service firm, free cashflows to equity are difficult to estimate.
 • The financial leverage is stable.

Background information:
 Current earnings/dividends:

 • Earnings per share in 1994 = $2.70
 • Dividends per share in 1994 = $.90

Inputs for the high-growth period:

Length of the high-growth period = 5 years
Beta during the high-growth period = 1.45
Long-Term Bond Rate = 7.50%
Cost of Equity during the high-growth period = 7.5%
$$+ (1.45 \times 5.5\%) = 15.48\%$$

 • Return on Assets during the high-growth period = 12.50% (slightly higher than the current 12.44%)
 • Dividend payout ratio remains at 33.33%.
 • Debt/Equity Ratio = 100% (slightly lower than the current 114.09%)
 • Interest rate on debt = 8.50% (tax rate = 36%)

Expected Growth Rate = b{ROA + D/E(ROA − i[1 − t])}
$$= .6667\{12.50\% + 1(12.50\% - 8.50\%[1 - .36])\}$$
$$= 13.04\%$$

Inputs for the stable-growth period:

 • Expected Growth Rate = 6%
 • Beta during the stable-growth period = 1.10

- Cost of Equity $= 7.50\% + (1.1 \times 5.5\%) = 13.55\%$
- The ROA, D/E ratio, and interest rate are assumed to remain unchanged during the stable-growth period.

Stable Payout Ratio $= 1 - g/\{ROA + D/E(ROA - i[1 - t])\}$

$\qquad\qquad\qquad = 1 - .06/\{12.50\% + 1(12.50\% - 8.50\%[1 - .36])\}$

$\qquad\qquad\qquad = 69.33\%$

Estimating the value: The first component of value is the present value of the expected dividends during the high-growth period. Based upon the current earnings ($2.70), the expected growth rate (13.04%), and the expected dividend payout ratio (33.33%), the expected dividends can be computed for each year in the high-growth period:

Year	EPS	DPS	Present Value
1	$3.05	$1.02	$0.88
2	3.45	1.15	.86
3	3.90	1.30	.84
4	4.41	1.47	.83
5	4.98	1.66	.81

Cumulative Present Value of Dividends (@15.48%)

$\qquad\qquad\qquad = \$.88 + \$.86 + \$.84 + \$.83 + \$.81 = \4.22

The present value of the dividends can also be computed in shorthand using the following computation:

$$\text{PV of Dividends} = \frac{\$.90 \times 1.1304 \times \left(1 - \dfrac{1.1304^5}{1.1548^5}\right)}{.1548 - .1304} = \$4.22$$

The price at the end of the high-growth phase (end of year 5) can be estimated using the constant growth model.

Terminal Price $=$ Expected Dividends per share$_{n+1}/(r - g_n)$

Expected Earnings per share$_6 = \$2.70 \times 1.1304^5 \times 1.06 = \5.28

Expected Dividends per share$_6 = \$5.28 \times .6933 = \3.66

Terminal Price $= \$3.66/(.1355 - .06) = \48.51

The present value of the terminal price can then be written as:

$$\text{PV of Terminal Price} = \frac{\$48.51}{1.1548^5} = \$23.62$$

The accumulated present value of dividends and the terminal price can then be calculated as follows:

$$P_0 = \frac{\$.90 \times 1.1304 \times \left(1 - \dfrac{1.1304^5}{1.1548^5}\right)}{.1548 - .1304} + \frac{\$48.51}{1.1548^5} = \$4.22 + \$23.62 = \$27.84$$

American Express was trading at $33.38 in March 1995, at the time of this analysis.

A Troubleshooting Guide: What is wrong with this valuation? Two-Stage Dividend Discount Model	
If this is your problem	*this may be the solution*
• If you get an extremely low value from this model, the likely culprits are:	
1. The stable period payout ratio is too low for a stable firm (<40%).	If using fundamentals, use a higher ROA; if entering directly, enter a higher payout.
2. The beta in the stable growth period is too high for a stable firm.	Use a three-stage model.
• If you get an extremely high value:	
1. The growth rate in the stable-growth period is too high for a stable firm.	Use a growth rate closer to GNP growth.

Illustration 10.6: Valuing a multinational consumer product company: Unilever

Unilever, a consumer product company with over 150 subsidiaries across the world, is headquartered in the Netherlands. It had earnings per share of 15 NG (Dutch guilders) in 1992 and paid out 4.30 NG as dividends. Its stock had a beta of 0.79, measured relative to the EOE index (Amsterdam). The ten-year bond rate in the Netherlands in July 1993 was 6.24% and the risk premium estimated for Dutch stocks relative to bonds was 4.50%.

The company's earnings per share grew at 10.97% between 1987 and 1992 and are expected to grow at 11.69% between 1993 and 1998. This growth rate is made feasible by the high return on assets (19.67%) earned by Unilever. Based upon fundamentals alone (D/E = 59.77%, retention ratio = 71.33%, and after-tax interest rate on debt = 4.43%), the expected growth rate would be much higher:

Expected growth rate = .7133(19.67% + .5977[19.67% − 4.43%]) = 20.52%

The increased competition that Unilever will face in many markets is expected to dampen this growth somewhat, leading to the lower growth rate estimate.

The growth rate after 1998 is expected to decline to 5%, while the payout ratio is estimated to increase to 69.74%, based on the assumption that the return on assets will be 12%, as the firm enters stable growth. The price at the end of the high-growth phase in 1993 can be estimated as follows:

15.00 NG × 1.1169⁵ × 1.05 × .6974/(.0980 − .05) = 398.23 NG

The present value of the expected dividends and the terminal price can then be written as:

$$P_0 = \frac{4.30 \text{ NG} \times 1.1169 \times \left(1 - \dfrac{1.1169^5}{1.0980^5}\right)}{.0980 - .1169} + \frac{398.23 \text{ NG}}{1.0980^5} = 272.23 \text{ NG}$$

The stock was trading at 191 NG in July 1993.

The Value of Growth Based on the Two-Stage Model

Investors pay a price premium when they acquire companies with high growth potential. This premium takes the form of higher price/earnings or price/book value ratios. While no one will contest the proposition that growth is valuable, it is possible to pay too much for growth. In fact, empirical studies that show low price/earnings ratio stocks earning return premiums over high price/earnings ratio stocks in the long term support the notion that investors overpay for growth. This section uses the two-stage dividend discount model to examine the value of growth, and it provides a benchmark that can be used to compare the actual prices paid for growth.

Estimating the Value of Growth. The value of the equity in any firm can be written in terms of three components:

$$P_0 = \underbrace{\left[\frac{DPS_0(1 + g)\left(1 - \dfrac{(1 + g)^n}{(1 + r)^n}\right)}{r - g} + \frac{DPS_{n+1}}{(r_n - g_n)(1 + r)^n} - \frac{DPS_1}{r_n - g_n}\right]}_{\text{Extraordinary Growth}}$$

$$+ \underbrace{\left[\frac{DPS_1}{r_n - g_n} - \frac{DPS_0}{r_n}\right]}_{\text{Stable Growth}} + \underbrace{\frac{DPS_0}{r_n}}_{\text{Assets in place}}$$

where DPS_t = expected dividends per share in year t

$\quad r$ = required rate of return in high-growth period

$\quad P_n$ = price at the end of year n

$\quad g_n$ = growth rate forever after year n

$\quad r_n$ = required rate of return in stable-growth period

Value of extraordinary growth = Value of firm with extraordinary growth

in first n years

− Value of firm as a stable-growth firm[4]

Value of stable growth = Value of firm as a stable-growth firm

− Value of firm with no growth

Assets in place = Value of firm with no growth

Illustration 10.7: An illustration of the value of growth: American Express and
 Unilever

Consider the example of American Express in March 1995:

Value of assets in place = Current EPS \times Payout ratio/r

$$= \$2.70 \times .3333/.1355 = \$6.64$$

The discount rate from the stable growth phase is used for this calculation.

Value of stable growth = Current EPS \times Payout ratio$(1 + g_n)/(r - g_n) - \$6.64$

$$= \$2.70 \times .3333 \times 1.06/(.1355 - .06) - \$6.64$$

$$= \$5.99$$

Value of extraordinary growth = $\$27.85 - \$6.64 + \$5.99 = \15.21

In the case of Unilever in 1993,

Value of assets in place = 15 NG \times .2867/.0980 = 43.90 NG

Value of stable growth = 15 NG \times .2867 \times 1.05/(.0980 - .05) - 43.90 NG

$$= 50.26 \text{ NG}$$

Value of extraordinary growth = 278.23 NG - 43.90 NG - 50.26 NG

$$= 178.07 \text{ NG}$$

The Determinants of the Value of Growth.

(a) *Growth rate during extraordinary period:* The higher the growth rate in the
extraordinary period, the higher is the estimated value of growth. If the growth
rate in the extraordinary-growth period had been raised to 20% for the Ameri-
can Express valuation, the value of extraordinary growth in American Express
would have increased from $15.21 to $24.27. Conversely, the value of high-
growth companies can drop precipitously if the expected growth rate is re-
duced, either because of disappointing earnings news from the firm or as a
consequence of external events. Figure 10.3 graphs the value of extraordinary
growth at American Express as a function of the expected growth rate.

(b) *Length of the extraordinary-growth period:* The longer the extraordinary-
growth period, the greater is the value of growth. At an intuitive level, this is
fairly simple to illustrate. The value of $15.21 obtained for extraordinary
growth in American Express is predicated on the assumption that high growth
will last for five years. If this is revised to last ten years, the value of extraordi-
nary growth will increase to $22.50.

(c) *Profitability of projects:* The profitability of projects determines both the
growth rate in the initial phase and the terminal value. As projects become
more profitable, they increase both growth rates, and the resulting value from
extraordinary growth will be greater.

(d) *Riskiness of the firm/equity:* The riskiness of a firm determines the discount
rate at which cashflows in the initial phase are discounted. Since the discount
rate increases as risk increases, the present value of the extraordinary growth
will decrease.

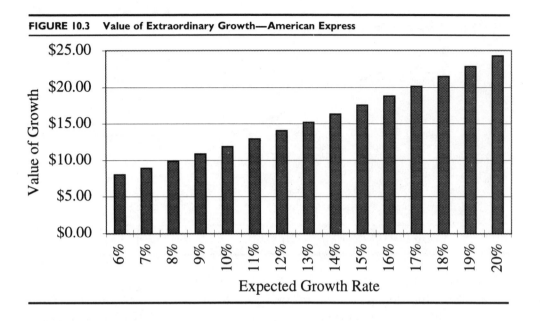

FIGURE 10.3 Value of Extraordinary Growth—American Express

The H Model for Valuing Growth

The H model is a two-stage model for growth, but unlike the classical two-stage model, the growth rate in the initial-growth phase is not constant but declines linearly over time to reach the stable-growth rate in steady state. This model was presented in Fuller and Hsia (1984).

The Model

The model is based upon the assumption that the earnings growth rate starts at a high initial rate (g_a) and declines linearly over the extraordinary-growth period (which is assumed to last 2H periods) to a stable growth rate (g_n). It also assumes that the dividend payout is constant over time and is not affected by the shifting growth rates. Figure 10.4 graphs the expected growth over time in the H model.

The value of expected dividends in the H model can be written as follows:

$$P_0 = \underbrace{\frac{DPS_0(1 + g_n)}{r - g_n}}_{\text{Stable Growth}} + \underbrace{\frac{DPS_0 \times H(g_a - g_n)}{r - g_n}}_{\text{Extraordinary Growth}}$$

where P_0 = value of the firm now per share
DPS_t = DPS in year t
r = required return to equity investor
g_a = growth rate initially
g_n = growth rate at the end of 2H years; applies forever after that

Limitations

This model avoids the problems associated with the growth rate dropping precipitously from the high-growth to the stable growth phase, but it does so at

FIGURE 10.4 Expected Growth in the H Model

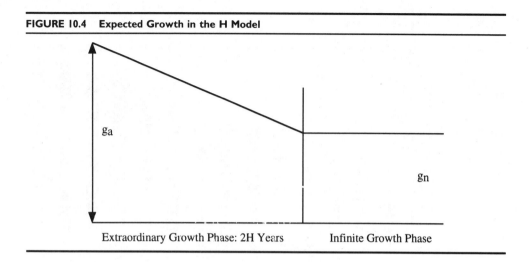

Extraordinary Growth Phase: 2H Years Infinite Growth Phase

a cost. First, the decline in the growth rate is expected to follow the strict structure laid out in the model—it drops in linear increments each year based upon the initial-growth rate, the stable-growth rate, and the length of the extraordinary-growth period. While small deviations from this assumption do not affect the value significantly, large deviations can cause problems. Second, the assumption that the payout ratio is constant through both phases of growth exposes the analyst to an inconsistency—as growth rates decline, the payout ratio remains unchanged (when it should be increasing).

Suitability of the Model

The allowance for a gradual decrease in growth rates over time may make this a useful model for firms that are growing rapidly right now but whose growth is expected to decline gradually over time as the firms get larger and the differential advantage they have over their competitors declines. The assumption that the payout ratio is constant, however, makes this an inappropriate model to use for any firm that has low or no dividends currently. Thus, the model, by requiring a combination of high growth and high payout, may be quite limited[5] in its applicability.

Illustration 10.8: Valuing with the H model: Syntex

Syntex Corporation was expected to have earnings per share of $2.15 in 1993 and to pay out dividends of $1.08 in the same year. The earnings had grown 18% a year for the previous five years, but this growth was expected to decline linearly (2% a year) over the next six years to a stable growth rate of 6%. The decline in growth can be attributed to three factors:

 (a) Declining profitability on two of the company's flagship products, Naprosyn and Anaprox (which generated almost half of all revenues in 1992), due to increased competition.

(b) Lower profitability in the health care sector overall.

(c) The fact that the firm has grown in size substantially, and maintaining high growth is getting progressively more difficult.

The beta for Syntex was 1.25, while the Treasury bond rate was 7%.

Current Earnings per share = $2.15

Current Dividends per share = $1.08

Current Growth Rate (g_a) = 18%

Length of transition period = 6 years

Stable Growth Rate (g_n) = 6%

Expected return on equity = 7% + 1.25 × 5.5% = 13.88%

$$\text{Value of Stable Growth} = \frac{\$1.08 \times 1.06}{.1388 - .06} = \$14.47$$

$$\text{Value of Extraordinary Growth} = \frac{\$1.08 \times 6/2 \times (.18 - .06)}{.1388 - .06} = \$4.91$$

$$\text{Value of Stock} = \$14.47 + \$4.91 = \$19.38$$

The stock was trading at $19.00 in May 1993.

Three-Stage Dividend Discount Model

The three-stage dividend discount model combines the features of the two-stage model and the H model. It allows for an initial period of high growth, a transitional period when growth declines, and a final stable-growth phase. It is the most general of the models because it does not impose any restrictions on the payout ratio.

The Model

This model assumes an initial period of stable high growth, a second period of declining growth, and a third period of stable low growth that lasts forever. Figure 10.5 graphs the expected growth over the three time periods.

The value of the stock is then the present value of expected dividends during the high-growth and the transitional periods, and of the terminal price at the start of the final stable-growth phase.

$$P_0 = \underbrace{\sum_{t=1}^{t=n1} \frac{EPS_0(1 + g_a)^t \times \Pi_a}{(1 + r)^t}}_{\text{High Growth}} + \underbrace{\sum_{t=n1+1}^{t=n2} \frac{DPS_t}{(1 + r)^t}}_{\text{Transition}} + \underbrace{\frac{EPS_{n2}(1 + g_n) \times \Pi_n}{(r - g_n)(1 + r)^n}}_{\text{Stable Growth}}$$

where EPS_t = earnings per share in year t

DPS_t = dividends per share in year t

g_a = growth rate in high-growth phase (lasts *n1* periods)

g_n = growth rate in stable-growth phase

Π_a = payout ratio in high-growth phase

Π_n = payout ratio in stable-growth phase

FIGURE 10.5 Expected Growth in the Three-Stage DDM

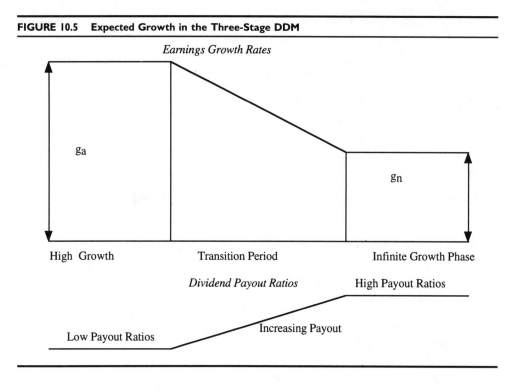

r = required rate of return on equity in high-growth period
r_n = required rate of return on equity in stable-growth period

The payment ratio will generally be low in the high-growth period, increase during the transition period, and be high in the stable-growth period.

Assumptions

This model removes many of the constraints imposed by other versions of the dividend discount model. In return, however, it requires a much larger number of inputs—year-specific payout ratios, growth rates, and betas. For firms where there is substantial noise in the estimation process, the errors in these inputs can overwhelm any benefits that accrue from the additional flexibility in the model.

Suitability of the Model

This model's flexibility makes it a useful model for any firm, which in addition to changing growth over time is expected to change on other dimensions as well—in particular, payout policies and risk. It is best suited for firms that are growing at an extraordinary rate now and are expected to maintain this rate for an initial period, after which the differential advantage of the firm is expected to deplete leading to gradual declines in the growth rate to a stable-growth rate. Practically speaking, this may be the more appropriate model to use for a firm whose earnings are growing at very high rates,[6] are expected to continue growing at those rates for an initial period, but are expected to start declining

gradually toward a stable rate as the firm becomes larger and loses its competitive advantages.

Illustration 10.9: Valuing with the three-stage DDM model: The Home Depot

The Home Depot is one of the great retailing success stories of the 1980s and early 1990s. It posted extraordinary growth both in revenues and profits and reaped its stockholders immense returns.

Rationale for using the model:
 • *Why three-stage?* The Home Depot is still in very high growth. Analysts project that its earnings per share will grow at 36% a year for the next five years.
 • *Why dividends?* The firm has had a track record of paying out dividends that roughly approximate free cashflows to equity.
 • The financial leverage is stable.

Background information:
 Current earnings/dividends:

 • Earnings per share in 1994 = $1.33
 • Dividends per share in 1994 = $0.16

 Inputs for the high-growth period:

 • Length of the high-growth period = 5 years
 • Expected Growth Rate = 36.00% (based upon analyst projections)
 • Beta during the high-growth period = 1.60
 • Cost of Equity during the high-growth period = 7.5% + 1.60(5.5%) = 16.30%
 • Long-Term Bond Rate = 7.5%
 • Dividend Payout Ratio = 12.03% (based on existing payout ratio)

 Inputs for the transition period:

 • Length of the transition period = 5 years
 • Growth rate in earnings will decline from 36% in year 5 to 6% in year 10 in linear increments.
 • Payout ratio will increase from 12.03% to 60% over the same period in linear increments.
 • Beta will drop from 1.60 to 1.00 over the same period in linear increments.

 Inputs for the stable-growth period:

 • Expected Growth Rate = 6%
 • Beta during the stable-growth period = 1.00
 • Cost of Equity = 7.50% + (1.0 × 5.5%) = 13.00%
 • Payout Ratio = 60%

Estimating the value: These inputs are used to estimated expected earnings per share, payout ratios, dividends per share, and costs of equity for the high-growth, transition, and stable-growth periods. The present values are also shown.

Period	EPS	Payout Ratio	DPS	Cost of Equity	Present Value
1	$1.81	12.03%	$0.22	16.30%	$0.19
2	2.46	12.03%	.30	16.30%	.22
3	3.35	12.03%	.40	16.30%	.26
4	4.55	12.03%	.55	16.30%	.30
5	6.19	12.03%	.74	16.30%	.35
6	8.04	21.62%	3.28	15.64%	1.33
7	9.97	31.22%	4.55	14.98%	1.61
8	11.77	40.81%	5.93	14.32%	1.83
9	13.18	50.41%	7.28	13.66%	1.98
10	13.97	60.00%	8.38	13.00%	2.02

Since the costs of equity change each year, the present value has to be calculated using the cumulated cost of equity. Thus, in year 7, the present value of dividends is

$$\text{PV of year 7 dividend} = \$4.55/(1.1630^5 \times 1.1564 \times 1.1498) = \$1.61$$

The terminal price at the end of year 10 can be calculated based upon the earnings per share in year 11, the stable-growth rate of 6%, a cost of equity of 13.00% (based upon the beta of 1), and the payout ratio of 60.00%:

$$\text{Terminal Price} = \$13.97 \times 1.06 \times .60/(.13 - .06) = \$126.96$$

FIGURE 10.6 Value vs. Expected Growth

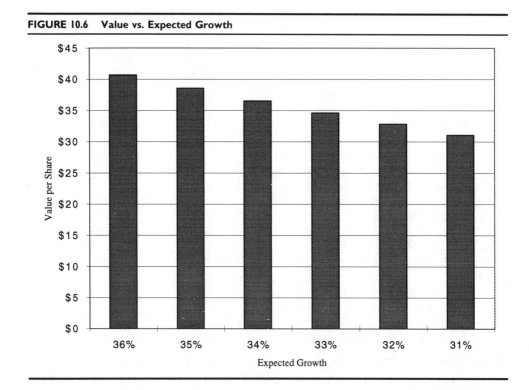

The components of value are as follows:

Present Value of dividends in high-growth phase = $1.31

Present Value of dividends in transition phase = $8.77

Present Value of terminal price at end of transition = $30.57

Value of Home Depot stock = $40.65

Home Depot stock was trading at $45 in February 1995.

The high growth rate embedded in the stock price also implies that the stock price will be sensitive to any information that may reflect on the sustainability of this growth. For instance, Figure 10.6 graphs out the value as a function of the expected growth.

A Troubleshooting Guide: What is wrong with this valuation? Three-Stage Dividend Discount Model	
If this is your problem	*this may be the solution*
• If you get an extremely low value from this model, the likely culprits are:	
The stable period payout ratio is too low for a stable firm (<40%).	If using fundamentals, use a higher ROA; if entering directly, enter a higher payout.
The beta in the stable period is too high for a stable firm.	Use a beta closer to 1.
• If you get an extremely high value:	
The growth rate in the stable-growth period is too high for a stable firm.	Use a growth rate closer to GNP growth.
The period of growth (high plus transition) is too long.	Use shorter high-growth and transition periods.

ISSUES IN USING THE DIVIDEND DISCOUNT MODEL

The dividend discount model's primary attraction is its simplicity and its intuitive logic. There are many analysts, however, who view its results with suspicion, because of limitations that they perceive it to possess. The model, they claim, is not really useful in valuation, except for a limited number of stable, high-dividend-paying stocks. This section examines some of the areas where the dividend discount model is perceived to fall short.

Valuing Non-Dividend-Paying or Low-Dividend-Paying Stocks

The conventional wisdom is that the dividend discount model cannot be used to value a stock that pays low or no dividends. This is incorrect. If the dividend payout ratio is adjusted to reflect changes in the expected growth rate, a reason-

able value can be obtained even for non-dividend-paying firms. Thus, a high-growth firm, paying no dividends currently, can still be valued based upon dividends that it is expected to pay out when the growth rate declines. If the payout ratio is not adjusted to reflect changes in the growth rate, however, the dividend discount model will underestimate the value of non-dividend-paying or low-dividend-paying stocks.

Is the Model Too Conservative in Estimating Value?

A standard criticism of the dividend discount model is that it provides too conservative an estimate of value. This criticism is predicated on the notion that the value is determined by more than the present value of expected dividends. For instance, it is argued that the dividend discount model does not reflect the value of "unutilized assets." There is no reason, however, that these unutilized assets cannot be valued separately and added on to the value from the dividend discount model. Some of the assets that are supposedly ignored by the dividend discount model, such as the value of brand names, can be dealt with fairly simply within the context of the model.

The Contrarian Nature of the Model

The dividend discount model is also considered by many to be a contrarian model. As the market rises, fewer and fewer stocks, they argue, will be found to be undervalued using the dividend discount model. This is not necessarily true. If the market increase is due to an improvement in economic fundamentals, such as higher expected growth in the economy and/or lower interest rates, there is no reason, a priori, to believe that the values from the dividend discount model will not increase by an equivalent amount. If the market increase is not due to fundamentals, the dividend discount model values will not follow suit, but that is more a sign of strength than weakness. The model is signaling that the market is overvalued relative to dividends and cashflows, and the cautious investor will pay heed.

TESTS OF THE DIVIDEND DISCOUNT MODEL

The ultimate test of a model lies in how well it works at identifying undervalued and overvalued stocks. The dividend discount model has been tested, and the results indicate that it does, in the long term, provide for excess returns. It is unclear, however, whether this is because the model is good at finding undervalued stocks or because it proxies for well-known empirical irregularities in returns relating to price/earnings ratios and dividend yields.

A Simple Test of the Dividend Discount Model

A simple study of the dividend discount model was conducted by Sorensen and Williamson (1985), where they valued 150 stocks from the Standard and

Poors 400 in December 1980, using the dividend discount model. They used the difference between the market price at that time and the model value to form five portfolios based upon the degree of under- or overvaluation. They made fairly broad assumptions in using the dividend discount model:

(a) The average of the earnings per share between 1976 and 1980 was used as the current earnings per share.
(b) The cost of equity was estimated using the capital asset pricing model.
(c) The extraordinary-growth period was assumed to be five years for all stocks, and the I/B/E/S consensus forecast of earnings growth was used as the growth rate for this period.
(d) The stable-growth rate, after the extraordinary-growth period, was assumed to be 8% for all stocks.
(e) The payout ratio was assumed to be 45% for all stocks.

The returns on these five portfolios were estimated for the following two years (January 1981 through January 1983), and excess returns were estimated relative to the S&P 500 index using the betas estimated at the first stage and the CAPM. Figure 10.7 illustrates the excess returns earned by the portfolio that was undervalued by the dividend discount model relative to both the market and the overvalued portfolio.

FIGURE 10.7 Performance of the Dividend Discount Model, 1981–1983

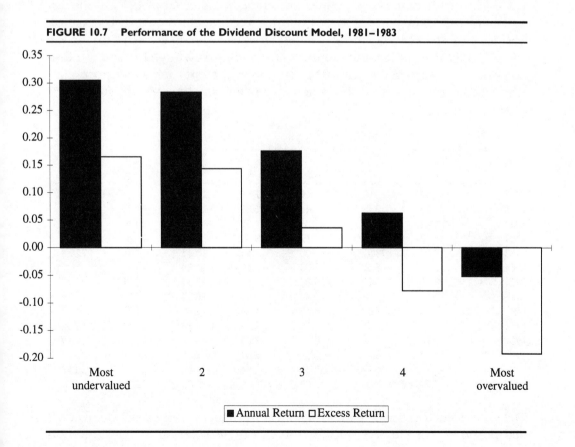

The undervalued portfolio had a positive excess return of 16% per year between 1981 and 1983, while the overvalued portfolio had a negative excess return of 15% per year during the same time period. Other studies that focus only on the dividend discount model come to similar conclusions. In the long term, undervalued (overvalued) stocks from the dividend discount model outperform (underperform) the market index on a risk-adjusted basis.

CAVEATS ON THE USE OF THE DIVIDEND DISCOUNT MODEL

The dividend discount model provides impressive results in the long term. There are, however, three considerations in generalizing the findings from these studies.

The dividend discount model does not beat the market every year.

The dividend discount model outperforms the market over five-year time periods, but there have been individual years when the model has significantly underperformed the market. Haugen (1993) reports on the results of a study that used the dividend discount model to analyze 250 large capitalization firms and to classify them into five quintiles from the first quarter of 1979 to the last quarter of 1991. The betas of these quintiles were roughly equal. The valuation was done by six analysts who estimated an extraordinary-growth rate for the initial high-growth phase, the duration of the high-growth phase, and a transitional phase for each of the firms. The returns (in percent) on the five portfolios, as well as the returns on the 250 stocks as a whole and the S&P 500 from 1979 to 1991, are as follows:

| | Quintile | | | | | | |
Year	Under-valued	2	3	4	Over-valued	250 Stocks	S&P 500
1979	35.07	25.92	18.49	17.55	20.06	23.21	18.57
1980	41.21	29.19	27.41	38.43	26.44	31.86	32.55
1981	12.12	10.89	1.25	−5.59	−8.51	28.41	24.55
1982	19.12	12.81	26.72	28.41	35.54	24.53	21.61
1983	34.18	21.27	25.00	24.55	14.35	24.10	22.54
1984	15.26	5.50	6.03	−4.20	−7.84	3.24	6.12
1985	38.91	32.22	35.83	29.29	23.43	33.80	31.59
1986	14.33	11.87	19.49	12.00	20.82	15.78	18.47
1987	.42	4.34	8.15	4.64	−2.41	2.71	5.23
1988	39.61	31.31	17.78	8.18	6.76	20.62	16.48
1989	26.36	23.54	30.76	32.60	35.07	29.33	31.49
1990	−17.32	−8.12	−5.81	2.09	−2.65	−6.18	−3.17
1991	47.68	26.34	33.38	34.91	31.64	34.34	30.57
1979–1991	1253.00%	657.00%	772.00%	605.00%	434.00%	722.00%	654.00%

The undervalued portfolio earned significantly higher returns than the overvalued portfolio and the S&P 500 for the 1979–1991 period, but it underper-

formed the market in five of the twelve years and the overvalued portfolio in four of the twelve years.

Is the model just proxying for low PE ratios and dividend yields?

The dividend discount model weights expected earnings and dividends in near periods more than earnings and dividends in far periods, and is biased toward finding low price/earnings ratio stocks with high dividend yields to be undervalued and high price/earnings ratio stocks with low or no dividend yields to be overvalued. Studies of market efficiency indicate that low-PE-ratio stocks have outperformed (in terms of excess returns) high-PE-ratio stocks over extended time periods. Similar conclusions have been drawn about high-dividend-yield stocks relative to low-dividend-yield stocks. Thus, the valuation findings of the model are consistent with empirical irregularities observed in the market.

It is unclear how much the model adds in value to investment strategies that use PE ratios or dividend yields to screen stocks. Jacobs and Levy (1988b) argue that the marginal gain is relatively small.

Attribute	Average Excess Return per Quarter: 1982–1987
Dividend discount model	0.06%
Low PE ratio	.92%
Book/price ratio	.01%
Cashflow/price ratio	.18%
Sales/price ratio	.96%
Dividend yield	−0.51%

This suggests that using low PE ratios to pick stocks adds 0.92% to quarterly returns, whereas using the dividend discount model adds only a further 0.06% to quarterly returns. If, in fact, the gain from using the dividend discount model is that small, screening stocks on the basis of observables (such as PE ratio or cashflow measures) may provide a much larger benefit in terms of excess returns.

There are tax disadvantages from high-dividend stocks.

Portfolios created with the dividend discount model are generally characterized by high dividend yield, which can create a tax disadvantage, if dividends are taxed at a rate greater than capital gains or if there is a substantial tax timing[7] liability associated with dividends. Since the excess returns uncovered in the studies presented above are pretax to the investor, the introduction of personal taxes may significantly reduce or even eliminate these excess returns.

In summary, the dividend discount model's impressive results in studies looking at past data have to be considered with caution. For a tax-exempt investment, with a long time horizon, the dividend discount model is a good tool, though it may not be the only one, to pick stocks. For a taxable investor, the benefits are murkier, since the tax consequences of the strategy have to be considered. For investors with shorter time horizons, the dividend discount model may not deliver on its promised excess returns, because of the year-to-year volatility in its performance.

CONCLUSION

The dividend discount model is a simple model for valuing equity and is based upon the assumption that the value of a stock is the present value of expected dividends. While the model is often criticized as being of limited value, it has proven to be surprisingly adaptable and useful in a wide range of circumstances. It may be a conservative model that finds fewer and fewer undervalued firms as market prices rise relative to fundamentals (earnings, dividends, etc.), but that can also be viewed as a strength. Tests of the model also seem to indicate its usefulness in gauging value, though much of its effectiveness may be derived from its finding low-PE-ratio, high-dividend-yield stocks to be undervalued.

QUESTIONS AND SHORT PROBLEMS

1. Respond true or false to the following statements relating to the dividend discount model:
 a. The dividend discount model cannot be used to value a high-growth company that pays no dividends.
 b. The dividend discount model will undervalue stocks, because it is too conservative.
 c. The dividend discount model will find more undervalued stocks when the overall stock market is depressed.
 d. Stocks that are undervalued using the dividend discount model have generally made significant positive excess returns over long periods (five years or more).
 e. Stocks that pay high dividends and have low price/earnings ratios are more likely to come out as undervalued using the dividend discount model.
2. Ameritech Corporation paid dividends per share of $3.56 in 1992, and dividends are expected to grow 5.5% a year forever. The stock has a beta of 0.90, and the treasury bond rate is 6.25%.
 a. What is the value per share, using the Gordon growth model?
 b. The stock is trading for $80 per share. What would the growth rate in dividends have to be to justify this price?
3. Church & Dwight, a large producer of sodium bicarbonate, reported earnings per share of $1.50 in 1993 and paid dividends per share of $0.42. In 1993, the firm also reported the following:

 Net Income = $30 million
 Interest Expense = $0.8 million
 Book Value of Debt = $7.6 million
 Book Value of Equity = $160 million

 The firm faced a corporate tax rate of 38.5%. (The market value debt/equity ratio is 5%.) The treasury bond rate is 7%.

 The firm expects to maintain these financial fundamentals from 1994 to 1988, after which it is expected to become a stable firm, with an earnings growth

rate of 6%. The firm's financial characteristics will approach industry averages after 1998. The industry averages are as follows:

> Return on Assets = 12.5%
> Debt/Equity Ratio = 25%
> Interest Rate on Debt = 7%

Church and Dwight had a beta of 0.85 in 1993, and the unlevered beta is not expected to change over time.

 a. What is the expected growth rate in earnings, based upon fundamentals, for the high-growth period (1994–1998)?

 b. What is the expected payout ratio after 1998?

 c. What is the expected beta after 1998?

 d. What is the expected price at the end of 1998?

 e. What is the value of the stock, using the two-stage dividend discount model?

 f. How much of this value can be attributed to extraordinary growth? to stable growth?

4. Oneida Inc., the world's largest producer of stainless steel and silverplated flatware, reported earnings per share of $0.80 in 1993 and paid dividends per share of $0.48 in that year. The firm is expected to report earnings growth of 25% in 1994, after which the growth rate is expected to decline linearly over the following six years to 7% in 1999. The stock is expected to have a beta of 0.85. (The treasury bond rate is 6.25%.)

 a. Estimate the value of stable growth, using the H model.

 b. Estimate the value of extraordinary growth, using the H model.

 c. What are the assumptions about dividend payout in the H model?

5. Medtronic Inc., the world's largest manufacturer of implantable biomedical devices, reported earnings per share in 1993 of $3.95 and paid dividends per share of $0.68. Its earnings are expected to grow 16% from 1994 to 1998, but the growth rate is expected to decline each year after that to a stable growth rate of 6% in 2003. The payout ratio is expected to remain unchanged from 1994 to 1998, after which it will increase each year to reach 60% in the steady state. The stock is expected to have a beta of 1.25 from 1994 to 1998, after which the beta will decline each year to reach 1.00 by the time the firm becomes stable. (The Treasury bond rate is 6.25%.)

 a. Assuming that the growth rate declines linearly (and the payout ratio increases linearly) from 1999 to 2003, estimate the dividends per share each year from 1994 to 2003.

 b. Estimate the expected price at the end of 2003.

 c. Estimate the value per share, using the three-stage dividend discount model.

ENDNOTES

1. There is no consensus on the best measure of expected inflation. There are several different choices. One simple measure is to use the Treasury bill rate as a predictor of short-term expected inflation. Another is to use surveys of economists on expected inflation to get an estimate. A third approach is to use inflation in the past as a measure of expected inflation in the future. This measure will depend upon the length of the historical period. For instance, the average

inflation from 1926–1990 is approximately 3.25% but it is much higher (5%) if only the 1981–1990 period is used.

2. The average real growth in the GNP of the United States has averaged 2–3% in the last thirty years. The growth rate in the 1981–1990 period is close to 2%.

3. The average payout ratio for large stable firms in the United States is about 60%.

4. The payout ratio used to calculate the value of the firm as a stable firm can be either the current payout ratio, if it is reasonable, or the new payout ratio calculated using the fundamental growth formula.

5. Proponents of the model would argue that using a steady-state payout ratio for firms that pay little or no dividends is likely to cause only small errors in the valuation.

6. The definition of a "very high" growth rate is largely subjective. As a rule of thumb, growth rates over 25% would qualify as very high, when the stable-growth rate is 6–8%.

7. Investors do not have a choice of when they receive dividends, whereas they have a choice on the timing of capital gains.

11

Free Cashflows to Equity Discount Models

The dividend discount model is based upon the premise that the only cashflows received by stockholders are dividends. This chapter uses a more expansive definition of cashflows to equity as the cashflows left over after meeting all financial obligations, including debt payments, and after covering capital expenditure and working capital needs. It discusses the reasons for differences between dividends and free cashflows to equity and presents the free cashflows to equity discount model for valuation.

FREE CASHFLOWS TO EQUITY VERSUS DIVIDENDS

This section lays out the methodology for calculating the free cashflows to equity (FCFE) and examines the reasons for and the implications of differences between FCFE discount models and dividend discount models.

Calculation of FCFE

The FCFE is the residual cashflows left over after meeting interest and principal payments and providing for capital expenditures to both maintain existing assets and create new assets for future growth. The FCFE is measured as follows:

$$\text{FCFE} = \text{Net Income} + \text{Depreciation} - \text{Capital Spending} - \triangle \text{ Working Capital}$$
$$- \text{ Principal Repayments} + \text{New Debt Issues}$$

In the special case where the capital expenditures and the working capital are expected to be financed at the target debt ratio δ and principal repayments are made from new debt issues, the FCFE is measured as follows:

$$\text{FCFE} = \text{Net Income} + (1 - \delta)(\text{Capital Expenditures} - \text{Depreciation})$$
$$+ (1 - \delta) \triangle \text{ Working Capital}$$

Why Are Dividends Different from FCFE?

The FCFE is a measure of what a firm can afford to pay out as dividends. There are few firms, however, that follow the policy of paying out their entire FCFE

as dividends. Many pay less, and some pay more, but the dividends paid are different from the FCFE for a number of reasons:

(a) *Desire for stability.* Firms are generally reluctant to change dividends, and dividends are considered "sticky" because the variability in dividends is significantly lower than the variability in earnings or cashflows. The unwillingness to change dividends is accentuated when firms have to reduce dividends, and empirically, increases in dividends outnumber cuts in dividends by at least a five-to-one margin in most periods. As a consequence of this reluctance to cut dividends, firms will often refuse to increase dividends even when earnings and FCFE go up, because they are uncertain about their capacity to maintain these higher dividends. This leads to a lag between earnings increases and dividend increases. Similarly, firms frequently keep dividends unchanged in the face of declining earnings and FCFE. Figure 11.1 reports the number of dividend changes (increases, decreases, no change) between 1981 and 1990.

The number of firms increasing dividends outnumbers those decreasing dividends seven to one. The number of firms, however, that do not change dividends outnumbers firms that do about four to one. Dividends are also less variable than either FCFE or earnings, but this reduced volatility is a result of keeping dividends significantly below the FCFE.

(b) *Future investment needs.* A firm might hold back on paying its entire FCFE as dividends if it expects substantial increases in capital expenditure needs in the future. Since issuing stocks is expensive (from a flotation cost standpoint), it may choose to keep the excess cash to finance these future needs.

FIGURE 11.1 Dividend Changes: Publicly Owned Firms, 1981–1990

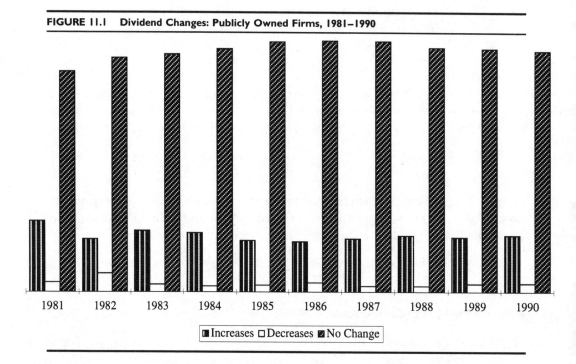

(c) *Tax factors.* If dividends are taxed at a higher tax rate than capital gains, a firm may choose to retain the excess cash and pay out much less in dividends than it has available. This is likely to be accentuated if the stockholders in the firm are in high tax brackets, as is the case with many family controlled firms. If, on the other hand, investors in the firm like dividends or tax laws favor dividends, the firm may pay more out in dividends than it has available in FCFE, often borrowing or issuing new stock to do so.

(d) *Signaling prerogatives.* Firms often use dividends as signals of future prospects, with increases in dividends being viewed as positive signals and decreases as negative signals. The empirical evidence is consistent with this signaling story, since stock prices generally go up on dividend increases and down on dividend decreases. The use of dividends as signals may lead to differences between dividends and FCFE.

The net effect is that dividends are sometimes higher than FCFE and sometimes lower. This is shown in Illustration 11.1.

Illustration 11.1: Firm that pays out less in dividends than it has available in FCFE: Merck

The free cashflows to equity for each year from 1990 to 1994 are calculated below for Merck and contrasted with the actual cash returned to stockholders, in the form of dividends and stock repurchases (amounts in millions)

	1990	1991	1992	1993	1994
Net Income	$1,207.00	$1,495.00	$1,781.00	$2,122.00	$2,485.00
−(Cap. Exp. − Depr.) × (1 − δ)	154.16	203.98	852.58	733.20	813.10
−∂ Working Capital × (1 − δ)	641.08	20.68	−529.22	523.58	356.26
=FCFE	$ 411.76	$1,270.34	$1,457.64	$ 865.22	$1,315.64
Dividends & Repurchases	$ 512.00	$ 652.00	$ 743.00	$ 893.00	$1,086.00

For Merck, the debt ratio (δ) (debt/capital) was 6% between 1989 and 1993.

The FCFE averaged $1,064 million a year between 1989 and 1993, while dividends and equity repurchases together averaged only $777 million a year, which works out to a dividend/FCFE ratio of 73.04%. In other words, Merck was retaining $287 million in cash each year that it could have paid out in dividends. This unpaid cash built up in the firm and is a major reason for the large cash balance that Merck had at the end of 1992.

FCFE VALUATION MODELS

The three versions of the FCFE valuation model presented in this section are simple variants on the dividend discount model, with one significant change—free cashflows to equity replace dividends in the models.

The Stable-Growth FCFE Model

The stable-growth FCFE model is designed to value firms that are growing at a stable growth rate and are hence in steady state.

The Model

The value of equity, under the stable-growth model, is a function of the expected FCFE in the next period, the stable-growth rate, and the required rate of return.

$$P_0 = \frac{FCFE_1}{r - g_n}$$

where P_0 = value of stock today
 $FCFE_1$ = expected FCFE next year
 r = cost of equity of the firm
 g_n = growth rate in FCFE for the firm forever

Caveats

The model is very similar to the Gordon growth model in its underlying assumptions and works under some of the same constraints. The growth rate used in the model has to be reasonable, relative to the nominal growth rate in the economy in which the firm operates. As a general rule, a "stable" growth rate cannot exceed the growth rate of the economy in which the firm operates by more than one or two percent.

 The assumption that a firm is in steady state also implies that it possesses other characteristics shared by stable firms. This would mean, for instance, that capital expenditures are not disproportionately large, relative to depreciation, and the firm is of "average" risk. (If the capital asset pricing model is used, the beta of the equity is not significantly different from 1.) While we would prefer to leave the analyst some leeway on both counts, a strict reading of these constraints would lead to stable firms possessing the following characteristics:

 (a) Capital expenditure is offset by depreciation.
 (b) The beta of the stock is 1. If an alternative model is used for the cost of equity, the resulting rate is close to the "average" rate for all stocks in the market.

Suitability of the Model

This model, like the Gordon growth model, is best suited for firms growing at a rate comparable to or lower than the nominal growth in the economy. It is, however, the better model to use for stable firms that pay out dividends that

are unsustainably high (because they exceed FCFE by a significant amount) or are significantly lower than the FCFE. Note, though, that if the firm is stable and pays out its FCFE as dividends, the value obtained from this model will be the same as the one obtained from the Gordon growth model.

Illustration 11.2: Stable-growth FCFE model: AT&T

Rationale for using the model:
- Given its size, it is unlikely that AT&T will be able to grow much faster than the economy in the long term.
- AT&T pays out much less in dividends than it generates in FCFE.

> Dividends per share in 1994 = $1.32
>
> FCFE per share in 1994 = $2.49

- The financial leverage is stable.

Background Information:
Current information:

- Earnings per share = $3.15
- Capital Expenditures per share = $3.15
- Depreciation per share = $2.78
- Change in Working Capital per share = $0.50
- Debt Financing Ratio = 25%

Earnings, capital expenditures, depreciation, and working capital are all expected to grow 6% a year.

The beta for the stock is 0.90, and the Treasury bond rate is 7.50%.

Estimating the Value:
Long-Term Bond Rate = 7.50%

Cost of Equity = 7.50% + (.90 × 5.50%) = 12.45%

Expected Growth Rate = 6.00%

Base-Year FCFE = Earnings per Share
 − (Capital Expenditures − Depreciation)(1 − Debt Ratio)
 − Change in Working Capital (1 − Debt Ratio)
 = $3.15 − ($3.15 − $2.78)(1 − .25) − $.50 (1 − .25)
 = $2.49

> Value per share = $2.49 × 1.06/(.1245 − .06) = $41.00

The stock was trading for $51.25 in March 1995.

A Troubleshooting Guide: What is wrong with this valuation? Stable-Growth FCFE Model

If this is your problem	*this may be the solution*
• If you get an extremely low value from this model, the likely culprits are:	
1. Capital expenditures are too high relative to depreciation.	Use smaller capital expenditures or use the two-stage FCFE model.
2. Working capital as a percentage of revenues is too high to sustain.	Normalize this ratio, using historical averages.
3. The beta is too high for a stable firm.	Use a beta closer to 1.
• If you get an extremely high value:	
1. Capital expenditures are lower than depreciation.	Set capital expenditures equal to depreciation.
2. Working capital as a percentage of revenues is negative.	Set equal to 0.
3. The expected growth rate is too high for a stable firm.	Use a growth rate closer to GNP growth.

The Two-Stage FCFE Model

The two-stage FCFE model is designed to value a firm that is expected to grow much faster than a stable firm in the initial period and at a stable rate after that.

The Model

The value of any stock is the present value of the FCFE per year for the extraordinary-growth period plus the present value of the terminal price at the end of the period.

$$\text{Value} = \text{PV of FCFE} \quad + \text{PV of Terminal Price}$$

$$= \sum_{t=1}^{t=n} \text{FCFE}_t/(1 + r)^t + P_n/(1 + r)^n$$

where FCFE_t = FCFE in year t

 P_n = price at the end of the extraordinary-growth period

 r = required rate of return to equity investors in the high-growth period

The terminal price is generally calculated using the infinite-growth-rate model:

$$P_n = \text{FCFE}_{n+1}/(r_n - g_n)$$

where g_n = growth rate after the terminal year forever

 r_n = required rate of return to equity investors in the stable-growth period

Calculating the Terminal Price

The same caveats apply here that apply to the growth rate for the stable-growth model, described in the previous section. In addition, the assumptions made to derive the FCFE after the terminal year have to be consistent with this as-

sumption of stability. For instance, while capital spending may be much greater than depreciation in the initial high-growth phase, the difference should narrow as the firm enters its stable-growth phase.

Illustration 11.3: Capital expenditure, depreciation, and growth rates

Assume that you have a firm with growth in earnings of 20% in the first five years and 8% per year in the stable period thereafter. The current earnings per share is $2.50. Current capital spending per share is $2.00 and current depreciation per share is $1.00. If we assume that capital spending and depreciation grow at the same rate as earnings,

$$\text{Earnings in year 5} = \$2.50 \times 1.20^5 = \$6.23$$
$$\text{Capital Spending in year 5} = \$2.00 \times 1.20^5 = \$4.98$$
$$\text{Depreciation in year 5} = \$1.00 \times 1.20^5 = \$2.49$$
$$\text{FCFE in year 5} = \$6.23 + \$2.49 - \$4.98 = \$3.74$$

If we use the infinite-growth-rate model, but fail to adjust the imbalance between capital expenditures and depreciation, the FCFE in the terminal year is

$$\text{FCFE in year 6} = \$3.74 \times 1.08 = \$4.04$$

This FCFE can then be used to compute the value per share at the end of year 5, but it will understate the true value.

One solution is to assume that capital spending is offset by depreciation during the stable period. With this assumption,

$$\text{FCFE in year 6} = \$6.23 \times 1.08 = \$6.73$$

This may be a radical assumption in some industries, where capital spending will have to exceed depreciation, even in "steady state."

An alternative approach is to set the growth rates in capital spending and depreciation for the first five years in such a way as to bring them into rough parity by year 6. For example, if the growth rate in capital spending over the first five years is 5% while the growth rate in depreciation is 20%,

$$\text{Capital Spending in year 5} = \$2.00 \times 1.05^5 = \$2.55$$
$$\text{Depreciation in year 5} = \$1.00 \times 1.20^5 = \$2.49$$
$$\text{FCFE in year 5} = \$6.23 + \$2.49 - \$2.55 = \$6.18$$

This cashflow can now grow at 8% forever.

Suitability of the Model

This model makes the same assumptions about growth as the two-stage dividend discount model, namely, that growth will be high and constant in the initial period and drop abruptly to stable growth after that. It is different because of its emphasis on FCFE rather than dividends. Consequently, it provides much better results than the dividend discount model when valuing firms that either have dividends that are unsustainable (because they are higher than FCFE) or pay less in dividends than they can afford to (i.e., dividends are less than FCFE).

Illustration 11.4: Two-stage FCFE model: Amgen

Amgen Inc., a leading biotechnology company, was the rumored target of a takeover attempt in 1995. The following is the valuation of the company.

Rationale for using the model:
- *Why two-stage?* While Amgen has had a history of extraordinary growth, its growth is moderating because (a) it is becoming a much larger company and (b) its products are maturing and may face competition soon.
- *Why FCFE?* Amgen does not pay dividends but has some FCFE. This FCFE is likely to increase as the growth rate moderates and the firm gets larger.
- The financial leverage is stable.

Background information:
 Current earnings/capital expenditures:

- Revenues per share in 1994 = $12.40
- Earnings per share in 1994 = $3.10
- Capital Expenditures per share in 1994 = $1.00
- Depreciation per share in 1994 = $.60

Inputs for the high-growth period:

- Length of the high-growth period = 5 years
- Return on Equity = 18.78% (This is much lower than the current ROE of about 28%; this ROE is going to be difficult to sustain as the firm gets larger.)
- Retention Ratio = 100% (The firm pays no dividends now and is unlikely to do so in the near future because its stockholders are more interested in price appreciation.)

> Expected Growth Rate = 1.00 × 18.78% = 18.78%

- The beta during the high-growth phase is expected to be 1.30.
- The long-term bond rate is 7.50%.

> Cost of Equity = 7.50% + 1.30(5.5%) = 14.65%

- Capital expenditures, depreciation, and revenues are expected to grow at the same rate as earnings (18.78%).
- Working capital is expected to be 20% of revenues.
- The debt ratio is approximately 18.01%.

Inputs for the stable-growth period:

- Expected Growth Rate = 6%
- Beta during the stable-growth period = 1.10

- Cost of Equity = 7.50% + (1.1 × 5.5%) = 13.55%
- Capital expenditures are assumed to be offset by depreciation.
- Working capital is expected to be 20% of revenues.
- The debt ratio is expected to remain at 18.01%.

Estimating the Value:
The first component of value is the present value of the expected FCFE during the high-growth period, calculated as follows (amounts are per share):

	Year				
	1	2	3	4	5
Earnings	$3.68	$4.37	$5.19	$6.17	$7.33
−(Cap. Ex. − Depr.) $(1 - \partial)$.39	.46	.55	.65	.78
−\triangle Working Capital $(1 - \partial)$.38	.45	.54	.64	.76
= FCFE	$2.91	$3.46	$4.11	$4.88	$5.79
Present Value (@14.65%)	$2.54	$2.63	$2.72	$2.82	$2.92

PV of FCFE during the high-growth phase = $2.54 + $2.63 + $2.72 + $2.82
+ $2.92 = $13.64

The terminal price at the end of the high-growth phase (end of year 5) can be estimated using the stable-growth model:

Terminal Price = Expected $FCFE_{n+1}/(r - g_n)$

Expected EPS_6 = $7.33 × 1.06 = $7.77

Expected $FCFE_6$ = EPS_6 − \triangle Working Capital(1 − Debt Ratio)

$\quad\quad$ = $7.77 − $.35(1 − .1801) = $7.48

Terminal price = $7.48/(.1355 − .06) = $99.07

[The change in working capital is 10% of the change in revenue in year 6.]
The present value of the terminal price can then be written as:

PV of Terminal Price = $\dfrac{\$99.07}{1.1465^5}$ = $50.01

The accumulated present value of dividends and the terminal price can then be calculated as follows:

PV today = PV of FCFE during the high-growth phase + PV of Terminal Price
$\quad\quad$ = $13.64 + $50.01 = $63.65

Amgen was trading at $60 in March 1995, at the time of this analysis.

A Troubleshooting Guide: What is wrong with this valuation? Two-Stage FCFE Model

If this is your problem	*this may be the solution*
• If you get an extremely low value from this model, the likely culprits are:	
1. Earnings are depressed due to some reason (economy, etc.).	Use normalized earnings.
2. Capital expenditures are significantly higher than depreciation in the stable-growth period.	Offset capital expenditures by depreciation; or reduce the difference for the stable-growth period.
3. The beta in the stable-growth period is too high for a stable firm.	Use a beta closer to 1.
4. Working capital as a percentage of revenues is too high to sustain.	Use a working capital ratio closer to industry.
5. The use of the two-stage model when the three-stage model is more appropriate.	Use a three-stage model.
• If you get an extremely high value:	
1. Earnings are inflated above normal levels.	Use normalized earnings.
2. Capital expenditures offset depreciation during the high-growth period.	Set capital expenditures higher.
3. Capital expenditures are lower than depreciation.	Set capital expenditures equal to depreciation.
4. The growth rate in the stable-growth period is too high for a stable firm.	Use a growth rate closer to GNP growth.

The E Model—A Three-Stage FCFE Model

The E model is designed to value firms that are expected to go through three stages of growth: an initial phase of high growth rates, a transition period where the growth rate declines, and a steady-state period where growth is stable.

The Model

The E model calculates the present value of expected FCFE over all three stages of growth:

$$P_0 = \sum_{t=1}^{t=n1} \frac{FCFE_t}{(1 + r)^t} + \sum_{t=n1+1}^{t=n2} \frac{FCFE_t}{(1 + r)^t} + \frac{P_{n2}}{(1 + r)^n}$$

where P_0 = value of the stock today
 $FCFE_t$ = FCFE in year t
 r = cost of equity
 P_{n2} = terminal price at the end of the transition period = $FCFE_{n2+1}/(r - g_n)$
 n1 = end of the initial high-growth period
 n2 = end of the transition period

Caveats

Since the model assumes that the growth rate goes through three distinct phases—high growth, transitional growth, and stable growth—it is important that assumptions about other variables be consistent with these assumptions about growth.

(a) *Capital spending versus depreciation.* It is reasonable to assume that as the firm goes from high growth to stable growth, the relationship between capital spending and depreciation will change. In the high-growth phase, capital spending is likely to be much larger than depreciation. In the transition phase, the difference is likely to narrow, and capital spending and depreciation should be in rough parity in the stable-growth phase. This is shown in Figure 11.2.

(b) *Risk.* As the growth characteristics of a firm change, so do its risk characteristics. In the context of the capital asset pricing model, as the growth rate declines, the beta of the firm can be expected to change. The tendency of betas to converge toward 1 in the long term has been confirmed by empirical observation of portfolios of firms with high betas. Over time, as these firms get larger and more diversified, the average betas of these portfolios move toward 1.

FIGURE 11.2 Three-Stage FCFE Model

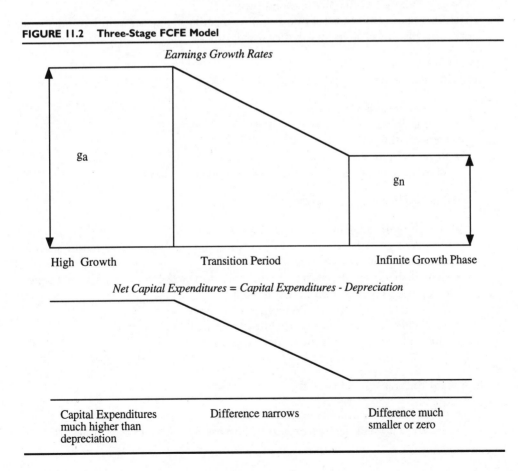

Suitability of the Model

Since the model allows for three stages of growth and for a gradual decline from high to stable growth, it is the appropriate model to use to value firms with very high growth rates currently. The assumptions about growth are similar to the ones made by the three-stage dividend discount model, but the focus is on FCFE instead of dividends, making it more suited to value firms whose dividends are significantly higher or lower than the FCFE.

Illustration 11.5: Valuation with the three-stage FCFE model: America Online

America Online provides computer online service to computer users in the United States. In February 1995, America Online entered into an agreement with Bertlesmann in Germany to extend its reach into Europe.

Rationale for using the model.
- *Why three-stage?* The expected growth rate in earnings is in excess of 50%, partly because of the growth in the overall market and partly because of the firm's position in the business.
- *Why FCFE?* The firm pays out no dividends, but has negative FCFE, largely as a consequence of large capital expenditures.
- The firm uses little debt (about 10%) in meeting financing requirements and does not plan to change this in the near future.

Background information:
 Current information:

 - Earnings per share = $.38
 - Capital Spending per share = $1.21
 - Depreciation per share = $.17
 - Revenues per share = $7.21
 - Working Capital as a percentage of revenues = 10.00%

 Inputs for the high-growth period:

 - Length of the high-growth period = 5 years.
 - Expected growth rate in earnings during the period = 52% (from analyst projections and market growth).
 - Capital spending, depreciation, and revenues will grow 20% a year during this period (based upon past growth).
 - Working capital will remain at 10% of revenues.
 - Approximately 10% of external financing will come from debt.
 - The beta for the high-growth period is 1.60.
 - The long-term bond rate is 7.50%.

 Inputs for the transitional period:

 - Length of the transition period = 5 years.
 - Growth rate will decline from 52% in year 5 to 6% in year 10 linearly.

- Capital spending will grow 6% a year in this period, while depreciation will continue to grow 12% a year.
- Revenues will increase 12% a year during this period; working capital will remain 10% of revenues.
- The debt ratio will remain at 10% during this period.
- The beta will decline linearly from 1.60 in year 5 to 1.20 in year 10.

Inputs for the stable-growth period:

- Earnings will grow 6% a year in perpetuity.
- Capital expenditures will be offset by depreciation.
- Revenues will also grow 6% a year; working capital will remain 10% of revenues.
- The debt ratio will remain at 10% during this period.
- The beta for the stock will be 1.20.

Estimating the value: The following are the expected cashflows over the first two periods (amounts are per share):

			Year		
High-Growth Period	1	2	3	4	5
Earnings	$0.58	$0.88	$1.33	$2.03	$3.08
−(Cap. Ex. − Depr.) (.09)	.12	1.34	1.61	1.94	2.32
− △ Working Capital (.09)	.13	.16	.19	.22	.27
= FCFE	− $0.67	− $0.62	− $0.47	− $0.13	$0.49
Present Value	− $0.58	− $0.46	− $0.30	− $0.07	− $0.23

			Year		
Transition Period	6	7	8	9	10
Growth Rate	42.80%	33.60%	24.40%	15.20%	6.00%
Earnings	$4.40	$5.88	$7.32	$8.43	$8.94
−(Cap. Ex. − Depr.) (.09)	2.44	2.56	2.68	2.81	2.95
− △ Working Capital (.09)	.19	.22	.24	.27	.30
= FCFE	$1.77	$3.11	$4.39	$5.34	$5.69
Beta	1.52	1.44	1.36	1.28	1.20
Cost of Equity	15.86%	15.42%	14.98%	14.54%	14.10%
Present Value	$.72	$1.09	$1.34	$1.43	$1.33

The FCFE in year 11, assuming that capital expenditures are offset by depreciation, is $9.15, yielding a terminal price of $112.94:

FCFE in year 11 $\quad\quad$ = EPS_{11} − ($Revenue_{11}$ − $Revenue_{10}$)(Working Capital as percentage of revenues)(1 − Debt Ratio)
$\quad\quad\quad\quad\quad\quad\quad\quad$ = ($8.94 × 1.06) − $.35(1 − .10) = $9.15

Cost of Equity in the \quad = 7.5% + (1.20 × 5.50%) = 14.10%
stable-growth phase
Terminal Price $\quad\quad\quad$ = $9.15/(.1410 − .06)
$\quad\quad\quad\quad\quad\quad\quad\quad$ = $112.94

The present values of the FCFE and the terminal price are as follows:

PV of FCFE in the high-growth phase = − $1.18
PV of FCFE in the transition phase = $5.91
PV of Terminal Price = $26.42
Value of Stock = $31.15

America Online was trading at $86.75 in March 1995.

A Troubleshooting Guide: What is wrong with this valuation?
Three-Stage FCFE Model

If this is your problem	*this may be the solution*
• If you get an extremely low value from this model, the likely culprits are:	
1. Capital expenditures are significantly higher than depreciation in the stable-growth phase.	Offset capital expenditures by depreciation; or capital expenditures grow more slowly than depreciation during the transition period to narrow the difference.
2. The beta in the stable-growth period is too high for a stable firm.	Use a beta closer to 1.
3. Working capital as a percentage of revenue is too high to sustain.	Use a working capital ratio closer to industry.
• If you get an extremely high value:	
1. Capital expenditures offset depreciation during the high-growth period.	Set capital expenditures higher.
2. Capital expenditures are less than depreciation.	Set capital expenditures equal to depreciation.
3. The growth period (high-growth plus transition) is too long.	Use a shorter growth period.
4. The growth rate in the stable-growth period is too high for a stable firm.	Use a growth rate closer to GNP growth.

FCFE MODEL VALUATION VERSUS DIVIDEND
DISCOUNT MODEL VALUATION

The discounted cashflow model which uses FCFE can be viewed as an alternative to the dividend discount model. Since the two approaches sometimes provide different estimates of value, it is worth examining when they provide similar estimates of value, when they provide different estimates of value, and what the difference tells us about the firm.

When They Are Similar

There are two conditions in which the value from using the FCFE in discounted cashflow valuation will be the same as the value obtained from using the dividend discount model. The first is the obvious one, where the dividends are equal to the FCFE. The second condition is more subtle, where the FCFE is greater than the dividends, but the excess cash (FCFE minus dividends) is invested in projects with net present value of 0. (For instance, investing in financial assets that are fairly priced should yield a net present value of 0.)

When They Are Different

There are several cases in which the two models will provide different estimates of value. First, when the FCFE is greater than the dividends and the excess cash either earns below-market interest rates or is invested in negative net present value projects, the value from the FCFE model will be greater than the value from the dividend discount model. There is reason to believe that this is not as unusual as it would seem at the outset. There are numerous case studies of firms that, having accumulated large cash balances by paying out low dividends relative to FCFE, have chosen to use this cash to finance unwise takeovers (where the price paid is greater than the value received from the takeover). In addition, the payment of smaller dividends than can be afforded to be paid out by a firm lowers debt/equity ratios and may lead the firm to become underleveraged, causing a loss in value.

In the cases where the dividends are greater than the FCFE, the firm will have to issue either new stock or new debt to pay these dividends, leading to at least three negative consequences for value. The flotation cost on these security issues, which can be substantial for equity issues, creates an unnecessary expenditure which decreases value. Second, if the firm borrows the money to pay the dividends, the firm may become overleveraged (relative to the optimal), leading to a loss in value. Finally, paying too much in dividends can lead to capital rationing constraints where good projects are rejected, resulting in a loss of wealth.

What Does It Mean When They Are Different?

When the value using the FCFE model is different from the value using the dividend discount model, with similar growth assumptions, there are two questions that need to be addressed: What does the difference between the two models tell us? Which of the two models is the appropriate one to use in evaluating the market price?

The more common occurrence is for the value from the FCFE model to exceed the value from the dividend discount model. The difference between the value from the FCFE model and the value using the dividend discount model can be considered one component of the value of controlling a firm—it measures the value of controlling dividend policy. In a hostile takeover, the bidder can expect to control the firm and change the dividend policy (to reflect FCFE), thus capturing the higher FCFE value. In the more infrequent case, where the value from the dividend discount model exceeds the value from the FCFE, the difference has less economic meaning but can be considered a warning on the sustainability of expected dividends.

As for which of the two values is the more appropriate one to use in evaluating the market price, the answer lies in the openness of the market for corporate control. If there is a sizable probability that a firm can be taken over or its management changed, the market price will reflect that likelihood, and the appropriate benchmark to use is the value from the FCFE model. As changes in corporate control become more difficult, either because of a firm's size and/or legal or market restrictions on takeovers, the value from the dividend discount model will provide the appropriate benchmark for comparison.

CONCLUSION

The primary difference between the dividend discount models described in the previous chapter and the free cashflows to equity models described in this chapter lies in the definition of cashflows: The dividend discount model uses a strict definition of cashflows to equity, that is, the expected dividends on the stock, while the FCFE model uses an expansive definition of cashflows to equity as the residual cashflows after meeting all financial obligations and investment needs. When firms have dividends that are different from the FCFE, the values from the two models will be different. In valuing firms for takeovers or where there is a reasonable chance of changing corporate control, the value from the FCFE provides the better estimate of value.

QUESTIONS AND SHORT PROBLEMS

1. Respond true or false to the following statements relating to the calculation and use of FCFE:
 a. The free cash flow to equity will generally be more volatile than dividends.
 b. The free cash flow to equity will always be higher than the dividends.

c. The free cash flow to equity will always be higher than net income.

d. The free cash flow to equity can never be negative.

2. Kimberly-Clark, a household product manufacturer, reported earnings per share of $3.20 in 1993, and paid dividends per share of $1.70 in that year. The firm reported depreciation of $315 million in 1993, and capital expenditures of $475 million. (There were 160 million shares outstanding, trading at $51 per share.) This ratio of capital expenditures to depreciation is expected to be maintained in the long term. The working capital needs are negligible. Kimberly-Clark had debt outstanding of $1.6 billion, and intends to maintain its current financing mix (of debt and equity) to finance future investment needs. The firm is in steady state and earnings are expected to grow 7% a year. The stock had a beta of 1.05. (The Treasury bond rate is 6.25%.)

 a. Estimate the value per share, using the Dividend Discount Model.

 b. Estimate the value per share, using the FCFE Model.

 c. How would you explain the difference between the two models, and which one would you use as your benchmark for comparison to the market price?

3. Ecolab Inc. sells chemicals and systems for cleaning, sanitizing and maintenance. It reported earnings per share of $2.35 in 1993, and expected earnings growth of 15.5% a year from 1994 to 1998, and 6% a year after that. The capital expenditure per share was $2.25, and depreciation was $1.125 per share in 1993. Both are expected to grow at the same rate as earnings from 1994 to 1998. Working capital is expected to remain at 5% of revenues, and revenues, which were $1,000 million in 1993, are expected to increase 6% a year from 1994 to 1998, and 4% a year after that. The firm currently has a debt ratio (D/(D + E)) of 5%, but plans to finance future investment needs (including working capital investments) using a debt ratio of 20%. The stock is expected to have a beta of 1.00 for the period of the analysis, and the Treasury bond rate is 6.50%. (There are 63 million shares outstanding)

 a. Assuming that capital expenditures and depreciation offset each other after 1998, estimate the value per share.

 b. Assuming that capital expenditures continue to be 200% of depreciation even after 1998, estimate the value per share.

 c. What would the value per share have been, if the firm had continued to finance new investments with its old financing mix (5%)? Is it fair to use the same beta for this analysis?

4. Dionex Corporation, a leader in the development and manufacture of ion chromography systems (used to identify contaminants in electronic devices), reported earnings per share of $2.02 in 1993, and paid no dividends. These earnings are expected to grow 14% a year for five years (1994 to 1998) and 7% a year after that. The firm reported depreciation of $2 million in 1993 and capital spending of $4.20 million, and had 7 million shares outstanding. The working capital is expected to remain at 50% of revenues, which were $106 million in 1993, and are expected to grow 6% a year from 1994 to 1998 and 4% a year after that. The firm is expected to finance 10% of its capital expenditures and working capital needs with debt. Dionex had a beta of 1.20 in 1993, and this beta is expected to drop to 1.10 after 1998. (The Treasury bond rate is 7%)

 a. Estimate the expected free cash flow to equity from 1994 to 1998, assuming that capital expenditures and depreciation grow at the same rate as earnings.

 b. Estimate the terminal price per share (at the end of 1998). Stable firms in this

industry have capital expenditures which are 150% of revenues, and maintain working capital at 25% of revenues.

c. Estimate the value per share today, based upon the FCFE model.

5. Biomet Inc, designs, manufactures and markets reconstructive and trauma devices, and reported earnings per share of $0.56 in 1993, on which it paid no dividends (It had revenues per share in 1993 of $2.91). It had capital expenditures of $0.13 per share in 1993, and depreciation in the same year of $0.08 per share. The working capital was 60% of revenues in 1993, and will remain at that level from 1994 to 1998, while earnings and revenues are expected to grow 17% a year. The earnings growth rate is expected to decline linearly over the following five years to a rate of 5% in 2003. During the high growth and transition periods, capital spending and depreciation are expected to grow at the same rate as earnings, but are expected to offset each other when the firm reaches steady state. Working capital is expected to drop from 60% of revenues during the 1994–1998 period to 30% of revenues after 2003. The firm has no debt currently, but plans to finance 10% of its net capital investment and working capital requirements with debt.

The stock is expected to have a beta of 1.45 for the high growth period (1994–1998), and it is expected to decline to 1.10 by the time the firm goes into steady state (in 2003). The Treasury bond rate is 7%.

a. Estimate the value per share, using the FCFE model.

b. Estimate the value per share, assuming that working capital stays at 60% of revenues forever.

c. Estimate the value per share, assuming that the beta remains unchanged at 1.45 forever.

6. Which of the following firms is likely to have a higher value from the dividend discount model, a higher value from the FCFE model or the same value from both models?

a. A firm that pays out less in dividends than it has available in FCFE, but which invests the balance in treasury bonds.

b. A firm which pays out more in dividends than it has available in FCFE, and then issues stock to cover the difference.

c. A firm which pays out, on average, its FCFE as dividends.

d. A firm which pays out less in dividends that it has available in FCFE, but which uses the cash at regular intervals to acquire other firms, with the intent of diversifying.

e. A firm which pays out more in dividends than it has available in FCFE, but borrows money to cover the difference. (The firm is over-levered to begin with.)

Valuing a Firm—The Free Cashflows to the Firm Approach

There are two approaches to valuing the equity in a firm—the dividend discount model and the FCFE valuation model. This chapter develops another approach to valuation where the entire firm is valued, by discounting the accumulated cashflows to all claimholders in the firm by the weighted average cost of capital, and it examines its limitations and applications.

FREE CASHFLOWS TO THE FIRM

The free cashflows to the firm are the sum of the cashflows to all claimholders in the firm, including stockholders, bondholders, and preferred stockholders.

Measuring Free Cashflows to the Firm

There are two ways of measuring the free cashflows to the firm (FCFF). One is to add up the cashflows to the claimholders:

FCFF = Free Cashflows to Equity + Interest Expense(1 − tax rate)
 + Principal Repayments − New Debt Issues + Preferred Dividends

The other way is to use earnings before interest and taxes (EBIT) as a basis for the calculation:

FCFF = EBIT(1 − tax rate) + Depreciation − Capital Expenditures
 − \triangle Working Capital

Both approaches should provide the same estimates of the cashflow.

FCFF and Other Cashflow Measures

The differences between FCFF and FCFE arise primarily from cashflows associated with debt—interest payments, principal repayments, and new debt is-

sues—and other nonequity claims, such as preferred dividends. For firms at their desired debt level, which finance their capital expenditures and working capital needs with this mix of debt and equity and use debt issues to finance principal repayments, the FCFF will exceed the FCFE.

One measure that is widely used in valuation is the earnings before interest, taxes, depreciation, and amortization (EBITDA). The FCFF is a closely related concept, but it takes into account the potential tax liability from the earnings as well as capital expenditures and working capital requirements.

Another measure used in valuation is the net operating income (NOI). The net operating income is defined to be the income from operations, prior to taxes and nonoperating expenses. If nonoperating expenses are deducted, the resulting figure is the earnings before interest and taxes (EBIT).

Each of these measures is used in valuation models, and each is a variant of the FCFF. Each, however, makes some assumptions about the relationship between depreciation and capital expenditures that are made explicit in the following table:

Cash flow Used	Definition	Caveats/Assumptions
FCFF	Free Cashflows to the Firm	• Use after-tax cost of capital as the discount rate.
FCFE	FCFF − Interest(1 − t) − Principal Repaid + New Debt Issued − Preferred Dividends	• Equity is being valued. • Cost of equity is the discount rate. • Adjust k_e for changing leverage.
EBITDA	FCFF + EBIT(t) +Depreciation + Capital Expenditures + ▲ Working Capital	• Use pretax cost of capital as the discount rate. • Assumes no capital expenditures. • Assumes no working capital.
NOI (1 − t)	FCFF + (Cap. Exp. − Depr.) + Nonoperating Exp. (1 − t) + Δ working capital	• Use after-tax cost of capital as the discount rate. • Assumes that capital expenditures are offset by depreciation. • Assumes that nonoperating expenses will not continue.
EBIT (1 − t)	FCFF + (Cap. Exp. − Depr.) + Δ working capital	• Use after-tax cost of capital as the discount rate. • Assumes that capital expenditures are offset by depreciation.

Note that

$$EBIT(1 − t) = EBITDA(1 − t) − (Depreciation)(1 − t)$$

$$EBIT = NOI − Nonoperating Expenses$$

Growth in FCFE versus Growth in FCFF

The primary reason for differences between the growth rate in the FCFF and the growth rate in the FCFE is the existence of leverage. Leverage generally

increases the growth rate in the FCFE relative to the growth rate in the FCFF. This can be illustrated using the formulation relating the growth rate to financial fundamentals. The growth rate in earnings per share is defined to be:

$$g_{EPS} = b\{ROA + D/E(ROA - i[1 - t])\}$$

where g_{EPS} = growth rate in earnings per share
b = retention ratio = 1 − Payout Ratio
ROA = (Net Income + Interest Expense[1 − t])/(BV of Debt + BV of Equity)
D/E = Book Value of Debt/Book Value of Equity
i = Interest Expense/Book Value of Debt

As long as the return on assets earned by a firm on its projects exceeds the after-tax interest rate, increasing leverage will increase the growth rate in earnings per share. The cashflow to the firm is a predebt cashflow and is not affected by increased leverage. Thus, the growth rate in EBIT, for the same firm, will be a function of only the retention ratio and the return on assets and will generally be lower:

$$g_{EBIT} = b(ROA)$$

The growth rates in capital expenditures, depreciation, and capital spending will be identical for purposes of calculating the FCFE and FCFF.

Illustration 12.1: Growth rate in FCFE and FCFF: The Home Depot

The Home Depot had earnings per share in 1992 of $0.82 and had registered growth in earnings per share of 45% in the prior five years. The firm had return on assets of 12.82%, a pretax interest rate of 7.7%, a debt/equity ratio of 36.59%, and a retention ratio of 91% in 1992 (the tax rate was 36%). Assuming that these levels will be sustained in the future, the growth rates in FCFE and FCFF will be as follows:

$$\text{Expected Growth Rate in FCFE} = b\{ROA + D/E(ROA - i[1 - t])\}$$
$$= .91\{12.82\% + .3659(12.82\% - 7.7\%$$
$$[1 - .36])\}$$
$$= 14.29\%$$
$$\text{Expected Growth Rate in FCFF} = b(ROA)$$
$$= .91 \times 12.82\% = 11.67\%$$

The growth rate in the FCFE is greater than the growth rate in the FCFF because of the leverage effect.

MODELS FOR VALUING THE FIRM

The value of the firm is obtained by discounting the FCFF at the weighted average cost of capital. Just as with the dividend discount model and the FCFE

model, the version of the model used will depend upon assumptions made about future growth.

Stable-Growth FCFF Model

A firm in steady state, with cashflows growing at a stable growth rate, can be valued using a variant of the infinite-growth model.

The Model

A firm with FCFF growing at a stable growth rate can be valued using the following model:

$$\text{Value of Firm} = FCFF_1/(WACC - g_n)$$

where $FCFF_1$ = expected FCFF next year
 WACC = weighted average cost of capital
 g_n = growth rate in the FCFF forever

Caveats

There are two conditions that need to be met in using this model. First, the growth rate used in the model has to be reasonable, relative to the nominal growth rate in the economy. Second, the relationship between capital expenditures and depreciation has to be consistent with assumptions of stable growth. A stable firm generally should not have capital expenditures that are significantly greater than depreciation, since there is no extraordinary growth and hence no need for additional capital investment. In fact, some analysts would argue that capital expenditures should offset depreciation in the steady state. These concerns mirror those raised in the Gordon growth model and the stable-growth version of the FCFE model.

Limitations

Like all stable-growth models, this one is sensitive to assumptions about the expected growth rate. This is accentuated, however, by the fact that the discount rate used in valuation is the weighted average cost of capital, which is significantly lower than the cost of equity for most firms. Furthermore, the model is sensitive to assumptions made about capital expenditures relative to depreciation. The FCFF can be inflated (deflated) by reducing (increasing) capital expenditures relative to depreciation.

Illustration 12.2: Valuing the food product division at RJR Nabisco

In early 1995, RJR Nabisco was actively seeking a buyer for its food products division to generate cash to pay off its debtholders.

Rationale for using the model:
- The division is in steady state; it is a large player in a stable market with strong competition. It cannot be expected to sustain high growth for any length of time.

- The division does not carry its own debt (though its parent company, RJR Nabisco, carries plenty). Thus, only the FCFF can be computed for the division.
- The entire division is up for sale, not just RJR's equity stake in the division.

Background information:
- In 1994, the food products division had revenues of $7 billion on which it earned $1.5 billion before interest and taxes.
- The division had capital expenditures of $660 million and depreciation of $550 million in 1994.
- Working capital as a percentage of revenues averaged 5% between 1993 and 1994. (Working capital increased $150 million in 1994.)
- The beta of comparable firms in the food products business is 1.05, and the average debt ratio of these firms is 23.67%. (The cost of debt at the largest of these firms is approximately 8.50%.)
- The tax rate is assumed to be 36%.
- The FCFF is expected to grow 5% a year in the long term.

Valuing the division:
The estimated FCFF of the division is as follows, in millions:

	Current	Next Year
EBIT$(1 - t)$	$960.00	$1,008.00
$-$(Cap. Ex. $-$ Depr.)	110.00	115.50
$- \Delta$ Working Capital	150.00	17.50
$=$ FCFF	$700.00	$875.00

The cost of capital is computed, based upon comparable firms in the food products business:

- Beta (based upon comparable firms) = 1.05
- Long-Term Bond Rate = 7.50%
- Cost of Equity (based upon comparable firms) = 7.5% + (1.05 × 5.50%) = 13.275%
- Pretax Cost of Debt = 8.50%; After-Tax Cost of Debt = 8.50%(1 − .36) = 5.44%
- Debt Ratio (based upon comparable firms) = 23.67%
- Cost of Capital (based upon comparable firms) = (13.275% × .7633) + (5.44% × .2367) = 11.42%

The value of the division, using this cost of capital and an expected growth rate of 5%, was estimated as follows:

Value of Division = $875/(.1142 − .05) = $13,629 million

General Version of the FCFF Model

The general version of the model can be used to value any firm, where sufficient information exists to forecast free cashflows to the firm.

The Model

The value of the firm, in the most general case, can be written as the present value of expected FCFF:

$$\text{Value of Firm} = \sum_{t=1}^{t=\infty} \frac{\text{FCFF}_t}{(1 + \text{WACC})^t}$$

where FCFF_t = FCFF in year t

If the firm reaches steady state after n years and starts growing at a stable growth rate g_n after that, the value of the firm can be written as:

$$\text{Value of Firm} = \sum_{t=1}^{t=n} \frac{\text{FCFF}_t}{(1 + \text{WACC})^t} + \frac{\text{FCFF}_{n+1}/(\text{WACC} - g_n)}{(1 + \text{WACC})^n}$$

where WACC_n = Weighted Average Cost of Capital in steady state

Firm Valuation versus Equity Valuation

This model, unlike the dividend discount model or the FCFE model, values the firm rather than equity. The value of equity, however, can be extracted from the value of the firm by subtracting out the market value of outstanding debt. Since it can be viewed as an alternative way of valuing equity, two questions arise: Why value the firm rather than equity? Will the values for equity obtained from the firm valuation approach be consistent with the values obtained from the equity valuation approaches described in the previous chapter?

The advantage of using the firm valuation approach is that cashflows relating to debt do not have to be considered explicitly, since the FCFF is a predebt cashflow, while they have to be taken into account in estimating FCFE. In cases where the leverage is expected to change significantly over time, this is a significant saving. The firm valuation approach does, however, require information about debt ratios and interest rates to estimate the weighted average cost of capital.

The value for equity obtained from the firm valuation and equity valuation approaches will be the same if:

(a) *Consistent assumptions are made about growth in the two approaches.* This does not mean that the same growth rate is used in both approaches, but may require that the growth rates in earnings be adjusted for the effect of leverage. This is especially true for the calculation of the terminal value, where a stable growth rate is assumed in both FCFE and FCFF models.

(b) *Bonds are correctly priced.* The value of equity in the FCFF approach is obtained by subtracting out the market value of the debt from the value of the firm. If the firm's debt is overvalued, the value of equity obtained from the FCFF model will be lower than the value obtained from the equity valuation approaches. The value of equity will be higher if the firm's debt is undervalued.

Suitability of the Model

Firms that either have very high leverage or are in the process of changing their leverage are best valued using the FCFF approach. The calculation of FCFE

is much more difficult in these cases because of the volatility induced by debt payments, and the value of equity, which is a small slice of the total value of the firm, is more sensitive to assumptions about growth and risk. Thus, this model may provide the most accurate estimates of value in a leveraged buyout, where the leverage of the firm is high initially but can be expected to change significantly over the next few years.

One of the primary problems with using cashflows to equity is the frequent occurrence of negative free cashflows to equity, especially for cyclical and highly leveraged firms. Since FCFF is before debt payments, it is much less likely to be negative and create problems in valuation.

Finally, if the FCFF approach is to be used to value the equity in a firm, the debt either has to trade at a "fair" price or has to be explicitly valued using updated interest rates that reflect the risk of the debt.

Illustration 12.3: Valuing an overleveraged firm using the FCFF approach: Federated Department Stores

Rationale for using the model:
- The earnings before interest and taxes at Federated in 1994, which amounted to $531 million, were still well below EBIT in 1988 of $628 million. The earnings are expected to grow at rates slightly above stable rates for the next five years as the firm recovers.
- The leverage in 1994 was still significantly above desirable levels, largely as a consequence of the leveraged buyout in the late 1980s. It was anticipated that this debt ratio would be lowered gradually over the next five years to acceptable levels.

Background information:
 Base year information:

- Earnings before interest and taxes in 1994 = $532 million
- Capital Expenditures in 1994 = $310 million
- Depreciation in 1994 = $207 million
- Revenues in 1994 = $7,230 million
- Working Capital as a percentage of revenues = 25.00%
- Tax Rate = 36%
- Long-Term Bond Rate = 7.50%

 Inputs for the high growth phase:

- Length of the high-growth phase = 5 years
- Expected Growth Rate in EBIT = 8%
- Beta = 1.25
- Cost of Debt = 9.50% (pretax)
- Debt Ratio = 50%
- Revenues, Capital Expenditures, and Depreciation will all grow at 8%

 Inputs for the stable-growth phase:

- Expected Growth Rate in FCFF = 5%
- Beta = 1.00

- Cost of Debt = 8.50%
- Debt Ratio = 25%
- Capital expenditures are offset by depreciation.

Estimating the value:
The forecasted free cashflows to the firm over the next five years are provided below, in millions:

	1	2	3	4	5	Terminal Year
EBIT	$574.45	$620.41	$670.04	$723.64	$781.54	$820.61
− t(EBIT)	206.80	223.35	241.21	260.51	281.35	295.42
−(Cap. Ex. − Depr.)	111.24	120.14	129.75	140.13	151.34	0.00
− Δ Working Capital	144.58	156.15	168.64	182.13	196.70	132.77
= FCFF	111.83	120.77	130.44	140.87	$152.15	$392.42

$$\text{Cost of Equity during the high-growth phase} = 7.5\% + (1.25 \times 5.5\%)$$
$$= 14.38\%$$
$$\text{Cost of Capital during the high-growth phase} = (14.38\% \times .5)$$
$$+ 9.50\%(1 - .36)(.5) = 10.23\%$$

The FCFF in the terminal year is estimated to be $392.42 million:

$$\text{FCFF in terminal year} = \text{EBIT}_6(1 - t) - (\text{Revenue}_6 - \text{Revenue}_5)$$
$$\times \text{Working Capital as a percentage of revenue}$$
$$= \$820.61(1 - .36) - \$132.77$$
$$= \$392.42 \text{ million}$$

$$\text{Cost of Equity during the stable-growth phase} = 7.50\% + (1.00 \times 5.50\%)$$
$$= 13.00\%$$

$$\text{Cost of Capital in the stable-growth phase} = (13.00\% \times .75)$$
$$+ 8.50\%(1 - .36)(.25)$$
$$= 11.11\%$$

$$\text{Terminal Value of the firm} = \$392.42/(.1111 - .05) = \$6,422 \text{ million}$$

The value of the firm is then the present value of the expected FCFF and the present value of the terminal value:

PV of FCFF =	$487.17 million
PV of Terminal Value =	$3,946.93 million
Value of Firm =	$4,434.11 million
Value of Debt =	$2,740.58 million
Value of Equity =	$1,693.52 million
Value per Share =	$13.38

Federated Department Stores was trading at $21 per share in March 1995.

Illustration 12.4: Valuing with the three-stage FCFF model: LIN Broadcasting

LIN Broadcasting was appraised in early 1995 by three investment bankers to determine the "appropriate price" per share on a takeover by AT&T. The three appraisals came in at $105 per share by Morgan Stanley for AT&T, $155 per share by Lehman Brothers for LIN Broadcasting, and a compromise valuation by Wasserstein Perella estimating the value to be $127.50 per share.

Rationale for using the model:

- *Why three-stage?* LIN Broadcasting is a fast-growing firm in a fast-growing industry segment. Revenues are expected to grow 30% a year for the next few years.
- *Why FCFF?* LIN Broadcasting has never made a profit after taxes, even though it has posted high growth, because it has had high leverage and nonoperating expenses. Prior to these charges, however, it earned a healthy operating income of $128 million in 1994. Thus, though FCFE is negative, FCFF is positive.
- The financial leverage is high but can be expected to decline as the industry stabilizes.

Background information:

Current inputs:

- EBIT in 1994 = $128.3 million
- Capital Expenditures in 1994 = $150.5 million
- Depreciation and Amortization in 1994 = $125.1 million
- Working Capital was about 10% of revenues in 1994.
- Revenues in 1994 = $688.6 million.
- Long-Term Bond Rate = 7.50%; Corporate Tax Rate = 36%.

Inputs for the high-growth period:

- Length of the high-growth period = 5 years
- Expected growth rate in Revenues/EBIT = 30.00%
- Beta = 1.60
- Cost of Equity = $7.5\% + (1.60 \times 5.5\%) = 16.30\%$
- Debt Ratio = 60% (The firm will continue to use debt heavily during this period, at a pretax cost of debt of 10%.)
- Capital expenditures and depreciation are expected to grow at the same rate as revenues and EBIT.
- Working capital will remain at 10% of revenues during this period.

$$\text{Weighted Average Cost of Capital} = (16.30\% \times .40) + (10\% \times .64 \times .60)$$
$$= 10.36\%$$

Inputs for the stable-growth period:

- Length of the transition period = 5 years
- Growth rate in EBIT will decline from 30% in year 5 to 5% in year 10 in linear increments.

- Capital expenditures will grow 8% a year and depreciation will grow 12% a year.
- Beta will drop to 1.25 for the entire transition period.
- The debt ratio will drop to 50%, and the pretax cost of debt will be 9%.
- Working capital will remain at 10% of revenues.

Weighted Average Cost of Capital $= (14.38\% \times .50) + (9\% \times .64 \times .50)$
$$= 10.07\%$$

Inputs for the stable-growth period:

- Expected growth rate in Revenues and EBIT $= 5\%$
- Capital expenditures and depreciation will grow at the same rate as EBIT.
- Beta $= 1.00$
- Cost of Equity $= 7.50\% + (1.0 \times 5.5\%) = 13\%$
- Debt Ratio $= 40\%$; Pretax Cost of Debt $= 8.5\%$

Estimating the value:
These inputs are used to estimated FCFF, the cost of capital, and the present values during the high-growth and transition periods:

Period	EBIT $(1 - t)$	Cap Exp	Depreciation	\triangle Working Cap.	FCFF	Debt Ratio	Beta	WACC	Present Value
1	$106.75	$195.65	$162.63	$20.66	$ 53.07	60.00%	1.60	10.36%	$ 48.09
2	138.77	254.35	211.42	26.86	68.99	60.00%	1.60	10.36%	56.64
3	180.40	330.65	274.84	34.91	89.68	60.00%	1.60	10.36%	66.72
4	234.52	429.84	357.30	45.39	116.59	60.00%	1.60	10.36%	78.60
5	304.88	558.80	464.49	59.00	151.57	60.00%	1.60	10.36%	92.59
6	381.10	603.50	520.23	63.92	233.90	50.00%	1.25	10.07%	129.81
7	457.31	651.78	582.65	63.92	324.27	50.00%	1.25	10.07%	163.50
8	525.91	703.92	652.57	57.53	417.03	50.00%	1.25	10.07%	191.05
9	578.50	760.24	730.88	44.10	505.04	50.00%	1.25	10.07%	210.20
10	607.43	821.05	818.59	24.26	580.70	50.00%	1.25	10.07%	219.58

The terminal value at the end of year 10 can be calculated based upon the FCFF in year 11, the stable growth rate of 5%, and the cost of capital in the stable-growth phase:

FCFF $=$ FCFF$_{10} \times 1.05 = \$580.70 \times 1.05 = \609.73 million

Cost of Capital in the stable-growth period $= (13.00\% \times .6)$
$$+ 8.5\%(1 - .36)(.4) = 9.98\%$$

Terminal Price $= \$609.73/(.0998 - .05) = \$12,253.55$ million

The components of value are as follows:

PV of FCFF in the high-growth phase =	$342.64 million
PV of FCFF in the transition phase =	$914.15 million
PV of terminal firm value at the end of transition =	$4,633.49 million
Value of firm =	$5,890.27 million
Value of Outstanding Debt =	$1,806.60 million
Value of Equity =	$4,083.67 million
Value per Share =	$79.29

FIRM VALUE AND LEVERAGE

The value of the firm is obtained by discounting the free cashflows to the firm at the weighted average cost of capital. While the FCFF is before debt payments and is hence unaffected by leverage, the weighted average cost of capital can change as the firm's leverage changes.

Why Minimize the Weighted Average Cost of Capital?

If the cashflows to the firm are unaffected by the debt/equity mix and the cost of capital is reduced, the value of the firm will increase. If the objective in choosing the financing mix for the firm is the maximization of firm value, this can be accomplished by minimizing the cost of capital.

The optimal financing mix for a firm is simple to compute if a schedule that relates the costs of equity and debt to leverage is provided.

Illustration 12.5: WACC, Firm Value, and Leverage

Assume that the costs of equity and debt at different debt levels are provided for a firm and that the cashflows to this firm are currently $200 million. These cashflows are expected to grow at 6% forever. The WACC schedule is provided below, together with the value of the firm (in millions) at each level of debt:

D/(D + E)	Cost of Equity	Cost of Debt	WACC	Firm Value
0%	10.50%	4.80%	10.50%	$4,711
10%	11.00%	5.10%	10.41%	4,807
20%	11.60%	5.40%	10.36%	4,862
30%	12.30%	5.52%	10.27%	4,970
40%	13.10%	5.70%	10.14%	5,121
50%	14.00%	6.30%	10.15%	5,108

D/(D + E)	Cost of Equity	Cost of Debt	WACC	Firm Value
60%	15.00%	7.20%	10.32%	4,907
70%	16.10%	8.10%	10.50%	4,711
80%	17.20%	9.00%	10.64%	4,569
90%	18.40%	10.20%	11.02%	4,223
100%	19.70%	11.40%	11.40%	3,926

Note that the Value of the Firm = FCFF(1 + g)/(WACC − g). Figure 12.1 graphs the WACC and firm value as a function of leverage.

FIGURE 12.1 WACC and Firm Value—Effects of Leverage: Boeing

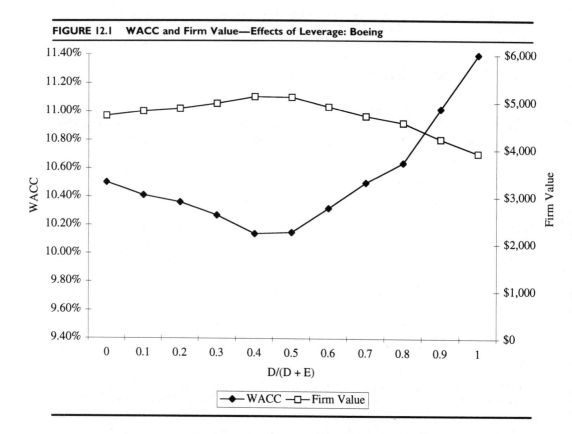

While this illustration makes the choice of an optimal financing mix seem trivial, it obscures some real problems that arise in applications. First, an analyst does not have the benefit of having the entire schedule of the costs of financing prior to an analysis. In most cases, the only level of debt about which there is any level of certainty about the cost of financing is the current level. Second, the analysis assumes implicitly that the level of cashflows to the firm is unaffected by the financing mix of the firm and, consequently, by the default risk (or bond rating) for the firm. While this may be reasonable in some cases, it might not be in others. For instance, a firm that manufacturers consumer durables might find that its sales drop off if its default risk increases,

because investors are reluctant to buy its products and risk not being able to obtain replacement parts for them down the road.

A Practical Framework for Analyzing Value and Leverage

There are compromises that have to be made in order to apply the cost of capital approach to "real world" problems. A general framework for analyzing these problems is provided in this section, with an extended illustration.

Cost of Equity

The primary task is to estimate the cost of equity at different levels of debt. The approach described below applies if the capital asset pricing model is used to estimate cost of equity. The approach can be modified if the arbitrage pricing model is used.

Step 1: Obtain a current estimate of the equity beta and the debt/equity ratio.

Step 2: Estimate the unlevered beta, that is, the beta the firm would have if it had no debt at all. If the relationship between beta and leverage is used, the unlevered beta can be written as:

$$\beta_u = \beta_{current}/(1 + [1 - t]D/E)$$

where β_u = unlevered beta of the firm
 $\beta_{current}$ = current equity beta of the firm
 t = tax rate for the firm
 D/E = current debt/equity ratio (in market value terms)

Step 3: Reestimate the levered betas for different levels of debt:

$$\beta_{levered} = \beta_u(1 + [1 - t]D/E)$$

where $\beta_{levered}$ = equity beta given new leverage
 D/E = debt/equity ratio

At each level of leverage, measured using the debt/equity ratio, reestimate the equity beta.

Step 4: Estimate the costs of equity using this levered beta:

$$k_e = R_f + \beta_{levered}(E[R_m] - R_f)$$

where k_e = cost of equity
 $E(R_m)$ = expected return on the market index
 R_f = current riskfree rate

Cost of Debt

The task here is to estimate the cost of debt of the firm at different levels of debt. As part of the background to estimating the cost of debt, two schedules will have to be developed:

(a) One schedule will lay out the relationship between default risk and a firm's underlying characteristics. For instance, if bond ratings are used to measure default risk, this schedule will describe the relationship between ratings and financial ratios, using either general information or information pertaining to a particular industry. If bond ratings are not available or are not used, as is the case in many markets outside the United States, general default risk classes[1] can be created to capture differences across firms, and related to firm characteristics.

(b) The other schedule will include current market interest rates on corporate bonds in each bond rating class or default risk class. These default premiums will change over time and will have to be updated on a regular basis.

Given this background, the cost of debt for a firm can be estimated at different levels of debt by first estimating the bond rating or default risk class for the firm at each debt level and then using the interest rate that corresponds to that rating.

Step 1: Prepare the latest income statement showing the current operating income and relevant financial ratios.

Step 2: Compute the current market value of the firm:

Market Value of Firm = Market Value of Equity + Market Value of Debt

Step 3: As the debt ratio is changed, compute the dollar value of debt:

Dollar Value of Debt = Debt/(Debt + Equity) × Current Market Value of Firm

Step 4: Compute the amount that will be paid as interest (Interest Rate × Dollar Value of Debt) and the financial ratios at each new debt ratio.

Step 5: Using the schedule developed relating bond ratings to financial ratios, estimate what the firm's rating (default class) will be at each new debt ratio and the market interest rate that would correspond to that rating (default class). This is the before-tax cost of debt.

Step 6: The after-tax cost of debt can then be computed using the firm's tax rate:

$$k_d = \text{After-Tax Cost of Debt} = \text{Before-Tax Cost of Debt}(1 - \text{Tax Rate})$$

Cost of Capital

With the costs of equity and debt at different levels of debt, the costs of capital for different levels of debt can be estimated. The debt ratio at which the cost of capital is minimized is the optimal debt ratio.

General Assumptions

The approach described above for estimating the cost of capital at different levels of debt rests on several assumptions. First, the effect on firm value of changing the capital structure is isolated by keeping the asset side fixed and

changing the liability side. In practical terms, this implies that the debt ratio is increased by issuing debt and repurchasing equity, and decreased by issuing equity and retiring debt. Can the optimal debt ratio obtained by doing this be generalized to cases where the firm plans to invest the new funds in projects rather than in buying back securities? As long as the firm continues to make investments in the same line of business or risk class it has operated in the past, the optimal debt ratio obtained from the analysis above can continue to be used. If the firm is planning to invest in new areas, with different risk profiles, the optimal debt ratio calculated, keeping the asset side fixed, may no longer be appropriate.

Second, the pretax operating income is assumed to be unaffected by the financing mix and, by extension, the default risk of the firm. If the operating income is a function of the firm's default risk, the basic framework will not change. However, minimizing the cost of capital may not be the optimal course of action since the value of the firm is determined both by the cashflows and the cost of capital. The value of the firm will have to be computed at each debt level, and the optimal debt ratio will be the one that maximizes firm value.

Illustration 12.6: Analyzing value and leverage: Boeing, March 1990

The general framework can be applied to find the optimal capital structure for a firm. The following section shows how the approach was used to analyze the optimal financing mix for Boeing Inc. in March 1990.

Boeing's Capital Structure on March 23, 1990

Boeing had only $277 million of debt[2] on its books in March 1990, while the market value of equity at the same point in time was $16,182 million (the market price per share was $69.75 and there were 232 million shares outstanding). In proportional terms, 1.68% of the overall financing mix was debt and the remaining 98.32% was equity.

The beta[3] for Boeing's stock in March 1990 was 0.95. The Treasury bond rate at that time was 9.00%. Boeing's senior debt was rated AA. While Boeing had no bonds outstanding, other long-term bonds with an AA rating were yielding 9.70%. The tax rate used for the analysis is 34%.

$$\text{Value of Firm} = \$16{,}182 + \$277 = \$16{,}459 \text{ million}$$

$$\text{Cost of Equity} = \text{Riskfree Rate} + (\text{Beta} \times \text{Market Premium})$$
$$= 9\% + (.95 \times 5.5\%) = 14.23\%$$

$$\text{Cost of Debt} = \text{Pretax Interest Rate} (1 - \text{Tax Rate})$$
$$= 9.70\%(1 - .34) = 6.40\%$$

$$\text{WACC} = 14.23\%(\$16{,}182/[\$16{,}182 + \$277])$$
$$+ 6.40\%(\$277/[\$16{,}182 + \$277]) = 14.09\%$$

Boeing: Cost of Equity and Leverage

Using the framework developed in the prior section, the unlevered beta is computed and then used to estimate levered betas at each level of debt. These betas are used to estimate the cost of equity. The Treasury bond rate was 9.00% in March 1990 and the historical market premium of 5.5% was used to compute the cost of equity.

$$\text{Unlevered Beta} = \text{Current Beta}/(1 + \text{Debt/Equity}[1 - t])$$
$$= .95/(1 + .0171[1 - .34]) = .94$$

The recomputed betas are reported in the following table:

Debt/(Debt + Equity)	Debt*	Levered Beta	Cost of Equity
0%	$ 0	0.94	14.17%
10%	1,646	1.01	14.55%
20%	3,292	1.09	15.02%
30%	4,938	1.21	15.63%
40%	6,584	1.35	16.44%
50%	8,230	1.56	17.58%
60%	9,876	1.87	19.67%
70%	11,522	2.39	23.48%
80%	13,168	3.42	30.72%
90%	14,814	6.52	52.44%

* Dollar Value of Debt = Debt/(Debt + Equity) × (Market Value of Eqity + Market Value of Debt)
 = Debt/(Debt + Dquity) × ($16,182 + $277)

Boeing: Cost of Debt and Leverage

Boeing: Bond Ratings and Financial Ratios. There are a number of financial ratios that are correlated with bond ratings, and a sophisticated model to predict ratings, using all these ratios, can be built. However, for purposes of this illustration, a much simpler version is used. The bond ratings are determined solely by the interest coverage ratio, which is defined as follows:

Interest Coverage Ratio = Earnings before interest and taxes/Interest Expense

While this may be simplistic, there are three reasons for choosing the interest coverage ratio. First, it is a ratio that is used by both Standard and Poor's and Moody's in coming up with a rating. Second, there is significant correlation not only between the interest coverage ratio and bond ratings but also between the interest coverage ratio and other ratios that are used in analysis, such as the debt coverage ratio and the fund flow ratios. Third, the interest coverage ratio changes as a firm changes its financing mix and becomes lower as the debt ratio increases.

Based upon an analysis of the financial ratios of manufacturing firms in different ratings classes, and extrapolating for those ratings where no firms were listed, the following chart was developed for March 1990:

Interest Coverage Ratio Range	Bond Rating
≥9.65	AAA
6.85–9.65	AA
5.65–6.85	A+
4.49–5.65	A
3.29–4.49	A−
2.76–3.29	BBB
2.18–2.76	BB
1.87–2.18	B+
1.57–1.87	B
1.27–1.57	B−
0.87–1.27	CCC
0.67–0.87	CC
0.25–0.67	C
<0.25	D

Using this chart as a guideline, then, a firm with an interest coverage ratio of 1.75 will be expected to have a rating of B for its bonds.

Boeing: Bond Ratings and Interest Rates. The relationship between bond ratings and interest rates in March 1990 was obtained by looking at yields of long-term bonds in each ratings class and averaging these yields. The following table summarizes the market interest rates/rating relationship and also reports the spread for these bonds over Treasury bonds. (The Treasury bond rate in March 1990 was 9%.)

Bond Rating	Interest Rate on Debt	Spread over Treasuries
AAA	9.30%	0.30%
AA	9.70%	0.70%
A+	10.00%	1.00%
A	10.25%	1.25%
A−	10.50%	1.50%
BBB	11.00%	2.00%
BB	11.50%	2.50%
B+	12.00%	3.00%
B	13.00%	4.00%
B−	14.00%	5.00%
CCC	15.00%	6.00%
CC	16.50%	7.50%
C	18.00%	9.00%
D	21.00%	12.00%

Boeing's Operating Income Statement, 1990. The following is Boeing's projected operating income statement (in millions) for the financial year 1989–1990. It shows that Boeing had earnings before interest, taxes, and depreciation of $2,063 million and paid out interest of only $23 million. The financial ratios provide evidence of the capability of Boeing to meet its debt obligations.

Income Statement, 1989–1990

Revenues	$27,500
− Operating Expenses	25,437
EBITDA	$ 2,063
− Depreciation	675
− Interest Expense	23
Income before Taxes	$ 1,365
− Taxes	396
Income after Taxes	$ 969
+ Depreciation	675
Fund Flow from Operations	$ 1,644

$$\text{Interest Coverage Ratio} = (\$1{,}365 + \$23)/\$23 = 60$$

$$\text{Fund flow interest coverage} = \$1{,}644/\$23 = 71$$

$$\text{Fund flow as a percentage of total debt} = \$1{,}644/\$277 = 5$$

Note that the interest coverage ratio is 60, but Boeing's current rating is AA. Based upon the coverage ratio alone, from the previous chart, Boeing should command a AAA rating. However, this fails to consider the fact that Boeing has almost no debt, and even small increases in dollar debt will lower the coverage ratio drastically.

Boeing: Effects of Leverage on Ratings. To compute the ratings for Boeing at different debt levels, the income statement is recomputed at each level of debt, the interest coverage ratio at that level of debt is estimated, and the rating that corresponds to that level of debt is obtained. For example, the following chart provides operating income statements (in millions) when the debt ratio is increased to 10% and 20% of the overall value of the firm.

	10% D/(D + E)	20% D/(D + E)
Debt*	$1,646	$3,292
EBITDA	$2,063	$2,063
− Depreciation	675	675
EBIT	1,388	1,388
− Interest Expense	160	346
Taxable Income	1,228	1,042
− Tax	418	354
Net Income	$ 811	$ 688
Interest Coverage Ratio	8.69	4.02
Likely Rating	AA	A −
Interest Rate	9.70%	10.50%
After-Tax Cost of Debt	6.40%	6.93%

* The value of the firm is $16,459 million. This is 10% and 20% of the value.

Note that there is an element of circular reasoning involved here. The interest rate is needed to calculate the interest coverage ratio, and the coverage ratio is necessary to compute the interest rate.[4]

This process is repeated for each level of debt from 10% to 90%, and the after-tax costs of debt are obtained.

Boeing: Effects of Leverage on Cost of Capital. With the cost of equity and the cost of debt estimated at each debt level, the cost of capital can be computed. The cost of capital, which is 14.17% when the firm is unlevered, decreases as the firm initially adds debt, reaches a minimum of 13.22% at 30% debt, and then starts to increase again. This is illustrated in graphic form in Figure 12.2.

Appendix 1 includes the details of the calculations.

Boeing: Firm Value and Cost of Capital. The rationale for minimizing the cost of capital is that this maximizes the value of the firm. To illustrate the effects on the firm value at Boeing of moving to the optimal, we start off with a simple formulation of firm value:

$$\text{Firm Value} = \text{FCFF}(1 + g)/(\text{WACC} - g)$$

where g = growth rate in the FCFF (steady state)

The current value (in March 1990) of the firm is $16,459 million, and the weighted average cost of capital is 14.09%. The current FCFF is:

$$\text{FCFF} = \text{EBIT}(1 - \text{tax rate}) + \text{Depreciation} - \text{Capital Expenditures}$$
$$= \$1,388(1 - .34) + \$675 - \$800 = \$791 \text{ million}$$

Solving for the implied growth rate:

$$\text{Growth Rate} = (\text{Firm Value} \times \text{WACC} - \text{FCFF})/(\text{Firm Value} + \text{FCFF})$$
$$= (\$16,459 \times .1409 - \$791)/(\$16,459 + \$791)$$
$$= 8.86\%$$

FIGURE 12.2 WACC and Debt Ratios: Boeing

Now assume that Boeing moves to a 30% debt ratio and a WACC of 13.22%. The firm can now be valued using the following parameters:

$$\text{FCFF} = \$791 \text{ million}$$
$$\text{WACC} = 13.22\%$$
$$\text{Growth Rate in FCFF} = 8.86\%$$
$$\text{Firm Value} = \$791 \times 1.0886/(.1322 - .0886) = \$19,772 \text{ million}$$

The value of the firm will increase from \$16,459 million to \$19,772 million if the firm moves to the optimal debt ratio:

$$\text{Increase in Firm Value} = \$19,772 - \$16,459 = \$3,313 \text{ million}$$

There are 232 million shares outstanding. Assuming that stockholders can rationally evaluate the effect of this refinancing, the increase in the stock price can be calculated:

$$\text{Increase in Stock Price} = \text{Increase in Firm Value/Number of Shares Outstanding}$$
$$= \$3,313/232 = \$14.78$$

Since the current stock price is \$69.75, the stock price can be expected to increase to \$84.53, which translates into a percentage price increase of 21.19%.

Since the assumption is that the asset side of the balance sheet is kept fixed and that changes in capital structure are made by borrowing funds and repurchasing stock, this would imply that the stock price would increase to \$84.53 upon the announcement of the stock repurchase.

Illustration 12.7: Optimal capital structure for Siemens (Germany)

In July 1993, Siemens AG had 55.8 million shares outstanding, and the shares traded at a price of 649.45 DM (deutsche marks) per share. The firm had debt outstanding of 4,244 million DM, resulting in a debt ratio of 10.48% in market value terms. The beta for the stock was 0.89, and the bonds were rated AAA, leading to a cost of debt of 6.72%. The ten-year bond rate in July 1993 was 6.42% in Germany, and the risk premium for stocks over bonds is assumed to be 3.50%. The weighted average cost of capital based upon these inputs is computed as follows:

	Debt	Equity
Market value weights	10.48%	89.52%
Cost of component	6.72%(1 − .38)	6.42% + (.89 × 3.5%)
	= 4.17%	= 9.54%

$$\boxed{\text{Cost of Capital} = (4.17\% \times .1048) + (9.54\% \times .8952) = 8.97\%}$$

Siemens reported earnings before interest, taxes, and depreciation of 8,095 million DM, with the depreciation amounting to 4,613 million DM in 1992. The firm also spent 5,560 million DM on capital investments in 1992.

$$\text{FCFF in 1992} = (8,095 - 4,613)(1 - .38) + 4,613 - 5,560$$
$$= 1,212 \text{ million DM}$$

The value of the firm in July 1993 was 40,483 million DM, leading to an implied growth rate in FCFF of 5.80%:

$$\text{Value of Firm} = \text{Expected FCFF next year}/(\text{WACC} - \text{Implied g}) \, 40{,}483$$
$$= 1{,}212(1 + g)/(.0897 - g)$$

Solving for g,

$$g = 5.80\%$$

Using the same framework employed for Boeing in the previous illustration, the costs of equity and debt are computed at different levels of debt for Siemens. Appendix 2 includes the complete analysis, and the following table provides a summary of the estimated costs of equity, debt, and capital at different levels of debt for Siemens, as well as an estimate of firm value at each level of debt:

Debt Ratio	Cost of Equity	Cost of Debt	Cost of Capital	Firm Value
0%	9.32%	4.17%	9.32%	$36,435
10%	9.52%	4.17%	8.99%	40,277
20%	9.77%	4.76%	8.77%	43,236
30%	10.10%	4.91%	8.54%	46,876
40%	10.52%	5.53%	8.53%	47,106
50%	11.12%	7.08%	9.10%	38,883
60%	12.02%	7.70%	9.43%	35,369
70%	13.55%	7.75%	9.49%	34,783
80%	17.53%	9.83%	11.37%	23,026
90%	29.31%	11.79%	13.54%	16,577

The cost of capital is minimized and the value of the firm is maximized at a debt ratio of 40%. If Siemens moves from its current debt ratio to its optimal, the cost of capital can be expected to decline from 8.97% to 8.53%. The value of the firm, as a consequence, can be expected to increase from 40,483 million DM to 47,106 million DM.

$$\text{Value of Firm (at optimal)} = 1{,}212 \text{ million DM}/(.0853 - .0580)$$
$$= 47{,}106 \text{ million DM}$$
$$\text{Increase in Value of Firm} = 47{,}106 \text{ million} - 40{,}483 \text{ million}$$
$$= 6{,}623 \text{ million DM}$$
$$\text{Increase in Price per Share} = 6{,}623 \text{ million DM}/55.80 \text{ million shares}$$
$$= 118.69 \text{ DM}$$
$$\text{Expected Price per Share at firm value} = 649.45 + 118.69 = 768.14 \text{ DM}$$

CONCLUSION

This chapter develops an alternative approach to discounted cashflow valuation. The cashflows to the firm are discounted at the weighted average cost of capital to obtain the value of the firm, which when reduced by the market value of

outstanding debt yields the value of equity. Since the cashflows to the firm are cashflows prior to debt payments, this approach is more straightforward to use when there is significant leverage or when leverage changes over time, though the weighted average cost of capital, used to discount free cashflows to the firm, has to be adjusted for changes in leverage.

QUESTIONS AND SHORT PROBLEMS

1. Respond true or false to the following statements about the free cashflow to the firm:
 a. The free cashflow to the firm is always higher than the free cashflow to equity.
 b. The free cashflow to the firm is the cumulated cashflow to all investors in the firm, although the form of their claims may be different.
 c. The free cashflow to the firm is a predebt, pretax cashflow.
 d. The free cashflow to the firm is an after-debt, after-tax cashflow.
 e. The free cashflow to the firm cannot be estimated without knowing interest and principal payments, for a firm with debt.

2. Union Pacific Railroad reported net income of $770 million in 1993 after interest expenses of $320 million. (The corporate tax rate was 36%.) It reported depreciation of $960 million in that year, and capital spending was $1.2 billion. The firm also had $4 billion in debt outstanding on the books, rated AA (carrying a yield to maturity of 8%), trading at par (up from $3.8 billion at the end of 1992). The beta of the stock is 1.05, and there were 200 million shares outstanding (trading at $60 per share), with a book value of $5 billion. Union Pacific paid 40% of its earnings as dividends, and working capital requirements are negligible. (The Treasury bond rate is 7%.)
 a. Estimate the free cashflow to the firm in 1993.
 b. Estimate the value of the firm at the end of 1993.
 c. Estimate the value of equity at the end of 1993 and the value per share, using the FCFF approach.

3. Lockheed Corporation, one of the largest defense contractors in the United States, reported EBITDA of $1,290 million in 1993 prior to interest expenses of $215 million and depreciation charges of $400 million. Capital expenditures in 1993 amounted to $450 million, and working capital was 7% of revenues (which were $13,500 million). The firm had debt outstanding of $3.068 billion (in book value terms), trading at a market value of $3.2 billion, and yielding a pretax interest rate of 8%. There were 62 million shares outstanding, trading at $64 per share, and the most recent beta is 1.10. The tax rate for the firm is 40%. (The Treasury bond rate is 7%.)

 The firm expects revenues, earnings, capital expenditures, and depreciation to grow at 9.5% a year from 1994 to 1998, after which the growth rate is expected to drop to 4%. (Capital spending will offset depreciation in the steady state period.) The company also plans to lower its debt/equity ratio to 50% for the steady state (which will result in the pretax interest rate dropping to 7.5%).
 a. Estimate the value of the firm.
 b. Estimate the value of the equity in the firm and the value per share.

4. In the face of disappointing earnings results and increasingly assertive institutional stockholders, Eastman Kodak was considering a major restructuring in 1993. As part of this restructuring, it was considering the sale of its health division, which earned $560 million in earnings before interest and taxes in 1993, on revenues of $5.285 billion. The expected growth in earnings was expected to moderate to 6% between 1994 and 1998 and to 4% after that. Capital expenditures in the health division amounted to $420 million in 1993, while depreciation was $350 million. Both are expected to grow 4% a year in the long term. Working capital requirements are negligible.

The average beta of firms competing with Eastman Kodak's health division is 1.15. While Eastman Kodak has a debt ratio (D/[D + E]) of 50%, the health division can sustain a debt ratio (D/[D + E]) of only 20%, which is similar to the average debt ratio of firms competing in the health sector. At this level of debt, the health division can expect to pay 7.5% on its debt before taxes. (The tax rate is 40%, and the Treasury bond rate is 7%.)
 a. Estimate the cost of capital for the division.
 b. Estimate the value of the division.
 c. Why might an acquirer pay more than this estimated value for the division?

5. You are analyzing a valuation done on a stable firm by a well-known analyst. Based upon the expected free cashflow to firm, next year, of $30 million and an expected growth rate of 5%, the analyst has estimated a value of $750 million. However, he has made the mistake of using the book values of debt and equity in his calculation. While you do not know the book value weights he used, you know that the firm has a cost of equity of 12%, and an after-tax cost of debt of 6%. You also know that the market value of equity is three times the book value of equity, while the market value of debt is equal to the book value of debt. Estimate the correct value for the firm.

6. Santa Fe Pacific, a major rail operator with diversified operations, had earnings before interest, taxes, and depreciation of $637 million in 1993, with depreciation amounting to $235 million (offset by capital expenditure of an equivalent amount). The firm is in a steady state and is expected to grow 6% a year in perpetuity. Santa Fe Pacific had a beta of 1.25 in 1993 and debt outstanding of $1.34 billion. The stock price was $18.25 at the end of 1993, and there were 183.1 million shares outstanding. The expected ratings and the costs of debt at different levels of debt for Santa Fe are shown in the following table (the Treasury bond rate is 7%, and the firm faced a tax rate of 40%):

D/(D + E)	Rating	Cost of Debt (Pretax)
0%	AAA	6.23%
10%	AAA	6.23%
20%	A+	6.93%
30%	A−	7.43%
40%	BB	8.43%
50%	B+	8.93%
60%	B−	10.93%
70%	CCC	11.93%
80%	CCC	11.93%
90%	CC	13.43%

The earnings before interest and taxes are expected to grow 3% a year in perpetuity, with capital expenditures offset by depreciation. (The tax rate is 40%, and the Treasury bond rate is 7%.)

a. Estimate the cost of capital at the current debt ratio.

b. Estimate the costs of capital at debt ratios ranging from 0% to 90%.

c. Estimate the value of the firm at debt ratios ranging from 0% to 90%.

ENDNOTES

1. For instance, firms in the market can be classified into five or seven groups, ranging from safest to riskiest, based upon financial fundamentals. These can be substitutes for ratings.

2. This is the book value of the outstanding debt. Since the debt was recent and small relative to the equity, we assumed that the book value was close to the market value.

3. This was the beta reported in Value Line for Boeing in March 1990. It is based upon a regression of five years of weekly returns for Boeing against the NYSE Composite.

4. This apparent problem is resolved by iterating until the interest rate used in calculating the interest expense is consistent with the interest rate from the rating at that level.

APPENDIX I. Analyzing Capital Structure for Boeing

Capital Structure

Inputs for Analysis

	Financial Market		Income Statement		
Current MV of Equity =	$16,182	Current Beta for Stock =	0.95	Current EBITDA =	$2,063
Current Outstanding Debt =	$ 277	Current Bond Rating =	AA	Current Depreciation =	$ 675
Number of Shares Outstanding =	232	Current T Bill Rate =	8.33%	Current Tax Rate =	34.00%
		Current T Bond Rate =	9.00%	Current Capital Spending =	$ 800
Risk Premium =	5.50%	Current Interest Rate =	9.70%	(Use default spreads given below.)	

Results from Analysis

	Current	Optimal	Change
D/(D + E) Ratio =	1.68%	30.00%	28.32%
Beta for the Stock =	0.95	1.21	0.26
Cost of Equity =	14.23%	15.63%	1.40%
AT Interest Rate on Debt =	6.40%	7.59%	1.19%
WACC	14.09%	13.22%	−0.88%
Implied Growth Rate =	8.86%	$19,772	$3,313
Market Value of Firm =	$16,459		
Market Price per share =	$ 69.75	$ 84.03	$ 14.28

We use the following default spreads in our analysis. Change them if necessary:

			Operating Income		
Rating	Spread	% Lower	Operating Income	Optimal D/(D + E)	
AAA	0.30%	−5%	$1,960	30.00%	
AA	0.70%	−10%	$1,857	20.00%	
A+	1.00%	−15%	$1,754	20.00%	
A	1.25%	−20%	$1,650	20.00%	

(continued)

APPENDIX I. (continued)

Rating	Spread		Operating Income		
			% Lower	Operating Income	Optimal D/(D+E)
A–	1.50%		–25%	$1,547	20.00%
BBB	2.00%		–30%	$1,444	20.00%
BB	2.50%		–40%	$1,238	10.00%
B+	3.00%		–50%	$1,032	10.00%
B	4.00%				
B–	5.00%				
CCC	6.00%				
CC	7.50%				
C	9.00%				
D	12.00%				

Current beta =	0.95	Current Equity =	$16,182
Current Debt =	$277	Current EBITDA =	$ 2,063
Tax rate =	34.00%	Current Rating =	AA

Current Depreciation =	$675
Current Interest rate (Company) =	9.70%
Current T Bond rate =	9.00%
Six-month T Bill rate =	8.33%

Worksheet for Estimating Ratings/Interest Rates

D/(D+E)	0.00%	10.00%	20.00%	30.00%	40.00%	50.00%	60.00%	70.00%	80.00%	90.00%
D/E	0.00%	11.11%	25.00%	42.86%	66.67%	100.00%	150.00%	233.33%	400.00%	900.00%
$ Debt	$0	$1,646	$3,292	$4,938	$6,584	$8,230	$9,875	$11,521	$13,167	$14,813
Beta	0.94	1.01	1.09	1.21	1.35	1.56	1.94	2.63	3.95	7.90
Cost of Equity	14.17%	14.55%	15.02%	15.63%	16.44%	17.58%	19.67%	23.48%	30.72%	52.44%
Operating Inc.	$2,063	$2,063	$2,063	$2,063	$2,063	$2,063	$2,063	$2,063	$2,063	$2,063
Depreciation	$675	$675	$675	$675	$675	$675	$675	$675	$675	$675
Interest	$0	$160	$346	$568	$922	$1,234	$1,629	$2,074	$2,370	$2,666
Taxable Income	$1,388	$1,228	$1,042	$820	$466	$154	($241)	($686)	($982)	($1,278)
Tax	$472	$418	$354	$279	$159	$52	($82)	($233)	($334)	($435)
Net Income	$916	$811	$688	$541	$308	$101	($159)	($453)	($648)	($844)

(+)Deprec'n	$675	$675	$675	$675	$675	$675	$675	$675	$675	$675
Funds from Op.	$1,591	$1,486	$1,363	$1,216	$983	$776	$516	$222	$27	($169)
Pre-tax Int. cov	8	8.69	4.02	2.44	1.51	1.12	0.85	0.67	0.59	0.52
Funds Int. Cov	8	9.31	3.94	2.14	1.07	0.63	0.32	0.11	0.01	–0.06
Funds/Debt	8	0.90	0.41	0.25	0.15	0.09	0.05	0.02	0.00	–0.01
Likely Rating	AA	AA	A–	BB	B–	CCC	CC	C	C	C
Interest Rate	9.70%	9.70%	10.50%	11.50%	14.00%	15.00%	16.50%	18.00%	18.00%	18.00%
Eff. Tax Rate	34.00%	34.00%	34.00%	34.00%	34.00%	34.00%	28.96%	22.76%	19.91%	17.70%

Worksheet for Calculating Weighted Average Cost of Capital

D/(D+E)	0.00%	10.00%	20.00%	30.00%	40.00%	50.00%	60.00%	70.00%	80.00%	90.00%
D/E	0.00%	11.11%	25.00%	42.86%	66.67%	100.00%	150.00%	233.33%	400.00%	900.00%
$ Debt	$0	$1,646	$3,292	$4,938	$6,584	$8,230	$9,875	$11,521	$13,167	$14,813
Cost of equity	14.17%	14.55%	15.02%	15.63%	16.44%	17.58%	19.67%	23.48%	30.72%	52.44%
Cost of debt	6.40%	6.40%	6.93%	7.59%	9.24%	9.90%	11.72%	13.90%	14.42%	14.81%
WACC	14.17%	13.73%	13.40%	13.22%	13.56%	13.74%	14.90%	16.78%	17.68%	18.58%
Firm Value	$16,232	$17,683	$18,968	$19,772	$18,327	$17,657	$14,257	$10,880	$9,769	$8,864

APPENDIX 2. Analyzing Capital Structure for Siemens

Inputs for Analysis

Capital Structure

Current MV of Equity =	DM36,239
Current Outstanding Debt =	DM4,244
Number of Shares Outstanding =	55.8
Risk Premium =	3.50%

Financial Market

Current Beta for Stock =	0.89
Current Bond Rating =	AAA
Current T Bill Rate =	5.80%
Current T Bond Rate =	6.42%
Current Interest Rate =	6.72%

Income Statement

Current EBITDA =	DM8,095
Current Depreciation =	DM4,613
Current Tax Rate =	38.00%
Current Capital Spending =	DM5,560
(Use default spreads given below.)	

Results from Analysis

	Current	Optimal	Change
D/(D + E) Ratio =	10.48%	40.00%	29.52%
Beta for the Stock =	0.89	1.17	0.28
Cost of Equity =	9.54%	10.52%	0.99%
AT Interest Rate on Debt =	4.17%	5.53%	1.36%
WACC	8.97%	8.53%	-0.45%
Implied Growth Rate =	5.80%		
Market Value of Firm =	DM40,483	DM47,106	DM6,623
Market Price per share =	DM649.44	DM768.14	DM118.70

We use the following default spreads in our analysis. Change them if necessary:

		Operating Income		
Rating	Spread	% Lower	Operating Income	Optimal D/(D + E)
AAA	0.30%	-5%	DM7,690	30.00%
AA	0.70%	-10%	DM7,286	20.00%
A+	1.00%	-15%	DM6,881	20.00%
A	1.25%	-20%	DM6,476	20.00%
A-	1.50%	-25%	DM6,071	20.00%
BBB	2.00%	-30%	DM5,667	20.00%

BB	2.50%		−40%	DM4,857	10.00%
B+	3.00%		−50%	DM4,048	10.00%
B	4.00%				
B−	5.00%				
CCC	6.00%				
CC	7.50%				
C	9.00%				
D	12.00%				

Current beta = 0.89
Current Debt = DM4,244
Tax rate = 38.00%

Current Equity = DM36,239
Current EBITDA = DM8,095
Current Rating = AAA

Current Depreciation = DM4,613
Current Interest rate (Company) = 6.72%
Current T Bond rate = 6.42%
Six-month T Bill rate = 5.80%

Worksheet for Estimating Ratings/Interest Rates

D/(D+E)	0.00%	10.00%	20.00%	30.00%	40.00%	50.00%	60.00%	70.00%	80.00%	90.00%
D/E	0.00%	11.11%	25.00%	42.86%	66.67%	100.00%	150.00%	233.33%	400.00%	900.00%
$ Debt	DM0	DM4,048	DM8,097	DM12,145	DM16,193	DM20,242	DM24,290	DM28,338	DM32,386	DM36,435
Beta	0.83	0.89	0.96	1.05	1.17	1.34	1.60	2.04	3.17	6.35
Cost of Equity	9.32%	9.52%	9.77%	10.10%	10.52%	11.12%	12.02%	13.55%	17.53%	28.64%
Operating Inc.	DM8,095	DM8,095	DM8,095	DM8,095	DM8,095	DM8,095	DM8,095	DM8,095	DM8,095	DM8,095
Depreciation	DM4,613	DM4,613	DM4,613	DM4,613	DM4,613	DM4,613	DM4,613	DM4,613	DM4,613	DM4,613
Interest	DM0	DM272	DM601	DM962	DM1,444	DM2,109	DM3,017	DM3,520	DM4,508	DM5,072
Taxable Income	DM3,482	DM3,210	DM2,881	DM2,520	DM2,038	DM1,373	DM465	(DM38)	(DM1,026)	(DM1,590)
Tax	DM1,323	DM1,220	DM1,095	DM958	DM774	DM522	DM177	(DM14)	(DM390)	(DM604)
Net Income	DM2,159	DM1,990	DM1,786	DM1,562	DM1,263	DM851	DM288	(DM23)	(DM636)	(DM986)
(+)Deprec'n	DM4,613	DM4,613	DM4,613	DM4,613	DM4,613	DM4,613	DM4,613	DM4,613	DM4,613	DM4,613
Funds from Op.	DM6,772	DM6,603	DM6,399	DM6,175	DM5,876	DM5,464	DM4,901	DM4,590	DM3,977	DM3,627
Pre-tax Int. cov	∞	12.80	5.80	3.62	2.41	1.65	1.15	0.99	0.77	0.69
Funds Int. Cov	∞	24.27	10.65	6.42	4.07	2.59	1.62	1.30	0.88	0.72
Funds/Debt	∞	1.63	0.79	0.51	0.36	0.27	0.20	0.16	0.12	0.10

(continued)

APPENDIX 2. (continued)

					Inputs for Analysis					
Likely Rating	AAA	AAA	A+	A−	BB	B	CCC	CCC	CC	CC
Interest Rate	6.72%	6.72%	7.42%	7.92%	8.92%	10.42%	12.42%	12.42%	13.92%	13.92%
Eff. Tax Rate	38.00%	38.00%	38.00%	38.00%	38.00%	38.00%	38.00%	37.59%	29.35%	26.09%

Worksheet for Calculating Weighted Average Cost of Capital

D/(D+E)	0.00%	10.00%	20.00%	30.00%	40.00%	50.00%	60.00%	70.00%	80.00%	90.00%
D/E	0.00%	11.11%	25.00%	42.86%	66.67%	100.00%	150.00%	233.33%	400.00%	900.00%
$ Debt	DM0	DM4,048	DM8,097	DM12,145	DM16,193	DM20,242	DM24,290	DM28,338	DM32,386	DM36,435
Cost of equity	9.32%	9.52%	9.77%	10.10%	10.52%	11.12%	12.02%	13.55%	17.53%	28.64%
Cost of debt	4.17%	4.17%	4.60%	4.91%	5.53%	6.46%	7.70%	7.75%	9.83%	10.29%
WACC	9.32%	8.99%	8.74%	8.54%	8.53%	8.79%	9.43%	9.49%	11.37%	12.12%
Firm Value	DM36,434	DM40,277	DM43,693	DM46,877	DM47,106	DM42,917	DM35,368	DM34,781	DM23,024	DM20,291

13

Special Cases in Discounted Cashflow Valuation

The standard discounted cashflow valuation (DCF) models have to be modified in special cases—for cyclical firms, for troubled firms, for firms with special product options, and for private firms. This chapter examines the problems associated with valuing these firms and suggests possible solutions.

CYCLICAL FIRMS

The earnings of cyclical firms are, by definition, volatile and depend upon the state of the economy. In economic booms, the earnings of these firms are likely to be inflated, while in recessions the earnings will be depressed. There are two basic issues that have to be addressed in applying DCF valuation to these firms: One relates to dealing with the cyclicality of earnings in the base year, and the second relates to incorporating the effects of earnings volatility on value.

Base-Year Earnings

In most DCF valuation, the current year is used as the base year and growth rates are used to project future earnings and cashflows. Depending upon at what stage of the economic cycle a valuation is done, the current year's earnings may be too low (if it is a recession) or too high (if the economy is at a peak) to use as a base year. The failure to adjust the base year's earnings for cyclical effects can lead to significant errors in valuation, since these effects are likely to dissipate as the economic cycle changes.

Illustration 13.1: Valuing a cyclical firm during a recession, using current earnings: Chesapeake Corp.

Chesapeake Corp., which makes recycled commercial and industrial tissue, is a cyclical firm in the paper products industry. It had a beta of 1.00 in 1992. The Treasury bond rate was 7% at the time of this analysis, and the risk premium of 5.5% for stocks over

bonds is used. It had earnings per share in 1992 of $0.63, down from $2.51 in 1988. If the current earnings per share is used as the base year's earnings, Chesapeake Corp. will be valued significantly below its true value, unless the growth rates are adjusted accordingly.

Current Earnings per share = $0.63

Current Depreciation per share = $2.93

Current Capital Expenditures per share = $3.63

Debt Ratio for financing capital expenditures = 45%

Long-term growth rate in earnings = 6%

Cost of Equity = 7% + (1 × 5.5%) = 12.5%

Free Cashflows to Equity in 1992 = $.63 + (1 − .45)($2.93 − $3.63)

 = $.245

Value per share = $.245 × 1.06/(.125 − .06) = $4.00

Chesapeake Corp. was trading at $20 per share in May 1993.

The problem can be accentuated if the firm has losses in the current year as a consequence of an economic downturn. There are three possible solutions to this problem; the first is useful when earnings are depressed but not negative, and the other two can be used for firms with negative earnings.

A. *Adjust the expected growth rate to reflect the economic cycle.* The simplest solution is to adjust the expected growth rate, especially in the near years, to reflect expected changes in the economic cycle. This would imply using a higher growth rate in the near years if current earnings are depressed (but not negative) because of an economic recession and if the economy is expected to recover. The strategy would be reversed if the current earnings are inflated because of an economic boom and if the economy is expected to slow down. The disadvantage of this approach is that it ties the accuracy of the estimate of value for a cyclical firm to the precision of the macroeconomic predictions of the analyst doing the valuation. The criticism, though, may not be avoidable since there is no way a cyclical firm can be valued without making assumptions about future economic growth.

The actual growth rate in earnings in "turning-point" years (years when the economy goes into or comes out of a recession) can be estimated by looking at the experience of this or similar firms in prior recessions.

Illustration 13.2: Valuing a cyclical firm, adjusting growth rates in near years: Chesapeake Corp.

Assume that the economy is expected to recover slowly in 1993 and much faster in 1994. As a consequence, the growth rates in earnings projected for Chesapeake Corp. (from the previous example) are as follows:

Year	Expected Growth Rate	Earnings per Share
1993	5%	$0.66
1994	100%	1.32
1995	50%	1.98
After 1996	6%	

Required Rate of Return on Equity = 7% + (1 × 5.5%) = 12.5%

The capital expenditures and depreciation are expected to grow at 6%. The free cashflows to equity can be estimated as follows:

	1993	1994	1995	1996
Earnings per share	$0.66	$1.32	$1.98	$2.10
−(Cap. Ex. − Deprecn.)(1 − ∂)	.42	.44	.47	.50
= FCFE	$0.24	$0.88	$1.51	$1.60

Terminal Price in 1995 = $1.60/(.125 − .06) = $24.62

Present Value per Share = $.24/1.125 + $.88/1.125^2

\qquad + ($1.51 + $24.62)/1.125^3 = $19.26

B. Use normalized (average) earnings for base-year earnings. The "adjusted growth rate" approach to valuation is not likely to provide a solution for those cyclical firms that have negative earnings as a consequence of a recession. One solution is to use an average earnings per share over a time period long enough to span an economic cycle as the earnings in the base year. This average earnings per share is considered "normalized" because it takes into account the cyclicality.

The implicit assumption in the use of normalized earnings as base-year earnings is that cyclical firms will revert quickly back to this level when the economic cycle turns, either from recession to recovery or from recovery to recession. If the firm's fundamentals have changed, this may be an unrealistic assumption that can lead to errors in valuation.

Ways of normalizing income: There is no right way of normalizing income, since what comprises a normal income is likely to vary from case to case. There are, however, some broad guidelines that can be used in income normalization.

(a) If earnings are depressed purely because of the economic cycle and are expected to rebound once the economy recovers: In this case, the standard approach is to average income over a period long enough to include an economic recovery and a recession. In some cases, the average dollar income is computed as the normal income, which may be inappropriate if either there is inflation or the size of the firm has changed significantly from the period over which income was averaged.

A variant on this approach that allows for scaling to size is to calculate the average return on equity or return on assets over the period. This return on

equity is applied to the current book value of equity to arrive at a standardized net income. Alternatively, the return on assets is applied to the current book value of assets to arrive at a standardized after-tax operating income.

Example: Daimler Benz reported earnings per share of $-\$3.03$ per share in 1993, in the midst of the recession. The following are estimated normalized earnings per share using both the average income and average return on assets approaches:

- Average Income Approach: Using EPS from 1988 to 1992 = $1.34
- Average Return on Assets Approach:

Average ROA from 1988 to 1992 = 7.00%

Total BV of Debt + BV of Equity = $20,000 million

Normalized EBIT$(1 - t)$ = $20,000 \times .07 = $1,400 million

Normalized Net Income = EBIT $(1 - t)$ − Interest Expense$)(1 - t)$

$\qquad\qquad$ = $1,400 − 900(1 - .38)$ = $842 million

Normalized EPS = $842/477.50 = $1.76

(There are 477.50 million shares outstanding.)

(b) If the earnings are depressed for firm-specific as well as cyclical reasons and/or the firm has changed significantly, by selling or adding assets, from the past: In this case, the past might not provide a reasonable basis for estimating normalized income. Instead, the analyst can estimate normalized income by estimating the average return on equity or assets earned by comparable firms in similar businesses and applying this average to the book value of the equity or the assets of the firm being valued to arrive at normalized earnings.

Example: General Motors reported a loss in 1992, due to both the recession and other firm-specific reasons. The following are estimated normalized earnings per share using the return on equity approach:

Average ROE for other automobile firms = 11.50%

Book Value of Equity per share for GM = $22.50

Normalized EPS = $22.50 \times .1150 = $2.58 million

(c) If the firm is rated, and the ratings agency has significantly more information to make a judgment of the firm's earning capacity: In this case, the rating assigned to the firm can be used as a basis for estimating operating income and normalized income. The linkage between operating income and the rating is made through the pretax interest coverage ratio, which is assumed to be known for all ratings classes. The procedure would take the following steps:

Step 1: Find the rating for the company.

Step 2: Find the median interest coverage ratio of all firms in that ratings class.

Step 3: Estimate the rating-based operating income for the company being analyzed:

Normalized Operating Income (EBIT) = Current Interest Expense

$\qquad\qquad\qquad\qquad\qquad\qquad\qquad\qquad$ × Interest Coverage Ratio

Step 4: Convert the pretax operating income into an after-tax operating income, if valuing the firm, or into a net income, by subtracting out interest expenses and calculating estimated taxes, if valuing the equity:

After-Tax Operating Income = Normalized EBIT(1 − tax rate)

Normalized net income = (Normalized EBIT − Interest Expense)

$\qquad\qquad\qquad\qquad\qquad$ × (1 − tax rate)

Example of a troubled firm, with negative earnings, no direct comparables, but a bond rating: Digital Equipment had negative earnings per share of $4.00 in 1993 and was assigned a bond rating of BBB by the ratings agencies. It had total interest expenses of $75 million in 1993.

Typical interest coverage ratio for BBB-rated company = 3.03

Normalized EBIT for Digital = 3.03 × $75 million = $226 million

Normalized Net Income = ($226 million − $75 million)(1 − .36)

$\qquad\qquad\qquad\qquad\qquad$ = $97 million

Normalized EPS = Normalized Net Income/No. of Shares

$\qquad\qquad\qquad\qquad$ = $97 million/135 million = $0.72

Whatever the approach used to normalize income, it is not necessary to normalize the other items in the analysis (depreciation, capital expenditures) unless they are skewed by the same factors that skew net income.

Illustration 13.3: Valuing a cyclical firm with normalized earnings per share: Ford

Ford Motor Company reported a deficit of $1.46 per share in 1992, largely as a consequence of the recession. It had capital expenditures of $10.40 per share and depreciation of $10.81 per share in 1992.

Normalized income: The average earnings per share over the period 1988–1992 was $3.14, which is used as a measure of normalized earnings.

Estimated growth: The projected growth rate in normalized earnings over the next five years is 21.23%, and it is expected to be 6% after that. Capital expenditures, depreciation, and revenues are expected to grow at 10% over the next five years and at 6% after that. The working capital is expected to be maintained at 40% of revenues.

Beta: The beta, which is currently 1.20, is expected to decline to 1.10 in the stable-growth period. The T Bond rate is 7%.

Financing mix: Ford plans to use a mix of equal parts debt and equity in financing its net capital expenditures and working capital needs.

Projected cashflows to equity: The projected free cashflows to equity for the next five years are as follows:

	1993	1994	1995	1996	1997
Earnings	$3.81	$4.61	$5.59	$6.78	$8.22
$-$(Cap. Exp. $-$ Depr.)$(1 - \partial)$	$-.23$	$-.25$	$-.27$	$-.30$	$-.33$
$-\triangle$ Working Capital$(1 - \partial)$	4.09	4.50	4.95	5.44	5.98
= FCFE	$-$ $.05	$.37	$.92	$1.64	$2.57
Present Value @ 13.60%	$-$ $.05	$.28	$.63	$.99	$1.36

Cost of Equity in the first five years = 7% + (1.2 × 5.5%) = 13.60%

Cost of Equity in the stable-growth period = 7% + (1.1 × 5.5%) = 13.05%

The free cashflows to equity in 1998 are expected to be $4.77, based upon the assumption that capital spending will offset depreciation:

$$FCFE_6 = EPS_6 - (Revenue_6 - Revenue_5)$$
$$\times \text{ (Working Capital as a percentage of revenue)}(1 - \partial)$$
$$= \$8.22 \times 1.06 - \$3.95 = \$4.77$$

This leads to a terminal value in 1997 of:

Terminal Price = $4.77/(.1305 $-$.06) = $67.66

The value per share can be written as the present value of the expected free cashflows to equity and the terminal value, discounted back at 13.60%.

Present Value of FCFE in the high-growth phase = $3.21

Present Value of Terminal Price = $35.76

Value per share = $38.97

Ford Motor Company was trading at $50 per share in May 1993.

Illustration 13.4: Valuation using normalized earnings per share: Volvo

The recession that depressed earnings at Ford in 1992 also affected automobile manufacturers in Europe and Japan. Volvo (Sweden) reported a loss of 31.60 Swedish kroners (SK) per share in 1992, though it continued to pay a dividend per share of 7.75 SK. The firm had depreciation per share of 25.31 SK and capital expenditures per share of 35.70 SK in 1992, and it finances its net capital expenditure with an equal mix of debt and equity. The average earnings per share between 1987 and 1991 was 33.92 SK, which is assumed to be a reasonable estimate of normalized earnings.

The beta of the stock, measured relative to the Swedish stock index (SWSMAFFR), is 1.27. The ten-year bond rate in July 1993 was 7.84% in Sweden, and the risk premium for stocks over bonds is assumed to be 4.50%.

The firm is expected to maintain an average growth rate in normalized earnings of 8.42% a year for the next five years, after which the growth rate is expected to decline to 5%. Based upon the normalized earnings, the expected free cashflows to equity for the high-growth period are as follows (in SK):

	1	2	3	4	5
Earnings	36.78	39.87	43.23	46.87	50.82
$-(\text{Cap. Ex.} - \text{Depr.})(1 - \partial)$	5.50	5.84	6.19	6.56	6.95
$-\partial \text{ Working Capital}(1 - \partial)$.91	.96	1.02	1.08	1.15
$= \text{FCFE}$	30.36	33.07	36.02	39.23	42.72
Present Value	26.74	25.65	24.60	23.59	22.62

The price at the end of the high-growth phase, based upon the assumption that the beta will decrease to 1.1 and capital expenditures offset depreciation for the stable-growth phase, is as follows:

$$\text{Terminal Price} = \text{FCFE}_6/(\text{Cost of Equity}_{stable} - \text{Stable Growth Rate})$$
$$= 52.34 \text{ SK}/(.1279 - .05) = 671.92 \text{ SK}$$

The present value of the expected free cashflows to equity in the high-growth phase and the terminal price are:

> Present Value of FCFE in the high-growth phase = 123.21 SK
>
> Present Value of Terminal Price = 355.87
>
> Value per share = 479.08 SK

The stock was trading at 448 SK per share in July 1993.

C. Estimate detailed cashflows during the transition period. Since the cyclicality in earnings is much greater than the cyclicality in revenues, the other solution is to estimate detailed cashflows, starting with revenues, for the transitional period from cyclical downturn to stability. Thus, a cyclical firm with negative earnings currently can expect to see its revenues increase more rapidly than its costs as the economy comes out of a recession, resulting in higher earnings and cashflows in the future.

Here again, the results of the valuation are tied to how good the underlying forecasts about the economy are. Analysts who are more optimistic about economic growth are likely to arrive at higher estimates of value for cyclical firms.

Illustration 13.5: Valuing a cyclical firm, using detailed cashflows: Ford

Ford Motor Company can also be valued using detailed projections of cashflows. The economy was expected to recover in 1993 and 1994, and the revenues were expected to grow faster in those years. Assume that revenues, which were $100,132 million in 1992, are expected to grow 10% in 1993 and 8% in 1994, 6% for the following three years, and 5% after that. The cost of goods sold (COGS) is expected to be 86% of revenues in 1993 (as in 1992), after which it is expected to be 85% of revenues. The working capital, which was $76,955 million in 1992, is expected to be 50% of additional revenues. In 1992, capital spending was $5,236 million and depreciation was $5,000 million, and both are expected to grow at 6% between 1993 and 1997. The equity

beta for Ford in 1992 was 1.20 while the cost of debt was 8.50%, and the market values of debt and equity were $100,000 million and $24,500 million. The following is the cost of capital for Ford Motor Company:

Cost of Equity = 13.60%

Equity/(Debt + Equity) = 19.68%

After-Tax Cost of Debt = 5.44%

Debt/(Debt + Equity) = 80.32%

Cost of Capital = 7.05%

The following are the projected free cashflows to the firm (in millions) between 1993 and 1997:

	1993	1994	1995	1996	1997
Revenues	$110,145	$118,957	$126,094	$133,660	$141,679
− COGS	94,725	101,113	107,180	113,611	120,428
− Depreciation	5,300	5,618	5,955	6,312	6,691
= EBIT	10,120	12,226	12,959	13,737	14,561
− EBIT(t)	3,643	4,401	4,665	4,945	5,242
= EBIT(1 − t)	6,477	7,824	8,294	8,791	9,319
+ Depreciation	5,300	5,618	5,955	6,312	6,691
− Capital Expenditures	5,550	5,883	6,236	6,610	7,007
− △ Working Capital	5,007	4,406	3,569	3,783	4,010
= FCFF	$ 1,220	$ 3,153	$ 4,444	$ 4,711	$ 4,993
Present Value	$ 1,140	$ 2,752	$ 3,623	$ 3,588	$ 3,553

The free cashflows to the firm in 1998 are expected to be $6,243 million. The cost of capital is projected to be 9.09%, as the debt ratio declines to 50%. This leads to a terminal value of:

Terminal Value of firm = $6,243/(.0909 − .06) = $152,824 million

The present value of the expected free cashflows to the firm and the terminal value (in millions) are as follows:

Present Value of FCFF in the high-growth phase = $14,654.95

Present Value of Terminal Value of Firm = $108,728.68

Value of the Firm = $123,383.64

Market Value of Debt = $100,000.00

Market Value of Equity = $23,383.64

Value of Equity per share = $23,383/490 = $47.72

Earnings Volatility

The other issue in valuing cyclical firms is how best to deal with earnings volatility. One way is to build expectations of future recessions and recoveries into the cashflows. This exercise is fraught with danger, since the error in such predictions is likely to be very large. The other way to incorporate earnings variability into the valuation is through the discount rate—cyclical firms tend to be more risky and require higher discount rates. Finally, a range of values can be obtained from a variety of scenarios, ranging from optimistic to pessimistic, for use in analysis.

FIRMS IN FINANCIAL DISTRESS

A firm in financial distress has some or all of the following characteristics: negative earnings and cashflows, an inability to meet debt payments, no dividends, and a high debt/equity ratio. This makes it difficult to apply discounted cashflow models to these firms. The solution to the problem depends, in large part, on how distressed the firm really is. If the distress is not expected to be fatal (in the sense of pushing the firm into liquidation), there are a variety of potential solutions. If, on the other hand, the distress is likely to be terminal, finding a solution is much more difficult.

If there is light at the end of the tunnel

A. Value the Firm rather than Equity

Firms that are distressed often are so because they have too much debt. By valuing the firm based upon the free cashflows to the firm, which is before debt payments, analysts can avoid some of the problems that they face when they have to value the equity directly, with negative free cashflows to equity and changing leverage.

Illustration 13.6: Valuing the firm rather than equity: American Airlines

American Airlines, in common with other airlines, had a bad year in 1992, losing $279 million in that year. The firm had earnings before interest and taxes of $300 million in 1992 and interest expenses of $540 million. An upturn in airline traffic and recent acquisitions is expected to create growth of 15% between 1993 and 1997 in earnings before interest and taxes, after which the growth is expected to decline to 6%. Capital expenditures, which amounted to $1,250 million in 1992, and depreciation, which was $1,041 million in 1992, were both expected to grow 6% a year starting in 1993. American Airlines had total debt of $8,283 million (with a market value of $8,000 million) and a market value of equity of $4,425 million in 1992. The cost of capital is as follows:

Cost of Equity = 14.43%

Equity/(Debt + Equity) = 35.61%

After-Tax Cost of Debt = 5.76%

Debt/(Debt + Equity) = 64.39%

Cost of Capital = 8.85%

The following are the projected free cashflows to the firm between 1993 and 1997:

	1993	1994	1995	1996	1997
EBIT(1 − t)	$257.60	$296.24	$340.68	$391.78	$450.54
−(Cap. Ex. − Depr.)	115.54	122.47	129.82	137.61	145.87
− △ Working Capital	0.00	0.00	0.00	0.00	0.00
= FCFF	$142.06	$173.77	$210.86	$254.17	$304.68
Present Value	$130.51	$146.67	$163.51	$181.08	$199.42

The expected free cashflows to the firm in 1998 are $477.58 million (assuming capital expenditures offset depreciation), and the cost or capital is projected to be 8.81%. The terminal value of the firm is:

Terminal Value of Firm = $477.58/(.0881 − .06) = $16,996 million

The present value of expected free cashflows to the firm and the terminal value (in millions), discounted at the cost of capital of 8.85%, are:

Present Value of FCFF in the high-growth phase = $821.20

Present Value of Terminal Value of Firm = $11,124.38

Value of the Firm = $11,945.58

Market Value of Outstanding Debt = $8,000.00

Market Value of Equity = $3,945.58

Market Value of Equity per Share = $52.61

The price per share in May 1993 was $59.

B. Use Normalized or Average Earnings

This approach, which is similar to that used for cyclical firms, uses an average earnings based upon a period where the earnings were healthier as the base-year earnings for analysis. The assumption is that the firm will revert back to health in the near future.

Illustration 13.7: Using normalized earnings for a troubled firm: American Airlines

American Airlines, which reported a loss of $3.72 per share in 1992, had average earnings per share between 1987 and 1991 of $2.84 (which is used as normalized earnings). The expected growth rate in normalized earnings is 15%. In 1992, the capital expenditure per share was $13.20 and the depreciation per share was $12.00, and both are expected to grow at 6% over time, and will be financed 50% with debt. The beta

for the stock was 1.35 (leading to a cost of equity of 14.43%), but it is expected to decline to 1.10 for the stable phase. The projected free cashflows to equity per share between 1993 and 1997 are as follows:

	1993	1994	1995	1996	1997
Earnings	$3.26	$3.75	$4.31	$4.96	$5.70
$-$(Cap. Ex. $-$ Depr.)$(1 - \partial)$.64	.67	.71	.76	.80
$-\triangle$ Working Capital$(1 - \partial)$	0	0	0	0	0
= FCFE	$2.63	$3.08	$3.60	$4.20	$4.90
Present Value	$2.29	$2.35	$2.40	$2.45	$2.50

The expected free cashflows to equity in 1998 are expected to be $6.05 (assuming capital expenditures offset depreciation), leading to a terminal value per share of:

Terminal Value = $6.05/(.1305 − .06) = $85.77

The present value of expected free cashflows to equity and the terminal value are:

Present Value of FCFE in the high-growth phase = $12.00

Present Value of Terminal Price = $43.72

Value of the Stock = $55.72

The stock was trading at $59 per share in May 1993.

C. Estimate Detailed Cashflows for Transition Period

The transition period for a distressed firm is the period over which it makes the shift from distress to financial health. If this transition period can be identified and detailed assumptions can be made about cashflows during this period, discounted cashflow valuation may still be feasible. The accuracy of the value obtained from the analysis is clearly linked to assumptions made about the probability of the transition from distress to health, the length of the transition period, and projections during the transition period.

Illustration 13.8: Using detailed cashflows for transition period: IBM

IBM reported earnings before interest and taxes in 1992, of $2.7 billion and had interest expenses of $2.5 billion. It had $29.32 billion of debt outstanding (with a market value of $27.5 billion) and 570 million shares outstanding, trading at $50 per share in May 1993. The cost of goods sold, not including depreciation, amounted to 88% of revenues in 1992, but it is expected to decline to 85% of revenues by 1997 and continue at that level. (Until the mid-1980s, the COGS as a percentage of revenues was generally below 80% at IBM.) The revenue in 1992 was $63 billion and is expected to grow 6% a year for the next five years and 5% a year after that. The working capital in 1992 was $2.3 billion but is expected to stay at 5% of revenues in the future. The capital

expenditure were expected to be $6 billion and depreciation was expected to be $6.625 billion in 1992. Both items are expected to grow 3% a year over the next five years, but are expected to offset each other after that. IBM had, and is expected to have, a beta of 0.95 and paid 8.50%, before tax, on its debt. The cost of capital for IBM is as follows:

Cost of Equity = 12.23%

Equity/(Debt + Equity) = 50.39%

After-Tax Cost of Debt = 5.44%

Debt/(Debt + Equity) = 49.61%

Cost of Capital = 8.86%

The projected free cashflows to the firm over the next five years (in millions) are as follows:

	1993	1994	1995	1996	1997
Revenues	$66,780.00	$70,786.80	$75,034.01	$79,536.05	$84,308.21
− COGS	58,766.40	61,584.52	64,529.25	67,605.64	71,661.98
− Depreciation	6,823.75	7,028.46	7,239.32	7,456.50	7,680.19
= EBIT	1,189.85	2,173.82	3,265.44	4,473.91	4,966.04
− EBIT(t)	428.35	782.58	1,175,56	1,610.61	1,787.77
= EBIT(1 − t)	761.50	1,391.25	2,089.88	2,863.30	3,178.27
+ Depreciation	6,823.75	7,028.46	7,239.32	7,456.50	7,680.19
− Capital Expenditures	6,180.00	6,365.40	6,556.36	6,753.05	6,955.64
− △ Working Capital	189.00	200.34	212.36	225.10	238.61
= FCFF	$ 1,216.25	$ 1,853.97	$ 2,560.48	$ 3,341.64	$ 3,664.20
Present Value	$ 1,117.28	$ 1,564.50	$ 1,984.86	$ 2,379.61	$ 2,396.96

The free cashflows to the firm in 1998 (the terminal year), assuming capital expenditures offset depreciation, are expected to be $3,126 million, and the cost of the capital is expected to be 8.70%. Coupled with the expected growth rate of 5%, this yields a terminal value of:

Terminal Value = $3,126/(.087 − .05) = $84,496 million

The present value of the expected free cashflows to the firm and the terminal value (in millions) are as follows:

Present Value of FCFF in the high-growth phase = $9,443.21

Present Value of Terminal Value of Firm = $55,273.77

Value of Firm = $64,716.99

Market Value of Debt = $27,500.00

Market Value of Equity = $37,216.99

Market Value of Equity per Share = $65.29

IBM was trading at $50 per share in May 1993.

This undervaluation of IBM is predicated on the assumption that the cost of goods sold can be reduced from 88% of revenues to 85% of revenues. To illustrate the

sensitivity of the valuation to this assumption, the COGS was kept at 87% after 1994. The comparable values (in millions) and the value per share for IBM are then:

Present Value of FCFF in the high-growth phase = $7,640.05

Present Value of Terminal Value of Firm = $35,240.94

Value of Firm = $42,880.99

Market Value of Debt = $27,500.00

Market Value of Equity = $15,380.99

Market Value of Equity per Share = $26.98

If there is no light at the end of the tunnel

Discounted cashflow valuation is conditioned on a "going concern" concept, with cashflows continuing into the future. As a consequence, other approaches may need to be used to value a firm where the distress is severe enough to be terminal. Two possible approaches that can be used to value these firms are discussed below.

A. Liquidation Value

The liquidation value of a firm is the aggregate of the value that the assets of the firm would command on the market, net of transactions and legal costs. The value of equity can be obtained by subtracting the value of the outstanding debt from the asset value.

Value of Equity = Liquidation Value of Assets − Outstanding Debt

Estimating liquidation value is complicated when the assets of the firm are not easily separated and thus cannot be valued individually. Furthermore, the likelihood that assets will fetch their fair market value will decrease as the urgency of the liquidation increases. A firm in a hurry to liquidate its assets may have to accept a discount on fair market value as a price for speedy execution.

B. Option Pricing Models

The liquidation value approach presumes that the market value of the assets currently exceeds the face value of outstanding debt. When this assumption is violated, the only approach left to value the equity in a distressed firm may be to use option pricing models. Equity in a heavily levered firm, where the value of the assets is lower than the face value of the debt, can be viewed as an out-of-the money call option on the underlying firm and can be valued as such.

FIRMS WITH PRODUCT OPTIONS

Discounted cashflow models estimate value on the basis of expected cashflows from assets. Some assets, which are valuable but are not producing cashflows currently and are not expected to do so in the near future, may not be valued fully in DCF models. One example of such an asset is a product option, that is, a patent or copyright on a product which may not be viable currently but will be valuable in the future.

DCF Valuation of Firms with Product Options

The value of a firm generally comes from two sources—assets in place and expected future growth opportunities. The value of the former is generally captured in current cashflows, while the value of the latter is reflected in the expected growth rate. In the case of product options, this is sometimes difficult to do, because the options may not be expected to pay off until well beyond the estimation period. If they are ignored, the value from the DCF model will be lower than the true value.

Illustration 13.9: DCF valuation of a firm with product options: Pfizer

Pfizer Inc. had earnings per share of $3.25 in 1992. The earnings had grown at 9.76% a year over the previous five years. The firm also paid dividends per share of $1.48 in 1992. While this growth rate was disappointing by pharmaceutical industry standards, Pfizer spent $4.8 billion on research and development and had a host of promising products—some of which are starting to produce cashflows (Procardia, Diflucan, and Cardura) and some of which are expected to produce significant cashflows in the future (Zithromax, Zoloft, and Norvasc).

 If Pfizer is valued based entirely on the basis of past growth and fundamentals, the DCF value is modest. The expected growth rate in the high-growth phase (expected to last from 1993 to 1997) is as follows:

Input	Estimate	Weight
Historical growth rate (1987–1992)	9.76%	50%
Growth rate from fundamentals	12.63%	50%
Weighted average growth rate	11.16%	

The expected growth rate after year 5 is 6%. In conjunction with the fundamentals, this yields a payout ratio of 68.02% after year 5 and a terminal value per share of $56.50. The present value of expected dividends per share during the high-growth phase and the terminal price are:

> Present Value of Dividends in the high-growth phase = $7.04
>
> Present Value of Terminal Price = $30.60
>
> Value of the Stock = $37.64

This value per share was significantly below the market price per share of $68 in May 1993. It can be argued that this is because the valuation, by focusing on current fundamentals and past growth, ignores the potential growth implicit in the product options that Pfizer owns.

Solutions

There are three possible solutions to the problems associated with valuing firms with product options:

(a) Value the product options on the open market and add them on to the value from DCF valuation; if there is an active market trading in product options, this offers a viable and simple way of valuing these options. In the absence of such a market, or when the product options are not separable and tradable, this approach becomes difficult to apply.

(b) Use a higher growth rate than the one justified by existing projects and assets, to capture the additional value from product options While this keeps the analysis within the traditional DCF valuation framework, the increase in the growth rate is essentially subjective, and it converts contingent cashflows (i.e., the product option will be exercised if and only if it makes economic sense) to expected cashflows.

(c) Use an option pricing model to value product options and add on the value to that obtained from DCF valuation. The advantage of this approach is that it mirrors the cashflow profile of a product option much more precisely by using contingent claim valuation. The problems with using any option pricing model, where the underlying asset is not traded, are well documented.

Caveats

The primary problem in valuing firms with product options is not that the options are ignored but that they are often double-counted. Analysts, all too frequently, use a higher growth rate to reflect the product options that a firm owns but then add on a premium to the DCF value for the same product options. It is this reasoning that was used to justify a stock price of $68 for Pfizer in 1993, when the growth rate projected from fundamentals would have justified a price of only $37.

Illustration 13.10: Double-counting product options: Pfizer

The valuation of Pfizer can be made more realistic by bringing in the effects of product options. Analysts forecast growth of 18.5% over the next five years, largely as a consequence of the promising products that Pfizer has in the pipeline. If this higher growth rate is used to value Pfizer, instead of the historical and fundamental growth rates, the value per share would be:

Present Value of Dividends in the high-growth phase = $8.54

Present Value of Terminal Price = $50.45

Value of the Stock = $50.00

Even with the higher growth rate, Pfizer's value is below its market price ($68). The difference cannot be justified on the basis of product options, since the expected growth rate reflects these product options already.

PRIVATE FIRMS

The basic discounted cashflow models for valuation should apply for any firm, whether public or private. Some of the critical inputs to the model, however, are easier to obtain for a publicly traded firm than for a private firm. This section examines some of the problems associated with valuing private firms and suggests solutions.

The Problems in Valuing Private Firms

The problems associated with valuing private firms can be classified under two categories.

Estimating Discount Rates

Models of risk and return used in estimating discount rates, including the capital asset pricing model and the arbitrage pricing model, use parameters estimated from past prices and/or returns. These traditional estimation procedures cannot be used for firms that are not traded or have been traded for only a short time period.

Estimating Cashflows

The estimation of both current cashflows and expected future growth rates is much more difficult to do for private firms than for publicly traded firms. In calculating current cashflows, for instance, it is often difficult, in private firms, to draw a distinction between management compensation and return on capital, since owners often also operate as managers. Thus, an owner-manager, who draws a low salary while owning the firm, may demand and deserve a much higher remuneration packet when the firm becomes public. The absence of the strict informational requirements that apply to publicly traded firms also makes the financial statements of private firms less reliable.

In estimating future growth for publicly traded firms, analysts have a rich information set—a long history of earnings and projections of future growth from other analysts. For private firms, there is substantially less information available. Past history is often unreliable, and there are few or no "outside" projections of growth rates. Consequently, estimates of future growth are likely to have much more error associated with them for private firms.

The Solutions

The problems associated with valuing private firms are not insurmountable. Some solutions are suggested below.

For Estimating Discount Rates

While traditional estimation procedures cannot be used to estimate betas, betas can still be estimated using one of three approaches.

(a) Comparable Firms. The betas of comparable firms can be used to estimate the beta of a nontraded or private firm. Given the determinants of betas, a comparable firm is one that is in the same business and has similar operating and financial leverage. The differences in betas, caused by differences in financial leverage, can be controlled for in this calculation.

Illustration 13.11: Using comparable firms to estimate betas

Assume that you have been asked to estimate the beta for American Casinos, a private firm that operates gaming facilities. American Casinos has outstanding debt with a book value of $50 million and equity with a book value of $100 million. The betas for public firms involved in gaming entertainment are as follows:

Firm	Beta	Debt/Equity
Aztar Corporation	1.35	66.73%
Bally Manufacturing	1.60	349.87%
Caesar's World	1.35	29.75%
Circus Circus	1.35	11.17%
International Game Technology	1.25	3.54%
Jackpot Enterprises	1.00	31.02%
Mirage Resorts	1.40	81.60%
Showboat Inc.	1.10	90.54%
Average	1.30	83.03%

Unlevered Beta for casino firms $= 1.30/(1 + .8303 [1 - .36]) = .85$

If the assumption is that American Casinos will operate at

- A market value debt ratio close to the industry average, the beta is 1.30.
- A market value debt ratio close to its current book value debt ratio, the appropriate beta is:

 Levered Beta $= .85(1 + .50[1 - .36]) = 1.12$

- Any other debt ratio, the beta can be estimated using the desired market value debt/equity ratio.

(b) Accounting Betas. An accounting beta is estimated from earnings rather than returns. The procedure followed is similar, and the periodic earnings of the firm are regressed against the aggregate earnings of the market to obtain a beta.

Illustration 13.12: Estimating an accounting beta

Assume that American Casinos has been in existence for ten years. The income that the firm has made in each of these ten years is available from income statements. The

percentage changes in aggregate earnings of all publicly traded firms are also available for the same period. The following table summarizes the data:

Year	American Casinos Earnings	Percentage Change	Percentage Change in Aggregate Market Earnings
1983	$11.00		
1984	18.50	68.18%	16.00%
1985	18.10	−2.16%	−12.00%
1986	18.30	1.10%	−1.00%
1987	22.80	24.59%	18.00%
1988	35.10	53.95%	30.00%
1989	37.50	6.84%	15.00%
1990	42.50	13.33%	10.00%
1991	42.00	−1.18%	−10.00%
1992	37.20	−11.43%	−15.00%

A regression of the percentage change in earnings for American Casinos against aggregate earnings yields the following (t statistics are in brackets):

$$\partial \text{ Earnings}_{\text{American Casinos}} = .0924 + 1,3734 \ \partial \text{ Earnings}_{\text{Market}}$$
$$(1.47) \quad (3.48)$$

The accounting beta from earnings is 1.37.

The primary problems with this approach are that earnings are measured much less frequently than returns (leading to fewer observations) and that they are subject to accounting measurement errors.

(c) *Using Financial Fundamentals.* In this approach, the betas of publicly traded firms are regressed against financial fundamentals, such as earnings variability, dividend payout, and leverage, and the relationship between betas and these variables is used to predict betas for private firms.

Illustration 13.13: Estimating betas from financial fundamentals

The following is an updated regression relating betas in 1991 to five variables: dividend yield, covariance in operating income, size, debt/equity ratio, and growth in earnings:

Beta = .9832 + .08 CV in Operating Income − .126 Dividend Yield
 + .15 Debt/Equity Ratio + .034 Growth in Earnings per Share
 − .00001 Total Assets

The values of each of these variables for American Casinos are as follows:

CV in Operating Income = 2.04

Dividend Yield = 3% (based upon the assumption that the free cashflows to
equity are paid out as dividends)

Debt/Equity Ratio = .5

Growth in Earnings = 10.29%

Total Assets = $300 million

Substituting into the regression, the beta for American Casinos can be written as follows:

$$\text{Beta} = .9832 + (.08 \times 2.04) - (.126 \times 3) + (.15 \times .5) + (.034 \times 10.29)$$
$$- (.00001 \times 300)$$
$$= 1.19$$

Alternative approaches to estimating betas offer estimates of varying precision, depending upon the circumstances. When there are a larger number of comparable firms, the first approach provides a fairly good estimate of beta. The quality of betas estimated from financial fundamentals is largely a function of the quality of the inputs and fit of the regression. The more general lesson is that betas can be estimated for nontraded assets and firms.

For Estimating Cashflows

There are no simple solutions to the problems associated with estimating the cashflows for a private firm. There are some precautions that can and should be taken:

(a) Any expenses associated with management salary or perquisites have to be scrutinized to see if they are, in fact, compensation for management services and not return on capital.

(b) If a private company is being taken public, the tax laws may change, and the effects of these changes on cashflows will have to be considered.

(c) A private firm may also face additional expenses in certain categories once it becomes a publicly traded firm. For instance, legal and recordkeeping costs will probably go up for a public firm. These increases in expenses will have to be considered in projecting future cashflows.

(d) The noise associated with past growth rates and the absence of estimates from other analysts add more weight to the growth rate obtained from fundamentals, for private firms.

Illustration 13.14: Valuing a private firm about to go public

Assume that American Casinos has current earnings of $37.2 million, and these earnings are expected to grow 15% a year over the next five years and 6% a year after that. The firm has capital expenditures of $15 million and depreciation of $8 million currently, and both items are expected to grow at 8% over the next five years. After year 5, the capital expenditures and depreciation are expected to grow 6% a year. The beta is expected to be 1.19 in the first five years and 1.10 after that. The projected free cashflows to equity over the next five years are as follows:

	1	2	3	4	5
Earnings	$42.78	$49.20	$56.58	$65.06	$74.82
$-(\text{Cap. Ex.} - \text{Depr.})(1 - \partial)$	5.04	5.44	5.88	6.35	6.86
$-\triangle \text{Working Capital}(1 - \partial)$	0	0	0	0	0
$= \text{FCFE}$	$37.74	$43.75	$50.70	$58.71	$67.97
Present Value	$33.22	$33.90	$34.58	$35.26	$35.93

The free cashflows to equity in year 6 are expected to be $72.04 million, leading to a terminal value of $1,021.89 million. The present value of the expected free cashflows to equity and the terminal value can be written as follows:

> Present Value of FCFE in the high-growth phase = $172.89
>
> Present Value of Terminal Price = $540.15
>
> Value of the Equity = $713.04

The value of the equity in American Casinos, based upon these expected cashflows, is $713.04 million. The price per share will depend upon the number of shares that the company decides to create.

The Special Problems Associated with "Privatizations"

Many of the issues raised in the previous section about valuing private firms are also issues in "privatizations," where government companies are valued and sold to the public or investors in the private sector. There are no past prices, the historical data is suspect, and the projection of future cashflows is difficult. The same solutions will apply as well. Measures of risk can be obtained by looking at firms in the same or similar lines of business, and cashflows can be estimated, albeit with error. The problems are accentuated, however, if

(a) *The firm being privatized is losing money.* The solutions suggested for troubled firms, including valuing the firm rather than equity and estimating detailed cashflows, may provide a way out.

(b) *The firm has operated in a noncompetitive environment historically but will be expected to operate in a competitive environment once it is privatized.* Historical results will mean very little in this case, since revenues and earnings will be overstated because of the absence of competition. Forecasts of revenues and cashflows will have to be based entirely upon the perceived quality of the products that the firm makes and their ability to command a market in the presence of competitors.

The standard critique of using discounted cashflow models to value "privatizations" is that there is too much uncertainty about the inputs for the value to have much meaning. This criticism is misdirected. The uncertainty is not caused by the model but is inherent in the firm being valued. No valuation

model will be free of it, though some approaches, such as multiples, evade the problem and create the illusion of accuracy.

Illustration 13.15: Valuing a privatization: Bancomer

Bancomer was one of Mexico's largest retail-oriented banks in 1991, when the Mexican government made the decision to privatize it, following the successful privatizations of other nationalized banks. The following table summarizes the results of these privatizations, in billions of pesos (MP):

Bank	Date of Sale	Price of Sale	Forecasted Earnings	PE Ratio
Mercantil	June 1991	611.20	62.20	12.73
Banpais	June 1991	544.99	30.70	17.73
Cremi	June 1991	748.29	51.30	21.87
Confia	August 1991	892.26	83.90	13.52
Banorie	August 1991	223.22	14.30	23.65
Bancreser	August 1991	425.13	8.40	50.48
Banamex	August 1991	9,744.98	1,233.00	11.18

Bancomer had net income of 634 billion pesos in 1990 and paid dividends of 116 billion pesos. The return on equity was 20% and is expected to remain high for the next ten years, as Bancomer takes advantage of the expected growth in income and demand for banking services. After that, the growth rate is expected to be 12% a year in the long term.

The average beta of financial service firms traded on the Mexican stock exchange was 0.90, and Bancomer was expected to have a similar beta. The ten-year bond rate was 12%, and the risk premium for stocks over bonds was expected to be 7.5%.

Required Rate of Return on Equity $= 12\% + 0.9(7.5\%) = 18.75\%$

Expected Growth Rate in Earnings for the next ten years $=$ Retention Ratio
$$\times \text{ ROE}$$
$$= .817 \times 20\%$$
$$= 16.34\%$$

Expected Payout Ratio in steady state (after year 10) $= 1 - g/\text{ROE}$
$$= 1 - 12\%/20\% = 40\%$$

The market value of equity can then be computed, using the two-stage dividend discount model:

$$P_0 = \frac{634 \text{ MP} \times .183 \times 1.1634 \left(1 - \dfrac{1.1634^{10}}{1.1875^{10}}\right)}{.1875 - .1634}$$
$$+ \frac{634 \text{ MP} \times 1.1634^{10} \times 1.12 \times .40}{(.1875 - .12) \times 1.1875^{10}} = 3{,}429 \text{ billion MP}$$

This works out to a price/earnings multiple of 7.04. A higher multiple can be justified only if the expected growth rate is higher than 16.34%.

In Summary

Valuing private firms clearly has its problems, but none of them are insurmountable. The paucity of reliable past information and of analyses by other analysts does create more estimation error in discounted cashflow valuation, but this error is likely to exist no matter which approach is used in valuation. We will return to this issue in Chapter 23.

CONCLUSION

There are many cases where traditional DCF valuation has to be modified or adapted to provide reasonable estimates of value. Some of these cases are presented in this chapter. Cyclical firms can be difficult to value because their earnings track the economy. A failure to adjust the earnings for these cyclical ups and downs can lead to significant undervaluation of these firms at the depth of a recession and significant overvaluation at the peak of a recovery. Troubled firms pose similar problems, but they are accentuated when earnings, cashflow, and book value all turn negative and there is little or no chance of the firm recovering. The primary problem in valuing private firms is the absence of information, especially market information, which is so readily available for publicly traded firms. In all these cases, DCF valuation is flexible enough to be used to estimate value.

QUESTIONS AND SHORT PROBLEMS

1. Intermet Corporation, the largest independent iron foundry organization in the country, reported a deficit per share of $0.15 in 1993. The earnings per share from 1984 to 1992 were as follows:

Year	EPS
1984	$0.69
1985	$0.71
1986	$0.90
1987	$1.00
1988	$0.76
1989	$0.68
1990	$0.09
1991	$0.16
1992	⟨$0.07⟩

The firm had capital expenditures of $1.60 per share, and depreciation per share of $1.20 in 1993. Working capital was expected to increase $0.10 per share in 1994. The stock has a beta of 1.2, which is expected to remain unchanged, and finances its capital expenditure and working capital requirements with 40% debt (D/[D + E]). The firm is expected, in the long term, to grow at the same rate as the economy (6%).

 a. Estimate the normalized earnings per share in 1994, using the average earnings approach.

 b. Estimate the normalized free cashflow to equity per share in 1994, using the average earnings approach.

2. General Motors Corporation reported a deficit per share in 1993 of $4.85, following losses in the two previous years. (The average earnings per share is negative.) The company had assets with a book value of $25 billion and spent almost $7 billion on capital expenditures in 1993, which was partially offset by a depreciation charge of $6 billion. The firm had $19 billion in debt outstanding, on which it paid interest expenses of $1.4 billion. It intends to maintain a debt ratio (D/[D + E]) of 50%. The working capital requirements of the firm are negligible, and the stock has a beta of 1.10. In the last normal period of operations for the firm between 1986 and 1989, the firm earned an average return on assets of 12%. (Return on Assets = Earnings before Interest and Taxes [1 − tax rate]/Total Assets; The tax rate was 40%.) The Treasury bond rate is 7%.

 Once earnings are normalized, GM expects them to grow 5% a year forever and capital expenditures and depreciation to keep track.

 a. Estimate the value per share for GM, assuming earnings are normalized instantaneously.

 b. How would your valuation be affected if GM were not going to reach its normalized earnings until 1995 (in two years)?

3. Toro Corporation, which manufactures lawn mowers and tractors, had revenues of $635 million in 1992, on which it reported a loss of $7 million (largely as a consequence of the recession). It had interest expenses of $17 million in 1992, and its bonds were rated BBB. (A typical BBB rated company had an interest coverage ratio (EBIT/Interest Expenses) of 3.10.) The company faced a 40% tax rate. The stock had a beta of 1.10. (The Treasury bond rate is 7%.)

 Toro spent $25 million on capital expenditures in 1992 and had depreciation of $20 million. Working capital amounted to 25% of sales. The company expects to maintain a debt ratio of 25%. In the long term, growth in revenues and profits is expected to be 4%, once earnings return to normal levels.

 a. Assuming that the bond rating reflects normalized earnings, estimate the normalized earnings for Toro Corporation.

 b. Allowing for the long-term growth rate on normalized earnings, estimate the value of equity for Toro Corporation.

4. Kollmorgen Corporation, a diversified technology company, reported sales of $194.9 million in 1992 and had a net loss of $1.9 million in that year. Its net income had traced a fairly volatile course over the previous five years:

Year	Net Income
1987	$ 0.3 million
1988	$11.5 million
1989	−$ 2.4 million
1990	$ 7.2 million
1991	−$ 4.6 million

The stock had a beta of 1.20, and the normalized net income is expected to increase 6% a year until 1996, after which the growth rate is expected to stabilize at 5% a year. (The beta will drop to 1.00.) The depreciation amounted to $8 million in 1992, and capital spending amounted to $10 million in that year. Both items are expected to grow 5% a year in the long term. The firm expects to maintain a debt ratio of 35%. (The Treasury bond rate is 7%.)

 a. Assuming that the average earnings from 1987 to 1992 represent the normalized earnings, estimate the normalized earnings and free cashflow to equity.
 b. Estimate the value per share.

5. OHM Corporation, an environmental service provider, had revenues of $209 million in 1992 and reported losses of $3.1 million. It had earnings before interest and taxes of $12.5 million in 1992 and debt outstanding of $104 million (in market value terms). There are 15.9 million shares outstanding, trading at $11 per share. The pretax interest rate on debt owed by the firm is 8.5%, and the stock has a beta of 1.15. The firm's EBIT is expected to increase 10% a year from 1993 to 1996, after which the growth rate is expected to drop to 4% in the long term. Capital expenditures will be offset by depreciation, and working capital needs are negligible. (The corporate tax rate is 40%, and the Treasury bond rate is 7%.)
 a. Estimate the cost of capital for OHM.
 b. Estimate the value of the firm.
 c. Estimate the value of equity (both total and on a per share basis).

6. You have been asked by the owner of a small firm that produces and sells computer software to come up with an estimate of value for the firm. The firm had revenues of $20 million in the most recent year, on which it made earnings before interest and taxes of $2 million. The firm had debt outstanding of $10 million, on which pretax interest expenses amounted to $1 million. The book value of equity is $10 million. The average beta of publicly traded firms that are in the same business is 1.30, and the average debt/equity ratio is 0.2 (based upon the market value of equity). The market value of equity of these firms is, on average, three times the book value of equity. All firms face a 40% tax rate. Capital expenditures amounted to $1 million in the most recent year and were twice the depreciation charge in that year. Both items are expected to grow at the same rate as revenues for the next five years and to offset each other in steady state.

 The revenues of this firm are expected to grow 20% a year for the next five years and 5% after that. Net income is expected to increase 25% a year for the next five years and 8% after that. (The Treasury bond rate is 7%.)
 a. Estimate the cost of equity for this private firm.
 b. Estimate the cost of capital for this private firm.
 c. Estimate the value of the owner's stake in this private firm, using both the firm approach and the equity approach.

Price/Earnings Multiples

T the price/earnings (PE) multiple or ratio is the most widely used and misused of all multiples. Its simplicity makes it an attractive choice in applications ranging from pricing initial public offerings to making judgments on relative value, but its relationship to a firm's financial fundamentals is often ignored, leading to significant errors in applications. This chapter will try to provide some insight into the determinants of price/earnings ratios.

THE USE AND MISUSE OF PE RATIOS

There are a number of reasons the price/earnings ratio is used so widely in valuation. First, it is an intuitively appealing statistic that relates the price paid to current earnings. Second, it is simple to compute for most stocks and is widely available, making comparisons across stocks simple. Third, it can be a proxy for a number of other characteristics of the firm including risk and growth.

While there are good reasons for using PE ratios, there is wide potential for misuse. One reason given for using PE ratios is that it eliminates the need to make assumptions about risk, growth, and payout ratios, all of which have to be estimated for discounted cashflow valuation. This is disingenuous, because PE ratios are ultimately determined by the very same parameters that determine value in discounted cashflow models. Thus, the use of PE ratios is a way, for some analysts, to avoid having to be explicit about their assumptions on risk, growth, and payout ratios. This may be convenient, but it is certainly not a legitimate reason for using PE ratios. Another reason for using the PE ratios of comparable firms is that they are much more likely to reflect market moods and perceptions. Thus, if investors are upbeat about retail stocks, the PE ratios of these stocks will be higher to reflect this optimism. Again, this can be viewed as a weakness, especially when markets make systematic errors in valuing entire sectors. In the example just used, if investors have overvalued retail stocks, on average, using the average PE ratio of these stocks will build that error into the valuation.

ESTIMATING PE RATIOS FROM FUNDAMENTALS

The price/earnings ratio can be related to the same fundamentals that determine value in discounted cashflow models—expected growth rates, payout ratios, and risk.

PE Ratio for a Stable Firm

A stable firm is a firm growing at a rate comparable to the nominal growth rate in the economy in which it operates. The value of equity for a stable firm, using the Gordon growth model described in Chapter 10, is:

$$P_0 = \frac{DPS_1}{r - g_n}$$

where P_0 = value of equity
DPS_1 = expected dividends per share next year
r = required rate of return on equity
g_n = growth rate in dividends (forever)

Since

$$DPS_1 = EPS_0(\text{Payout Ratio})(1 + g_n)$$

the value of the equity can be written as:

$$P_0 = \frac{EPS_0(\text{Payout Ratio})(1 + g_n)}{r - g_n}$$

Rearranging to yield the PE ratio:

$$\frac{P_0}{EPS_0} = PE = \frac{\text{Payout Ratio}(1 + g_n)}{r - g_n}$$

If the PE ratio is stated in terms of expected earnings in the next time period, this can be simplified to:

$$\frac{P_0}{EPS_1} = PE_1 = \frac{\text{Payout Ratio}}{r - g_n}$$

The PE ratio is an increasing function of the payout ratio and the growth rate, and a decreasing function of the riskiness of the firm.

Table 14.1 provides approximate PE ratios for stable firms for a range of discount rates and growth rates.

Illustration 14.1: Estimating the PE ratio for a stable firm: Deutsche Bank

Deutsche Bank AG had earnings per share of 46.38 DM in 1994 and paid out 16.50 DM as dividends per share that year. The growth rate in earnings and dividends, in the long term, is expected to be 6%. The beta for Deutsche Bank is 0.92, and the long-term bond rate in Germany is 7.50%. (The premium used for German stocks is 4.5%.)

TABLE 14.1 PE Ratios for Stable Firms

Multiply the firm's payout ratio by the following number

Discount Rate	Expected Growth Rate								
	0.00%	1.00%	2.00%	3.00%	4.00%	5.00%	6.00%	7.00%	8.00%
12%	8.33	9.18	10.20	11.44	13.00	15.00	17.67	21.40	27.00
13%	7.69	8.42	9.27	10.30	11.56	13.13	15.14	17.83	21.60
14%	7.14	7.77	8.50	9.36	10.40	11.67	13.25	15.29	18.00
15%	6.67	7.21	7.85	8.58	9.45	10.50	11.78	13.38	15.43
16%	6.25	6.73	7.29	7.92	8.67	9.55	10.60	11.89	13.50
17%	5.88	6.31	6.80	7.36	8.00	8.75	9.64	10.70	12.00
18%	5.56	5.94	6.38	6.87	7.43	8.08	8.83	9.73	10.80
19%	5.26	5.61	6.00	6.44	6.93	7.50	8.15	8.92	9.82
20%	5.00	5.32	5.67	6.06	6.50	7.00	7.57	8.23	9.00

Current Dividend Payout Ratio = 16.50/46.38 = 35.58%

Cost of Equity = 7.50% + (.92 × 4.5%) = 11.64%

PE Ratio based on fundamentals = .3558 × 1.06/(.1164 − .06) = 6.69

Deutsche Bank was selling at a PE ratio of 13.50 at the time of this analysis.

It could be argued that the low PE ratio of Deutsche Bank is more a consequence of Deutsche Bank not paying out what it can afford to as dividends. If this is the source of the problem, the dividend payout ratio can be replaced with the FCFE as a proportion of the earnings of the firm. The following analysis illustrates this point.

Illustration 14.2: Estimating the PE ratio for a stable firm using FCFE: Siemens

Siemens AG had earnings per share of 32.76 DM and paid dividends per share of 13 DM in 1994. The beta for the stock was 0.93. The ten-year bond rate in Germany was 7.5%, and the risk premium for stocks over bonds is assumed to be 4.5%. The company had FCFE in 1994 of 20 DM per share.

FCFE Payout Ratio = 20 DM/32.76 DM = 61.05%

Dividend Payout Ratio = 39.68%

Expected Growth Rate in Earnings and Dividends in the long term = 6%

Cost of Equity = 7.50% (+ .93 × 4.5%) = 11.69%

PE Ratio based on fundamentals = .6105 × 1.06/(.1169 − .06) = 11.37

Siemens was selling at a price/earnings multiple of 16.68. In this illustration, the low dividends cannot be blamed for the low valuation.

PE Ratio for a High-Growth Firm

The price/earnings ratio for a high-growth firm can also be related to fundamentals. In the special case of the two-stage dividend discount model, this relationship can be made explicit fairly simply. When the growth rate and payout ratios are known, the dividend discount model can be written as follows:

$$P_0 = \frac{EPS_0(Payout\ Ratio)(1 + g)\left(1 - \dfrac{(1 + g)^n}{(1 + r)^n}\right)}{r_n - g} + \frac{EPS_0(Payout\ Ratio_n)(1 + g)^n(1 + g_n)}{(r - g_n)(1 + r)^n}$$

where EPS_0 = earnings per share in year 0 (current year)

g = growth rate in the first n years

r = required rate of return on equity in the first n years

Payout Ratio = payout ratio in the first n years

g_n = growth rate after n years, forever (stable growth rate)

$Payout\ Ratio_n$ = payout ratio after n years, forever (stable growth rate)

r_n = required rate of return on equity after n years

Rearranging to yield the PE ratio:

$$\frac{P_0}{EPS_0} = PE = \frac{Payout\ Ratio(1 + g)\left(1 - \dfrac{1 + g)^n}{(1 + r)^n}\right)}{r - g} + \frac{Payout\ Ratio_n(1 + g)^n(1 + g_n)}{(r_n - g_n)(1 + r)^n}$$

The price/earnings ratio is determined by:

(a) *Payout ratio during the high-growth and stable periods:* The PE ratio increases as the payout ratio increases.

(b) *Riskiness (through the discount rate r):* The PE ratio becomes lower as riskiness increases.

(c) *Expected growth rate in earnings, in both the high-growth and stable periods:* The PE ratio increases as the growth rate increases, in either period.

This formula is general enough to be applied to any firm, even one that is not paying dividends right now. In fact, the ratio of free cashflows to equity to earnings can be substituted for the payout ratio for firms that pay significantly less in dividends than they can afford to.

Illustration 14.3: Estimating the PE ratio for a high-growth firm using the two-stage model

Assume that you have been asked to estimate the PE ratio for a firm that has the following characteristics:

Growth rate in first 5 years = 25%

Growth rate after 5 years = 8%

Beta $= 1.0$

Payout ratio in first 5 years $= 20\%$

Payout ratio after 5 years $= 50\%$

Riskfree rate $=$ Treasury bond rate $= 6\%$

Required rate of return $= 6\% + (1 \times 5.5\%) = 11.5\%$

$$PE = \frac{.2 \times 1.25 \times \left(1 - \dfrac{1.25^5}{1.115^5}\right)}{(.115 - .25)} + \frac{.5 \times 1.25^5 \times 1.08}{(.115 - .08) \times 1.115^5} = 28.75$$

The estimated PE ratio for this firm is 28.75.

Illustration 14.4: Estimating the PE ratio: Nike

The following is an estimation of the appropriate PE ratio for Nike in March 1995. It is assumed to have five years of high growth left, after which the firm is expected to be in steady state.

High-growth period:

Expected Return on Equity $= 18\%$ (This is slightly lower than the ROE in 1994 of 19.5%.)

Expected Payout Ratio $= 20\%$ (This is the current payout ratio.)

> Growth Rate in the high-growth period $=$ ROE$(1 - $ Payout Ratio$)$
> $= .18(1 - .2) = 14.4\%$

The beta of Nike currently is 1.45, and the Treasury bond rate is 7.5%, yielding a cost of equity of:

Cost of Equity $= 7.5\% + (1.45 \times 5.5\%) = 15.48\%$

Stable-growth period:

Expected Growth Rate $= 6\%$

Expected Return on Equity $= 15.00\%$

> Expected Payout Ratio in the stable-growth period $= 1 - 6\%/15\% = 60\%$

Cost of Equity $= 7.5\% + (1.1 \times 5.5\%) = 13.55\%$

The price/earnings ratio can be estimated based upon these inputs:

$$PE = \frac{.20 \times 1.144 \times \left(1 - \dfrac{1.144^5}{1.1548^5}\right)}{.1548 - .144} + \frac{.60 \times 1.44^5 \times 1.06}{1.1548^5(.1355 - .06)} = 9.01$$

Nike was trading at a price/earnings ratio of 14 in March 1995.

PE Ratios and Expected Extraordinary Growth

The PE ratio of a high-growth firm is a function of the expected extraordinary growth rate; the higher the expected growth, the higher the PE ratio for the firm. In Illustration 14.3, for instance, the PE ratio can be graphed as a function of the extraordinary growth rate. As the firm's anticipated extraordinary growth rate in the first five years declines from 25% to 8%, the PE ratio for the firm also decreases from 28.75 to 15.

Investment Strategies that Compare PE to the Expected Growth Rate

Portfolio managers and analysts sometimes compare PE ratios to the expected growth rate to identify undervalued and overvalued stocks. In the simplest form of this approach, firms with PE ratios less than their expected growth rate are viewed as undervalued. In its more general form, the ratio of PE ratio to growth is used as a measure of relative value, with lower values believed to indicate undervaluation relative to other firms. Peters (1991) provides a simple test of this proposition by classifying firms into deciles based upon the ratio of PE ratio to expected long-term growth, for every quarter from January 1982 to June 1989. The lowest PE/growth decile outperformed the market in 26 out of the 30 quarters for which returns were measured and earned significantly higher returns than the Standard and Poors 500. The compounded return over the period was 1,536% for the lowest PE/growth decile, while the return on the S&P 500 index over the same period was 356%.

In its simple form, there is no basis for believing that a firm is undervalued just because it has a PE ratio less than its expected growth rate. This relationship may be consistent with a fairly valued or even an overvalued firm, if interest rates are high or if a firm is of high risk. The following example expands on

FIGURE 14.1 PE Ratios and Extraordinary Growth

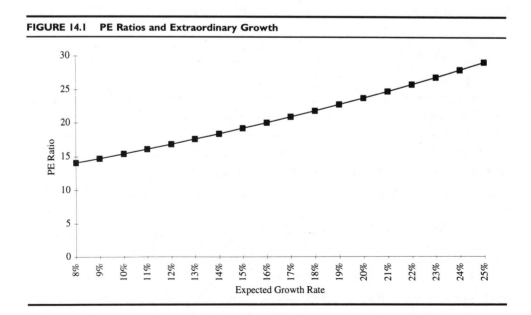

the firm described in Illustration 14.3, where under the initial assumptions about interest rates and risk, the firm had a PE ratio of 28.75, which was greater than the expected growth rate. It evaluates the PE ratio as a function of the level of interest rates and of risk, as measured by betas.

Illustration 14.5: PE Ratio versus growth: The effect of interest rates and risk

In Illustration 14.3, the Treasury bond rate used is 6%. The effects of increasing the Treasury bond rate on PE ratios is examined in Figure 14.2. As illustrated in the graph, the PE ratio for this firm is lower than the expected growth rate when the Treasury bond rate is greater than 7%, though it is not undervalued. For instance, the PE ratio will drop to 11.96 if the Treasury bond rate increases to 10%, well below the expected growth rate of 25% in the first five years but still correctly valued.

A similar analysis can be done relating the PE ratio to the beta of the firm. In Illustration 14.3, the PE ratio will decline as the beta is increased, and this relationship is summarized in Figure 14.3. In this graph, as well, the PE ratio for the firm will be lower than the expected growth rate if the beta of the firm exceeds 1.10, even though it is not undervalued.

The danger of concluding that a firm is undervalued just because its PE ratio is less than its expected growth rate is that it may be the wrong conclusion for high-risk (high-beta) firms or when interest rates are high.

In its relative form, where firms are ranked on the basis of the ratio of PE

FIGURE 14.2 PE Ratios and Treasury Bond Rates

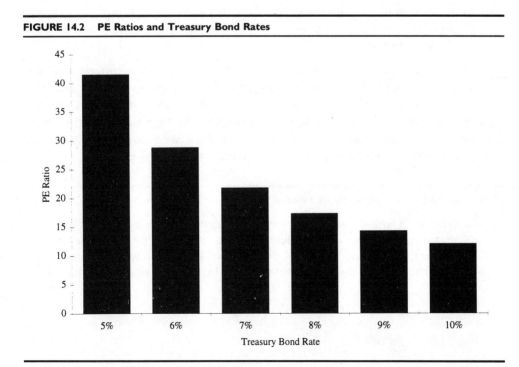

FIGURE 14.3 PE Ratios and Betas

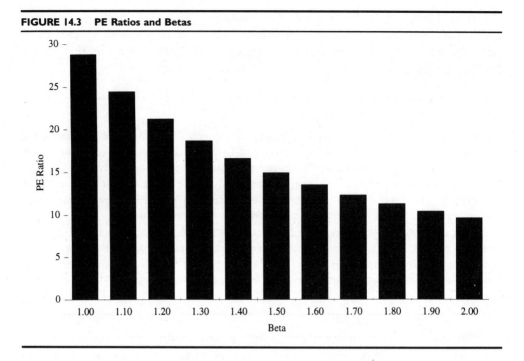

ratio to expected growth, the rankings will provide a measure of relative value, if:

(a) The length of the high-growth period is the same for all firms.
(b) All firms are of equivalent risk. If the model used is the CAPM, all firms have the same betas.

If these assumptions are not fulfilled, however, a direct comparison of the ratio of PE to expected growth may not be justified because a higher-risk firm should be expected to have a lower PE ratio than another firm with the same expected growth rate but much less risk. Similarly, the PE ratio for a firm where high growth is expected to last five years will be lower than the PE ratio for a firm where the same high growth is expected to last ten years.

Illustration 14.6: Comparing the PE ratios of firms with different risk levels

Consider two firms with the same expected growth rates of 25% for the first five years and 8% after that, the same payout policies (payout ratio in the first five years of 20%; 50% thereafter), but different levels of risk (beta of 1.0 for the first firm and 1.5 for the second). The PE ratio for the riskier firm will be lower than the PE ratio for the safer firm.

The PE ratio of the safer firm is:

$$PE = \frac{.2 \times 1.25 \times \left(1 - \dfrac{1.25^5}{1.115^5}\right)}{.115 - .25} + \frac{.5 \times 1.25^5 \times 1.08}{1.115^5(.115 - .08)} = 28.75$$

FIGURE 14.4 PE Ratios and Expected Growth: High-Risk vs. Low-Risk

The PE ratio of the riskier firm is:

$$PE = \frac{.2 \times 1.25 \times \left(1 - \dfrac{1.25^5}{1.1425^5}\right)}{.1425 - .25} + \frac{.5 \times 1.25^5 \times 1.08}{1.1425^5(.1425 - .08)} = 14.87$$

The PE ratio of the safer firm will be higher than the PE ratio of the riskier firm at every level of growth, as illustrated in Figure 14.4.

COMPARISONS OF PE RATIOS

Price/earnings ratios are often compared across countries, across companies, and across time. While these comparisons can yield valuable information, they often fail to control for changes in the fundamentals that affect these multiples.

Comparisons across Countries

Comparisons are often made between PE ratios in different countries with the intention of finding undervalued and overvalued markets. It is clearly misleading in these cases to compare PE ratios across different markets without controlling for differences in the underlying variables. This is illustrated in the following example.

Illustration 14.7: PE ratios in markets with different fundamentals

The following are the summary economic statistics for stock markets in two different countries—Country 1 and Country 2. The key difference between the two countries is that interest rates are much higher in Country 1.

	Country 1	Country 2
Treasury bond rate	10.00%	5.00%
Market premium	4.00%	5.50%
Expected inflation	4.00%	4.00%
Expected growth in real GNP	2.00%	3.00%
Average payout ratio	50.00%	50.00%
Expected PE ratio	$.5 \times 1.06/$ $(.14 - .06)$ $= 6.625$	$.5 \times 1.07/$ $(.105\)\ .07)$ $= 15.29$

In this case, the PE ratio in Country 2 will be significantly higher than the PE ratio in Country 1, but it can be justified on the basis of differences in financial fundamentals.

This principle can be extended to broader comparisons of PE ratios across countries. The following table summarizes PE ratios across different countries at the end of 1992, together with interest rates (short term and long term) and expected growth in the gross domestic product for 1993. A naive comparison of PE ratios suggests that Japanese stocks, with a PE ratio of 38.2, are overvalued, while Dutch stocks, with a PE ratio of 12.8, are undervalued. There is, however, a strong positive correlation between PE ratios and expected GDP growth, and a negative correlation between PE ratios and interest rates.

Correlation between PE ratios and short-term interest rates $= -.883$

Correlation between PE ratios and long-term interest rates $= -.183$

Correlation between PE ratios and expected growth rate in GDP $= .767$

TABLE 14.2 PE Ratios for Several Countries, Yearend 1992

Country	PE Ratio	Interest Rate		Expected Growth Rate in GDP, 1993
		Short Term	Long Term	
Australia	20.1	5.65%	8.67%	3.0%
Canada	17.2	6.36%	8.69%	2.7%
France	14.9	12.31%	7.94%	.6%
Germany	14.4	8.45%	7.01%	− .8%
Japan	38.2	3.46%	4.28%	1.7%
Netherlands	12.8	9.05%	8.55%	.5%
Switzerland	15.2	5.75%	5.34%	.4%
United Kingdom	18.9	6.19%	8.54%	1.1%
United States (S&P 500)	24.0	3.21%	7.25%	2.9%

A cross-sectional regression of PE ratios on interest rates and expected growth yields the following:

> PE Ratio = 41.85 − .20 Short-Term Rate − 3.44 Long-Term Rate
> + 3.21 Growth in GDP

The three variables used in this regression explain a significant proportion (85%) of the differences in PE ratios across countries.

Based upon this regression, the predicted PE ratios for the countries are as follows:

Country	Actual PE	Predicted PE	Over/Undervalued by
Australia	20.1	20.56	−.46
Canada	17.2	19.38	−2.18
France	14.9	14.04	.86
Germany	14.4	13.51	.89
Japan	38.2	31.91	6.29
Netherlands	12.8	12.27	.53
Switzerland	15.2	23.64	−8.44
United Kingdom	18.9	14.80	4.10
United States (S&P 500)	24.0	25.60	−1.60

From this comparison, Dutch stocks, which have the lowest PE ratio, would have been considered overvalued after controlling for differences in interest rates and GDP growth, while Canadian, Swiss, and U.S. stocks would have been considered undervalued.

Comparisons among Emerging Markets

The following table summarizes PE ratio differences across emerging markets early in 1995. In this table, the country risk factor is that estimated by *The Economist* for these emerging markets [it is scaled from 0 (safest) to 100 (riskiest)].

Country	PE Ratio	Interest Rate (Short-Term)	GDP Nominal Growth	Country Risk
Peru	63	15.00%	22.00%	20
South Korea	38	16.55%	17.70%	20
Malaysia	36	5.67%	12.10%	30
Singapore	35	3.25%	13.60%	5
Philippines	34	9.06%	14.10%	55
India	33	11.48%	16.20%	45
Pakistan	32	12.50%	16.50%	50
Turkey	30	70.00%	79.00%	55
Thailand	30	12.75%	13.20%	30
Chile	28	13.35%	12.40%	25
Brazil	26	1,680.00%	1,675.20%	60
Argentina	24	12.70%	11.00%	55
Indonesia	22	16.00%	15.20%	40
Hong Kong	20	6.64%	10.60%	15
Venezuela	20	15.00%	15.70%	75
Mexico	19	50.50%	44.00%	70

The regression of PE ratios on these variables provides the following:

PE = 33.52 − 103.5 Interest Rate + 103.85 Nominal GNP Growth
 − .143 Country Risk R^2 = 36.80

This would lead to the following predicted PE ratios:

Country	PE Ratio	Predicted PE	Over/Undervalued by
Peru	63	37.98	65.88%
South Korea	38	31.91	19.09%
Malaysia	36	35.92	.21%
Singapore	35	43.56	−19.65%
Philippines	34	30.92	9.97%
India	33	32.02	3.05%
Pakistan	32	30.56	4.70%
Turkey	30	35.24	−14.88%
Thailand	30	29.74	.88%
Chile	28	29.00	−3.46%
Brazil	26	25.83	.65%
Argentina	24	23.93	.29%
Indonesia	22	27.02	−18.59%
Hong Kong	20	35.51	−43.67%
Venezuela	20	23.57	−15.15%
Mexico	19	16.93	12.20%

This analysis would suggest that Chile, Hong Kong, Indonesia, Singapore, Turkey, and Venezuela are undervalued, while the rest of the markets would be considered overvalued.

Comparisons across Time

Another comparison that is often made using PE ratios is across different time periods. As the fundamentals (interest rates and expected growth) change over time, the PE ratio will also change. A more appropriate comparison is therefore not between PE ratios across time, but between the actual PE ratio and the predicted PE ratio based upon fundamentals existing at that time. This is illustrated in the following example.

Illustration 14.8: PE ratios across time

The following are the summary economic statistics at two points in time for the same stock market. The interest rates in the first period were significantly higher than the interest rates in the second period.

	Period 1	Period 2
Treasury bond rate	11.00%	6.00%
Market premium	5.50%	5.50%
Expected inflation	5.00%	4.00%
Expected growth in real GNP	3.00%	2.50%

	Period 1	Period 2
Average payout ratio	50%	50%
Expected PE ratio	$.5 \times 1.08/$	$.5 \times 1.065/$
	$(.165 - .08)$	$(.115 - .065)$
	$= 6.35$	$= 10.65$

The PE ratio in the second time period will be significantly higher than the PE ratio in the first period, largely because of the drop in interest rates.

Figure 14.5 summarizes the earnings/price ratios for the average stock in the market and Treasury bond rates in each year from 1960 to 1994.

There is a strong positive relationship between EP ratios and Treasury bond rates, as evidenced by the correlation of 0.67 between the two variables. In addition, there is evidence that the term structure also affects the PE (or EP) ratio. In the following regression, we regress EP ratios against the level of Treasury bond rates and a term structure variable Treasury bond minus Treasury bill rate):

$$EP = 3.34\% + .7160 \, T \, Bond \, Rate - .9039 (T \, Bond \, Rate - T \, Bill \, Rate) R^2 = .795$$
$$\quad (3.52) \quad (6.57) \quad\quad\quad\quad (-4.03)$$

FIGURE 14.5 Earnings/Price Ratios and Treasury Bond Rates, 1960–1994

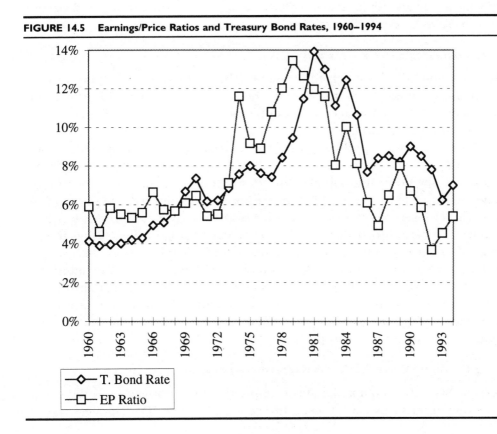

Other things remaining equal, this regression suggests that:

- Every 1% increase in the Treasury bond rate increases the EP ratio by 0.716%.
- Every 1% increase in the difference between Treasury bond and Treasury bill rates reduces the EP ratio by 0.90%. (As the term structure flattens out, EP ratios should increase; PE ratios should decrease.)
- Based upon this regression, the predicted EP ratio at the beginning of 1995, with the Treasury bill rate at 5.8% and the Treasury bond rate at 7.5%, would have been:

$$EP_{1995} = 3.34\% + (.7160 \times 7.50\%) - .9039(7.50\% - 5.80\%)$$
$$= 7.17\%$$
$$PE_{1995} = 1/EP_{1995} = 1/.0717 = 13.94$$

- The actual PE ratio in January 1995 was 16.58.

This regression can be enriched by adding other variables that should be correlated to the price/earnings ratio, such as expected growth in GNP and payout ratios, as independent variables.

Comparing PE Ratios across Firms

PE ratios vary across industries and across firms because of differences in fundamentals—higher growth generally translates into higher PE ratios. When comparisons are made across firms, differences in risk, growth rates, and payout ratios have to be controlled for explicitly.

Using Comparable Firms: Pros and Cons

The most common approach to estimating the PE ratio for a firm is choose a group of comparable firms, to calculate the average PE ratio for this group, and to subjectively adjust this average for differences between the firm being valued and the comparable firms.

There are several problems with this approach. First, the definition of a "comparable" firm is essentially a subjective one. The use of other firms in the industry as the control group is often not a solution because firms within the same industry can have very different business mixes and risk and growth profiles. There is also plenty of potential for bias. One clear example of this is in takeovers, where a high PE ratio for the target firm is justified using the PE ratios of a control group of other firms that have been taken over. This group is designed to give an upwardly biased estimate of the PE ratio and other multiples. Second, even when a legitimate group of comparable firms can be constructed, differences will continue to persist in fundamentals between the firm being valued and this group. Adjusting for differences subjectively does not provide a satisfactory solution to this problem.

Using the Entire Cross-Section: A Regression Approach

In contrast to the "comparable firm" approach, the information in the entire cross-section of firms can be used to predict PE ratios. The simplest way of

summarizing this information is with a multiple regression, with the PE ratio as the dependent variable and proxies for risk, growth, and payout forming the independent variables.

Past Studies. This approach is not new. One of the earliest studies was done by Kisor and Whitbeck (1963). Using data from the Bank of New York as of June 1962 for 135 stocks, they arrived at the following regression:

PE = 8.2 + 1.5 Growth Rate in Earnings + 6.7 Payout Ratio
 − .2 Standard Deviation in EPS Changes

Malkiel and Cragg (1968) followed up by estimating the coefficients for a regression of the PE ratio on the growth rate, the payout ratio, and the beta for stocks for the time period from 1961 to 1965.

Year	Regression	R^2
1961	$PE = 4.73 + 3.28g + 2.05\pi - .85\beta$.70
1962	$PE = 11.06 + 1.75g + .78\pi - 1.61\beta$.70
1963	$PE = 2.94 + 2.55g + 7.62\pi - .27\beta$.75
1964	$PE = 6.71 + 2.05g + 5.23\pi - .89\beta$.75
1965	$PE = .96 + 2.74g + 5.01\pi - .35\beta$.85

where PE = PE ratio at the start of the year
 g = growth rate in earnings
 π = earnings payout ratio at the start of the year
 β = beta of the stock

They concluded that while such models were useful in explaining PE ratios, they were of little use in predicting performance.

Fuller, Huberts, and Levinson (1992) took a different tack and regressed earnings/price ratios of firms on the COMPUSTAT databases against the growth rate in earnings in the subsequent eight years. They found that stocks with high EP ratios (low PE ratios) have significantly lower growth in the subsequent period than stocks with low EP ratios (high PE ratios), suggesting that EP ratios do convey information about future earnings growth.

More Recent Regressions. These PE ratio regressions have been updated in the following section using data from 1987 to 1991. The COMPUSTAT database was used to extract information on PE ratios, payout ratios, and earnings growth rates[1] (for the preceding five years) for all NYSE and AMEX firms with data available in each year. The betas were obtained from the Center for Research in Securities Prices (CRSP) tape for each year. All firms with negative earnings were eliminated from the sample, and the regression of PE on the independent variable yielded the following results:

Year	Regression	R^2
1987	PE = 7.1839 + 13.05 Payout − .6259 Beta + 6.5659 EGR	.9287
1988	PE = 2.5848 + 29.91 Payout − 4.5157 Beta + 19.9143 EGR	.9465
1989	PE = 4.6122 + 59.74 Payout − .7546 Beta + 9.0072 EGR	.5613
1990	PE = 3.5955 + 10.88 Payout − .2801 Beta + 5.4573 EGR	.3497
1991	PE = 2.7711 + 22.89 Payout − .1326 Beta + 13.8653 EGR	.3217

where PE = PE ratio at the end of the year
 Payout = dividend payout ratio at the end of the year
 Beta = beta of the stock, using returns from the previous five years
 EGR = earnings growth rate over the previous five years

1995 regression:

PE = 19.77 − 12.54 Payout − .4122 Beta + 15.19 EGR R^2 = .2794

where EGR = Expected earnings growth rate over next five years

Problems with the Regression Methodology. The regression methodology is a convenient way of compressing large amounts of data into one equation capturing the relationship between PE ratios and financial fundamentals. But it does have its limitations. First, the basic regression assumes a linear relationship between PE ratios and the financial proxies, and that might not be appropriate. An analysis of the residuals from a regression may suggest transformations of the independent variables (squared, natural logs) that work better in explaining PE ratios. Second, the independent variables are correlated with each other. For example, high-growth firms tend to have high risk. This multicollinearity makes the coefficients of the regressions unreliable and may explain the "wrong" signs on the coefficients and the large changes in these coefficients from period to period. Third, the basic relationship between PE ratios and financial variables itself might not be stable, and if it shifts from year to year, the predictions from the model may not be reliable. For instance, the R-squared in the regressions reported above declines from 0.93 in 1987 to 0.32 in 1991, and the coefficients change dramatically over time. Part of the reason for this is that earnings are volatile, and PE ratios reflect this volatility. The low R-squared for the 1991 regression can be ascribed to the recession's effects on earnings in that year.

Illustration 14.9: Valuing a private firm using the cross-sectional regression: Auntie Anne's

Auntie Anne's is a private business that sells pretzels and makes its revenue by franchis-

ing (with each franchise costing about $15,000 in 1995). The following is some of the information available on the company:

Net income in 1994 = $350,000

Growth rate in net income over previous five years = 100%

Growth rate anticipated over next five years in net income = 70%

In 1994: Capital Expenditures = $250,000; Depreciation = $50,000; \triangleWorking

Capital = $50,000

Free cashflows to equity in 1994 = Net Income

$-$ (Capital Expenditure $-$ Depreciation)

$- \triangle$ Working Capital

= $350,000 $-$ ($250,000 $-$ $50,000) $-$ $50,000

= $100,000

(The firm used no debt.)

Beta based upon comparable firms = 1.10 (The comparable firms used were

franchisors in the food business.)

To find the value, first compute the variables in the desired units:

Payout ratio = 100/350 = 28.57%

Earnings growth rate = 70%

Beta = 1.10

Based upon the PE ratio regression reported for 1995:

Predicted PE Ratio = 19.77 $-$ (12.54 \times .2857) $-$ (.4122 \times 1.10)

+ (15.19 \times .70) = 26.37

Predicted Market Value of Equity = Net Income \times PE Ratio

= $350,000 \times 26.37 = $9,228,416

PROBLEMS WITH PE RATIOS

There are general problems associated with the estimation of PE ratios that make its use troublesome. First, PE ratios are not meaningful when the earnings per share is negative. While this can be partially overcome by using a normalized or average earnings per share, the problem cannot be eliminated. Second, the volatility of earnings can cause the PE ratio to change dramatically from period to period. For cyclical firms, earnings will follow the economy, whereas the prices reflect expectations about the future. Thus it is not uncommon for the PE ratio of a cyclical firm to peak at the depths of a recession and bottom out at the peak of an economic boom.

Illustration 14.10: Valuing an initial public offering using PE ratios

Consider the hypothetical example of American Casinos, valued in the previous chapter using discounted cashflow valuation. American Casinos has current earnings of $37.20

million and is expected to register growth in earnings of 15% over the next five years. The PE ratios for firms involved in gaming entertainment are as follows:

Firm	Beta	Debt/ Equity	PE Ratio	Payout Ratio	Expected Growth
Aztar Corporation	1.35	66.73%	14.70	5.00%	6.00%
Bally Manufacturing	1.60	349.87%	24.33	14.00%	20.00%
Caesar's World	1.35	29.75%	15.50	0%	14.50%
Circus Circus	1.35	11.17%	25.40	0%	16.50%
International Game Tech.	1.25	3.54%	52.90	0%	34.00%
Jackpot Enterprises	1.00	31.02%	22.30	58.00%	32.50%
Mirage Resorts	1.40	81.60%	30.40	0%	17.50%
Showboat Inc.	1.10	90.54%	16.10	7.00%	32.00%
Average	1.30	83.03%	25.20	10.50%	21.63%
American Casinos	1.19	50.00%	?	0%	15.00%

The average PE ratio for firms in the gaming entertainment business is 25.20. Applying this PE ratio to value the equity in American Casinos:

> Value of Equity in American Casinos = $37.20 × 25.20 = $937.58 million

This is much greater than the value of equity obtained from discounted cashflow valuation, which is $713.04 million.

One reason for the higher valuation using the average PE ratio from comparable firms may be that publicly traded firms in gaming entertainment are overvalued. Another possible reason for the higher valuation may be that the public firms that form the comparable firm sample have higher expected growth than American Casinos.

A regression of PE ratios on fundamentals can also be done, using only the firms in the gaming entertainment business:

PE = $-31.59 - 20.11$ Payout Ratio $+ 107.80$ Expected Growth $+ 27.38$ Beta

Substituting the values for American Casinos:

$$\text{Predicted PE} = -31.59 - (20.11 \times 0) + (107.80 \times .15) + (27.38 \times 1.19)$$
$$= 17.16$$

Using this predicted PE ratio yields a value of equity of:

> Value of Equity = $37.20 × 17.16 = $638.35 million

This value is much closer to the value obtained from discounted cashflow valuation.

VARIANTS OF THE PE RATIO

There are several variants of earnings multiples in use—some use accounting earnings while others use cashflows; some are based upon pretax earnings while others use after-tax earnings. Most of these variants can be analyzed using the same framework used for analyzing the PE ratio.

Price/FCFE Multiple

There are some analysts who prefer to use price/FCFE ratios to value firms because of well-documented problems with accounting measures of earnings. In order to analyze the determinants of price/FCFE ratios, consider the FCFE two-stage model:

$$P_0 = \frac{FCFE_0(1 + g)\left(1 - \dfrac{1 + g)^n}{(1 + r)^n}\right)}{r - g} + \frac{FCFE_0(1 + g)^n(1 + g_n)}{(r_n - g_n)(1 + r)^n}$$

where P_0 = value of the stock now
$FCFE_0$ = free Cashflows to equity in year 0
g = expected growth rate during the extraordinary-growth period (first n years)
r = required rate of return on equity for the extraordinary-growth period
g_n = expected growth rate in the stable-growth period (after n years)
r_n = required rate of return on equity for the stable-growth period

Rearranging terms:

$$\frac{P_0}{FCFE_0} = \frac{(1 + g)\left(1 - \dfrac{(1 + g)^n}{(1 + r)^n}\right)}{r - g} + \frac{(1 + g)^n(1 + g_n)}{(r_n - g_n)(1 + r)^n}$$

The determinants of price/FCFE ratios are similar to the determinants of PE ratios—they include the expected growth rate in the initial high-growth period, the expected growth rate during the stable-growth period, and the relationship between capital expenditures and depreciation.

Note that a common variant of this multiple which uses the cashflows prior to capital expenditures and working capital needs overestimates the cashflows to equity investors in the firm and may lead to misleading estimates of value.

Illustration 14.11: Use of Price/FCFE ratios: Intel

Intel Inc. is expected to maintain a growth rate of 22.09% over the next five years in earnings. After five years, the growth rate in earnings is expected to be 6%. The capital spending, depreciation, and revenue are expected to grow at the same rate as earnings, and the working capital as a percent of revenues is expected to remain unchanged at 40%. Intel has a beta of 1.30 currently but is expected to have a beta of 1.1 in the stable period. The Treasury bond rate is 7%.

The projected price/FCFE ratio based upon these fundamentals is as follows:

$$\frac{P_0}{FCFE_0} = \frac{1.2209 \times \left(1 - \frac{1.2209^5}{1.1415^n}\right)}{.1415 - .2209} + \frac{1.2209^5 \times 1.06}{1.1415^5(.1305 - .06)} = 27.19$$

Value of Firm/Free Cashflows to the Firm

The multiples specified so far in this chapter relate specifically to valuing equity. An alternative ratio yields the value of the firm as a multiple of the free cashflows to the firm (FCFF), that is, the cashflows before debt payments. Again, the multiple can be written as follows:

$$V_0 = \frac{FCFF_0(1 + g)\left(1 - \frac{(1 + g)^n}{(1 + WACC)^n}\right)}{WACC - g} + \frac{FCFF_0(1 + g)^n(1 + g_n)}{(WACC - g_n)(1 + WACC)^n}$$

where V_0 = value of the firm (today)
 $FCFF_0$ = free cashflows to the firm in the current year
 g = expected growth rate in FCFF in the extraordinary-growth period (first n years)
 $WACC$ = weighted average cost of capital in the extraordinary-growth period
 g_n = expected growth rate in FCFF in the stable-growth period (after n years)
 $WACC_n$ = weight average cost of capital in the stable-growth period

Rearranging terms:

$$\frac{V_0}{FCFF_0} = \frac{(1 + g)\left(1 - \frac{1 + g)^n}{(1 + WACC)^n}\right)}{WACC - g} + \frac{(1 + g)^n(1 + g_n)}{(WACC - g_n)(1 + WACC)^n}$$

Again, this assumes that the FCFF is stated, after taxes, to the firm. Multiples of pretax free cashflows to the firm (or earnings before interest and taxes) can be similarly computed from the after-tax multiple:

$$\frac{V_0}{EBIT} = \frac{V_0}{FCFF_0}(1 - tax\ rate)$$

This multiple can be further depressed by adding depreciation back to the pretax earnings (EBITDA), especially for capital-intensive firms.

The advantage of using this approach for highly levered firms is that it examines the entire firm and may provide more reasonable estimates of value than looking at equity, which is only a small slice of the overall firm. The market value of the outstanding debt can be subtracted from the value of the firm to value equity.

A Note on Multiples of Pretax Cashflows

Multiples of pretax cashflows will always be lower than multiples of after-tax cashflows. For a firm with a tax rate of 40%, the pretax multiple will be only 60% of the after-tax multiple (using the equation above). For investors used to dealing with after-tax multiples, pretax multiples often seem low. This "illusory reasonableness" is part of the reason why they are used to justify large premiums in takeovers.

Illustration 14.12: Using value/FCFF approaches to value a firm: MCI Communications

MCI Communications had earnings before interest and taxes of $3,356 million in 1994 (its net income after taxes was $855 million). It had capital expenditures of $2,500 million in 1994, and depreciation of $1,100 million; working capital increased by $250 million. It expects free cashflows to the firm to grow 15% a year for the next five years and 5% a year after that. The cost of capital is 10.50% for the next five years and 10% after that. The company faces a tax rate of 36%. The predicted value/free cashflows to the firm ratio for MCI Communications is as follows:

$$\frac{V_0}{FCFF_0} = \frac{(1.15)\left(1 - \dfrac{1.15^5}{1.105^5}\right)}{.105 - .15} + \frac{(1.15^5 \times 1.05)}{1.105^5(.10 - .05)} = 31.28$$

Use of shortcuts: after-tax EBIT, EBIT, and EBITDA: In the case of MCI, there is a big difference between the FCFF and other cashflow measures. For instance, the table below illustrates the appropriate multiple using other cashflow measures and the amount by which you would overpay if you used the FCFF multiple.

$$\text{Free Cashflows to the Firm} = \text{EBIT}(1 - t) + \text{Depreciation} - \text{Capital Spending}$$
$$- \triangle \text{ Working Capital}$$
$$= \$3,356(1 - .36) + \$1,100 - \$2,500 - \$250$$
$$= \$498 \text{ million}$$

	Value	Correct Multiple	Error on Value if FCFF Multiple is Used
FCFF	$498	31.28382355	0%
EBIT $(1 - t)$	2,148	7.251163362	431%
EBIT	3,356	4.640744552	674%
EBITDA	4,456	3.49513885	895%
Net Income	855	14.58636107	This is the PE ratio

Thus, a multiple of 3.50 on EBITDA may seem low, but it is in fact the right multiple for a firm like MCI that has huge capital expenditures.

A Note of Caution

When valuations are based upon multiples of EBIT or EBITDA, they have to be used cautiously. A "low" multiple may in fact be hopelessly over-optimistic for a firm where the EBIT is significantly higher than the FCFF (because of capital spending or working capital needs) and for capital-intensive firms that may generate large capital expenditures.

PRICE/DIVIDEND RATIOS AND DIVIDEND YIELDS

Investors have relied on the dividend yields of stocks, to varying degree, in constructing investment strategies. For value investors of the Graham-Dodd school and to the Dow theorists,[2] a high dividend yield has been a reliable indicator of success, both for the overall market and for individual stocks.

Determinants of Price/Dividend Ratios and Dividend Yields

The price/dividend ratio is the inverse of the dividend yield, and the determinants of this ratio can be obtained using the simple Gordon growth model:

$$\frac{P_0}{DPS_1} = \frac{1}{r - g_n}$$

where r = required rate of return on equity

g_n = expected growth rate in dividends (and earnings) in the long term

The dividend yield can then be written as:

Dividend Yield $= r - g_n$ for a stable firm

Thus the dividend yield for a stable firm should be the difference between the required rate of return on equity and the expected growth rate in dividends in the long term.

Dividend Yields versus Treasury Rates

The Proposition

A common approach to finding under- or overvaluation in the market is to compare the dividend yield to the interest rate on Treasury bonds, with high dividend yields relative to Treasury bond rates being considered a sign of undervaluation and low yields of overvaluation. The argument is generally couched in opportunity cost terms. Stocks, it is argued, become better bargains when their dividend yields are high relative to the offerings on their prime competitors—bonds. Bonds become better investments as Treasury bond rates rise relative to dividend yields.

A Test of the Proposition

Figure 14.6 reports statistics on the dividend yield and Treasury bond rates from 1960 to 1994. Does the difference between the average dividend yield on the market and the Treasury bond rate have any power in predicting future stock returns? Does a low dividend yield, relative to the Treasury bond rate, suggest that stocks are overvalued? To answer these questions, a regression of stock market returns, in annual periods from 1960 to 1994, against the difference between the dividend yield and the Treasury bond rate was run. The result of the regression is reported below:

$$XRET_t = .0647 - 1.3662 \ (DYLD_{t-1} - TBOND_{t-1})$$
$$(1.18) \quad (1.06)$$

where $XRET_t$ = stock market returns in period t
$DYLD_{t-1}$ = dividend yield at the end of period $t - 1$
$TBOND_{t-1}$ = Treasury bond rate at the end of period $t - 1$

There is no evidence to suggest that the difference between the dividend yields and Treasury bonds has any power in predicting stock returns in the next period. (The t statistics are insignificant, and the coefficient has the wrong sign.)

FIGURE 14.6 Treasury Bond Rates and Dividend Yields, 1960–1994

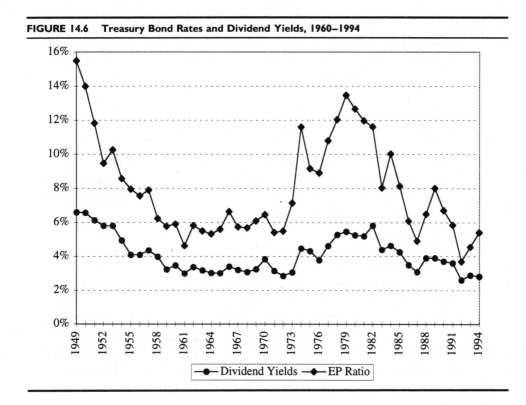

The Determinants

If the difference between the dividend yield and the Treasury bond rate does not have any predictive power in explaining future stock returns, what, if anything, does it say about market conditions? The appropriate comparisons can be obtained by manipulating the equation for dividend yield:

$$\text{Dividend yield} = r - g_n$$
$$= (\text{Treasury Bond Rate} + \text{Risk Premium}) - g_n$$
$$\text{Dividend Yield} - \text{Treasury Bond Rate} = \text{Risk Premium} - g_n$$

In general, the difference between the average dividend yield in the market and the Treasury bond rate will be equal to the difference between the risk premium for investing in stocks and the expected growth rate in corporate dividends (and earnings) in the long term. If the risk premium increases, either because investors become more risk averse or the uncertainty in the underlying economy increases, dividend yields will increase relative to the Treasury bond rate. Conversely if the expected growth rate increases or the risk premium decreases, Treasury bond rates will increase relative to dividend yields.

PE RATIOS AND STOCK RETURNS

One of the enduring irregularities that has been noted in tests of the capital asset pricing model is the tendency of low-price/earnings-ratio stocks to outperform the market and high-price/earnings-ratio stocks to underperform the market on a risk-adjusted basis. This has been established using a variety of different approaches. Basu (1977) used the CAPM framework to show that low-PE-ratio stocks earn positive excess returns relative to the market and that high-PE-ratio stocks underperform the market. Goodman and Peavy (1983) used industry-relative PE ratios and concluded that stocks with low PE ratios relative to the industry in which they operate earn excess returns. Levy and Lerman (1985) came to the same conclusions using stochastic dominance rather than the CAPM.

Practitioners recognized the value of low PE ratios well before these academic studies were published. One of the key criteria used by Ben Graham (1949) to pick undervalued stocks was a low PE ratio. Low PE ratios also form an integral part of many contrarian strategies.

There are several competing rationale advanced for this phenomenon. One is that the CAPM does not adequately measure risk and that betas are underestimated for low-PE-ratio stocks and overestimated for high-PE-ratio stocks. Given that low-PE-ratio stocks are usually large stable firms with high dividends, there seems to be little basis for this argument. The second is that the model's focus on pretax returns obscures the higher tax liability that will be faced by the investor buying the low-PE-ratio stocks and getting higher dividends. While this critique may be justifiable when tax rates on dividends are significantly higher than capital gains tax rates, it becomes less sustainable when the tax rates on the two types of income are similar and when investors are tax exempt.

The third possibility is that investors consistently overestimate the value of growth and pay too much for high-growth firms and too little for stable firms. This would be a clear violation of market efficiency and could provide opportunities for excess returns for investors who go against the grain and buy portfolios of low-PE-ratio stocks.

CONCLUSION

The price/earnings ratio and other earnings multiples, which are widely used in valuation, have the potential to be misused. These multiples are ultimately determined by the same fundamentals that determine discounted cashflow value—expected growth, risk, and payout ratios. To the extent that there are differences in fundamentals across countries, across time, and across companies, the multiples will also be different. A failure to control for these differences in fundamentals can lead to erroneous conclusions based purely upon a direct comparison of multiples.

QUESTIONS AND SHORT PROBLEMS

1. National City Corporation, a bank holding company, reported earnings per share of $2.40 in 1993 and paid dividends per share of $1.06. The earnings had grown 7.5% a year over the prior five years and were expected to grow 6% a year in the long term (starting in 1994). The stock had a beta of 1.05 and traded for ten times earnings. (The Treasury bond rate was 7%.)
 a. Estimate the PE Ratio for National City Corporation.
 b. What long-term growth rate is implied in the firm's current PE ratio?
2. On March 11, 1994, the New York Stock Exchange Composite was trading at 16.9 times earnings, and the average dividend yield across stocks on the exchange was 2.5%. The Treasury bond rate on March 11, 1994, was 6.95%. The economy was expected to grow 2.5% a year (in real terms) in the long term, and the consensus estimate for inflation in the long term was 3.5%.
 a. Based upon these inputs, estimate the "appropriate" PE ratio for the exchange.
 b. What growth rate in dividends/earnings would justify the PE ratio on March 11, 1994?
 c. Would it matter whether this higher growth came from higher inflation or higher real growth? Why?
3. International Flavors and Fragrances, a leading creator and manufacturer of flavors and fragrances, paid out dividends of $0.91 per share on earnings per share of $1.64 in 1992. The firm is expected to have a return on equity of 20% between 1993 and 1997, after which the firm is expected to have stable growth of 6% a year. (The return on equity is expected to drop to 15% in the stable growth phase.) The dividend payout ratio is expected to remain at the current level from 1993 to 1997. The stock has a beta of 1.10, which is not expected to change. (The Treasury bond rate is 7%.)
 a. Estimate the PE ratio for International Flavors, based upon fundamentals.

b. Estimate how much of the PE ratio can be ascribed to the extraordinary growth in earnings that the firm expects to have between 1993 and 1997.

4. Cracker Barrel, which operates restaurants and gift shops, reported dramatic growth in earnings and revenues between 1983 and 1993. During this period, earnings grew from $0.08 per share in 1983 to $0.78 per share in 1993. The dividends paid in 1993 amounted to only $0.02 per share. The earnings growth rate was expected to ease to 15% a year from 1994 to 1998, and to 6% a year after that. The payout ratio is expected to increase to 10% from 1994 to 1998, and to 50% after that. The beta of the stock is currently 1.55, but it is expected to decline to 1.25 for the 1994–1998 time period and to 1.10 after that. (The Treasury bond rate is 7%.)

 a. Estimate the PE ratio for Cracker Barrel.
 b. Estimate how much higher the PE ratio would have been, if it had been able to maintain the growth rate in earnings that it had posted between 1983 and 1993. (Assume that the dividend payout ratios are unaffected.)
 c. Now assume that disappointing earnings reports in the near future lower the expected growth rate between 1994 and 1998 to 10%. Estimate the PE ratio. (Again, assume that the dividend payout ratio is unaffected.)

5. The S&P 500 was trading at 21.2 times earnings on December 31, 1993. On the same day, the dividend yield on the index was 2.74%, and the Treasury bond rate was 6%. The expected growth rate in real GNP was 2.5%.

 a. Assuming that the S&P 500 was correctly priced, what is the inflation rate implied in the PE ratio?
 b. By February 1994, Treasury bond rates had increased to 7%. If payout ratios and expected growth remain unchanged, what would the effect on the PE ratio be?
 c. Does an increase in interest rates always imply lower prices (and PE ratios)?

6. The following were the PE ratios of firms in the aerospace/defense industry at the end of December, 1993, with additional data on expected growth and risk:

Company	PE Ratio	Expected Growth	Beta	Payout
Boeing	17.3	3.5%	1.10	28%
General Dynamics	15.5	11.5%	1.25	40%
General Motors—Hughes	16.5	13.0%	0.85	41%
Grumman	11.4	10.5%	0.80	37%
Lockheed Corporation	10.2	9.5%	0.85	37%
Logicon	12.4	14.0%	0.85	11%
Loral Corporation	13.3	16.5%	0.75	23%
Martin Marietta	11.0	8.0%	0.85	22%
McDonnell Douglas	22.6	13.0%	1.15	37%
Northrop	9.5	9.0%	1.05	47%
Raytheon	12.1	9.5%	0.75	28%
Rockwell	13.9	11.5%	1.00	38%
Thiokol	8.7	5.5%	0.95	15%
United Industrial	10.4	4.5%	0.70	50%

 a. Estimate the average and median PE ratios. What, if anything, would these averages tell you?

b. An analyst concludes that Thiokol is undervalued, because its PE ratio is lower than the industry average. Under what conditions is this statement true? Would you agree with it here?

c. Using a regression, control for differences across firms on risk, growth, and payout. Specify how you would use this regression to spot under- and over-valued stocks. What are the limitations of this approach?

7. The following was the result of a regression of PE ratios on growth rates, betas, and payout ratios for stocks listed on the Value Line Database in April 1993:

$$PE = 18.69 + 0.0695 \text{ GROWTH} - 0.5082 \text{ BETA} - 0.4262 \text{ PAYOUT}$$
$$R^2 = 0.35$$

Thus, a stock, with an earnings growth rate of 20%, a beta of 1.15, and a payout ratio of 40% would have had an expected PE ratio of:

$$PE = 18.69 + 0.0695 \times 20 - 0.5082(1.15) - 0.4262 \times 0.40 = 19.33$$

You are attempting to value a private firm with the following characteristics:

a. The firm had net profits of $10 million. It did not pay dividends, but had depreciation allowances of $5 million and capital expenditures of $12 million in the most recent year. Working capital requirements were negligible.

b. The earnings had grown 25% over the previous five years and are expected to grow at the same rate over the next five years.

c. The average beta of publicly traded firms in the same line of business is 1.15, and the average debt/equity ratio of these firms is 25%. (The tax rate is 40%.) The private firm is an all-equity financed firm, with no debt.

(1) Estimate the appropriate PE ratio for this private firm, using the regression.

(2) What would some of your concerns be in using this regression in valuation?

ENDNOTES

1. The use of past growth rates in the regression is not the preferred option. If projected growth rates had been available on the COMPUSTAT database, as they are on the I/B/E/S tape, they would have been used instead.

2. Charles H. Dow suggested that stocks selling at a dividend yield less than 3.5% were overvalued. Dow theorists have remained faithful to the founder's concept of value and argue that investors sell stocks when the dividend yield drops below 3.5% and buy stocks when the yield rises above 6%.

15

Price/Book Value Multiples

The relationship between price and book value has always attracted the attention of investors. Stocks selling for well below the book value of equity have generally been considered good candidates for undervalued portfolios, while those selling for more than book value have been targets for overvalued portfolios. This chapter examines the price/book value (PBV) ratio in more detail and considers the determinants of this ratio and how best to evaluate or estimate the ratio.

GENERAL ISSUES IN ESTIMATING AND USING PBV RATIOS

Measurement

The book value of equity is the difference between the book value of assets and the book value of liabilities. The measurement of the book value of assets is largely determined by accounting convention. In the United States, it is the original price paid for the assets reduced by any allowable depreciation on the assets. Consequently, the book value of an asset decreases as it ages. The book value of liabilities similarly reflects the "at-issue" value of the liabilities.

Book Value versus Market Value

The market value of an asset reflects its earning power and expected cashflows. Since the book value of an asset reflects its original cost, it might deviate significantly from market value if the earning power of the asset has increased or declined significantly since its acquisition.

Advantages of Using PBV Ratios

There are several reasons why investors find the price/book value ratio useful in investment analysis. The first is that the book value provides a relatively stable, intuitive measure of value which can be compared to the market price. For investors who instinctively mistrust discounted cashflow estimates of value, it is a much simpler benchmark for comparison. The second is that, given

reasonably consistent accounting standards across firms, PBV ratios can be compared across similar firms for signs of under- or overvaluation. Finally, even firms with negative earnings, which cannot be valued using price/earnings ratios, can be evaluated using PBV ratios.

Disadvantages of Using PBV Ratios

There are several disadvantages associated with measuring and using price/book value ratios. First, book values, like earnings, are affected by accounting decisions on depreciation and other variables. When accounting standards vary widely across firms, the PBV ratios may not be comparable across firms. A similar statement can be made about comparing PBV ratios across countries with different accounting standards. Second, book value may not carry much meaning for service firms that do not have significant fixed assets. Third, the book value of equity can become negative if a firm has a sustained string of negative earnings reports, leading to a negative PBV ratio.

ESTIMATING PBV RATIOS FROM FUNDAMENTALS

The price/book value ratio can be related to the same fundamentals that determine value in discounted cashflow models.

PBV Ratio for a Stable Firm

A stable firm is a firm growing at a rate comparable or lower than the nominal growth rate in the economy in which it operates. The value of equity for a stable firm, using the Gordon growth model, is:

$$P_0 = \frac{DPS_1}{r - g_n}$$

where P_0 = value of equity

$\quad DPS_1$ = expected dividends per share next year

$\quad\quad r$ = required rate of return on equity

$\quad\quad g_n$ = growth rate in dividends (forever)

Substituting EPS_0 (Payout Ratio $[1 + g_n]$) for DPS_1, the value of the equity can be written as:

$$P_0 = \frac{EPS_0 \times \text{Payout Ratio} \times (1 + g_n)}{r - g_n}$$

Defining the return on equity (ROE) as EPS_0/Book Value of Equity, the value of equity can be written as:

$$P_0 = \frac{BV_0 \times ROE \times \text{Payout Ratio} \times (1 + g_n)}{r - g_n}$$

Rewriting in terms of the PBV ratio:

$$\frac{P_0}{BV_0} = PBV = \frac{ROE \times \text{Payout Ratio} \times (1 + g_n)}{r - g_n}$$

If the return on equity is based upon expected earnings in the next time period, this can be simplified to:

$$\frac{P_0}{BV_0} = PBV = \frac{ROE \times \text{Payout Ratio}}{r - g_n}$$

The PBV ratio is an increasing function of the return on equity, the payout ratio, and the growth rate, and a decreasing function of the riskiness of the firm.

This formulation can be simplified even further by relating growth to the return on equity:

$$g = ROE(1 - \text{Payout Ratio})$$

Substituting back into the PBV equation:

$$\frac{P_0}{BV_0} = PBV = \frac{ROE - g_n}{r - g_n}$$

The PBV ratio of a stable firm is determined by the differential between the return on equity and the required rate of return on its projects. If the return on equity exceeds the required rate of return, the price will exceed the book value of equity; if the return on equity is lower than the required rate of return, it will be lower than the book value of equity. The advantage of this formulation is that it can be used to estimate PBV ratios for firms that do not pay out dividends.

Illustration 15.1: Estimating the PBV ratio for a stable firm with dividends: Amoco

Amoco had earnings per share of $3.82 in 1994 and paid out 60% of its earnings as dividends that year. The growth rate in earnings and dividends, in the long term, is expected to be 6%. The return on equity at Amoco in 1994 was 15%. The beta for Amoco was 0.65, and the Treasury bond rate was 7.5%.

Current Dividend Payout Ratio = 60%

Expected Growth Rate in Earnings and Dividends = 6%

Return on Equity = 15%

Cost of Equity = 7.5% + (.65 × 5.5%) = 11.08%

PBV Ratio based on fundamentals = .15 × .60 × 1.06/(.1108 − .06) = 1.88

PBV Ratio based on return differential = (.15 − .06)/(.1108 − .06) = 1.77

Amoco was selling at a PBV ratio of just about 2.00 in March 1995. The following

table shows the relationship of the PBV ratio to the return on equity for oil companies in 1995:

Company	Price per Share	BV per Share	PBV	ROE
Elf Aquitane	36	29.6	1.22	5.0%
Amerada Hess	45	32.65	1.38	3.5%
Getty	12	8.15	1.47	11.0%
Murphy Oil	42	27.95	1.50	7.5%
Ashland Oil	34	21.23	1.60	12.4%
Repsol	27	15.35	1.76	15.5%
Royal Dutch	107	58.95	1.82	12.0%
Texaco	61	33.15	1.84	11.0%
Occidental Pete	19	9.95	1.91	9.5%
Mobil	85	44.5	1.91	13.0%
Chevron	44	22.2	1.98	13.0%
Amoco	59	28.85	2.05	15.0%
Exxon	62	28.3	2.19	15.0%
British Petroleum	80	33.6	2.38	15.0%
Unocal	27	11.3	2.39	13.0%
Atlantic Richfield	103	38.9	2.65	16.0%

Correlation between PBV ratios and ROE = .78
Regression:

PBV = .91 + 8.26 (ROE)

R^2 = .61

This regression would suggest that every 1% increase in the return on equity would increase the PBV ratio by 0.0826.

Valuing a Privatization Candidate (Oil)

Assume that you have been asked to value PEMEX, the nationalized Mexican oil company for the Mexican government; all you know is that it has earned a return on equity of 14% last year. The appropriate PBV ratio can be estimated in one of two ways:

Beta based upon international oil companies = .70

Cost of Equity = 7.50% + (.70 × 5.50%) = 11.35%

PBV Ratio (based on fundamentals) = (.14 − .06)/(.1135 − .06) = 1.50

PBV Ratio (based on regression) = .91 + (8.26 × 0.14) = 2.07

Illustration 15.2: Estimating the PBV ratio for a "privatization" candidate: Jenapharm (Germany)

One of the byproducts of German reunification was the Treuhandanstalt, the German privatization agency set up to sell hundreds of East German firms to other German

companies, individual investors, and the public. One of the handful of firms that seemed to be a viable candidate for privatization was Jenapharm, the most respected pharmaceutical manufacturer in East Germany. Jenapharm, which was expected to have revenues of 230 million DM in 1991, also was expected to make earnings before interest and taxes of 30 million DM. The firm had a book value of assets of 110 million DM and a book value of equity of 58 million DM. The interest expenses in 1990 amounted to 15 million DM.

The firm was expected to maintain sales in its niche product, a contraceptive pill, and grow at 5% a year in the long term, primarily by expanding into the generic drug market.

The average beta of pharmaceutical firms traded on the Frankfurt Stock Exchange was 1.05, though many of these firms had much more diversified product portfolios and less volatile cashflows. Allowing for the higher leverage and risk in Jenapharm, a beta of 1.25 was used for Jenapharm. The ten-year bond rate in Germany at the time of this valuation was 7%, and the risk premium for stocks over bonds is assumed to be 3.5%.

$$\text{Expected Net Income} = (\text{EBIT} - \text{Interest Expense})(1 - t)$$
$$= (30 - 15)(1 - .4) = 9 \text{ million DM}$$
$$\text{Return on Equity} = \text{Expected Net Income/Book Value of Equity}$$
$$= 9/58 = 15.52\%$$
$$\text{Required Return on Equity} = 7\% + (1.25 \times 3.5\%) = 11.375\%$$
$$\text{PBV Ratio} = (\text{ROE} - g)/(r - g) = (.1552 - .05)/(.11375 - .05) = 1.65$$
$$\text{Estimated MV of Equity} = \text{BV of Equity} \times \text{PBV Ratio} = 58 \times 1.65$$
$$= 95.70 \text{ million DM}$$

PBV Ratio for a High-Growth Firm

The price/book value ratio for a high-growth firm can also be related to fundamentals. In the special case of the two-stage dividend discount model, this relationship can be made explicit fairly simply. The value of equity of a high-growth firm in the two-stage dividend discount model can be written as:

$$\text{Value of Equity} = \text{Present Value of expected dividends}$$
$$+ \text{Present value of terminal price}$$

When the growth rate is assumed to be constant after the initial high-growth phase, the dividend discount model can be written as follows:

$$P_0 = \frac{\text{EPS}_0 \times \text{Payout Ratio} \times (1 + g) \times \left(1 - \dfrac{(1 + g)^n}{(1 + r)^n}\right)}{r - g}$$
$$+ \frac{\text{EPS}_0 \times \text{Payout Ratio}_n \times (1 + g)^n (1 - g_n)}{(r_n - g_n)(1 + r)^n}$$

where g = growth rate in the first n years
$ r$ = required return on equity in first n years

$\text{Payout} = \text{payout ratio in the first } n \text{ years}$

$g_n = \text{growth rate after } n \text{ years forever (stable growth rate)}$

$\text{Payout Ratio}_n = \text{payout ratio after } n \text{ years (stable growth rate)}$

$r_n = \text{required return on equity after } n \text{ years}$

Substituting $BV_0 \times ROE$ for EPS_0 and rearranging, we get:

$$\frac{P_0}{BV_0} = PBV = ROE$$

$$\times \left\{ \frac{\text{Payout Ratio}(1 + g)\left(1 - \frac{[1 + g]^n}{[1 + r]^n}\right)}{r - g} + \frac{\text{Payout Ratio}_n(1 - g)^n(1 + g_n)}{(r_n - g_n)(1 + r)^n} \right\}$$

The PBV ratio is determined by:

(a) *Return on equity:* Earning per share/Book Value per share. The price-book value ratio is an increasing function of the return on equity.

(b) *Payout ratio, in both the high-growth and stable-growth periods:* The PBV ratio increases as the payout ratio increases.

(c) *Riskiness (through the discount rate* r*):* The PBV ratio becomes lower as riskiness increases.

(d) *Growth rate in earnings, in both the high-growth and stable-growth periods:* The PBV ratio increases as the growth rate increases, in either period.

This formula is general enough to be applied to any firm, even one that is not paying dividends right now.

Illustration 15.3: Estimating the PBV ratio for a high-growth firm in the two-stage model

Assume that you have been asked to estimate the PBV ratio for a firm with the following characteristics:

Growth rate in first five years = 20%

Growth rate after five years = 8%

Beta = 1.0

Return on equity = 25%

Payout ratio in first five years = 20%

Payout ratio after five years = 68%

Riskfree rate = Treasury bond rate = 6%

Required rate of return = 6% + (1 × 5.5%) = 11.5%

$$PBV = .25 \left(\frac{.2 \times 1.20 \times \left[1 - \frac{1.20^5}{1.115^5}\right]}{.115 - .20} + \frac{.68 \times 1.20^5 \times 1.08}{[.115 - .08] \times 1.115^5} \right) = 7.89$$

The estimated PBV ratio for this firm is 7.89.

Illustration 15.4: Estimating the PBV ratio for a high-growth firm: Bertelsmann

Bertelsmann AG is a German publishing company that is involved in a wide range of media enterprises around the world. It is also unusual because of its emphasis on maintaining a high return on equity. The following are some of the inputs used to examine the payoffs from this emphasis:

High-Growth Period	Stable-Growth Period
Expected length = 10 years	
Growth Rate = 20%	Growth Rate = 6%
Payout Ratio = 30%	Payout Ratio = 60%
Return on Equity = 28.57%	Return on Equity = 15%

The beta in both periods is 0.90. The German long bond rate was approximately 7.50%.

> Note: Expected Growth Rate = ROE(1 − Payout Ratio)

Cost of Equity = 7.50% + (.90 × 5.5%) = 12.45%

The PBV ratio, based upon these inputs, is calculated below:

$$
\text{PBV} = \left(.2857 \times \frac{.30 \times 1.20 \times \left[1 - \dfrac{1.20^{10}}{1.1254^{10}} \right]}{.1245 - .20} + .15 \times \frac{.60 \times 1.20^{10} \times 1.06}{[.1245 - .06] \times 1.1245^{10}} \right)
$$

$$
= 4.08
$$

Bertelsmann AG traded at a PBV ratio of 3.50 in March 1995.

PBV Ratios and Return on Equity

The ratio of price to book value is strongly influenced by the return on equity. A lower return on equity affects the PBV ratio directly through the formulation specified in the prior section and, indirectly, by lowering the expected growth or payout. A simple way of relating the return on equity to growth is the following:

Expected Growth Rate = Retention Ratio × Return on Equity

The effects of lower return on equity on the PBV ratio are shown in the following example.

Illustration 15.5: Return on equity and PBV ratio

Assume that a firm has the following characteristics:

Return on Equity = 25%
Growth Rate in first five years = 20%
Growth Rate after five years = 8%
Payout Ratio in first five years = 20%
Payout Ratio after five years = 68%
Required Rate of Return = 11.5%

Note that the growth rate in the first five years is:

g = Retention Ratio × ROE = .8 × 25% = 20%

and the growth rate after year five is:

g = Retention Ratio × ROE = .32 × 25% = 8%

$$PBV = .25 \left(\frac{.2 \times 1.20 \times \left[1 - \dfrac{1.20^5}{1.115^5} \right]}{.115 - .20} + \frac{.68 \times 1.20^5 \times 1.08}{(.115 - .08) \times 1.115^5} \right) = 7.89$$

If the firm's return on equity drops to 12%, the PBV ratio will reflect the drop. The lower return on equity will also lower expected growth in the initial high-growth period:

Expected Growth Rate (first five years) = Retention Ratio × Return on Equity
= .80 × 12% = 9.6%

After year five, either the retention ratio has to increase or the expected growth rate has to be lower than 8%. If the retention ratio is adjusted,

New Retention Ratio after year 5 = Expected Growth/ROE = 8%/12%
= 66.67%
New Payout Ratio after year 5 = 1 − Retention Ratio = 33.33%

The new PBV ratio can then be calculated as follows:

$$PBV = .12 \left(\frac{.2 \times 1.096 \times \left[1 - \dfrac{1.096^5}{1.115^5} \right]}{.115 - .096} + \frac{.333 \times 1.096^5 \times 1.08}{(.115 - .08) \times 1.115^5} \right) = 1.25$$

The drop in the ROE has a two-layered impact. First, it lowers the growth rate in

earnings and/or the expected payout ratio, thus having an indirect effect on the PBV ratio. Second, it reduces the PBV ratio directly.

The PBV ratio is also influenced by the required rate of return, with higher required rates of return leading to lower PBV ratios. The influence of the return on equity and the required rate of return can be consolidated in one measure by taking the difference between the two rates. The larger the return on equity relative to the required rate of return, the greater the PBV ratio. In Illustration 15.5, for instance, the firm, which had a required rate of return of 11.5%, went from having a return on equity that was 13.5% greater than the required rate of return to a return on equity that barely broke even (0.5% greater than the required rate of return). Consequently, its PBV ratio declined from 7.89 to 1.25. Figure 15.1 shows the PBV ratio as a function of the difference between the return on equity and the required rate of return. Note that when the return on equity is equal to the required return, the price is equal to the book value.

Illustration 15.6: ROE and PBV Ratios: IBM

IBM provides a classic example of the effects of lower returns on equity on PBV ratios. In 1983, IBM had a price that was three times its book value, one of the highest PBV multiples among the Dow 30 stocks at that time. By 1992, the PBV ratio for IBM had declined to 1, significantly lower than the average ratio for Dow 30 stocks. This decline in the PBV ratio was triggered by the decline in return on equity at IBM, from 25% in 1983 and 1984 to about 5% in 1992. Figure 15.2 illustrates both variables between 1982 and 1992 for IBM.

FIGURE 15.1 **PBV Ratio as a Function of the Return Differential**

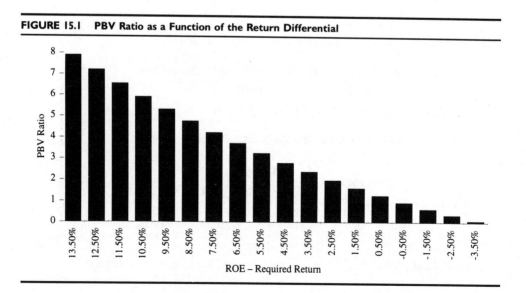

FIGURE 15.2 PBV Ratios and Return on Equity: IBM, 1982–1992

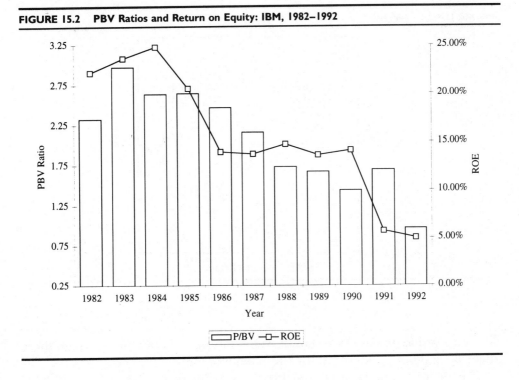

Looking for Undervalued Securities—PBV Ratios and ROE

Given the relationship between PBV ratios and returns on equity, it is not surprising to see firms that have high returns on equity selling for well above book value and firms that have low returns on equity selling at or below book value. The firms that should draw attention from investors are those that provide mismatches of PBV ratios and returns on equity—low PBV ratios and high ROE or high PBV ratios and low ROE. This is illustrated in Figure 15.3.

Figure 15.4 graphs financial service stocks in March 1995 on this matrix, using PBV ratios as of March 1995 and returns on equity in the latest financial year (1994).

A Simple Control for ROE: PBV/ROE Ratio

A simple way of controlling for differences in return on equity is to calculate the ratio of PBV ratios to return on equity, and ranking firms on that basis. Using that approach, the financial service firms that had the lowest PBV/ROE ratios were:

Company	PBV	ROE	PBV/ROE
J. P. Morgan	1.15	17.5	0.06571429
PNC Bank Corp.	1.18	17.2	.06860465
Chemical Bank	.97	14.1	.06879433
Bankamerica	1.00	11.4	.0877193
First Union Corp.	1.38	15.7	.08789809

FIGURE 15.3 Undervalued and Overvalued Securities

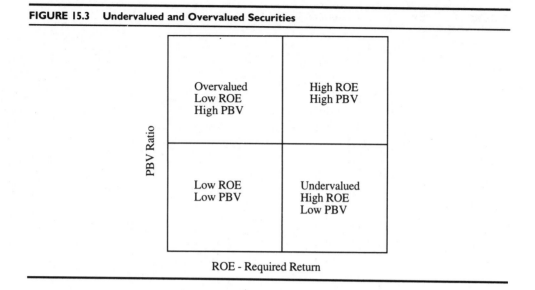

The firms would be considered undervalued using this approach, though there might be another explanation for the phenomenon.

The firms that had the highest PBV/ROE ratios were:

Company	PBV	ROE	PBV/ROE
Midlantic Corp.	1.28	6.5	0.19692308
Chase Manhattan	.95	5.7	.16666667
Wells Fargo	2.2	14.2	.15492958
U.S. Trust	2.56	18.5	.13837838
Suntrust Banks	1.64	13.1	.21519084

These firms would be considered overvalued.

The Determinants of Return on Equity

The emphasis placed on historical or current returns on equity in the analysis of the Dow 30 stocks should not obscure the fact that the price is determined by expectations of future returns in equity. To the extent that there is a correlation between past and future returns on equity, the historical measures matter. Focusing on the current return on equity can be dangerous, however, when the competitive environment is changing and can lead to significant errors in valuation (as evidenced in the earlier illustration of IBM).

The difference between return on equity and the required rate of return is a measure of a firm's capacity to earn super-normal profits in the business in which it operates. Corporate strategists have examined the determinants of the size and expected duration of these excess profits (and high return on equity) using a variety of frameworks. One of the better known is the "five forces of competition" framework developed by Porter (see Figure 15.5). In

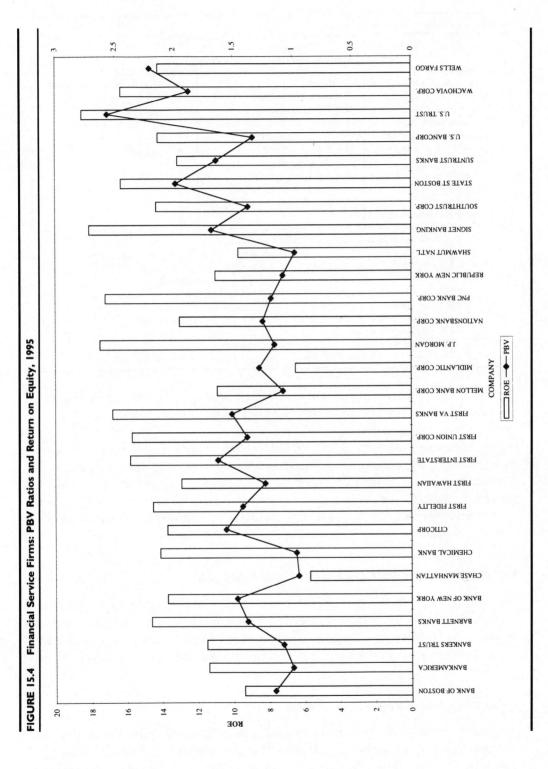

FIGURE 15.4 Financial Service Firms: PBV Ratios and Return on Equity, 1995

329

FIGURE 15.5 Determinants of Return on Equity

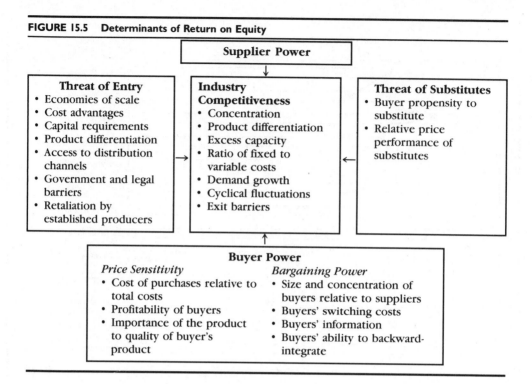

his approach, competition arises not only from established producers producing the same product but also from suppliers of substitutes and from potential new entrants into the market.

In Porter's framework, firms are able to maintain a high return on equity because there are significant barriers to entry by new firms or by competitors. The analysis of the return on equity of a firm can be made richer and much more informative by examining the competitive environment in which it operates. There may also be clues in this analysis to the future direction of the return on equity.

ESTIMATING PBV RATIOS FROM COMPARABLES

Price/book value ratios vary across firms for a number of reasons: different expected growth, different payout ratios, different risk levels, and, most importantly, different returns on equity. Comparisons of PBV ratios across firms and/or across time that do not take into account these differences are likely to be flawed.

Using Comparable Firms: Pros and Cons

The most common approach to estimating PBV ratios for a firm is to choose a group of comparable firms, calculate the average PBV ratio for this group, and base the PBV ratio estimate for a firm on this average. The adjustments made to reflect differences in fundamentals between the firm being valued and the comparable group are usually made subjectively.

There are several problems with this approach. First, the definition of a "comparable" firm is essentially a subjective one. The use of other firms in the industry as the control group is often not a solution because firms within the same industry can have very different business mixes and risk and growth profiles. There is also plenty of potential for bias. Second, even when a legitimate group of comparable firms can be constructed, differences will persist in fundamentals between the firm being valued and this group. Adjusting for differences subjectively does not provide a satisfactory solution to this problem, since these judgments are only as good as the analysts making them.

Using the Entire Cross-Section—A Cross-Sectional Regression

In contrast to the "comparable firm" approach, the information in the entire cross-section of firms can be used to predict PBV ratios. The simplest way of summarizing this information is with a multiple regression, with the PBV ratio as the dependent variable and proxies for risk, growth, return on equity, and payout forming the independent variables.

Past Studies

The relationship between price/book value ratios and the return on equity has been highlighted in other studies. Wilcox (1984) posited a strong linear relationship between PBV ratio (plotted on a logarithmic scale) and return on equity. Using data from 1981 for 949 Value Line stocks, he arrived at the following equation:

$$\log(PBV) = -1.00 + 7.51(\text{Return on Equity})$$

He also found that this regression has much smaller mean-squared error than competing models using price/earnings ratios and/or growth rates.

Updated Regressions

These PBV ratio regressions have been updated in the following section using data from 1987 to 1991. The COMPUSTAT database was used to extract information on PBV ratios, return on equity, payout ratios, and earnings growth rates (for the preceding five years) for all NYSE and AMEX firms with data available in each year. The betas were obtained from the CRSP tape for each year. All firms with negative book values were eliminated from the sample, and the regression of PBV on the independent variables yielded the following for each year:

Year	Regression	R^2
1987	PBV = .1841 + .00200 Payout − .3940 Beta + 1.3389 EGR + 9.35 ROE	.8617
1988	PBV = .7113 + .00007 Payout − .5082 Beta + .4605 EGR + 6.9374 ROE	.8405

(continued)

Year	Regression	R^2
1989	PBV = .4119 + .0063 Payout − .6406 Beta + 1.0038 EGR + 9.55 ROE	.8851
1990	PBV = .8124 + .0099 Payout − .1857 Beta + 1.1130 EGR + 6.61 ROE	.8846
1991	PBV = 1.1065 + .3505 Payout − .6471 Beta + 1.0087 EGR + 10.51 ROE	.8601

where PBV = PBV ratio at yearend
 Payout = dividend payout ratio at yearend
 Beta = beta of the stock
 EGR = earnings growth rate over the preceding five years
 ROE = Net Income/Book Value of Equity

1995 regression

PBV = .4138 + .3194 Payout − .3418 Beta + .3549 EGR + 14.75 ROE

 R^2 = .7726

EGR = expected earnings growth rate over the next five years

Illustration 15.7: Valuing an initial public offering using the cross-sectional regression

Assume that you have been asked to value Semitool Inc., a company that manufactures equipment used in the fabrication of semiconductors, early in 1995 and that you have obtained the following data on the company:

 Book Value of Equity = $29.60 million

 Net Income in 1994 = $3.60 million

 Beta based on comparable firms = 1.40 (This is the average beta for
 comparable firms.)

 Free Cashflows to Equity in 1994 = − $2.50 million

 Expected Growth Rate over the next five years = 20%

First compute the variables in the desired units:

 Payout = 0% (Assume that this company will not pay dividends)

 Earnings Growth Rate = 20%

 Return on Equity = 3.60/29.60 = 12.16%

 Beta = 1.40

Then compute the value as follows:

 Predicted PBV Ratio = .4138 + (.3194 × 0) − (.3418 × 1.40)
 + (.3549 × .20) + (14.75 × .1216) = 1.80

 Predicted Market Value of Equity in Semitool = 1.80 × $29.60
 = $53.28 million

PBV RATIOS AND INVESTMENT STRATEGIES

Investors have used the relationship between price and book value in a number of investment strategies, ranging from the simple to the sophisticated. Some have used low price/book value ratios as a screen to pick undervalued stocks.

PBV Ratios and Excess Returns

Several studies have established a relationship between PBV ratios and excess returns. Rosenberg, Reid, and Lanstein (1985) found that the average returns on U.S. stocks are positively related to the ratio of a firm's book value to market value. Between 1973 and 1984, the strategy of picking stocks with high book value/price ratios (low price/book value ratios) yielded an excess return of 36 basis points a month. Fama and French (1992), in examining the cross-section of expected stock returns between 1963 and 1990, established that the positive relationship between book value/price ratios and average returns persists in both the univariate and multivariate tests, and is even stronger than the size effect in explaining returns. When they classified firms on the basis of book value/price ratios into twelve portfolios, firms in the lowest book value/price (higher PBV) class earned an average monthly return of 0.30%, while firms in the highest book value/price (lowest PBV) class earned an average monthly return of 1.83% for the 1963–1990 period.

Chan, Hamao, and Lakonishok (1991) found that the book value/market value ratio has a strong role in explaining the cross-section of average returns on Japanese stocks. Capaul, Rowley, and Sharpe (1993) extended the analysis of price/book value ratios across other international markets and conclude that value stocks, that is, stocks with low PBV ratios, earned excess returns in every market that they analyzed, between 1981 and 1992. Their annualized estimates of the return differential earned by stocks with low PBV ratios, over the market index, were as follows:

Country	Added Return to Low PBV Portfolio
France	3.26%
Germany	1.39%
Switzerland	1.17%
United Kingdom	1.09%
Japan	3.43%
United States	1.06%
Europe	1.30%
Global	1.88%

A caveat is in order. Fama and French point out that low PBV ratios may operate as a measure of risk, since firms with prices well below book value are more likely to be in trouble and go out of business. Investors therefore have to evaluate for themselves whether the additional returns made by such firms justify the additional risk taken on by investing in them.

Using PBV Ratios as an Investment Screen

The excess returns earned by firms with low PBV ratios has been exploited by investment strategies that use PBV ratios as a screen. Ben Graham, for instance, listed price being less than two-thirds of book value as one of the criteria to be used to pick stocks.

The discussion in the preceding section emphasized the importance of return on equity in determining the PBV ratio and noted that only firms with high return on equity and a low PBV ratio could be considered undervalued. This proposition was tested by screening all NYSE stocks from 1981 to 1990 on the basis of both PBV ratios and returns on equity and creating two portfolios—an "undervalued" portfolio with low PBV ratios (in the bottom 25% of the universe) and high returns on equity (in the top 25% of the universe), and an "overvalued" portfolio with high PBV ratios (in the top 25% of the universe) and low returns on equity (in the bottom 25% of the universe)—each year, and then estimating excess returns on each portfolio in the following year. The following table summarizes returns on these two portfolios for each year from 1982 to 1991.

Year	Undervalued Portfolio	Overvalued Portfolio	S&P 500
1982	37.64%	14.64%	40.35%
1983	34.89%	3.07%	.68%
1984	20.52%	−28.82%	15.43%
1985	46.55%	30.22%	30.97%
1986	33.61%	.60%	24.44%
1987	−8.80%	−.56%	−2.69%
1988	23.52%	7.21%	9.67%
1989	37.50%	16.55%	18.11%
1990	−26.71%	−10.98%	6.18%
1991	74.22%	28.76%	31.74%
1982–1991	25.60%	10.61%	17.49%

The undervalued portfolios significantly outperformed the overvalued portfolios in eight out of ten years, earning an average of 14.99% more per year between 1982 and 1991, and also had an average return significantly higher than the Standard and Poors 500.

VARIANTS ON PBV RATIOS

Tobin's Q: Market Value/Replacement Cost

Definition

Tobin's Q provides an alternative to the price/book value ratio, by relating the market value of the firm to the replacement value of the assets in place. In cases where inflation has pushed up the price of the assets or where technology has reduced the price of the assets, this measure may provide a better measure of undervaluation.

Tobin's Q = Market Value of Assets/Replacement Value of Assets in Place

While this measure has some advantages in theory, it does have some practical problems. The first is that the replacement value of some assets may be difficult to estimate, largely because they are so firm specific. The second is that, even where replacement values are available, substantially more information is needed to construct this measure than the traditional PBV ratio.

In practice, analysts often use shortcuts to arrive at Tobin's Q, using book value of assets as a proxy for replacement value. In these cases, the only distinction between this measure and the PBV ratio is that this ratio is stated in terms of the entire firm (rather than just the equity).

Determinants

The value obtained from Tobin's Q is determined by two variables—the market value of the firm and the replacement cost of assets in place. In inflationary times, where the cost of replacing assets increases significantly, Tobin's Q will generally be lower than the unadjusted PBV ratio. Conversely, if the cost of replacing assets declines much faster than the book value (computers might be a good example), Tobin's Q will generally be higher than the unadjusted PBV ratio.

Link to Takeovers

Many studies in recent years have suggested that a low Tobin's Q is indicative of an undervalued or a poorly managed firm, which is more likely to be taken over. Lang, Stulz, and Walkling (1989) concluded that firms with low Tobin's Q are more likely to be taken over for purposes of restructuring and increasing value. They also found that shareholders of high q bidders gain significantly more from successful tender offers than shareholders of low q bidders.

The Estep T Score

The Estep T model takes into account three variables—return on equity, growth, and PBV ratios—that have been emphasized in this chapter, and consolidates them into one measure. Estep (1985, 1987) provides a simple derivation of this model, which yields the following:

$$T = g + \frac{(ROE - g)}{PBV} + \frac{\triangle PBV}{PBV}(1 + g)$$

where T = Estep T = total return
 g = growth of stockholders' book value of equity over the period
 ROE = return on equity
 PBV = price/book value ratio of equity
 \triangle PBV = change in PBV ratio over the period

This approach can then be used to decompose actual returns from past periods into three components—growth, cashflow yield, and valuation change. More importantly, this approach can also be used to predict future returns and pick undervalued and overvalued securities. Estep tests out the performance of a portfolio, created on the basis of the highest expected return, as measured by

the T score, and concludes that for the period 1982–1986 this portfolio would have earned an excess return of 5.2% over the S&P 500.

CONCLUSION

The relationship between price and book value is much more complex than most investors realize. The PBV ratio of a firm is determined by its expected payout ratio, its expected growth rate in earnings, and its riskiness. The most important determinant, however, is the return on equity earned by the firm—higher (lower) returns lead to higher (lower) PBV ratios. The mismatch that should draw investor attention is the one between return on equity and PBV ratios—high PBV ratios with low returns on equity (overvalued) and low PBV ratios with high returns on equity (undervalued).

QUESTIONS AND SHORT PROBLEMS

1. Answer true or false to the following statements, with a short explanation.
 a. A stock that sells for less than book value is undervalued.
 b. If a company's return on equity drops, its price/book value (PBV) ratio will generally drop more than proportionately—that is, if the return on equity drops by half, the PBV ratio will drop by more than half.
 c. A combination of a low PBV ratio and a high expected return on equity suggests that a stock is undervalued.
 d. Other things remaining equal, a higher growth stock will have a higher PBV ratio than a lower growth stock.
 e. In the Gordon growth model, firms with higher dividend payout ratios will have higher PBV ratios.
2. NCH Corporation, which markets cleaning chemicals, insecticides, and other products, paid dividends of $2.00 per share in 1993 on earnings of $4.00 per share. The book value of equity per share was $40.00, and earnings are expected to grow 6% a year in the long term. The stock has a beta of 0.85 and sells for $60 per share. (The Treasury bond rate is 7%.)
 a. Based upon these inputs, estimate the price/book value ratio for NCH.
 b. How much would the return on equity have to increase to justify the PBV ratio that NCH sells for currently?
3. You are analyzing the price/book value ratios for firms in the trucking industry relative to returns on equity and required rates of return. The data on the companies are as follows:

Company	PBV	ROE	Beta
Builders Transport	2.00	11.5%	1.00
Carolina Freight	0.60	5.5%	1.20
Consolidated Freight	2.60	12.0%	1.15
J. B. Hunt	2.50	14.5%	1.00
M. S. Carriers	2.50	12.5%	1.15
Roadway Services	3.00	14.0%	1.15
Ryder System	2.25	13.0%	1.05
Xtra Corporation	2.80	16.5%	1.10

(The Treasury bond rate is 7%.)
 a. Compute the average PBV ratio, return on equity, and beta for the industry.
 b. Based upon these averages, are stocks in the industry under- or overvalued relative to book values?
4. United Healthcare, a health maintenance organization, is expected to have earnings growth of 30% for the next five years and of 6% after that. The dividend payout ratio will be only 10% during the high growth phase but will increase to 60% in steady state. The return on equity was 21% in the most recent time period. The stock has a beta of 1.65 currently, but the beta is expected to drop to 1.10 in steady state. (The Treasury bond rate is 7.25%.)
 a. Estimate the PBV ratio for United Healthcare, given the inputs provided here.
 b. How sensitive is the PBV ratio to estimates of growth during the high growth period?
 c. United Healthcare trades at a PBV ratio of 7.00. How long would extraordinary growth have to last (at a 30% annual rate) to justify this PBV ratio?
5. Johnson and Johnson, a leading manufacturer of health care products, had a return on equity of 31.5% in 1993 and paid out 37% of its earnings as dividends. The stock had a beta of 1.25. (The Treasury bond rate is 6%.) The extraordinary growth is expected to last for ten years, after which the growth rate is expected to drop to 6% and the return on equity to 15%. (The beta will move to 1.)
 a. Assuming the return on equity and dividend payout ratio continue at current levels for the high growth period, estimate the PBV ratio for Johnson and Johnson.
 b. If health care reform passes, it is believed that Johnson and Johnson's return on equity will drop to 20% for the high growth phase. If they choose to maintain their existing dividend payout ratio, estimate the new PBV ratio for Johnson and Johnson. (You can assume that the inputs for the steady state period are unaffected.)
6. Assume that you have done a regression of PBV ratios for all firms on the New York Stock Exchange and arrived at the following result:

PBV = 0.88 + 0.82 PAYOUT + 7.79 GROWTH − 0.41 BETA
 + 13.81 ROE $\{R^2 = 0.65\}$

where Payout = Dividend payout ratio during most recent period
 Beta = Beta of the stock in most current period
 Growth = Projected growth rate in earnings over next five years
To illustrate, a firm with a payout ratio of 40%, a beta of 1.25, a ROE of 25%, and expected growth rate of 15% would have had a price/book value ratio of:

PBV = 0.88 + 0.82(0.4) + 7.79(.15) − 0.41(1.25)+ 13.81(.25)
 = 5.3165

 a. What, if any, use would you put the R squared of the regression to?
 b. Consider the initial public offering in the previous example. Estimate the predicted PBV ratio for this initial public offering using the cross-sectional regression. Why might this result be different from the peer group regression done in the prior problem?

16

Price/Sales Multiples

The price/earnings and price/book value multiples remain the most widely used of the multiples in valuation. In recent years, however, analysts have increasingly turned to value as a multiple of sales. This chapter describes some of the advantages associated with using this multiple, its determinants, and how it can be used to examine the effects of corporate strategy and to assess the value of brand names.

ISSUES IN USING PS MULTIPLES

Advantages

The ratio of price to sales has proved attractive to analysts for a number of reasons. First, unlike PE and PBV ratios, which can become negative and not meaningful, the price/sales multiple is available even for the most troubled firms. Second, unlike earnings and book value, which are heavily influenced by accounting decisions on depreciation, inventory, and extraordinary charges, revenue is relatively difficult to manipulate. Third, PS multiples are not as volatile as PE multiples and hence may be more reliable for use in valuation. For instance, the PE ratio of a cyclical firm changes much more than its PS ratio, because earnings are much more sensitive to economic changes than revenue. Fourth, the PS multiple provides a convenient handle for examining the effects of changes in pricing policy and other corporate strategic decisions.

Disadvantages

One of the advantages of using revenue instead of earnings and book value is its stability. This stability can also become a disadvantage, when the firm's problems lie in cost control. In such cases, the revenues may not decline even though the earnings and value drop precipitously. Thus, while it is tempting to use PS multiples to value troubled firms with negative earnings and book value, the failure to control for differences across firms in costs and profit margins can lead to very misleading valuations.

PS RATIOS AND FUNDAMENTALS

The price/sales ratio can be related to the same fundamentals that determine value in discounted cashflow models—earnings growth rates, the payout ratio, and risk.

PS Ratio for a Stable Firm

A stable firm is a firm growing at a rate comparable to or lower than the nominal growth rate in the economy in which it operates. The value of equity for a stable firm, using the Gordon growth model, is:

$$P_0 = \frac{DPS_1}{r - g_n}$$

where P_0 = value of equity

DPS_1 = expected dividends per share next year

r = required rate of return on equity

g_n = growth rate in dividends (forever)

Substituting EPS_0 (Payout Ratio) $(1 + g_n)$ for DPS, the value of the equity can be written as:

$$P_0 = \frac{EPS_0 \times \text{Payout Ratio} \times (1 + g_n)}{r - g_n}$$

Using the definition Profit Margin = EPS_0/Sales per Share, the value of equity can be written as:

$$P_0 = \frac{\text{Sales}_0 \times \text{Profit Margin} \times \text{Payout Ratio} \times (1 + g_n)}{r - g_n}$$

Rewriting in terms of the price/sales ratio,

$$\frac{P_0}{\text{Sales}_0} = PS = \frac{\text{Profit Margin} \times \text{Payout Ratio} \times (1 + g_n)}{r - g_n}$$

If the profit margin is based upon expected earnings in the next time period, this can be simplified to:

$$\frac{P_0}{\text{Sales}_0} = PS = \frac{\text{Profit Margin} \times \text{Payout Ratio}}{r - g_n}$$

The PS ratio is an increasing function of the profit margin, the payout ratio, and the growth rate, and a decreasing function of the riskiness of the firm.

Illustration 16.1: Estimating the PS ratio for a stable firm: International Multifoods

International Multifoods had revenues per share of $134.70 in 1994, earnings per share of $1.50, and paid out 55% of its earnings as dividends. The growth rate in earnings and dividends, in the long term, is expected to be 6%. The beta is 0.80, and the Treasury bond rate was 7.5% in 1994.

Net Profit Margin = Net Income/Revenues = \$1.50/\$134.70 = 1.11%
Cost of Equity = 7.5% + (.8 × 5.5%) = 11.90%

PS Ratio based on fundamentals = .011 × .55 × 1.06/(.119 − .06) = .1097

International Multifoods was selling at a PS ratio of 0.14 at the time of this analysis.

PS Ratio for a High-Growth Firm

The price/sales ratio for a high-growth firm can also be related to fundamentals. In the special case of the two-stage dividend discount model, this relationship can be made explicit fairly simply. The value of equity of a high-growth firm in this model can be written as:

P_0 = Present Value of Expected Dividends in the high-growth period
+ Present Value of Terminal Price

When the growth rate is assumed to be constant forever, the value can be written as follows:

$$P_0 = \frac{EPS_0 \times \text{Payout Ratio} \times (1 + g)\left(1 - \frac{[1 + g]^n}{[1 + r]^n}\right)}{r - g} + \frac{EPS_0 \times \text{Payout Ratio}_n \times (1 + g)^n(1 + g_n)}{(r - g_n)(1 + r)^n}$$

where g = growth rate in the first n years
Payout Ratio = payout ratio in the first n years
g_n = growth rate after n years, forever (stable growth rate)
Payout Ratio$_n$ = payout ratio after n years, forever (stable growth rate)

Substituting Sales$_0$ × Profit Margin for EPS_0 and rearranging, we get:

$$\frac{P_0}{\text{Sales}_0} = PS = \text{Profit Margin}$$

$$\times \left\{ \frac{\text{Payout Ratio}(1 + g)\left(1 - \frac{[1 + g]^n}{[1 + r]^n}\right)}{r - g} + \frac{\text{Payout Ratio}_n(1 + g)^n(1 + g_n)}{(r_n - g_n)(1 + r)^n} \right\}$$

The PS ratio is determined by:

(a) *Net profit margin:* The PS ratio is an increasing function of the net profit margin, or Earnings per share/Revenue per share.
(b) *Payout ratio in both the high-growth period and the stable-growth period:* The PS ratio increases as the payout ratio increases.

(c) *Riskiness (through the discount rate r):* The PS ratio becomes lower as riskiness increases.

(d) *Expected growth rate in earnings, in both the high-growth and stable-growth periods:* The PS ratio increases as the growth rate increases, in either period.

This formula is general enough to be applied to any firm, even one that is not paying dividends right now.

Illustration 16.2: Estimating the PS ratio for a high-growth firm in the two-stage model

Assume that you have been asked to estimate the PS ratio for a firm with the following characteristics:

Growth Rate in the first five years = 20%

Growth Rate after five years = 8%

Beta = 1.0

Payout Ratio in the first five years = 20%

Payout Ratio after five years = 68%

Riskfree Rate = Treasury bond rate = 6%

Net Profit Margin = 10%

Required Rate of Return = 6% + (1 × 5.5%) = 11.5%

$$PS = .10 \left(\frac{.2 \times 1.20 \times \left[1 - \frac{1.20^5}{1.115^5}\right]}{.115 - .20} + \frac{.68 \times 1.20^5 \times 1.08}{(.115 - .08) \times 1.115^5} \right) = 3.16$$

The estimated PS ratio for this firm is 3.16.

Illustration 16.3: Estimating the PS ratio: Marks & Spencer

Marks & Spencer is a leading British retailer, which sells consumer goods under the name "St. Michael" and markets its wares internationally through Brooks Brothers and Kings Supermarkets in the United States and through chains of retail stores in Canada, Europe, and Hong Kong. The following are the estimates in 1994 for the high-growth and stable-growth periods:

High-Growth Period

Expected length of the period = 10 years (longer because of international growth prospects)

Expected Growth Rate = 16.00%

Net Profit Margin = Net Profits/Revenues = 8.88% (expected to remain unchanged)

Payout Ratio = 44.29% (expected to remain unchanged)

Beta = .99 (expected to remain unchanged)

Stable-Growth Period

Expected Growth Rate = 6.00%

Expected Payout Ratio = 65.00%

Beta is expected to remain unchanged.

The long-term gilt (government bond) rate in the United Kingdom was 8.50% at the time of this analysis, and a risk premium of 5.50% was used.

Cost of Equity = 8.5% + (.99 × 5.5%) = 13.95%

$$PS = .0888 \left(\frac{.4429 \times 1.16 \times \left[1 - \frac{1.16^{10}}{1.1395^{10}} \right]}{.1395 - .16} + \frac{.65 \times 1.16^{10} \times 1.06}{(.1395 - .06) \times 1.1395^{10}} \right)$$

$$= 1.35$$

The market value of Marks & Spencer was 1.68 times revenues in March 1995.

PS RATIOS AND PROFIT MARGINS

The key determinant of price/sales ratios is the profit margin. Firms involved in businesses that have high margins can expect to sell for much higher multiples of sales. A decline in profit margins has a twofold effect. First, the reduction in profit margins reduces the PS ratio directly. Second, the lower profit margin can lead to lower growth and hence lower PS ratios.

The profit margin can be linked to expected growth fairly easily if an additional term is defined—the ratio of sales per share to book value per share. Using a relationship developed between growth rates and fundamentals, the expected growth rate can be written as:

Expected Growth Rate = Retention Ratio × Return on Equity

= Retention Ratio(Net Profit/Sales)(Sales/BV of Equity)

= Retention Ratio × Profit Margin × Sales/BV of Equity

As the profit margin is reduced, the expected growth rate will decrease, if the sales do not increase proportionately.

Illustration 16.4: Estimating the effect of lower profit margins on PS ratios

Consider a firm with the following characteristics:

Growth Rate in the first five years = 20%

Growth Rate after five years = 8%

Beta = 1.00

Payout Ratio in the first five years = 20%

Payout Ratio after five years = 50%

Required Return = 11.5%

Profit Margin = 10%

Sales/BV Ratio = 2.50

$$PS = .10 \left(\frac{.2 \times 1.20 \times \left[1 - \frac{1.20^5}{1.115^5} \right]}{.115 - .20} + \frac{.50 \times 1.20^5 \times 1.08}{(.115 - .08) \times 1.115^5} \right) = 2.35$$

If the firm's profit margin declines and total revenue remains unchanged, the PS ratio for the firm will decline with it. For instance, if the firm's profit margin declines from 10% to 5% and the Sales/BV ratio remains unchanged:

New Growth Rate in the first five years = Retention Ratio × Profit Margin

$$\times \text{ (Sales/BV)}$$

$$= .8 \times .05 \times 2.50 = 10\%$$

The new PS ratio can then be calculated as follows:

$$PS = .05 \left(\frac{.2 \times 1.10 \times \left[1 - \frac{1.10^5}{1.115^5} \right]}{.115 - .10} + \frac{.50 \times 1.10^5 \times 1.08}{(.115 - .08) \times 1.115^5} \right) = .77$$

The relationship between profit margins and the PS ratio is illustrated more comprehensively in the graph in Figure 16.1. The PS ratio is estimated as a function of the profit margin, keeping the sales/book value of equity ratio fixed.

This linkage of PS ratios and profit margins can be utilized to analyze the value effects of changes in corporate strategy as well as the value of a "brand name."

Valuation Effects of Changing from High-Margin to Low-Margin Strategy

Porter (1980) in his examination of generic strategies, suggests that firms can follow one of two strategies to gain competitive advantage. In the first, the firm offers a product similar to that offered by its competitors, but at a much lower price, and hopes to establish cost leadership. In the second strategy, the firm attempts to differentiate its product from its competitors and charge a price premium. The choice between a "high margin, low volume" strategy (differentiation) and a "low margin, high volume" strategy (cost leadership) can be examined using the PS multiple. This is illustrated in the following example:

FIGURE 16.1 PS Ratios and Profit Margins

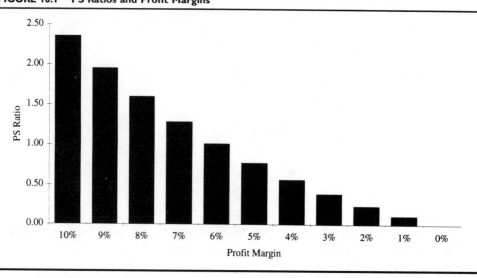

Illustration 16.5: Choosing between a high-margin and a low-margin strategy

Assume that a firm has to choose between the two strategies:

	High-Margin/ Low-Volume	Low-Margin/ High-Volume
Profit Margin	10%	5%
Sales/Book Value	2.5	4.0

Assume, in addition, that the firm is expected to pay out 20% of its earnings as dividends over the next five years and 50% of earnings as dividends after that. The growth rate after year five is expected to be 8%. The book value of equity per share is $10. The beta of the firm is 1.0. The Treasury bond rate is 6%, and the risk premium is 5.5%.

Expected Return = 6% + (1 × 5.5%) = 11.5%

High-Margin Strategy

Expected Growth Rate in the first five years = Profit Margin × (Sales/BV)

$$\times \text{ Retention Ratio}$$

$$= .10 \times 2.5 \times .8 = 20\%$$

$$\text{PS Ratio} = .10 \left(\frac{.2 \times 1.20 \times \left[1 - \dfrac{1.20^5}{1.115^5} \right]}{.115 - .20} + \frac{.50 \times 1.20^5 \times 1.08}{(.115 - .08) \times 1.115^5} \right)$$

$$= 2.35$$

Sales/Book Value = 2.50

Price = PS Ratio × (Sales/BV) × BV = 2.35 × 2.5 × $10 = $58.75

Low-Margin Strategy

Expected Growth Rate in the first five years = Profit Margin \times (Sales/BV)

$$\times \text{ Retention Ratio}$$

$$= .05 \times 4 \times .8 = 16\%$$

$$\text{PS Ratio} = .05 \left(\frac{.2 \times 1.16 \times \left[1 - \dfrac{1.16^5}{1.115^5} \right]}{.115 - .16} + \frac{.50 \times 1.16^5 \times 1.08}{(.115 - .08) \times 1.115^5} \right)$$

$$= .9966$$

Sales/Book Value = 4.00

Price = PS Ratio \times (Sales/BV) \times BV = .9966 \times 4 \times \$10 = \$39.86

The high-margin strategy is clearly the better one to follow here, if the objective is value maximization.

Illustration 16.6: Examining the effects of moving to a lower-margin, high-volume strategy: Philip Morris

Philip Morris had sales of \$59,131 million, earned \$4,939 million in net income, and had a book value of equity of \$12,563 million in 1992. The firm paid 42% of its earnings as dividends. The beta for the stock was 1.10.

Based upon 1992 figures, the inputs for the PS ratio calculation would be:

Profit Margin = 8.35%

Sales/Book Value of Equity = 4.71

Book Value per share = \$14.10

Retention Ratio = 58%

Expected Return = 7% + (1.1 \times 5.5%) = 13.05%

Expected Growth Rate over the next five years = Retention Ratio

$$\times \text{ Profit Margin}$$

$$\times \text{ (Sales/Book Value)}$$

$$= .58 \times .0835 \times 4.71$$

$$= 22.80\%$$

Expected Growth Rate after five years = 6%

Expected payout ratio after five years = 65%

$$\text{PS Ratio} = .0835 \left(\frac{.42 \times 1.2280 \times \left[1 - \dfrac{1.2280^5}{1.1305^5} \right]}{.1305 - .2280} + \frac{.65 \times 1.2280^5 \times 1.06}{(.1305 - .06) \times 1.1305^5} \right)$$

$$= 1.46$$

In April 1993, Philip Morris announced that it was cutting prices on its Marlboro brand of cigarettes because of increasing competition from low-priced competitors.

This was viewed by many analysts as a precursor of further price cuts and a signal of a move to a lower-margin strategy. Assume that the profit margin will decline to 7% from 8.35% as a consequence. All the other inputs are unchanged.

$$\text{Expected Growth Rate over the next five years} = \text{Retention Ratio}$$
$$\times \text{ Profit Margin}$$
$$\times \text{ (Sales/Book Value)}$$
$$= .58 \times .07 \times 4.71 = 19.12\%$$

$$\text{PS Ratio} = .07 \left(\frac{.42 \times 1.1912 \times \left[1 - \frac{1.1912^5}{1.1305^5} \right]}{.1305 - .1912} + \frac{.65 \times 1.1912^5 \times 1.06}{(.1305 - .06) \times 1.1305^5} \right)$$

$$= 1.06$$

As a consequence of the new lower-price strategy, the PS ratio will decline from 1.46 to 1.06. Unless the sales/book value ratio increases by an equivalent margin (27.40%), the value of Philip Morris will decrease. In the case where profit margins decline by this magnitude and the sales/book value is not expected to increase, the value will decline by 27.40%.

The market reacted negatively to the announcement of price cuts, and the stock price dropped approximately 20% on the announcement.

An Aside on Market Share
There are some firms that have focused on maximizing market share as their primary objective function. The linkage between increased market share and market value is a tenuous one and can be examined using the profit margin/PS ratio framework suggested above. If increasing market share leads to higher margins, either because of economies of scale driving down costs or increased market power driving out competitors, it will lead to higher value. If the increase in the market share is accompanied by lower prices and profit margins, the net effect on value can be negative.

The Value of a Brand Name

One of the critiques of traditional valuation is that it fails to consider the value of brand names and other intangibles. Hiroyumi Itami, in his book *Mobilizing Invisible Assets,* provides a summary of this criticism. He says:

Analysts have tended to define assets too narrowly, identifying only those that can be measured, such as plant and equipment. Yet the intangible assets, such as a particular technology, accumulated consumer information, brand name, reputation and corporate culture, are invaluable to the firm's competitive power. In fact, these invisible assets are the only real source of competitive edge that can be sustained over time.

While this criticism is clearly overstated, the approaches used by analysts to value brand names are often ad hoc and may significantly overstate or understate their value. Firms with well-known brand names often sell for higher multiples than lesser-known firms. The standard practice of adding on a "brand name premium," often set arbitrarily, to discounted cashflow value, can lead to erroneous estimates. Instead, the value of a brand name can be estimated using the approach that relates profit margins to PS ratios.

One of the benefits of having a well-known and respected brand name is that firms can charge higher prices for the same products, leading to higher profit margins and hence to higher PS ratios and firm value. The larger the price premium that a firm can charge, the greater is the value of the brand name. The value of a brand name can be written, in terms of equity, as:

$$\text{Value of brand name} = (PS_b - PS_g) \times \text{Sales}$$

where PS_b = PS ratio of the firm with the benefit of the brand name
PS_g = PS ratio of a firm with a generic product

More generally, the value of a brand name can also be written in terms of firm value:

$$\text{Value of Brand Name} = \{(V/S)_b - (V/S)_g\} \times \text{Sales}$$

where $(V/S)_b$ = Value of Firm/Sales ratio of the firm with brand name
$(V/S)_g$ = Value of Firm/Sales ratio

Illustration 16.8: Valuing a brand name: Kellogg

The following is an analysis of brand name value at Kellogg Corporation. The estimates for Kellogg were obtained from 1994 financial statements. The after-tax operating margin for the generic equivalent was obtained by looking at a private brand cereal manufacturer. The expected growth is assumed to be:

Expected Growth in After-Tax Operating Income = Retention Ratio
× Return on Assets

	Kellogg	Generic
Pretax Operating Margin	22.00%	10.50%
After-Tax Operating Margin	14.08%	6.72%
Return on Assets	32.60%	15.00%
Retention Ratio	56.00%	56.00%
Expected Growth	18.26%	8.40%
Length of high-growth period	5 yr.	5 yr.
Cost of Equity	13.00%	13.00%
E/(D + E)	92.16%	92.16%
Cost of Debt	8.50%	8.50%
D/(D + E)	7.84%	7.84%
Cost of Capital	12.41%	12.41%
Value/Sales Ratio	3.39	1.10

Value of Kellogg brand name = (3.39 − 1.10) × $6,562 million

= $15,026 million

Value of Kellogg as a company = 3.39 × $6,562 million = $22,271 million

Approximately 67.70% ($15,026/$22,271) of the value of the company can be traced to brand name value.

The Danger of Double-Counting the Value of a Brand Name

The value of a brand name results in higher growth and higher value for the firm owning it. There are some analyses where the brand name value is double-counted. To provide an illustration of how this could happen, assume that Kellogg is valued using a discounted cashflow model and that the expected growth rate used in the valuation is 18.26%. This value already incorporates the value of the brand name through the use of the high growth rate. If an additional value is now assigned to the brand name, the brand name value is double-counted.

From Net Income to Operating Income and from Equity to Value

The profits margins for firms can be stated in terms of net income (as they have in all the examples so far) or in terms of operating income (EBIT). If pretax operating margins are used, the appropriate value estimate is that of the

FIGURE 16.2 Undervalued and Overvalued Securities

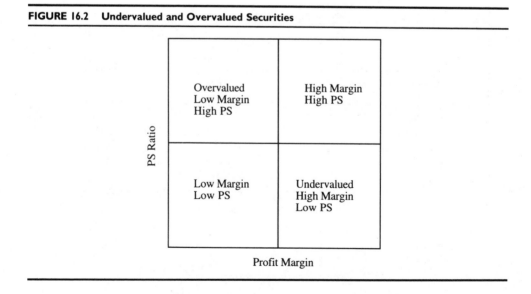

FIGURE 16.3 Profit Margins and PS Ratios—Largest U.S. Companies

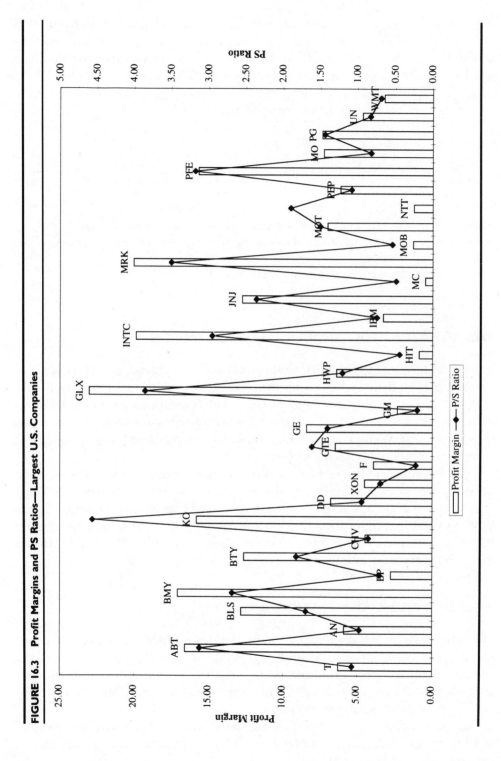

349

firm. In particular, if one makes the assumption that free cashflows to the firm are equal to EBIT($1 -$ tax rate) (and net capital expenditures and working capital requirements are 0), then the value of the firm can be written as a function of the after-tax operating margin, which is EBIT($1 - t$)/Sales:

$$\frac{\text{Value of Firm}_0}{\text{Sales}_0} = \text{After-tax Operating Margin}$$

$$\times \left\{ \frac{(1 + g)\left(1 - \dfrac{[1 + g]^n}{[1 + \text{WACC}]^n}\right)}{\text{WACC} - g} + \frac{(1 + g)^n(1 + g_n)}{(\text{WACC}_n - g_n)(1 + \text{WACC})^n} \right\}$$

where g = growth rate in after-tax operating income for the first n years

g_n = growth rate in after-tax operating income after n years, forever (stable growth rate)

WACC = weighted average cost of capital

WACC_n = weighted average cost of capital after n years

THE MISMATCH THAT SHOULD DRAW ATTENTION

The key determinant of the price/sales ratio is the profit margin. Thus, it is not surprising to find firms with low profit margins and low PS ratios and firms with high profit margins and high PS ratios. However, firms with high PS ratios and low profit margins as well as firms with low PS ratios and high profit margins should attract investors' attention as potentially overvalued and undervalued securities, respectively (see Figure 16.2).

The PS ratios and profit margins of the largest (in market value terms) firms on the NYSE in March 1995 are plotted on the matrix in Figure 16.3. From Figure 16.3, it is clear that the companies with the highest profit margins (Coca Cola [KO], Glaxo [GLX], Intel [INTC], and Merck [MRK]) also have the highest PS ratios. Companies with low profit margins (Matsushita ADR [MC], Hitachi ADR [HIT]) trade at low PS ratios.

PS RATIOS AND CROSS-SECTIONAL DATA

The other approach to estimating the price/sales multiple draws on the cross-sectional determinants of the multiple. While it is legitimate to look at the average PS ratios of comparable firms operating in the same industry, differences in profit margins have to be taken into consideration before any comparisons can be made or conclusions drawn.

In this approach, the cross-sectional data is used to estimate the PS ratio as a function of fundamental variables—dividend payout, beta, growth rate in earnings, and profit margin.

PS = a + b Payout + c Beta + d Earnings Growth Rate + e Profit Margin

The following represent regressions of PS ratios on the fundamentals for each year from 1987 to 1991.

Year	Regression	R^2
1987	PS = .7894 + .0008 Payout − .2734 Beta + .5022 EGR + 6.46 Margin	.4434
1988	PS = .1660 + .0006 Payout − .0692 Beta + .5504 EGR + 10.31 Margin	.7856
1989	PS = .4911 + .0393 Payout − .0282 Beta + .2836 EGR + 10.25 Margin	.4601
1990	PS = .0826 + .0105 Payout − .1073 Beta + .5449 EGR + 10.36 Margin	.8885
1991	PS = .5189 + .2749 Payout − .2485 Beta + .4948 EGR + 8.17 Margin	.4853

where PS = PS Ratio at yearend
 Margin = profit margin for the year = Net Income/Sales for the year (in percent)
 Payout = payout ratio = Dividends/Earnings at yearend
 EGR = Earnings Growth Rate over the previous five years

1995 regression

PS = −.1967 + .4503Payout − .1769Beta + .0820EGR + 13.02Margin

R^2 = .7726

EGR = expected Earnings Growth Rate over the next five years

Illustration 16.9: Valuing an acquisition target using PS ratio regressions

Assume that you have been asked to value Wellcome Inc. and that you have obtained the following 1994 data on the company:

Sales = $4,350 million

Net Income = $845 million

Beta = .60

Earnings Growth Rate = 10%

Dividend Payout Ratio = 50%

First compute the profit margin in the desired unit:

Profit Margin = $845/$4,350 = 19.43%

Using the regression estimated for the end of 1994:

Predicted PS Ratio = −.1967 + (.4503 × .50) − (.1769 × .60) + (.0820 × .10) + (13.02 × .1943) = 2.46

Predicted Market Value of Equity = 2.46 × $4,350 = $10,701 million

USING PS RATIOS IN INVESTMENT STRATEGIES

Screening stocks on the basis of price/sales multiples has been incorporated by some investors into their investment strategies. There is relatively little empirical evidence either for or against the proposition that low-PS-ratio stocks are more likely to be undervalued. In one of the few direct tests of the PS ratio, Senchack and Martin (1987) compared the performance of low-PS-ratio portfolios with low-PE-ratio portfolios and concluded that the low-PS-ratio portfolio outperformed the market but not the low-PE-ratio portfolio. They also found that the low-PE-ratio strategy earned more consistent returns than did a low-PS-ratio strategy and that a low-PS-ratio strategy was more biased toward picking smaller firms. Jacobs and Levy (1988a) tested the value of low PS ratios (standardized by the PS ratios of the industries in which the firms operated) as part of a general effort to disentangle the forces influencing equity returns. They concluded that low-PS-ratio stocks, by themselves, yielded an excess return of 0.17% a month between 1978 and 1986, which was statistically significant. Even when other factors were thrown into the analysis,[1] the PS ratio remained a significant factor in explaining excess returns (together with PE ratio and size).

The significance of profit margins in explaining PS ratios suggests that screening on the basis of both PS ratios and profit margins should be more successful at identifying undervalued securities. To test this proposition, the stocks on the NYSE were screened on the basis of PS ratios and profit margins to create "undervalued" portfolios (PS ratios in the lowest quartile and profit margins in the highest quartile) and "overvalued" portfolios (PS ratios in the highest quartile and profit margins in the lowest quartile) at the end of each year from 1981 to 1990. The returns on these portfolios in the following year are summarized in the following table:

Year	Undervalued Portfolio	Overvalued Portfolio	S&P 500
1982	50.34%	17.72%	40.35%
1983	31.04%	6.18%	.68%
1984	12.33%	−25.81%	15.43%
1985	53.75%	28.21%	30.97%
1986	27.54%	3.48%	24.44%
1987	−2.28%	8.63%	−2.69%
1988	24.96%	16.24%	9.67%
1989	16.64%	17.00%	18.11%
1990	−30.35%	−17.46%	6.18%
1991	91.20%	55.13%	31.74%
1982–1991	23.76%	15.48%	17.49%

During the period, the undervalued portfolios outperformed the overvalued portfolios in six out of the ten years, earning an average of 8.28% more per year, and averaged a significantly higher return than the Standard and Poors 500.

CONCLUSION

The price/sales multiple is widely used to value private firms and to compare value across publicly traded firms. An analysis of the fundamentals highlights the importance of profit margins in determining this multiple, in addition to the standard variables—the dividend payout ratio, the required rate of return, and the expected growth rate. Comparisons of PS multiples across firms have to take into account differences in profit margins. One approach that controls for differences in fundamentals is the cross-sectional regression approach, which is described and presented in this chapter.

QUESTIONS AND SHORT PROBLEMS

1. Longs Drug, a large drugstore chain operating primarily in Northern California, had sales per share of $122 in 1993, on which it reported earnings per share of $2.45 and it paid a dividend per share of $1.12. The company is expected to grow 6% in the long term, and has a beta of 0.90. (The Treasury bond rate is 7%.)
 a. Estimate the appropriate price/sales multiple for Longs Drug.
 b. The stock is currently trading for $34 per share. Assuming the growth rate is estimated correctly, what would the profit margin need to be to justify this price per share?
2. You are examining the wide differences in PS ratios that you can observe among firms in the retail store industry and are trying to come up with a rationale to explain these differences.

Company	Price	Per Share Sales	Per Share Earnings	Expected Growth	Beta	Payout
Bombay Company	$38	$ 9.70	$0.68	29.00%	1.45	0%
Bradlees	15	168.60	1.75	12.00%	1.15	34
Caldor	32	147.45	2.70	12.50%	1.55	0
Consolidated Store	21	23.00	0.95	26.50%	1.35	0
Dayton Hudson	73	272.90	4.65	12.50%	1.30	38
Federated	22	58.90	1.40	10.00%	1.45	0
Kmart	23	101.45	1.75	11.50%	1.30	59
Nordstrom	36	43.85	1.60	11.50%	1.45	20
Penney	54	81.05	3.50	10.50%	1.10	41
Sears	57	150.00	4.55	11.00%	1.35	36
Tiffany's	32	35.65	1.50	10.50%	1.50	19
Wal-Mart	30	29.35	1.05	18.50%	1.30	11
Woolworth	23	74.15	1.35	13.00%	1.25	65

 a. There are two companies that sell for more than revenues, the Bombay Company and Wal-Mart. Why?
 b. What is the variable that is most highly correlated with price/sales ratios?
 c. Which of these companies is most likely to be over- or undervalued? How did you arrive at this judgment?
3. Walgreen, a large retail drugstore chain in the United States, reported net income

of $221 million in 1993 on revenues of $8,298 million. It paid out 31% of its earnings as dividends, a payout ratio it is expected to maintain between 1994 and 1998, during which period earnings growth is expected to be 13.5%. After 1998, earnings growth is expected to decline to 6%, and the dividend payout ratio is expected to increase to 60%. The beta is 1.15 currently and is expected to remain unchanged. (The Treasury bond rate is 7%.)

 a. Estimate the price/sales ratio for Walgreen, assuming its profit margin remains unchanged at 1993 levels.

 b. How much of this PS ratio can be attributed to extraordinary growth?

4. Tambrands, a leading producer of tampons, reported net income of $122 million on revenues of $684 million in 1992. Earnings growth was anticipated to be 11% over the next five years, after which it was expected to be 6%. The firm paid out 45% of its earnings as dividends in 1992, and this payout ratio was expected to increase to 60% during the stable period. The beta of the stock was 1.00.

 During the course of 1993, erosion of brand loyalty and increasing competition for generic brands led to a drop in net income to $100 million on revenues of $700 million. The sales/book value ratio was comparable to 1992 levels. (The Treasury bond rate in 1992 and 1993 was 7%.)

 a. Estimate the PS ratio based upon 1992 profit margins and expected growth.

 b. Estimate the PS ratio based upon 1993 profit margins and expected growth. (Assume that the extraordinary growth period remains five years, but that the growth rate will be impacted by the lower margins.)

5. Gillette Inc., the leading producer of grooming aids, was faced with a significant corporate strategy decision early in 1994 on whether it would continue its high-margin strategy or shift to a lower margin to increase sales revenues in the face of intense generic competition. The two strategies being considered were as follows:

 Status Quo High-Margin Strategy

 • Maintain profit margins at 1993 levels (In 1993, net income was $575 million on revenues of $5,750 million.) from 1994 to 2003.

 • The sales/book value ratio, which was 3 in 1993, can then be expected to decline to 2.5, between 1994 and 2003.

 Low-Margin Higher Sales Strategy

 • Reduce net profit margin to 8% from 1994 to 2003.

 • The sales/book value ratio will then stay at 1993 levels from 1994 to 2003.

The book value per share at the end of 1993 was $9.75. The dividend payout ratio, which was 33% in 1993, is expected to remain unchanged from 1994 to 2003 under either strategy, as is the beta, which was 1.30 in 1993. (The Treasury Bond rate is 7%.)

 After 2003, the earnings growth rate is expected to drop to 6% and the dividend payout ratio is expected to be 60% under either strategy. The beta will decline to 1.0.

 a. Estimate the PS ratio under the status quo strategy.

 b. Estimate the PS ratio under the low margin strategy.

c. Which strategy would you recommend, and why?

d. How much would sales have to drop under the status quo strategy for the two strategies to be equivalent?

6. You have regressed price/sales ratios against fundamentals for NYSE stocks in 1994 and come up with the following regression:

PS = 0.42 + 0.33 PAYOUT + 0.73 GROWTH − 0.43 BETA
 + 7.91 MARGIN

For instance, a firm with a 35% payout, a 15% growth rate, a beta of 1.25, and a profit margin of 10% would have had a price/sales ratio of:

PS = 0.42 + 0.33*0.35 + 0.73*0.15 − 0.43*125 + 7.91*0.10

 = 0.8985

a. What do the coefficients on this regression tell you about the independent variables relationship with the dependent variable? What statistical concerns might you have with this regression?

b. Estimate the PS ratios for all the retail chains described in question 2. Why might this answer be different from the one obtained from the regression of only the drugstore firms? Which one would you consider more reliable and why?

ENDNOTE

1. Jacobs and Levy considered 25 different anomaly measures, based upon past studies, including size, PE ratio, PBV ratio, earnings momentum measures, relative strength, and neglect.

Option Pricing Theory

Options are derivative securities, that is, they are securities that derive their value from an underlying asset. Though traded options are of comparatively recent origin, option-like securities have existed for much longer. The technology available for valuing options has expanded dramatically in the last 25 years, especially since the development of the basic option pricing model by Black and Scholes. Their model, while setting the general framework for valuing options, has been modified to work in a variety of settings. An alternative model for option pricing, the binomial model, also provides more insight into the determinants of option value. This chapter examines the characteristics of options, the determinants of option value, and the basic option pricing models as a prelude to the application of these models to valuation.

WHAT IS AN OPTION?

An option provides the holder with the right to buy or sell a specified quantity of an underlying asset at a fixed price (called a strike price or an exercise price) at or before the expiration date of the option. Since it is a right and not an obligation, the holder can choose not to exercise the right and allow the option to expire. There are two types of options—call options and put options.

Call Options

A call option gives the buyer of the option the right to buy the underlying asset at a fixed price at any time prior to the expiration date of the option. The buyer pays a price for this right.

Summary of Transactions in a Call Option

	Now	At Expiration
Buyer of call	pays the call price and gets the right to exercise.	If asset value (S) > strike price (K), buyer exercises. Gross Profit = S − K Net Profit = S − K − Call Price

	Now	*At Expiration*
Seller of call	receives the call price and agrees to deliver the asset at the exercise price if the buyer demands it any time before expiration.	If S < K, buyer does not exercise. Call Price = Buyer's Loss = Seller's Gain

A Payoff Diagram

A call payoff diagram (see Figure 17.1) illustrates the cash payoff on a call option at expiration. For a call, the net payoff is negative (and equal to the price paid for the call) if the value of the underlying asset is less than the strike price. If the price of the underlying asset exceeds the strike price, the gross payoff is the difference between the value of the underlying asset and the strike price, and the net payoff is the difference between the gross payoff and the price of the call.

Put Options

A put option gives the buyer of the option the right to sell the underlying asset at a fixed price at any time prior to the expiration date of the option. The buyer pays a price for this right.

Summary of Transactions in a Put Option

	Now	*At Expiration*
Buyer of put	pays the put price and gets the right to exercise.	If asset value (S) < strike price (K), buyer exercises. Gross Profit = K − S Net Profit = K − S − Put Price (*continued*)

FIGURE 17.1 Call Option Payoff Diagram

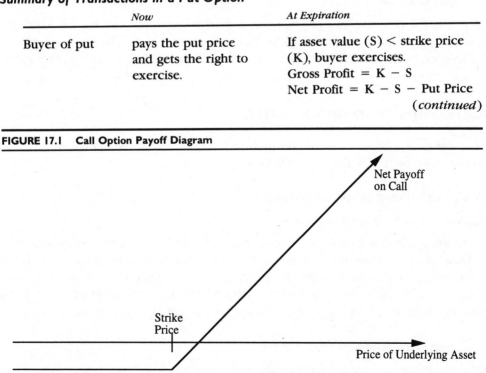

FIGURE 17.2 Put Option Payoff Diagram

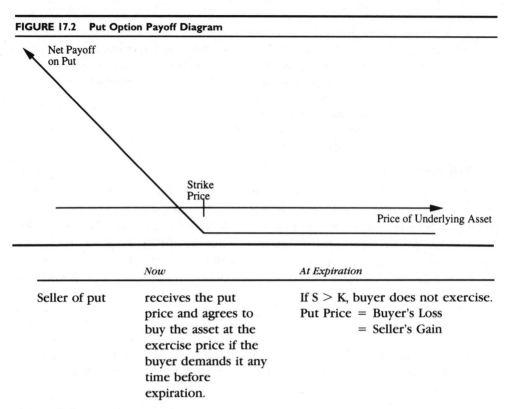

	Now	*At Expiration*
Seller of put	receives the put price and agrees to buy the asset at the exercise price if the buyer demands it any time before expiration.	If S > K, buyer does not exercise. Put Price = Buyer's Loss = Seller's Gain

A Payoff Diagram

A put has a negative net payoff (equal to the put price) if the value of the underlying asset exceeds the strike price and has a gross payoff equal to the difference between the strike price and the value of the underlying asset if the asset value is less than the strike price. This is shown in Figure 17.2.

DETERMINANTS OF OPTION VALUE

The value of an option is determined by a number of variables relating to the underlying asset and financial markets.

Variables relating to the Underlying Asset

Current Value of Underlying Asset

Options are assets that derive value from an underlying asset. Consequently, changes in the value of the underlying asset affect the value of the options on that asset. Since calls provide the right to buy the underlying asset at a fixed price, an increase in the value of the asset will make calls more valuable. Puts, on the other hand, become less valuable as the value of the asset increases.

Variance in Value of Underlying Asset

The buyer of an option acquires the right to buy or sell the underlying asset at a fixed price. The higher the variance in the value of the underlying asset,

the greater is the value of the option. This is true for both calls and puts. While it may seem counterintuitive that an increase in a risk measure (variance) should increase value, options are different from other securities since the buyers of options can never lose more than the price they pay for them, and can potentially earn significant returns from large price movements.

Dividends Paid on the Underlying Asset

The value of the underlying asset can be expected to decrease if there are dividend payments on the asset during the life of the option. As a consequence, the value of a call on the asset is a decreasing function of the size of expected dividend payments, and the value of a put is an increasing function of expected dividend payments.

Variables Relating to the Option Characteristics

Strike Price of the Option

A key characteristic that describes the option is the strike price. In the case of calls, where the holder acquires the right to buy at a fixed price, the value of the call will decline as the strike price increases. In the case of puts, where the holder has the right to sell at a fixed price, the value will increase as the strike price increases.

Time to Expiration on the Option

Both calls and puts become more valuable as the time to expiration on them increases. The longer time to expiration provides more time for the value of the underlying asset to move, increasing the value of both types of options. There is an additional effect on option value. In the case of a call, where the buyer has to pay a fixed price at expiration, the present value of this fixed price decreases as the life of the option increases, and this increases the value of the call. In the case of a put, the present value of the expected proceeds from the sale of the asset at the exercise price at expiration decreases as the time to expiration is extended.

Variables Relating to Financial Markets

Riskless Interest Rate Corresponding to the Life of the Option

Since the buyer of an option pays the price of the option up front, there is an opportunity cost involved. This opportunity cost will depend upon the level of interest rates and the time to expiration on the option. The riskless interest rate also enters into the valuation of options when the present value of the exercise price is calculated, since the exercise price does not have to be paid (received) until expiration on calls (puts). Increases in the interest rate will increase the value of calls and reduce the value of puts.

American Versus European Options: Variables Relating to Early Exercise

An American option can be exercised at any time prior to its expiration, while a European option can be exercised only at expiration. The possibility of early exercise makes American options more valuable than otherwise-similar European options and also makes them more difficult to value. There is one compensating factor, which enables the former to be valued using models designed for the latter. In most cases, the time premium associated with the remaining life of an option makes early exercise suboptimal.

While early exercise is generally not optimal, there are at least two exceptions to this rule. One is where the underlying asset pays large dividends, thus reducing the value of the asset and of call options on it. In these cases, call options may be exercised just before an ex-dividend date, if the time premium on the options is less than the expected decline in asset value as a consequence of the dividend payment. The other is where an investor holds both the underlying asset and deep in-the-money puts on that asset, at a time when interest rates are high. The time premium on the put may be less than the potential gain from exercising the put early and earning interest on the exercise price.

A Summary of the Determinants of Option Value

The following table summarizes the variables and their predicted effects on call and put prices:

	Effect on	
Factor	Call Value	Put Value
Increase in stock price	Increases	Decreases
Increase in strike price	Decreases	Increases
Increase in variance of underlying asset	Increases	Increases
Increase in time to expiration	Increases	Increases
Increase in interest rates	Increases	Decreases
Increase in dividends paid	Decreases	Increases

OPTION PRICING MODELS

Option pricing theory has made vast strides since 1972, when Black and Scholes published their path-breaking paper providing a model for valuing dividend-protected European options. They used a "replicating portfolio," that is, a portfolio composed of the underlying asset and the riskfree asset that had the same cashflows as the option being valued, to come up with their final formulation. While their derivation is mathematically complicated, there is a simpler binomial model for valuing options that draws on the same wellspring of logic. This chapter provides a short introduction to both the binomial and the Black-Scholes models.

The Binomial Model

The binomial option pricing model is based upon a simple formulation for the asset price process, where the asset, in any time period, can move to one of two possible prices.

Describing a Binomial Process

The general formulation of a stock price process that follows the binomial model is as follows:

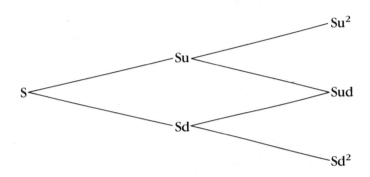

where S is the current stock price and the price moves up to Su with probability p and down to Sd with probability $1 - p$ in any time period.

Creating a Replicating Portfolio

The objective in creating a replicating portfolio is to use a combination of riskfree borrowing/lending and the underlying asset to create the same cashflows as the option being valued. The principles of arbitrage then apply, and the value of the option has to be equal to the value of the replicating portfolio. In the case of the general formulation above, where stock prices can move up to Su or down to Sd in any time period, the replicating portfolio for a call with strike price K will involve borrowing \$B and acquiring Δ of the underlying asset, where,

$$\Delta = \text{number of units of the underlying asset bought} = (C_u - C_d)/(Su - Sd)$$

where C_u = value of the call if the stock price is Su
 C_d = value of the call if the stock price is Sd

The Iterative Process of Valuation

In a multiperiod binomial process, the valuation has to proceed iteratively, starting with the last time period and moving backward in time until the current point in time. The portfolios replicating the option are created at each step and valued, providing the values for the option in that time period. The final output from the binomial option pricing model is that the value of the option can be stated in terms of the replicating portfolio, composed of Δ shares (option delta) of the underlying asset and riskfree borrowing/lending.

> Value of the call = Current Value of the underlying asset × Option Delta
> − Borrowing needed to replicate the option

Illustration 17.1: An example of binomial valuation

Assume that the objective is to value a call with a strike price of $50, which is expected to expire in two time periods, on an underlying asset whose price currently is $50, and is expected to follow a binomial process.

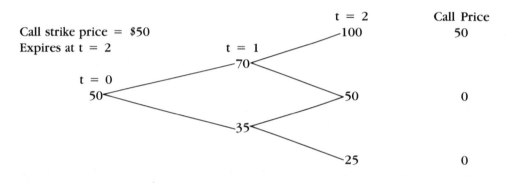

Now assume that the interest rate is 11%. In addition, define:

Δ = number of shares in the replicating portfolio

B = dollars of borrowing in the recursive portfolio

Objective: Combine Δ shares of stock and B dollars of borrowing to replicate the cashflows from the call with a strike price of $50.

Step 1: Start with the end nodes and work backward.

Implication: If the stock price is $70 at $t = 1$, borrowing $45 and buying 1 share of the stock will give the same cashflows as buying the call. The value of the call at $t = 1$, if the stock price is $70, is therefore:

$$70\Delta - B = 70 - 45 = \$25$$

Implication: If the stock price is $35 at $t = 1$, then the call is worth nothing.

Step 2: Move backward to the earlier time period and create a replicating portfolio that will provide the cashflows that the option will provide.

Implication: Borrowing $22.50 and buying $5/7$ of a share will provide the same cashflows as a call with a strike price of $50. The value of the call therefore has to be the same as the value of this position:

Value = $5/7$ × Current Stock Price − $22.5 = $13.20

The Determinants of Value

The binomial model provides insight into the determinants of option value. The value of an option is not determined by the expected price of the asset but by its current price, which, of course, reflects expectations about the future. This is a direct consequence of arbitrage. If the option value deviates from the value of the replicating portfolio, investors can create an arbitrage position, that is, a position that requires no investment, involves no risk, and delivers positive returns. The option value increases as the time to expiration is extended, as the price movements (u and d) get larger, and with increases in the interest rate.

The Black-Scholes Model

The binomial model provides an intuitive feel for the determinants of option value, but it does require a large number of inputs, in terms of expected future prices at each node. The Black-Scholes is not a different model for modeling

options. It is one limiting case of the binomial, but it reduces the informational requirements substantially.

The Linkage to the Binomial

The binomial model is a discrete-time model for asset price movements, with a time interval (t) between price movements. As the time interval is shortened, the limiting distribution, as t approaches 0, can take one of two forms. If, as t approaches 0, price changes become smaller, the limiting distribution is the normal distribution and the price process is a continuous one. If, as t approaches 0, price changes remain large, the limiting distribution is the Poisson distribution, that is, a distribution that allows for price jumps.

The Black-Scholes model applies when the limiting distribution is the normal distribution,[1] and explicitly assumes that the price process is continuous and that there are no jumps in asset prices.

The Model

The version of the model presented by Black and Scholes was designed to value European options, which were dividend-protected. Thus neither the possibility of early exercise nor the payment of dividends affects the value of options in this model.

The value of a call option in the Black-Scholes model can be written as a function of the following variables:

S = current value of the underlying asset

K = strike price of the option

t = life to expiration of the option

r = riskless interest rate corresponding to the life of the option

σ^2 = variance in the ln(value) of the underlying asset

The model itself can be written as:

$$\text{Value of the call} = SN(d_1) - Ke^{-rt}N(d_2)$$

where

$$d_1 = \frac{\ln\left(\frac{S}{K}\right) + \left(r + \frac{\sigma^2}{2}\right)t}{\sigma\sqrt{t}}$$

$$d_2 = d_1 - \sigma\sqrt{t}$$

The process of valuation of options using the Black-Scholes involves the following steps:

Step 1: The inputs to the Black-Scholes are used to estimate d_1 and d_2.

Step 2: The cumulative normal distribution functions, $N(d_1)$ and $N(d_2)$, corresponding to these standardized normal variables are estimated.

Step 3: The present value of the exercise price is estimated, using the continuous time version of the present value formulation:

Present Value of the exercise price $= Ke^{-rt}$

Step 4: The value of the call is estimated from the Black-Scholes model.

The Determinants of Value

The determinants of value in the Black-Scholes are the same as the determinants in the binomial—the current value of the stock price, the variability in stock prices, the time to expiration on the option, the strike price, and the riskless interest rate. The principle of replicating portfolios that is used in binomial valuation also underlies the Black-Scholes. The following table provides the replicating portfolios for calls and puts, using the binomial and the Black-Scholes models, where B, B', \triangle, and \triangle' are estimated from the binomial process.

	Replicating Portfolio	
Option Position	with Binomial	with Black-Scholes
Buy call option	Borrow $B. Buy \triangle shares of stock.	Borrow $Ke^{-rt}N(d_2)$. Buy $N(d_1)$ shares of stock.
Sell call option	Lend $B. Sell short \triangle shares.	Lend $Ke^{-rt}N(d_2)$. Sell short $N(d_1)$ shares.
Buy put option	Lend $B'. Sell short \triangle' shares.	Lend $Ke^{-rt}(1 - N[d_2])$. Sell short $(1 - N[d_1])$ shares.
Sell put option	Borrow $B'. Buy \triangle' shares.	Borrow $Ke^{-rt}(1 - N[d_2])$. Buy $(1 - N[d_1])$ shares.

Model Limitations and Fixes

The version of the Black-Scholes model presented above does not take into account the possibility of early exercise or the payment of dividends. Both impact the value of options, and there are adjustments which, while not perfect, provide partial corrections to value.

Dividends

The payment of dividends reduces the stock price. Consequently, call options will become less valuable and put options more valuable as dividend payments are increased. There are two possible adjustments for dividends, one for short-term options and the other for long-term options.

Short-Term Options. When options have only a short time to expiration (less than a year), the present value of the expected dividends during the life of the option can be estimated and subtracted from the current value of the asset to obtain a "dividend-adjusted value." This dividend-adjusted value can be used as the input for S in the Black-Scholes model.

$$\text{Adjusted Stock Price} = S' = S - \sum \frac{Div_t}{(1 + r)^t}$$

Value of the call $= S'N(d_1) - Ke^{-rt}N(d_2)$

where

$$d_1 = \frac{\ln\left(\dfrac{S'}{K}\right) + \left(r + \dfrac{\sigma^2}{2}\right)t}{\sigma\sqrt{t}}$$

$$d_2 = d_1 - \sigma\sqrt{t}$$

Illustration 17.2: Valuing a short-term option with dividend adjustments: IBM

Consider a call option on IBM with a strike price of $45 and four months to expiration. The stock is trading at $50. Using past stock prices, the variance in the log of stock prices for IBM is estimated at 0.06. There is one dividend, amounting to $0.56, and it is expected to be paid in two months. The riskless rate is 3%.

Present Value of Expected Dividend $= \$.56/1.03^{2/12} = \$.5572$

Dividend-Adjusted Stock Price $= \$50 - \$.56 = \$49.44$

Other inputs for the Black-Scholes:

Strike Price $= \$45$

Variance in log(stock prices) $= .06$

Time to expiration $= 4$ months $= \frac{4}{12}$

Riskless Rate $= 3\%$

The value from the Black-Scholes is:

$d_1 = .8072$

$d_2 = .6658$

$N(d_1) = .7901$

$N(d_2) = .7472$

Value of the call $= (\$49.44 \times .7901) - \$45\, e^{-(.03 \times 4/12)}(.7472) = \5.78

A Note on Estimating the Inputs to the Black-Scholes Model
The Black-Scholes model requires inputs that are consistent on time measurement. As presented here, all the inputs have to be annualized. The variance, estimated from ln(asset prices), can be annualized easily because variances are linear in time if the serial correlation is 0. Thus, if monthly (weekly) prices are used to estimate variance, the variance is annualized by multiplying by 12 (52).

Long-Term Options. The present-value approach to dealing with dividends becomes tedious and difficult to apply for long-term options. If the dividend yield ($y =$ Dividends/Current Value of the asset) of the underlying asset is expected

to remain unchanged during the life of the option, the Black-Scholes model can be modified to take dividends into account.

$$C = Se^{-yt}N(d_1) - Ke^{-rt}N(d_2)$$

where

$$d_1 = \frac{\ln\left(\frac{S}{K}\right) + \left(r - y + \frac{\sigma^2}{2}\right)t}{\sigma\sqrt{t}}$$

$$d_2 = d_1 - \sigma\sqrt{t}$$

From an intuitive standpoint, the adjustments have two effects. First, the value of the asset is discounted back to the present at the dividend yield to take into account the expected drop in value from dividend payments. Second, the interest rate is offset by the dividend yield to reflect the lower carrying cost from holding the stock (in the replicating portfolio).

Illustration 17.3: Valuing a long-term option with dividend adjustments—primes and scores: IBM

Primes and scores are securities traded on the American Stock Exchange. A score entitles the holder to all price appreciation on an underlying traded stock over the life of the score, while the prime entitles the holder to all dividends (and the stock price, capped at the current level). Thus the score is a long-term call option on the underlying stock.

Consider primes and scores on IBM with a five-year lifetime. The current price of the stock is $50, and the stock is expected to maintain its current dividend yield (y = $2.26/$50 = 4.52%). The five-year bond rate is 5.5%. The inputs to the Black-Scholes model are:

S = current asset value = $50

K = strike price = $50

Riskless rate = 5.5%

Time to expiration = 5 years

Variance in log(stock prices) = .06

Dividend yield = 4.52%

The value from the Black-Scholes is:

d_1 = .3633 $N(d_1)$ = .6418

d_2 = −.1844 $N(d_2)$ = .4268

Value of score = $50 e^{-(.0452 \times 5)}(.6418) − $50 e^{-(.055 \times 5)}(.4268) = $9.39

Since the holder of the prime is entitled to all cashflows other than the price appreciation, the value of a prime can be estimated as follows:

Value of Prime = Value of Stock − Value of Score = $50 − $9.39 = $40.61

Early Exercise

There are two basic approaches for dealing with the possibility of early exercise. One approach values the option to each ex-dividend day and chooses the maximum of the estimated call values. The other approach uses a modified version of the binomial to consider the possibility of early exercise.

Approach 1: Pseudo-American Valuation.

Step 1: Define when dividends will be paid and how much the dividends will be.

Step 2: Value the call option to each ex-dividend date using the dividend-adjusted approach described above, where the stock price is reduced by the present value of expected dividends.

Step 3: Choose the maximum of the call values estimated for each ex-dividend day.

Illustration 17.4: Using Pseudo-American option valuation to adjust for early exercise

Consider an option with a strike price of $35 on a stock trading at $40. The variance in the log(stock prices) is 0.05, and the riskless rate is 4%. The option has a remaining life of eight months, and there are three dividends expected during this period:

Expected Dividend	Ex-Dividend Day
$0.80	In 1 month
.80	In 4 months
.80	In 7 months

The call option is first valued to just before the first ex-dividend date:

$$S = \$40 \qquad K = \$35 \qquad t = \tfrac{1}{12} \qquad \sigma^2 = .05 \qquad r = .04$$

The value from the Black-Scholes model is:

Value of Call = $5.132

The call option is then valued to before the second ex-dividend date:

Adjusted Stock Price = $40 − $.80/1.04$^{1/12}$ = $39.20

$$K = \$35 \qquad t = \tfrac{4}{12} \qquad \sigma^2 = .05 \qquad r = .04$$

The value of the call based upon these parameters is:

Value of Call = $5.07

The call option is then valued to before the third ex-dividend date:

Adjusted Stock Price = $40 − $.80/1.04$^{1/12}$ − $.80/1.04$^{4/12}$ = $38.41

$$K = \$35 \qquad t = \tfrac{7}{12} \qquad \sigma^2 = .05 \qquad r = .04$$

The value of the call based upon these parameters is:

Value of Call = $5.128

The call option is then valued to expiration:

Adjusted Stock Price = $40 − $.80/1.04$^{1/12}$ − $.80/1.04$^{4/12}$ − $.80/1.04$^{7/12}$

= $37.63

K = $35 t = $^{8}/_{12}$ σ^2 = .05 r = .04

The value of the call based upon these parameters is:

Value of Call = $4.76

Pseudo-American Value of the Call = Maximum ($5.132, $5.07, $5.128, $4.76)
= $5.132

Approach 2: Using the Binomial.

Step 1: If the variance in log(stock prices) has been estimated for the Black-Scholes, convert these into inputs for the binomial model:

$$u = \exp([r − \sigma^2/2][T/m] + \sqrt{[\sigma^2 T/m]})$$

$$d = \exp([r − \sigma^2/2][T/m] − \sqrt{[\sigma^2 T/m]})$$

where u and d are the up and down movements per unit time for the binomial, T is the life of the option, and m is the number of periods within that lifetime.

Step 2: Specify the period in which the dividends will be paid and make the assumption that the price will drop by the amount of the dividend in that period.

Step 3: Value the call at each node of the tree, allowing for the possibility of early exercise just before ex-dividend dates. There will be early exercise if the remaining time premium on the option is less than the expected drop in option value as a consequence of the dividend payment.

Step 4: Value the call at time 0, using the standard binomial approach.

The Impact of Exercise on the Value of the Underlying Asset

The derivation of the Black-Scholes model is based upon the assumption that exercising an option does not affect the value of the underlying asset. This may be true for listed options on stocks, but it is not true for some types of options. For instance, the exercise of warrants[2] increases the number of shares outstanding and brings in fresh cash into the firm, both of which will affect the stock price. The expected negative impact (dilution) of exercise will make warrants less valuable than otherwise similar call options. The adjustment for dilution in the Black-Scholes to the stock price involves three steps:

Step 1: The stock price is adjusted for the expected dilution from warrant exercise:

Dilution-adjusted S = (S n$_s$ + W n$_w$)/n$_s$

where S = current value of the stock

n_w = number of warrants outstanding
W = market value of warrants outstanding
n_s = number of shares outstanding

When the warrants are exercised, the number of shares outstanding will increase, reducing the stock price. The numerator reflects the market value of equity, including both stocks and warrants outstanding.

Step 2: The variance used in the option pricing formula is the variance in the value of the equity in the company (i.e., the value of stocks plus warrants, not just the stocks).

Step 3: Once the call is valued using the option pricing model, the option value is adjusted to reflect dilution:

Dilution-adjusted Value = Call Value from model $\times n_s/(n_w + n_s)$

Illustration 17.5: Valuing a warrant with dilution

MN Corporation has 1 million shares of stock trading at $50, and it is considering an issue of 500,000 warrants with an exercise price of $60 to raise fresh equity for the firm. The warrants will have a five-year lifetime. The standard deviation in the value of equity has been 20%, and the five-year riskless bond rate is 10%. The stock is expected to pay $1 in dividends per share this year, and is expected to maintain this dividend yield for the next five years.

The inputs to the warrant valuation model are as follows:

$S = (1,000,000 \times \$50 + 500,000 \times \$W)/(1,000,000 + 500,000)$

K = exercise price on warrant = $60

t = time to expiration on warrant = 5 years

σ^2 = variance in value of equity = $.2^2$ = .04

y = dividend yield on stock = $1/$50 = 2%

Since the value of the warrant is needed as an input to the process, there is an element of circularity in reasoning. After a series of iterations where the warrant value was used to reestimate S, the results of the Black-Scholes valuation of this option are:

d_1 = −.1435 $N(d_1)$ = .4430

d_2 = −.5907 $N(d_2)$ = .2774

Value of Call = $50 $e^{-(.02 \times 5)}$(.4430) − $60 $e^{-(.10 \times 5)}$(.2774) = $3.59

Value of Warrant = Value of Call $\times n_s/(n_w + n_s)$ = $3.59(1,000,000/1,500,000)
= $2.39

Illustration 17.6: Valuing a warrant: Siemens

In July 1993, Siemens AG (Germany) had 3 million warrants outstanding that expire in five years (in 1998), with an exercise price of 693 DM. There were 55.80 million shares outstanding in the company, and the stock was trading at 657.50 DM in July 1993, with a dividend yield of 1.98%. The five-year bond rate in Germany was 5.88%. The annualized variance in the value of equity for Siemens was 13.89%.

The inputs to the warrant valuation model are as follows:

S = (55.80 × 657.50 + 3.0 × W)/(55.80 + 3.0)

K = exercise price on warrant = 693 DM

t = time to expiration on warrant = 5 years

r = riskless rate corresponding to life of option = 5.88%

σ^2 = variance in value of stock = .1389

y = dividend yield on stock = 1.98%

The results of the Black-Scholes valuation of this option are:

d_1 = .5438 $N(d_1)$ = .7067

d_2 = −.2896 $N(d_2)$ = .3861

$$\text{Value of Warrant} = 657.50\, e^{-(.0198 \times 5)}(.7067) - 693\, e^{-(.0588 \times 5)}(.3861)$$
$$\times (55.80/58.80) = 195.81\ \text{DM}$$

The warrants were trading at 120.5 DM in July 1993.

Valuing Puts

The value of a put is related to the value of a call with the same strike price and the same expiration date through an arbitrage relationship that specifies that:

C − P = S − Ke^{-rt}

where C is the value of the call and P is the value of the put (with the same life and exercise price).

This arbitrage relationship can be derived fairly easily and is called put-call parity. To see why put-call parity holds, consider creating the following portfolio:

(a) Sell a call and buy a put with exercise price K
(b) Buy the stock at current stock price S.

The payoff from this position is riskless and always yields K at expiration (t). To see this, assume that the stock price at expiration is S:

Position	Payoffs at t if S* > K	Payoffs at t if S* < K
Sell call	−(S* − K)	0
Buy put	0	K − S*
Buy stock	S*	S*
Total	K	K

Since this position always yields K risklessly, its value must be equal to the present value of K at the riskless rate (Ke^{-rt}).

$$S + P - C = Ke^{-rt}$$
$$C - P = S - Ke^{-rt}$$

This relationship can be used to value puts. Substituting the Black-Scholes for-mulation for the value of an equivalent call:

$$\text{Value of Put} = Se^{-yt}(N[d_1] - 1) - Ke^{-rt}(N[d_2] - 1)$$

where

$$d_1 = \frac{\ln\left(\frac{S}{K}\right) + \left(r - y + \frac{\sigma^2}{2}\right)t}{\sigma\sqrt{t}}$$

$$d_2 = d_1 - \sigma\sqrt{t}$$

CONCLUSION

An option is an asset with payoffs that are contingent on the value of an underly-ing asset. A call option provides its holder with the right to buy the underlying asset at a fixed price, whereas a put option provides its holder with the right to sell at a fixed price, both at any time before the expiration of the option. The value of an option is determined by six variables—the current value of the underlying asset, the variance in this value, the strike price and the life of the option, the riskless interest rate, and the expected dividends on the asset. This is illustrated in both the binomial and the Black-Scholes models, which value options by creating replicating portfolios, composed of the underlying asset and riskless lending or borrowing. These models can be used to value assets that have option-like characteristics.

QUESTIONS AND SHORT PROBLEMS

1. The following are prices of options traded on Microsoft Corporation, which pays no dividends.

	Call		Put	
	K = 85	K = 90	K = 85	K = 90
I month	2.75	1.00	4.50	7.50
3 month	4.00	2.75	5.75	9.00
6 month	7.75	6.00	8.00	12.00

The stock is trading at $83, and the annualized riskless rate is 3.8%. The standard deviation in log stock prices (based upon historical data) is 30%.
a. Estimate the value of a three-month call, with a strike price of $85.
b. Using the inputs from the Black-Scholes model, specify how you would repli-cate this call.

 c. What is the implied standard deviation in this call?

 d. Assume now that you buy a call with a strike price of $85 and sell a call with a strike price of $90. Draw the payoff diagram on this position.

 e. Using put-call parity, estimate the value of a three-month put with a strike price of $85.

2. You are trying to value three-month call and put options on Merck, with a strike price of $30. The stock is trading at $28.75 and is expected to pay a quarterly dividend per share of $0.28 in two months. The annualized riskless interest rate is 3.6%, and the standard deviation in log stock prices is 20%.

 a. Estimate the value of the call and put options using the Black-Scholes.

 b. What effect does the expected dividend payment have on call values? On put values? Why?

3. There is the possibility that the options on Merck described above could be exercised early.

 a. Use the pseudo-American call option technique to determine whether this will affect the value of the call.

 b. Why does the possibility of early exercise exist? What types of options are most likely to be exercised early?

4. You have been provided the following information on a three-month call:

$$S = 95 \quad K = 90 \quad t = 0.25 \quad r = 0.04$$

$$N(d1) = 0.5750 \quad N(d2) = 0.4500$$

 a. If you wanted to replicate buying this call, how much money would you need to borrow?

 b. If you wanted to replicate buying this call, how many shares of stock would you need to buy?

5. Go Video, a manufacturer of video recorders, was trading at $4 per share in May 1994. There were 11 million shares outstanding. At the same time, it had 550,000 one-year warrants outstanding, with a strike price of $4.25. The stock has had a standard deviation (in log stock prices) of 60%. The stock does not pay a dividend. The riskless rate is 5%.

 a. Estimate the value of the warrants, ignoring dilution.

 b. Estimate the value of the warrants, allowing for dilution.

 c. Why does dilution reduce the value of the warrants?

6. You are trying to value a long-term call option on the NYSE Composite Index, expiring in five years, with a strike price of $275. The index is currently at 250, and the annualized standard deviation in stock prices is 15%. The average dividend yield on the index is 3%, and it is expected to remain unchanged over the next five years. (The five-year Treasury bond rate is 5%.)

 a. Estimate the value of the long-term call option.

 b. Estimate the value of a put option, with the same parameters.

 c. What are the implicit assumptions you are making when you use the Black-Scholes model to value this option? Which of these assumptions are likely to be violated? What are the consequences of your valuation?

7. A new security on AT&T will entitle the investor to all dividends on AT&T over the next three years, limit upside potential to 20%, but also provide downside protection below 10%. AT&T stock is trading at $50, and three-year call and put options are traded on the exchange at the following prices:

	Call Options		Put Options	
K	1 year	3 year	1 year	3 year
45	$8.69	$13.34	$1.99	$ 3.55
50	$5.86	$10.89	$3.92	$ 5.40
55	$3.78	$ 8.82	$6.59	$ 7.63
60	$2.35	$ 7.11	$9.92	$10.23

How much would you be willing to pay for this security?

ENDNOTES

1. Stock prices cannot drop below 0, because of the limited liability of stockholders in publicly listed firms. Hence stock prices, by themselves, cannot be normally distributed, since a normal distribution requires some probability of infinitely negative values. The distribution of the natural logs of stock prices is assumed to follow a log-normal distribution in the Black-Scholes. This is why the variance used in the Black-Scholes is the variance in the log of stock prices.

2. Warrants are call options issued by firms, either as part of management compensation contracts or to raise equity.

18

Applications of Option Pricing Theory to Equity Valuation

Most readers of this chapter probably do not associate option pricing theory with equity or asset valuation. This chapter will aim to show that option pricing theory has an important role to play in valuation and that it provides a very different perspective that can be useful in understanding and analyzing troubled firms, natural resource firms, and high-technology firms.

APPLICATION OF OPTION PRICING MODELS TO VALUATION

The option pricing models described in the preceding chapter can be used to value any asset that has the characteristics of an option, with some caveats. In this section, option pricing theory will be applied to valuation in three areas: Equity will be valued as a call option on the firm, natural resource assets will be analyzed as options, and a patent will be valued as an option on a product.

A Few Caveats on Applying Option Pricing Models

When option pricing theory is applied to real options, as it is in this chapter, there are several potential problems that need to be addressed.

1. The underlying asset is not traded. Option pricing theory, as presented in the binomial and the Black-Scholes models, is built on the premise that a replicating portfolio can be created using the underlying asset and riskless lending and borrowing. While this is perfectly justifiable in the context of listed options on traded stocks, it becomes less defensible when the underlying asset is not traded and arbitrage is therefore not feasible. The options presented in this section are on assets that are not traded, and the value from option pricing models have to be interpreted with caution.

2. The price of the asset follows a continuous process. The Black-Scholes option pricing model is derived under the assumption that the underlying asset's price process is continuous, that is, there are no price jumps. If this assumption is violated, as it is with most real options, the model will underestimate the value of deep out-of-the-money options. One solution is to use a higher variance estimate to value deep out-of-the-money options and lower variance estimates for at-the-money or in-the-money options. Another is to use an option pricing model that explicitly allows for price jumps, though the inputs to these models are often difficult to estimate.[1]

3. The variance is known and does not change over the life of the option. The assumption that option pricing models make—that the variance is known and does not change over the option lifetime—is not unreasonable when applied to listed short-term options on traded stocks. When option pricing theory is applied to long-term real options, there are problems with this assumption, since the variance is unlikely to remain constant over extended periods of time and may in fact be difficult to estimate in the first place. Again, there are modified versions of the option pricing model that allow for changing variances, but they do require that the process by which variance changes be modeled explicitly.

4. Exercise is instantaneous. The option pricing models are based upon the premise that the exercise of an option is instantaneous. This assumption may be difficult to justify with real options, where exercise may require the building of a plant or the construction of an oil rig, actions that are unlikely to happen in an instant. The fact that exercise takes time also implies that the true life of a real option is often less than the stated life. Thus, while a firm may own the rights to an oil reserve for the next ten years, the fact that it takes several years to get the oil out reduces the life of the natural resource option that the firm owns.

VALUING EQUITY AS AN OPTION

The traditional approaches to valuing equity have been described in detail in earlier chapters. Discounted cashflow valuation is based upon forecasted cashflows, and the present value of these cashflows, at the appropriate discount rate, provides an estimate of the value of the equity or the firm. Multiples, on the other hand, value equity by looking at comparable firms and adjusting for differences between firms. This section offers an alternative view of equity and may provide a useful perspective when a troubled firm has to be valued.

The General Framework

The equity in a firm is a residual claim; that is, equity holders lay claim to all cashflows left over after other financial claimholders (debt, preferred stock, etc.) have been satisfied. If a firm is liquidated, the same principle applies, with equity investors receiving whatever is left over in the firm after all outstanding

debts and other financial claims are paid off. The principle of limited liability, however, protects equity investors in publicly traded firms if the value of the firm is less than the value of the outstanding debt, and they cannot lose more than their investment in the firm. The payoff to equity investors, on liquidation, can therefore be written as:

$$\text{Payoff to equity on liquidation} = V - D \qquad \text{if } V > D$$
$$= 0 \qquad \text{if } V \le D$$

where V = value of the firm

D = face value of the outstanding debt and other external claims

A call option with a strike price of K on an asset with a current value of S has the following payoffs:

$$\text{Payoff on exercise} = S - K \qquad \text{if } S > K$$
$$= 0 \qquad \text{if } S \le K$$

Equity can thus be viewed as a call option on the firm, where exercising the option requires that the firm be liquidated and the face value of the debt (which corresponds to the exercise price) be paid off.

If the debt in the firm is a single issue of zero-coupon bonds with a fixed lifetime and the firm can be liquidated by equity investors at any time prior, the life of the equity as a call option corresponds to the life of the bonds.

Illustration 18.1: Application to valuation: A simple example

Assume a firm whose assets are currently valued at $100 million and that the standard deviation in this asset value is 40%. Further, assume that the face value of debt is $80 million. (It is zero-coupon debt with ten years left to maturity). If the ten-year Treasury

FIGURE 18.1 Payoff Diagram: Net Payoff on Equity

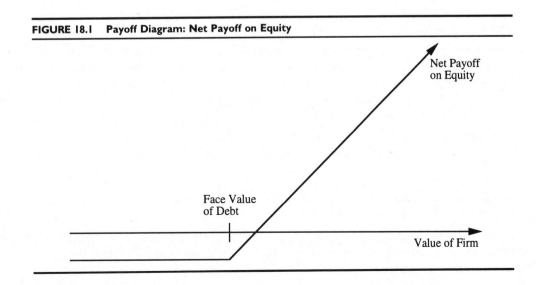

bond rate is 10%, how much is the equity worth? What should the interest rate on debt be?

At the outset, the information provided may seem inadequate to answer these questions. The use of the option pricing approach provides a solution.

The parameters of equity as a call option are as follows:

Value of the underlying asset = S = Value of the firm = $100 million

Exercise Price = K = Face Value of outstanding debt = $80 million

Life of the option = t = Life of zero-coupon debt = 10 years

Variance in the value of the underlying asset = σ^2 = Variance in firm value
= .16

Riskless Rate = r = Treasury bond rate corresponding to option life = 10%

Based upon these inputs, the Black-Scholes model provides the following value for the call:

d_1 = 1.5994 $\qquad\qquad$ $N(d_1)$ = .9451

d_2 = .3345 $\qquad\qquad$ $N(d_2)$ = .6310

Value of the call = ($100 × .9451) − ($80 $e^{-.10 \times 10}$ × .6310) = $75.94 million

Value of the outstanding debt = $100 − $75.94 = $24.06 million

Interest rate on debt = ($80/$24.06)$^{1/10}$ − 1 = 12.77%

Implications of Viewing Equity as a Call Option

There are some valuable insights that can be obtained by viewing equity as a call option.

Valuing Equity in a Troubled Firm

The first implication is that equity will have value, even if the value of the firm falls well below the face value of the outstanding debt. Such a firm will be viewed as troubled by investors, accountants, and analysts, but that does not mean that its equity is worthless. In fact, just as deep out-of-the money traded options command value because of the possibility that the value of the underlying asset may increase above the strike price in the remaining lifetime of the option, equity will command value because of the time premium on the option (the time until the bonds mature and come due) and the possibility that the value of the assets may increase above the face value of the bonds before they come due.

Illustration 18.2: Value of a troubled firm

In the preceding example, assume that the value of the firm is only $50 million, well below the face value of the outstanding debt ($80 million). Assume that all the other inputs remain unchanged.

The parameters of equity as a call option are as follows:

Value of the underlying asset $= S =$ Value of the firm $= \$50$ million

Exercise Price $= K =$ Face Value of outstanding debt $= \$80$ million

Life of the option $= t =$ Life of zero-coupon debt $= 10$ years

Variance in the value of the underlying asset $= \sigma^2 =$ Variance in firm value
$$= .16$$

Riskless Rate $= r =$ Treasury bond rate corresponding to option life $= 10\%$

Based upon these inputs, the Black-Scholes model provides the following value for the call:

$d_1 = 1.0515$ $N(d_1) = .8534$

$d_2 = -.2135$ $N(d_2) = .4155$

> Value of the call $= (\$50 \times .8534) - (\$80\,e^{-.10 \times 10} \times .4155) = \30.44 million
> Value of the bond $= \$50 - \$30.44 = \$19.56$ million

The equity in this firm has substantial value, because of the option characteristics of equity. This might explain why stock in firms that are in "Chapter 11" and essentially bankrupt still has value.

The Conflict between Bondholders and Stockholders

Stockholders and bondholders have different objective functions, and this can lead to agency problems, where stockholders can expropriate wealth from bondholders. The conflict can manifest itself in a number of ways—for instance, stockholders have an incentive to take riskier projects than bondholders do and to pay more out in dividends than bondholders would like them to. This conflict between bondholders and stockholders can be illustrated dramatically using the option pricing model. Since equity is a call option on the value of the firm, an increase in the variance in the firm value, other things remaining equal, will lead to an increase in the value of equity. It is therefore conceivable that stockholders can take risky projects with negative net present values, which, while making them better off, may make the bondholders and the firm less valuable. This is illustrated in the following example:

Illustration 18.3: Effect on value of the conflict between stockholders and bondholders

Consider again the firm described in Illustration 18.1, with a value of assets of $100 million, a face value of zero-coupon, ten-year debt of $80 million, and a standard deviation in the value of the firm of 40%. The equity and debt in this firm were valued as follows:

Value of Equity = $75.94 million

Value of Debt = $24.06 million

Value of the Firm = $100 million

Now assume that the stockholders have the opportunity to take a project with a negative net present value of − $2 million, but assume that this project is a very risky project that will push up the standard deviation in firm value to 50%. The equity as a call option can then be valued using the following inputs:

Value of the underlying asset = S = Value of the firm = $100 million − $2 million = $98 million (The value of the firm is lowered because of the negative net present value project.)

Exercise Price = K = Face Value of outstanding debt = $80 million

Life of the option = t = Life of zero-coupon debt = 10 years

Variance in the value of the underlying asset = σ^2 = Variance in firm value

$$= .25$$

Riskless Rate = r = Treasury bond rate corresponding to option life = 10%

Based upon these inputs, the Black-Scholes model provides the following value for the equity and debt in this firm:

Value of Equity = $77.71 million

Value of Debt = $20.29 million

Value of Firm = $98.00 million

The value of equity rises from $75.94 million to $77.71 million, even though the firm value declines by $2 million. The increase in equity value comes at the expense of bondholders, who see their wealth decline from $24.06 million to $20.19 million.

Another case where there might be a conflict between stockholders and bondholders is in the case of conglomerate mergers, where the variance in earnings and cashflows of the combined firm can be expected to decline because the merging firms have earning streams that are not perfectly correlated. In these mergers, the value of the combined equity in the firm will decrease after the merger because of the decline in variance, and bondholders will gain. Stockholders can reclaim some or all of this lost wealth by utilizing their higher debt capacity and issuing new debt.

Illustration 18.4: Effects on equity of a conglomerate merger

You are provided information on two firms, which operate in unrelated businesses and hope to merge.

	Firm A	Firm B
Value of the firm	$100 million	$150 million
Face Value of debt	$80 million	$50 million
		(zero-coupon debt)

	Firm A	Firm B
Maturity of debt	10 years	10 years
Standard Deviation in firm value	40%	50%
Correlation between firm cashflows	.4	

The ten-year bond rate is 10%.

The variance in the value of the firm after the acquisition can be calculated as follows:

$$\text{Variance in combined firm value} = w_1^2\sigma_1^2 + w_2^2\sigma_2^2 + 2w_1w_2\rho_{1\,2}\sigma_1\sigma_2$$
$$= (.4^2 \times .16) + (.6^2 \times .25)$$
$$+ (2 \times .4 \times .6 \times .4 \times .4 \times .5)$$
$$= .154$$

The values of equity and debt in the individual firms and the combined firm can then be estimated using the option pricing model:

	Firm A	Firm B	Combined Firm
Value of equity in the firm	$75.94	$134.47	$207.43
Value of debt in the firm	24.06	15.53	42.57
Value of the firm	100.00	150.00	250.00

The combined value of the equity prior to the merger is $210.41 million, and it declines to $207.43 million after. The wealth of the bondholders increases by an equal amount. There is a transfer of wealth from stockholders to bondholders, as a consequence of the merger. Thus, conglomerate mergers that are not followed by increases in leverage are likely to see this redistribution of wealth occur across claimholders in the firm.

Obtaining Option Pricing Inputs: Some Real World Problems

The examples that have been used to illustrate the use of option pricing theory to value equity have made some simplifying assumptions. Among them are the following:

(1) There are only two claimholders in the firm—debt and equity.
(2) There is only one issue of debt outstanding, and it can be retired at face value.
(3) The debt has a zero coupon and no special features (convertibility, put clauses, etc.).
(4) The value of the firm and the variance in that value can be estimated.

Each of these assumptions is made with a reason. By restricting the claimholders to two, the problem is made more tractable. Introducing other claimholders, such as preferred stock, will make it difficult to arrive at a result, albeit not impossible. By assuming only one zero-coupon debt issue, which can be retired at face value any time prior to maturity, the features of the debt are made to correspond closely to the features of the strike price on a standard option. If the debt is coupon debt, or more than one debt issue is outstanding, the equity

investors can be forced to exercize (liquidate the firm) at these earlier coupon dates, if they do not have the cashflows to meet their coupon obligations. Finally, knowing the value of the firm and the variance in that value makes the option pricing possible, but it also raises an interesting question about the usefulness of option pricing in the valuation context. If the bonds of the firm are publicly traded, the market value of the debt can be subtracted from the value of the firm to obtain the value of equity much more directly. In defense of the option pricing approach, it does have its advantages. When the debt of a firm is not publicly traded, using option pricing theory can provide an estimate of value for the equity in the firm. Even when the debt is publicly traded, the bonds may not be correctly valued, and the option pricing framework can be useful in evaluating the values of debt and equity. Finally, by relating the values of debt and equity to the variance in firm value, it provides some insight into the redistributive effects of actions taken by the firm.

Applicability in Valuation

Since most firms do not fall into the neat framework developed above of having only one zero-coupon bond outstanding, there are compromises that have to be made to use this model in valuation.

1. Value of the Firm. The value of the firm can be obtained in one of two ways. In the first, the market values of outstanding debt and equity are accumulated, assuming that all debt and equity are traded, to obtain firm value. The option pricing model then reallocates the firm value between debt and equity. In the second, the market values of the assets of the firm are estimated, either by discounting expected cashflows at the weighted average cost of capital or by using prices from a market that exists for these assets.

2. Variance in Firm Value. The variance in firm value can be obtained directly if both stocks and bonds in the firm trade in the marketplace. Defining σ_e^2 to be the variance in the stock price and σ_d^2 to be the variance in the bond price, w_e to be the market-value weight of equity and w_d to be the market-value weight of debt, the variance in firm value can be written as:[2]

$$\sigma_{firm}^2 = w_e^2 \sigma_e^2 + w_d^2 \sigma_d^2 + 2 w_e w_d \rho_{e\,d} \sigma_e \sigma_d$$

where $\rho_{e\,d}$ is the correlation between the stock and the bond prices.

When the bonds of the firm are not traded, the variance of similarly rated bonds is used as the estimate of σ_d^2, and the correlation between similarly rated bonds and the firm's stock is used as the estimate of $\rho_{e\,d}$.

3. Maturity of the Debt. In contrast with the assumption that a firm has one zero-coupon bond outstanding, most firms have more than one debt issue on their books, and much of the debt comes with coupons. Since the option pricing model allows for only one input for the time to expiration, these multiple bonds issues and coupon payments have to be compressed into one measure; that is, these multiple issues have to be converted into one equivalent zero-coupon

bond. One solution that takes into account both the coupon payments and the maturity of the bonds is to estimate the duration of each debt issue and calculate a face-value-weighted average of the durations of the different issues. This value-weighted duration is then used as a measure of the time to expiration of the option.

Illustration 18.5: Valuing equity as an option: The example of an airline

Assume that you have been asked to value an airline. The airline owns routes in North America, Europe, and South America, with the following estimates of current market value:

North America	$400 million
Europe	500 million
South America	100 million

The airline has considerable debt outstanding. It has four debt issues outstanding, with the following characteristics:

Maturity	Face Value (millions)	Coupon	Duration (years)
20-year debt	$100	11%	14.1
15-year debt	100	12%	10.2
10-year debt	200	12%	7.5
1-year debt	800	12.5%	1.0

The stock of the airline has been trading on the NYSE. The annualized standard deviation in ln(stock prices) has been 25%, and the firm's debt has been approximately 90% of the firm value (during the variance estimation period). The firm is rated B. Though its bonds are not traded, other B-rated bonds have had an annualized standard deviation of 10% (in ln[bond prices]). The correlation between B-rated bonds and this airline's stock price is 0.3. The firm pays not dividends. The current Treasury bond rate is 8%.

Step 1: Find the value of the firm by adding up the value of its assets:

Value of the firm = $400 + $500 + $100 = $1,000 million

Step 2: Find the face value of debt outstanding:

Value of the debt = $100 + $100 + $200 + $800 = $1,200 million

Step 3: Find the average duration of the debt outstanding:

Average duration = ($100/$1,200) × 14.1 + ($100/$1,200) × 10.2
 + ($200/$1,200) × 7.5 + ($800/$1,200) × 1
 = 3.9417 years

Step 4: Estimate the variance in the value of the firm by finding the weighted average of the variances in stock and bond prices:

$$\text{Variance of the firm} = (E/[D + E])^{-2}\sigma_e^2 + (D/[D + E])^2\sigma_d^2$$
$$+ 2(E/[D + E])(D/[D + E])\rho_{e\,d}\sigma_e\sigma_d$$

$$= (.1^2 \times .25^2) + (.9^2 \times .10^2)$$
$$+ (2 \times .1 \times .9 \times .3 \times .25 \times .10)$$
$$= .010075$$

Step 5: Value equity as an option:

$d_1 = .7671$ $\qquad\qquad\qquad$ $N(d_1) = .7784$

$d_2 = .5678$ $\qquad\qquad\qquad$ $N(d_2) = .7148$

Value of the call $= (\$1,000 \times .7784) - (\$1,200\, e^{-.08 \times 3.9417} \times .7148)$
$$= \$152.63 \text{ million}$$

Illustration 18.6: Valuing equity as an option: Wang Labs

Wang Labs was a firm in trouble in March 1993. It was officially in "Chapter 11," and had debt outstanding with a face value of $529.40 million. The weighted average duration of this debt was 5.1 years (the weighted average maturity of the debt was 8.7 years). The present value of the firm estimated using projected cashflows to the firm, discounted at the weighted average cost of capital of 10%, was $410 million.

	1993	1994	1995	1996	1997
Revenues	$1,300	$1,010	$1,067	$1,121	$1,177
− COGS	1,000	658	705	741	778
− SG & A	750	279	267	269	282
= EBIT	(450)	73	95	111	117
− EBIT(t)	(162)	26	34	40	42
= EBIT(1 − t)	(288)	47	61	71	75

Terminal Value $= \$794$ million

The cashflows to the firm are expected to stay constant after 1997. There are no working capital requirements, and capital expenditures are offset by depreciation.

The stock has been traded on the NYSE, and the variance based upon monthly prices between 1987 and 1991 is 0.0262. There are Wang Lab bonds, due in 2008, that have been traded from 1987 to 1991, and the variance in monthly prices for these bonds is 0.0126. The correlation between stock price and bond price changes has been 0.27. The proportion of debt in the capital structure during the period 1987–1991 was 86.1%.

Step 1: Find the annualized variance in the stock and bond prices:

Annualized Variance in stock price $= .0262 \times 12 = .3144$

Standard Deviation $= .5607$

Annualized Variance in bond price $= .0126 \times 12 = .1518$

Standard Deviation $= .3896$

Step 2: Find the annualized variance in firm value:

Annualized Variance in firm value $= (.139^2 \times .3144) + (.861^2 \times .1518)$
$$+ (2 \times .139 \times .861 \times .27$$
$$\times .5607 \times .3896)$$
$$= .1326$$

The five-year bond rate (corresponding to the weighted average duration of 5.1 years) is 6%.

Step 3: Find the value of the call based upon the following parameters of equity as a call option:

Value of the underlying asset = S = Value of the firm = $410 million

Exercise Price = K = Face Value of outstanding debt = $529.4 million

Life of the option = t = Weighted average duration of debt = 5.1 years

Variance in the value of the underlying asset = σ^2 = Variance in firm value

$$= .1326$$

Riskless Rate = r = Treasury bond rate corresponding to option life = 6%

Based upon these inputs, the Black-Scholes model provides the following value for the call:

$d_1 = .4725$ $\qquad\qquad\qquad$ $N(d_1) = .6816$

$d_2 = .3499$ $\qquad\qquad\qquad$ $N(d_2) = .3632$

Value of the call = ($410 × .6816) − (529.4 $e^{-.06 \times 5.1}$ × .3632)

$\qquad\qquad\qquad = \$137.87$ million

Wang's equity was trading at $85 million in March 1993.

VALUING NATURAL RESOURCE OPTIONS/FIRMS

Firms that have made natural resource investments (mines, oil reserves, etc.) have traditionally been evaluated using discounted cashflow techniques. The use of these techniques may not be appropriate, given the options that these firms possess to leave the investments untouched, if the price of the resource declines and, to exploit them fully, if the price rises. This section uses option pricing theory to value not only individual natural resource investments but also firms that own portfolios of natural resource investments (such as oil companies).

The General Framework

In a natural resource investment, the underlying asset is the resource, and the value of the asset is based upon two variables: the quantity of the resource that is available in the investment and the price of the resource. Thus, in a gold mine, the underlying asset is the value of the estimated gold reserves in the mine, based upon the current price of gold. In most such investments, there is a cost associated with developing the resource, and the difference between the value of the asset extracted and the cost of the development is the profit to the owner of the resource. Defining the cost of development as X and the estimated value of the resource as V, the potential payoffs on a natural resource option can be written as follows:

Payoff on natural resource investment $= V - X$ if $V > X$

$\qquad\qquad\qquad\qquad\qquad\qquad\qquad\quad\; = 0$ if $V \leq X$

Thus, the investment in a natural resource option has a payoff function similar to that of a call option (see Figure 18.2).

Obtaining the Inputs for Valuing Natural Resource Options

To value a natural resource investment as an option requires assumptions about a number of variables:

1. *Available reserves of the resource:* Since this is not known with certainty at the outset, it has to be estimated. In an oil tract, for instance, geologists can provide reasonably accurate estimates of the quantity of oil available in the tract.
2. *Estimated cost of developing the resource:* The estimated development cost is the exercise price of the option. Again, a combination of knowledge about past costs and the specifics of the investment have to be used to come up with a reasonable measure of development cost.
3. *Time to expiration of the option:* The life of a natural resource option can be defined in one of two ways. If the ownership of the investment has to be relinquished at the end of a fixed period of time, that will be the life of the option. In many offshore oil leases, for instance, the oil tracts are leased to the oil company for five to ten years. The second approach is based upon the inventory of the resource and the capacity output rate, and estimates of the number of years it would take to exhaust the inventory. Thus, a gold mine with a mine inventory of 3 million ounces and a capacity output rate of 150,000 ounces a year will be exhausted in 20 years, which is defined to be the life of the natural resource option.
4. *Variance in value of the underlying asset:* The variance in the value of the underlying asset is determined by two factors: variability in the price of the

FIGURE 18.2 Payoff Diagram: Net Payoff on Extracting Reserve

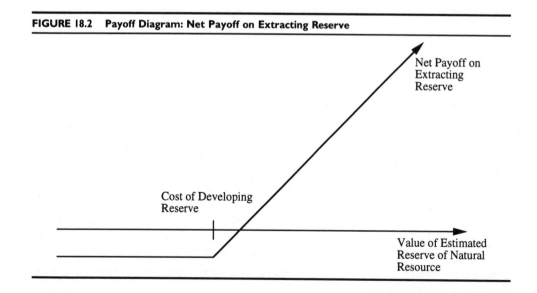

resource and variability in the estimate of available reserves. In the special case where the quantity of the reserve is known with certainty, the variance in the underlying asset's value will depend entirely upon the variance in the price of the natural resource.

5. Just as dividends reduce the value of a stock and produce a cashflow to stockholders, production on an annual basis depletes the value of the underlying natural resource asset and provides a cashflow on the asset. The net production revenue as a percentage of the market value of the reserve is the equivalent of the dividend yield and is treated the same way in calculating option values.

An important issue in using option pricing models to value natural resource options is the effect of development lags on the value of these options. Since the resources cannot be extracted instantaneously, a time lag has to be allowed between the decision to extract the resources and the actual extraction. A simple adjustment for this lag is to discount the present value of developed reserve based upon the length of the lag. Thus, if there is a one-year lag in development, the current value of the developed reserve will be discounted back one year at the "cashflow/asset value" ratio (dividend yield).

This approach to applying option pricing models to valuing natural resource investments is examined in much more detail in Brennan and Schwartz (1985) and Siegel, Smith, and Paddock (1993), with the former applying it to value a gold mine and the latter to value an oil tract.

Illustration 18.7: Application to valuation: A gold mine

The following is a simpler version of the example presented in Brennan and Schwartz, applying option pricing theory to value a gold mine.

Consider a gold mine with an estimated inventory of 1 million ounces and a capacity output rate of 50,000 ounces per year. The price of gold is expected to grow 3% a year. The firm owns the rights to this mine for the next 20 years. The cost of opening the mine is $10 million, and the average production cost is $250 per ounce. This production cost, once initiated, is expected to grow 5% a year. The standard deviation in gold prices is 20%, and the current price of gold is $375 per ounce. The riskless rate is 9%. The inputs to the model are as follows:

Value of the underlying asset = Present Value of expected gold sales at 50,000 ounces a year = $(50{,}000 \times \$375) \times (1 - [1.03^{20}/1.09^{20}])/(.09 - .03) = \211.79 million

Exercise Price = Cost of opening mine

+ Present Value of the cost of producing gold

$= \$10 \text{ million} + (50{,}000 \times \$250)$

$\times (1 - [1.05^{20}/1.09^{20}])/(.09 - .05) = \174.55 million

Variance in ln(gold price) = .04

Time to expiration on the option = 20 years

Riskless interest rate = 9%

Dividend Yield = Loss in production for each year of delay = $\frac{1}{20}$ = 5%

(Note: It will take 20 years to empty the mine, and the firm owns the rights for 20 years. Every year of delay implies a loss of one year of production.)

Based upon these inputs, the Black-Scholes model provides the following value for the call:

$$d_1 = 1.5578 \qquad\qquad N(d_1) = .9403$$
$$d_2 = .6634 \qquad\qquad N(d_2) = .7464$$
$$\text{Value of the call} = (\$211.79\,e^{-.05 \times 20} \times .9403) - (\$174.55\,e^{-.09 \times 20} \times .7464)$$
$$= \$51.73 \text{ million}$$

The value of the mine as an option is $51.73 million, in contrast to the static capital budgeting analysis which would have yielded a net present value of $37.24 million ($211.79 million − $174.55 million). The additional value accrues directly from the mine's option characteristics.

Illustration 18.8: Application to valuation: An oil reserve

The following is a simplified version of the illustration provided by Siegel, Smith, and Paddock to value an offshore oil property.

Consider an offshore oil property with an estimated oil reserve of 50 million barrels of oil, where the present value of the development cost is $12 per barrel and the development lag is two years. The firm has the rights to exploit this reserve for the next 20 years, and the marginal value per barrel of oil is $12 per barrel currently (price per barrel − marginal cost per barrel). Once developed, the net production revenue each year will be 5% of the value of the reserves. The riskless rate is 8%, and the variance in ln(oil price) is 0.03.

Given this information, the inputs to the Black-Scholes can be estimated as follows:

Current Value of the asset = S = Value of the developed reserve discounted back the length of the development lag at the dividend yield = $12 × 50/1.05^2 = $544.22 million

(If development is started today, the oil will not be available for sale until two years from now. The estimated opportunity cost of this delay is the lost production revenue over the delay period. Hence the discounting of the reserve back at the dividend yield.)

Exercise Price = Present Value of development cost = $12 × 50 = $600 million

Time to expiration on the option = 20 years

Variance in the value of the underlying asset = .03

Riskless Rate = 8%

Dividend Yield = Net Production Revenue/Value of reserve = 5%

Based upon these inputs, the Black-Scholes model provides the following value for the call:

$$d_1 = 1.0359 \qquad\qquad N(d_1) = .8498$$
$$d_2 = .2613 \qquad\qquad N(d_2) = .6030$$
$$\text{Value call of the} = (\$544.22\,e^{-.05 \times 20} \times .8498) - (\$600\,e^{-.08 \times 20} \times .6030)$$
$$= \$97.08 \text{ million}$$

This oil reserve, though not viable at current prices, still is a valuable property because of its potential to create value if oil prices go up.

Extending the Option Pricing Approach to Value Natural Resource Firms

The examples provided above illustrate the use of option pricing theory in valuing individual mines and oil tracts. Since the assets owned by a natural resource firm can be viewed primarily as options, the firm itself can be valued using option pricing theory. The preferred approach would be to consider each option separately, value it, and accumulate the values of the options to get the value of the firm. Since this information is likely to be difficult to obtain for large natural resource firms such as oil companies, which own hundreds of such assets, a variant of this approach is to value the entire firm as one option. A purist would probably disagree, arguing that valuing an option on a portfolio of assets (as in this approach) will provide a lower value than valuing a portfolio of options (which is what the natural resource firm really owns). Nevertheless, the value obtained from the model still provides an interesting perspective on the determinants of the value of natural resource firms.

The inputs to the option pricing model, when applied to valuing a natural resource firm, can be summarized as follows:

Input to Model	Corresponding Input for Valuing Natural Resource Firm
Value of underlying asset	Value of accumulated estimated reserves of the resource owned by the firm, discounted back the length of the development lag at the dividend yield.
Exercise Price	Estimated accumulated cost of developing estimated reserves.
Time to expiration on option	Average relinquishment period across all reserves owned by the firm (if known), or estimate of when reserves will be exhausted, given current production rates.
Riskless Rate	Riskless rate corresponding to the life of the option.
Variance in value of asset	Variance in the price of the natural resource.
Dividend Yield	Estimated annual net production revenue as a percentage of the value of the reserve.

Illustration 18.9: Valuing an oil company: Gulf Oil, 1984

Gulf Oil was the target of a takeover in early 1984 at $70 per share. (It had 165.30 million shares outstanding and total debt of $9.9 billion.) It had estimated reserves of 3,038 million barrels of oil, and the average cost of developing these reserves was estimated to be $10 a barrel in present value dollars. (The development lag is approximately two years.) The average relinquishment life of the reserves is 12 years. The price of oil was $22.38 per barrel, and the production cost, taxes, and royalties were estimated at $7 per barrel. The bond rate at the time of the analysis was 9.00%. Gulf

Oil was expected to have net production revenues each year of approximately 5% of the value of the developed reserves. The variance in oil prices is 0.03.

Value of underlying asset = Value of estimated reserves discounted back for period of development lag

$$= 3,038(\$22.38 - \$7)/1.05^2$$

$$= \$42,380.44 \text{ million}$$

Exercise Price = Estimated Development Cost of reserves = $3,038 \times \$10$

$$= \$30,380 \text{ million}$$

Time to expiration = Average length of relinquishment option = 12 years

Variance in value of asset = Variance in oil prices = .03

Riskless Interest Rate = 9%

Dividend Yield = Net Production Revenue/Value of developed reserves = 5%

Based upon these inputs, the Black-Scholes model provides the following value for the call:

$d_1 = 1.6548$ $N(d_1) = .9510$

$d_2 = 1.0548$ $N(d_2) = .8542$

Value of the call = $(\$42,380.44 \ e^{-.05 \times 12} \times .9510)$

$$- (\$30,380 \ e^{-.09 \times 12} \times .8542) = \$13,306 \text{ million}$$

This represents the value of the undeveloped reserves of oil owned by Gulf Oil. In addition, Gulf Oil had free cashflows to the firm from its oil and gas production of $915 million from already developed reserves, and these cashflows are likely to continue for ten years (the remaining lifetime of developed reserves). The present value of these developed reserves, discounted at the weighted average cost of capital of 12.5%, yields:

Value of already developed reserves = $\$915(1 - 1.125^{-10})/.125$

$$= \$5,065.83 \text{ million}$$

Adding the value of the developed and undeveloped reserves of Gulf Oil provides the value of the firm:

Value of the undeveloped reserves	= $13,306 million
Plus Value of production in place	+ 5,066 million
Equals Total Value of firm	= 18,372 million
Less Outstanding Debt	− 9,900 million
Value of equity	= 8,472 million
Value per share	= $8,472/165.3 = $51.25

This analysis would suggest that Gulf Oil was overvalued at $70 per share.

VALUING PRODUCT PATENTS AS OPTIONS

One of the limitations of discounted cashflow valuation is its failure to adequately consider assets that do not produce cashflows currently, are not ex-

pected to produce cashflows in the near future, but are valuable nevertheless because of their potential to produce value for the firm. A firm with valuable product patents that are unutilized currently but could produce significant cashflows in the future may therefore be undervalued using traditional valuation techniques. Using an option pricing approach to value these product patents may provide insight into the value that they add to the firm.

The General Framework

A product patent provides the firm with the right to develop the product and market it. It will do so only if the present value of the expected cashflows from the product sales exceed the cost of development. If this does not occur, the firm can shelve the patent and not incur any further costs. If I is the present value of the costs of developing the product and V is the present value of the expected cashflows from development, the payoffs from owning a product patent can be written as:

$$\text{Payoff from owning a product patent} = V - I \quad \text{if } V > I$$
$$= 0 \quad \text{if } V \leq I$$

Thus, a product patent can be viewed as a call option, where the product itself is the underlying asset, and has a payoff function similar to that of a call option (see Figure 18.3).

Obtaining the Inputs for Option Valuation

The inputs needed to apply option pricing theory to valuing product patents are, at the surface, the same as those needed for any application—the value of the underlying asset, the variance in the value, the time to expiration on the option, the strike price, the riskless rate, and the equivalent of the dividend

FIGURE 18.3 Payoff Diagram: Net Payoff on Introducing a Product

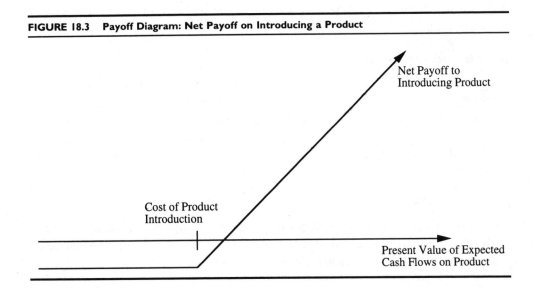

Net Payoff to Introducing Product

Cost of Product Introduction

Present Value of Expected Cash Flows on Product

yield. The actual estimation of these inputs, however, for product patent valuation can be difficult.

Value of the Underlying Asset

The underlying asset, in the case of product patents, is the product itself, and the current value of this asset is the present value of expected cashflows from introducing the product now, which can be obtained by doing a standard capital budgeting analysis. Given that patents are on products that are not available in the market right now, there is likely to be a substantial amount of noise in the cashflow estimates and the present value. This uncertainty, rather than being viewed as a problem, should be viewed as the reason why the product patent option has value. If the expected cashflows on the product were known with certainty and were not expected to change, there would be no need to adopt an option pricing framework, since there would be no value to the option.

Variance in the Value of the Asset

As noted in the prior section, there is likely to be considerable uncertainty associated with the cashflow estimates and the present value that measures the value of the asset now, partly because the potential market size for the product is unknown and partly because technological shifts can change the cost structure and profitability of the product. The variance in the present value of cashflows from the project can be estimated in one of two ways. If similar products have been introduced in the past, the variance in the cashflows from these products can be used as an estimate. Alternatively, probabilities can be assigned to various market scenarios, cashflows estimated under each scenario, and the variance estimated across present values.

The value of the option is largely derived from the variance in cashflows—the higher the variance, the higher the value of the product patent. Thus, the value of a product patent in a stable business will be less than the value of one in an environment where technology, competition, and markets all change rapidly.

Exercise Price on Option

A product option is exercised when the firm owning the option decides to invest in the resources needed to produce and market the product. The cost of making this investment is the equivalent of the exercise price of the option. The underlying assumption is that this cost remains constant (in present-value dollars) and that any uncertainty associated with the product is reflected in the present value of cashflows on the product.

Expiration of the Option

The product option expires when the product patent ends, and investments made after the patent expiration are assumed to deliver a net present value of 0 as competition drives returns down to the required rate.

Dividend Yield

There is a cost to delay in a product option. Since the patent expires after a fixed period and excess profits (which are the source of positive present value) are assumed to disappear after that as new competitors emerge, each year of delay translates into one less year of value-creating cashflows.[3] If the cashflows are evenly distributed over time and the life of the patent is n years, then the cost of delay can be written as:

$$\text{Annual Cost of delay} = \frac{1}{n}$$

Thus, if the product patent is for 20 years, the annual cost of delay works out to 5% a year.

Illustration 18.10: Valuing a product option

Assume that a firm has the patent rights, for the next 20 years, to a product that requires an initial investment of $1.5 billion to develop and a present value, right now, of cash inflows of only $1 billion. The technology is rapidly evolving, however, and there is a possibility that this will become a valuable project in the future. Assume that a simulation of the project under a variety of technological and competitive scenarios yields a variance in the present value of inflows of 0.03. The current riskless 20-year bond rate is 10%.

The inputs to the option pricing model are as follows:

Value of the underlying asset = Present Value of inflows (current)

= $1,000 million

Exercise Price = Present Value of cost of developing product = $1,500 million

Time to expiration = Life of the patent = 20 years

Variance in value of underlying asset = Variance in PV of inflows = .03

Riskless Rate = 10%

Based upon these inputs, the Black-Scholes model provides the following value for the call:

$d_1 = 1.1548$ $N(d_1) = .8759$

$d_2 = .3802$ $N(d_2) = .6481$

Value of the call = ($1,000 $e^{-.05 \times 20}$ × .8759) − ($1,500 $e^{-.10 \times 20}$ × .6481)

= $190.66 million

This suggests that though this product has a negative net present value currently, it is a valuable product when viewed as an option. This value can then be added to the value of the other assets that the firm possesses, and provides a useful framework for incorporating the value of product options and patents.

A specialized case of this application is when a firm has no assets that produce cashflows currently, but it is composed entirely of product options. Then the accumulated value of these options is the value of the firm.

Illustration 18.11: Valuing a firm with only product options

Consider a biotechnology firm, which has no cashflow-producing assets currently but has one product in the pipeline that has much promise in providing a treatment for diabetes. The product has not been approved by the FDA, and, even if approved, it could be faced with competition from similar products being worked on by other firms. The firm, however, would hold the patent rights to this product for the next 25 years. After a series of simulations, under a variety of technological and competitive environments, the expected present value of the cash inflows is estimated to be $500 million, with a variance of 0.20 (signifying the uncertainty of the process). The expected present value of the cost of developing the product is estimated to be $400 million. The annual cashflows on the product, once developed, are expected to be 4% of the present value of the inflows. The 25-year bond rate is 7%.

The inputs to the option pricing model are as follows:

Value of underlying asset = Present Value of expected cashflows = $500 million

Exercise Price = Present Value of cost of developing product for commercial use

$$= \$400 \text{ million}$$

Time to expiration on the option = Time to expiration on patent rights

$$= 25 \text{ years}$$

Variance in value of underlying asset = .20

Riskless Rate = 7%

Dividend Yield = Expected Annual Cashflow/PV of cash inflows = 4%

Based upon these inputs, the Black-Scholes model provides the following value for the call:

$d_1 = 1.5532$ $N(d_1) = .9398$

$d_2 = .6828$ $N(d_2) = .2474$

Value of the call $= (\$500 \ e^{-.04 \times 25} \times .9398) - (\$400 \ e^{-.07 \times 25} \times .2474)$

$$= \$155.66 \text{ million}$$

The estimated value of this firm, based upon an option pricing approach, is $155.66 million. This is a more realistic measure of value than traditional discounted cashflow valuation (that would have provided a value of $100 million) because it reflects the underlying uncertainty in the technology and in competition.

CONCLUSION

Option pricing theory has wide applicability in valuation, especially in contexts where traditional discounted cashflow valuation and multiples do not work. Even in cases where they do, option pricing models provide another perspective that can be useful. This chapter examines three specific applications of option pricing theory. In the first, equity is analyzed as a call option on the underlying firm. In the second, the value of a natural resource asset, such as a

mine or an oil tract, is viewed as a call option. In the third, the value of a product patent is estimated, on the assumption that a patent provides a call option on the underlying product.

QUESTIONS AND SHORT PROBLEMS

1. XYZ Corporation has $500 million in zero-coupon debt outstanding, due in five years. The firm had earnings before interest and taxes of $40 million in the most recent year (the tax rate is 40%). These earnings are expected to grow 5% a year in perpetuity, and the firm paid no dividends. The firm had a cost of equity of 12% and a cost of capital of 10%. The annualized standard deviation in firm values of comparable firms is 12.5%. (The five-year Treasury bond rate is 5%.)
 a. Estimate the value of the firm.
 b. Estimate the value of equity, using an option pricing model.
 c. Estimate the market value of debt and the appropriate interest rate on the debt.
2. McCaw Cellular Communications reported earnings before interest and taxes of $850 million in 1993, and had a depreciation allowance of $400 million in that year (which was offset by capital spending of an equivalent amount). The earnings before interest and taxes are expected to grow 20% a year for the next five years and 5% a year after that. The cost of capital is 10%. The firm has $10 billion in debt outstanding with the following characteristics:

Duration	Debt
1 year	$2 billion
2 years	$4 billion
5 years	$4 billion

The annualized standard deviation in the firm's stock price is 35%, whereas the annualized standard deviation in the traded bonds is 15%. The correlation between stock and bond prices has been 0.5. The firm has a debt/equity ratio of 50%, and the after-tax cost of debt is 6%. (The beta of the stock is 1.50; the 30-year treasury bond rate is 7%.) The three-year Treasury bond rate is 5%.
 a. Estimate the value of the firm.
 b. Estimate the value of the equity.
 c. The stock was trading at $60 and there were 210 million shares outstanding in January 1994. Estimate the implied standard deviation in firm value.
3. You are examining the financial viability of investing in some abandoned copper mines in Chile that still have significant copper deposits in them. A geological survey suggests that there might be 10 million pounds of copper still in the mines and that the cost of opening up the mines will be $3 million (in present value dollars). The capacity output rate is 400,000 pounds a year, and the price of copper is expected to increase 4% a year. The Chilean government is willing to grant a 25-year lease on the mine. The average production cost is expected to be 40 cents a pound, and the current price per pound of copper is 85 cents. (The production cost is expected to grow 3% a year, once initiated.) The annual-

ized standard deviation in copper prices is 25%, and the 25-year Treasury bond rate is 7%.

 a. Estimate the value of the mine using traditional capital budgeting techniques.

 b. Estimate the value of the mine based upon an option pricing model.

 c. How would you explain the difference between the two values?

4. You have been asked to analyze the value of an oil company with substantial oil reserves. The estimated reserves amount to 10 million barrels, and the estimated present value of the development cost for each barrel is $12. The current price of oil is $20 per barrel, and the average production cost is estimated to be $6 per barrel. The company has the rights to these reserves for the next twenty years, and the 20-year bond rate is 7%. The company also proposes to extract 4% of its reserves each year to meet cashflow needs. The annualized standard deviation in the price of the oil is 20%.

What is the value of this oil company?

5. You are analyzing a capital budgeting project. The project is expected to have a PV of cash inflows of $250 million and will cost $200 million (in present value dollars) to take on. You have done a simulation of the project cashflows, and the simulation yields a variance in present value of cash inflows of 0.04. You have the rights to this project for the next five years, during which period you have to pay $12.5 million a year to retain the project rights. (The five-year Treasury bond rate is 8%.)

 a. What is the value of the project, based upon traditional NPV?

 b. What is the value of the project as an option?

 c. Why are the two values different? What factor or factors determine the magnitude of this difference?

6. Cyclops Inc., a high-technology company specializing in state-of-the-art visual technology, is considering going public. While the company has no revenues or profits yet on its products, it has a ten-year patent to a product that will enable contact lens users to get no-maintenance lens that will last for years. While the product is technically viable, it is exorbitantly expensive to manufacture, and the potential market for it will be relatively small currently. (A cashflow analysis of the project suggests that the present value of the cash inflows on the project, if adopted now, would be $250 million, while the cost of the project will be $500 million.) The technology is rapidly evolving, and a simulation of alternative scenarios yields a wide range of present values, with an annualized standard deviation of 60%. To move toward this adoption, the company will have to continue to invest $10 million a year in research. (The ten-year Treasury bond rate is 6%.)

 a. Estimate the value of this company.

 b. How sensitive is this value estimate to the variance in projected cashflows? What broader lessons would you draw from this analysis?

ENDNOTES

1. Jump process models that incorporate the Poisson process require inputs on the probability of price jumps, the average magnitude, and the variance, which can all be estimated but with a significant amount of noise.

2. This is an extension of the variance formula for a two-asset portfolio.

3. A value-creating cashflow is one that adds to the net present value because it is in excess of the required return for investments of equivalent risk.

19

The Determinants of
Interest Rates

The value of a bond is the present value of the expected cashflows on the bond, discounted at an interest rate that is appropriate to the riskiness of that bond. Since the cashflows on a straight bond are fixed at issue, the value of a bond is inversely related to the interest rate that investors demand for that bond. The interest rate charged on a bond is determined by both the general level of interest rates, which applies to all bonds and financial investments, and the default premium specific to the entity issuing the bond.

This chapter examines the determinants of both the general level of interest rates and the magnitude of the default premiums on specific bonds. The general level of interest rates incorporates expected inflation and a measure of real return and reflects the term structure, with bonds of different maturities carrying different interest rates. The default premium varies across time, depending in large part on the health of the economy and investors' risk preferences.

BOND PRICES AND INTEREST RATES

The value of a straight bond is determined by the level of and changes in interest rates. As interest rates rise, the price of a bond will decrease, and vice versa. This inverse relationship between bond prices and interest rates arises directly from the present value relationship that governs bond prices.

The Present Value Relationship

The value of a bond, like all financial investments, is derived from the present value of the expected cashflows on that bond, discounted at an interest rate that reflects the default risk associated with the cashflows. There are two features that set bonds apart from equity investments. First, the cashflows on a bond, that is, the coupon payments and the face value of the bond, are usually set at issue and do not change during the life of the bond. Even when they do change, as in the case of floating-rate bonds, the changes are generally linked to changes in interest rates. Second, bonds usually have fixed lifetimes, unlike stocks, since most bonds[1] specify a maturity date. As a consequence, the present

value of a "straight bond" with fixed coupons and specified maturity is determined entirely by changes in the discount rate, which incorporates both the general level of interest rates and the specific default risk of the bond being valued.

The present value of a bond, expected to mature in N time periods, with coupons in every period, can be written as:

$$\text{PV of Bond} = \sum_{t=1}^{t=N} \frac{\text{Coupon}_t}{(1 + r)^t} + \frac{\text{Face Value}}{(1 + r)^N}$$

where Coupon$_t$ = coupon expected in period t
Face Value = face value of the bond
r = discount rate for the cashflows

The discount rate used to calculate the present value of the bond will vary from bond to bond, depending upon default risk, with higher rates used for riskier bonds and lower rates for safer ones.

If the bond is traded, and a market price is therefore available for it, the internal rate of return can be computed for the bond—that is, the discount rate at which the present value of the coupons and the face value is equal to the market price. This internal rate of return is called the yield to maturity on the bond.

There are several details relating to both the magnitude and timing of cashflows that can affect the value of a bond and its yield to maturity. First, the coupon payment on a bond may be semiannual, in which case the discounting has to allow for the semiannual cashflows. (The first coupon will be discounted back half a year; the second one, one year; the third, a year and a half; and so on.) Second, once a bond has been issued, it accrues coupon interest between coupon payments, and this accrued interest has to be added on to the price of the bond when valuing the bond.

Illustration 19.1: Valuing a straight bond at issue

The following is a valuation of a 30-year U.S. government bond at the time of issue. The coupon rate on the bond is 7.50%, and the market interest rate is 7.75%. The price of the bond can be calculated thus:

$$\text{PV of Bond} = \sum_{t=1}^{t=30} \frac{75.00}{1.0775^t} + \frac{1,000}{1.0775^{30}} = \$971.18$$

This is based upon annual coupons. If the calculation is based upon semiannual coupons, and the annual percentage rate remains 7.75%, the value of the bond is:

$$\text{PV of Bond} = \sum_{t=1}^{t=60} \frac{37.50}{1.03875^t} + \frac{1,000}{1.03875^{60}} = \$971.03$$

Illustration 19.2: Valuing a seasoned straight bond

The following is a valuation of a seasoned U.S. government bond, with 19 years and 8 months left to expiration and a coupon rate of 11.75%. The next coupon is due in two months. The current 20-year bond rate is 7.5%. The value of the bond can be calculated as follows:

$$\text{PV of Bond} = \sum_{t=1}^{t=39} \frac{58.75}{1.0375^t} + \frac{58.75}{1.0375^{2/6}} + \frac{1,000}{1.0375^{40}} = \$1,487.36$$

This bond trades at well above face value, because of its high coupon. Note that the second term of the equation is the present value of the next coupon.

A Measure of Interest Rate Risk in Bonds

When the fact that the cashflows on a bond are fixed at issue is combined with the present value relationship governing bond prices, there is a clear rationale for why interest changes affect bond prices so directly. Any increase in interest rates, either at the economywide level or because of an increase in the default risk of the company issuing the bond, will lower the present value of the stream of expected cashflows and hence the value of the bond. Any decrease in interest rates will have the opposite impact.

The effect of interest rate changes on bond prices will vary from bond to bond and will depend upon a number of characteristics of the bond:

The Maturity of the Bond. Holding coupon rates and default risk constant, increasing the maturity of a straight bond will increase its sensitivity to interest rate changes. The present value of cashflows changes much more for cashflows further in the future, as interest rates change, than for cashflows nearer in time. Figure 19.1 illustrates the present values of six bonds: a 5-year, a 10-year, a 15-year, a 20-year, a 30-year, and a 50-year bond, all with 8% coupons for a range of interest rates.

The longer-term bonds are much more sensitive to interest rate changes than the shorter-term bonds. For instance, an increase in interest rates from 8% to 10% results in a decline in value of 7.61% for the 5-year bond and of 19.83% for the 50-year bonds.

The Coupon Rate of the Bond. Holding maturity and default risk constant, increasing the coupon rate of a straight bond will decrease its sensitivity to interest rate changes. Since higher coupons result in more cashflows earlier in the bond's life, the present value will change less as interest rates change. At the extreme, if the bond is a "zero-coupon" bond, the only cashflow is the face value at maturity, and the present value is likely to vary much more as a function of interest rates. Figure 19.2 illustrates the percentage changes in bond values for six 30-year bonds with coupon rates ranging from 0% to 10% for a range of interest rates.

FIGURE 19.1 Bond Values and Bond Maturity

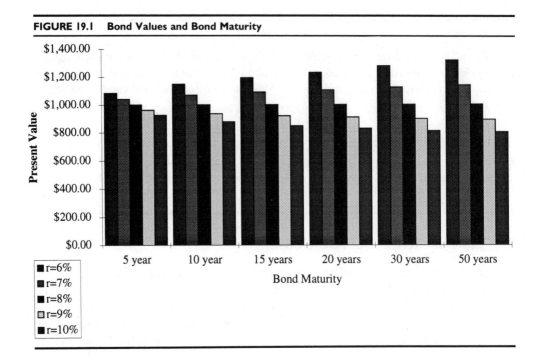

FIGURE 19.2 Bond Values and Coupon Rates

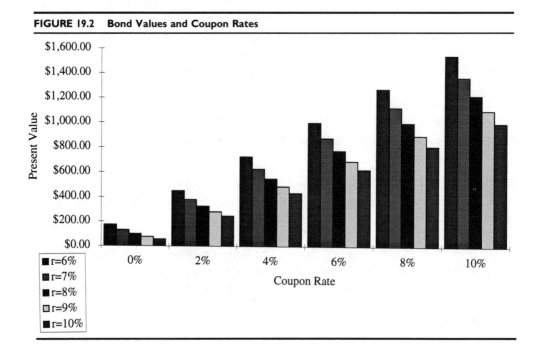

The bonds with the lower coupons are much more sensitive, in percentage terms, to interest rate changes than those with higher coupons.

While the maturity and the coupon rate are the key determinants of how sensitive the price of a bond is to interest rate changes, a number of other factors impinge on this sensitivity. Any special features that the bond has, including convertibility and callability, make the maturity of the bond less definite and can therefore affect the bond price's sensitivity to interest rate changes. If there is any relationship between the level of interest rates and the default premium on bonds, the default risk of a bond can affect its price sensitivity. See Figure 19.3.

FIGURE 19.3 Interest Rates and Bond Maturities: The 1993 Experience

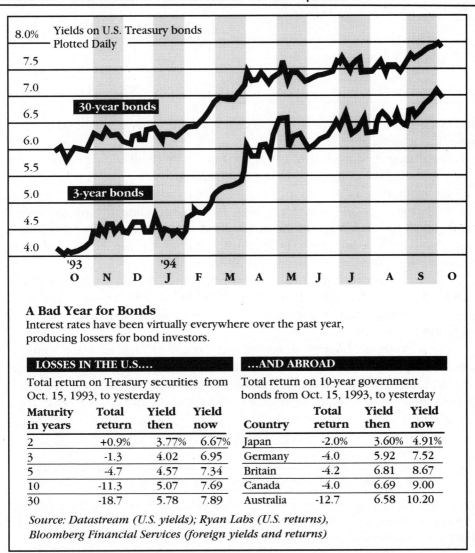

A Bad Year for Bonds
Interest rates have been virtually everywhere over the past year, producing lossers for bond investors.

LOSSES IN THE U.S....				...AND ABROAD			
Total return on Treasury securities from Oct. 15, 1993, to yesterday				Total return on 10-year government bonds from Oct. 15, 1993, to yesterday			
Maturity in years	Total return	Yield then	Yield now	Country	Total return	Yield then	Yield now
2	+0.9%	3.77%	6.67%	Japan	-2.0%	3.60%	4.91%
3	-1.3	4.02	6.95	Germany	-4.0	5.92	7.52
5	-4.7	4.57	7.34	Britain	-4.2	6.81	8.67
10	-11.3	5.07	7.69	Canada	-4.0	6.69	9.00
30	-18.7	5.78	7.89	Australia	-12.7	6.58	10.20

Source: Datastream (U.S. yields); Ryan Labs (U.S. returns), Bloomberg Financial Services (foreign yields and returns)

A More Formal Measure of Interest Rate Risk: Duration

Since the interest rate risk of a bond is a significant component of its total risk, a more formal measure of interest risk is needed, which consolidates the effects of maturity, coupon rates, and the bond's special features. To arrive at this measure, consider the present value relationship developed earlier in this chapter:

$$\text{PV of Bond} = \sum_{t=1}^{t=N} \frac{\text{Coupon}_t}{(1+r)^t} + \frac{\text{Face Value}}{(1+r)^N}$$

Differentiating the bond price with respect to interest rate should provide a formal measure of bond price sensitivity to interest rate changes:

$$\text{Duration of Bond} = dP/dr = \frac{\displaystyle\sum_{t=1}^{t=N} \frac{t \times \text{Coupon}_t}{(1+r)^t} + \frac{N \times \text{Face Value}}{(1+r)^N}}{\displaystyle\sum_{t=1}^{t=N} \frac{\text{Coupon}_t}{(1+r)^t} + \frac{\text{Face Value}}{(1+r)^N}}$$

The bond price differential, dP/dr, is called the duration of the bond and measures the interest rate sensitivity of the bond.

The duration of a bond is a weighted maturity of all the cashflows on the bond including the coupons, where the weights are based upon both the timing and the magnitude of the cashflows. Larger and earlier cashflows are weighted more than smaller and later cashflows. By incorporating the magnitude and timing of all the cashflows on the bond, duration captures all the variables that affect bond price sensitivity to interest rates. The higher the duration of a bond, the more sensitive it is to changes in interest rates.

The duration of a bond will always be less than the maturity for a coupon bond and equal to the maturity for a zero-coupon bond with no special features. In general, the duration of a bond will decrease as the coupon rate on the bond increases.

The measure of duration described here is called "Macaulay duration" and it is the simplest version, based upon yields to maturity and upon the assumption of a flat term structure. Modified versions of duration, which are more flexible in their assumptions about the term structure and its shifts over time exist and are widely used.

Illustration 19.3: Estimating durations for coupon bonds

The following is a duration of a seasoned government bond, with 20 years left to expiration and a coupon rate of 11.75%. The interest rate is 7.5%. The duration of the bond, assuming annual coupon payments, can be calculated as:

t	Cashflows	PV of Cashflows	t × PV of Cashflow
1	$117.50	$109.30	$109.30
2	117.50	101.68	203.35
3	117.50	94.58	283.75
4	117.50	87.98	351.94
5	117.50	81.85	409.23
6	117.50	76.14	456.81
7	117.50	70.82	495.77
8	117.50	65.88	527.06
9	117.50	61.29	551.57
10	117.50	57.01	570.10
11	117.50	53.03	583.36
12	117.50	49.33	591.99
13	117.50	45.89	596.58
14	117.50	42.69	597.65
15	117.50	39.71	595.67
16	117.50	36.94	591.05
17	117.50	34.36	584.17
18	117.50	31.97	575.38
19	117.50	29.74	564.98
20	1,117.50	263.07	5,261.48
		$1,433.27	$14,501.21

Duration of the Bond = $14,501/$1,433 = 10.12

DETERMINANTS OF INTEREST RATES

The discount rate used to discount cashflows on a bond is determined by a number of variables—the general level of interest rates in the economy, the term structure of interest rates, and the default risk of the bond. Figure 19.4 provides the building blocks for arriving at the interest rate on a straight corporate bond.

The first block is the level of short-term default-free interest rates, and it captures the overall level of rates in the economy. The second block is a maturity premium, which reflects the difference between longer-term default-free rates and short-term rates, and is generally positive. The third block is a default premium, which is related to the default risk of the bond in question. This section takes a closer look at these blocks.

Level of Interest Rates

The short-term default-free rate can be decomposed into two components—an expected inflation rate during the period and an expected real rate of return.

FIGURE 19.4 Building Blocks for Interest Rates

Long-Term Corporate Rate—Long Term Government Rate	Default Premium
Long-Term Government Rate—Short-Term Government Rate	Maturity Premium
Short-Term Government Security Rate	Instantaneous (Short-Term Default-Free Rate)

> Short-term default-free rate = Expected Inflation
> + Expected Real Rate of Return

This identity is known as the Fisher equation and essentially implies that changes in short-term rates can be traced to changes in either expected inflation or the expected real rate of return. The more precise version of the Fisher equation allows for the compounding effect:

$$1 + r = (1 + I)(1 + R)$$

where r = nominal interest rate
 I = expected inflation
 R = expected real rate of return

It should be emphasized that the Fisher equation is an identity and there is no question of it being proved or disproved. The real questions that arise from the equation arise as a consequence of specific assumptions made about the expected inflation and real rate of return.

Expected Inflation

Expected inflation is clearly the dominant variable determining interest rates. Generally speaking, a forecaster who can predict changes in inflation well should also be able to post a good track record in predicting interest rate changes. The first step in forecasting inflation is understanding its determinants.

The Determinants of Inflation. There is consensus on the determinants of inflation, though there is little agreement about the consequences of specific actions on inflation. To understand both the determinants of inflation and the sources of disagreement between the different schools of thought on inflation, consider another identity:

$$P = MV/Y$$

where P = price level
 M = money supply in the economy
 V = velocity of money circulation in the economy
 Y = real output in the economy

The velocity of money measures how often the currency, used to define the money supply M, circulates in the economy and how much is created in terms of transactions for every unit of currency created. Thus, if \$1 in additional currency created \$3 in transactions, the velocity of money is 3. While the money supply used in the equation can be defined in a number of different ways, ranging from just currency to broader aggregates, the velocity has to be defined consistently.

This identity can be stated in terms of changes as follows:

$$dP = (dM)(dV)/dY$$

The lefthand side of this identity is the inflation rate, and the righthand side provides the three determinants of the inflation rate:

(a) *The change in the money supply:* If the money supply increases, with no concurrent change in real output and money velocity, the inflation rate will increase. This is the basis for the argument by many monetarists, who believe that there is no linkage between real output and money supply, that money velocity is stable over long periods, and that loose monetary policy (increasing the money supply) is the reason for high inflation. While some monetarists will concede that monetary policy can have short-term effects on real output, most argue that it cannot impact real output in the long term. They also argue that while money velocity may change over time, these changes occur over the very long term and are unlikely to have a major impact on inflation.

(b) *The change in money velocity:* If the money velocity increases, with no concurrent change in money supply and real output, the inflation rate will increase. Economists have long debated why money velocity changes over time. One determinant is technology, since changes in the way people save (from checking accounts to money market accounts) and in the way they spend (from cash transactions to credit card transactions) affect the money velocity. Another is the faith the public has in the currency. In hyperinflationary environments, individuals are much less willing to hold currency (because it depreciates in value so quickly) and therefore attempt to convert the currency into real goods. This unwillingness to hold currency translates into higher money velocity. Thus, if the central bank is viewed as having eased the reins on the money supply, there is often a concurrent increase in money velocity, leading to a surge in inflation.

(c) *The change in real output:* If the real output increases, with no concurrent increase in money supply and money velocity, the inflation rate will decrease. This is often the basis of the argument used by Keynesians for easing monetary policy during economic downturns. Increasing the money supply, they argue, results in a concomitant increase in real output, since there is excess capacity, and the effects on inflation are therefore muted or nonexistent.

Measuring Inflation. A true measure of inflation would consider changes in the prices of all goods and services used in an economy, weighted by their usage values. The reported measures of inflation, either at the consumer or the producer level, attempt to do so but often lag changes in true inflation for a number of reasons. The first is that not all goods and services are traded in a marketplace

where prices are easily available and goods are fairly standardized. Thus, it is easy to gauge the inflation in medical prescription prices but much more difficult to gauge the inflation in the prices of medical services. The second is that all inflation indices are based upon samplings of prices of goods, rather than the universe of all goods traded. Even if the sample is not biased, there is the possibility of sampling error that enters into the numbers. The third is the issue of weighting on the basis of usage value. Due to practical considerations of time and resources, the weights are not adjusted every time the inflation index is computed to allow for changes in usage. Instead, index weights are adjusted infrequently, leading to biases in the measured inflation. Thus, the inflation indices that kept the usage of gasoline by households constant in the late 1970s while oil prices were climbing (and people were cutting back on the use of gasoline) tended to overstate the inflation rate. The final consideration is about the level at which inflation is to be measured, since counting goods at every level of the process (from commodity to manufactured good to retailed good) would result in double- or even triple-counting the same good. Different inflation indices examine inflation at different stages in the process and can lead to different conclusions about whether inflation is increasing, decreasing, or staying unchanged. There are three widely reported indices of inflation in the United States: the consumer price index (CPI), the producer price index (PPI), and the GNP price deflator. The CPI measures inflation at the level of the consumer, while the PPI measures it at the production stage. The GNP deflator looks at overall price movements in one economy. While the first two are measured monthly, the last is measured quarterly.

Forecasting Inflation. Since changes in inflation signal changes in interest rates, economists and analysts have expended considerable time and resources forecasting inflation, with mixed results. The forecasting models used range from the naive to the sophisticated and are based upon everything from gut feeling to elaborate econometrics. The output from these models can be contrasted with predictions based purely upon past inflation—either the inflation in the last time period or time-series models that examine trends and shifts in past inflation—and the results, for the most part, are mixed. Elaborate forecasting models do no better than time-series models in the short term but may better capture changes in inflation in the long term because they consider information beyond that available in past inflation rates.

Testing the Fisher Equation. As mentioned earlier, the Fisher equation is an identity that cannot be proved or disproved. There have, however, been numerous attempts to impose additional constraints on the model, to test the usefulness of the model in explaining changes in interest rates over time. These studies go back to Fisher's own work on interest rates and inflation, where he found that the correlation between the rate of inflation and the commercial paper rate was low in both his sample periods—1890 to 1914 and 1915 to 1927. The correlation between inflation and the commercial paper rate did not improve as various leads and lags on inflation were tried.

Fama (1976) made the assumption that real rates do not change much over time and that changes in interest rates should therefore almost entirely be caused by changes in inflation. He tested this proposition by regressing interest rates against expected inflation:

$$I_t = a + bR_t$$

where R_t = nominal interest rate during period t
I_t = expected inflation during period t

He argued that if his initial assumption about constant real rates was true, this regression would yield the following:

(a) The intercept would be equal to the constant real rate over the period.
(b) The slope of the regression would be 1, since all changes in interest rates would be a consequence of changes in inflation.

Lacking an adequate measure of expected inflation, he used the one-month Treasury bill rate at the start of each month as a measure of expected inflation during the month and the one- and three-month Treasury bill rates as measures of nominal rates. His results, for the period 1953 to 1971, were as follows:

CPI regressed against one-month Treasury bills:

$$I_t = .0007 - .98R_t \qquad R^2 = .29$$
$$\quad\; (.0003) \quad (.10)$$

CPI regressed against three-month Treasury bills:

$$I_t = .0023 - .92R_t \qquad R^2 = .48$$
$$\quad\; (.0011) \quad (.11)$$

Based upon this regression, he concluded that the hypothesis of constant real rates was supported and that the slope was statistically indistinguishable from 1, suggesting that there is a one-to-one relationship between changes in interest rates and expected inflation.

The studies that followed up on this one have generally not been as encouraging. Wood (1985), for instance, updates Fama's regression, after adding a lagged measure of inflation to it, and contrasts the results for two periods—1953 to 1971 and 1974 to 1981.

$$I_t = a + bR_t + cI_{t-1}$$

Period	Regression	R^2
1953–1971	$I_t = .0006 - .84R_t + .09I_{t-1}$ $(.0003)\;\;(.111)\quad(.064)$.309
1974–1981	$I_t = .0023 - .25R_t + .47I_{t-1}$ $(.0008)\;\;(.12)\quad(.11)$.371

The coefficient on nominal interest rates (R_t) which was close to 1 (as used

by Fama in his study) for the 1953–1971 time period drops to 0.25 for the 1974–1981 time period.

The reason for the surprisingly good results from 1953 to 1971 may be traceable to the fact that inflation was very stable during this period and that changes in inflation tended to be small. The stability in inflation during this period is contrasted with other periods in U.S. financial history in Figure 19.5.

Thus, it seems likely that the hypothesis of stable real rates and a one-to-one relationship between interest rates and inflation will be rejected in any period or any economy where there is volatility in interest rates and inflation. Since the importance of forecasting increases with the volatility in interest rates and inflation, the cautionary notes on forecasting short-term interest rates based only upon expected inflation should be taken to heart.

Expected Real Rate of Return

The other component of the Fisher equation is the expected real rate of return. On an intuitive level, the expected real rate of return is the rate at which individuals are willing to trade off current consumption for future consumption. Given the human preference for present consumption, the expected real rate of return should be positive, but can vary widely across time and across economies. If individuals in a society have a strong desire for current consumption, the expected real rate of return will have to be high to induce them to defer consumption.

Realized Real Rates of Return. Since the expected real rate of return is based upon the preference functions of individuals, which are difficult to observe, we are reduced to observing realized real rates of return, which can be defined to be:

$$\text{Realized Real Rate of Return} = \text{Nominal Interest Rate}_t - \text{Actual Inflation}_t$$

where Nominal Interest Rate$_t$ = nominal interest rate at the beginning of period t
Actual Inflation$_t$ = actual inflation during period t

While the expected real rate of return should be positive, the realized real rate of return can be positive or negative, depending upon the period under observation. Figure 19.6 summarizes the realized real rates of return for the United States from 1926 to 1990. The average realized real rate of return over the entire period was 0.61%, but there were periods where the real rate of return deviated significantly from the mean.

Expected Real Return and Expected Real Growth. Ultimately, real returns to investors in an economy come from real growth in the economy. One way to approach the estimation of expected real return is to estimate the expected real growth rate in the economy. Thus, the expected real return in an economy growing in the long term at 2.5% a year should be approximately 2.5%. If the expected real return increases above the long-term growth rate in the economy, the imbalance will lead to a depletion of savings and a shortfall in investments.

FIGURE 19.5 Inflation Rates from 1890 to 1982

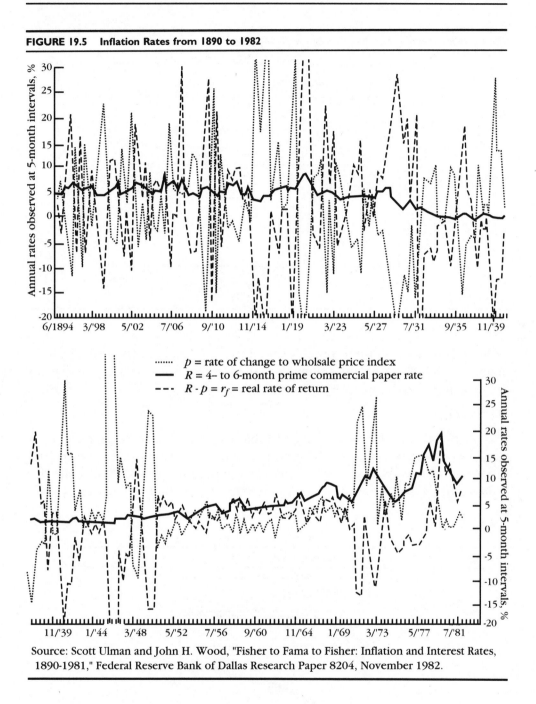

Source: Scott Ulman and John H. Wood, "Fisher to Fama to Fisher: Inflation and Interest Rates, 1890-1981," Federal Reserve Bank of Dallas Research Paper 8204, November 1982.

Alternatively, if the real return decreases below the long-term growth rate, the imbalance will lead to an accumulation of savings and overinvestment.

Maturity Premium

The maturity premium refers to the difference in interest rates between a short-term (or instantaneous) default-free interest rate and an interest rate for a

FIGURE 19.6 Realized Real Rates of Return, 1926–1990

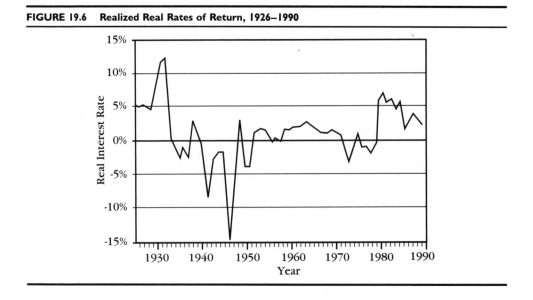

longer-maturity default-free bond. In the following section, the maturity premium is clarified further and a number of different theories designed to explain the magnitude of the maturity premium are examined.

The Yield Curve

The relationship between maturity and interest rates is usually captured by a yield curve, which graphs yields on bonds against bond maturities. Figure 19.7 summarizes Treasury bond yield curves in the last quarter of 1994. While the yield curve is generally upward sloping, as in this figure, there have been periods

FIGURE 19.7 Yield Curves, Last Quarter of 1994

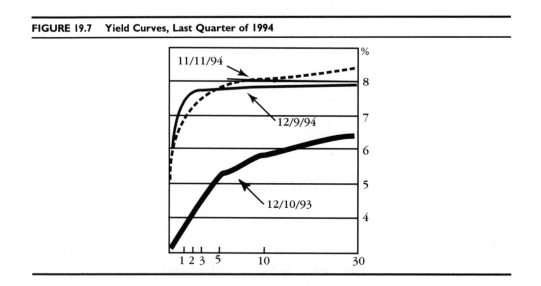

FIGURE 19.8 Yield Curves from 1971 to 1990

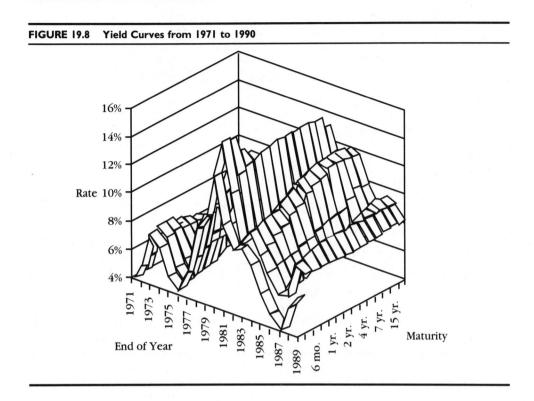

where the yield curve has been downward sloping. Figure 19.8 shows the yield curves from 1971 to 1989.

While the yield curves are usually constructed using the yields to maturity of government bonds, the presence of coupons on these bond results affects the calculated yield to maturity. This limitation can be overcome in one of two ways. The first is to construct a yield curve using only zero-coupon government coupon bonds of different maturities. The second is to extract spot interest rates from the yields to maturity of coupon bonds and to plot the spot rates against maturities. The following example illustrates the process of extracting spot rates.

Illustration 19.4: Yields to maturity and spot rates

The following table provides yields to maturity on one- to five-year bonds and extracts spot rates from the yields to maturity:

Maturity	Yield to Maturity	Spot Rate
1 year	4.00%	4.00%
2 year	4.25%	4.26%
3 year	4.40%	4.41%
4 year	4.50%	4.514%
5 year	4.58%	4.60%

The spot rate is estimated from the two-year rate as follows:

Price of two-year bond $=$ $Coupon_1/(1 + {_0}r_1)$
$+ (Face\ Value + Coupon_2)/(1 + {_0}r_2)^2$

Assuming that the bond is priced at par:

$1,000 = 42.50/1.04 + 1,042.50/(1 + {_0}r_2)^2$

Solving for ${_0}r_2$:

${_0}r_2 = (1,042.50/[1,000 - 42.50/1.04])^{.5} - 1 = 4.26\%$

The other rates are extracted using a similar process:

$1,000 = 44/1.04 + 44/1.0426^2 + 1,044/(1 + {_0}r_3)^3$
$1,000 = 45/1.04 + 45/1.0426^2 + 45/1.0441^3 + 1,045/(1 + {_0}r_4)^4$
$1,000 = 45.80/1.04 + 45.80/1.0426^2 + 45.80/1.0441^3 + 45.80/1.0451^4$
$+ 1,045.80/(1 + {_0}r_5)^5$

The difference between yields to maturity and spot rates increases as the bond maturity increases.

Spot and Forward Rates

The spot rate on a multiperiod bond is an average rate that applies over the periods. The forward rate is a one-period rate for a future period, and can be extracted from the spot rates. For instance, if ${_0}S_2$ is the two-period spot rate and ${_0}S_1$ is the one-period spot rate, the forward rate for the second period, ${_1}F_2$, can be obtained as follows:

$${_1}F_2 = (1 + {_0}S_2)^2/(1 + {_0}S_1)$$

The forward rate for period 3 can be extracted using the spot rates for periods 2 and 3, and in general, the forward rate for period n can be written as:

$${_{n-1}}F_n = (1 + {_0}S_n)^n/(1 + {_0}S_{n-1})^{n-1}$$

If the yield curve for spot rates is upward sloping, the yield curve using forward rates will be even more so. Alternatively, if the spot rate yield curve is downward sloping, the forward rate yield curve will be even more so. The following illustration builds on the previous one, and extracts forward rates from spot rates.

Illustration 19.5: Spot rates and forward rates

The forward rates are extracted from the spot rates for one- to five-year bonds. This is illustrated in the following table:

	Yield to Maturity	Spot Rate	Forward Rate
1	4.00%	4.00%	4.00%
2	4.25%	4.26%	4.52%
3	4.40%	4.41%	4.71%
4	4.50%	4.51%	4.81%
5	4.58%	4.60%	4.96%

Forward rate for year 2 $= 1.0426^2/1.04 - 1 = 4.52\%$

Forward rate for year 3 $= 1..0441^3/1.0426^2 - 1 = 4.71\%$

Forward rate for year 4 $= 1.0451^4/1.0441^3 - 1 = 4.81\%$

Forward rate for year 5 $= 1.0458^5/1.0451^4 - 1 = 4.96\%$

Determinants of the Maturity Premium

The magnitude of the maturity premium is determined by a number of factors including expectations about inflation, investor preferences for liquidity, and demands from specific market segments. Each of these factors is examined in more detail.

Expected Inflation. Expectations about future inflation are a key determinant of longer-term rates. In general, if inflation is expected to go up in future periods, longer-term rates will be higher than shorter-term rates. Alternatively, if inflation is expected to go down in future periods, longer-term rates may be lower than shorter-term rates.

An extreme version of this story is the "pure expectations hypothesis," where the term structure is driven entirely by expectations about inflation. Under this hypothesis, the yield curve will be upward sloping if investors expect inflation to rise in future periods, flat if investors expect inflation to remain unchanged in future periods, and downward sloping if investors expect inflation to decline in future periods. This is illustrated in Figure 19.9.

The pure expectations hypothesis can also be stated in terms of forward rates and expected spot rates. If the hypothesis is correct, the forward rate for period n should be the best predictor of the expected spot rate in that period; that is:

$$_{n-1}F_n = Exp(_{n-1}S_n)$$

where $_{n-1}F_n$ = forward rate for period n

$Exp(_{n-1}S_n)$ = expected one-period spot rate in period n

While the pure expectations hypothesis may be extreme in assuming that forward rates are determined entirely by expected spot rates, it does highlight the importance of expected inflation in determining the maturity premium.

Liquidity Preference. The liquidity preference theory is not an alternative to the pure expectations theory. It builds on expectations by taking into account

FIGURE 19.9 Pure Expectations Hypothesis

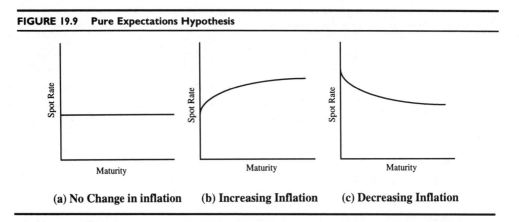

(a) No Change in inflation (b) Increasing Inflation (c) Decreasing Inflation

uncertainty and risk aversion. In the form in which it was originally developed by Hicks (1946), the uncertainty was seen as accruing to the lender who concurrently charged a liquidity premium for lending for longer time periods. This uncertainty can also be stated in terms of bond prices, with long-term bonds being viewed as more volatile than short-term bonds, as interest rates change. Under this theory, holding expectations of inflation constant, longer-term rates will be higher than shorter-term rates. Stated in terms of forward rates and expected spot rates:

$$_{n-1}F_n = Exp(_{n-1}S_n) + L_t$$

where L_t = liquidity premium corresponding to a bond maturity of t periods

Figure 19.10 illustrates how the liquidity premium builds on top of the pure expectations hypothesis. While the traditional theory assumes a positive liquidity premium (L_t), the assumption that all lenders prefer to lend short term over long term may not always be appropriate. For instance, a lender with fixed liabilities 20 years from now may view a 20-year zero-coupon bond as less risky than a Treasury bill, because it matches cash inflows to cash outflows. The question therefore becomes an empirical one: Does the average lender prefer to lend short or long term?

McCulloch (1975) attempted to estimate term premiums for different time periods and arrived at the following estimates:

Maturity	6-month	1-year	5-year	10-year	20-year	30-year
Estimate	0.41%	0.43%	0.43%	0.43%	0.43%	0.43%
Standard Error	.06%	.07%	.07%	.07%	.07%	.07%

There are two key findings that emerge from this study. The positive term premiums suggest that, on average at least, lenders prefer lending short to long term. The term premiums also do not seem sensitive to bond maturity. The

FIGURE 19.10 Term Structure with Liquidity Premium

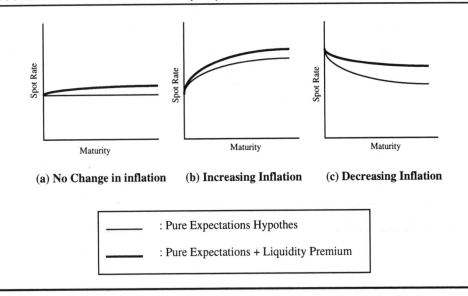

(a) No Change in inflation (b) Increasing Inflation (c) Decreasing Inflation

————— : Pure Expectations Hypothes

———— : Pure Expectations + Liquidity Premium

second result has been challenged in a number of studies. Van Horne (1965) finds term premiums increasing, albeit at a decreasing rate, with bond maturity.

Demands from Specific Market Segments. The price of bonds, like any other security, is determined by demand and supply. If the market is segmented and there are sizable groups of investors whose demand is for a specific maturity, the term structure will be affected by these groups. Again, considering the extreme case, where investors will lend and borrow only for specific maturities, the interest rate at each maturity will be determined by demand and supply at that maturity. This is illustrated in Figure 19.11. Under this scenario, the term structure can take any shape, depending upon the demand and supply at each maturity.

The assumption that investors will lend or borrow only for specific maturities and not substitute other maturities even when it is very favorable for them to do so is an extreme one. In reality, market segments do exist and do affect the term structure, but only at the margin and for one or two maturities. For instance, the demand from Japanese investors in the late 1980s for just-issued 30-year bonds resulted in a slight kink in the term structure, where 30-year bond rates were slightly lower than 29-year bond rates, even though the rest of the yield curve was upward sloping.

The Empirical Evidence on Maturity Premiums. Empirical studies of the term structure have examined several questions including the relative frequency of upward- and downward-sloping term structures, the magnitude of liquidity premiums, and the presence of market segments. The evidence can be summarized as follows:

FIGURE 19.11 Market Segmentation and Term Structure

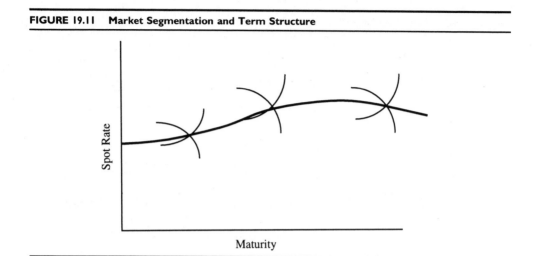

- The yield curve, at least in this century, has been more likely to be upward sloping than downward sloping. Examining yield curves at the beginning of each year from 1900 to 1992, the yield curve has been downward sloping in only 28 of the 93 years. This is inconsistent[2] with a pure expectations hypothesis, where downward-sloping yield curves should be just as likely as flat or upward-sloping yield curves. It is, however, consistent with a combination of expectations and liquidity preference hypotheses, where positive liquidity premiums are demanded over and above expected inflation.
- The term structure is much more likely to be downward sloping when the level of interest rates is high, relative to historical rates. The following table[3] summarizes the frequency of downward-sloping yield curves as a function of the level of interest rates:

Time Period	1-Year Corporate Bond Rate	Slope of Yield Curve		
		Positive	Flat	Negative
1900–1970	Above 4.40%	0	0	20
	3.25%–4.40%	10	10	5
	Below 3.25%	26	0	0
1971–1992	Above 8.00%	4	1	3
	Below 8.00%	10	4	0

This evidence is consistent with the expectations and liquidity preference hypotheses, but it is also consistent with a hypothesis that interest rates move within a normal range. When they approach the upper end (lower end) of the normal range, the yield curve is more likely to be downward sloping (upward sloping).
- Studies have generally found that expectations about future interest rates are important in shaping the term structure. Meiselman (1962) computed high positive correlations between forecasting errors and changes in various forward rates, and stable term premiums. In contrast, there are many researchers who argue that the volatility in interest rates is much too great to be explained by just

expectations about future rates and constant term premiums. Shiller (1979) concludes that the greater the volatility in interest rates, the larger the term premium.

- Attempts by the government to alter the shape of the yield curve by adjusting the maturity of government bond/bill issues have largely been unsuccessful in the long term. For instance, "Operation Twist" in 1962 was designed to make the yield curve flatter[4] by lowering long-term rates and raising short-term rates, by issuing short-term debt to finance deficits. Though the yield curve did flatten, long-term yields did not decline. This can be viewed as evidence of the weakness of the market segmentation hypothesis.
- There is evidence that the shape of the term structure has strong predictive power for future changes in the real economy. Harvey (1991) examined the G–7 countries (Canada, France, Germany, Italy, Japan, the United Kingdom and the United States) and concluded that 54% of world economic growth could be explained by the term structure.

Default Premium

While there is no possibility of default for bond issues made by the United States Treasury, corporate bonds or state/local bonds can default on interest or principal payments. If there is any possibility of default on a bond, there will be a default premium in addition to the maturity premium on the bond. The default premium will increase with the perceived default risk of the bond and is generally also a function of the maturity and terms of the specific bond.

Empirical Evidence on Bond Defaults

The most direct measure of bond defaults is the default rate—defaulted issues as a percentage of the par value of debt outstanding. Hickman (1958) investigated the default experience of fixed-income corporate bonds between 1900 and 1943, as a function of the bond rating:

Size of Issue	Ratings					
	I	II	III	IV	V–IX	No Rating
>$5 million	5.9%	6.0%	13.4%	19.1%	42.4%	28.6%
≤$5 million	10.2%	15.5%	9.9%	25.2%	32.6%	27.0%

Hickman's study was corrected by Fraine and Mills (1961) for differences in call provisions and biases introduced by the period of World War II. Hempel (1971) did an even more extensive study of default rates from 1837 to 1965 and found, not surprisingly, that default rates increased dramatically during depressions. Atkinson (1967) extended Hickman's study through 1965 and computed the average annual default rate at only 0.1% a year from 1944 to 1965. While not directly comparable to the earlier studies, Altman (1994) computed default rates for high-yield bonds from 1970 to 1993. Figure 19.12 reports the default rates on these bonds. The evidence indicates that corporate bonds do default and that they are more likely to default during economic recessions/depressions. There is also clear evidence that the default rates are higher for higher-risk bonds and lower for safer bonds.

FIGURE 19.12 Historical Default Rates, 1970 to 1993 (excluding defaulted issues in par value outstanding)

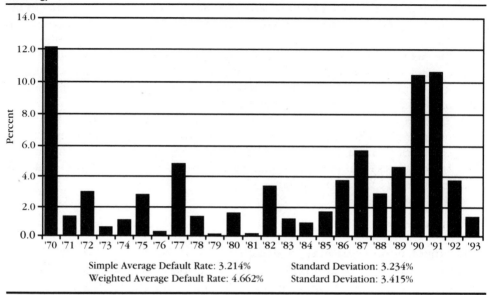

Simple Average Default Rate: 3.214% Standard Deviation: 3.234%
Weighted Average Default Rate: 4.662% Standard Deviation: 3.415%

Measures of Default Risk

Bond ratings represent one approach to measuring the default risk on bonds. The process of rating a bond is described in more detail in Chapter 3, and it incorporates both public and private information about the entity issuing the bond. The following listing summarizes the ratings used by Moody's and Standard and Poor's for corporate and state/local bonds:

Moody's

Rating	Explanation
Aaa	Best quality
Aa	High quality
A	Upper-medium grade
Baa	Medium grade
Ba	Possess speculative elements
B	Generally lack characteristics of desirable investment
Caa	Poor standing; may be in default
Ca	Speculative in a high degree; often in default
C	Lowest grade; very poor prospects

Standard and Poor's

Rating	Explanation
AAA	Highest grade
AA	High grade
A	Upper-medium grade
BBB	Medium grade

<div align="center">Standard and Poor's</div>

Rating	Explanation
BB	Lower-medium grade
B	Speculative
CCC–CC	Outright speculation
C	Reserved for income bonds
DDD–D	In default, with rating indicating relative salvage value

While bond ratings provide a convenient and easily accessible measure of default risk, the default risk can also be measured using publicly available financial data on the firm. A combination of financial ratios, described in Chapter 5, can be used to arrive at a measure of default risk. In some cases, a number of financial ratios can be consolidated into a numerical measure[5] of default risk.

The Determinants of the Default Premiums

If the bond ratings are a measure of default risk, the interest rates on corporate bonds should be determined, at least partially, by their bond ratings. The difference between a corporate bond and a Treasury bond, of equivalent maturity, is referred to as the default premium, and it should increase as the bond rating decreases. The default premium does vary over time, over bonds of different maturities, and is affected by investor restrictions and special features in bonds.

Cyclical Effects. In general, the default premiums can be expected to increase during periods of economic recession and to decrease during periods of economic expansion. This can be attributed to a couple of reasons. During recessions, investors become more risk averse and have to be offered larger risk premiums for investing in riskier bonds. A second rationale is the increased desire for liquidity[6] and marketability during recessions, leading to wider risk premiums.

Figure 19.13 graphs out the differential between Aaa corporate and Baa corporate bonds from 1946 to 1992, with recessions indicated in the shaded areas. The widening in risk premiums is particularly visible during the 1974–1975 and 1981–1982 recessions.

Recessions have a secondary effect on default risk, because the default risk of some firms, especially cyclical ones, tends to increase as their earnings and cashflows decrease. If ratings agencies factor in the cyclical effects, they might not adjust the bond ratings accordingly.

Term Structure of Default Premiums. The risk of default on a bond is generally a function of its maturity—the default risk on a short-term bond may be different from the default risk on a longer-term bond. Though it may seem logical to argue that default premiums should increase with maturity, there may be specific circumstances where the reverse is true. Johnson (1967) defines a "crisis-at-maturity" scenario, usually in the midst of a recession or a depression, where a firm is perceived to have insufficient funds to meet its immediate debt servicing needs, though it is expected to revert to health in the long term. In this scenario, the default premiums will be lower for longer-maturity bonds than for shorter-

FIGURE 19.13 Aaa Versus Baa Corporate Bonds, 1946–1992

maturity bonds. Johnson found evidence of inverted default premium term structures during 1934, in the midst of the Great Depression.

The other evidence on the term structure of default premiums is mixed. Sarig and Warga (1989) found evidence of declining default premiums with maturity for the lowest-grade issues, which they attribute to the option features embedded in longer-term issues. Litterman and Iben (1991) offered limited empirical evidence to the contrary and argue that default premiums increase with maturity.

CONCLUSION

Figure 19.14 brings together the components discussed above—the instantaneous interest rate, the maturity premium, and the default premium, in analyzing the interest rate on a corporate bond with no special features. The presence of special features such as callability and convertibility in a bond clearly affects its price and the interest rate on the bond. These special features are examined in more detail in the next chapter.

QUESTIONS AND SHORT PROBLEMS

1. Estimate the value of a just-issued 20-year government bond with an 8% coupon rate if interest rates are at 9%. How much will this value change if interest rates go up by 2%? If they go down by 2%? (Coupons are paid semi-annually.)

FIGURE 19.14 The Determinants of Interest Rates

Special Features	1. Convertibility to common stock 2. Callability: Usually by issuer at fixed price 3. Floating rate: Coupon rate varies with market interest rate 4. Zero-coupon features	1. Lowers interest rate on bond. 2. Increases interest rate on bond. 3. Lower than fixed rate when issued. 4. May lower interest rate on bond.
Default Premium	The default risk of a bond is a function of: • the riskiness of the issuer's business • the predictability of cashflows from the business • the amount of debt that the issuer already has outstanding • the size of the company and the value of securable assets Ratings agencies try to summarize this risk in a rating. The default premium itself changes with the business cycle, increasing during recessions and decreasing in recoveries.	The default premium increases with the default risk. In terms of ratings, this means that bonds with lower ratings have higher interest rates. (Even within the same rating, markets will grade bonds much more finely based upon risk.) During recessions, the default premium will increase.
Maturity Premium	In general, the maturity premium is determined by: • expectations of future interest rates: If rates are expected to go down (up) in the future, the maturity premium will be positive (negative). • liquidity premium: In order to induce investors to buy longer-term bonds you have to offer them a positive premium. • market segments: The preferences of certain groups of investors for fixed maturities will affect the rates for those bonds.	The combined maturity premium (Expectations + Liquidity Premium + Market Preferences) determines the shape of the yield curve. In most periods this yield curve is upward sloping. (Longer-term bonds have higher rates than shorter-term bonds.) In a few periods the expectation of lower rates may dominate and result in a downward-sloping yield curve.
Expected Inflation	Expected inflation is a function of: • growth in base money supply • growth in real output • changes in money velocity (how quickly it changes hands) Other things being equal, increases in money supply and money velocity increase inflation and increases in real output decrease it. $\text{Expected Inflation} = \dfrac{\% \text{ Money Growth} \times \% \text{ Change in Velocity}}{\% \text{ Change in Real Output}}$	Pure monetarists believe that velocity is stable and that real output is unaffected by monetary policy. In their world, increases in money supply result in inflation. Hence the calls for a stable monetary policy (with low money growth). Keynesians, on the other hand, suggest that real output will increase when monetary policy eases and that velocity will decline. They therefore conclude that increased money growth will not cause inflation.
Real Interest Rate	The real interest rate is a function of: • investor's preferences for current/future consumption • technology	Real interest rates are presumed to be stable over time and about 2–3%.

2. Estimate the value of a seasoned government bond with a 7.5% coupon rate and 12 years to maturity if interest rates are at 8.0%. (Coupons are paid semi-annually, and the next coupon is due in three months.)

3. Estimate the duration of a government bond with a coupon rate of 10% and a five-year maturity if the yield to maturity on the bond is 8%. (You can assume, for purposes of simplicity, that the coupons are paid annually.)

4. Why are longer-term bonds more sensitive to a given change in interest rates than shorter-term bonds? Why are zero-coupon bonds more sensitive than coupon bonds of equal maturity?

5. If the nominal interest rate is 8%, and expected inflation is 5%, estimate the expected real rate of return. Why might the actual real rate of return deviate from this expectation?

6. You are provided with the following information on government bonds of different maturities:

Maturity	Yield to Maturity
1 year	5.0%
2 years	5.5%
3 years	6.0%
4 years	6.5%
5 years	7.0%

You can assume that the bonds are trading at par, and that therefore the coupon rates are equal to the yields to maturity.

a. Plot the yield curve using the yields to maturity.
b. Estimate the spot rates for the different maturities.
c. Estimate the forward rates for each of the five years.

7. If lenders demand a liquidity premium for lending long term, yield curves will always be upward sloping. Is this statement true? Why or why not?

8. Some studies that looked at low-rated bonds in the 1980s found that the default premiums received on these bonds were much larger than the default rate on them. (In other words, investors in these bonds made more over the period, even after adjusting for actual defaults, than investors in higher-rated or default-free bonds.) They then concluded that the default premiums were too high. Would you agree? Why or why not?

ENDNOTES

1. Console bonds are the exception to this rule, since they are perpetuities.

2. Prior to the abandonment of the gold standard, negatively sloped yield curves were just as likely to occur as positively sloped yield curves.

3. Some of this table is extracted from Wood (1984).

4. A similar, though less formal, attempt was made in 1993 by the Treasury Department to raise short-term rates and lower long-term rates by issuing more short-term bonds and fewer long-term bonds. It was successful at raising short-term rates, but long-term rates increased concomitantly.

5. One example of this is the Altman Z score, which is obtained by doing a multiple discriminant analysis of bankrupt firms. It is described in more detail in Chapter 3.

6. An extreme case of this is the flight to quality that occurs during crises, which also leads to higher risk premiums.

20

Special Features in Bonds

Fixed-income securities often have special features embedded in them that have to be factored into the value. Some of these features are options—to convert into stock (convertible bonds), to call the bond back if interest rates go down (callable bonds), and to put the bond back to the issuer at a fixed price under specific circumstances (putable bonds). Other bond characteristics, such as interest rate caps and floors, have option features. Some of these options reside with the issuer of the bond, some with the buyer of the bond, but they all have to be priced. Option pricing models can be used to value these special features and to price complex fixed-income securities. Some special features in bonds such as sinking funds, subordination of further debt, and the type of collateral may affect the prices of bonds as well.

CONVERTIBILITY

A convertible bond is a bond that can be converted into a predetermined number of shares, at the option of the bondholder. While it generally does not pay to convert at the time of the bond issue, conversion becomes a more attractive option as stock prices increase. Firms generally add conversion options to bonds to lower the interest rate paid on the bonds.

The Conversion Option

In a typical convertible bond, the bondholder is given the option to convert the bond into a specified number of shares of stock. The conversion ratio measures the number of shares of stock for which each bond may be exchanged. Stated differently, the market conversion value is the current value of the shares for which the bonds can be exchanged. The conversion premium is the excess of the bond value over the conversion value of the bond.

Thus, a convertible bond with a par value of $1,000 that is convertible into 50 shares of stock has a conversion ratio of 50. The conversion ratio can also be used to compute a conversion price—the par value divided by the conversion ratio, yielding a conversion price of $20. If the current stock price is $25, the market conversion value is $1,250 (50 × $25). If the convertible bond is trading at $1,300, the conversion premium is $50.

The effect of including a conversion option in a bond is illustrated in Figure 20.1.

Determinants of Value

The conversion option is a call option on the underlying stock, and its value is therefore determined by the variables that affect call option values—the underlying stock price, the conversion ratio (which determines the strike price), the life of the convertible bond, the variance in the stock price, and the level of interest rates. The payoff diagrams on a call option and on the conversion option in a convertible bond are illustrated in Figure 20.2.

Like a call option, the value of the conversion option will increase with the price of the underlying stock, the variance of the stock, and the life of the conversion option, and decrease with the exercise price (determined by the conversion option).

The effects of increased risk in the firm can cut both ways in a convertible bond—it will decrease the value of the straight bond portion while increasing the value of the conversion option. These offsetting effects will generally mean that convertible bonds will be less exposed to changes in the firm's risk than are other types of securities.

Option pricing models can be used to value the conversion option with three caveats: Conversion options are *long term,* making the assumptions about constant variance and constant dividend yields much shakier; conversion options result in *stock dilution;* and conversion options are often *exercised before expiration,* making it dangerous to use European option pricing models. These

FIGURE 20.1 Bond Value and Conversion Option

FIGURE 20.2 Call Option and Conversion Option: Comparison of Payoffs

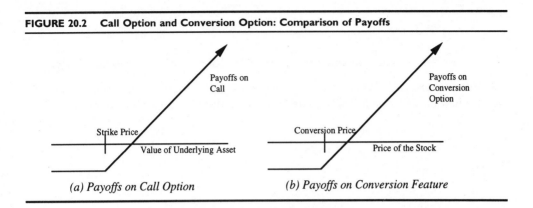

(a) Payoffs on Call Option (b) Payoffs on Conversion Feature

problems can be partially alleviated by using a binomial option pricing model, allowing for shifts in variance and early exercise, and factoring in the dilution effect. These changes are described in more detail in Chapter 17. Illustration 20.1 provides an example of the use of option pricing models in valuing a conversion option in a convertible bond.

The value of a convertible bond is also affected by a feature shared by most convertible bonds which allow for the adjustment of the conversion ratio (and price) if the firm issues new stock below the conversion price or has a stock split or dividend. In some cases, the conversion price has to be lowered to the price at which new stock is issued. This is designed to protect the convertible bondholder from misappropriation by the firm.

Illustration 20.1: Valuing a conversion option/convertible bond: General Signal

In December 1994, General Signal had convertible bonds outstanding with the following features:

- The bonds matured in June 2002. There were 100,000 shares outstanding.
- They had a face value of $1,000 and were convertible into 25.32 shares per bond until June 2002.
- The coupon rate on the bond was set at 5.75%.
- The company was rated A −. Straight bonds of similar rating and similar maturity were yielding 9.00%.
- The stock price in December 1994 was $32.50. The volatility (standard deviation in log stock prices) based upon historical data was 50.00%.
- There were 47.35 million shares outstanding. Exercising the convertible bonds will create 2.532 million additional shares (100,000 × 25.32 shares).
- The dividend yield on the stock was $3%. (The T Bond rate was 7.75%.)

The two components of the convertible bond can be valued as follows:

Straight Bond Component. If this bond had been a straight bond, with a coupon rate of 5.75% and a yield to maturity of 9.00% (based upon the bond rating), the value of this straight bond would have been:

$$\text{PV of Bond} = \sum_{t=1}^{t=15} \frac{28.75}{1.045^t} + \frac{1,000}{1.09^{7.5}} = \$832.73$$

This is based upon semiannual coupon payments (of \$28.75 for semiannual periods).

Conversion Option. The value of the conversion option is estimated using the Black-Scholes model, with the following parameters for the conversion option:

Type of option = Call

Number of calls per bond = 25.32

Stock Price = \$32.50

Strike Price = \$1,000/25.32 = \$39.49

Standard Deviation in stock prices(ln) = .5

Time to expiration = 7.5 years

Riskless Rate = 7.75% (rate on 7.5-year Treasury bond)

Dividend Yield on stock = 3.00%

Allowing for the dilution inherent in the exercise (see section on warrant pricing for details on the valuation correction):

Value of one call = \$12.85

Value of the conversion option = \$12.85 × 25.32 = \$325.36

Convertible Bond. The value of the convertible bond is the sum of the straight bond and conversion option components:

Value of Convertible Bond = Value of Straight Bond

+ Value of Conversion Option

= \$832.73 + \$325.43 = \$1,158.09

This valuation is based upon the assumption that the conversion option is unconstrained and that the bonds are not callable. The effects of introducing these changes into the analysis will be examined in the following sections.

The Effect of Forced Conversion

Companies that issue convertible bonds sometimes have the right to force conversion if the stock price rises to a specified level. This right to force conversion caps the profit that can be made on the conversion option and hence affects its value. Figure 20.3 illustrates the effect of forced conversion on the expected payoffs.

The value of a capped call, with an exercise price of K_1 and a cap of K_2, can be calculated as follows:

Value of Capped Call(K_1, K_2) = Value of Call(K_1) − Value of Call(K_2)

This is because the cashflows on a capped call can be replicated by buying the call with a strike price of K_1 and selling the call with a strike price of K_2.

FIGURE 20.3 Value of a Capped Call

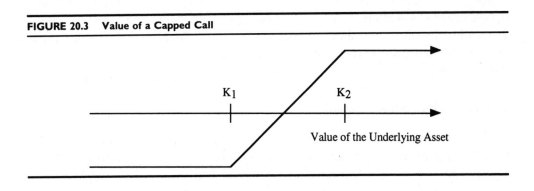

K_1 K_2

Value of the Underlying Asset

CALLABILITY

The issuer of a callable bond preserves the right to call back the bond and pay a fixed price (generally at a premium over the par value) for it. Thus, if interest rates decline (bond prices rise) after the initial issue, the firm can refund the bonds at the fixed price instead of the market value. Adding the call option to a bond should make it less attractive to buyers, since it reduces the potential upside on the bond. As interest rates go down and the bond price increases, the bonds are more likely to be called back.

The distinction between a straight bond and a callable bond are illustrated in Figure 20.4. The difference in the upside between straight and callable bonds is quite clearly illustrated. As interest rates decline, the values of the two bonds diverge, whereas they converge as interest rates increase.

There are several common features shared by most callable bonds. Most callable bonds come with an initial period of *call protection,* during which the

FIGURE 20.4 Callable and Noncallable Bonds

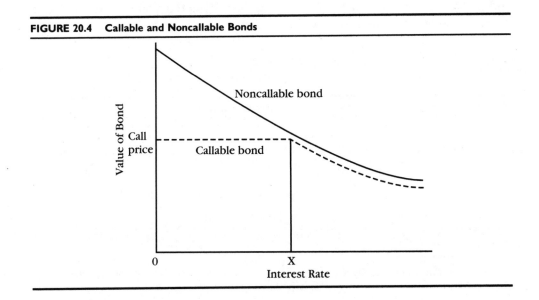

bonds cannot be called back. Such bonds are called deferred callable bonds. The call price on most callable bonds is set at an initial level above par value plus one annual coupon payment, but it declines as time passes and approaches the par value.

Valuing the Callability Option

The issuer's right to call back a bond if interest rates drop (or bond prices rise) to an attractive level is a call option on the bond and can be valued as such. The payoffs on a callable bond are shown in Figure 20.5. The value of the callable feature on a callable bond will increase as interest rates decline and as the volatility of interest rates increases.

Since the callable feature is held by the issuer of the bond, the value of a callable bond can be written as follows:

Value of Callable Bond = Value of Straight Bond
 − Value of Call Feature on Bond

A callable bond should therefore sell for less than an otherwise similar straight bond.

Traditional Analysis

The traditional approach to analyzing callable bonds is to estimate yields to call as well as yields to maturity. The former is based upon the assumption that the bond will be called at the first call date while the latter assumes holding the bond until maturity. The two yields are compared, and the investor chooses the lower of the two as a measure of the expected return on the bond. This approach can also be extended to calculate the yield to all possible call dates and picking the lowest of these yields as the expected yield on the callable bond. This yield is called the yield to worst.

FIGURE 20.5 Payoffs on Call Feature on Bond to Seller of Bond

(a) Payoffs on Call Option (b) Payoffs on Call Feature on Bond

While this approach may give the investor some sense of the potential downside from the callability of the bond, it suffers from all the standard problems of the "yield to maturity" calculation. First, it assumes that the investor can reinvest all coupons until the bond is called at the yield to call, which is not a realistic assumption since calls are much more likely if interest rates go down. Second, it does not examine the rate at which the proceeds from the called bond can be reinvested by the investor. Thirdly, it assumes that the bond will be called on the call date, which takes away the option characteristics of the call feature.

Illustration 20.2: Estimating yields to maturity and call on a callable bond

Consider a corporate bond with 20 years to maturity and a 12% coupon rate that is callable in two years at 105% of the face value. The bond is trading at $980 currently. The yield to maturity and the yield to call on the corporate bond are as follows:

$$\text{Yield to Maturity: } \sum_{t=1}^{t=40} \frac{60.00}{(1+r/2)^t} + \frac{1,000}{(1+r)^{20}} = \$980$$

Solving for r, the yield to maturity is approximately 12.26%.

$$\text{Yield to Call: } \sum_{t=1}^{t=4} \frac{60.00}{(1+r/2)^t} + \frac{1,050}{(1+r/2)^4} = \$980$$

Solving for r, the yield to call is approximately 13.25%.

Price/Yield Relationship for a Callable Bond

The price/yield relationship on a callable bond is different because the potential that the bond will be called back puts an upper limit on the price, making the relationship between price and yield convex, for some range of the yields. The difference is illustrated in Figure 20.6. The section of the price/yield relationship on the callable bond when the yield falls below y^* has negative convexity—that is, the price appreciation on this bond will be less than the price depreciation for a given change (down or up) in interest rates.

Determinants of Value—Option Pricing Approach

The call feature in a callable bond can be valued using option pricing models. It is a series of call options on the underlying bond, and its value is determined by the level and volatility of interest rates. There are some modifications that need to be made to the standard option pricing models before they can be applied in this context.

Once the call feature is valued as a series of options, the yield on a callable bond can be adjusted for the option features, and the difference between this adjusted yield and Treasuries of equivalent maturity is called the option-

FIGURE 20.6 Price vs. Yield: Callable and Noncallable Bonds

adjusted spread. This approach is a more realistic way of considering the effects of the call feature on expected yields than the traditional yield to call approach. The following illustration values the call feature on a callable bond.

Illustration 20.3: Valuing a callable bond

The following analysis, based upon Fabozzi (1994), values a 17-year callable bond with a coupon rate of 12% by valuing the straight bond, the call feature on the straight bond, and the value of the callable bond as a function of the yield on the bond. The actual option valuation was done using a binomial option pricing model, with an interest rate volatility of 12% and a short-term interest rate of 6%

Yield	Value of Straight Bond	Value of Call Feature	Value of Callable Bond
20.51%	60.00	$ 0	$ 60.00
19.55%	63.00	0	63.00
18.66%	66.00	0	66.00
17.59%	70.00	0	70.00
16.63%	74.00	0	74.00
15.54%	79.00	.02	78.98
14.56%	84.00	.06	83.94
13.51%	90.00	.22	89.78
12.57%	96.00	.67	95.33
11.46%	104.00	2.11	101.89

Yield	Value of Straight Bond	Value of Call Feature	Value of Callable Bond
10.59%	111.00	4.60	106.40
9.59%	120.00	9.80	110.20
8.60%	130.00	17.81	112.19
7.73%	140.00	27.21	112.79

While the value of the straight bond increases as the yield drops, the callable bond's value stops increasing because the call feature becomes more and more valuable as the yield becomes lower. In fact the value of the callable bond is maximized at $112.94.

Effective Duration and Effective Convexity

In the previous chapter we defined duration to be a measure of a bond's sensitivity to interest rate changes. While doing so, it was assumed that cashflows did not change as interest rates changed. This assumption is clearly violated for callable bonds, where the cashflows on the bond are influenced by the level of rates—if interest rates drop enough, the bond will be called. For bonds such as these, there is a different measure of duration that is more appropriate called the effective duration. The duration of any bond can be approximated as follows, for a small change in interest rates:

$$\text{Duration} = (P_- - P_+)/P_0(y_+ - y_-)$$

where P_- = price of the bond if yield decreases by x basis points
P_+ = price of the bond if yield increases by x points
P_0 = price of the bond initially
y_+ = initial yield + x basis points
y_- = initial yield − x basis points

This approach can be used to estimate the effective duration of callable bonds for any segment of the yield curve. It can also be used for any other bonds with embedded options such as putable bonds or mortgage-backed securities, which have the prepayment option embedded in them.

A similar adjustment can be made to the standard convexity measure to arrive at the *effective convexity* of any bond with embedded options:

$$\text{Effective Convexity} = (P_+ - P_- - 2P_0)/P_0(.5[y_+ - y_-])^2$$

Valuing a Callable Convertible Bond

Many convertible bonds have embedded call features. The presence of two options in the bond, one possessed by the buyer of the bond and the other possessed by the seller of the bond, and the interaction between the two options implies that the two options have to be valued together. Brennan and Schwartz (1977, 1980) provide an analysis of convertible bonds with call features, default

risk, and stock price dilution. The simplest approach for illustrating the interaction between the various options is a binomial option pricing model.

Empirical Evidence on Call Feature

When a convertible bond is callable, holders of the convertible bond lose the opportunity to make further returns on the bond as stock prices increase. Companies can establish a variety of call policies such as calling the instant the market value of the convertible rises above the call price or waiting until the market value is well in excess of the call price. Ingersoll (1977) argued that a bond should be called when its conversion value equals its call price. Given that a 30-day notice has to be given to bondholders of a call, firms may prefer to build a cushion to protect against risk during this period.

The empirical evidence, however, suggests that firms do not usually follow the optimal policy. Ingersoll, for instance, found that between 1968 and 1975, the average conversion value was 43.9% above the call price for bonds and 38.5% for preferred stocks. The call policy chosen by a firm and communicated to financial markets implicitly through its actions has an effect on the value of the convertible bond.

PREPAYMENT OPTION

Mortgage-backed securities, which came of age in the 1980s, securitized residential mortgages, by packaging them and issuing marketable securities of various types on them—either as flowthrough investments, where holders receive a share of the total cashflows on the pool of mortgages, or as derivative products, where holders receive customized packages of cashflows, depending upon their preferences. The latter, called collateralized mortgage obligations (CMOs), in their simplest form divide cashflows on the mortgage pool into four tranches, with cashflows on each tranche starting as the cashflows on the previous tranche are completed. Figure 20.7 illustrates this type of security.

In recent years, CMOs have been refined further, and even more-specialized products have been created, including stripped mortgage-backed securities (where cashflows are divided on the basis of principal and interest), floating-rate classes, and inverse floaters (where the interest rate on the security increases as the index rate decreases).

Mortgages can be prepaid by borrowers, if interest rates decline. This prepayment option that resides with borrowers affects the cashflows, and therefore the value, of all mortgage-backed securities.

The Prepayment Option

The homeowner may prepay a loan for any number of reasons, but the level of interest rates is a critical variable. If interest rates decline sufficiently, the potential gain from prepayment may exceed the cost of prepayment. The graph

FIGURE 20.7 Cashflows on CMOs

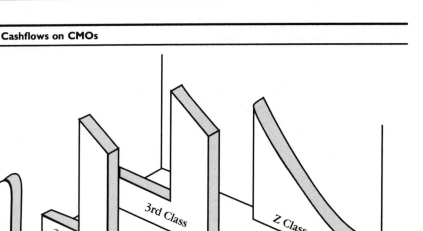

in Figure 20.8 illustrates the percentage of homeowners who prepay as a function of the difference between the interest rate and the coupon rate, based upon historical data.

If the level of interest rates was the only determinant of prepayment and homeowners were rational about prepayment decisions, the prepayment option could be valued very similarly to the call option in a callable bond (as a function of the level and volatility of interest rates).

There are, however, other variables besides the level of interest rates that determine whether homeowners prepay. For instance, there is a correlation between prepayment and the age of a mortgage, irrespective of interest rates. Furthermore, some homeowners may never prepay their mortgages no matter how much interest rates drop. There are also seasonal factors that affect prepayment. Consequently, option pricing models alone fall short in pricing prepayment options in mortgage-backed securities.

A number of researchers have attempted to develop models that explain prepayment, as a basis for pricing the prepayment option, with characteristics such as age and coupon rate as inputs, in addition to specific characteristics of the borrowers in the pool. In cases where a specific rather than a generic pool of mortgages is being priced, the historical payment record of the specific[1] pool is useful and is often the basis for estimating prepayments.

FIGURE 20.8　Prepayments and Interest Rates

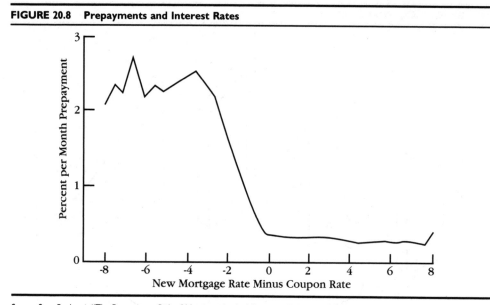

Source: Sean Becketti, "The Prepayment Risk of Mortgage-backed Securities," *Economic Review of the Federal Reserve Bank of Kansas City* (February 1989), 53.

FIGURE 20.9　Interest-Only and Principal-Only Securities

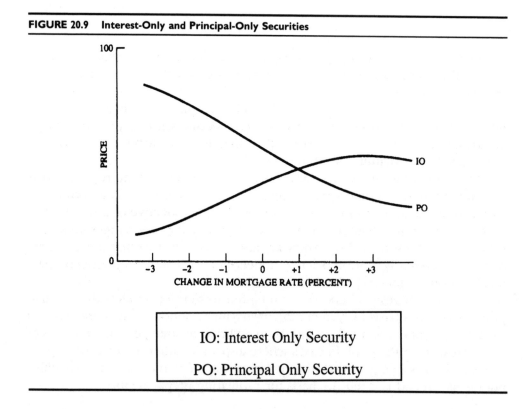

IO: Interest Only Security

PO: Principal Only Security

Valuing the Prepayment Option

The effect of the prepayment option on value will vary with the type of mortgage-backed security. Consider, for instance, the price behavior of interest-only and principal-only securities, as interest rates change. As interest rates increase, the interest payments on the interest-only securities go up, leading to a higher value for the security, at least initially, though the present value effects (which are negative) start to dominate beyond a certain point. As interest rates decrease, the prepayments lead to lower interest payments and a lower value for the security. The principal-only securities behave more like conventional bonds, increasing in value as interest rates decline and decreasing in value as they increase. Figure 20.9 illustrates this relationship.

INTEREST RATE CAPS AND FLOORS

A floating-rate bond is a bond that has an interest rate linked up to an index—either a government bond rate (Treasury bond or bill) or the LIBOR. The rationale for issuing such bonds is to reduce the interest rate risk for both the issuer and the buyer of the bond. Most floating-rate bond issuers, however, *cap* their floating-rate obligations to ensure that interest rates do not rise above a prespecified rate (the cap). Some floating-rate bonds offer buyers some compensation by providing a *floor,* below which interest rates will not decline. If a floating-rate bond has a cap and a floor, a *collar* is created.

Caps, Floors, and Collars

The presence of a cap on a floating-rate bond can be illustrated best by contrasting a bond with a cap with a floating-rate bond without one. This is done in Figure 20.10. The cap on a floating-rate bond has the same effect as a call option on interest rates with a strike price of K_c, with the issuer of the bond holding the option. A call option on interest rates translates[2] into a put option on the underlying bond. The price of a floating-rate bond with a cap can then be written as:

Price of floating-rate bond with cap = Price of floating-rate bond without cap

− Value of put on bond

The presence of a floor on interest rates can be illustrated using a similar comparison of a bond with a floor with a bond without one, as in Figure 20.11. The floor on a floating-rate bond has the same effect as adding a put option on interest rates with a strike price of K_f, with the buyer of the bond holding the put. A put option on interest rates can be translated into a call option on the underlying bond. The price of a floating-rate bond with a floor can then be written as:

Price of floating-rate bond with floor = Price of floating-rate bond without floor

+ Value of call on bond

FIGURE 20.10 Effects of Caps on Floating-Rate Loans

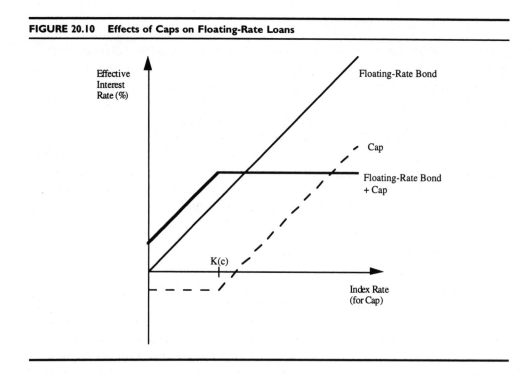

FIGURE 20.11 Effects of a Floor on Floating-Rate Loans

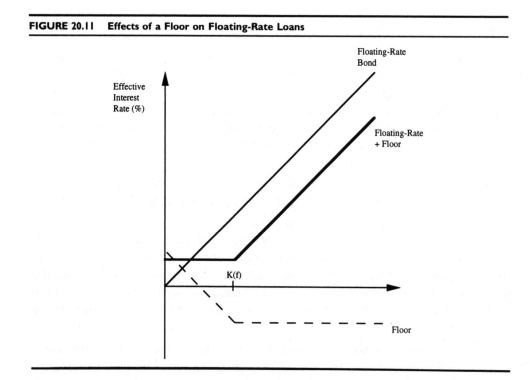

Finally, the presence of both a cap and a floor can be illustrated as in Figure 20.12. The presence of a collar on a floating-rate bond creates two options—a call option with a strike price of K_c for the issuer of the bond and a put option with a strike price of K_f for the buyer of the bond. These options on interest rates can be stated again in terms of options on the underlying bond:

Price of floating-rate bond with collar = Price of floating-rate bond without collar
+ Value of call on bond
− Value of put on bond

Valuing Caps and Floors

Option pricing models can be used to value caps, floors, and collars with some caveats. The key assumption in the Black-Scholes model of constant volatility over the life of the option is likely to be violated for interest rate options, both because of the long-term nature of these options and because the variance in the bond price is likely to change as the bond maturity declines. There have been attempts to use yield instead of price and assume that it conforms to a lognormal distribution.

Subrahmanyam (1990) noted that the value of a cap on interest rates can be written as a series of put options on the price of an equivalent bill or bond.

FIGURE 20.12 Effect of a Collar on a Floating-Rate Loan

Briys, Crouhy, and Schobel (1991) provided a framework for pricing caps, floors, and collars. They argued that caps and floors can be modeled as a series of independent options on zero-coupon bonds. They allowed for the fact that bond prices do not follow the geometric Brownian motion used by Black and Scholes (1973), but adopted a different stochastic process to price caps, floors, and collars. Subrahmanyam and Park (1990) used the call/put approach to value caps and floors on 6-month LIBOR, and the illustration below is based on their analysis.

Illustration 20.4: Valuing a two-year cap/floor on six-month LIBOR

Assume that the current 6-month LIBOR rate is 8% and that the cap/floor has an exercisable price of 8%. The cap consists of three options, which are exercisable at the end of 6 months (183 days), 12 months (365 days), and 18 months (548 days). Each of these options is on the \$LIBOR rate (of 183 days for the first, 182 days for the second, and 183 days for the third).

The options can be valued using the bill prices (rather than interest rates), and the inputs used in the Black-Scholes model are as follows:

Option Maturity	Bill Price	Exercise Price	Forward Price	Volatility
183	0.9609	0.9611	0.9626	0.0100
365	.9250	.9609	.9609	.0100
548	.8890	.9611	.9615	.0100

The first column provides the maturity period for each of the three options. The second column is the value of a zero-coupon bond with a maturity equal to the maturity of the zero-coupon bond— \$1 discounted back 183 days at 8% is \$0.9609; \$1 discounted back 365 days at 8% is \$0.9250, and so on. The third column is the strike price, based upon the cap rate, for each option. The fourth column is the forward price of the bill at the option expiration date. The final column is the assumed annualized volatility in bill prices of 1%.

The values of the call and put options with these maturities on bills is provided in the following table in basis points. These can be converted into option values for options on interest rates by multiplying by the number of put options on bills that is equivalent to one call option on the interest rate.

Adjustment factor $= \alpha =$ 1/Exercise Price of equivalent bill option

	Treasury Bill Options		Interest Rate Options	
	Put	Call	Call	Put
183	19.6133	33.6639	20.4065	35.0254
365	34.6903	36.4439	36.1010	37.9259
548	39.8620	43.5135	41.4742	45.2734

Value of the cap =		97.9817
Value of the floor =		120.2237

To illustrate the calculation, the values of the interest rate options for the 183-day option can be estimated as follows:

Adjustment factor for 183-day option = 1/.9611 = 1.0405

Value of 183-day put on Treasury bill = 19.6133

Value of 183-day call on interest rate = 19.6133 × 1.0405 = 20.4076

OTHER FEATURES

There are a number of other bond features that affect the value of the bond: a sinking fund provision, where the firm plans to retire a specified face value of the bonds outstanding each year; provisions relating to the subordination of future debt issues; and bond covenants on investment and dividend policy.

Sinking Funds

Most industrial bond issues come with sinking fund provisions, requiring the issuer to retire a specified portion of the bond issue each year, starting a period of time (five or ten years) after the initial issue. The sinking fund provision can take one of two forms:

(a) A trustee collects a cash payment from the bond issuer and calls bonds for redemption at the sinking fund call price, usually based upon a lottery.
(b) The bond issuer can buy back bonds in the open market and deliver the specified number of bonds to the trustee in the period specified.

If the bond issuer has the option to do the latter, bonds will be bought back and delivered if the market price is less than the call price, and cash will be delivered to the trustee to make the call if the market price is greater than the call price.

Sinking funds usually relate to a single issue, but they can sometimes cover multiple issues ("funnel sinking fund"). Most sinking funds also allow the bond issuer to accelerate callbacks if it is in the issuer's favor to do so (i.e., interest rates have gone down since the issue).

A sinking fund has two effects, one of which benefits the issuer of the bond and the other which benefits the buyer of the bond. The issuer of the bond gets a delivery option, because he or she has an option to either deliver the cash for the call price or buy the bonds at the market price. The value of this call option (similar to the option in a callable bond) will increase with the volatility of interest rates and decrease with the level of interest rates. The buyer of the bond has less default risk because of the requirement that some of the debt be retired each period. The net effect will determine whether a sinking fund provision adds or detracts from the value of a bond.

The empirical evidence on the sinking fund provision is mixed. While some of the earlier studies concluded that a sinking fund provision added to bond

value, Ho and Lee (1985) found that its net value is insignificant overall but that it adds more value as default risk increases than it does as interest rate volatility increases.

Subordination of Further Debt and Collateral

Existing debt holders are negatively affected by the issue of new debt, especially if the new debt has superior claims on the assets of the issuer. Therefore, some bond issues have *subordination clauses,* which put restrictions on the issue of additional debt. Additional debt might have to be subordinated to existing debt; that is, in the event of bankruptcy, subordinated debt will be paid off after existing debt is fully paid. The presence of subordination clauses in a bond agreement should make it less risky and therefore more valuable.

Some bonds are issued with specific collateral issued behind them, with a specific asset of the firm backing up the promised payments on the bond. If the collateral is property, the bond is called a mortgage bond, whereas if it is securities, it is a collateral trust bond. Other bonds are issued without specific collateral and are called unsecured bonds. Other things remaining equal, secured bonds should be viewed as less risky and more valuable than equivalent unsecured bonds.

The Effect of Bond Covenants

Most bond issues are accompanied by a set of covenants that restrict the investment and dividend policies of the firm. These covenants are designed to protect bondholders from stockholders, who might try to expropriate wealth from them by

(a) taking on much riskier projects, especially if the firm is highly levered.
(b) paying significantly higher dividends than expected.

Bond covenants should reduce the risk of expropriation on a bond and increase the value of the bond.

CONCLUSION

Bonds become increasingly complex as special features are added to them, since these special features affect the cashflows, risk, and value of these bonds. Many of these special features have option characteristics—the chance to convert the bond into other securities or assets, the option to call the bond back if interest rates go down, and the option to put the bond back to the issuer if contractual obligations are not met. Traditional option pricing models can be used to value these options, some of which reside with the buyer (thus increasing the value of the bond) and some of which are held by the seller (which would reduce value). The presence of more than one of these options in the

same bond (for example, a callable convertible bond) does add to the complexity of the process, but it can be overcome.

QUESTIONS AND SHORT PROBLEMS

1. You are analyzing a convertible bond with a face value of $1,000 and an annual coupon of 4%, which is convertible into 30 shares of stock any time over the next 20 years. The current stock price is $27, and the convertible is trading at $1,177.
 a. Estimate the conversion ratio and conversion price.
 b. Estimate the conversion premium.
 c. If the interest rate on straight bonds issued by the same company is 8%, estimate the value of the conversion option.

2. ITC Corporation has convertible bonds outstanding with the following features:
 - The bonds mature in 15 years; there are 100,000 bonds outstanding.
 - Each bond can be converted into 50 shares of stock any time until expiration.
 - The coupon rate on the bond is 5%; straight bonds issued by the company are yielding 10%.
 - The current stock price is $15 per share, and the standard deviation in ln (stock prices) is 40%.
 - There are 20 million shares outstanding.
 a. Value the conversion option.
 b. Estimate the value of the straight bond portion.
 c. If these bonds were issued at par, who would be gaining? Who would be losing?
 d. What impact would forced conversion have on the value of this convertible bond?

3. A company has two issues of bonds outstanding. They both have the same maturities and coupon rates, but they differ in one respect: The first issue (Issue A) is callable, while the second is not. Respond true or false to the following statements:
 a. The callable bonds will trade for a higher price than the noncallable bonds.
 b. The callable bonds have a shorter duration than the noncallable bonds.
 c. The callable bonds will have a higher yield than the noncallable bonds.
 d. The callable bonds will be more sensitive to interest rate changes than the noncallable bonds.

4. You are evaluating the yield on a callable bond with a 10-year maturity and a 9% coupon rate. The bond can be called back at 110% of par in three years. The bond is trading at $950.
 a. Estimate the yield to maturity.
 b. Estimate the yield to call.
 c. Which of the two would you use in analyzing the bond?

5. Collateralized Mortgage Obligations (CMOs) provide investors with the opportunity to invest in cashflows from mortgage obligations. These cashflows are affected by mortgage prepayments. Assume that you have valued (and bought) CMOs on the assumption that homeowners will prepay as soon as it is rational for them to do so. What would be the effect on your returns if:

- homeowners consistently waited too long before prepaying mortgages?
- homeowners consistently prepaid mortgages at the right time?

6. Answer true or false to the following statements and explain your answers.

 a. A floating-rate loan with no cap or floor has very low or no duration.

 b. A floating-rate loan with a cap will have a higher interest rate than a similar floating-rate loan with no cap.

 c. A floating-rate loan with a floor will have a higher interest rate than a similar floating-rate loan with no floor.

 d. A loan with a sinking fund provision will have a lower interest rate than a similar loan with no sinking fund provision.

ENDNOTES

1. A number of variables have been found to be useful in explaining prepayments—the market price relative to the original purchase price and geographical differences, for instance.

2. The translation is not one to one. A call option on interest rates is the equivalent of α options on the underlying bill or bond, where $\alpha = 1/\text{Exercise price of equivalent bill}$.

21

Valuing Futures Contracts

A futures contract is a contract between two parties to exchange assets or services at a specified time in the future at a price agreed upon at the time of the contract. In most conventionally traded futures contracts, one party agrees to deliver a commodity or security at some time in the future, in return for an agreement from the other party to pay an agreed-upon price on delivery. The former is the seller of the futures contract, while the latter is the buyer.

This chapter explores the pricing of futures contracts on a number of different assets—perishable commodities, storable commodities, and financial assets, by setting up the basic arbitrage relationship between the futures contract and the underlying asset. It also examines the effects of transactions costs and trading restrictions on this relationship and on future prices. Finally, the chapter reviews some of the evidence on the pricing of futures contracts.

FUTURES, FORWARD, AND OPTION CONTRACTS

Futures, forward, and option contracts are all viewed as derivative contracts because they derive their value from an underlying asset. There are, however, some key differences in the workings of these contracts.

How a Futures Contract Works

There are two parties to every futures contract—the seller of the contract, who agrees to deliver the asset at the specified time in the future, and the buyer of the contract, who agrees to pay a fixed price and take delivery of the asset. While a futures contract may be used by a buyer or seller to hedge other positions in the same asset, price changes in the asset after the futures contract agreement is made provide gains to one party at the expense of the other. If the price of the underlying asset increases after the agreement is made, the buyer gains at the expense of the seller. If the price of the asset drops, the seller gains at the expense of the buyer.

FIGURE 21.1 Cashflows on Futures Contracts

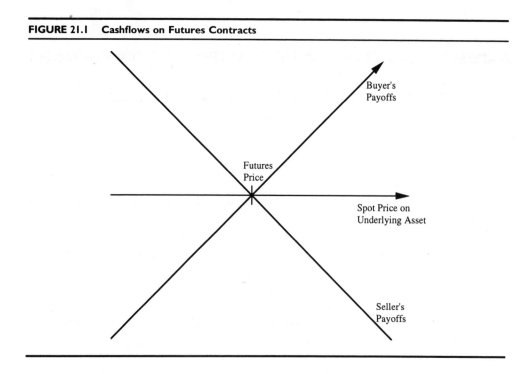

Futures versus Forward Contracts

While futures and forward contracts are similar in terms of their final results, a forward contract does not require that the parties to the contract settle up until the expiration of the contract. Settling up usually involves the loser (i.e., the party that guessed wrong on the direction of the price) paying the winner the difference between the contract price and the actual price. In a futures contract, the differences are settled every period, with the winner's account being credited with the difference, while the loser's account is reduced. This process is called marking to the market. While the net settlement is the same under the two approaches, the timing of the settlements is different and can lead to different prices for the two types of contracts. The difference is illustrated in the following example, using a futures contract in gold.

Illustration 21.1: Futures versus forward contracts: Gold futures contract

Assume that the spot price of gold is $400 and that a three-period futures contract on gold has a price of $415. The following table summarizes the cashflow to the buyer and seller of this contract on a futures and forward contract over the next three time periods, as the price of the gold futures contract changes.

Time Period	Gold Futures Contract	Forward		Futures	
		Buyer's Cashflow	Seller's Cashflow	Buyer's Cashflow	Seller's Cashflow
1	$420	$ 0	$ 0	$ 5	$ −5
2	430	0	0	10	−10
3	425	10	−10	−5	5

The net cashflow from the seller to the buyer is $10 in both cases, but the timing of the cashflows is different.

Futures and Forward Contracts versus Option Contracts

While the difference between a futures and a forward contract may be subtle, the difference between these contracts and option contracts is much greater. In an options contract, the buyer is not obligated to fulfill his or her side of the bargain, which is to buy the asset at the agreed-upon strike price in the case of a call option and to sell the asset at the strike price in the case of a put option. Consequently, the buyer of an option will exercise the option only if it is in his or her best interests to do so, that is, if the asset price exceeds the

FIGURE 21.2 Buying a Futures Contract vs. Buying a Call Option

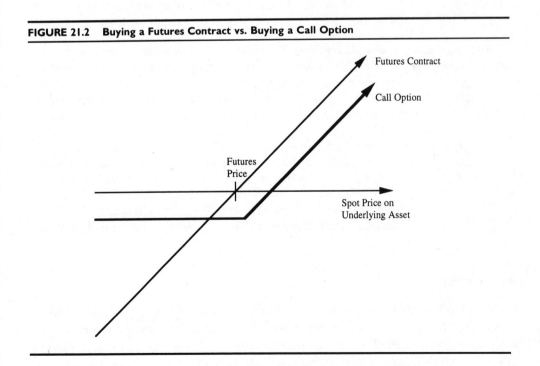

striking price in a call option and vice versa in a put option. The buyer of the option, of course, pays for this privilege up front. In a futures contract, both the buyer and the seller are obligated to fulfill their sides of the agreement. Consequently, the buyer does not gain an advantage over the seller and should not have to pay an up-front price for the futures contract itself. Figure 21.2 summarizes the differences in payoff on the two types of contracts in a payoff diagram.

TRADED FUTURES CONTRACTS—INSTITUTIONAL DETAILS

A futures contract is an agreement between two parties. In a traded futures contract, an exchange acts as an intermediary and guarantor, and also standardizes and regulates how the contract is created and traded.

| Buyer of Contract | → | Futures Exchange | ← | Seller of Contract |

In this section, we will examine some of the institutional features of traded futures contracts.

Standardization

Traded futures contracts are standardized to ensure that contracts can be easily traded and priced. The standardization occurs at a number of levels:

(a) *Asset quality and description:* The type of asset that can be covered by the contract is clearly defined. For instance, a lumber futures contract traded on the Chicago Board of Trade (CBOT) allows for the delivery of 130,000 board feet of lumber per contract. A Treasury bond futures contract traded on the same exchange requires the delivery of bonds with a maturity of greater than 15 years.[1]

(b) *Asset quantity:* Each traded futures contract on an asset provides for the delivery of a specified quantity of the asset. For instance, a gold futures contract traded on the CBOT requires the delivery of 100 ounces of gold at the contract's expiration. The purpose of the standardization is to ensure that the futures contracts on an asset are perfect substitutes for each other. This allows for liquidity and also allows parties to a futures contract to get out of positions easily.

Price Limits

Futures exchanges generally impose "price movement limits" on futures contracts. For instance, the daily price movement limit on orange juice futures contracts on the CBOT is 5¢ per pound or $750 per contract (which covers 15,000 pounds). If the price of the contract drops or increases by the amount of the price limit, trading is generally suspended for the day, though the ex-

change has the discretion to reopen trading in the contract later in the day. The table in Figure 21.3 summarizes the price limits on different traded futures contracts.

The radionale for introducing price limits is to prevent panic buying and selling on an asset, based upon faulty information or rumors, and to prevent

FIGURE 21.3 Commodity Trading Limits

Commodity and Exchange	Trading Hours (Local Time)	Contract Unit	Per Unit	Per Contract	1¢/1$ Move
United States Commodities Exchanges					
Cattle feeder (CME)	9:05–12:45	44,000 lb	$.000025 lb	$ 11	$440
Cattle (CME)	9:05–12:45	40,000 lb	2½ 100¢ lb	10	$400
Cattle (MACE)	9:05– 1:00	20,000 lb	.00025 lb	5	$200
Certificates of deposit (CBOT)	7:30– 2:00	$1,000,000	1 BP .01	25	100 BP = $2500
Certificates of deposit (IMM)	7:30– 2:00	$1,000,000	1 BP .01	15	100 BP = $2500
Citrus (FCOJ) (NYCE)	10:15– 2:45	15,000 lb	5/100¢ lb	7.50	$150
Cocoa (NYCSC)	9:30– 3:00	10 t	$1 t	10	$10
Coffee C (NYCSC)	9:45– 2:28	37,500 lb	1/100¢ lb	3.75	$375
Copper (COMEX)	9:50– 2:00	25,000 lb	.05/100¢ lb	12.50	$250
Corn (CBOT)	9:30– 1:15	5,000 bu	1/4¢ bu	12.50	$50
Corn (MACE)	9:30– 1:15	1,000 bu	1/8¢ bu	1.25	$10
Cotton (NYCE)	10:30– 3:00	50,000 lb	1/100¢ lb	5	$500
Cotton (NOCE)	9:15– 2:00	50,000 lb	$.0001 lb	5	$500
Currencies, foreign (IMM)					
British pound	7:30– 1:24	25,000	.0005	12.50	
Canadian dollar	– 1:26	100,000	.0001	10	
Deutschemark	– 1:20	125,000	.0001	12.50	
Dutch guilder	– 1:30	125,000	.0001	12.50	
French franc	– 1:28	250,000	.0005	12.50	
Japanese yen	– 1:22	12,500,000	.00001	12.50	
Swiss franc	– 1:16	125,000	.0001	12.50	
Eurodollar CDs	7:30– 2:00	$1,000,000	1 BP .01	25	100 BP = $2500
Crude oil, sour (NYMEX)		1,000 bbl	$.01 bbl	10	$10
Crude oil, sweet (NYMEX)		1,000 bbl	$.01 bbl	10	$10
Crude oil, sweet (CBOT)		1,000 bbl	$.01 bbl	10	$10
Gasoline, leaded NY (NYMEX)	9:30– 3:30	42,000 gal	$.001	4.20	$420
Gasoline, leaded (CBOT)		42,000 gal	$.00025 gal	10.50	$420
Gasoline, unleaded Gulf (CBOT)	8:30– 2:30	42,000 gal	$.00025 gal	10.50	$420
Gasoline, leaded (CME)		42,000 gal	$.00025 gal	10.50	$420
Gasoline, unleaded (CME)		42,000 gal	$.00025 gal	10.50	$420
Gold (CBOT)	8:00– 1:30	100 oz t	10¢ oz	10	$100
Gold (COMEX)	9:00– 2:30	100 oz t	10¢ oz	10	$100
Gold (IMM)	8:00– 1:30	100 oz t	10¢ oz	10	$100
Gold (MACE)	8:00– 1:40	33.2 oz t	2.5¢ oz	83¢	$33.20
GNMA CDR (CBOT)	8:00– 2:00	$100,000	1/32 pt	31.25	1 pt = $1000
Heating oil, no. 2 NY (NYMEX)	10:00– 2:45	42,000 US gal	$.0001 gal	4.20	$420
Heating oil, no. 2 (CBOT)		42,000 US gal	$.00025 gal	10.50	$420
Hogs, live (CME)	9:10– 1:00	30,000 lb	2½/100¢ lb	7.50	$300
Hogs, live (MACE)	9:10– 1:15	15,000 lb	.025¢ lb	3.75	$150
Lumber (CME)	9:00– 1:05	130,000 board ft	10¢ MBF	13.00	$1.30
NYSE composite index (NYFE)	10:00– 4:15	$500 × futures price	.05	25.00	
Oats (CBOT)	9:30– 1:15	5,000 bu	1/4 bu	12.50	$50
Oats (MACE)	9:30– 1:30	5,000 bu	1/8¢ bu	6.25	$50
Palladium (NYMEX)	9:00– 2:20	100 oz t	5¢ oz t	5.00	$100
Platinum (NYMEX)	9:10– 2:30	50 oz t	10¢ oz t	5.00	$50
Plywood, western (CBOT)	9:00– 1:05	76,032 ft²	10¢ MSF	7.60	$76
Pork bellies (CME)	9:10– 1:00	38,000 lb	$.00025 lb	9.50	$380
Potatoes, white round (NYME)	9:45– 2:00	50,000 lb	1¢ cwt	5.00	$5
Propane (LPG) (NYCE)	9:45– 2:35	42,000 gal	$.001	42.0	$420
Rice, milled (NOCE)	9:45– 1:45	1,200 cwt	$.005 cwt	6.00	

overreaction to real information. By allowing investors more time to react to extreme information, it is argued, the price reaction will be more rational and reasoned.

Margin Requirements for Trading

In a futures agreement, there is no payment made by the buyer to the seller, nor does the seller have to show proof of physical ownership of the asset at the time of the agreement. In order to ensure, however, that the parties to the futures contract fulfill their sides of the agreement, they are required to deposit funds in a margin account. The amount that has to be deposited at the time of the contract is called the initial margin. As prices move subsequently, the contracts are marked to market, and the profits or losses are posted to the investor's account. The investor is allowed to withdraw any funds in the margin account in excess of the initial margin.

 If the investor has a string of losses, because of adverse price movements, the margin account will be depleted. To ensure that there are always funds in the account, the investor is expected to maintain a *maintenance margin,* which is generally lower than the initial margin. If the funds in the margin account fall below the maintenance margin, the investor will receive a *margin call* to replenish the funds in the account. These extra funds that have to be brought in are known as a variation margin.

PRICING OF FUTURES CONTRACTS

Most futures contracts can be priced on the basis of arbitrage; that is, a price or range of prices can be derived at which investors will not be able to create positions involving the futures contract and the underlying asset that make riskless profits with no initial investment. The following sections examine the pricing relationships for a number of futures contracts.

Perishable Commodities

Perishable commodities offer the exception to the rule that futures contracts are priced on the basis of arbitrage, since the commodity has to be storable for arbitrage to be feasible. On a perishable futures contract, the futures price will be influenced by

 (a) *the expected spot price of the underlying commodity:* If the spot price on the underlying commodity is expected to increase before the expiration of the futures contract, the futures prices will be greater than the current spot price of the commodity. If the spot price is expected to decrease, the futures price will be lower than the spot price.
 (b) *any risk premium associated with taking the futures position:* Since there is a buyer and a seller on a futures contract, the size and the direction of the risk premium will vary from case to case and will depend upon whether the buyer is viewed as providing a service to the seller or vice versa.

In an agricultural futures contract, where farmers or producers are the primary sellers of futures contracts and individual investors are the buyers, it can be argued that the latter are providing a service to the former and thus should be rewarded. In this scenario, the futures price will be lower than the expected spot price.

$$\text{Futures Price} = \text{Spot Price} - \text{Expected Risk Premium}$$

In this type of relationship between futures and spot prices, prices are said to exhibit "normal backwardation."

In a futures contract where buyers of the futures contract are industrial users (a good example would be Hershey's, a chocolate manufacturer, buying sugar futures to lock in favorable prices) and the sellers are individual investors, the buyers are being provided the service, and the sellers could demand a reward, leading to a risk premium that is positive. In this case, the futures price will be greater than the expected spot price (assuming flat expectations), and futures prices are said to exhibit "normal contango."

In most modern commodity futures markets, neither sellers nor buyers are likely to be dominated by users or producers, and the net benefit can accrue to either buyers of sellers and there is no a priori reason to believe that risk premiums have to be positive or negative. In fact, if buyers and sellers are both speculating on the price, rather than hedging output or input needs, the net benefit can be 0, leading to a risk premium of 0. In such a case the futures price should be equal to the expected spot price.

These three possible scenarios for the futures price, relative to the expected spot price, are graphed in Figure 21.4.

The empirical evidence from commodity futures markets is mixed. An early study by Houthaker (1957) found that futures prices for commodities were generally lower than the expected spot prices, a finding that is consistent with a "normal backwardation." Telser (1958) and Gray (1961), however, reported contradictory evidence from the wheat and corn futures markets.

Storable Commodities

The distinction between storable and perishable goods is that storable goods can be acquired at the spot price and stored till the expiration of the futures contract, which is the practical equivalent of buying a futures contract and taking delivery at expiration. Since the two approaches provide the same result, in terms of having possession of the commodity at expiration, the futures contract, if priced right, should cost the same as a strategy of buying and storing the commodity. The two additional costs of the latter strategy are as follows:

(a) Since the commodity has to be acquired now, rather than at expiration, there is an added financing cost associated with borrowing the funds needed for the acquisition now:

$$\text{Added Interest Cost} = \text{Spot Price} ([1 + \text{Interest Rate}]^{\text{Life of futures contract}} - 1)$$

FIGURE 21.4 **Futures on Perishable Commodities**

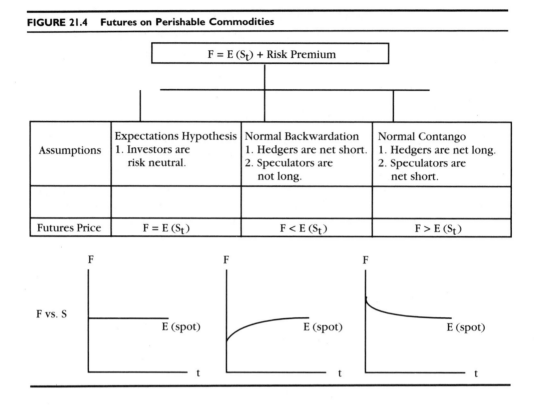

(b) If there is a storage cost associated with storing the commodity until the expiration of the futures contract, this cost has to be reflected in the strategy as well. In addition, there may be a benefit to having physical ownership of the commodity. This benefit is called the convenience yield and will reduce the futures price. The net storage cost is defined to be the difference between the total storage cost and the convenience yield.

If F is the futures contract price, S is the spot price, r is the annualized interest rate, t is the life of the futures contract, and k is the net annual storage costs (as a percentage of the spot price) for the commodity, the two equivalent strategies and their costs can be written as follows:

Strategy 1: Buy the futures contract; take delivery at expiration; pay F.

Strategy 2: Borrow the spot price of the commodity (S) and buy the commodity; pay the additional costs:

 (a) Interest Cost $= S([1 + r]^t - 1)$
 (b) Storage Cost, net of convenience yield $= S\,k\,t$

If the two strategies have the same costs:

$$F^* = S + S([1 + r]^t - 1) + S\,k\,t$$
$$= S([1 + r]^t + k\,t)$$

This is the basic arbitrage relationship between futures and spot prices. Any

deviation from this arbitrage relationship should provide an opportunity for arbitrage; that is, a strategy with no risk and no initial investment will provide positive profits. These arbitrage opportunities are described in Figure 21.5.

This arbitrage is based upon several assumptions. First, investors are assumed to borrow and lend at the same rate, which is the riskless rate. Second, when the futures contract is overpriced, it is assumed that the seller of the futures contract (the arbitrageur) can sell short on the commodity and can recover, from the owner of the commodity, the storage costs that are saved as a consequence. To the extent that these assumptions are unrealistic, the bounds on prices within which arbitrage is not feasible expand. Assume, for instance, that the rate of borrowing is r_b and the rate of lending is r_a, and that the short seller cannot recover any of the saved storage costs and has to pay a transactions cost of t_s. The futures price will then fall within a bound:

$$(S - t_s)(1 + r_a)^t < F^* < S([1 + r_b]^t + kt)$$

If the futures price falls outside this bound, there is a possibility of arbitrage, and this is illustrated in Figure 21.6.

Stock Index Futures

Futures on stock indices have become an important and growing part of most financial markets. An index future entitles the buyer to any appreciation in the index over and above the index futures price and the seller to any depreciation in the index from the same benchmark. To evaluate the arbitrage pricing of an index future, consider the following strategies:

> *Strategy 1:* Sell short on the stocks in the index for the duration of the index futures contract; invest the proceeds at the riskless rate. (This strategy requires that the owners of the index be compensated for the dividends they would have received on the stocks.)
>
> *Strategy 2:* Sell the index futures contract.

Both strategies require the same initial investment, have the same risk, and should provide the same proceeds. Again, if S is the spot price of the index, F is the futures prices, y is the annualized dividend yield on the stock, and r is the riskless rate, the cashflows from the two contracts at expiration can be written as follows:

$$F^* = S(1 + r - y)^t$$

If the futures price deviates from this arbitrage price, there should be an opportunity for arbitrage. This is illustrated in Figure 21.7. This arbitrage is conditioned on several assumptions. First, it, like the commodity futures arbitrage, assumes that investors can lend and borrow at the riskless rate. Second, it ignores transactions costs on both buying stock and selling short on stocks. Third, it assumes that the dividends paid on the stocks in the index are known

FIGURE 21.5 Storable Commodity Futures—Pricing and Arbitrage

$$F^* = S([1 + r]^t + k\,t)$$

	If F > F*	
Time	*Action*	*Cashflows*
Now:	1. Sell futures contract	0
	2. Borrow spot price at riskfree rate	S
	3. Buy spot commodity	−S
At t:	1. Collect commodity; pay storage cost	−S k t
	2. Deliver on futures contract	F
	3. Pay back loan	−S$(1 + r)^t$
NCF =		F − S$([1 + r]^t - k\,t)$ > 0

	If F < F*	
Time	*Action*	*Cashflows*
Now:	1. Buy futures contract	0
	2. Sell short on commodity	S
	3. Lend money at riskfree rate	−S
At t:	1. Collect on loan	S$(1 + r)^t$
	2. Take delivery of futures contract	−F
	3. Return borrowed commodity; collect storage costs	+S k t
NCF =		S$([1 + r]^t + k\,t)$ − F > 0

Key Inputs:

F* = theoretical futures price r = riskless rate of interest (annualized)

F = actual futures price t = time to expiration on futures contract

S = spot price of commodity k = annualized carrying cost, net of convenience yield (as percentage of spot price)

Key Assumptions:

1. The investor can lend and borrow at the riskless rate.
2. There are no transactions costs associated with buying or selling short the commodity.
3. The short seller can collect all storage costs saved because of the short selling.

FIGURE 21.6 Storable Commodity Futures—Pricing and Arbitrage with Modified Assumptions

$$F_h^* = S[(1 + r_b]^t + k t]$$
$$F_l^* = (S - t_s)(1 + r_a)^t$$

If $F > F_h^*$

Time	Action	Cashflows
Now:	1. Sell futures contract	0
	2. Borrow spot price at r_b	S
	3. Buy spot commodity	−S
At t:	1. Collect commodity from storage	−S k t
	2. Deliver on futures contract	F
	3. Pay back loan	−S(1 + r_b)^t
NCF =		$F - S[(1 + r_b]^t - k t > 0$

If $F < F_l^*$

Time	Action	Cashflows
Now:	1. Buy futures contract	0
	2. Sell short on commodity	S − t_s
	3. Lend money at r_a	−(S − t_s)
At t:	1. Collect on loan	(S − t_s)(1 + r_a)^t
	2. Take delivery of futures contract	−F
	3. Return borrowed commodity; collect storage costs	0
NCF =		$(S - t_s)(1 + r_a)^t - F > 0$

Additional Key Inputs:

F_h = upper limit for arbitrage bound on futures prices

F_l = lower limit for arbitrage bound on futures prices

Modified Assumptions:

1. Investor can borrow at r_b ($r_b > r$) and lend at r_a ($r_a < r$).
2. The transactions costs associated with selling short are t_s (where t_s is the dollar transactions costs).
3. The short seller does not collect any of the storage costs saved by the short selling.

453

FIGURE 21.7 Stock Index Futures—Pricing and Arbitrage

$$F^* = S([1 + r - y])^t$$

If F > F*

Time	Action	Cashflows
Now:	1. Sell futures contract	0
	2. Borrow spot price of index at riskfree rate	S
	3. Buy stocks in index	$-S$
At t:	1. Collect dividends on stocks	$S((1 + y)^t - 1)$
	2. Deliver on futures contract	F
	3. Pay back loan	$-S(1 + r)^t$
NCF =		$F - S([1 + r - y]^t) > 0$

If F < F*

Time	Action	Cashflows
Now:	1. Buy futures contract	0
	2. Sell short stocks in the index	S
	3. Lend money at riskfree rate	$-S$
At t:	1. Collect on loan	$S(1 + r)^t$
	2. Take delivery of futures contract	$-F$
	3. Return borrowed stocks; pay forgone dividends	$-S((1 + y)^t - 1)$
NCF =		$S([1 + r - y]^t - F > 0$

Key Inputs:

F* = theoretical futures price r = riskless rate of interest (annualized)

F = actual futures price t = time to expiration on futures contract

S = spot level of index y = dividend yield over lifetime of futures contracts (as percentage of current index level)

Key Assumptions:

1. The investor can lend and borrow at the riskless rate.
2. There are no transactions costs associated with buying or selling short stocks.
3. Dividends are known with certainty.

454

with certainty at the start of the period. If these assumptions are unrealistic, the index futures arbitrage will be feasible only if prices fall outside a band, the size of which will depend upon the seriousness of the violations of the assumptions.

Assume that investors can borrow money at r_b and lend money at r_a, and that the transactions costs of buying stock are t_c and of selling short are t_s. The band within which the futures price must stay can be written as follows:

$$(S - t_s)(1 + r_a - y)^t < F^* < (S + t_c)(1 + r_b - y)^t$$

The arbitrage that is possible if the futures price strays outside this band is illustrated in Figures 21.8.

Treasury Bond Futures

The Treasury bond futures traded on the CBOT require the delivery of any government bond with a maturity greater than 15 years, with a no-call feature for at least the first 15 years. Since bonds of different maturities and coupons will have different prices, the CBOT has a procedure for adjusting the price of the bond for its characteristics. The conversion factor itself is fairly simple to compute and is based upon the value of the bond on the first day of the delivery month, with the assumption that the interest rate for all maturities equals 8% per annum (with semiannual compounding). The following example calculates the conversion factor for a 9% coupon bond with 18 years to maturity.

Illustration 21.2: Calculation of conversion factors for Treasury bond futures

Consider a 9% coupon bond with 20 years to maturity. Working in terms of a $100 face value of the bond, the value of the bond can be written as follows, using the interest rate of 8%:

$$\text{PV of Bond} = \sum_{t=1}^{t=40} \frac{4.50}{(1.04)^t} + \frac{100}{(1.04)^{40}} = \$109.90$$

The conversion factor for this bond is 109.90. Generally speaking, the conversion factor will increase as the coupon rate increases and with the maturity of the delivered bond.

The Delivery Option and the Wild Card Play

This feature of Treasury bond futures, that is, that any one of a menu of Treasury bonds can be delivered to fulfill the oblidation on the bond, provides an advantage to the seller of the futures contract. Naturally, the cheapest bond on the menu, after adjusting for the conversion factor, will be delivered. This *delivery option* has to be priced into the futures contract.

There is an additional option embedded in Treasury bond futures contracts that arises from the fact that the Treasury bond futures market closes at 2:00 P.M., whereas the bonds themselves continue trading until 4:00 P.M. The seller

FIGURE 21.8 Stock Index Futures—Pricing and Arbitrage with Modified Assumptions

$$F_h^* = (S + t_c)(1 + r_b - y)^t$$
$$F_l^* = (S - t_s)(1 + r_a - y)^t$$

If $F > F_h^*$

Time	Action	Cashflows
Now:	1. Sell futures contract	0
	2. Borrow spot price at r_b	$S + t_c$
	3. Buy stocks in the index	$-(S - t_c)$
At t:	1. Collect dividends on stocks	$S([1 + y]^t - 1)$
	2. Deliver on futures contract	F
	3. Pay back loan	$-(S + t_c)(1 + r_b)^t$
NCF =		$F - (S + t_c)(1 + r_b - y)^t > 0$

If $F < F_l^*$

Time	Action	Cashflows
Now:	1. Buy futures contract	0
	2. Sell short stocks in the index	$S - t_s$
	3. Lend money at r_a	$-(S - t_s)$
At t:	1. Collect on loan	$(S - t_s)(1 + r_a)^t$
	2. Take delivery of futures contract	$-F$
	3. Return borrowed stocks; pay forgone dividends	$-S([1 + y]^t - 1)$
NCF =		$(S - t_s)(1 + r_a - y)^t - F > 0$

Additional Key Inputs:

F_h = upper limit for arbitrage bound on futures prices

F_l = lower limit for arbitrage bound on futures prices

Modified Assumptions:

1. Investor can borrow at r_b ($r_b > r$) and lend at r_a ($r_a < r$).

2. The transactions costs associated with selling short are t_s (where t_s is the dollar transactions costs), and the transactions costs associated with buying the stocks in the index are t_c.

FIGURE 21.9 Treasury Bond Futures—Pricing and Arbitrage

$$F^* = (S - PVC)(1 + r)^t$$

	If F > F*	
Time	Action	Cashflows
Now:	1. Sell futures contract	0
	2. Borrow spot price of bond at riskfree rate	S
	3. Buy Treasury bonds	$-S$
Till t:	1. Collect dividends on bonds; invest	$PVC(1 + r)^t$
	2. Deliver the cheapest bond on contract	F
	3. Pay back loan	$-S(1 + r)^t$
NCF =		$F - (S - PVC)(1 + r)^t > 0$

	If F < F*	
Time	Action	Cashflows
Now:	1. Buy futures contract	0
	2. Sell short Treasury bonds	S
	3. Lend money at riskfree rate	$-S$
Till t:	1. Collect on loan	$S(1 + r)^t$
	2. Take delivery of futures contract	$-F$
	3. Return borrowed bonds; pay forgone coupons with interest	$-PVC(1 + r)^t$
NCF =		$(S - PVC)(1 + r)^t - F > 0$

Key Inputs:

F* = theoretical futures price
F = actual futures price
S = spot price of Treasury bond

r = riskless rate of interest (annualized)
t = time to expiration on futures contract
PVC = present value of coupons on bond during life of futures contract

Key Assumptions:
1. The investor can lend and borrow at the riskless rate.
2. There are no transactions costs associated with buying or selling short bonds.

does not have to notify the clearinghouse until 8:00 P.M. about his or her intention to deliver. If bond prices decline after 2:00 P.M., the seller can notify the clearinghouse of intention to deliver the cheapest bond that day. If not, the seller can wait for the next day. This option is called the *wild card play*.

Valuing a Treasury Bond Futures Contract

The valuation of a Treasury bond futures contract follows the same lines as the valuation of a stock index future, with the coupons of the Treasury bond replacing the dividend yield of the stock index. The theoretical value of a futures contract should be:

$$F^* = (S - PVC)(1 + r)^t$$

where F^* = theoretical futures price for Treasury bond futures contract
\quad S = spot price of Treasury bond
\quad PVC = present value of coupons during life of futures contract
\quad r = riskfree interest rate corresponding to futures life
\quad t = life of futures contract

If the futures price deviates from this theoretical price, there should be opportunity for arbitrage. These arbitrage opportunities are illustrated in Figure 21.9. This valuation ignores the two options described above—the option to deliver the cheapest-to-deliver bond and the option to have a wild card play. These give an advantage to the seller of the futures contract and should be priced into the futures contract. One way to build this into the valuation is to use the cheapest deliverable bond to calculate both the current spot price and the present value of the coupons. Once the futures price is estimated, it can be divided by the conversion factor to arrive at the standardized futures price.

Currency Futures

In a currency futures contract, the current spot price (S) is the price of one unit of the foreign currency in dollars, and F is the futures price. Holding the foreign currency enables the investor to earn the riskfree interest rate (r_f) prevailing in that country. Assuming that the local riskfree rate is r, the theoretical value of a futures contract on a currency should be:

$$F^* = S(1 + r - r_f)$$

If the actual futures price deviates from F^*, there should be opportunity for arbitrage.

EFFECTS OF SPECIAL FEATURES IN FUTURES CONTRACTS

The arbitrage relationship provides a measure of the determinants of future prices on a wide range of assets. There are, however, some special features that

affect futures prices. One is the fact that futures contracts require marking to the market, while forward contracts do not. Another is the existence of trading restrictions, such as price limits on futures contracts. This section examines the pricing effects of each of these special features.

Futures versus Forward Contracts

As described earlier in this chapter, futures contracts require marking to the market while forward contracts do not. If interest rates are constant and the same for all maturities, there should be no difference between the value of a futures contract and the value of an equivalent forward contract. When interest rates vary unpredictably, forward prices can be different from future prices. This is because of the reinvestment assumptions that have to be made for intermediate profits on a futures contract and the borrowing rate assumptions that have to be made for intermediate losses. The effect of this interest-rate-induced volatility on futures prices will depend upon the relationship between spot prices and interest rates. If they move in opposite directions (as is the case with stock indices and Treasury bonds), the interest rate risk will make futures prices greater than forward prices. If they move together (as is the case with some real assets), the interest rate risk can actually counter price risk and make futures prices less than forward prices.

In most real-world scenarios, and in empirical studies, the difference between futures and forward prices is fairly small and can be ignored.

Trading Restrictions

The existence of price limits and margin requirements on futures contract are generally ignored in the valuation and arbitrage conditions described in this chapter. It is, however, possible that these restrictions on trading, if onerous enough, could impact value. The existence of price limits, for instance, has two effects. One is that it might reduce the volatility in prices, by protecting against market overreaction to information, and thus make futures contracts more valuable. The other is that it makes futures contracts less liquid, and this may make them less valuable. The net effect could be positive or negative.

CONCLUSION

The value of a futures contract is derived from the value of the underlying asset. The opportunity for arbitrage will create a strong linkage between the futures and spot prices, and the actual relationship will depend upon the level of interest rates, the cost of storing the underlying asset, and any yield that can be made by holding the asset. In addition, the institutional characteristics of the futures markets, such as price limits and "marking to the market," as well as any delivery option, can affect the futures price.

QUESTIONS AND SHORT PROBLEMS

1. The following is an excerpt from *The Wall Street Journal* futures page. It includes the futures prices of gold. The current cash (spot) price of gold if $403.25. Make your best estimates of the implied interest rates (from the arbitrage relationship) in the futures prices. (You can assume zero carrying costs for gold.)

Contract Expiring In	Trading At
1 month	$404.62
2 months	$406.11
3 months	$407.70
6 months	$412.51
12 months	$422.62

2. You are a portfolio manager who has just been exposed to the possibilities of stock index futures. Respond to the following situations:
 a. Assume that you have the resources to buy and hold the stocks in the S&P 500. You are given the following data (assume that this is January 1):

 Level of the S&P 500 index = 258.90
 June S&P 500 futures contract = 260.15
 Annualized Rate on T bill expiring June 26 (expiration date) = 6%
 Annualized dividend yield on S&P 500 stocks = 3%

 Assume that dividends are paid out continuously over the year. Is there potential for arbitrage? How would you go about setting up the arbitrage?
 b. Assume now that you are known for your stock selection skills. You have 10,000 shares of Texaco in your portfolio (now selling for $38) and are extremely worried about the direction of the market until June. You would like to protect yourself against market risk by using the December S&P 500 futures contract (which is at $260.15). If Texaco's beta is .8, how would you go about creating this protection?

3. Assume that you are a mutual fund manager with a total portfolio value of $100 million. You estimate the beta of the fund to be 1.25. You would like to hedge against market movements by using stock index futures. You observe that the S&P 500 June futures are selling for $260.15 and that the index is at $258.90. Answer the following questions:
 a. How many stock index futures would you have to sell to protect against market risk? (3 points)
 b. If the risk free rate is 6% and the market risk premium is 8%, what return would you expect to make on the mutual fund (assuming you don't hedge)? (1 point)
 c. How much would you expect to make if you hedge away all market risk? (1 point)

4. Given the following information on gold futures prices, the spot price of gold, the riskless interest rate, and the carrying cost of gold, construct an arbitrage position. (Assume that it is December 1987 now.)

 December 1988 futures contract price = 515.60/troy oz

Spot price of gold = 481.40/troy oz

Interest rate (annualized) = 6%

Carrying cost (annualized) = 2%

 a. What would you have to do right now to set up the arbitrage?

 b. What would you have to do in December to unwind the position? How much arbitrage profit would you expect to make?

 c. Assume now that you can borrow at 8%, but you can lend at only 6%. Establish a price band for the futures contract within which arbitrage is not feasible.

5. The following is a set of prices for stock index futures on the S&P 500.

Maturity	Futures Price
March	$246.25
June	247.75

The current level of the index is $245.82, and the current annualized T bill rate is 6%. The annualized dividend yield is 3%. (Today is January 14. The March futures expire on March 18 and the June futures on June 17.)

 a. Estimate the theory basis and the actual basis in each of these contracts.

 b. Using one of the two contracts, set up an arbitrage. Also, show how the arbitrage will be resolved at expiration. (You can assume that you can lend or borrow at the riskfree rate and that you have no transaction costs or margins.)

 c. Assume that a good economic report comes out on the wire. The stock index goes up to $247.82 and the T bill rate drops to 5%. Assuming that arbitrage relationships hold and that the dollar dividends paid do not change, how much will the March future go up by? (2 points)

6. You are provided the following information:

Current price of wheat = $19,000 for 5,000 bushels

Riskless rate = 10% (annualized)

Cost of storage = $200 a year for 5,000 bushels

One-year futures contract price = $20,400 (for a contract for 5,000 bushels)

 a. What is F* (the theoretical price)?

 b. How would you arbitrage the difference between F and F*? (Specify what you will do now and at expiration, and what your arbitrage profits will be.)

 c. If you can sell short (cost $100 for 5,000 bushels) and cannot claim any of the storage cost for yourself on short sales, at what rate would you have to be able to lend for this arbitrage to be feasible?

ENDNOTE

1. The reason the exchange allows equivalents is to prevent investors from buying a significant portion of the specified Treasury bonds and cornering the market.

22

Valuing Real Estate

The valuation models developed for financial assets—primarily stocks and bonds—are applicable for real assets, as well. Real estate investments comprise the most significant component of real asset investments. This chapter explores the application of discounted and relative valuation models to real estate investments.

REAL VERSUS FINANCIAL ASSETS

Real estate and financial assets share several common characteristics: Their value is determined by the cashflows they generate, the uncertainty associated with these cashflows, and the expected growth in the cashflows. Ceteris paribus, the higher the level and growth in the cashflows and the lower the risk associated with the cashflows, the greater is the value of the asset.

There are also significant differences between the two classes of assets. There are differences in liquidity across the two markets and in the types of investors in each market. There are also differences in the nature of the cashflows generated by financial and real estate investments. In particular, real asset investments often have finite lives and have to be valued accordingly. Many financial assets, such as stocks, have infinite lives. These differences in asset lives manifest themselves in the value assigned to these assets at the end of the "estimation period." The values of infinite-lived assets, like stocks, tend to increase over time. The terminal value of a real asset may be lower than its current value because the usage of the asset might depreciate its value. In the case of real estate, the building component will have a finite life while the land component will have an infinite life.

DISCOUNTED CASHFLOW VALUATION

The value of any asset that is producing/generating a cashflow is the present value of its expected cashflows. Just as discounted cashflow valuation models—such as the dividend discount model—can be used to value financial assets, they can also be used to value real estate investments.

To use the discounted cashflow valuation methodology to value real estate investments, it is necessary

- to measure the riskiness of real estate investments, and to estimate a discount rate based on that riskiness.
- to estimate the expected cashflows on the real estate investment for the life of the asset.

The following sections examine these issues.

Estimating Discount Rates

The fundamental propositions developed in Chapters 3 and 4 regarding risk and return can be applied to real estate investments. There are, however, several measurement issues that are specific to these investments. Questions also remain about whether these models adequately capture the risk involved in these investments and, if not, how to incorporate these additional risk factors.

Propositions about Risk

The two basic models used to analyze financial assets are the capital asset and the arbitrage pricing models. In both models, the risk of any asset, real or financial, is defined to be that portion of the asset's variance that cannot be diversified away. This nondiversifiable risk is measured by the market beta in the capital asset pricing model (CAPM) and by multiple factor betas in the arbitrage pricing model (APM). The primary assumptions that both models make to arrive at these conclusions are that the marginal investor in the asset is well diversified and that the risk is measured in terms of the variability of returns.

If one assumes that these models apply for real assets as well, the risk of a real asset should be measured by its beta relative to the market portfolio in the CAPM and by its factor betas in the APM.

Measuring Risk for Real Assets in Asset Pricing Models

Even if it is accepted that the risk of a real asset is its market beta in the CAPM and its factor betas in the APM, there are several issues related to the measurement and use of these risk parameters that need to be examined. To provide some insight into the measurement problems associated with real assets, consider the standard approach to estimating betas for a publicly traded stock. First, the prices of the stock are collected from historical data and returns are computed on a periodic basis (daily, weekly, or monthly). Second, these stock returns are regressed against returns on a stock index over the same period to obtain the beta. For nontraded or infrequently traded real assets, these steps are not as straightforward.

Individual Assets: Prices and Risk Parameters. The betas of individual stocks can be estimated fairly simply because stock prices are available for extended time

periods. The same cannot be said for individual real estate investments. A piece of property does not get bought and sold very frequently, though similar properties might. Consequently, price indices are available for classes of assets (example: Downtown Manhattan Office Buildings), and risk parameters can be estimated for these classes.

Even when price indices are available for classes of real estate investments, questions remain about the comparability of assets within a class (Is one downtown building the same as any other? How does one control for differences in age and quality of construction? What about location?) and about the categorization itself (Office Buildings versus Residential Buildings; Single Family versus Multi-Family Residences).

There have been attempts to estimate market indices and risk parameters for classes of real estate investments. The obvious and imperfect solution to the nontrading problem in real estate is to construct indices of real estate investment trusts (REITs) that are traded and have market prices. The reason this might not be satisfactory is that the properties owned by real estate investment trusts may not be representative of the real estate property market, and the securitization of real estate may result in differences between real estate and REIT returns. An alternative solution is The Frank Russell Company Index of real estate values which is based upon approximately 1,000 commingled properties owned by real estate equity funds (CREFs). While many of these properties are not traded in every period, the index is based upon appraised values for these properties.[1] In addition, Ibbotson and Siegal (I&S) have estimated annual returns on an index of unlevered properties. Finally, Case and Shiller (C&S) constructed an index using actual transactions prices, rather than appraised values, to estimate the value of residential real estate. Table 22.1

TABLE 22.1 Returns on Real Estate, Stocks, and Bonds

Series	Period	Compound Annual Return (%)	Arithmetic Mean Return (%)	Standard Deviation (%)	Serial Correlation
CREF (commercial)	1969–87	10.8	10.9	2.6	.43
REIT (commercial)	1972–87	14.2	15.7	15.4	.11
I&S (commercial)	1960–89	8.7	8.8	4.9	.73
C&S (residential)	1970–86	8.5	8.6	3.0	.17
Home (residential)	1947–89	9.8	9.9	4.7	.54
Harris (residential)	1926–89	8.5	8.7	5.4	.55
Farm (farmland)	1947–89	9.9	10.2	7.8	.64
S&P 500	1947–89	12.3	13.5	16.7	−.10
Long-term government bonds	1947–89	4.6	5.0	10.0	.16
U.S. Treasury bills	1947–89	4.9	4.9	3.3	.86
Inflation	1947–89	4.2	4.3	3.5	.66

Source: The CREF, REIT, and C&S summary statistics are from William N. Goetzmann and Roger G. Ibbotson, "The Performance of Real Estate as an Asset Class," *Journal of Applied Corporate Finance*, Fall 1990. All other series are from *I/IDEAS United States Capital Markets* data module, Ibbotson Associates, Inc., Chicago, 1991.

summarizes the returns on real estate indices, the S&P 500, and an index of bonds.

There are several interesting results that emerge from this table. First, not all real estate series behave the same way. The returns on CREFs have much lower volatility associated with them than REITs, because of the associated appraisal smoothing bias. Second, REITs seem to have more in common with returns on the stock market than returns on other real estate indices. There is high positive serial correlation in many of the real estate return series, especially those based upon appraised data. This is attributed to the smoothing of appraisals that are used in these series.

The Market Portfolio. In estimating the betas of stocks, it is generally assumed that a stock index is used as a proxy for the market portfolio. In theory, however, the market portfolio should include all assets in the economy, in proportion to their market values. This is of particular significance when the market portfolio is used to estimate the risk parameters of real estate investments. The use of a stock index as the market portfolio will result in the marginalization[2] of real estate investments and the underestimation of risk for these assets.

The differences between a stock and an "all-asset" portfolio can be large because the market value of real estate investments not included in the stock index is significant. Figure 22.1 summarizes the approximate worldwide market values of different asset classes available to U.S. investors in 1990 (from Ibbotson).

The differences in returns between an all-stock portfolio and a portfolio composed of different asset classes are illustrated in the graph in Figure 22.2, tracing returns on the S&P 500 index, a balanced portfolio manager index (SEI),

FIGURE 22.1 Market Values of Different Asset Classes

FIGURE 22.2 Returns on Stock Index Versus All-Asset Index

	BB&K Diversified	S&P 500	SEI Median
Cumulative return	854.4%	659.1%	446.0%
Annual return	10.3%	9.2%	7.7%
Standard deviation	7.7%	16.5%	11.4%

Bailand, Biehl and Kaiser diversified portfolio index

Standard and Poor's 500 stock index

Professional balanced portfolio manager, SEI Corp. median

and an index that includes real estate investments (B, B & K) from 1967 to 1990.

There is also evidence that real estate investments and stocks do not move together in reaction to larger economic events. This is illustrated in Table 22.2.

The differences between real asset and financial asset returns are accentuated when inflation rates change. Fama and Schwert (1976), for instance, examined returns on different asset classes and concluded that real estate investments react positively to unanticipated increases in inflation while financial assets react negatively. Figure 22.3 (from Ibbotson) illustrates nominal and real returns on real estate from 1978 to 1990. Because of these differences, the returns on a market portfolio inclusive of real assets can be very different from the returns on a market portfolio composed entirely of stocks.

While few economists would argue with the value of incorporating real estate investments into the market portfolio, most are stymied by the measurement problems. These problems, insurmountable until recently, are becoming more approachable as real estate investments get securitized and traded. For instance, exchanges that trade real estate master limited partnerships and real estate business trusts have opened.

Some Practical Solutions. If one accepts the proposition that the risk of a real estate investment should be measured using traditional risk and return models, there are some practical approaches that can be used to estimate risk parameters:

- The risk of a class of real estate investments can be obtained by regressing returns on the class (using the Ibbotson series, for instance, on commercial and residen-

TABLE 22.2 Correlations Across Asset Classes

	I&S	CREF	Home	C&S	Farm	S&P	Long-term Government Bonds	Treasury Bills	Inflation
I&S	1.00								
CREF	.79	1.00							
Home	.52	.12	1.00						
C&S	.26	.16	.82	1.00					
Farm	.06	−.06	.51	.49	1.00				
S&P	.16	.25	−.13	−.20	−.10	1.00			
Long-term government bonds	−.04	.01	−.22	−.54	−.44	.11	1.00		
Treasury bills	.53	.42	.13	−.56	−.32	−.07	.48	1.00	
Inflation	.70	.35	.77	.56	.49	−.02	−.17	.26	1.00

tial property) against returns on a consolidated market portfolio. The primary problems with this approach are: (a) These returns series are based upon smoothed appraisals and may understate the true volatility in the market, and (b) the returns are available only for longer return intervals (annual or quarterly).
- The risk parameters of traded real estate securities (REITs and Master Limited Partnerships) can be used as a proxy for the risk in real estate investment. The limitations of this approach are that securitized real estate investments may behave differently from direct investments and that it is much more difficult to estimate risk parameters for different classes of real estate investment (unless one can find REITs that restrict themselves to one class of investments—such as commercial property).
- The demand for real estate is in some cases a derived demand. For instance, the value of a shopping mall is derived from the value of retail space, which should be a function of how well retailing is doing as a business. It can be argued, in such a case, that the risk parameters of a mall should be related to the risk parameters of publicly traded retail stores. Corrections should obviously be made for differences in operating and financial leverage.

Other Risk Factors

Does investing in real estate investments expose investors to more (and different) types of risk than investing in financial assets? If so, how is this risk measured and is it rewarded? The following are some of the issues related to real estate investments that might affect the risk and expected returns.

Diversifiable versus Nondiversifiable Risk. It is argued that some investments (such as real estate) may require capital outlays that are so large that investors may not be able to diversify sufficiently. Consequently, the use of the CAPM or APM, which assume that only nondiversifiable risk is rewarded, will lead to underestimation of risk.

This argument, however, can be countered fairly easily by noting that:

- Many investors who concentrate their holdings in real estate do so by choice. They see it as a way of leveraging their specialized knowledge of real estate.

FIGURE 22.3 Nominal and Real Returns on Real Estates

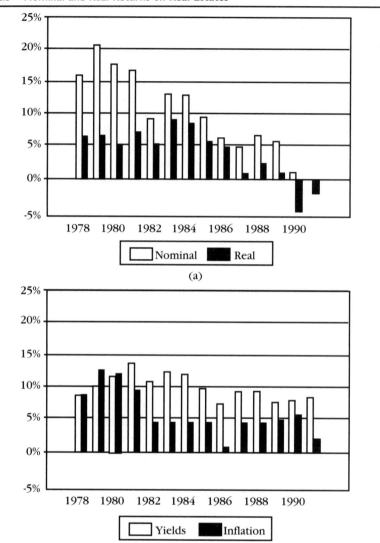

_(a)

- Even large real estate investments can be broken up into smaller pieces, allowing investors the option of holding real estate investments in conjunction with financial assets.
- Just as the marginal investor in stocks is often an institutional investor, with the resources to diversify and keep transactions costs low, the marginal investor in many real estate markets today has sufficient resources to diversify.

Lack of Liquidity. A more relevant critique of traditional risk measures is that they assume that all assets are liquid (or, at least, that there are no differences in liquidity across assets). The markets for many real estate investments are less liquid than markets for financial assets—transactions occur less frequently,

transactions costs are higher, and there are far fewer buyers and sellers. The less liquid an asset, it is argued, the more risky it is.

The link between lack of liquidity and risk is much more difficult to quantify for several reasons. One is that this link depends upon the time horizon of the investor. An investor who intends to hold long term will care less about liquidity than one who is uncertain about his or her time horizon or wants to trade short term. Another is that such a link is affected by the external economic conditions. For instance, real estate is much more liquid during economic booms, when prices are rising, than during recessions, when prices are depressed.

The alternative to trying to view the absence of liquidity as an additional risk factor and building it into discount rates is to value the illiquid asset conventionally (as if it were liquid) and then to apply a liquidity discount to it. This is often the practice in valuing closely held and illiquid businesses and allows for the liquidity discount to be a function of the investor and external economic conditions at the time of the valuation.

Exposure to Legal Changes. The value of all investments is affected by changes in the tax law—changes in depreciation methods and changes in tax rates on ordinary income and capital gains. Real estate investments are particularly exposed to changes in the tax law, because they derive a significant portion of their value from cashflows driven by the tax code.

Unlike corporations, which issue financial assets and which can move operations from one locale to another to take advantage of locational differences in tax rates and other legal restrictions, real estate is not mobile and is therefore much more exposed to changes in local laws (such as zoning requirements, property taxes, and rent control).

The question becomes whether this additional sensitivity to changes in tax and local laws is an additional source of risk and, if so, how this risk should be priced in.

Information Costs and Risk. Real estate investments often require specific information about local conditions that is difficult (and costly) to obtain. The information is also likely to contain more noise. There are some who argue that this higher cost of acquiring information and the greater noise in this information should be built into the risk and discount rates used to value real estate. This argument, however, is not restricted to real estate. It has been used as an explanation for the small stock premium—that is, small stocks make higher returns than larger stocks, after adjusting for risk (using the CAPM). Small stocks, it is argued, generally have less information available on them than larger stocks, and the information tends to be more noisy.

An Alternative Approach to Estimating Discount Rates: The Survey Approach

The problems with the assumptions of traditional risk and return models (that investors are well diversified, that assets are liquid, that transactions costs are

low, and so on) and the difficulties associated with the measurement of risk for nontraded real assets in these models have led to alternative approaches to estimating discount rates for these real assets. In the context of real estate, for instance, the cost of equity is often obtained by surveying potential investors in real estate on what rate of return they would demand for investing in different types of property investments. Table 22.3 summarizes an excerpt of the results of such a survey done by Cushman and Wakefield, a national/nationwide real estate firm, of investors in various real estate properties.

This approach is justified on the following grounds:

- These surveys are not based upon some abstract models of risk and return (which may ignore risk characteristics that are unique to the real estate market) but on what actual investors in real estate want to make as a return.
- These surveys allow for the estimation of discount rates for specific categories of properties (hotels, apartments, etc.) by region and by type of investor, without requiring a dependence upon past prices like risk and return models.
- There are relatively few large investors who invest directly in real estate (rather than in securitized real estate). It is therefore feasible to do such a survey.

There are, however, grounds for contesting this approach, as well:

- Surveys, by their very nature, yield different "desired rates of return" for different investors for the same property class. Assuming that a range of desired returns can be obtained for a class of investments, it is not clear where one goes next. Presumably, those investors who demand returns at the high end of the scale will find themselves priced out of the market and those whose desired returns are at the low end of the scale will find plenty of undervalued properties. The

TABLE 22.3 Survey Results from Cushman and Wakefield

Interviewee	Geographic Areas of Investment	Property Type Preference	Overall Rates	
			Going-in	Terminal
Apartment Investor	Southwest	Apartments	10%	10–11%
Apartment Investor	Pacific Northwest	Apartments	9.25%	9.25%
Bank (Mortgage Broker)	Pacific Northwest	Apartments	9.25–9.75%	9.5–10.25%
		Office-Urban (A)	8.25–8.5%	8.5%
		Office-Suburban	9%	9.5%
		Business Parks	9–9.5%	9.5–10%
		Industrial	9–9.5%	9.5–10%
		Regional Malls	8.25–8.5%	8.5%
		Neighborhood	9.75–10%	10.25%

Cushman & Wakefield Appraisal Division National Investor Survey—May1991

question of who the marginal investor in an investment should be is not answered in these surveys.

- The survey approach bypasses the issue of risk but it does not really eliminate it. Clearly, investors demand the returns that they do on different property classes because they perceive them to have different levels of risk.
- The survey approach works reasonably well when there are relatively few and fairly homogeneous investors in the market. While this might have been the case a decade ago, it is becoming less so as new institutional investors enter the market and the number of investors increases and investors become more heterogeneous.
- The survey approach also becomes suspect when the investors who are surveyed act as pass-throughs—they invest in real estate, securitize their investments, sell them to others, and move on. If they do so, it is the desired returns of the ultimate investor (the buyer of the securitized real estate) that should determine value, not the desired returns of the intermediate investor.

There are several advantages to using a model that measures risk and estimates a discount rate based on the risk measure, rather than using a survey.

- A risk and return model, properly constructed, sets reasonable bounds for the expected returns. For instance, the expected return on a risky asset in both the CAPM and the APM will exceed the expected return on a riskless asset. There is no such constraint on survey responses.
- A risk and return model, by relating expected return to risk and risk to prespecified factors, allows an analyst to be proactive in estimating discount rates rather than reactive. For instance, in the context of the CAPM, the expected return on an investment is determined by its beta, which in turn is determined by the cyclicality of the business (in which the investment is made) and the financial

| Internal Rate of Return | Growth Rates | | Typical Holding Period | Decision Priorities | Remarks |
	Income	Expense			
13–15%	0–4.5%	4–5%	6	1) 35% CA 2) 35% OAR 3) 30% IRR	(a) Cap actual NOT, not potential.
N/A	5%	4%	5–7	1) 40% OAR 2) ATCF+DR+AVE 3) 20% Ca 4) 10% GIM 5) $/SF	Buys new and existing projects with 60 unit minimum size.
11–12%	4–5%	4–5%	10	1) OAR	
11%	4–5%	4–5%	10	2) $/SF	
11.5–12%	4–5%	4–5%	10	3) CA	
11.5%	4–5%	4–5%	10		
11.5%	4–5%	4–5%	10		
11%	4–5%	4–5%	10		
12–13%	4–5%	4–5%	10		

leverage taken on. Thus, an analyst who knows how the financial leverage in an investment is expected to change over time can adjust the beta of that investment accordingly and use it in valuation. There is no such mechanism available when the survey approach is used.

- Where the ultimate investor is not known at the time of the analysis, as is the case in real estate investments that are securitized, a risk and return model provides the framework for estimating the discount rate for a hypothetical marginal investor.

As real estate markets become more accessible to institutional investors and more investments are made with the objective of eventual securitization, the need for a good risk and return model will become more acute. These same trends will also make real estate investments more like financial investments (by making them more liquid). Sooner rather than later, the same models used to estimate risk and discount rates for financial assets will be used to estimate risk and discount rates for real estate investments.

Cost of Equity and Cost of Capital

The distinction between cost of equity and cost of capital, drawn in Chapter 4, is significant. If the cashflows being discounted on a real estate deal are cashflows to equity, the appropriate discount rate is the cost of equity. If the cashflows being discounted are predebt cashflows, that is, cashflows to the firm, the appropriate discount rate is the cost of capital. The preceding discussion on risk and discount rates is relevant to the measurement of the cost of equity. The cost of capital is the average of the cost of equity and the after-tax cost of debt, weighted by their market value proportions. The after-tax cost of debt in a real estate investment is a function of

- (a) the default risk in the investment, which determines the rate of borrowing,[3] and
- (b) the tax rate of the investor, which determines the tax benefit from borrowing.

$$\text{Cost of Capital} = \text{Cost of Equity} \ (E/[D + E])$$
$$+ \ \text{Interest Rate}(1 - t)(D/[D + E])$$

Given the high leverage associated with real estate investments, it can be argued that the better approach is to value the property and then subtract out the value of the outstanding debt to arrive at the value of the equity in the real estate investment.

Estimating Cashflows

Not all real estate investments generate cashflows. For those that do, cashflows can be estimated in much the same way that they can be estimated for financial investments. The ultimate objective is to estimate cashflows after taxes. Just as with financial assets, these cashflows can be estimated for equity investors in the real asset. These are the cashflows left over after meeting all operating

expenses, debt obligations (interest expenses and principal payments), and capital expenditures. The cashflows can also be estimated for all investors in the real estate investment. This is the equivalent of cashflows to the firm, which is the cashflow prior to meeting debt obligations.

Many real estate investments generate cashflows in the form of lease revenues and rents and can be valued using discounted cashflow models. In estimating these cashflows, the following points have to be addressed.

Cash Inflows

The cashflows from a real estate investment generally take the form of rents and lease payments. In estimating rents for future years, several factors have to be considered, including: (a) past trends in rents, (b) demand and supply conditions for space provided by the property, and (c) general economic conditions. The impact of rent control laws on rent increases also have to be factored in.

In office/multiple residential buildings, all space may not be rented at a particular time. Thus, the vacancy rate (i.e., the percentage of the space that will not be rented out at any point in time) has to be projected in conjunction with market rents. Even in tight markets, there will be periods of time when space cannot be rented out, leading to a vacancy rate.

With new buildings, the projections have to factor in how long it will take initially to get occupants to rent/lease space. Clearly, the longer it takes, the less is the discounted cashflow value of the building.

In the case of leased property, the terms of the lease can affect the projected lease revenues. If income properties are subject to existing leases, the terms of the lease such as the length of the lease, the contracted lease payments with future increases, additional reimbursable expenses, and provisions on lease renewal will determine cashflow estimates. The leases may also be net leases, where the tenant is responsible for paying taxes, insurance, and maintenance.

Cash Outflows

Expenses on real estate investments include items—such as property taxes, insurance, repairs and maintenance, and advertising—that are unrelated to occupancy and are fixed, as well as items—such as utility expenses—that are a function of occupancy and are variable.

In addition, the following factors will affect projected expenses:

- *Reimbursability:* Some expenses incurred in connection with a property by the owner may be reimbursed by the tenant, as part of a contractual agreement.
- *Expenses Stops:* Many office leases include provisions to protect the owner from increases in operating expenses beyond an agreed-upon level. Any increases beyond that level have to be paid by the tenant.

Expected Growth

A key input in estimating cashflows is the expected growth rate in both rents/leases and expenses. A key factor in estimating the growth rate is the expected

inflation rate. In a stable real estate market, the expected growth in cashflows should be close to the expected inflation rate. In tight markets with low vacancy rates, it is possible for the expected growth rate in rents to be higher than the expected inflation rate, at least until the market shortages disappear. The reverse is likely to be true in markets with high vacancy rates.

The surveys used to estimate discount rates, reported in Table 22.3, also collect information on investors' expectations of expected growth. It is interesting that while there are significant differences among investors on discount rates, the expected growth rates in cash inflows and outflows fall within a tight band. In 1989, for instance, the Cushman and Wakefield survey of investors in a wide range of markets found that they all estimated expected growth in cashflows to be between 4 and 6%.

Terminal Value

In all discounted cashflow valuation models, a key input is the estimate of terminal value, that is, the value of the asset at the end of the investment time horizon. There are three basic approaches that can be used to estimate the terminal value:

(a) The current value of the property can be assumed to increase at the expected inflation rate to arrive at a terminal value. Thus, the terminal value of a property, worth $10 million now, in ten years will be $13.44 million if the expected inflation rate is 3% (Terminal Value = 10×1.03^{10}). The danger of this approach is that it starts off with the assumption that the current value of the asset is reasonable, and tries to then assess the true value of the asset.

(b) An alternative to this approach is to assume that the cashflows in the terminal year (the last year of the investment horizon) will continue to grow at a constant rate forever after that. If this assumption is made, the terminal value of the asset is:

$$\text{Terminal Value of Equity/Asset}_n = \text{Expected CF}_{n+1}/(r - g)$$

where r is the discount rate (cost of equity if it is the terminal value of equity, and cost of capital if it is the terminal value of the asset), and CF_t is the cashflow (cashflow to equity if terminal value is for equity and to firm if terminal value is total terminal value).

Thus, if the property described in the previous example had produced a net cashflow, prior to debt payments, of $1.2 million in year 10, if this cashflow was expected to grow 3% a year forever after that, and if the cost of capital was 13%, the terminal value of the property can be written as follows:

$$\text{Terminal Value of Asset} = \text{FCFF}_{11}/(\text{WACC} - g)$$
$$= \$1.2 \times 1.03/(.13 - .03) = \$12.36 \text{ million}$$

(c) A close variation on the infinite growth model is the "capitalization rate" (cap rate) used by many real estate appraisers to value properties. In its most general form, the cap rate is the rate by which operating income is divided to get the value of the property. To see the linkage with the infinite-growth model, assume that the net operating income (prior to debt payments) is also the free

cashflows to the firm. Then the capitalization rate can be written as a function of the discount rate and the expected growth rate:

Capitalization Rate = (r − g)/(1 + g)

where *r* is the discount rate (the cost of equity if net income is being capitalized and the cost of capital if net operating income is being capitalized) and *g* is the expected growth rate forever. In the above example, the capitalization rate would have been:

Capitalization Rate = (.13 − .03)/1.03 = 9.70%

As an approximation, the denominator is usually ignored, leading to a cap rate of 10%.

DCF Valuation Models

Once a discount rate has been chosen and cashflows estimated, the value of an income-producing real asset can be estimated either in whole (by discounting cashflows to the firm at the weighted average cost of capital) or to its equity investors (by discounting cashflows to equity at the cost of equity). The following illustration provides an example of discounted cashflow valuation in real estate.

Illustration 22.1: Valuing an office building: 90 Trinity Place

The following was a valuation at the end of 1994 of 90 Trinity Place, a 14-story building owned and operated by New York University in downtown Manhattan with the following features:

- The building was designed and built in 1973 and has 84,628 square feet of rentable area.
- There was an estimated initial construction and renovation cost of $2.5 million.
- It was assumed for purposes of this analysis that the rental space would not be fully rented out for three years. The expected vacancy rates in the first three years are as follows:

Year	Vacancy Rate
1995	25%
1996	15%
1997	10%
After 1997	5%

The vacancy rate in downtown Manhattan at the time of the valuation in similar buildings was 15%.
- The market rents in the building were expected to average $30.00 per square foot in 1994 based upon average rents in the surrounding buildings.
- The market rents were assumed to grow 4% a year for five years and 3% a year after that forever.
- The variable operating expenses were assumed to be $5.00 per square foot and

are expected to grow at the same rate as rents. The fixed operating expense in 1994 amounted to $200,000 and was expected to grow at 3% forever.

- The real estate taxes were based upon the following assessed values from 1995 to 1998 and were assumed to grow 3% a year after that:

Year	Assessed Value	Real Estate Tax (Property Tax)
1985	$4,969,200	$ 642,613
1996	6,123,800	831,521
1997	7,278,400	1,037,714
1998	8,433,000	1,262,447

It is assumed that all tenants will pay their pro rata share of increases in real estate taxes that exceed 3% a year.

- The first year of operation for the valuation was assumed to be 1995.
- The tax rate on income was assumed to be 35%.
- The cost of borrowing[4] was assumed to be 9.00%, pretax. It is also assumed that the building would be financed with 20% equity and 80% debt.

Estimating Discount Rates

Cost of equity: The cost of equity could have been estimated using one of three approaches:

(a) Surveys of real estate investors by Cushman and Wakefield in 1994 found that the median return expected by these investors on their equity investment was 12%.

(b) The realized internal rate of return on buildings bought and sold in downtown Manhattan, prior to the real crisis of 1989–1993, was approximately 11%.

(c) A beta estimated by regressing the "Office Buildings" return series against a consolidated market portfolio[5] was 0.80. This beta, in conjunction with a 30-year Treasury bond rate of 8%, yields a cost of equity of:

$$\text{Cost of Equity} = \text{Riskfree Rate} + \text{Beta} \times \text{Risk Premium}$$
$$= 8\% + 0.8\,(5.5\%)$$
$$= 12.4\%$$

The last approach has been used in this analysis as the cost of equity.

Cost of capital: The cost of capital is the average of the cost of equity and the cost of debt, weighted by their proportions in the financing mix:

$$\text{Weighted Average Cost of Capital} = 12.40\%(.2) + 9.00\%(1 - .35)(.8)$$
$$= 7.16\%$$

Estimating Cashflows for the Extraordinary-Growth Period. The following table projects cashflows on the building prior to debt payments from 1995 to 1999:

	1995	1996	1997	1998	1999
Rentable space	84,628	84,628	84,628	84,268	84,628
Vacancy rate	25 %	15%	10%	5%	5%
Rented space	63,471	71,934	76,165	80,397	80,397
Rent per square foot	$31.20	$32.45	$33.75	$35.10	$36.50
Rental revenue	$1,980,295	$2,334,108	$2,570,265	$2,821,580	$2,934,443
Real estate tax escalation	$158,718	$169,619	$181,247	$193,602	$0
Total income	$2,139,013	$2,503,727	$2,751,512	$3,015,181	$2,934,443
Fixed operating expenses	$206,000	$212,180	$218,545	$225,102	$231,855
Variable operating expenses	$253,884	$287,735	$304,661	$321,586	$321,586
Real estate taxes	$642,623	$831,521	$1,037,714	$1,262,447	$1,300,320
Operating expenses	$1,102,507	$1,331,436	$1,560,920	$1,809,135	$1,853,762
Operating income	$1,036,506	$1,172,291	$1,190,592	$1,206,046	$1,080,681
Tax	$362,777	$410,302	$416,707	$422,116	$378,238
Operating income after tax	$673,729	$761,989	$773,885	$783,930	$702,443
Renovation (cap. ex.)	($2,500,000)	$0	$0	$0	$0
Free cashflows on building	($1,826,271)	$761,989	$773,885	$783,930	$702,443

Estimating a Terminal Value. The terminal value is estimated using the infinite-growth model. The cashflows on the building are estimated for the terminal year (2000) to be $729,787. These cashflows are expected to grow 3% a year forever. The terminal value of the building is then:

$$\text{Terminal Value of the building} = \text{FCF}_{2000}/(\text{WACC} - g)$$
$$= \$729,787/(.0716 - .03) = \$17,542,955$$

Estimating the Value of the Building. The value of the building today can be estimated by taking the present value of the cashflows to the building and the terminal value of the building at the weighted average cost of capital.

$$\text{Present Value of building} = -\$1,826,271/1.0716 + \$761,989/1.0716^2$$
$$+ \$773,885/1.0716^3 + \$783,930/1.0716^4$$
$$+ (\$702,443 + \$17,542,955)/1.0716^5$$
$$= \$13,094,596$$

Based upon the projected cashflows to the firm and the estimated discount rates, the building should be valued at $13,094,596.

Illustration 22.2: Valuing the equity stake in a building: 90 Trinity Place

The analysis above can be done for just the equity stake in 90 Trinity Place. To do so, assume that the amount borrowed is $10 million, at an interest rate of 9%, and that the loan is a balloon payment loan, with the principal due at the end of 1999.

Discount Rate. The appropriate discount rate to use while valuing the equity stake in the building is the cost of equity, estimated to be 12.40% in this analysis.

Estimating Cashflows to Equity in the High-Growth Period. The estimated cashflows to equity are estimated from 1995 to 1999 in the following table, by estimating interest expenses on the debt (9% of $10 million) and calculating cashflows to equity after these payments.

	1995	1996	1997	1998	1999
Rentable space	84,628	84,628	84,628	84,628	84,628
Vacancy rate	25 %	15%	10%	5%	5%
Rented space	63,471	71,934	76,165	80,397	80,397
Rent per square foot	$31.20	$32.45	$33.75	$35.10	$36.50
Rental revenue	$1,980,295	$2,334,108	$2,570.265	$2,821,580	$2,934,443
Real estate tax escalation	$158,718	$169,619	$181,247	$193,602	$0
Total income	$2,139,013	$2,503,727	$2,751,512	$3,015,181	$2,934,443
Fixed operating expenses	$206,000	$212,180	$218,545	$225,102	$231,855
Variable operating expenses	$253,884	$287,735	$304,661	$321,586	$321,586
Real estate taxes	$642,623	$831,521	$1,037,714	$1,262,447	$1,300,320
Operating expenses	$1,102,507	$1,331,436	$1,560,920	$1,809,135	$1,853,762
Operating income	$1,036,506	$1,172,291	$1,190,592	$1,206,046	$1,080,681
Interest expenses	$900,000	$900,000	$900,000	$900,000	$900,000
Tax	$47,777	$95,302	$101,707	$107,116	$63,238
Net income	$88,279	$176,989	$188,885	$198,930	$117,443
Renovation (cap. ex.)	($2,500,000)	$0	$0	$0	$0
Free cashflows on equity in building	($2,411,271)	$176,989	$188,885	$198,930	$117,443

Estimated Terminal Value of Equity in Building. The terminal value of equity in the building is estimated by subtracting the principal due on the balloon payment loan ($10 million) from the terminal value of the building:

Terminal Value of building = $17,542,955

Principal due on loan = $10,000,000

Terminal Value of equity = $7,542,955

Estimating the Value of the Equity Stake in the building. The value of equity in 90 Trinity Place can be estimated by discounting the cashflows to equity and the terminal value of equity at the cost of equity:

$$Present\ Value\ of\ equity = -\$2,411,271/1.124 + \$176,989/1.124^2$$
$$+ \$188,885/1.124^3 + \$198,930/1.124^4$$
$$+ (\$117,443 + \$7,542,955)/1.124^5$$
$$= \$2,522,402$$

The value of the equity in the building is $2,522,402.

Limitations of DCF Valuation

There are many reasons given for why discounted cashflow valuation is not appropriate for real estate. First, it is argued that discount rates are difficult, if not impossible, to estimate for most real estate investments. In the discussion of this topic, we have pointed out that this is not necessarily true. Second, it is argued that estimating cashflows for the time horizon is tedious and difficult to do, as is the estimation of the terminal value. We would argue that it is much easier to estimate cashflows for real estate than for some financial investments (for instance, a high-growth stock). Third, it is argued that DCF valuation does not reflect market conditions—that the market is strong or weak at the time of valuation. We would reject this argument at two levels. On one level, the cashflows should reflect the market conditions, since they will be higher (higher rents and lower vacancy rates) and grow faster in strong market conditions. On the other level, any additional value being assigned by the market beyond the cashflow levels can be considered to be "overvaluation" and should not be built into the appraised value in the first place.

COMPARABLE/RELATIVE VALUATION

Just as price/earnings and price/book value ratios are used to value financial assets, real estate investments can be valued using standardized value measures and comparable assets. There are several reasons for doing so:

- It provides a mechanism for valuing non-cashflow-producing assets. For instance, the value of a single family residential building bought as a primary residence can be estimated by looking at similar properties in the same area.
- It takes into account market trends that might not be reflected in the cashflows yet for a number of reasons. Leases might have frozen lease payments in place while market values have risen, and rent control laws might prevent rents from rising with market values.
- It is also argued that valuing based upon comparables is much simpler to do than DCF valuation since it does not require, at least explicitly, the estimation of discount rates and cashflows.

What Is a Comparable Asset?

The key limitation of all comparable-based approaches is in the definition of *comparable*. In the case of stocks, differences in growth, risk, and payout ratios between stocks have to be adjusted for before price/earnings ratios are compared. Many analysts choose to restrict their comparisons of stocks to those within the same industry group, to keep it relatively homogeneous. In the case of real estate, differences in size, scale, location, age, and quality of construction have to be accounted for before comparisons are made. Some of these adjustments are straightforward and objective (such as differences in size) and others are subjective (such as differences in location).

Use of Standardized Value Estimates

When valuing assets based upon comparable assets, the value has to be standardized for the comparison. In stocks, this standardization is often done by dividing the price per share by the earnings per share (PE) or the book value per share (PBV). In the case of real estate, this adjustment is made by:

(a) *Size:* The simplest standardized measure is the price per square foot,[6] which standardizes value using the size of the building. In office rentals, where square footage is a key factor determining rental revenues, this may be a useful adjustment. It does not, however, factor in differences in any of the other dimensions.

(b) *Income:* The value of an asset can be standardized using its income. For instance, the gross income multiplier (price of property divided by gross annual income) is an income-standardized value measure. The advantage of this approach is that the income incorporates differences in scale, construction quality, and location.[7] The gross income should be prior to debt payments, since differences in leverage can cause large differences in the income available to equity investors.

Why Comparables May Work Better for Real Estate Than Stocks

One of the difficulties in using comparables to value stocks is that risk and growth characteristics can vary widely across stocks even in the same industry class. In the case of real estate properties in the same locale, the argument can be made that the growth and risk characteristics are very similar across these properties and that the only differences are therefore differences in the capacity to generate income.

Illustration 22.3: Valuing a property based upon comparables

Consider the property at 90 Trinity Place that was valued using discounted cashflow valuation. Assume that there were five other properties that were sold in 1994 in downtown Manhattan, with the following parameters:

Property	Sale Price	Size (sq. ft.)	Price per Square Foot	Gross Rent	Price/Gross Rent
A	$ 79,638,900	757,692	$105.11	$14,479,800	5.50
B	88,949,722	643,887	138.14	13,276,078	6.70
C	65,671,680	1,010,000	65.02	12,876,800	5.10
D	158,405,669	880,105	179.98	22,629,381	7.00
E	215,265,423	1,900,320	113.28	43,931,719	4.90
Average			120.31		5.84

The property at 90 Trinity Place has 84,628 square feet of rental space. Based upon the average price per square foot, the value of the property is:

Value of 90 Trinity Place = 84,628 sq. ft. × $120.31/sq. ft. = $10.18 million

The estimated gross rent in 1996 is $2,334,108. Based upon the price/gross rent multiple estimated from comparable properties:

Value of 90 Trinity Place = $2,334,108 × 5.84 = $13.63 million

The 1996 gross rents are used rather than 1995 rents, because there will be a high vacancy rate in 1995 as new tenants are sought for the building.

A REGRESSION APPROACH

One of the approaches used to extend the reach of relative valuation for stocks is the regression approach, where price/earnings or price/book value multiples were regressed against independent variables that cause differences in these multiples—risk, growth, and payout. Since the variables causing differences in real estate values in a locale are fairly obvious—vacancy rates, size, and the capacity to generate income, among others, it should be relatively simple to extend this approach to analyze properties.

CONCLUSION

There is much that is said in this chapter that repeats what was said in earlier chapters on stock valuation. This is because a real estate investment can (and, in our view, should) be valued with the same approaches used to value financial assets. While the structure and caveats of discounted cashflow models remain unchanged for real estate investments, there are some practical problems that have to be faced and overcome. In particular, some real assets do not trade regularly and risk parameters (and discount rates) are difficult to estimate. A real asset can also be valued using comparable real assets, but the difficulties in identifying "comparable" assets, and controlling for differences across them, remain significant problems.

QUESTIONS AND SHORT PROBLEMS

1. An analyst who looks at real estate decides to apply the capital asset pricing model to estimate the risk (beta) for real estate. He regresses returns on a real estate index (based upon appraised values) against returns on a stock index, and estimates a beta of 0.20 for real estate. Would you agree with this estimate? If you do not, what might be the sources of your disagreement?

2. An alternative way of estimating risk for real estate is to use prices on traded REITs to compute returns, and to regress these returns against a stock index to arrive at a beta estimate. Would this beta be a more reliable estimate of risk? Why or why not?

3. The risk for real estate can be viewed as a derived demand. If this is the case, the risk of real estate can be estimated from the underlying business it supports. Under this view, what would be the appropriate proxy to use for risk in the following types of real estate investments:

 a. Commercial real estate in New York.

 b. Commercial real estate in Houston.

 c. Commercial real estate in San Jose (Silicon Valley).

 d. Hotel complex in Orlando.

4. Would your valuation of real estate be affected by who the potential investors in the property are? For instance, would your analysis be any different if the primary investors were individuals, involved primarily in real estate, or if they were institutional investors?

5. How would you factor in the absence of liquidity into your valuation?

6. You have been asked to value an office building in Orlando, Florida, with the following characteristics:

 • The building was built in 1988 and has 300,000 square feet of rentable area.

 • There would be an initial construction and renovation cost of $3 million.

 • It will take two years to fill the building. The expected vacancy rates in the first two years are as follows:

Year	Vacancy Rate
I	30%
2	20%
After year 2	10%

 • The market rents in the building were expected to average $15 per square foot in the current year based upon average rents in the surrounding buildings.

 • The market rents were assumed to grow 5% a year for five years at 3% a year after that forever.

 • The variable operating expenses were assumed to be $3 per square foot and are expected to grow at the same rate as rents. The fixed operating expense in 1994 amounted to $300,000 and was expected to grow at 3% forever.

 • The real estate taxes are expected to amount to $300,000 in the first year, and grow 3% a year after that. It is assumed that all tenants will pay their prorated share of increases in real estate taxes that exceed 3% a year.

 • The tax rate on income was assumed to be 42%.

 • The cost of borrowing was assumed to be 8.25%, pretax. It was also assumed that the building would be financed with 30% equity and 70% debt.

 • A survey suggests that equity investors in real estate require a return of 12.5% of their investments.

 a. Estimate the value of the building, based upon expected cashflows.

 b. Estimate the value of just the equity stake in this building.

7. You are trying to value the same building based upon comparable properties sold in recent years. There have been six property sales of buildings of comparable size in the surrounding area.

Property	Sale Price	Size (Sq. Ft.)	Gross Rent
A	$20,000,000	400,000	$5,000,000
B	18,000,000	425,000	4,750,000
C	22,000,000	450,000	5,100,000
D	25,000,000	400,000	5,500,000
E	15,000,000	350,000	4,000,000
F	12,000,000	300,000	3,000,000

 a. Estimate the value of the building, based upon price per square foot.

 b. Estimate the value of the building, based upon price/gross rent.

 c. What are some of the assumptions you make when you value a building based upon comparable buildings?

ENDNOTES

1. There is only one quarter each year in which each property is appraised by an independent outside appraiser. For the other 3 quarters, an internal appraisal is done. Studies have shown that the major jump in value occurs in the quarter when the independent appraisal takes place.

2. When the beta of an asset is estimated relative to a stock index, the underlying assumption is that the marginal investor has the bulk of his or her portfolio (97% or 98%) in stocks, and measures risk relative this portfolio.

3. The cost of borrowing can be estimated in a number of ways, including the yield to maturity on debt and the mortgage constant to recognize the amortization factor.

4. The yield to maturity on commercial mortgages is published in Barron's.

5. This market portfolio has real estate as one of its weighted components.

6. More generally, it is price per spatial unit—beds in hospitals, seats in restaurants, units in apartments, etc.

7. Buildings of better quality in better locations should command higher rents/leases and higher expected income than other buildings.

23

Valuing Other Assets

O ne of the fundamental precepts of this book is that all assets, financial and real, can be valued systematically using discounted cashflow valuation, relative valuation, or contingent claim valuation models. The bulk of this book examines the valuation of stocks, but the last few chapters have extended the reach of valuation models to include fixed-income securities, options, futures, and real estate. In this chapter, we examine how to value a wide range of assets, from sports franchises to restaurants to cab medallions.

CLASSIFYING ASSETS

While the assets covered in this chapter come from very different backgrounds and attract different investors, they can be broadly classified into three categories:

(a) Assets that are expected to generate cashflows over time and can be valued with discounted cashflow models.

(b) Assets that do not generate cashflows but attain value because they are scarce and either are perceived to be valuable (collectibles, coins) and/or generate utility to their owners (antiques, paintings). These assets can be valued using "comparable" assets.

(c) Assets that do not generate cashflows but could be valuable in the event of a contingency—they have option characteristics. These assets can be valued using contingent claim valuation models.

Within each category, there are a surprising number of commonalities both across different assets and with the financial assets described in the earlier chapter.

CASHFLOW-PRODUCING ASSETS

A number of assets derive their value from their capacity to generate cashflows to their owners. For instance, the value of a private business is a function of its capacity to generate cashflows and the uncertainty associated with these cashflows. The basic principles of DCF valuation, described in earlier chapters, apply for any of these assets and require the following steps:

- Estimate cashflows on the asset for the estimation period. These cashflows can either be predebt (cashflows to the firm) or after-debt cashflows (cashflows to equity).
- Estimate the value of the asset, if any, at the end of the estimation period. This value will decline over time if the asset loses value with use or has a limited life, but may increase if it is an ongoing business.
- Estimate a discount rate that reflects the riskiness of the cashflows. This discount rate will be the cost of equity if the cashflows discounted are cashflows to equity and the cost of capital if the cashflows are cashflows to the firm.
- Calculate the present value of the cashflows to arrive at the value of the asset or the value of the equity in the assets.

There are several practical problems associated with applying these steps to assets when cashflows are difficult to estimate and risk cannot be easily quantified (and converted into a discount rate). In most cases, these problems are not insurmountable. Since the problems and the solutions vary from case to case, we consider a series of examples, ranging from the valuation of a simple franchise to more complex businesses.

Valuing a Franchise

The acquisition of a franchise provides the franchisee with the opportunity to earn above-market returns for the life of the franchise. While the sources of these above-market returns vary from case to case, they can arise from a number of different factors:

- *Brand name value:* The franchise might have a brand name value that enables the franchisee to charge higher prices and attract more customers than an otherwise similar business. Thus, an investor may be willing to pay a significant up-front fee to acquire a McDonald's franchise, in order to take advantage of the brand name value, which in turn is partly a function of history and partly a function of advertising expenditures.
- *Patent protection:* In some cases, a franchise has value because it enables a franchisee to produce a product, the rights to which are owned by the franchise. For instance, an investor may pay a fee to Disney for the right to manufacture Mickey Mouse watches or toys, and hope to recoup the fee by selling more of the product or charging a higher price for it.
- *Legal monopolies:* Sometimes, a franchise may have value because the franchisee is given the exclusive right to provide a service. For instance, a company may pay a large fee for the right to operate concession stands in a baseball stadium, knowing that they will face no competition within the stadium on sales of items in the stands. In a milder variant of this, multiple franchises are sometimes sold but the number of franchises is kept limited to ensure that the franchisees earn excess returns. New York City, for example, sells cab medallions that are a prerequisite for operating a Yellow Cab in the city. They also have tight restrictions on nonmedallion owners offering the same service. Consequently, a market where cab medallions are bought and sold exists.

Illustration 23.1: Valuing a limited franchise: New York City cab medallions

Background:
- In 1994, New York City had 11,787 cab medallions outstanding.[1] The owner of a cab medallion has the right to operate a Yellow Cab in the five boroughs of New York City—Manhattan, Brooklyn, the Bronx, Queens, and Staten Island.
- New York City restricts nonmedallion owners from picking up customers on the street, though they can still be summoned in other ways.
- All Yellow Cabs in the city are regulated by the Taxi and Limousine Commission, which sets fares and reserves the right to fine owners who do not follow its numerous requirements.

Cashflows on a Cab Medallion
- The typical New York City cab is a Chevrolet Caprice. The cost of acquiring one in 1994 was approximately $15,000, and it has an expected life of ten years. The cab can be depreciated over the life down to a salvage value of zero.
- A cab can be expected to be on the road 330 days of the year, with an expected down time (for maintenance) of 35 days, and make $250 a day prior to meeting operating expenses, maintenance expenses, and the cost of time for the driver.
- The annual cost of fuel and operating expenses is expected to be 25% of revenues, and the maintenance expenses are expected to amount to $1,500 a year.
- The cost of automobile insurance, covering the cost of collision, theft, and bodily harm, is $2,000 a year.
- The annual fee to be paid to the Taxi and Limousine Commission is $500. Other licensing costs are expected to amount to $500 a year.
- The total cost per day, inclusive of benefits, of the driver of the cab is expected to amount to $100. (This includes the 35 days when the car is down for maintenance.)

Estimating Risk and Discount Rates. The capacity of a cab to pull in the expected revenues is a function of several variables:

- *The state of the city's economy:* The more buoyant the economy of the city, the greater are the potential revenues from owning and operating a cab in it. Since the state of New York City's economy is, in large part, driven by the state of the financial services sector, there is in all likelihood a positive correlation between cab revenues and financial services sector health.
- *The scarcity of cabs:* The value of a cab medallion is derived directly from the fact that there are only a limited number of medallions that are sold. To the extent that the city either can issue more medallions or allows gypsy cabs (unlicensed taxis) to operate within the environs of the city, it can affect the expected revenues.
- *The fare structure:* Since the fare structure is regulated, the expected revenues from owning a cab in the future will be dependent on the generosity of raises that the Taxi and Limousine Commission allows.

There are a number of other potential sources of risk including collision and theft that have already been built into the cost structure. To the extent that these are estimates, they could also create swings in the cashflows.

> Assuming that the expected revenues factors in the number of medallions outstanding and the expected changes in the fare structure already, the primary source of risk in owning a cab medallion is assumed to be shifts in the city's economy. If the health of the city's economy is a function of the financial services sector, the risk of owning a cab medallion should be similar to the risk of investing in a financial service firm.

The average beta of financial service firms headquartered in New York City is 1.25. At the end of 1994, with Treasury bond rates at 8%, the cost of equity would have been:

$$\text{Cost of Equity} = 8\% + (1.25 \times 5.5\%) = 14.88\%$$

This will be used as the cost of equity in valuing a cab medallion.

Financing Mix. Assume that the medallion will be financed half with equity and half with debt and that the debt will carry an interest rate of 10% per annum. Allowing for a marginal tax rate (federal, state, and city) of 40%, the cost of capital for valuing the medallion is:

$$\text{Cost of Capital} = (14.88\% \times .5) + 10\%(1 - .4)(.5) = 10.44\%$$

Estimating Future Growth and Value. It is assumed that the expected operating income from owning a cab will keep up with expected inflation, which is assumed to be 3% in the long term. The predebt cashflow from owning a cab medallion is provided below:

Item	Calculation	Amount
Revenues	330 × $250	$82,500
Expenses:		
Driver	365 × $100	36,500
Fuel & Operating	25% of Revenues	20,625
Maintenance	$1,500/year	1,500
Depreciation	$1,500/year	1,500
Fees & License Costs	$1,000/year	1,000
EBIT		21,375
Taxes	40% of EBIT	8,550
EBIT(1 − t)		12,825
+ Depreciation		1,500
− Capital Expenditure	For replacement	1,500
Free Cash Flow from Operations		12,825

The cashflow from depreciation is set aside to meet the eventual expense of replacing the car at the end of the tenth year.

Based upon the expected cashflows from operations of $12,825, the expected

growth rate of 3% in the long term, and the cost of capital of 10.44%, the value of owning a medallion is:

> Value of a New York City cab medallion = $12,825 \times 1.03/(.1044 - .03)$
> $= \$177,550$

Other Factors. This valuation is based upon the presumption that a cab driver is hired to drive the cab. If the driver owns and operates the cab, this is still the appropriate way to approach the valuation, since the time of the driver has to be priced in. Failing to do so will inflate the expected after-tax cashflows and the value of the medallion unjustly. The other issue that is not resolved in this valuation is whether there are any economies of scale involved in owning more than one medallion, in terms of reduced insurance costs or downtime. To the extent that there is, medallions will be more likely to be sold to existing owners of medallions than to new investors.

Valuing Sports Franchises

Sports franchises offer a specialized example of franchise valuation. Their uniqueness arises from several factors. First, they tend to be significantly more valuable than most other franchises, with values running into the hundreds of millions for some teams. Second, the success of a sports franchise is judged not only in economic terms but also in terms of winning and losing—though winning teams tend to gain in economic terms as well. Third, the strong local connections that these teams have and the intense emotions they evoke in their fans make them different from a typical business.

Steps in Valuing a Sports Franchise. The steps in valuing a sports franchise trace the steps in any valuation—cashflows from owning the franchise have to be estimated in conjunction with a discount rate that reflects the uncertainty associated with these cashflows.

(a) *Estimating cashflows:* The cashflows from owning a sports franchise will depend a great deal on the contractual agreement on the sharing of gate receipts in that sport and the magnitude of cable and television revenues. Even within the same sport, different leagues may have different arrangements. There are several other factors that can affect these cashflows, including:

- *Stadium ownership/special terms:* Some franchises own the stadiums that they play in and pay little or no additional cost for using them. Others lease their stadiums from the cities that they play in and pay an annual revenue. One of the ways cities have attempted to attract franchises from other locales is by offering extremely lenient terms for those franchises to move and play in them.
- *Size of the local market:* Not all sports franchises are created equal, especially in this age when the revenues from cable and television contracts can be a significant proportion of total revenues. A team playing in a large media market, like New York City or Los Angeles, has a decided advantage over a team playing in a small market, like Pittsburgh.

- *Success/failure of the team:* There is clearly a monetary payoff to being a successful team, both in terms of being on television and sharing in the revenues that come from the playoffs and also in terms of merchandising. The Dallas Cowboys, for instance, used their success during the 1970s as a springboard to becoming "America's team" and profiting from it.
- *Size of the payroll/player expenses:* The primary expense in most sports franchises is the player payroll, which has climbed dramatically over the last two decades in most sports. The average major league baseball player in 1994 was paid $1.2 million, and the average NHL player was paid $560,000. There are player development expenses, as well, associated with the ownership of minor league teams in baseball, that can contribute significantly to the bottom line.

(b) *Estimating discount rates:* The discount rate is more difficult to estimate. There are very few sports franchises that are publicly traded, with estimated betas. This estimation problem can be approached in a number of different ways:

- Professional sports is part of the professional entertainment business. Thus, it can be argued that the New York Yankees have more in common with Time Warner than with a typical New York City business.
- While not many professional franchises are publicly traded, there are a number of businesses whose revenues are derived from sports merchandising that are publicly traded. For instance, sportswear companies such as Nike and Russell Athletic are listed and traded on the stock exchange and have risk parameters estimated for them. To the extent that their profits are linked up to the popularity of professional sports, there should be some information in their risk estimates.
- The risk of these franchises can be estimated using the financial information they reveal about their revenues and profits over time and relating these numbers to earnings performance in the marketplace. Thus, sports franchises whose revenues and income swing more dramatically than overall market revenue and income would be considered more risky and deserving of higher discount rates.

Illustration 23.2: Valuing baseball franchises

Background. Major league baseball came to a grinding halt in September 1994 as owners and players disagreed about whether player expenses were getting out of control. Owners argued that they were and that most teams were losing money, though they refused to share their financial statements. The players argued that the teams were in fact making money but using creative bookkeeping[2] to report losses.

While the owners and the players wrangled over the state of finances in the game, the Baltimore Orioles franchise was sold for $173 million to a new owner, Peter Angelos, after having been bought by Edward Bennett Williams for $12 million 20 years earlier. In 1992, Bob Lurie managed to get $100 million from local interests for the financially troubled San Francisco Giants, and actually turned down an offer of $115 million to move them to Tampa/St. Petersburg. Of course, these transactions do not imply that these franchises were worth this much in terms of revenue-generating power, since there are substantial side benefits to owning a sports franchise, especially for a publicity-seeking owner.[3]

In the following analysis, we will attempt to value three baseball franchises as of September 1994, before the players' strike. We will consider one National League team—the Pittsburgh Pirates—and two American League teams—the New York Yankees and the Baltimore Orioles.

Cashflows on a Baseball Franchise

(a) *Revenues:* A major league baseball franchise has several sources of revenues, though the magnitude of the revenue is affected by the revenue-sharing arrangement within the league. The two leagues that comprise major league baseball—the National League and the American League—have very different revenue-sharing arrangements among themselves.

(1) *Home game receipts:* The first and most obvious source of revenues for a major league team is the receipts at the 81 home games that it plays as part of a regular baseball season. In the American League, the home team and the visiting team split gate receipts on an 80–20 basis, while the National League allows home teams to keep approximately 95% of the home gate receipts. Luxury box receipts can be kept by the home team.

(2) *Road game receipts:* This is the flip side of home game receipts. While National League teams get to keep most of their home game receipts, they receive relatively small amounts (about 43¢ a ticket or 5% of gate receipts) from the 81 road games that they play. The American League teams keep 20% of their road game revenues.

(3) *Concessions and parking:* The sales from concession stands of souvenirs, food, soft drinks, and beer can be a source of profit to the team, either directly or through the sale of the concession rights to outsiders. Since there need to be fans in the stands for these sales to happen, these revenues are correlated with the home game attendance and receipts.

(4) *National TV revenues:* The leagues have contracts with national TV networks allowing them to carry some of the regular season games, the playoffs, and the World Series. These revenues are shared equally among the different franchises. One of the criticisms mounted against major league baseball in 1994 was that it had allowed a lucrative contract for $1 billion with CBS to expire and replaced it with one with ABC, NBC, and ESPN for about half that. This led to a drop in each team's share from $14 million in 1993 to about $7.5 million in 1994.

(5) *Local TV revenues:* The local television revenues are determined by the size of the local media market. The New York Yankees, playing in the largest media market in the nation, signed a contract with MSG Network for $486 million over 12 years. The Seattle Mariners, on the other hand, signed a three-year contract in 1994 with KIRO–TV for $7 million. Under the revenue-sharing arrangement, about 25% of cable revenues have to be shared with the rest of the league,[4] while local broadcast TV revenues belong entirely to the home team.

(6) *National licensing:* The major league clubs also make revenues from the national licensing of the club's name, which can be very large for known franchises like the Yankees and Dodgers and smaller for lesser-known franchises like the Mariners.

(7) *Stadium advertising:* The billboards around the stadium and the giant television screens in most stadiums provide an avenue for advertisers to get their messages to fans, and the revenues from the advertising may accrue to the club.

(8) *Other revenues:* This covers all other sources of revenues. For instance, the Baltimore Orioles, in the new stadium built for them by the city, received almost $5.374 million in revenues from club seats and private suites and $3.633 million in unidentified other revenues.

The following table provides estimates for each of these categories in 1993 for the three teams:

	Pittsburgh Pirates	Baltimore Orioles	New York Yankees
Net home game receipts	$15,116,398	$29,596,120	$ 26,000,000
Road receipts	806,586	4,556,488	5,000,000
Concessions and parking	2,209,391	13,367,911	15,000,000
National TV revenues	12,500,000	12,500,000	12,500,000
Local TV revenues	7,500,000	14,183,000	44,000,000
National licensing	4,162,747	3,050,949	6,000,000
Stadium advertising	100,000	4,391,383	5,500,000
Other revenues	1,000,000	9,200,000	6,000,000
Total revenues	$43,395,122	$90,845,851	$120,000,000

The lucrative television contract signed by the New York Yankees gives them the edge in terms of revenues over the other two teams.

(b) Expenses: The primary expenditure incurred by baseball teams is the cost of player salaries and other related expenses (including the cost of operating the minor league teams). This varies from team to team and from year to year. In addition, there are expenses associated with the contractual obligations from releasing players. There are a number of other categories of expenditure as well:

- There is a fairly large cost associated with both team operations (travel, lodging, etc.) and operating the stadium.
- For teams that rent their stadiums from the cities they play in, there is a cost associated with this action. For teams that own their own stadiums, there might be a depreciation or amortization charge if the stadium was built recently.
- The most troublesome category is the general administrative cost, since many team owners have been accused of nepotism in hiring—relatives have been hired on the teams' payrolls at inflated salaries. If this is the case, these salaries should be treated as dividends to the owner rather than expenditures.

The following table summarizes the expenses faced by the Pittsburgh Pirates, the Baltimore Orioles, and the New York Yankees in 1993:

	Pittsburgh Pirates	Baltimore Orioles	New York Yankees
Player salaries	$26,188,403	$27,771,482	$45,000,000
Team operating expenses	6,239,025	3,803,907	6,000,000
Player development	9,163,095	8,768,399	12,000,000
Stadium and game operations	4,370,986	3,269,790	5,000,000
Other player costs	1,991,000	4,795,751	5,500,000
General and administrative costs	5,267,617	7,921,151	9,000,000
Broadcasting	1,250,000	0	0
Rent and amortization	0	6,252,151	0
Total operating expenses	$54,470,126	$62,582,631	$82,500,000

(c) *Discount rates:* The betas to be used in the valuation are estimated by using a firm that derives much of its revenues from baseball—Topps. Topps, which manufactures Bazooka bubblegum and baseball cards, is publicly traded on the New York Stock Exchange and had an estimated[5] beta of 1.10 in 1994. This beta yields a cost of equity of

Cost of Equity $= 8.00\% + (1.1 \times 5.5\%) = 14.05\%$

The financial leverage used varies substantially from team to team. Allowing for a mix of 75% equity and 25% debt in the financing and a pretax cost of debt of 9%, the cost of capital can be estimated as follows (assume that the tax rate is 44%):

$$\text{Cost of Capital} = (14.05\% \times .75) + 9\%(1 - .44)(.25)$$
$$= 11.80\%$$

Valuation. The operating after-tax cashflows to owning the three teams highlighted above can be estimated as follows:

	Pittsburgh Pirates	Baltimore Orioles	New York Yankees
Total revenues	$43,395,122	$90,845,851	$120,000,000
Total operating expenses	54,470,126	62,582,631	82,500,000
EBIT	(11,075,004)	28,263,220	37,500,000
Taxes (at 44%)	(4,873,002)	12,435,817	16,500,000
EBIT(1 − tax rate)	(6,202,002)	15,827,403	21,000,000

The Pittsburgh Pirates have negative earnings before interest and taxes, partly as a result of losing key players to the free agent market after 1992. If the average revenues from 1990 to 1992 were used instead of the current year numbers, the after-tax operating income for the Pirates is closer to $5 million. (This is a normalized operating income.)

Allowing for a growth of 3% in the long term in these after-tax operating incomes and factoring in the cost of capital of 11.80%, the values of the three teams are as follows:

Value of the Pittsburgh Pirates = $5,000,000 × 1.03/(.1180 − .03)
= $58.5 million

Value of the Baltimore Orioles = $15,827,403 × 1.03/(.1180 − .03)
= $185.3 million

Value of the New York Yankees = $21,000,000 × 1.03/(.1180 − .03)
= $245.8 million

Special Factors. There are several interesting issues that arise in the context of valuing a sports franchise. One is the *potential for moving a team to another market.* As the example above illustrates, there are significant differences between teams in terms of their potential to sign lucrative television contracts and attract large crowds to home games. Thus the Pittsburgh Pirates may be worth more as the Phoenix Pirates. Consequently, teams that are losing significant amounts may still sell for high prices because of the possibility that they could be worth more in another market. Another is the *effect of signing or failing to sign a star player,* for instance, Bobby Bonilla and the Pittsburgh Pirates. While there may be an immediate effect on cashflows, the value of the franchise itself should be relatively unaffected because it is determined by the cashflows in the long term.

Valuing Businesses with a Personal Component

Many businesses derive a significant portion of their value from a "key person," who is often the owner, and may be worth significantly less if run by someone else. In these cases, it is important that the consequences of losing this key person be built into the valuation. It is also important than the additional risk associated with the dependence upon an individual be factored into the analysis. In the following analysis, we will value such a restaurant.

Illustration 23.3: Valuing a key player business: Lutece

Lutece is a renowned restaurant located at 249 East 50th Street in Manhattan. In 1994, Lutece was sold by its owner/chef Andre Soltner to Ark Restaurants, a publicly traded restaurant chain, for an undisclosed amount. *The New York Times,* blanching as a result of the sale, ran the headline "Lutece, a Dining Landmark, Is Sold to a Chain Operator," which was followed by an article detailing the surprise marriage of the classic French restaurant to Ark, a company largely known for operating theme concepts. Bryan Miller, the *Times'* former restaurant reviewer and writer of the piece, likened the addition of Lutece to Ark's portfolio to "hanging a Van Gogh in a community art exhibit."

Background. Lutece was founded in 1961 by Andre Soltner and quickly acquired a reputation for serving food of exceptional quality. It has received a five-star rating from Mobil for 24 consecutive years and is one of five New York City restaurants that gets

a four-star rating (the highest) from *The New York Times*. In a sign of slippage, however, its ranking in the Zagat Survey of New York City restaurants dropped to eighth in 1994 from being perennially at or near the top for much of the 1970s and 1980s.

Estimating Cashflows. Following are some of the pertinent facts on Lutece:

- The restaurant can seat 92 diners. It has one seating for lunch and two seatings for dinner. It fills 70% of its seats at lunchtime and 80% of its seats at dinner.
- The restaurant is open 340 days every year and closed for the remaining 25 days.
- The average price of a lunch is $30, and the average price of a dinner is $66. Approximately one third of this is for liquor.
- There are 42 employees on the staff of the restaurant. The cost of food is approximately 30% of the price of the meal, and the payroll amounts to $800,000 a year.
- The annual rent for the space used by Lutece is $600,000.

The following is an estimation of the after-tax operating cashflows in 1994 for Lutece:

	Assumption	Base Year
Revenues:		
Lunch	70% occupancy; $30 per person	$ 656,880
Dinner	80% occupancy; $66 per person	1,651,584
Total		2,308,464
Expenses:		
Food	30% of revenues	692,539
Staff	$800,000 for staff expenses	800,000
Rent		600,000
Total		2,092,539
EBIT		215,925
Taxes	Assumed tax rate of 40%	86,370
EBIT(1 − t)		129,555

These cashflows are expected to grow 6% a year for three years and 3% a year after that. The following table summarizes the expected cashflows over the next three years:

	Base Year	1	2	3
Revenues	2,308,464	$2,446,972	$2,593,790	$2,749,418
Expenses	2,092,539	2,218,092	2,351,177	2,492,248
EBIT	215,925	228,880	242,613	257,170
Taxes	86,370	91,552	97,045	102,868
EBIT(1 − t)	129,555	137,328	145,568	154,302

Estimating Discount Rates. The acquirer in this case, Ark Restaurants, has a relatively low beta (0.7) and gets only about 10% of its financing needs from debt. Assuming that the underlying risk in investing in Lutece is similar, the cost of equity can be estimated as follows (assuming that the long-term Treasury bond rate is 8%):

$$\text{Cost of Equity} = 8\% + (.7 \times 5.5\%) = 11.85\%$$

If Ark Restaurants can borrow money at 9% and faces a 40% tax rate, the cost of capital can be calculated as follows:

$$\text{Cost of Capital} = (11.85\% \times .90) + 9\%(1 - .04)(.10)$$
$$= 11.20\%$$

Estimating Value. The value of Lutece can be estimated by discounting the cashflows at the weighted average cost of capital. Allowing for a growth rate of 6% over the next three years and 3% after that, the value of the restaurant can be estimated as follows:

$$\text{Value at the end of the high-growth period} = \text{EBIT}_4((1 - t)/(\text{WACC} - g_n))$$
$$= \$257,170 \times 1.03$$
$$\times .6/(.112 - .03)$$
$$= \$1,937,002$$

$$\text{Value of Lutece} = \$137,328/1.112 + \$145,568/1.112^2$$
$$+ (\$154,302 + \$1,937,002)/1.112^3 = \$1,762,125$$

Valuing the Key Person. There probably would be no argument that some of Lutece's value derives from Andre Soltner's presence as chef. It would be worth examining how much this value would change if he were to be replaced by somebody else. The simplest way to evaluate this effect is to

- estimate the effect on occupancy and through this on cashflows of replacing Mr. Soltner with another chef. To the extent that occupancy and cashflows decline, the value of the restaurant will decline.
- calculate the value of the restaurant based on the discounted cashflows.

In extreme cases, where the entire value of an enterprise depends upon one person, the value can drop to essentially 0 if the key person were to leave or die. In less extreme cases, the value of the key person can be estimated to be the difference between the values of the enterprise with and without that person in place.[6]

Analyzing the Effect of Illiquidity on Value

Private businesses and some categories of investments (real estate, precious gems, fine art) cannot be bought and sold as easily as publicly traded securities. This lack of liquidity makes these investments less attractive, and therefore less valuable, than otherwise similar investments which are more liquid.

Determinants of the Liquidity Discount

The size of the liquidity discount assigned to a business or an asset will depend upon a number of factors, some of which would include the following:

(a) *Type of assets owned by the firm.* Even if a business is not liquid, its assets may be. The more liquid the assets owned by the firm, the lower should be the liquidity discount assigned in valuing that firm or its securities. Thus, a business that has a substantial proportion of its assets in cash and marketable securities should have less of a liquidity discount than one that is made up primarily of plant and equipment.

(b) *Size of the business.* One of the ways in which businesses can bypass the absence of liquidity is by borrowing on their assets. From a practical stand-point, this is more feasible for larger businesses than for smaller ones. Conse-quently, the larger the firm, the smaller should be size of the liquidity discount.

(c) *Health of the business.* Building on the notion that businesses can borrow on their assets and bypass the lack of liquidity, it is quite clear that the owners of healthy businesses, which make substantial profits, suffer less of a liquidity problem than the owners of troubled businesses. Healthier businesses should sell at smaller discounts than troubled ones.

(d) *Cashflow-generating capacity.* Businesses that generate substantial cashflows should have smaller liquidity discounts associated with them than businesses that do not have that capacity to generate cashflows.

Empirical Evidence

Restricted securities are securities issued by a company, but not registered with the SEC, that can be sold through private placements to investors but cannot be resold in the open market, except under provisions of SEC's rule 144. They cannot be sold for a two-year holding period, and limited amounts can be sold after that. In studies of these securities going back to 1966, there have been several consistent findings.

Restricted securities trade at significant discounts on publicly traded shares in the same company. Maher (1975) examined restricted stock purchases made by four mutual funds in the period 1969–1973 and concluded that they traded at an average discount of 35.43% on publicly traded stock in the same compa-nies. Moroney (1971) reported a mean discount of 35% for acquisitions of 146 restricted stock issues by 10 investment companies, using data from 1970. In a recent study of this phenomenon, Silber (1991) found that the median dis-count for restricted stock is 33.75%. Silber reported that the discounts tend to be smaller for larger and more diversified companies and larger for companies in trouble. Silber developed the following relationship between the size of the discount and the characteristics of the firm issuing the registered stock:

$$LN(RPRS) = 4.33 + 0.036\ LN(REV) - 0.142\ LN(RBRT) + 0.174\ DERN$$
$$+ 0.332\ DCUST$$

where RPRS = Relative price of restricted stock (to publicly traded stock)

REV = Revenues of the private firm (in millions of dollars)

RBRT = Restricted Block relative to Total Common Stock in %

DERN = 1 if earnings are positive; 0 if earnings are negative

DCUST = 1 if there is a customer relationship with the investor;
0 otherwise

From Concept to Practice

There are two basic approaches to estimating the liquidity discount for a private business.

- *Approach 1:* Use the average liquidity discount, based upon past studies, of 30% for private firms. Adjust subjectively for size; make the discount smaller for larger firms.
- *Approach 2:* Estimate the discount as a function of the determinants—the size of the firm, the stability of cashflows, the type of assets, and cashflow-generating capacity of the liquidity discount.

For instance, the Silber study suggests a relationship between the amount of revenues and the liquidity discount as shown in Figure 23.1. Thus, if an analyst has to estimate the liquidity discount for a private business with revenues of $120 million, the graph shown in Figure 23.1 could be used to arrive at an estimate.

> Liquidity Discount for small firm with negligible revenues = 30%
>
> Liquidity Discount for this business = 30% − 6% = 24%
>
> (The 6% comes from the graph in Figure 23.1; it is the reduction in liquidity discount as a function of the revenues.)

FIGURE 23.1 Effects of Increasing Revenues on Liquidity Discounts: Estimated from Silber Regression

Revenues (in millions of dollars)

☐ Marginal Reduction in Liquidity Discount ■ Cumulative Reduction on Liquidity Discount

NON-CASHFLOW-PRODUCING ASSETS

Assets that do not produce cashflows cannot be valued using discounted cash-flow models. They derive their value from a combination of factors—a scarcity of supply relative to demand, consumption utility, and individual perceptions. While they can be valued relative to comparables, their values are also much more volatile since they are based upon perceptions. There are a wide range of assets that fall under this category, from limited edition Barbie dolls to rare coins to wine.

Special Issues in Valuing Non-Cashflow-Producing Assets

The process of using comparables in valuing an asset is fairly straightforward, at least in the abstract. The first step in the process is to collect a group of comparable assets. The second is to estimate a measure of standardized value for this group. The third is to control for differences between assets in this group and the asset being valued to arrive at a measure of reasonable value for the asset. The problems in applying this approach to some of the assets described in this chapter are as follows:

- Finding comparable assets may be difficult to do for some non-cashflow-producing assets. While there are indices compiled on various unconventional assets, there are substantial differences between the assets within each index.
- The markets for many of these assets are neither liquid nor public. Many transactions are not arm's-length, and the prices are therefore unreliable.
- It is not clear how one controls for differences across assets that are comparable, when these differences are not quantitative but relate to perception.

One case where a model for comparables seems to have fared remarkably well is in the area of valuing wine vintages. Professor Orley Ashenfelter at Princeton University has developed a regression model that factors in temperature and rainfall in wine-growing regions to evaluate wine vintages (Bordeaux, California cabernet sauvignon, red Burgundy, Sauternes, and Port wines) and come up with estimates of value per bottle, which is published in his newsletter titled "Liquid Assets." The analog from stock valuation would be to compare price/earnings ratios across firms, controlling for risk and growth characteristics.

ASSETS WITH OPTION CHARACTERISTICS

Some assets derive their value not from the cashflows they generate or from highly valued comparables but from the potential they possess to be valuable some time in the future. One example of this would be the "undeveloped land" in an unsought area that has low value now but could have an explosive increase in value if the area is developed. Another example would be art produced by

an unknown artist that could be very valuable if the artist is discovered. These assets have option characteristics.

The practical problems with applying this approach are manifold. First, in many cases the underlying asset is not clearly defined and has no traded market value. Second, the absence of trading in these assets makes it difficult to estimate a volatility measure to use in valuing the options. Third, many of these assets do not have a clearly defined lifetime, though there are reasonable constraints on how long they can be expected to last.

CONCLUSION

This chapter provides an insight into the breadth of use that valuation models can be put to, ranging from valuing a New York City cab medallion to a five-star restaurant. The basic models remain unchanged, but the inputs may be more difficult to get and have more noise associated with them. That should not, however, be viewed as a barrier to their use.

QUESTIONS AND SHORT PROBLEMS

1. You have been asked to value Barrista Espresso, a chain of espresso coffee shops that have opened on the east coast of the United States. You have collected the following information:
 * The company had earnings before interest and taxes of $10.5 million in the most recent year. However, the founders of the company had never charged themselves a salary, which would have amounted to $1 million based upon comparable companies.
 * The tax rate is 36%.
 * The capital expenditures in the most recent year amounted to $4.5 million, while depreciation was only $1 million.
 * Working capital is expected to remain at 10% of revenues.
 * Earnings, revenues, and net capital expenditures are expected to grow 30% a year for five years, and 6% after that forever.
 * There are three comparable companies that are publicly traded:

	Beta	D/E	k_d
Starbucks:	1.74	9.53%	9.00%
Au Bon Pain:	1.21	31.43%	8.50%
Sbarro:	1.12	0.00%	NA

 Barrista Espresso is expected to maintain a debt ratio of 12% and face a cost of debt of 8.75%.
 a. Estimate the value of Barrista Espresso, as a firm.
 b. Estimate the value of equity in Barrista Espresso.
 c. Would your valuation be any different if you were valuing the company for an initial public offering rather than a private valuation?
2. What are some of the determinants of the size of the liquidity discount? Answer true or false to the following statements:

 a. There should be no liquidity discount attached to the value if the valuation is being done for an initial public offering.
 b. The liquidity discount should be larger for a high-growth firm with no current cashflows than for a stable firm with positive cashflows.
 c. The liquidity discount will become smaller for firms when they start losing money.
 d. The size of the liquidity discount will depend partly upon the buyer's characteristics.
3. You have valued a business, using discounted cashflow models, at $250 million for a private sale. The business, which does make money, had revenues of $200 million in the most recent year. How much of a liquidity discount would you apply to this firm:
 a. based upon the Silber regression?
 b. based upon correcting the average discount (25%) for the size of the firm?
4. You are trying to value a bed-and-breakfast business in Vermont for its owner based upon the following information:
 • The business had pretax operating income of $100,000 in the most recent year. This income has grown 5% a year for the last three years and is expected to continue growing at that rate for the foreseeable future.
 • About 40% of this operating income can be attributed to the fact that the owner is a master chef. He does not plan to stay on if the business is sold.
 • The business is financed equally with debt and equity. The pretax cost of borrowing is 8%. The beta for publicly traded firms in the hospitality business is 1.10. (The Treasury bond rate is 7%.)
 • The capital maintenance expenditure, net of depreciation, was $10,000 in the most recent year, and it is expected to grow at the same rate as operating income.
 • The business is expected to have an operating life of 10 years, after which the building will be sold at an anticipated price of $1.5 million, net of capital gains taxes.
 a. Value the business for sale.
 b. How much would the value change if the owner offered to stay on for the next three years?

ENDNOTES

1. The number of cab medallions had been frozen at this level since 1937. A proposal in 1995 proposed raising this number by 400, and faced stiff opposition from existing medallion owners.

2. Roger Noll, a Stanford economist, argued that a number of team owners were intermingling expenses from other businesses that they owned with those of their baseball franchises and were paying exorbitant salaries to themselves and their kin from the franchises.

3. Witness George Steinbrenner . . . need I say more!

4. The Yankees, for instance, did not sign a single contract with MSG Network. Instead, they signed several contracts, which pay the team unusually large fees for rights to videos, film libraries, and other services, to shield the revenues from revenue sharing.

5. This beta was estimated using 60 months of price data using the S&P 500 as the index.

6. Consider the value of David Letterman to CBS. One estimate in *The New York Times* claimed that 20% of the profits at CBS in 1993 could be traced to the success of David Letterman's show. If this is true, CBS may be getting an incredible bargain, even at $5 million a year.

24

Overview and Conclusion

The problem in valuation is not that there are not enough models to value an asset, it is that there are too many. Choosing the right model to use in valuation is as critical to arriving at a reasonable value as understanding how to use the model. This chapter attempts to provide an overview of the valuation models introduced in this book and a general framework that can be used to pick the right model for any task.

CHOICES IN VALUATION MODELS

In the broadest possible terms, firms or assets can be valued in one of three ways: approaches that discount cashflows to arrive at a present value of equity or of the firm, approaches that base value upon multiples, and approaches that use contingent claim valuation (or option pricing models). Within each of these approaches, there are further choices that help determine the final value.

In the context of discounted cashflow valuation, either cashflows to equity can be discounted at the cost of equity to arrive at a value of equity or cashflows to the firm can be discounted at the cost of capital to arrive at the value of the firm. The cashflows to equity themselves can be defined in the strictest sense as dividends or in a more expansive sense as free cashflows to equity. These models can be further categorized on the basis of assumptions about growth into stable-growth, two-stage, and three-stage models. Finally, the measurement of earnings and cashflows may be modified to match the special characteristics of the firm/asset—current earnings for firms/assets that have normal earnings, or normalized earnings for firms/assets whose current earnings may be distorted either by temporary factors or cyclical effects.

In the context of multiples, the price of a stock can be expressed in terms of a number of firm-specific variables—earnings, cashflows, book value, and sales. The multiples themselves can be estimated by using comparable firms in the same business, from cross-sectional regressions that use the broader universe, or from fundamentals. For other assets, such as real estate, the price can be similarly expressed as a function of gross income or income per square foot of space. Here, the comparables would be other properties in the same locale with similar characteristics.

The chart in Figure 24.1 categorizes the choices in valuation models avail-

FIGURE 24.1 Summary of Valuation Models

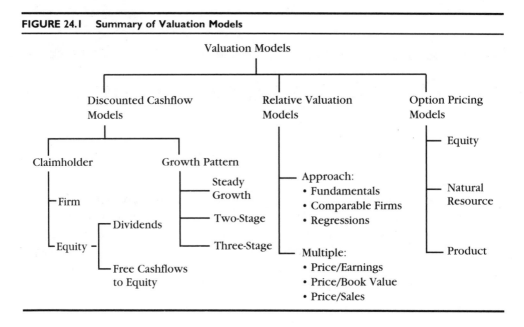

able to an analyst. The choice of a model often has much more far-reaching consequences in terms of value than the actual inputs to the model. Choosing the wrong model can result in large errors in valuation.

DETERMINANTS OF CHOICE

Discounted Cashflow Models

At the risk of stating the obvious, the model used in valuation should be tailored to match the characteristics of the asset being valued. The unfortunate truth is that the reverse is often true. Time and resources are wasted trying to make assets fit a prespecified valuation model, either because it is considered to be the "best" model or because not enough thought goes into the process of model choice.

There is no one "best" model. The appropriate model to use in a particular setting will depend upon a number of the characteristics of the asset or firm being valued.

Level of Earnings

The most basic issue that affects model choice is whether the firm made or lost money. At a practical level, firms with positive earnings are easier to value than firms with negative earnings. Even within the subgroup of positive earnings, a firm's earnings can be classified as either normal or abnormal. A firm's earnings are abnormal if temporary events, either marketwide or firm-specific, affect the measured earnings. For instance:

(a) A cyclical firm will generally report depressed earnings during an economic downturn and high earnings during an economic boom. Neither may properly capture the true earnings potential of the firm.

(b) A firm may report abnormally low earnings in a period during which it takes an extraordinary charge.

(c) A firm in the process of restructuring may report low earnings during the restructuring period as the changes made to improve firm performance are put into effect.

The earnings should be cleansed of temporary effects, or normalized, before being used in valuation.

While negative earnings almost always make the process of valuation more complex, the prescription for fixing the problem will vary depending upon why the firm lost money in the first place. There are at least three classes of firms that report negative earnings:

(a) *Cyclical firms* often report losses during economic recessions, as revenues decline and costs do not. The normalization of earnings here is a fairly simple process and requires the consideration of earnings across the entire economic cycle, adjusted for inflation.

(b) *Troubled firms* are firms that have lost and continue to lose money because of firm-specific or industry-specific factors. For example, the well-documented woes of the airline industry across the world in 1991 and 1992 resulted in most airlines making significant losses in those years. The solution here will depend upon whether there is light at the end of the tunnel. If a firm seems to be in a hopeless state and likely to go bankrupt, the only models that are likely to provide meaningful measures of value are the option pricing model and a model based upon liquidation value. If, on the other hand, the firm is troubled but unlikely to go bankrupt, it can be valued using the firm valuation approach, with free cashflows to the firm projected for the transition period to financial health.

(c) A *start-up firm* may report negative earnings in its initial periods of growth, not because it is unhealthy but because the investments it has made take time to pay off. The cashflows to the firm and to equity are often also negative, because the capital expenditure needs for this type of firm tend to be disproportionately large relative to depreciation. If this firm's expected future profit is based upon a single product line, its value can be estimated using the option pricing approach. If the firm's future is based upon multiple product lines, the value can be estimated using the firm value approach, with free cashflows to the firm projected into the future until the growth in capital expenditures slackens (as investment opportunities dry up and competition enters the fray) and cashflows turn positive.

Current Growth Rate in Earnings

The choice of discounted cashflow model will also be influenced by the level of current growth in earnings. For purposes of classification, the current growth rate in earnings can be classified into three broad levels:

(a) Firms growing at or below the nominal growth rate in the economy that they operate in. These firms are categorized as growing at a *stable* rate.
(b) Firms growing at a rate moderately higher than the nominal growth rate in the economy. These firms are classified as *moderate-growth* firms.
(c) Firms growing at a rate much higher than the nominal growth rate in the economy. These firms are grouped as *high-growth* firms.

For firms growing at the stable rate, the steady-state models that assume constant growth provide good estimates of value (Gordon growth model, stable FCFE model, and stable FCFF model). The choice between these models will be determined by the firm's dividend policy and leverage. For firms growing at a "moderate" rate, the two-stage discounted cashflow models should provide enough flexibility in terms of capturing the underlying characteristics of the firm, while a three-stage model may be needed to capture the longer transitions to stable growth that are inherent in "high-growth-rate" firms.

The question of what level of growth separates moderate- from high-growth firms can only be answered after examining the overall economy and the industry in which the firm operates. In general, the growth rate that would be needed to be a high-growth firm will be higher in faster-growing economies and in industries that are in flux.

Source of Growth

The higher expected growth for a firm can come from either "general" competitive advantages acquired over time by building up a brand name or reducing costs of production (from economies of scale), or "specific" advantages that are the result of legal barriers to entry or product patents. The former are likely to dissipate over time as new competitors enter the marketplace, while the latter are more likely to disappear abruptly when the legal barriers to entry are removed. The expected growth rate for a firm that has "specific" sources of growth is likely to follow the two-stage process where growth is high for a certain period (for instance, the period of the patent) and drops abruptly to a stable rate after that. The expected growth rate for a firm that has "general" sources of growth is more likely to decline gradually over time, as new competitors come in. The speed with which this competitive advantage is expected to be lost is a function of several factors, including:

(a) *The competence of the firm's management.* More competent management will be able to slow, though not stop, the loss of competitive advantage over time, by creating strategies that find new markets in which to exploit the firm's current competitive advantage (as in Coca Cola entering the Eastern European and Soviet markets) and that attempt to find new sources of competitive advantage.
(b) *Ease of entry into the firm's business.* The greater the barriers to industry in entering the firm's business, either because of capital requirements or technological factors, the slower will be the loss of competitive advantage.

Dividends Versus Free Cashflows to Equity

In valuing equity, using steady-state, two-stage, or three-stage models, an analyst can either discount dividends or free cashflows to equity. In an environment where there are significant limits on the market for corporate control (takeover restrictions) or where the free cashflows to equity, over time, are fully paid out as dividends, the dividend discount model should provide the benchmark for comparison to the market prices. In any other environment, the free cashflows to equity, which may be greater than or lower than the dividend but which are actually much more representative of the firm's true capacity to general cashflows, will provide the more reasonable estimate of value.

Stability of Leverage

The process of valuation can either focus on cashflows to equity (and value equity) or cashflows to the firm (and value the firm). Since both approaches should provide consistent estimates of value, with similar assumptions, the choice between them will be largely determined by the ease of use of the models. For firms that have stable leverage (i.e., they have debt ratios that are not expected to change during the period of the valuation), there is little to choose between the models. For firms that have unstable leverage (i.e., they have too much or too little debt and want to move toward their optimum during the period of the valuation), the firm valuation approach is much simpler to use because it does not require cashflow projections from interest and principal payments and is much less sensitive to errors in estimating leverage changes. (The calculation of the cost of capital requires an estimate of the debt ratio, but the cost of capital itself does not change as much as a consequence of changing leverage as does the cost of equity.)

While much of this discussion has been presented in terms of financial assets, the same factors also apply for real assets. Questions about whether earnings from the asset are normal or abnormal and whether growth is likely to be high, moderate, or tied to the inflation rate will drive the choice of a model. If the leverage in a real asset investment is high and changing (as it is in most real estate investments), it would make more sense to value the asset itself rather than just the equity stake in the asset.

These factors are summarized and presented in Table 24.1, with the appropriate discounted cashflow model highlighted for each combination of the factors.

Relative Valuation Models

Many analysts choose to value assets using relative valuation models. In making this choice, two basic questions have to be answered: Which multiple will be used in the valuation? Will this multiple be arrived at using fundamentals, comparable firms/assets, or a cross-sectional regression? The following factors will play a role in answering these questions.

TABLE 24.1 Firm Characteristics and DCF Model Choice

| Sign | Earnings | | Source of Growth | Dividends vs. FCFE | Leverage | Other Factors | Appropriate Model |
	Normalcy	Growth					
Positive	Normal	Stable	NA	= FCFE	Stable	NA	Gordon Growth
Positive	Normal	Stable	NA	≠ FCFE	Stable	NA	FCFE Stable
Positive	Normal	Stable	NA	NA	Unstable	NA	FCFF Stable
Positive	Normal	Moderate	General	= FCFE	Stable	NA	H
Positive	Normal	Moderate	Specific	= FCFE	Stable	NA	2-stage DDM
Positive	Normal	Moderate	Specific	≠ FCFE	Stable	NA	2-staeg FCFE
Positive	Normal	Moderate	Either	NA	Unstable	NA	2-stage FCFF
Positive	Normal	High	Either	= FCFE	Stable	NA	3-stage DDM
Positive	Normal	High	Either	≠ FCFE	Stable	NA	3-stage FCFE
Positive	Normal	High	Either	NA	Unstable	NA	3-stage FCFF
Positive	Abnormal	NA	NA	NA	Stable	NA	Normalized EPS
Positive	Abnormal	NA	NA	NA	Unstable	NA	Normalized FCFF
Negative	Cyclical	NA	NA	NA	Stable	NA	Normalized EPS
Negative	Cyclical	NA	NA	NA	Unstable	NA	Normalized FCFF
Negative	Troubled	NA	NA	NA	Either	Turn around	FCFF
Negative	Troubled	NA	NA	NA	Either	Bankruptcy	Option
Negative	Start-up	NA	NA	NA	Either	Many lines	FCFF
Negative	Start-up	NA	NA	NA	Either	Single line	Option

NA Not applicable.

Level of Earnings

The price/earnings multiple remains the most widely used relative valuation technique. Due to its dependence on current earnings, its use is circumscribed by whether these earnings are measured correctly and are normal. Furthermore, the price/earnings ratio is meaningless when earnings are negative. If the firm being valued has a current loss or if its earnings are distorted because of firm-specific actions (such as a restructuring) or macroeconomic factors (such as a recession), a multiple that is not directly impacted by current income may be more appropriate (price/book value or price/sales ratios).

Number of Comparable Firms/Assets

The preferred option in most relative valuation is to find a group of comparable firms,[1] estimate the chosen multiple for this group, and adjust the estimate for differences between the firm being valued and the group. The key step in this process is finding the comparable firms. In theory, a "comparable" firm is in the same line of business and has a similar growth and risk profile as the firm being valued. In practice, we find that analysts often have to stretch the limits of comparability. The firms that are finally classified as comparable often have very different business mixes and are significantly different from the firm being valued in risk and growth characteristics.

 If a large number of firms similar to the one being valued exist and are traded on financial markets, this approach to valuation is justifiable. To the extent that such a group is difficult to put together, either because the firm

TABLE 24.2 Firm Characteristics and Relative Valuation Model Choice

Earnings		Number of Comparable Firms	Market Valuation	Type of Business	Appropriate Model
Sign	Level				
Positive	Normal	Many	Correct for sector	Either	PE/Comparable firms
Positive	Normal	Few	Correct for market	Either	PE/Regression
Positive	Normal	Either	Incorrect	Either	PE/Fundamentals
Negative or	Abnormal	Many	Correct for sector	Manufacturing	PBV/Comparable firms
Negative or	Abnormal	Few	Correct for market	Manufacturing	PBV/Regression
Negative or	Abnormal	Either	Incorrect	Manufacturing	PBV/fundamentals
Negative or	Abnormal	Many	Correct for sector	Service	PS/Comparable firms
Negative or	Abnormal	Few	Correct for market	Service	PS/Regression
Negative or	Abnormal	Either	Incorrect	Service	PS/Fundamentals

being valued is unique or because the overall market has limited listings, it may be more appropriate to use a cross-sectional regression to estimate the multiple. Such a regression can use all the firms in the universe and control for differences in the underlying characteristics.

Market Valuation

When multiples are estimated using either the comparable firm approach or from a cross-sectional regression, there is the implicit assumption that the market correctly values firms in aggregate, though it may make errors in valuing individual firms. If the market can incorrectly value entire sectors, these approaches will build the errors into the valuation. In those cases, it may be better to estimate multiples from fundamentals.

Type of Business

The book value of assets measures something tangible in a manufacturing firm but does not mean much in a service firm. Thus, price/book value ratios are more meaningful for the former. For the latter, price/sales ratios, which draw on revenues and profit margins, may be more useful as a measure of relative value.

Table 24.2 relates the choice of relative valuation model to these characteristics.

CONCLUSION

The analyst faced with the task of valuing a firm/asset or its equity has to choose between three different approaches—discounted cashflow valuation, relative valuation, and option pricing models—and within each approach, between different models. This choice will be driven largely by the characteristics of the firm/asset being valued—the level of its earnings, its growth potential, the sources of earnings growth, the stability of its leverage, and its dividend policy.

Matching the valuation model to the asset or firm being valued is as important a part of valuation as understanding the models and having the right inputs.

QUESTIONS AND SHORT PROBLEMS

1. What discounted cashflow model would you use to value the following businesses?
 a. A firm that has negative net income currently, primarily because it has high leverage. (It plans to reduce leverage over time.)
 b. A firm that pays out as much in dividends as it can afford to and is in stable growth.
 c. A high-growth firm that makes money and has no debt.
 d. A high-technology firm that has no revenues currently but has a valuable patent.
 e. A bankrupt firm with negative net income and book value of equity.
2. You have been asked to value a cyclical firm at the business cycle's peak. How would you reflect this fact in your valuation?
3. An analyst uses five different discounted cashflow models to estimate value and then averages them out to arrive at a final estimate. Do you agree with this approach?
4. When would you use "comparables" to value a firm instead of discounted cashflow valuation? What are the advantages and disadvantages of doing so?

ENDNOTE

1. If a real asset is being valued, the same reasoning would apply, with data on comparable assets being compiled and used as a basis for valuation.

References

Altman, E. I. 1968. Financial ratios, discriminant analysis and the prediction of corporate bankruptcy. *Journal of Finance* 23:589–609.

Altman, E. I. 1994. *Defaults and returns on high yield bonds.* Working paper. Salomon Center, New York University.

Amihud, Y.; B. Christensen; and H. Mendelson. 1992. *Further evidence on the risk-return relationship.* Working paper. New York University.

Arnott, R. D. 1985. The use and misuse of consensus earnings. *Journal of Portfolio Management* 11:18–27.

Atkinson, T. R. 1967. *Trends in corporate bond quality.* New York: National Bureau of Economic Research.

Basu, S. 1977. The investment performance of common stocks in relation to their price-earnings: A test of the efficient market hypothesis. *Journal of Finance* 32:663–682.

Bathke, A. W., Jr., and K. S. Lorek. 1984. The relationship between time-series models and the security market's expectation of quarterly earnings. *The Accounting Review* 59:163–176.

Bernstein, L. A., and J. G. Siegel. 1979. The concept of earnings quality. *Financial Analysts Journal* 35:72–75.

Bethke, W. M., and S. E. Boyd. 1983. Should dividend discount models be yield-tilted? *Journal of Portfolio Management* 9:23–27.

Black, F., and M. Scholes. 1972. The valuation of option contracts and a test of market efficiency. *Journal of Finance* 27:399–417.

Box, G., and G. Jenkins. 1976. *Time series analysis: forecasting and control.* Oakland, CA: Holden-Day.

Brennan, M. J. 1970. Taxes, market valuation and corporation financial policy. *National Tax Journal* 23:417–427.

Brennan, M. J., and E. S. Schwartz. 1977. Savings bonds, retractable bonds and callable bonds. *Journal of Financial Economics* 5:67–88.

Brennan, M. J., and E. S. Schwartz. 1980. Analyzing convertible bonds. *Journal of Financial and Quantitative Analysis* 15:907–929.

Brennan, M. J., and E. S. Schwartz. 1985. Evaluating natural resource investments. *Journal of Business* 58:135–158.

Brown, L. D., and M. S. Rozeff. 1979. Univariate time series models of quarterly accounting earnings per share: A proposed model. *Journal of Accounting Research* 19: 178–189.

Brown, L. D., and M. S. Rozeff. 1980. Analysts can forecast accurately! *Journal of Portfolio Management* 6:31–34.

Capaul, C.; I. Rowley; and W. F. Sharpe. 1993. International value and growth stock returns. *Financial Analysts Journal* 49:27–36.

Chan, L. K., and J. Lakonishok. 1992. *Are the reports of Beta's death premature?* Working paper. University of Illinois—Champaign-Urbana.

Chan, L. K.; Y. Hamao; and J. Lakonishok. 1991. Fundamentals and stock returns in Japan. *Journal of Finance* 46:1739–1789.

Chen, N.; R. Roll; and S. A. Ross. 1986. Economic forces and the stock market. *Journal of Business* 59:383–404.

Choi, F. D. S., and R. M. Levich. 1990. *The capital market effects of international accounting diversity.* Homewood, Ill.: Dow Jones-Irwin.

Collins, W., and W. Hopwood. 1980. A multivariate analysis of annual earnings forecasts generated from quarterly forecasts of financial analysts and univariate time series models. *Journal of Accounting Research* 20:390–406.

Conrad, J. 1989. The price effect of option introduction. *Journal of Finance* 44: 487–498.

Copeland, T. E.; T. Koller; and J. Murrin. 1990. *Valuation: measuring and managing the value of companies.* New York: Wiley.

Cottle, S.; R. Murray; and F. Bloch. 1988. *Security analysis.* New York: McGraw-Hill.

Cragg, J. G., and B. G. Malkiel. 1968. The consensus and accuracy of predictions of the growth of corporate earnings. *Journal of Finance* 23:67–84.

Crichfield, T.; T. Dyckman; and J. Lakonishok. 1978. An evaluation of security analysts' forecasts. *The Accounting Review* 53:651–668.

Dann, L. Y., and H. DeAngelo. 1983. Standstill agreements, privately negotiated stock repurchases, and the market for corporate control. *Journal of Financial Economics* 11:275–300.

DeBondt, W. F. M., and R. Thaler. 1985. Does the stock market overreact? *Journal of Finance* 40:793–805.

DeBondt, W. F. M., and R. Thaler. 1987. Further evidence on investor overreaction and stock market seasonality. *Journal of Finance* 42:557–581.

Estep, T. 1985. A new method for valuing common stocks. *Financial Analysts Journal* 41:26, 27, 30–33.

Estep, T. 1987. Security analysis and stock selection: Turning financial information into return forecasts. *Financial Analysts Journal* 43:34–43.

Fabozzi, F. J. 1994. *Investment management.* Englewood Cliffs, N.J.: Prentice Hall.

Fama, E. F. 1965. The behavior of stock market prices. *Journal of Business* 38:34–105.

Fama, E. F. 1970. Efficient capital markets: A review of theory and empirical work. *Journal of Finance* 25:383–417.

Fama, E. F. 1975. Short-Term interest rates as predictors of inflation. *American Economic Review* 65:269–282.

Fama, E. F., and K. R. French. 1992. The cross-section of expected returns. *Journal of Finance* 47:427–466.

Foster, G. 1977. Quarterly accounting data: Time series properties and predictive ability results. *The Accounting Review* 52:1–31.

Fraine, H. G., and R. H. Mills. 1961. Effect of defaults and credit deterioration on yields of corporate bonds. *Journal of Finance* 16:423–434.

Fried, D., and D. Givoly. 1982. Financial analysts forecasts of earnings: A better surrogate for earnings expectations. *Journal of Accounting and Economics* 4:85–107.

Fruhan, W. E. 1979. *Financial strategy: Studies in the creation, transfer and destruction of shareholder value.* Homewood, Ill.: Irwin.

Fruhan, W. E.; W. C. Kester; S. P. Mason; T. R. Piper; and R. S. Ruback. 1992. *Case Problems in Finance.* Homewood, Ill.: Irwin.

Fuller, R. J., and C. Hsia. 1984. A simplified common stock valuation model. *Financial Analysts Journal* 40:49–56.

Fuller, R. J.; L. C. Huberts; and M. Levinson. 1992. It's not Higgledy-Piggledy growth! *Journal of Portfolio Management* 18:38–46.

Givoly, D., and J. Lakonishok. 1984. The quality of analysts' forecasts of earnings. *Financial Analysts Journal* 40:40–47.

Goodman, D. A., and J. W. Peavy, III. 1983. Industry relative price-earnings ratios as indicators of investment returns. *Financial Analysts Journal* 39:60–66.

Gordon, M. 1962. *The investment, financing and valuation of the corporation.* Homewood, Ill.: Irwin.

Graham, B.; D. L. Dodd; and S. Cottle. 1962. *Security analysis,* 4th ed. New York: McGraw-Hill.

Griffin, P. 1977. The time-series behavior of quarterly earnings: Preliminary evidence. *Journal of Accounting Research* 17:71–83.

Harvey, C. R. 1988. The real term structure and consumption growth. *Journal of Financial Economics* 22:305–333.

Haugen, R. A. 1990. *Modern investment theory.* Englewood Cliffs, N.J.: Prentice Hall.

Haugen, R. A., and J. Lakonishok. 1988. The incredible January effect. Homewood, Ill.: Dow Jones-Irwin.

Hawkins, E. H.; S. C. Chamberlin; and W. E. Daniel. 1984. Earnings expectations and security prices. *Financial Analysts Journal* 40:24–27, 30–38, 74.

Hempel, G. H. 1971. *The postwar quality of state and local debt.* New York: National Bureau of Economic Research.

Hickman, W. B. 1958. *Corporate bond quality and investor experience.* New York: National Bureau of Economic Research.

Hicks, J. R. 1946. *The value of capital.* New York: Oxford University Press.

Hiroyumi, Itami. 1987. *Mobilizing invisible assets.* Boston: Harvard University Press.

Ho, T. S. Y., and S. B. Lee. 1989. Pricing of the call and sinking fund provisions on corporate bonds under interest rate risk: Empirical evidence. *International Journal of Finance* 2:1–17.

Ibbotson, R. G., and G. P. Brinson. 1993. *Global investing.* New York: McGraw Hill.

Ingersoll, J. 1977. An examination of corporate call policies on convertible securities. *Journal of Finance* 32:463–478.

Jacobs, B. I., and K. N. Levy. 1988a. Disentangling equity return irregularities: New insights and investment opportunities. *Financial Analysts Journal* 44:18–44.

Jacobs, B. I., and K. N. Levy. 1988b. On the value of "Value." *Financial Analysts Journal* 44:47–62.

Jaffe, J. 1974. Special information and insider trading. *Journal of Business* 47:410–428.

Jensen, M. C. 1969. Risk, the pricing of capital assets, and the evaluation of investment portfolios. *Journal of Business* 42:167–247.

Jensen, M. C. 1986. Agency costs of free cashflow, corporate finance and takeovers. *American Economic Review* 76:323–329.

Johnson, R. E. 1967. Term structures of corporate bond yields as a function of the risk of default. *Journal of Finance* 22:313–345.

Kaplan, R. S., and R. Roll. 1972. Investor evaluation of accounting information: Some empirical evidence. *Journal of Business* 45:225–257.

Kisor, M., Jr., and V. S. Whitbeck. 1963. A new tool in investment decision-making. *Financial Analysts Journal* 19:55–62.

Levy, H., and Z. Lerman. Testing P/E ratio filters with stochastic dominance. *Journal of Portfolio Management* 11:31–40.

Little, I. M. D. 1962. *Higgledy Piggledy growth.* Oxford: Institute of Statistics.

Litzenberger, R. H., and K. Ramaswamy. 1979. The effect of personal taxes and dividends on capital asset prices: Theory and empirical evidence. *Journal of Financial Economics* 7:163–196.

McConnell, J. J., and C. J. Muscarella. 1985. Corporate capital expenditure decisions and the market value of the firm. *Journal of Financial Economics* 14:399–422.

McCulloch, J. H. 1975. An estimate of the liquidity premium. *Journal of Political Economy* 83:95–119.

Meiselman, D. 1962. *The term structure of interest rates.* Englewood Cliffs, N.J.: Prentice Hall.

O'Brien, P. 1988. Analysts' forecasts as earnings expectation. *Journal of Accounting and Economics* 10:53–83.

Park, S. Y., and M. G. Subrahmanyam. 1990. Option features of corporate securities. In *Financial Options,* ed. S. Figlewski et al. Homewood, Ill.: Business One Irwin.

Peters, D. J. 1991. Valuing a growth stock. *Journal of Portfolio Management* 17:49–51.

Peters, E. E. 1991. *Chaos and order in the capital markets.* New York: Wiley.

Porter, M. E. 1980. *Competitive strategy: Techniques for analyzing industries and competitors.* New York: Free Press.

Richards, R. M., and J. D. Martin. 1979. Revisions in earnings forecasts: How much response? *Journal of Portfolio Management* 5:47–52.

Roll, R. 1977. A critique of the asset pricing theory's tests: Part I: On past and potential testability of theory. *Journal of Financial Economics* 4:129–176.

Roll, R. 1984. A simple implicit measure of the bid-ask spread in an efficient market. *Journal of Finance* 39:1127–1139.

Rosenberg, B.; K. Reid; and R. Lanstein. 1985. Persuasive evidence of market inefficiency. *Journal of Portfolio Management* 11:9–17.

Rosenberg, B., and V. Marathe. 1979. Tests of capital asset pricing hypotheses. *Research in Finance* 1:115–124.

Sarig, O., and A. Warga. 1989. Some empirical estimates of the term structure of interest rates. *Journal of Finance* 44:1351–1360.

Schipper, K., and A. Smith. 1983. Effects of recontracting on shareholder wealth: The case of voluntary spin-offs. *Journal of Financial Economics* 12:437–468.

Schipper, K., and A. Smith. 1986. A comparison of equity carve-outs and seasoned equity offerings: Share price effects and corporate restructuring. *Journal of Financial Economics* 15:153–186.

Senchack, A. J., Jr., and J. D. Martin. 1987. The relative performance of the PSR and PER investment strategies. *Financial Analysts Journal* 43:46–56.

Seyhun, H. N. 1986. Insiders' profits, costs of trading and market efficiency. *Journal of Financial Economics* 16:189–212.

Shapiro, A. 1985. Corporate strategy and the capital budgeting decision. *Midland Corporate Finance Journal,* 3:22–36.

Shapiro, A. 1989. *Modern corporate finance.* New York: Macmillan.

Siegel, D.; J. Smith; and J. Paddock. 1993. Valuing offshore oil properties with option pricing models. In *The new corporate finance,* ed. D. H. Chew, Jr. New York: McGraw-Hill.

Silber, W. L. 1991. Discounts on restricted stock: The impact of illiquidity on stock prices. *Financial Analysts Journal,* 47:60–64.

Sorensen, E. H., and D. A. Williamson. 1985. Some evidence on the value of the dividend discount model. *Financial Analysts Journal* 41: 60–69.

Stapleton, R. C. 1985. A note on default risk, leverage and the MM theorem. *Journal of Financial Economics* 2:377–381.

Sunder, S. 1973. Relationship between accounting changes and stock prices: Problems of measurement and some empirical evidence. In *Empirical Research in Accounting: Selected Studies:* 1–45. Toronto: Lexington.

Sunder, S. 1975. Stock price and risk related accounting changes in inventory valuation. *The Accounting Review:* 305–315.

Takeover legislation. 1995. *Journal of Financial Economics* 25:291–322.

Van Horne, J. C. 1965. Interest-rate risk and the term structure of interest rates. *Journal of Political Economy* 73:344–351.

Vander Weide, J. H., and W. T. Carleton. 1988. Investor growth expectations: Analysts vs. history. *Journal of Portfolio Management* 14:78–83.

Watts, R. 1975. *The time series behavior of quarterly earnings.* Working paper. University of Newcastle.

Weston, J. F., and T. E. Copeland. 1992. Orlando: *Managerial finance,* 9th ed. Harcourt Brace Jovanovich.

Wilcox, J. W. 1984. The P/B-ROE valuation model. *Financial Analysts Journal* 40: 58–66.

Wood, J. H., and N. L. Wood. 1985. *Financial markets.* Orlando: Harcourt Brace Jovanovich.

Woolridge, R. 1993. Competitive decline and corporate restructuring. In *The new corporate finance,* ed. D. H. Chew, Jr. New York: McGraw-Hill.

Index